W9-BZI-103

DATE DUE			
OCT 1			
OCT 28			
NOV 26			

74194
Endleman

St. Procopius College Library
Maple Ave. and College Rd.
Lisle, Illinois

Personality and social life   TEXT AND READINGS

Consulting Editor: C H A R L E S H. P A G E
University of California, Santa Cruz

Personality

and social life TEXT AND READINGS

ROBERT ENDLEMAN

Adelphi University

RANDOM HOUSE   NEW YORK

137.33
E56p

First Printing

© *Copyright, 1967, by Random House, Inc.*
All rights reserved under International and Pan-American
Copyright Conventions. Published in New York by Random House, Inc.
and simultaneously in Toronto, Canada,
by Random House of Canada Limited.

Library of Congress Catalog Card Number: 67–10908
Manufactured in the United States of America by H. Wolff

74194

To
J. *and* L.

Preface

This is a book on personality in its connections with social structure and culture. While I trust that professionals in the relevant fields as well as literate layman will find value and illumination in these pages, the book was written primarily for use as a combination text and collection of readings for university courses at the advanced undergraduate and graduate level. The courses for which it would be used are variously entitled Personality and Social Structure, Personality and Culture, the Individual and Society, Social Forces and the Individual, Human Growth and Social Environment, and even Social Psychology (though the content here fits only particular versions of the latter). The work attempts to combine something of the range of findings and perspectives typical of a collection of readings with the unitary viewpoint and continuity of a single-author text—necessarily with some sacrifice of each. A particular personal viewpoint serves as the selective principle in choosing the readings by other authors (a few of which were written especially for this volume) as well as informing the parts written by myself. The psychological grounding is explicitly psychoanalytic and within that perspective, Freudian rather than neo-Freudian. My exemplars for a psychoanalytic anthropology are Weston La Barre, George Devereux, and Géza Róheim, to name only the most important. I have attempted to carry that kind of analysis into several pan-human problems and then explicitly into the study of large-scale modern societies, which have typically been the province of sociologists more than anthropologists. (The disciplinary boundaries are given no explicit reference at all in the book: such barriers are intrinsically irrelevant, even inimical, to the subject matter at hand. We need to learn whatever we can about personality and social life, regardless of the provenience of the ideas.)

This book had its origins in the need that I felt for a collection of instructional materials in personality and society coherent with my own particular way of viewing this subject matter. Hence, the book has an emphasis of its own, and does not attempt to be comprehensive, nor to represent all the possible relevant studies or views on each problem considered, nor necessarily to include at each point "obvious" conflicting material that would readily come to mind to many professional readers. Since some parts of the book of my own authorship derive from earlier works of mine cast in a framework not entirely consonant with the main perspective of the book, some unevenness (or "openness") has been allowed in the total structure of the work. In any case, some loose-ness at the edges, so to speak, is in the nature of the subject matter. The form of the whole, and of the various parts (see especially Chapter Five) I would call "configurational" rather than "systematic," and I shall leave it to the professional reader to determine the value of such a design. In the making of the book, it has allowed me a certain amount of controlled free association and excursions into a few areas not as yet, to my knowl-edge, very much developed in this personality-culture kind of way—for example, the problem of play and its relationship to work, to culture generally, to the problem of transitions, and to the question of trans-cultural standards of normality. These are areas to which I hope that my efforts will lead other scholars to devote more sustained attention.

A book such as this derives, of course, from the whole recent develop-ment of the studies of man and society, filtered by the accidents of biography of the principal author. Besides those already mentioned, my intellectual debts in the literature of psychoanalysis, anthropology, and sociology will be apparent to the professional reader. Formal instruction by illuminating mentors, the adrenalin of dialogue with challenging col-leagues, private study and self-exploration, critical reflection stimulated by teaching a multitude and variety of university students over many years, all have, of course, contributed. Hence, in the larger sense the "debts" and "influences" are innumerable, and any particular list neces-sarily invidious. Still, acknowledgment to a few persons who have helped especially on this particular book is in order. The other authors whose work is presented or adapted in the book, were of course indispensable for the book. Special thanks go to Henry Carsch of Carleton College (Minnesota), Victor Gioscia of Adelphi University and Jewish Family Service (New York), to Aaron and Joan Katcher of the University of Pennsylvania, and Michael Parenti of Sarah Lawrence College, for their original papers, and for their patience in waiting out the successive delays in publication. Critical reading of different portions of the manu-script was given as follows: by Anne Roe, of my condensation-adaptation of her three long papers on the psychology of scientists; by Melford Spiro, of my essay on the Kibbutz; by Dennis Wrong, of Chapter Seven. For permissions to reprint in original or condensed form, or to adapt freely, as acknowledged at specific points in the book, I wish to thank all the respective authors.

Adelphi University facilitated the work on the book in many ways, tangible and otherwise; and Carl Backman and the University of Nevada helped with hospitality and facilities during a period of work there. Gratitude is due also to Helen Slavin and Linda LoDuca for typing portions of the manuscript; and to Marion Guest, David Jaffe, Richard LaRocca, Philip Leonhard, Brian McBride, Carl Schmidt, and Marsha Troum, who as student assistants at Adelphi University in successive periods assisted in many ways with the preparation of the manuscript. For the preparation of the index, I am indebted to Laurin Raiken. A special note of recognition to Ralph Romanelli, who refracted the very process of the work through the vision of the artist and sustained my trust in the creative unconscious.

The responsibility for the resulting form of the book, and for the content of those portions of my authorship or adaptation, is of course my own.

Finally, my thanks to Random House for undertaking publication of this work, and for all their help along the way; for the counsel of sociology editor Charles Page who struggled valorously with portions of a frequently turgid earlier draft; and especially, for the exuberant encouragement of college editor Theodore Caris, whose faith in my getting the book completed so frequently far exceeded my own.

R. E.

New York
December, 1966

Contents

Personality and social life   TEXT AND READINGS

Introduction

Man is a creature and creator of man. Come into the world a mewling helpless little animal, driven by diffuse stirrings of a peculiar body, he is totally dependent on human warmth and care to survive and be. At once he is enmeshed in social life, at once begins to learn and share in culture. Dualities and paradox pervade his life: instincts and culture, the separate being and the vital social ties, the truly felt and the way to be, uniqueness of oneself and the sameness with all mankind. Social bonds imprison and also liberate. Culture shows the world and also makes man blind and deaf. We are vastly various and laughably alike. Bodily kin to aeons of life, man yet richly creates what no animal can match. Helpless yet vastly powerful, driven by irrational passions yet open to gigantic rationality, able at Olympian detachment and prone as well to boundaryless immersion in depths of oceanic feeling, of oneness with the herd or with ineffable mysteries of the universe—all of these is man. Within himself as well, each man is divided in countless ways: drives against drives, a knowing, sensing self and yet another darker inner nameless being, a striving and a slothful self, a self of control and one of indulgence, a demanding or forbidding voice, an answer defiant or pleasure bound, a doer, actor, mover, a luxuriant in reverie, a feeler of love and bliss and hate. Bodily female or bodily male, a part of oneself is the other sex, or no sex at all. The world of others, one's ties with them, are ordered and chaotic both. Landscapes, events, the ways of men, make sense and yet absurdity. Grown, we yet feel an infant's rage or fear, at times a child's exuberant joy. Another's plight evokes a cold, unfeeling stare, another's still an anguished desperation.

Man becomes a human personality only through the joys and pains of human contact, care and giving and taking, and only through learning the ways of that small portion of mankind that is his tribe or community or nation at a particular time in history—in other words, through culture, and through a particular culture. Thus we are something more and something less than the human animal seen as the potential of man. More because no human animal could invent even the simplest of human cultures alone; less because no human culture could respond to, foster, and develop anything like the full range of the potentialities of this human animal. Hence there is a fundamental tension built into the very process of becoming human, one which no culture and no separate personality, can ever fully resolve.

We are all creatures of culture—of the accumulated ways of mankind, of the capacities the human animal has developed to tame or cope with the world of nature and the world of his own kind. We are also all creatures of the particular culture of our own time and tribe and place. Thus each personality is doubly related to culture: first, we cannot be human at all without culture, in the large sense, being imbedded in our personalities; second, we become particular personalities through the particularities of a specific culture, in the narrow sense, in which we grow up. These are commonplaces, to be sure, but within them lie a host of puzzles and ambiguities. It is these, or some of them, we shall try to explore in this book. While we are all creatures of culture, and of particular cultures, we are not all equally so or similarly so. Each personality can be viewed as having a unique core of potentialities. Since we are widely, though not infinitely, various in the natures of our bodies and our bodily drives and in that intricate interplay of our chemistry and our personal histories, of genes and the "accidents" of our situations, no particular set of culture patterns can be experienced with the same ease, or comfort, or satisfaction by all of its participants. Some persons are bound to be acutely distressed, even at war, in their particular place or age. These are the "costs and casualties" of the culture. Some of this will occur in any culture. While some cultures may offer a greater scope for diversity, none is likely to approach anything like the whole range of human potentiality—what Ruth Benedict imaginatively called "the great arc of human experience"—or, otherwise put, the polymorphism of instinctual possibility. There is not only a duality, but a perpetual interplay, a dialectic, between man and culture. Man is ever living culture and in tension with it. He can never fully live without it, yet he can never fully be at ease with it.

Man does not become a culture-being by diffuse acquisition from the world around him. He does so rather by his social life. This means he acquires the ways of his society through the persons important in his early life, and this usually means primarily through the family, in a process we call socialization. Though other arrangements are possible and have been tried, the ways of most of the world have been to link the biological process of reproduction with the social process of care and response and socialization. The social arrangement of the family probably antedates biological humanity, and seems from the evidence to have very strong roots in the basic evolutionary situation of man. This is one sense of the universal commonalities of all mankind, and its general outlines will be examined in Chapter One. The residential-social unit of mother and immature offspring, with "father" (mother's mate) "coming home to stay" is a prototype of all human experience. Here we find the complex of sex and dependency in this primal situation where love and hate are learned—the family as the crucible of human experience—as the scene of the deepest roots of the personality. The relation of personality to the family and its patterned relationships can be seen as having three levels: what is universal for all of mankind (the common biological and prototypical social elements); what is commonly experienced in a particular society and culture, but different from others; and what is unique to a particular person or a particular family, making them distinctive from all others even in the same society or community. Chapter One will concern elements universal for all mankind; later chapters will explore some of the variations and their relevance for different kinds of personality functioning.

We have not as yet attempted any definition of "personality"— and in a sense there is no one definition that will satisfactorily deal with all possible questions one can raise about the nature of the individual person. We shall essay only some preliminary characterizations at this point, for in a sense, the development of its meaning is the subject of the whole book. One may talk, for example, about personality as an individual person's unique way of living in the world—he is unique in that no other person has had exactly his combination of genetic endowment, life experiences, and exposures to the intricacies of culture. To refer to a "way of living in the world" of course implies that there is something patterned and both internally and temporally *consistent* in the individual. One may also refer to the patterned and persistent ways in which the individual person experiences the interplay between his bodily drives, his relationships with crucial other persons, and the regulative, restrictive, or permissive forces of the culture in which he lives—again with an assumption of some kind or degree of long-term *continuity* in his "ways." One may go further still and ask about patterned, consistent, and persistent ways in which the individual person deals with those forces within himself which are not ordinarily accessible to his conscious awareness, but some aspects of which might be brought to awareness under special circumstances—in other words, the unconscious forces, and their relationship to the conscious. One may then extend this kind of exploration into the kinds of methods or techniques the individual regularly or repeatedly employs—what in psychodynamic analysis is called "mechanisms." Another dimension we can explore is the way the individual plays the various social *roles* he is "assigned" or "takes on himself" in the social world of human relationships, and we can relate this way in turn to his "inner dynamics"—the interplay of conscious and unconscious forces, of instinct and controlled, aware behavior. In each area an individual is unique. He also shares areas of commonality with others who are like himself in some important dimension. For example, they share with him the same culture or subculture, the same type of family situation, certain temperamental drives, or some similar social placement in the world via age, sex, occupation, or religion. On the third level, the universal, any individual is like all other human beings in encountering certain prototypical human experiences, having common biologically-based drives, or using part or all of the definable human repertory of psychodynamic "mechanisms."

A central question about personality, whether unique, communally shared, or universal, is the manner of development. How does a personality become the way it is? What universal patterns of growth and development are traversed, and what variations within them? How do the biological underpinnings interplay with the social facts of relationships to significant other persons in the family or other social settings? Just how is "socialization" involved in the process of personality development? How variably complete or incomplete can the socialization process be in a particular society? What typical conflicts or dilemmas are experienced in the impact of socialization on the developing personality? Which of these are universal, rooted either in biology or universal human situations (or both); which are traceable to the particular arrangements of a certain society or tribe or community, or kind of family setting determined by such elements as the occupation of the "breadwinner" of the family?

How differently does this whole process go on in different societies? In Chapters Two and Three we shall explore some of these variations, using detailed case studies of four distinct communities, examined for their cultures and subcultures in general, their social structural patterns, their socialization, and the typical patterns of personality development that evidently derive from and also probably contribute to the social and cultural patterns.

It may appear, so far, that "personality" is being viewed primarily as a social *product*. What of the other side of the relationship? To what extent can the social structural arrangements of a particular society or community, and its culture, be derived from the personality trends that are common to the members of the community? What happens in the process of growing up? To what extent and in what ways do the early experiences in socialization, and the ways the personality has reacted to these experiences, persist into the later years of the individual? How does the special infancy and childhood of man, of that time and place, live on in institutions, in work and play, in art and ritual, in social loves and hates?

TRANSITIONS

How does child become man or woman? What are the special problems of transitions? How differently do different societies deal with these problems, and how alike? What are the costs and benefits for the personality, and for the society or community? What is universal about this special phase of burgeoning sexuality in the transition from childhood to adulthood, and what is culture-bound? How does infantile sexuality, as channeled in the society, impinge upon this transitional stage? Why are some cultures richer, more elaborate, more convoluted, in ritual and imagery than others during this phase? What are the special needs of such transitional stages in a large complex society like our own, with its bureaucratization, mechanization, and rapid rate of secular change? What special forms of such transition develop in such a society? How are they in turn related to the dynamic trends and tensions of such a society?

WORK, PLAY AND PERSONALITY

What is the relationship of work and play in different kinds of personalities and in different kinds of cultures? How does each draw upon the resources, the potentialities, the conflicts and tensions of different personality types, or personalities as structured by different kinds of societies? How do different kinds of work roles channelize different kinds of personalities, or different personality mechanisms and trends, and in turn consolidate or expand certain psychic orientations at the expense of other possibilities into a way of living in the world? What kinds of work roles have deep effect on a personality, have greater centrality and resonance, while other roles touch only superficial features of the self? What are the special psychodynamic qualities of such deeply resonant roles as scientist, artist, poet, and healer, and how do these in turn relate to the deeper forces unleashed in play? How in turn is play related to the sacred, in the dynamics of personality, or to the assumption of deviant roles, as in crime and delinquency?

PERSONALITY IN EXTREME SITUATIONS

Cultures, no matter how peculiar, assume some ongoing continuity. But there are many ways such continuity and order may be drastically broken: suddenly, violently, in disasters or violent revolutions; in semi-institutional forms which nevertheless mark a radical rupture between culture and man, and man and man, situations like the horrors of the concentration camps of the twentieth century; and, on a less ghastly scale, the "total institutions" such as prisons and insane asylums. These various frames have in common: man in extremity, man in situations so fraught with catastrophe that culture all but ceases to be his support or guide, and man struggles alone. What happens then? How do any men survive at all in concentration camps? And of those who do, how do they "adapt" or "adjust" to the routinization of horror that the camps represent? What happens to people—socially and dynamically—in disasters, natural or manmade? How do they cope with the extremity of the situation, and assuming they survive the initial impact, how do they react afterward? How do they play their usual and unusual roles, deal with loss, with stricken neighbors and kin? What psychodynamic elements does the disaster unleash in the victim-survivors, the "near-misses" and the "remote-misses," the visitors from near and far who flock to the scene for voyeuristic thrills? What relevance do such extreme situations have for understanding man faced with the more pervasive extremities of life in an increasingly dangerous and complex world?

SHARED DYNAMICS AND PSYCHOPATHOLOGY

Culture is built upon the sharing of sense and feeling about the world and the sharing of illusions. Any culture is "crazy" from the perspective of any other sufficiently different in its basic premises. Moreover, some social scientists suggest that at the unconscious root of *any* culture are elemental emotional presuppositions that are false to harsh reality, at least to the extent that they partake of the basic illogic, wishful distortion, magic, and megalomania characteristic of the id forces of all human beings. The superficial forms this illogic takes vary greatly from one culture to the next, but the substructures tend to be essentially the same. The eternal magic denial of death is but one poignant example. Shared psychodynamics, then, may be regarded as shared psychopathology. How does this develop and form in concrete instances? Will examination of cults, sects, social movements, variations on the forms of leadership, add to our understanding of these processes? Do different subcultures, for example ethnic ones, create distinctive styles of psychopathology? How are illusion, culture, and psychopathology interrelated? Can we perceive a psychodynamic pattern in the illusions of Western man? Can we formulate some notions of "normality" that do not fall into the trap of elevating the biases of one particular cultural tradition into eternals of mankind, nor the trap of infinite cultural relativism where "all things are possible" and man seems to be infinitely plastic in his possibilities? What can we learn from psychoanalytic sociology and anthropology that will enable us to pose a universalist conception of normality and pathology, "beyond cultural relativism" in a perspective that unites the scientism of the social sciences with the humanism of the humanities, sets man in all his potential as a measure of man and of culture, and serves as a basis for not only analysis but also critique of the extant social order?

APPROACH

The range of studies that can be drawn upon for this book is almost as broad as all of the behavioral and social sciences and much of the humanities as well. To attempt a comprehensive coverage would be hopeless. Instead the approach is frankly and drastically selective, emphasizing those studies and points of view this author has found most enlightening or most provocative in raising crucial questions. As will be evident, however, the selectivity pays no obeisances to formal academic discipline lines; sociology, anthropology, psychology and psychoanalysis, as well as philosophical and literary sources, are tapped wherever they seemed relevant to the problem at hand. Also, in a subject so large and so riddled with unresolved problems, I have not attempted to maintain the most rigorous standards of organization of materials (though my systematic theoretical biases will be evident to the professional reader, and will no doubt appear to those who do not share them, to be an arbitrarily restrictive influence). Rather the effort is to keep open the sense of tension and ambiguity suggested in the opening passage. Inevitably I see a number of large questions as open and problematical which other scholars may regard as more settled than this book suggests, and I have taken as settled many questions which other scholars regard as problematic.

ONE

Fundamentals: personality, family, society

1. UNIVERSALS OF MANKIND: ROOTS IN EVOLUTION

Personality and social life involve us in the great universals and manifold diversities of man. What are the common strands in personality development, anywhere in time and place, that make it possible for us to recognize and understand the human personality, in all its various guises, in all the diverse costumes and decorations of culture anywhere in the world? What is common to human culture, to all human cultures? What common problems are intrinsic to patterns of social life in all of history, in all the various climes? In short, what makes us human, as physical animals, as psychological beings, as players of roles, and as bearers of cultural traditions?

Biologically we are all one: one species, *homo sapiens*, the only species of this genus known to have survived on this planet into (geologically) modern times.[1] This means we have one basic physiology

Much of what follows in this chapter is heavily indebted to the formulations of Weston La Barre, in The Human Animal *(Chicago: University of Chicago Press, 1954), a remarkable synthesis of physical and cultural anthropology, psychoanalysis, and linguistics. The impact of this work on my thinking is gratefully acknowledged. Needless to add, the responsibility for what has been done here with La Barre's ideas is solely my own.*

[1] That is, the postglacial age, or roughly the past 25,000 years. Not that very-close-to-manlike animals date only from this geologically recent period: only that other hominids, classifiable as other species of *homo* (such as the Neanderthals, Java Man, Peking Man) give no indication of having survived on earth beyond that time. Manlike animals, with erect posture, bipedal gait, complex brain, rudiments of culture and probably also language, go back, by current estimates, at least to the early Pleistocene period, as much as a million years ago, or more. (The hesitancy and qualification of such statements is

for all of mankind with only local variation in miniscule and largely non-adaptive details.

What kind of animal is man? In terms of evolution, this:

Man is a *vertebrate*—an animal that has solved the combined problems of support, protection, and speed-and-mobility by the development of an internal bony segmented skeleton, a necessary condition for the later development of larger-sized land-living animals.

Man is a *mammal*—the animal that "invented" warm-bloodedness, the placenta, and mammary glands. That is, he is a land-living animal adapted by its warm-bloodedness to many different climes; versatile in diet; multiplying, with great economy, by dimorphous sexual reproduction, protecting and feeding the developing young in the intra-uterine unity of mother and child, then violently expelling the neonate into the strange and different world, re-establishing the unity (only in part) in the suckling at the breast; then succoring the young through a relatively long learning-dependency period. This is an animal that has embarked upon much greater interindividual dependency than to be found in "lower" forms of vertebrates. Further, it is an animal with a much larger brain, both absolutely and relatively to body size, a vastly greater speed of nervous impulses, and greater complexity of nervous coordination, than its evolutionary predecessors. Together these mean vastly greater awareness and reactivity.

Among the mammals, man is a *primate*. These mammals developed, probably originally as protection against land-living reptilian predators, a tree-living mode of life and adaptations to it that were enormously significant in the development of man; the tree-living primate is a brachiating, handed, vertical animal, the hands becoming important not only for locomotion through the trees, but also for feeding a no-longer grasping mouth. The snout recedes, the sense of smell declines, the face becomes relatively vertical and flat, and sight becomes the great significant sense: eyes become frontal and on the same plane, and stereoscopic and color vision appear. The teats, reduced to two, are now in breasts in a chest position, the infant clings to its mother's torso to feed, and the mother can now feed the single baby in her arms, as no non-primate mammalian mother can. Fewer

necessary. Physical anthropology is riddled with controversies about the exact relationship of the various "fossil men" to each other and to the ancestry of modern man, as a comparison of any three or four current general texts in physical anthropology will readily reveal.)

young are born (multiple births are rare), and better care of them (an evolutionary necessity) is associated with a lengthening of the period of dependency of the young and with attendance on and protection of mother and young by the adult male, due to non-seasonal sexual interest in the female, which in turn is related to the year-round availability of food supply in the tropical forest environment for these largely vegetarian animals. In the evolution of the primates, from lemurs to monkeys to apes to man, we find a number of trends significant for the nature of the human animal. The period of gestation gets longer; the young at birth are progessively smaller, more helpless, and more immature; the length of the period of dependency on the mother increases; a longer time is needed before the young are able to locomote on their own; the suckling period gets longer and longer; more time is needed for the young to achieve social independence from the adults; sexual maturity is progressively delayed; and the life span of the individual animal constantly increases. Correspondingly, as the brain further increases in size and complexity, we have animals more interindividually dependent and with a generally more complicated and sensitive responsiveness to the world around them, including, ever more importantly, other members of the species.

Man is a very special *kind* of primate, abandoning tree life but keeping its special "gains," developing a fully erect posture and two-footed gait with specialized walking feet. He is subject to an even more infantile vulnerability. Most important, man is the first in evolution with a very special power, *speech*.

How, when, and where this all happened, expert interpreters are not at all agreed, since the fossil and related evidence is scattered and meager and open to multiple reconstructions. According to one recent and highly imaginative and integrative interpretation,[2] the process may have been something like this:

Tree-living primate ancestors of both the modern apes and man living in the East African forests faced an ecological crisis in the Miocene age (the geological period estimated as about 28 to 12 million years ago). Due to climatic changes, the forests receded and gave way to open grassy savanna. In the competitive struggle for the declining forest territories, weaker bands of these apes ("proto-hominoids") were forced to the edges of the groves and thence to

[2] Charles Hockett and Robert Ascher, "The Human Revolution," *Current Anthropology*, Vol. 5, No. 3, June 1964, pp. 135-47.

migrate across open savanna in quest of other grove territory in which to continue their traditional arboreal and vegetarian existence. With the further recession of the forests, such grove-to-grove treks became progressively longer, producing an increasing premium on these apes' developing a more fully bipedal mode of locomotion (possible but only intermittently used by their ancestors) and hence on the development of the characteristically human foot (the only important human bodily specialization). This bipedality and the related fully erect posture were adaptive not only for locomotion, but also for two other significant reasons: the value of being able to see predators over the savanna grasses, and of being able to free the already prehensile hands for carrying weapons, first of defense against the existing larger mammal predators, later of offense against other (especially large) animals now objects of predation. As the forests continued to recede, the "failures" who were forced out had in time to accept the savannas as their necessary habitat, and therefore to adapt to it, and the predatory conditions in it. Occasional tool- and weapon-carrying of the tree ancestors and relatives now became a constant necessity, and weapons of defense became weapons of offense as these "waifs," to survive in the new environment, became hunters themselves and changed from the vegetarian diet of the trees to the carnivorous or omnivorous diet of the new life. *Carrying* thus produced the "hunting revolution," and the "failures" of the forest struggle were on their way to evolving into men. Carrying of weapons, and carrying of food, frees the mouth and the teeth, an essential for the development of language. The hunting of larger animals, made possible by the carrying of first ad-hoc then deliberately manufactured weapons, in turn requires social cooperation and coordination. Hand-signaling is not feasible if hands are carrying weapons or food or infants. Meanwhile visual attention is focused on the prey and on other hunters. Therefore, the most feasible communication must be *auditory*. Hence, selective survival chances go to those bands who further develop an already existing primate system of vocal *calls* (something like that of the present-day gibbon). Why would such a system of calls need to be further elaborated, in a direction that leads to language? Because social organization would necessarily have become more complex under conditions of collective hunting of larger game animals, with its concomitant of a larger range of food-sharing, and hence a wider range of "socialization" among the band members. It is assumed that these members would have to have moved in bands of some size (ten to thirty or so), for singly or in very small groups they would have had very poor chances of surviving against larger and more powerful predators better adapted to the savanna environment. They would also have transferred to the new environment habits of territoriality that such apes tend to have in the trees: that is, a safe home base surrounded by a not clearly bounded food-getting territory. Further, the adaptive development of fully erect posture (that is, those who developed this feature had a better chance of surviving than those who did not) also brought about physical changes in the structure of the head, brain, face, jaws, and "organs of speech" that made distinctively human speech possible.

The development of true language from an ape-type call system might have occurred in the following fashion: Calls are discrete vocal signals, each communicating a total Gestalt of a situation, such as food, danger, location of the caller. The first step would be the *blending* of two different calls into a new composite, for example a new call indicating food *and* danger, using one constituent part of each of the old calls. While such blending must have occurred fortuitously thousands of times in the earlier tree life, without being taken up and transmitted through the band, the new and socially more complex savanna life would put a premium upon the development of such innovations. Blending then institutes a process of *building* composite signals out of separate meaningful parts. (Linguists call this changing a *closed* system into an *open* one.) This opening up must have taken thousands of years, but once accomplished, it is revolutionary. Now communication demands detailed conventions that cannot possibly be transmitted through the genes (presumably the main mechanism in earlier systems) and *must* be learned. Therefore, there is natural selection for greater learning capacity, hence of the bases, in brain structure, for such capacity. Opening up the system also involves *displacement*: that is, it makes possible (something increasingly *necessary* in more complex social life) talking about things out of sight, in the past or future, or purely hypothetical, which is parallel to the elements of foresight and memory involved in carrying a weapon for which one has no immediate use. Each of these mental habits reinforces the other, and each is reciprocally related to the process of tool or weapon *manufacture*, as distinct from carrying sticks or stones used as tools. During this process, probably taking hundreds of generations, the head-face-vocal apparatus structure is changed to a form like that of modern man, the use of such blended-call pre-language increases the innervation of the vocal tract and enriches the cortical representation of that region. This sets the stage for the final development to language.

As pre-language develops, the number of different call-blends increases to a point where it becomes difficult to distinguish some of them from others. Then by mutation some individuals start to listen to and to articulate these call-Gestalten not as total units, but in terms of smaller constituent elements, discretely produced and heard, in varying arrangements. Thus, the distinction between sound units (what linguists call "phonemes") and collections of sound units that have minimum unit of *meaning* ("morphemes") is made. With this we have true language.

We now have man: the creator and creature of *culture*, man the animal with *language*, and, hence, man the animal who has gone *beyond* biological evolution.

The last stage in the development from an apelike ancestor to man is both a biological and a cultural process and involves in a complex intercausality all the elements that make man distinctively "human": the use of hands to carry and use things like sticks and stones as tools and weapons and then to *make* tools and weapons, with which in turn man *transforms* the environment rather than merely adapting to it; the freeing of the hands by the development of the specialized human foot; the transformation of man's ecological place dependent on both of these and the whole complex of hunting, its social organization, and the related social and sexual band relationships; the transformation and freeing of the face and mouth and head and brain; the development of more complex cortical processes; the increased duration and dependency of human infancy and the relation of this to the whole complex learning process that makes human beings human.

Another important by-product of man's erect posture, the change from a dorsal to a frontal position in sexual intercourse,[3] has profound implications for human sexuality and the psychosexual development of the child, with which we shall be much concerned in the sections that follow. This change is related to the sheer engineering changes in man's body that the bipedal erect posture produced.

[3] Of course, various positions have been retained by man, but it is probably true that only man among the mammals uses the frontal position.

(Presumably the enlargement of the gluteus maximus thus produced made the old primate dorsal position awkward and fostered the invention of the frontal position, probably unique to human beings). This position puts the adult male mate in the same position to the female as the suckling infant, and probably thereby enhances the diffusion and complication of the two kinds of sexual feelings of the female—toward infant and toward mate—which had probably already begun with the non-seasonal year-round sexuality of primates in tree life. The importance of this phenomenon for the Oedipus complex is one of the great pan-human problems. On the part of the adult male, the changed coital position probably has a great bearing on the characteristically human development of *paternal* feelings toward the offspring, the like of which we find in no other mammals. And it is patently important in the phenomenon of Oedipal rivalries, from the point of view of the *husband-father*.

La Barre[4] also suggests, that the changed coital position also means a change in the role of the female in controlling the situation of sexual encounter. Whereas the primate female in dorsal position in effect controls the sexual situation, the human female in supine frontal position, if solitary, is vulnerable to any sexual encounter with the (usually) physically stronger male. This would help to explain the development of institutions of male dominance, sexual possessiveness, familial "protectiveness" of the male toward the mate as well as the offspring and also the necessity for sexual rules. Hunting males need social cooperation, which unregulated sexuality would easily disrupt.

The implications of the evolution toward modern man ramify in all directions.[5]

When was this process completed? The scholars whose work we have just summarized suggest by the *beginning* of the Pleistocene period (that is, roughly a million years ago).[6] That is, *man* had

[4] Weston La Barre, "Comment on Hockett-Ascher's paper on 'The Human Revolution,'" *Current Anthropology*, Vol. 5, No. 3, June 1964, p. 148.

[5] For a further discussion of implications of the Hockett-Ascher theory, see Robert Endleman, "Reflections on The Human Revolution," *The Psychoanalytic Review*, Summer 1966, Vol. 53, No. 2, pp. 1-24.

[6] It is to be noted that other experts disagree. Leakey, for example, who made many of the most important recent fossil finds in Africa, including Zinjanthropus, estimates a date of around one and three-quarters to *two* million years ago, for a being that is *essentially* man (though the fossil finds cannot give conclusive evidence about speech). Other authorities, by contrast, think that full human language may not have developed until as late as 40,000 years ago. See, for

evolved by that time, taking as man: a generalized primate with one specialization (the human foot), with fully erect posture and two-footed gait, stereoscopic and color vision, very complex hand-eye-brain coordinations, a large, complex brain, great learning capacity, the use and manufacture of tools, and *language*.

This, then, is an "ape with a difference"—an ape even more attuned to social life, an ape born even more vulnerable and in need of succor and care and teaching, an ape even more sociable than his forebears and cousins, an ape even more dependent, during an infancy and childhood even more prolonged.

At the same time, strangely enough, this is an ape that seems to be *arrested* at a more infantile stage and, paradoxically, because of this, open to far greater possibilities of learning and intricacies of response. This "infantilized ape" preserves into adulthood, even into old age, features that in his evolutionary forebears appeared in embryo or in postpartum infancy but then disappeared. This ape has remained more generalized, more primitive, than his contemporary collateral relatives (chimpanzee, gorilla, orangutan, and perhaps gibbon) and at the same time become much more complex, rich in potential, and more vulnerable than they. His infancy is even more prolonged than theirs and increasingly vulnerable to the vicissitudes of getting along with one's kin and kind. This is an ape who depends throughout his life, more than any ape before, on his *group* existence. We need each other, and our common life, as no other animals have ever needed each other before. We need each other just to survive, we need each other to be human. More than any other animal, man continues to depend on the network of cooperation and mutual aid of others of his species, through all his achievements and masteries. Man is the most social of animals—out of desperate need and exuberant play. Alone as neonate, he could never survive. Alone, even as adult, the cumulations of a culture inside his skull, he would still find survival tough. Bodily he has none of the protections and offensive weapons other animals have evolved for themselves in nature's grim struggle for the scarcities of the universe. His strength is puny beside the boar; his speed a snail's beside the mountain cat; in sea to sharks he's easy prey; an eagle's claws, a rattler's fangs, even

---

a stimulating discussion by many anthropologists, all in one place, the various commentaries on the Hockett-Ascher paper in the same issue of *Current Anthropology* in which their paper appeared (Vol. 5, No. 3, June 1964, pp. 147-68).

the quills of porcupine can maim or quite demolish him. Yet he has more than survived; he has all but conquered a planet. Social life and culture have taken man *beyond* biological evolution.

Man is an infantilized ape in two senses: one, the extraordinary prolongation of infancy and childhood dependency in man; two, the retention into adulthood, in the human animal, of traits that are infantile or embryonic in lower species, in particular in the other higher primates. In the progression from other mammals to other primates to man the duration of gestation increases, the typical number of offspring per birth declines, the period from birth to sexual maturity increases, and even more dramatically, the period from birth to full adult growth increases. Furthermore, the long prenatal period and the protracted and helpless infancy are prerequisites for the ultimately high development of the nervous system and mental powers.

With man's great reproductive economy, heightened further by the advancements of culture, his precocious and lifelong sexuality must be seen as a kind of "surplus sexuality" or "discretionary sexuality" (to borrow concepts from economics) and, as La Barre points out, very significantly so for the *social* life of man. Freud, of course, has taught us to see this close linkage of the social and the sexual, the simplified formulation of which is to say *all* social ties are basically libidinal ties. Sexuality, including the basic components of adult sexuality, is present at birth and persists as a lifelong component of what makes us human. It is probable that man's further development of primate verticality (derived from the conditions of arboreal life) into a more completely frontal approach to the world (the totally upright posture and gait), extending this to the frontal position in coitus, so that *all* relationships, mate to mate as well as parent to child are face-to-face relationships, are in the background of man's particularly polymorphous *sexual-sociality*. These connections, in turn, are linked with two other human phenomena: *language* and *play*. Language is an oral activity, most intensively developed in face-to-face contacts (in contrast with a call system, which operates primarily at a distance). Perhaps then the frontal position in coitus has as much to do with the development of language, as the savanna hunting organization. In turn, language is linked to the development of human sexuality through the phenomenon of *play*. Man's infantile sexuality is more persistent and consequential through life than the sexuality of any other animal. Other animals grow up, *un*learn to play; *man never does*. This is his burden and his glory. And too, this is another meaning of man's being an infantilized ape.

Compared to other mammals, other primates, man has a peculiar sexuality. Infancy is polymorphous. At five, children are capable of adult genital acts and the female of producing ova. However, reproduction almost always waits for nubility. Besides, the sexual drive is extravagantly out of line with reproductive necessity (especially in this reproductively very efficient and economical animal)—only a very minute portion of it being requisite for the continuity of the species. The rest (most of it) is in effect a "surplus" open to multiple forms and potentially in the realm of freedom—that is, *play*. Eros binds us each to all, in possibility. But everywhere we find it formed, shaped, narrowed, directed, and tied in multiple and divergent ways to many different *social* forms. The peculiar hiatus between the genitally capable five-year-old and the turbulent adolescent (a gap peculiar to man) stands as a specially human juvenile age, a span a tenth to an eighth of the total human span of life, when the child turns from more direct sexuality to the learnings of the objective and social world, his capacities especially open to the secular world of man. This is the time when a vast amount of the apparatus of culture is learned and the child becomes the kind of human being that is his culture's own.

The late Géza Róheim, one of the rare scholars who has actively combined psychoanalysis and anthropology, states the case for considering man an "infantilized ape" in the following passage:

Man as an Infantilized Ape

GÉZA RÓHEIM

The enormous discrepancy in the age of *sexual maturity* and full growth is striking when we compare man to the other animals. . . . If human development is slowed down as compared to other animals, the ultimate effect of the slowing down would be that certain infantile traits are permanently retained. . . . [The] Dutch anatomist L. Bolk . . . believes that he has found a new evolutionary principle valid for other beings as well but which he applies specifically to human. . . . Some aspects of human anatomy are adaptive. . . . Others he calls primary, and he enumerates orthognathy, hairlessness, loss of pigmentation in skin, hair and eyes, the shape of the ear, the "mongoloid fold," the central position

Reprinted with permission from Géza Róheim, Psychoanalysis and Anthropology *(New York: International Universities Press, 1950), pp. 400-04.*

of the foramen magnum, weight of the brain, persistence of sutures, the labia majora of the woman, the construction of hand and foot, the form of the pelvis, the ventral position of the vagina, and certain variations of the jaw and the sutures. "Considering these variations in the light of the ontogeny of the primates, we come to the conclusion that they all represent fetal states that have been retained by mankind. Phenomena that were transitory in the ape have become permanent in man. The other primates go through periods in their evolution in which they are not followed by man. . . ." (L. Bolk, *Das Problem der Menschwerdung*, Jena, 1926, pp. 1-6.) In a somewhat condensed form, Bolk's thesis is that man is a primate foetus that has attained sexual maturity. If a fetal quality becomes gradually permanent, there must be an inhibitory factor that prevents the normal process of ontogenesis. . . . Bolk assumes that the cause must be endocrinological. The hormones that increase or decrease growth function differently in human beings and in anthropoid apes. "A hippopotamus is mature at the age of four before humans have shed their milk teeth. *In the prolonged symbiosis of the child with his parents we have the reason why human beings live in families, and in this prolonged co-existence of two generations we have the biological basis of social life.*" (Bolk, p. 20; Róheim's italics). . . . Most significant, however, is the fact that the Soma is more retarded than the Germa, so that within the frame of our general retardation *our sexuality is relatively precocious.*

The sexual pattern is present in infants before the gonadal hormone is produced in adequate quantities. Perloff tells us that the sexual pattern of infants includes the three important patterns of adult sexual behavior, tumescence of the organ, rhythmic pelvic thrusts and the intense neuromuscular reaction known as orgasm. These patterns must therefore be present in the infant at birth. [W. H. Perloff, "Role of the Hormones in Human Sexuality," *Psychosomatic Medicine*, XI (1949) p. 138.]

The female ovum is practically fully developed at the early age of five, but the body is not ready yet to live up to the consequences of this development. Whereas, in general, the achievement of maturity in sex means also that the organism has completed its growth, there is a very different situation in mankind, where the body lags behind the sex impulse. The fact that the female ovum is ready at the age of five, which corresponds to the sexual maturation of anthropoid apes, indicates that there must have been a period in the life of our pre-human ancestors in which they were fully mature at this early age. (Bolk, *op. cit.*, pp. 24, 25). A change in nourishment, such as a transition from the herbivorous to the omnivorous or carnivorous stage, may have led to modifications of the endocrine system. We represent our ancestors in their infant stage and the process of retardation is still going on. (Bolk, pp. 40, 44). . . .

[J]uvenilization is a necessary condition but not a complete explanation of civilization.

DISCUSSION

Note, in the above passage, "Bolk assumes that the cause [of the inhibitory factor responsible for the fetalization of man] must be endocrinological." The basis for such endocrine change could be a change in *diet*. And a change of diet is precisely what the apelike ancestors of man must have undergone in their transformation from the Miocene "rejects" to man: that is, a change from the herbivorous diet of the tree-living primates to the carnivorous or omnivorous one of our more human ancestors. This diet change, of course, did not just happen. It was itself a product of the whole complex of ecological, social, and body-structural changes outlined above.

2. LANGUAGE AND SYMBOLS

Man is the *talking* animal. Speech, symbolizing, consciousness, and history—these are especially human gifts. Man is an animal gloried and burdened with the problem of *consciousness*: we think; therefore we are. He also is an animal gloried and burdened with *history*: an ape who remembers and misremembers, tells and retells his story in all its ever-changing versions, exulting and agonizing both. Consciousness and history are, of course, impossible without *language*.

In the outline sketch above, we drew upon the recent work of two scholars who trace the evolution of man, with special reference to language. Language was traced to the blending of different items of a system of vocal calls, such as those of the present-day gibbons. This hypothetical picture, however, is incomplete. A lot of infra-human vocal communication is not by calls at all—for those are signals over a *distance*—but rather by a kind of "feckless play-chattering" [7] between individuals who are physically close, even in contact with each other. And these vocalizations are typically at much lower frequencies (pitch) and much lower amplitude (volume) than are call signals. Along with the blending of distance signal calls leading toward language, there must also have been a blending of elements from the

[7] The phrase is Weston La Barre's. See his "Comment" on the paper by Hockett and Ascher, "The Human Revolution," *op. cit.*, p. 150.

play chattering of our not-yet-human ancestors. The word "play" is used here advisedly. Play—the special arena in which so much of man's "surplus sexuality" can be expressed—was probably as vitally involved in the evolution of language as any harsh necessities such as an "emergency" requiring a call signaling the presence of both food and danger in the same situation. In the heightened interindividual dependency of our primate ancestors who came back down to the ground, and had to work out a new ecological adaptation to a different environment, interindividual empathy and communicability must have greatly increased and contexts of play must have been greatly extended and elaborated. This is the same period in which the becoming-human animal became progressively more juvenilized. Then the range, number, and variety of vocalizations increased, and play increased the chances for innovations among these vocalizations, in the form of blendings and recombinations. And the needs of the new situation "selected for" such innovations.

There are many kinds of pre-linguistic vocalization, and each of these has been adduced by one theorist or another as a candidate for *the* origin of language. One is imitation of sounds heard in the environment (the "bow-wow" theory of language origin). Another is emotive ejaculation (the "pooh-pooh" or "ai-yai-yai!" theory). Then there are expiratory sounds made to the accompaniment of physical exertions (the "yo-he-ho" theory). Another consists of exclamations in singsong spontaneously made in exultation of a successful feat (the "ta-ra-ra-boom-te-day!" theory). Still another includes sounds made by infants sucking or chewing at the mother's breast (the "chew" theory). To these can be added the whole repertory of non-linguistic sounds and exclamations any animals at all like human beings may make in carrying out any of the body processes (eating, eliminating, copulating, to name the classical Freudian triad, but also including scratching, rubbing, grooming the body). Any and all of these could have, in fact must have, contributed to the repertory of sounds in early proto-language. One of the processes by which these can develop into language is blending, as already discussed. Another is conventionalization. A particular sound comes to be regularly associated with a particular referent, at first by the close affinity between the sound and the activity or thing referred to. Later, when such phatic elements are blended and combined in ever more complex ways, the relationship between the sound combination and the thing referred to becomes purely conventional. There is no longer any obvious connection, and the association of sound and "thing" has to be learned.

Language is a product of the whole complex of body-structural and ecological adaptational habit changes that our proto-human primate ancestors must have undergone after being forced out of the trees by some such process as was postulated in the foregoing account. It is interrelated with the progressive juvenilization of man, the increase and generalization of sexuality, the increased interdependency and the corresponding premium on cooperation and communication, the great elaboration of the role of play, in turn connected with infantilization and with the increased parent-child ties.

Language is also importantly related to a specially human phenomenon, *repression*. For language introduces the concept of *negation* into vocal communication. For example, a call signal indicating food may have the elements ABCD. Another signifying danger may have the elements EFGH. A new situation including the presence of both food and danger may elicit a new blend call with the elements ABGH. Then ABCD comes to mean "food and *no* danger" and EFGH to mean "danger and *no* food." Thus, CD signifies "no danger" and EF signifies "no food." This is a radical innovation in communication. Since the concept of negation ("*no* food") does not exist in the unconscious,[8] we may hypothesize that it must have required some important psychic changes in our more apelike ancestors to enable this kind of conceptualization. Such change can be described as the capacity for *repression*. This may have been learned in the context of this changing animal's burgeoning sexuality, for the diffusion of sexual feelings from mother-infant to mate-mate, heightened by the new frontal position in copulation, could be expected to produce rivalries between the generations in the emerging proto-human family, requiring a strong internal mechanism for keeping in check or denying the sexual impulses involved—that is, repression.

Aside from the concept of negation, language is repressive in other ways. Language represents a codification of reality, the classification of experiences into a conventional set of categories which, in any one language, may be very different from those of another language. Such codifications represent a constriction upon experience, and a reduction and flattening of spontaneity of feeling. Every language constitutes a formal system of constructs and categories that constrain and

[8] See Sigmund Freud, "On Negation," *Collected Papers*, Vol. V, pp. 181-85.

channelize the confrontation with "reality" and makes difficult, if not impossible, certain kinds of playful verbal elaborations or recombinations. Therefore, language, though owing much to play in both its origins and in its later elaborations, is also antithetical to play, or put more broadly, to Eros, to the expression of basic libidinal feelings. (Poetry and myth do attempt to come to the rescue, showing Eros and play struggling to remold language more to their liking.) Hence language is a great liberating as well as constraining force on man.

Language, in effect, propels the ape into *consciousness*, and with consciousness, man begins to have a *history*.

Consciousness and history are themselves the *products* of group life, as they are part of its *conditions* in its human form. There is a progressive interplay here: more complex group life demands and creates more complex communication. Emotive cries of gibbon's hoots are added to, reinforced, enlarged, and modified by the special human gift, the ability to symbolize. This requires a more developed brain, with cortex rich and convolute. Symbolizing represents a giant leap from biological evolution to culture as the unique way of man. It gives man a store of learning vastly greater than ever possible before. It frees man from the tyranny of the here and now. Signs are rooted to their attendant scene. Symbols open up communication about past and future, about absent, hypothetical, contingent, or merely imagined events. Symbolic learning also releases man from depending on the immediate personal teachers in the here and now, the common situation of infant mammals learning from adults in other species.

Man is the *talking* animal—the infantilized ape orally instructing and admonishing his even more infantile young. Here is the ape who has learned to tell tales—of man and other animals; the world around; of the mysterious, terrifying, and wonderful forces in the world; of love and hate and need and satisfaction; of fear and joy; of life and death; of yearning, disappointment, grief, and play; of sun and moon and stars and tides, desert, forest, sea and polar wastes; of rain and drought, of snows and cloudless skies; of the brilliance of day and fearsome dark of night; of the changing of the seasons; of gods and heroes, and devils and fools among men and their animal kin; of strange and terrible and funny events; of the intriguing chanciness of life; of mating-love, of carrying and birth; of growth and the mysterious ripening of breasts and loins, of the awesome, funny and ever-intriguing bonds and rifts between the female and the male. Here emerges man, a very special ape, the first animal to *tell* about himself, make and create and invent a history, see the world and tell it true and askew, the first animal capable of telling his offspring all manner of stories, truths and lies, jokes and solemn absurdities. This verbal world is entwined and mixed forever with experience, molding and distorting memory and anticipation.

Humanity can be said to begin with the *cultural* crystallization of the pre-human family of mother, offspring, and the attendant sexually interested male, through symbolic learning. Speech and verbal consciousness infinitely extended the domain of mastery and experience achieved by our tool-making man-ape ancestors.

There are interconnections among a number of conditions that characterize specifically human existence. Biologically man is extremely dependent, as neonate, as infant, as child, and also as adult. Man's sexuality is precocious, persistent, non-seasonal, and lifelong, and is the fulcrum of his social life. With his complex brain and neural system, man has enormous learning potentiality. Language and symbolism gives him great potential for extending himself. With tools and fire, he can use and remake the world of earth, of other animals, and others of himself. He has capacity to invent, to master, to fantasize, to make up tales, to create a past, to imagine a future. He can play with thought and words, gambol with the exuberance of possibility, cry a defiant denial to death. And he can and does band together in a great variety of social forms, achieving in collectives what individual could do alone.

Man's infantilization, his permanent sexuality, ever taking him back to infancy (ontogenetic and phylogenetic both), and the peculiar di-phasic onset of this sexuality, infantile and pubertal, with the important latency phase between: these are tied up with the *social* and *cultural* nature of man. Other animals have social organization. Some at much lower evolutionary levels have a rather complex one, such as termites and ants, and some have forms suggestive of man, with a certain degree of intercommunication approaching a human quality, as in the other primates. But man is eminent in the combination of social organization and *learned* culture: acquired symbolic learning created and re-created and perpetually both renewed and transformed from generation to generation. The pressing interindividual dependency of man—his weakness—has its other side of strength: the enormous learning potential and the great if not infinite variability of social and cultural forms open to man's possibility.

3. CULTURE AND THE FAMILY DRAMA

Culture is the pan-human universal. It is the *ways* in which the pan-human unconscious core is expressed in an array of superficial variations that come down to a very limited number of underlying typical patterns, and these are carried through from generation to generation. Such continuity derives not only from the deliberate and conscious teaching of new generations by the older generations, but also, and more significantly, from the deeper communication of unspoken feelings, assumptions and premises about the world, carried on from parent to child, especially during the pre-verbal period of infancy. Communication of that kind occurs before the child has a chance to learn to mouth the culturally patterned ideas of our conscious verbalizations. It relies instead upon the deeper unspoken communication of body and emotion, in the way a mother holds a child, the joy or anger in her voice, the body postures and gestures, the touch-feeling of bodies to each other, the thousand physical signs of tension or relaxation.

Culture, in its most general sense, is a universal human phenomenon. Culture is both persistence and transcendence of human limitations. It shows persistence in the ways in which all cultures are manifestations of and ways of dealing with the crying dependencies and frustrations of the infantile situation, which stay with us in some forms throughout our lives and continue to be expressed through the mazes of specific cultural manifestations. Culture is also transcendence: man's evolutionary jump, man's stretching of himself to be something beyond the infant, something reaching for that omnipotence which is the other side of the infantile helplessness and the persistent and sustaining fantasy of man as a striving, creating being. Cultures are of course vastly (though not infinitely) diverse, as Ruth Benedict and other anthropologists have so eloquently demonstrated. But beneath this great diversity there are also remarkable similarities. It is these universal elements we want to emphasize here, for they push us back to the problem of universal human nature the relativists have been trying to avoid. The universals of culture deal with pan-human existential problems rooted in human biology, the place of man in evolution, the universal features of dealing with physical environments on this particular planet, and most importantly of all, the universal severely limited set of human relationships that human beings face everywhere in time and place.

Culture means complex adaptations to difficult situations and contingencies. It means the creation of special "worlds" of experience that are not given or predetermined by the terrain of the surrounding natural non-human world. Only man creates this special world—and all the special problems it entails. Culture means the creation of myths and lies, poetry and science, distortions and illusions, which "are" reality for the communicants. Man is pre-eminent in his capacity to tell himself things that are not so, and to make himself psychically ill. He is unique in his capacities for irrational ferocity as in his accumulated destructive power. These are fruits and costs of culture. Without culture, however, he is nothing, an animal uniquely unprotected against ferocities in the rest of nature and without resources to survive and build.

INFANCY AND THE FAMILY*

Culture sets the scene of the infancy situation and in turn is molded by it. The universality of the human infancy situation includes these elements: dependency, the push of sexual need, and some degree of frustration, rivalry, and conflict. The parents themselves are rooted, intrapsychically, in their own childhood experiences of dependency, rivalry and frustration. This continuity gives to all children a common unconscious core and common, pan-human social dilemmas. Consequently, these problems persist from generation to generation.

Because of the extreme dependency of the infant on the primary

* A note to professional readers: In this section and the following we present some basic propositions about the psychic, social, and cultural nature of the situation of infancy and childhood that have universal or nearly universal application. Of necessity the formulations are broad and leave aside many empirical variations and (at least apparent) contradictions, many of which are however dealt with in discussions of empirical case studies in the later chapters of the book. The formulations given here are this author's attempt at a distillation of several decades of work by psychoanalysts and anthropologists. Some professional readers may of course find such statements assertive or dogmatic: I would refer them to the relevant literature and point out that this present work makes no claim to final and definitive formulations. Nor is an attempt being made to include all possible conflicting views. Rather there is an attempt to offer a provisional synthesis of those lines of work this writer has found most fruitful in understanding the puzzles of personality and society. In this chapter reference is made to one major anthropological argument with the Freudian view—that of Malinowski on the Oedipus complex—and an attempt is made to confront its propositions. The discussion is not, of course, to be taken as a comprehensive account of anthropological discussions on this matter, but only to indicate the main lines of the confrontation; specific issues involved are explored from several different angles through the case studies and discussions in later chapters of the book.

social objects, the ways of becoming a social being (one meaning of "human nature") are developed in the infant's social relations with the crucial persons in the infant's life—typically, the members of the nuclear family. The nuclear family—mother and children and mother's current mate—is found in nearly all known societies. For all practical purposes it is a universal feature of human societies.[9] Of course, in many (primarily primitive) societies there are important kin ties for the child in addition to the nuclear family, such as uni-lineal kin groups (clans) or extended family structures of varying kinds. But even in these cases the nuclear family tends to be the *primary* setting for the earliest care and nurturing of the infant, the later infancy socialization, and much if not most of the later child-hood training. First and foremost, the family is the *emotional* crucible for the child.

Here the infant enters from birth into a highly intense emotional relationship with a very small number of important persons, mother and father[10] and a limited number of siblings. These are the "significant others" of his early life. As such they are likely to be significant to him in his own inner functioning for the rest of his life.

[9] Anthropologists have found a few apparent exceptions. See E. Kathleen Gough, "Is the Family Universal?—The Nayar Case," *Journal of the Royal Anthropological Institute*, Vol. LXXXIX, 1959, Part I. Reprinted in Norman W. Bell and Ezra F. Vogel (eds.), *A Modern Introduction to the Family* (New York: Free Press of Glencoe, 1960) pp. 76-92. "The Nayars . . . had a kin-ship system in which the elementary family of father, mother and children was not institutionalized as a legal, productive, distributive, residential, social-izing, or consumption unit. . . . Even when physiological paternity was known with reasonable certainty, the genitor had no economic, social, legal or ritual rights in, nor obligations to, his children, after he had once paid the fees of their births." (The genitor was a temporary visiting mate of the woman, not the ritual husband she acquired at puberty.) Even this case, however, is not an exception to the generalization that there are some adult males important in the socialization of the child: in this case, they are the menfolk of the mother's matrilineal clan. A recent, modern and well-known instance of severe limitation (though not abolition) of the nuclear family's functions is that of the Kibbutz communal agricultural settlements in Israel, discussed in detail in Chapter Two of this book.

[10] For purposes of this analysis "mother" should be read to refer to "mother-surrogate" if any adult female other than the biological mother actually carries on the mothering role to the child; the term "mother" is used simply to avoid having to repeat the awkward phrase "mother or mother-surrogate" or some such term as "mothering-person" (which could in fact refer to a male). Similarly "father" stands for "father or father-surrogate" (often a stepfather) but means specifically the *sexual mate* of the mother, and will not be used to refer simply to a male who has *authority* over the child—for example, a mother's brother in matrilineal systems, if he is not also the mate of the mother.

This nuclear family is rooted in the biology of man: in the double sexuality of the mother—toward husband and toward child; in her relative incapacity for other tasks such as getting food or shelter during pregnancy and the early period of infant care; in her relative unproductiveness and vulnerability during these periods; and in the male's constant non-seasonal sexual interest in the female, most conveniently and consistently satisfied by a particular constant mate. The specific tasks of child care may be delegated and diffused in a variety of ways. The "mother" for the child may in fact be a series of "surrogates" rather than the biological mother, or a group of related females including the biological mother, for example, a group of co-wives in a polygynous household, or a group of female kin of the mother. Still in most cases there is one adult female who is the *central* or *focal* "mother" for the child—and typically society has explicitly linked biological motherhood with the mothering tasks of care and emotional loving response to the infant and child.[11]

Motherhood is a certainty; fatherhood only a probability. Still, *social* fatherhood—defined most generally as being the mate of the mother—is a very definite and well-nigh universal fact of human societies. That this has no necessary connection with biological paternity can be seen in those societies like the Trobriand Islanders and the aboriginal tribes of Australia where the connection between copulation and conception is not recognized.[12] There, in what seems to be an inconsistency, we find disapproval of illegitimate birth and a great importance attached to the role of the father in family life.

The nuclear family has persisted through all of known human history, and probably all the way from our proto-human ancestors, to guess from other primates, and from primitive societies at the lowest technological levels. It has persisted through all kinds of supplementary variations (clan organizations, extended families), through the

[11] While it is partly an ethnocentric bias of our system to regard the claims of the "natural" mother who has been separated from her child, as superior to those of a foster mother who has actually "raised" the child, this may in fact not be far from the statistical norm for all human societies. There are tribes, for example, where a group of sisters united in matrilineal descent and matrilocal residence, share much of each other's child rearing, and are called "mother" by the children of all of them. Even in these instances a clear distinction is made for and by the child between the "real" (biological) mother and the "clan" (classificatory) mothers.

[12] See Bronislaw Malinowski, *The Sexual Life of Savages in Northwest Melanesia* (London: Routledge & Kegan Paul, 1929) and Géza Róheim, *Psychoanalysis and Anthropology* (New York: International Universities Press, 1950).

whole range of marriage forms (polygyny, polyandry, even combinations of both, as well as monogamy), and through many apparent
abolitions (Kibbutz, "free love" in the post-revolutionary Soviet
Union, "children for the State" in Nazi Germany, to mention only
recent examples). This persistence should lead us to be skeptical of
predictions of any radical changes in humanity in this sphere.

The nuclear family (or some very good "functional equivalent")
seems to be necessary for the neonate human animal to *become* a
human being. Not only physical survival, but also the development
of distinctively human characteristics of emotional responsiveness
and communication depend on the intense "phatic" [13] ties of parents
and child—as the negative cases of isolated children[14] make abundantly clear.

The child must become human as a member of one sex in a two-
sex human world. He does this through intense relationships with a
critical adult of each sex in his infancy and childhood. The number
of combinations of family composition is extremely limited, and the
basic situation is a triangle of child, same-sex parent, and opposite-
sex parent.

As Freud has taught us, the intense feelings of dependency, longing, and "love" of the child toward the parent (either sex), as well
as the positive feelings of parent toward child, are erotic in nature,
and the "family drama" (or otherwise viewed, the personality development of the child) is an erotic one. Freud also showed us that the
sexuality of the infant is "polymorphous-perverse"—that is, like
other aspects of the infant's drives and wishes, diffuse, global, undifferentiated, involving the whole organism, attachable to *any* kind
of object, human of either sex and any age, other animal or in fact
inanimate objects or forces as well, and capable of being gratified by
almost any kind of contact with any part of the body of the child.
This infantile diffuseness and versatility in sexuality is part of the

[13] I have adopted this useful term in the sense given it by Weston La
Barre: "Phatic communication . . . communicates a generalized emotional
tone [rather than making] . . . genuine or verifiable statements about the
structure of the universe." La Barre, *op. cit.* pp. 57-58. Gibbons' cries are
phatic, so is human babbling at a cocktail party, as well as most of the human
mother's vocalizations to her infant. La Barre elaborates the significance of
this kind of communication at many points throughout his book.

[14] See, for the best authenticated case, Kingsley Davis, "Extreme Social
Isolation of a Child," *American Journal of Sociology*, Vol. 45, 554-65, and
"Final Note on a Case of Extreme Isolation," *American Journal of Sociology*,
Vol. 52, 1947, pp. 432-37.

basic heritage of man, contributing to his complex elaborations of culture and social organization—and at the same time contributing to conflict, unreason, and tension in social life. Both clinical and comparative anthropological findings abound with evidence that the infantilism of this earliest stage of life persists in us all (in all societies, no matter how "advanced") as the underlife of culture and as the underpinnings of all man's vitality, creativity, and play. This is another meaning of the statement that "Man is an infantilized ape."

The infant's demands are total, immediate, and absolutistic: "All I want is all there is and then some—and right now!" An infant lives in a world of both helplessness and omnipotence. The fantasy of magical control over the universe (a recurrent dream of adult men and cultures throughout the world) lives side by side with the infant's extreme dependency—again echoed in the recurrent cultural wish to be totally taken care of by an infinitely benevolent and nurturant parent-deity who will right all the wrongs of the world, erase all pains and ills, and save us all.

The absolutism of the infant's dependency wishes produces a universal dilemma. No society in the world has ever been able to satisfy such absolutistic wish, and none ever could. Hence, no matter what efforts may be made in particular societies to attend to the infant's "needs" as fully as possible, there is bound to be some element of frustration. A primary frustration is, of course, the one Freud emphasized: that the libidinal ties of parent and child conflict with the libidinal ties of the parental pair. The basic triangle of the human drama is child–mother–and mother's mate. Put another way, at the roots of human experience is the conflict of dependency-sexuality and sharing-sexuality. It is also doubtful that sharing-sexuality of mature adults can ever be completely free of elements of the dependency-sexuality of parent-child, for the parents themselves must have become human through the dramatic encounters of the early childhood ties, with their great overloading on the side of dependency.

SEXUALITY AND THE NUCLEAR FAMILY

The sexuality-dependency dilemmas of the child may be summarized as follows:

The male child is involved in a deep sex-dependency relationship with the mother. The father in sexual possession of the mother (albeit in a different, adult, mode of sexual expression) detracts from the mother's sexual-nurturing attentions to the son and is thus a rival for the mother's attentions. This is a scarcity situation. The mother has only so much "love" to pass around: the more the father gets, the less the son gets, and vice versa. (At least this is, deductively, the way the child sees the situation, and often enough the father, even consciously, defines it this way.) The wish of the son is to have the mother exclusively, and the way to accomplish this is to get rid of the father. The incest taboo intervenes and suppresses and mitigates the extremity of the mother's expression of sexual feeling toward the son, and in time *he* must learn to abandon the wish for exclusive sexual rights to the mother—and, in a sense, to sexual rights to her altogether. He must learn, however, to maintain the *sex* of the libidinal object but to change the *form of expression* from oral-dependent to genital-sharing and also, partially, to reverse the dependency roles so that as husband or lover *he* is nurturer as well as nurtured. The conflict created by the infantile desire to sexually monopolize the mother and kill the father, with the culture's taboos on incest and parricide, Freud called the Oedipus Complex, and he regarded it as universal for mankind.

The problem for the *female child* is different. She may maintain the dependency *mode* of the relationship in learning adult ways of sexuality, but she must change not only the person but also the sex of the person who is the object of the sexuality. Probably aided by sexual responsiveness of the father to her, which in most cultures is regarded more permissively than the sexual responsiveness of mother toward son, the female child in the "normal" path of development transfers her dependency-sexual cravings from the mother to the father and later on from him to other men. In the stage of cravings for the father, and consequent sexual rivalry to the mother, the girl undergoes the female version of the Oedipus complex. This, as for the boy, must be repressed as the cultural taboos on incest and matricide are imposed.

In each case, the child has to learn to give up a specific person who is the sexual object and later transfer these feelings to another person of that sex but distinguished from the earlier object in two important ways: it must be someone outside the nuclear family and outside any extended kin lines that are defined in that society, and it must be someone of the child's own generation. The cultural formulation of these controls is known as the "incest taboo."

THE INCEST TABOO

The incest taboo, in most general terms, means a culturally enforced prohibition against sexual relations between two persons socially defined as close kin. The specification of *who* precisely are socially defined as close kin varies from one society to another, but certain relationships are so defined in all societies. Therefore, for our purposes we can distinguish "primary" from "secondary" incest taboos. The primary taboos involve relationships within the nuclear family: mother-son, brother-sister, and father-daughter. The secondary incest taboos involve extensions of such taboos to specified additional relatives beyond the nuclear family, variable according to the nature of the kinship system of the particular society. They would include, for example, for a male in a matrilineal clan system his mother's sisters and their daughters, his mother's mother and her sisters and any of their female descendants in the female line, and so on. In some societies "incest" may include relationships with various in-law kin as well; in some, collateral relatives up to a certain "degree of consanguinity," such as a third cousin, may be included. There are great variations, and no one rule has anything near universal application. Because of this variability, and the probability that such extensions are psychologically displacements of feelings aroused in relation to primary—that is, nuclear-family—relatives, we may omit them from the present discussion and concentrate on those that concern the nuclear family.

The primary incest taboos, against mother-son, brother-sister, and father-daughter sex relations, are found to be almost completely universal for human societies.[15]

[15] Apparent exceptions, such as permitted (even required) royal brother-sister marriages in Pharaonic Egypt, Inca Peru, and pre-European-contact Hawaii, have been written off by anthropologists, since they applied *only* to royalty in those societies and indicated a way of asserting and perpetuating the divine character of the royalty as opposed to the "commoner" population, precisely by *requiring* what is forbidden to the commoner. Hence they can be seen as accentuating the incest taboos that apply to the general population. However, recent researches by Russell Middleton purport that in certain periods, for ancient Egypt at least, father-daughter and brother-sister marriages were allowed, for the *commoner* population as well. (Interestingly not mother-son marriages, which suggests that that is the most profound taboo.) See Russell Middleton, "Brother-Sister and Father-Daughter Marriage in Ancient Egypt," *American Sociological Review*, Vol. 27, 1962, pp. 603-11.

Other researches indicate possible father-daughter marriages occurring in ancient Iran. See J. S. Slotkin, "On a Possible Lack of Incest Regulations in Old Iran," *American Anthropologist*, Vol. 49, 1947, pp. 612-17; and subsequent exchange with Ward Goodenough, *American Anthropologist*, Vol. 51, 1949, pp. 326-28, and 531-32. A technical point should be included here: strictly, rules against marriage of close kin (exogamy rules) are distinct from rules against *sex relations* between close kin (incest taboos) since the latter may occur without marriage, and even one form of incestuous relationship, the most com-

Primary incest taboos do several things. They propel the child to seek new objects outside the nuclear family, hence engage him in the wider world of his society, and provide the base for that wider cooperation and division of labor that make more complex cultures possible. It is probable that in the cultural evolution of man incest taboos have had adaptive significance so that a selective process went on. Those bands of early men who did institute such taboos enforced contact, cooperation, and exchange with other bands through intermarriage. With such a wider pool of both genetic and cultural materials they were better able to survive in competition for the same territory than other bands that inbred in the absence of incest taboos.

Incest taboos also function to help the child maintain emotional boundaries between himself and the most affectively charged others of his early world. The maintenance of such boundaries can be seen as an important element in ego strength. Without such boundaries the individual is likely to remain rooted in infantile and magical ways of dealing with the world. Let us apply this understanding to the evolutionary situation of early man. Bands of early man who developed and practiced incest taboos would develop greater ego strength, greater capacity to move outward into the world and manipulate it in more realistic (less magic-ridden) ways, and hence have a selective advantage over those bands who did not have the incest taboo. Simultaneously the outbreeding of the bands who did have the taboo would give them a genetic advantage of adaptation by giving them a wider pool of genetic materials, and hence of possi-

---

mon and likely, that is, father-daughter incest, may occur *with* marriage without technically violating the exogamy rule, if the kinship system is matrilineal, thus making father and daughter members of different clans. However, for our purposes, the major concern is with marriages that not only violate the incest taboo, but also violate *primary* incest taboos, for example, those involving co-members of the nuclear family rather than the more variable, and less emotionally charged, extensions to unilineal kin and the like.

The Egyptian and Iranian cases require us to prefix the world "almost" to the term universal in regard to primary incest taboos. I do not think this is a serious qualification. Cultures seem to have great possibilities for weaving exotic elaborations around the basic themes dictated by human biology and the pan-human tasks of *becoming* human—yet in time returning to the "more nearly universal" forms and solutions. The few known "exceptions" of this sort do not release us from the necessity of explaining and understanding why it is that all the rest *do* follow certain lines. Thus, the near-universality of primary incest taboos, through the otherwise large variability of social forms in other aspects of culture, is still an impressive fact and still needs to be interpreted, as is being attempted here.

bilities. Correspondingly, the contacts involved in outbreeding would broaden the range of available *cultural* solutions to environmental problems. Thus, "outbreeding producing hybrid vigor" can be seen as both a genetic and a cultural process.

Primary incest taboos, most centrally, function to limit the role of eroticism in the relationship of the child of either sex to the crucial persons of his growing-up years, that is, the other members of the nuclear family. These fateful emotional ties are both an essential condition for the socialization of the child and a serious danger if they persist too long or too strongly. They must be kept under control. They can never be extinguished entirely and will inevitably, through the unconscious and in transformed guises in consciousness and overt behavior, suffuse the ways in which the child, when grown, will enter into any significant affective relationship, particularly those of marriage and parenthood. If the erotic component of the infantile relationship is not later strenuously denied, (that is, repressed) by the imposition of the incest taboo, a reasonably effective assumption of adult relationships as spouse and as parent will become difficult to the point of impossibility. This is a universal human dilemma. What is widely variable is the degree and intensity with which it is experienced and the ways in which it is handled. These may vary widely from one individual to another and from one culture to another, to the extent that a culture predisposes toward some common ways of meeting the conflict.

OEDIPAL CONFLICT

Intrinsically related to the problem of the incest taboo is the problem of Oedipal conflict. The context for the acceptance of the incest taboo—the renunciation of the sexual component in the relationship to the opposite-sex parent—is the situation of sexual monopoly of the parental pair, to the exclusion of the child of either sex. Consequently, there arises the intrinsic rivalry of the child with the same-sex parent for the parent of opposite sex (and incidentally, alongside of this, the homosexual analogue, rivalry with the opposite-sex parent for the same-sex parent.) An important aspect of these triangular dramas is that there is typically strong *positive* feeling toward either of the parents which conflicts with rivalrous hostile feelings. The formulation of the Oedipus *complex* as simply the boy's desire to sexually possess the mother and kill the father, or the girl's desire to possess the father and kill the mother, is very much an oversimplification. There are again a great variety of ways this basic sexual-scarcity and taboo situation may be experienced and resolved. The essential element in the Freudian understanding is that intrinsically —therefore universally—in the human nuclear family situation there will exist this problem of sexuality, scarcity, and the need to overcome the infantile extremity of dependency. Of course, in different particular families, and in the different kinship structures of different societies, the precise version of this dilemma and the ways of meeting it may vary. It is unnecessary to argue that the particular constellation to which Freud gave the name Oedipus complex for Western culture of the early twentieth century is uni-versal for all societies (we know that in all its particularities it is not) in order to recognize the basic elements of Oedipal conflict as occur-ring in any society where the nuclear family is the basic setting for the child to grow up.

In this light, the attempt to refute the universality of the Oedipus complex by the anthropologist Malinowski in his study of the matri-lineal Trobriand Islanders[16] is unsuccessful. Malinowski argued that the "complex" of the Trobrianders consisted of the desire to kill the mother's brother and to marry the sister. He asserted that this was congruent with the fact that the main male authority over a boy is not the father but the mother's brother, and that brother-sister in-cest taboo is strongly expressed. Malinowski neglected the element of sexual rivalry (crucial to the Freudian view); neglected the fact that the Trobriand mother's brother is definitely not the sexual pos-sessor of the mother, while the boy's father is. Malinowski portrays the Trobriand father as a positive, loving, playful figure toward the boy, therefore not the object of the boy's hostility. But the uncle as disciplinarian and authority over the boy, by Malinowski's own ac-count, does not enter the boy's life in this role until the boy is from five to seven years old, that is, *after* the boy would have gone through the postulated Oedipal phase. Therefore, it is reasonable to suppose that expressed hostility toward mother's brother is at least in part a displacement from the father, and expressible precisely be-cause it both has a "realistic" basis and does not arouse a conflict between sexual rivalry for the mother and positive feeling toward the playful, indulgent father.

Though understandably polemical in the context of the period,

[16] Bronislaw Malinowski, *Sex and Repression in Savage Society* (London: Routledge & Kegan Paul, 1927).

and extremely weak in its reasoning and conclusions, Malinowski's work is valuable in retrospect, not because he "proved" the non-universality of the Oedipus complex, but rather because his work opened the way for anthropological studies that could probe into the variety of ways conflicts revolving around the sex-rivalry-dependency struggle may be structured in significantly different kinship and other social structures.[17] This theme will be pursued in context in the case studies of the following chapter and some of its ramifications in transition rituals will be considered in Chapter Four.

The task, then, is to study the variabilities and uniformities of the ways in which sexuality, as a central element of personality, develops in different kinds of family settings—thence to the reciprocities between sexual and personality development, on the one hand, and the forms of social organization and culture, on the other.

Man everywhere becomes human by becoming a *particular* version of humanity, molded toward the image and by the mechanisms of a particular society and its cultural forms. We are nowhere only exemplars of basic "human nature." At the same time, while molded in certain directions by a particular society and culture, and especially by the particular forms of nuclear family and extended kin relationships prevailing in that society, we are individually never only a product of these forms. Rather, each individual personality is a particular form of *tension* between his particular version of "basic human nature" (in terms of biologically given drives and genetically given temperamental potential) and the particular version of the societally determined and culturally patterned socialization he has undergone, and continues to undergo, in a particular society. This formulation attempts to avoid both human nature determinism on the one hand and social or cultural determinism on the other. It pays attention to these elements: (1) universals of human nature, the biological and social nature of man; (2) the variability (large but finite) of social and cultural forms, especially as these concern the socialization process; and (3) the idiosyncratic variability of individual personalities, in terms of genetic endowment, "accidents" of biography, and range of responsiveness to common social pressure. True, it is *generally* the case that most societies tend to social-

17 Róheim, *op. cit.*, for an extended discussion of the bases for accepting the universality of the Oedipal constellation and for a specific challenge to Malinowski's interpretation of the Trobriand case. Unlike Malinowski, Róheim finds in Malinowski's own data sufficient documentation of father-son Oedipal themes in Trobriand culture. See pp. 167, 191, and Chapter III generally.

ize their young in such a way that they will basically conform to the norms of the culture and basically fulfill the roles of the social system, thus perpetuating it into the next generation. However, we must not assume that this process works smoothly and automatically and without difficulties in all societies. Nor must we assume that it is equally effective in all, nor that it does so without sizable costs, different in different societies, nor that it works equally or even similarly well for all individuals in that society. Rather, all these are questions to be raised about each particular society and culture: How well does it work? What kinds of personalities does it in fact produce? What range? What psychic costs does it entail? For what kinds of personalities?

4. OVERSOCIALIZED MAN?

Although our central interest here is not argumentation about various social science theories, but rather confrontation with the substance of human problems and dilemmas, our understanding is often sharpened and clarified by writings which were originally *polemical* in intent. Such an essay is the following one by the contemporary sociologist Dennis H. Wrong.

The Oversocialized Conception of Man in Modern Sociology

DENNIS H. WRONG

Gertrude Stein, bed-ridden with a fatal illness, is reported to have suddenly muttered, "What, then, is the answer?" Pausing, she raised her head, murmured, "But what is the question?" and died. Miss Stein presumably was pondering the ultimate meaning of human life, but her brief final soliloquy has a broader and humbler relevance. Its point is that answers are meaningless apart from questions. If we forget the questions, even while remembering the answers, our knowledge of them will subtly deteriorate, becoming rigid, formal, and catechistic as the sense of indeterminacy, of rival possibilities, implied by the very putting of a question is lost.

Reprinted with permission of the author and the American Sociological Association from American Sociological Review, *Vol. 26, No. 2, April 1961, pp. 183-93. (Footnotes omitted).*

Social theory must be seen primarily as a set of answers to questions we ask of social reality. If the initiating questions are forgotten, we readily misconstrue the task of theory, and the answers previous thinkers have given become narrowly confining conceptual prisons, degenerating into little more than a special, professional vocabulary applied to situations and events that can be described with equal or greater precision in ordinary language. Forgetfulness of the questions that are the starting points of inquiry leads us to ignore the substantive assumptions "buried" in our concepts and commits us to a one-sided view of reality.

Perhaps this is simply an elaborate way of saying that sociological theory can never afford to lose what is usually called a "sense of significance;" or, as it is sometimes put, that sociological theory must be "problem-conscious." I choose instead to speak of theory as a set of answers to questions because reference to "problems" may seem to suggest too close a linkage with social criticism or reform. My primary reason for insisting on the necessity of holding constantly in mind the questions that our concepts and theories are designed to answer is to preclude defining the goal of sociological theory as the creation of a formal body of knowledge satisfying the logical criteria of scientific theory set up by philosophers and methodologists of natural science. Needless to say, this is the way theory is often defined by contemporary sociologists.

Yet to speak of theory as interrogatory may suggest too self-sufficiently intellectual an enterprise. Cannot questions be satisfactorily answered and then forgotten, the answers becoming the assumptions from which we start in framing new questions? It may convey my view of theory more adequately to say that sociological theory concerns itself with questions arising out of problems that are inherent in the very existence of human societies and that cannot therefore be finally "solved" in the way that particular social problems perhaps can be. The "problems" theory concerns itself with are problems *for* human societies, which, because of their universality, become intellectually problematic for sociological theorists.

Essentially, the historicist conception of sociological knowledge that is central to the thought of Max Weber and has recently been ably restated by Barrington Moore, Jr., and C. Wright Mills is a sound one. The most fruitful questions for sociology are always questions referring to the realities of a particular historical situation. Yet both of these writers, especially Mills, have a tendency to underemphasize the degree to which we genuinely wish and seek answers to trans-historical and universal questions," nor the even more formalistic effort to construct all-encompassing in mind the formalistic quest for social "laws" or "universal propositions," nor the even more formalistic effort to construct all-encompassing "conceptual schemes." Moore and Mills are rightly critical of such efforts. I am thinking of such questions as, "How are men capable of uniting to form enduring societies in the first place?"; "Why and to what degree is change inherent in human societies and what are the sources of change?"; "How is man's animal nature domesticated by society?"

Such questions—and they are existential as well as intellectual questions—are the *raison d'être* of social theory. They were asked by men long before the rise of sociology. Sociology itself is an effort, under new and unprecedented historical conditions, to find novel answers to them. They are not questions which lend themselves to successively more precise answers as a result of cumulative empirical research, for they remain eternally problematic. Social theory is necessarily an interminable dialogue. "True understanding," Hannah Arendt has written, "does not tire of interminable dialogue and 'vicious circles' because it trusts that imagination will eventually catch at least a glimpse of the always frightening light of truth."

I wish briefly to review the answers modern sociological theory offers to one such question, or rather to one aspect of one question. The question may be variously phrased as, "What are the sources of social cohesion?"; or "How is social order possible?"; or, stated in social-psychological terms, "How is it that man becomes tractable to social discipline?" I shall call this question in its social-psychological aspect the "Hobbesian question" and in its more strictly sociological aspect the "Marxist question." The Hobbesian question asks how men are capable of the guidance by social norms and goals that makes possible an enduring society, while the Marxist question asks how, assuming this capability, complex societies manage to regulate and restrain destructive conflicts between groups. Much of our current theory offers an oversocialized view of man in answering the Hobbesian question and an overintegrated view of society in answering the Marxist question.

A number of writers have recently challenged the overintegrated view of society in contemporary theory. In addition to Moore and Mills, the names of Bendix, Coser, Dahrendorf, and Lockwood come to mind. My intention, therefore, is to concentrate on the answers to the Hobbesian question in an effort to disclose the oversocialized view of man which they seem to imply.

Since my view of theory is obviously very different from that of Talcott Parsons and has, in fact, been developed in opposition to his, let me pay tribute to his recognition of the importance of the Hobbesian question—the "problem of order," as he calls it—at the very beginning of his first book, *The Structure of Social Action*. Parsons correctly credits Hobbes with being the first thinker to see the necessity of explaining why human society is not a "war of all against all"; why, if man is simply a gifted animal, men refrain from unlimited resort to fraud and violence in pursuit of their ends and maintain a stable society at all. There is even a sense in which, as Coser and Mills have both noted, Parsons' entire work represents an effort to solve the Hobbesian problem of order. His solution, however, has tended to become precisely the kind of elaboration of a set of answers in abstraction from questions that is so characteristic of contemporary sociological theory.

We need not be greatly concerned with Hobbes' own solution to the problem of order he saw with such unsurpassed clarity. Whatever interest his famous theory of the origin of the state may still hold for political scientists, it is clearly inadequate as an explanation of the origin of society. Yet the pattern as opposed to the details of Hobbes' thought bears closer examination.

The polar terms in Hobbes' theory are the state of nature, where the war of all against all prevails, and the authority of Leviathan, created by social contract. But the war of all against all is not simply effaced with the creation of political authority: it remains an ever-present potentiality in human society, at times quiescent, at times erupting into open violence. Whether Hobbes believed that the state of nature and the social contract were ever historical realities—and there is evidence that he was not that simple-minded and unsociological, even in the seventeenth century—is unimportant; the whole tenor of his thought is to see that war of all against all and Leviathan dialectically, as coexisting and interacting opposites. As R. G. Collingwood has observed, "According to Hobbes . . . *a body politic is a dialectical thing*, a Heraclitean world in which at any given time there is a negative element." The first secular social theorist in the history of Western thought, and one of the first clearly to discern and define the problem of order in human society long before Darwinism made awareness of it a commonplace, Hobbes was a dialectical thinker who refused to separate answers from questions, solutions to society's enduring problems from the conditions creating the problems.

What is the answer of contemporary sociological theory to the Hobbesian question? There are two main answers, each of which has come to be understood in a way that denies the reality and meaningfulness of the question. Together they constitute a model of human nature, sometimes clearly stated, more often implicit in accepted concepts, that pervades modern sociology. The first answer is summed up in the notion of the "internalization of social norms." The second, more commonly employed or assumed in empirical research, is the view that man is essentially motivated by the desire to achieve a positive image of self by winning acceptance or status in the eyes of others.

The following statement represents, briefly and broadly, what is probably the most influential contemporary sociological conception—and dismissal—of the Hobbesian problem: "to a modern sociologist imbued with the conception that action follows institutionalized patterns, opposition of individual and common interests has only a very limited relevance or is thoroughly unsound." From this writer's perspective, the problem is an unreal one: human conduct is totally shaped by common norms or "institutionalized patterns." Sheer ignorance must have led people who were unfortunate enough not to be modern sociologists to ask, "How is order possible?" A thoughtful bee or ant would never inquire, "How is the social order of the hive or ant-hill possible?" for the opposite of that order is unimaginable when the instinctive endowment of the insects ensures its stability and built-in harmony between "individual and common interests." Human society, we are assured, is not essentially different, although conformity and stability are there maintained by non-instinctive processes. Modern sociologists believe that they have understood these processes and that they have not merely answered but disposed of the Hobbesian question showing that, far from expressing a valid intimation of the tensions and possibilities of social life, it can only be asked out of ignorance.

It would be hard to find a better illustration of what Collingwood, following Plato, calls *eristical* as opposed to dialectical thinking: the answer destroys the question, or rather destroys the awareness of rival possibilities suggested by the question which accounts for its having been asked in the first place. A reversal of perspective now takes place and we are moved to ask the opposite question: "How is it that violence, conflict, revolution, and the individual's sense of coercion by society manage to exist at all, if this view is correct?" Whenever a one-sided answer to a question compels us to raise the opposite question, we are caught up in a dialectic of concepts which reflects a dialectic in things. But let us examine the particular processes sociologists appeal to in order to account for the elimination from human society of the war of all against all.

THE CHANGING MEANING OF INTERNALIZATION

A well-known section of *The Structure of Social Action*, devoted to the interpretation of Durkheim's thought, is entitled "The Changing Meaning of Constraint." Parsons argues that Durkheim originally conceived of society as controlling the individual from the outside by imposing constraints on him through sanctions, best illustrated by codes of law. But in Durkheim's later work he began to see that social rules do not "merely regulate 'externally' . . . they enter directly into the constitution of the actors' ends themselves." Constraint, therefore, is more than an environmental obstacle which the actor must take into account in pursuit of his goals in the same way that he takes into account physical laws: it becomes internal, psychological, and self-imposed as well. Parsons developed this view that social norms are constitutive rather than merely regulative of human nature before he was influenced by psychoanalytic theory, but Freud's theory of the superego has become the source and model for the conception of the internalization of social norms that today plays so important a part in sociological thinking. The use some sociologists have made of Freud's idea, however, might well inspire an essay entitled, "The Changing Meaning of Internalization," although, in contrast to the shift in Durkheim's view of constraint, this change has been a change for the worse.

What has happened is that internalization has imperceptibly been equated with "learning," or even with "habit-formation" in the simplest sense. Thus when a norm is said to have been "internalized" by an individual, what is frequently meant is that he habitually both affirms it and conforms to it in his conduct. The whole stress on inner conflict, on the tension between powerful impulses and superego controls, the behavioral outcome of which cannot be prejudged, drops out of the picture. And it is this that is central to Freud's view, for in psychoanalytic terms to say that a norm has been internalized, or introjected to become part of the superego, is to say no more than that a person will suffer guilt-feelings if he fails to live up to it, not that he will in fact live up to it in his behavior.

The relation between internalization and conformity assumed by most sociologists is suggested by the following passage from a recent, highly-praised advanced textbook: "Conformity to institutionalized norms is, of course, 'normal.' The actor, having internalized the norms, feels something like a need to conform. His conscience would bother him if he did not." What is overlooked here is that the person who conforms may be even more "bothered," that is, subject to guilt and neurosis, than the person who violates what are not only society's norms but his own as well. To Freud, it is precisely the man with the strictest superego, he who has most thoroughly internalized and conformed to the norms of his society, who is most wracked with guilt and anxiety.

Paul Kecskemeti, to whose discussion I owe initial recognition of the erroneous view of internalization held by sociologists, argues that the relations between social norms, the individual's selection from them, his conduct, and his feelings about his conduct are far from self-evident. "It is by no means true," he writes, "to say that acting counter to one's own norms always or almost always leads to neurosis. One might assume that neurosis develops even more easily in persons who *never* violate the moral code they recognize as valid but repress and frustrate some strong instinctual motive. A person who 'succumbs to temptation,' feels guilt, and then 'purges himself' of his guilt in some reliable way (e.g., by confession) may achieve in this way a better balance, and be less neurotic, than a person who never violates his 'norms' and never feels conscious guilt."

Recent discussions of "deviant behavior" have been compelled to recognize these distinctions between social demands, personal attitudes toward them, and actual conduct, although they have done so in a laboriously taxonomic fashion. They represent, however, largely the rediscovery of what was always central to the Freudian concept of the superego. The main explanatory function of the concept is to show how people repress themselves, imposing checks on their own desires and thus turning the inner life into a battlefield of conflicting motives, no matter which side "wins," by successfully dictating overt action. So far as behavior is concerned, the psychoanalytic view of man is less deterministic than the sociological. For psychoanalysis is primarily concerned with the inner life, not with overt behavior, and its most fundamental insight is that the wish, the emotion, and the fantasy are as important as the act in man's experience.

Sociologists have appropriated the superego concept, but have separated it from any equivalent of the Freudian id. So long as most individuals are "socialized" that is, internalize the norms and conform to them in conduct, the Hobbesian problem is not even perceived as a latent reality. Deviant behavior is accounted for by special circumstances: ambiguous norms, anomie, role conflict, or greater cultural stress on valued goals than on the approved means for attaining them. Tendencies to deviant behavior are not seen as dialectically related to conformity. The presence in man of motivational forces bucking against the hold social discipline has over him is denied.

Nor does the assumption that internalization of norms and roles is the essence of socialization allow for a sufficient range of motives underlying conformity. It fails to allow for variable "tonicity of the superego," in Kardiner's phrase. The degree to which conformity is frequently the result of coercion rather than conviction is minimized. Either someone has internalized the norms, or he is "unsocialized," a feral or socially isolated child, or a psychopath. Yet Freud recognized that many people, conceivably a majority, fail to acquire superegos. "Such people," he wrote, "habitually permit themselves to do any bad deed that procures them something they want, if only they are sure that no authority will discover it or make them suffer for it; their anxiety relates only to the possibility of detection. Present-day society has to take into account the prevalence of this state of mind." The last sentence suggests that Freud was aware of the decline of "inner-direction," of the Protestant conscience, about which we have heard so much lately. So let us turn to the other elements of human nature that sociologists appeal to in order to explain, or rather explain away, the Hobbesian problem.

MAN THE ACCEPTANCE-SEEKER

The superego concept is too inflexible, too bound to the past and to individual biography, to be of service in relating conduct to the pressures of the immediate situation in which it takes place. Sociologists rely more heavily therefore on an alternative notion, here stated—or, to be fair, overstated—in its baldest form: "People are so profoundly sensitive to the expectations of others that all action is inevitably guided by these expectations."

Parsons' model of the "complementarity of expectations," the view that in social interaction men mutually seek approval from one another by conforming to shared norms, is a formalized version of what has tended to become a distinctive sociological perspective on human motivation. Ralph Linton states it in explicit psychological terms: "The need for eliciting favorable responses from others is an almost constant component of [personality]. Indeed, it is not too much to say that there is very little organized human behavior which is not directed toward its satisfaction in at least some degree."

The insistence of sociologists on the importance of "social factors" easily leads them to stress the priority of such socialized or socializing motives in human behavior. It is frequently the task of the sociologist to call attention to the intensity with which men desire and strive for the good opinion of their immediate associates in a variety of situations, particularly those where received theories or ideologies have unduly emphasized other motives such as financial gain, commitment to ideals, or the effects on energies and aspirations of arduous physical conditions. Thus sociologists have shown that factory workers are more sensitive to the attitudes of their fellow-workers than to purely economic incentives; that voters are more influenced by the preferences of their relatives and friends than by campaign debates on the "issues"; that soldiers, whatever their ideological commitment to their nation's cause, fight more bravely when their platoons are intact and they stand side by side with their "buddies."

It is certainly not my intention to criticize the findings of such studies. My objection is that their particular selective emphasis is generalized— explicitly or, more often, implicitly—to provide apparent empirical support for an extremely one-sided view of human nature. Although sociologists have criticized past efforts to single out one fundamental motive in human conduct, the desire to achieve a favorable self-image by winning approval from others frequently occupies such a position in their own thinking. The following "theorem" has been, in fact, openly put forward by Hans Zetterberg as "a strong contender for the position as the major Motivational Theorem in sociology":

An actor's actions have a tendency to become dispositions that are related to the occurence [sic] of favored uniform evaluations of the actor and-or his actions in his action system.

Now Zetterberg is not necessarily maintaining that this theorem is an accurate factual statement of the basic psychological roots of social behavior. He is, characteristically, far too self-conscious about the logic of theorizing and "concept formation" for that. He goes on to remark that "the maximization of favorable attitudes from others would thus be the counterpart in sociological theory to the maximization of profit in economic theory." If by this it is meant that the theorem is to be understood as a heuristic rather than an empirical assumption, that sociology has a selective point of view which is just as abstract and partial as that of economics and the other social sciences, and if his view of theory as a set of logically connected formal propositions is granted provisional acceptance, I am in agreement. (Actually, the view of theory suggested at the beginning of this paper is a quite different one.)

But there is a further point to be made. Ralf Dahrendorf has observed that structural-functional theorists do not "claim that order is *based on* a general consensus of values, but that it *can be conceived of in terms of* such consensus and that, if it is conceived of in these terms, certain propositions follow which are subject to the test of specific observations." The same may be said of the assumption that people seek to maximize favorable evaluations by others; indeed this assumption has already fathered such additional concepts as "reference group" and "circle of significant others." Yet the question must be raised as to whether we really wish to, in effect, define sociology by such partial perspectives. The assumption of the maximization of approval from others is the psychological complement to the sociological assumption of a general value consensus. And the former is as selective and one-sided a way of looking at motivation as Dahrendorf and others have argued the latter to be when it determines our way of looking at social structure. The oversocialized view of man of the one is a counterpart to the overintegrated view of society of the other.

Modern sociology, after all, originated as a protest against the partial view of man contained in such doctrines as utilitarianism, classical economics, social Darwinism, and vulgar Marxism. All of the great nineteenth and early twentieth century sociologists saw it as one of their major tasks to expose the unreality of such abstractions as economic man, the gain-seeker, of the classical economists; political man, the power-seeker of the Machiavellian tradition in political science; self-preserving man, the security-seeker of Hobbes and Darwin; sexual or libidinal man, the pleasure-seeker of doctrinaire Freudianism; and even religious man, the God-seeker of the theologians. It would be ironical if it should turn out that they have merely contributed to the creation of yet another reified abstraction in socialized man, the status-seeker of our contemporary sociologists.

Of course, such an image of man is, like all the others mentioned, valuable for limited purposes so long as it is not taken for the whole truth. What are some of its deficiencies? To begin with, it neglects the other half of the model of human nature presupposed by current theory: moral man, guided by his built-in superego and beckoning ego-ideal. In recent years sociologists have been less interested than they once were in culture and national character as backgrounds to conduct, partly because stress on the concept of "role" as the crucial link between the individual and the social structure has directed their attention to the immediate situation in which social interaction takes place. Man is increasingly seen as a "role-playing" creature, responding eagerly or anxiously to the expectations of other role-players in the multiple group settings in which he finds himself. Such an approach, while valuable in helping us grasp the complexity of a highly differentiated social structure such as our own, is far too often generalized to serve as a kind of *ad hoc* social psychology, easily adaptable to particular sociological purposes.

But it is not enough to concede that men often pursue "internalized values" remaining indifferent to what others think of them, particularly when, as I have previously argued, the idea of internalization has been "hollowed out" to make it more useful as an explanation of conformity. What of desire for material and sensual satisfactions? Can we really dispense with the venerable notion of material "interests" and invariably replace it with the blander, more integrative "social values"? And what of striving for power, not necessarily for its own sake—that may be rare and pathological—but as a means by which men are able to *impose* a normative definition of reality on others? That material interests, sexual drives, and the quest for power have often been overestimated as human motives is no reason to deny their reality. To do so is to suppress one term of the dialectic between conformity and rebellion, social norms and their violation, man and social order, as completely as the other term is suppressed by those who deny the reality of Man's "normative orientation" or reduce it to the effect of coercion, rational calculation, or mechanical conditioning.

The view that man is invariably pushed by internalized norms or pulled by the lure of self-validation by others ignores—to speak archaically for a moment—both the highest and the lowest, both beast and angel, in his nature. Durkheim, from whom so much of the modern sociological point of view derives, recognized that the very existence of a social norm implies and even creates the possibility of its violation. This is the meaning of his famous dictum that crime is a "normal phenomenon." He maintained that "for the originality of the idealist whose dreams transcend his century to find expression, it is necessary that the originality of the criminal, who is below the level of his time, shall also be possible. One does not occur without the other." Yet Durkheim lacked an adequate psychology and formulated his insight in terms of the actor's cognitive awareness rather than in motivational terms. We do not have Durkheim's excuse for falling back on what Homans has called a "social mold theory" of human nature.

SOCIAL BUT NOT ENTIRELY SOCIALIZED

I have referred to forces in man that are resistant to socialization. It is not my purpose to explore the nature of these forces or to suggest how we ought best conceive of them as sociologists—that would be a most ambitious undertaking. A few remarks will have to suffice. I think we must start with the recognition that *in the beginning there is the body.* As soon as the body is mentioned the specter of "biological determinism" raises its head and sociologists draw back in fright. And certainly their view of man is sufficiently disembodied and non-materialistic to satisfy Bishop Berkeley, as well as being de-sexualized enough to please Mrs. Grundy.

Am I, then, urging us to return to the older view of a human nature divided between a "social man" and a "natural man" who is either benevolent, Rousseau's Noble Savage, or sinister and destructive, as Hobbes regarded him? Freud is usually represented, or misrepresented, as the chief modern proponent of this dualistic conception which assigns to the social order the purely negative role of blocking and re-directing men's "imperious biological drives." I say "misrepresented" because, although Freud often said things supporting such an interpretation, other and more fundamental strains in his thinking suggest a different conclusion. John Dollard, certainly not a writer who is oblivious to social and cultural "factors," saw this twenty-five years ago: "It is quite clear," he wrote, ". . . that he [Freud] does not regard the instincts as having a fixed social goal; rather, indeed, in the case of the sexual instinct he has stressed the vague but powerful and impulsive nature of the drive and has emphasized that its proper social object is not picked out in advance. His seems to be a drive concept which is not at variance with our knowledge from comparative cultural studies, since his theory does not demand that the 'instinct' work itself out with mechanical certainty alike in every varying culture."

So much for Freud's "imperious biological drives!" When Freud defined psychoanalysis as the study of the "vicissitudes of the instincts," he was confirming, not denying, the "plasticity" of human nature insisted on by social scientists. The drives or "instincts" of psychoanalysis, far from being fixed dispositions to behave in a particular way, are utterly subject to social channeling and transformation and could not even reveal themselves in behavior without social molding any more than our vocal cords can produce articulate speech if we have not learned a language. To psychoanalysis man is indeed a social animal; his social nature is profoundly reflected in his bodily structure.

But there is a difference between the Freudian view on the one hand and both sociological and neo-Freudian conceptions of man on the other. To Freud man is a *social* animal without being entirely a *socialized* animal. His very social nature is the source of conflicts and antagonisms that create resistance to socialization by the norms of any of the societies which have existed in the course of human history. "Socialization" may mean two quite distinct things; when they are confused, an oversocialized view of man is the result. On the one hand socialization means the "transmission of the culture," the particular culture of the society an individual enters at birth; on the other hand the term is used to mean the "process of becoming human," of acquiring uniquely human attributes from interaction with others. All men are socialized in the latter sense, but this does not mean that they have been completely molded by the particular norms and values of their culture. All cultures, as Freud contended, do violence to man's socialized bodily drives, but this in no sense means that men could possibly exist without culture or independently of society. From such a standpoint, man may properly be called as Norman Brown has called him, the "neurotic" or the "discontented" animal and repression may be seen as the main characteristic of human nature as we have known it in history.

But isn't this psychology and haven't sociologists been taught to foreswear psychology, to look with suspicion on what are called "psychological variables" in contradiction to the institutional and historical forces with which they are properly concerned? There is, indeed, as recent critics have complained, too much "psychologism" in contemporary sociology, largely, I think, because of the bias inherent in our favored research techniques. But I do not see how, at the level of theory, sociologists can fail to make assumptions about human nature. If our assumptions are left implicit, we will inevitably presuppose a view of man that is tailor-made to our special needs; when our sociological theory overstresses the stability and integration of society, we will end up imagining that man is the disembodied, conscience-driven, status-seeking phantom of current theory. We must do better if we really wish to win credit outside of our ranks for special understanding of man, that plausible creature whose wagging tongue so often hides the despair and darkness in his heart.

DISCUSSION

As Wrong shows in the foregoing paper, society is never entirely ordered and cohesive. Conflict is a perennial potential. And man is never totally "at home" in society. He is *social* by nature, but never entirely socialized. His being social is a product of his being a human animal—in all the senses of this term that we have been developing in the preceding pages. The motives of man in society are not singular. He may strive for material well-being or wealth or for power. He may seek sensual pleasures, or God or the ultimate, or mere acceptance by his fellows. He may strive for equilibrium or its opposite—the attainment of extreme states. To paraphrase P. T.

Barnum: all of these motives operate in some men some of the time; some of them in some men most of the time; some of them in all men some of the time. But no one of them is *the* key to "human nature." Similarly, society is a mechanism of social cohesion, some of the time. Society is an arena of enormous conflict, some of the time. Society is a self-perpetuating conserving system—again, partially, or some of the time. Society is a system driving toward constant change —again, some of the time, or in some cases. Both society and culture, on one side, and individual personality, on another, are riddled with persistent *internal conflict*—and what is going on at any particular time is a working out of the *vicissitudes* of the individual or of the society or culture. The "working out" is never a final solution, for conflicts are recurrent and inevitable.

5. PSYCHODYNAMICS IN SOCIAL LIFE

Social organization is never absolute. Neither is socialization. Culture is open to change. Change is possible because of the built-in tensions of any society. Culture can be seen as the way men have developed, in a particular society, of dealing with their intrapsychic dilemmas, in their universal aspects and in the aspects particular to that society. These dilemmas refer back to the infantile situation and the problems of the "family drama," for the effects of these primary experiences ramify into many, or even all, spheres of social life. Thus social life in general can be seen as a set of collective transformations of intrapsychic "solutions" of the family drama, played out on a variety of larger stages. The kind of people we are is determined by the interplay of pan-human unconscious forces, the universal and the specific infantile experiences we have had, the universal and specific family dramas we have undergone, and the kind of resolutions of these family dramas,—especially the common and unconscious elements in these resolutions. All these forces will inevitably shape, mold, change, or perpetuate the institutions by which we live. These institutions are "given" only in the sense that the infant and child encounter them as a "there" reality, full-blown and operating. But the institutions are themselves the products of prior generations including the one that is parental to this child. The institutions are subject to change, especially where they are or become incongruent with the psychic needs—including the unconscious ones —of new generations. Institutions both shape and are shaped by the psychic experience of the people of the society. For this reason they can seldom be exported to or imposed upon other societies without encountering considerable, often fundamental, change to suit the psychic qualities of the recipient population. Social institutions are psychic products, just as personality is a social product.

This intrepretation is at odds with a viewpoint on the origin or source of institutions, or of institutional change, prevalent among many sociologists and anthropologists today. For example, Yehudi Cohen, an extremely perceptive anthropologist who has contributed greatly to the personality-and-culture literature, writes:[18]

> There are many pitfalls in attempts to move directly from unconscious processes to cultural institutions. Unconscious conflict produces symptoms of idiosyncratic or even shared pathology, but not institutions. It is demonstrable that the institutions under which people live can engender or acerbate conflict, but the institutions of society arise out of ecological and historical factors, out of economic and adaptational necessity, out of pressures of warfare and conquest and the like. They do not arise out of personality or out of conflict as such.

These last two sentences require comment and modification. Consider Max Weber's famous thesis linking Protestantism and modern capitalism.[19] Weber's thesis can be restated in psychodynamic terms: Many ecological, economic, technological, and political conditions in many advanced cultures seem to have provided the necessary backgrounds for the development of modern industrial capitalism; yet these societies (for example, ancient Rome, classical China, premodern India) did not produce the institutions of industrial capitalism. What was crucially lacking in these societies, and was present in the West from the time of the Protestant Reformation, was a *spirit* (*Geist*) which enjoined rationally ordered, self-disciplined activity toward transcendental goals. What was required for this activity was a suppression or repression of hedonistic impulses and a thorough-going, unrelenting calculation in the process of self-mastery.

---

18 Yehudi Cohen, "The Establishment of Identity in a Social Nexus: The Special Case of Initiation Ceremonies . . . ," *American Anthropologist*, 66, No. 3, Part 1, June 1964, p. 532.

19 Max Weber, *The Protestant Ethic and the Spirit of Capitalism* (original, German 1920), English translation, T. Parsons London: George Allen & Unwin, 1930).

No such spirit was part of the value-system of these other societies, and, correspondingly, we can deduce that appropriate socialization toward the realization of such value was lacking. When this is translated into psychodynamic terms, it appears that one of the conditions for the Western world's development of modern industrial capitalism was the institutionalization of what is essentially the *anal-compulsive character*,[20] exalting it by the value-system of disciplined ascetic mastery (first developed in religious terms by the "Protestant ethic," then secularized and universalized.) This kind of character formation, by contrast, does not seem to have been institutionalized in the other large-scale civilizations that Weber studied (Rome, China, India),[21] and this fact evidently prevented the otherwise "favorable" economic, ecological, military, and other conditions from resulting in industrial capitalism as an institutional system in those societies.

This interpretation would certainly seem to call into question a statement such as Cohen's, that "institutions arise out of ecological and historical factors, out of economic and adaptational necessity, out of pressures of warfare and the like . . . *not* out of personality or out of conflict as such."

Not that the anal-compulsive character produced industrial capitalism in a simple one-to-one causal relationship, as though the anal character appeared out of nowhere and the rest followed. Rather, even though there may *appear* to be—from a distance of time and space—some "adaptational necessity" for certain institutions to appear, there is no certainty that they will appear, or if adopted from other cultures by contact, no certainty that they will work in the way they do elsewhere, *unless* there is some congruence between the institution and the psychodynamic needs of the people of that society. And the Weber case seems to document this argument.[22] The char-

[20] A character formation whose central drives are determined by reactions against anal eroticism in the form of excessive control, routinization, orderliness, miserliness (withholding) and work as a defense against anxiety. The compulsive quality is indicated by the relevant activities and avoidances going beyond realistic outside demands and the inability to avoid or "let up" on such actions without strong anxiety reactions.

[21] Admittedly, the historical evidence does not permit making a categorically negative statement on this point; however, the statement does not argue that no anal-compulsive characters ever appeared in those societies, but only that such a character type was not institutionalized as the *ideal*.

[22] Anthropologists have noted instances from societies that they have studied where there seemed to be an "adaptational necessity" for, for example, some "obvious" technological change, which, however was *not* introduced, to the

acter trends, or the psychodynamic needs, are not something *sui generis*. They are themselves a product of a convergence of different institutional forces as transmitted by the similarities in the socialization process throughout a society or section of it—but this element must be there. It is the *dynamic* by which institutional continuity or change can work at all. The term "institutions" is simply a shorthand way of referring to commonalities, convergences, and consequences, intended and otherwise, in the ways *persons* in the given society, think, feel, and act, and they do think, feel, and act in terms of their own individual intrapsychic processes.

The issues raised here are basic problems of the relationship of psychodynamic forces to the operation of institutional structures. My position is this: Institutional structures *require* certain *motivational* forces to be in operation, and these in turn depend on certain kinds of psychodynamic processes being at work in the individuals involved in fulfilling the roles which keep these institutions functioning. This does not mean, necessarily, that only one kind of character structure can provide the necessary psychodynamic and hence the motivating forces. Rather, it is possible that the similar or functionally equivalent motivational forces may be imbedded in several different kinds of character structure. (My hypothesis is that their *number* is likely to be rather small, since a type of character structure generally tends to operate to limit the range of alternative motivations and to bind in and rigidify the person's actions and wishes into a range that can appear extremely constricted from the viewpoint of persons of other character types.)

---

detriment of the survival value of the society. Commonly these are explained away as cases where "the force of traditionalism was too strong." The obvious question is, "*Why* was it too strong in that case, while it was overridden in others?" For example, compare Mead's discussion of the technological changes in Manus between her first and second visits, where the impetus toward such technological "adaptations" was not only the contact with American GI's during World War II—contact that many other tribal societies also had—but the pre-existent character structure that involved elements very much like Protestant asceticism. (See Margaret Mead, *New Lives for Old*, New York: William Morrow and Company, 1956.)

Anthropological studies of acculturation repeatedly demonstrate that this process is a highly selective one, and the selection is not according to what Europeans would consider as "obvious" rational or utilitarian grounds. For example, M. J. Herskovits, a noted specialist on that topic, notes that: "In Africa, attempts to induce natives to improve their techniques of cultivation by changing from hoe to plow have met with great resistance. Yet in most of Africa, cotton prints for clothing have been taken over with avidity." Melville J. Herskovits, *Man and His Works* (New York: Alfred A. Knopf, 1948), p. 530.

The range of personalities evident in a modern society would indicate that it is unlikely that a whole society will produce only one
personality type, which in turn has the psychodynamics necessary for
the fulfillment of the various kinds of roles developed by that society. However, certain psychodynamic *mechanisms* must be available
to a large proportion of the persons in the society, disregarding their
differences in other personality dimensions, to ensure that the system does in fact work. For example, the persistence of self-disciplining ascetic mechanisms in a large part of modern society enables the
work of modern industry to get done, with some approximation of
the rational scheduling and bureaucratic ordering that this system
demands. For contrast we may consider cultures newly undergoing
industrialization, where such self-disciplining asceticism is lacking in
the basic personality dynamics of the population. For example, in
parts of Latin America the pace and effectiveness of the industrialization process is subverted precisely by the lack of these driving
forces within the population that is being recruited into the industrial proletariat. This contrasts greatly with the character of the
Anglo-American and West European labor forces. Another example
can be seen in the difficulties encountered by the Soviet Union in
deliberately trying to create a new type of basic character in line with
the demands of a modern industrialized society in opposition to the
older type of "Russian character." Aspects of this struggle are explored in the interesting paper of Inkeles, Hanfmann, and Beier presented in Chapter Three.

The complexities of any large-scale society, and the incongruities
and puzzles to be found within even some very "simple" primitive
societies, should lead us to conclude that there is simply no direct,
rudimentary relationship between the over-all institutions of a society, its family and socialization patterns and the personality development of the members of the society. Probably the most we can
say is that there is a general strain toward congruence. We could
hypothesize an extreme case as follows: Other institutions have a
very high congruence with the family patterns. Socialization processes are consistent with both family and other institutions. Therefore, the personality structure is consistent with the institutional demands in all spheres, with a minimum of conflict; hence life has a
simple, "natural," un-self-conscious quality, providing persons with a
sense of ease and fulfillment and, in effect, *freedom*. However, no
society that we have record of, fits such a model. There was a period

when some of the nonliterate societies, such as the Pueblo Indians or some of the Polynesian tribes, were pictured in such terms. But the more that anthropologists learned about those tribes, and particularly the greater the number of different anthropologists who studied the same tribes, the more blurred and conflicting the pictures became, and the more even those societies appeared to be ridden by many different internal strains, conflicts, and inconsistencies.[23]

However, we may posit a "strain toward congruence" as a kind of hypothetical model. In that context we may ask questions about particular institutional systems and their related personality types. What does an institutional system *in fact* do to promote, encourage, and create the relevant kinds of personality patterns? How does an institutional system, in working *toward* certain psychodynamic patterns, in fact also promote, usually without intending, certain other psychological forces and conflicts, which work in different, perhaps conflicting directions, from the personality trends the system seems to "need?" How in turn are these institutional directions reflections of, or products of, other psychic forces in the molders and perpetuators of these institutions, forces hidden from awareness or derived from deeper conflicts in these individuals, which, again, may be related to general institutional drifts of the society?

This image of society sees economic, technological, political, and psychological forces simultaneously interacting in a variety of ways, much of this hidden from the awareness of the participating actors. That we know not what we do, that "history goes on behind our backs," that we are pushed and pulled by many real forces both inside and outside ourselves, that it is immensely difficult to calculate the whole range of consequences of any deliberate purposive action or policy—all these are the axiomatic lessons of modern social science. Freud took us the first steps in that hard and liberating journey inside our separate selves. Marx and Weber provided some big steps in a different revealing journey into the unseen forces of society and history. These roads converge. The Puritan, seeking salvation, created modern capitalism. Americans, seeking secular order, promote enactment of such a vast complexity of laws and ordinances that agents of law and order cannot possibly enforce them all, and hence resort to discretion, corruption, and a host of morally ques-

[23] See for example, the now extensive anthropological literature debating the peacefulness and coherence, of the Pueblo societies, demolishing the "myth of the happy Hopi."

tionable compromises. About any such important sociological statements—documentations of the theme of the "unintended consequences of purposive social action"—we need to ask such questions as: What drove the Puritan? What were his intrapsychic conflicts? How did his early socialization make him the kind of person he was, with those historically fateful drives? Or *was* it early socialization? *Why* are Americans so intent on creating, then scoffing at, secular law? What psychic conflicts are pushing them? What anxieties? What uncertainties?

Personality, character, the psychodynamics of the individual, these are social products, to be sure—but not in any simple direct way. For how do you get the occasional Puritan in an erotically permissive, indulgent, hedonistically anti-work-oriented, normatively chaotic matrifocal Negro lower-class family? How the child who resists or ignores the allurements of mass-media popular culture and its pervasive fun morality? How the libertine from the philistine family? We are not simply carbon copies of either the older generation or the models of our own generation. Socialization is never complete, and never totally effective. Situational aspects—"chance" events (not predictable from the system)—and the great variability possible in *how* even the most common socialization efforts are carried on, (not to mention individual differences in genetically or uterine-derived temperamental characteristics) all make a difference in the total complex that goes to make up an individual personality. Fill out this picture, and we see the personalities of a society as being infinitely variable, each unique. But that picture is distorted too. There *are* commonalities, there are similarities in the way all these different original temperaments are molded to be more alike than different, for the Samoan to be more like another Samoan than like a Chinese or a Bantu. The socialization within a society, or a distinguishable subgroup within a society, does in fact follow patterns, and much of this process we can trace and explain. The socializers, though different from each other each as unique individual personalities, are not really so very different. Moreover, whatever their own biographies, they are subject to very similar *contemporary* pressures and problems when functioning as parents, teachers, club leaders and so on in socializing the child. Also, under the surface variability, they may be more alike at the deeper underlying levels of their personalities—the levels of the unconscious, of the intrapsychic conflicts—than they are themselves aware. And it is *particularly* at these levels that they

can impose great similarities in socialization upon a younger generation. It has already been stressed that the child learns more and is
molded more intensely by the non-verbal, phatic, unconscious, communications of the parent than by what is consciously taught.

For example, a generation of mothers angry and frustrated with
their housewifely lot, sexually unfulfilled by busy success-striving
husbands, communicates this driven frustrated quality directly to
their children. And a generation of children have experienced these
same or similar communications, as their experience of mother and
mothering, in common, usually unconscious ways. The daughters of
these mothers will, in turn, develop their ways of being female, being
wives and being mothers, that reflect these deeper intrapsychic realities, whether or not they ever verbalize a sense of tension about their
female roles. The sons, in turn, will develop similar unconscious
images of the female emphasizing the denying, deceiving, frustrating
"bitch" qualities, react in turn in their expectancies in courting,
marriage, fatherhood, and other masculine roles.

Personality is social product, yes, but that means product of the
whole entanglement of social and psychic forces of all the individuals involved in the growing of the child as each reacts to the others
and to his own inner self. The social forces of which personality is a
product *include* the personalities—all the intrapsychic conflicts, tensions, doubts, as well as strengths, joys, and capacities—of each of
the "others" in the child's social world. The cultural dimension includes all those norms of how the family is structured—monogamous or polygamous marriage, nuclear or extended family, bilateral
or unilineal descent groups; the economic roles of husbands and
wives and children; the legal position of different familial roles; the
norms expanding or contracting the prescriptions and proscriptions
of all the various family roles. These constitute the *frame*, within
which the particular psychic reactions and counterreactions go on,
among the various players. The frame makes for a push toward certain kinds of intense involvements and not, or less, toward others, as
for example, the difference between the intense and exclusive emotional ties among the very small number of members of the American nuclear family, in contrast to the diffuse, extensive, non-exclu-
sive, and relatively mild emotional ties of the Arapesh child toward
the great number and variety of kin. Further, besides direct influence of the kind just mentioned, the cultural frame produces consequences, not necessarily intended, to which the psychic structures of

the individual personalities react, and these reactions take on certain intrapsychic patterns (some unconscious), which are important for the relationships of the child.

Two contradictory statements may be made about the continuity of culture and the forms of social life. First, there is a strain toward continuity (analogous to the strain toward congruence): a culture *tends* to reproduce itself from generation to generation. Second, the continuity of the same forms is not always assured: it is precarious. The patterns of culture, the forms of social organization, can be changed, often drastically, within a generation. Most forms of social life, most cultures, no matter how well patterned, do have areas of looseness, of incongruity, of internal conflict, of discrepancy between the standard ways and some aspects of the psychodynamics of the participants, which make it uncertain that the patterns will have continuity from generation to generation. The psychodynamics of personality development always produce *latent* potentialities which may go relatively unexpressed in a particular historical period, but which may be suddenly tapped by changes in some aspect of culture or situation, sometimes with explosive creative or destructive effect.[24] Complexity, the internal conflicts and inconsistencies, and the sheer variety of temperaments upon which similar socialization and situational pressures are imposed, make room for some innovation and change. Thus a special convergence of unique personalities, culture crisis, and an unprepared-for situation may produce a drastic change so that something apparently entirely new emerges. This may mean liberation, or it may mean new and different constraints. These elements of looseness and variability are tremendously important, in large-scale modern societies, with their great complexity and special premium upon change, and in previously less complex societies undergoing technological transformation and its consequences. Such systems have areas of *play*.[25] A system that has "room for play" —and all do to some extent—has chances for transformation, with all its awesome potential for both greater freedom and more and different conflicts.

[24] For example Manus from 1928 to 1953. See Margaret Mead, *New Lives for Old, op. cit.*

[25] A deliberate play on words is intended, for "play" means energies not committed to required tasks, "play" means release of the imagination—more deeply, release of some of the most powerful forces of the unconscious, of the repressed erotic and aggressive potentialities. Such release produces activities that are allowed because they apparently "don't count."

SELECTED BIBLIOGRAPHY

Aberle, D. F., *et al.* "The Incest Taboo and the Mating Habits of Animals," *American Anthropologist.* Vol. 65, 1963, pp. 253-65.
An excellent critical review of theories of the origin and persistence of the incest taboo.

Barnouw, Victor. *Culture and Personality.* Homewood, Ill.: Dorsey Press, 1963.
A simply written introductory text representing the prevailing trends in anthropological culture-personality studies, including lucid discussion of methods.

Benedict, Ruth. *Patterns of Culture.* Boston: Houghton Mifflin, 1934, and many later editions.
In effect, the "manifesto" of cultural relativism dominant in anthropology of the second quarter of the twentieth century, and probably the most influential single book in anthropology of the period.

Brown, Norman O. *Life Against Death.* Middletown, Conn.: Wesleyan University Press, 1959.
A penetrating analysis of the culture of the West, seen as a product of, as well as producing, distinctive forms of the "universal neurosis" of man. A radical Freudian view as distinct from the neo-Freudianism of Erich Fromm.

Calhoun, D., *et al.* (eds.). *Personality, Work, Community: An Introduction to Social Science.* Philadelphia: J. B. Lippincott, 1953, and later editions.
The first part, "Personality," a stimulating and intriguing collection of papers and excerpts from a great variety of sources on the relationship of personality to society and culture.

Cohen, Yehudi A. *Social Structure and Personality.* New York: Holt, Rinehart and Winston, 1961.
A thoughtful "casebook" containing many important contributions.

Erikson, Erik. *Childhood and Society.* New York: W. W. Norton & Co., 1950.
A masterful development of neo-Freudian "revision" highlighting an influential revision and broadening of the Freudian "psychosexual stages," with a shift of emphasis from libidinal problems to ego psychology.

Ford, C. and A. Beach. *Patterns of Sexual Behavior.* New York: Harper & Row, Publishers, 1951.
Both cross-cultural and cross-species comparative study of sexual behavior, providing wider perspectives on human sexuality.

Freud, Sigmund.
Annotation is scarcely necessary in this Freudian age.
Among the major writings, in English translation, are:
————. *Beyond the Pleasure Principle.* New York: Liveright Publishing Corp., 1950.

————. *Collected Papers*. 5 Volumes. London: Hogarth Press and the Institute of Psychoanalysis, 1953.

————. *The Ego and the Id*. London: Hogarth Press and the Institute of Psychoanalysis, 1949.

————. *A General Introduction to Psychoanalysis*. New York: Liveright Publishing Corp., 1935.

————. *Three Contributions to a Theory of Sex*. New York: E. P. Dutton & Co., 1962.

————. *Totem and Taboo*. New York: W. W. Norton & Co., 1952. Probably the most controversial and "disputed" of Freud's writings. Anthropologically considered fantastic and untenable at the time of its original publication in 1913 and for long afterward, it has come to be re-evaluated with greater respect (see Margaret Mead).

Fromm, Erich. *Escape from Freedom*. New York: Holt, Rinehart and Winston, 1941. Attempts a psychodynamic interpretation of the rise of Protestantism and the modern secular order of the West, in effect linking the analyses of Weber and Freud.

Hockett, Charles and Robert Ascher. "The Human Revolution," *Current Anthropology*. Vol. 5, No. 3, June 1964, pp. 135-47; followed by illuminating commentary by other major anthropologists. Significant new theory of human origins, linking language, culture and ecological adaptation to evolutionary analysis.

Hsu, Francis (ed.). *Psychological Anthropology*. Homewood, Ill.: Dorsey Press, 1961. An important source book of critical articles surveying the anthropological literature in this field. For the advanced student.

Inkeles, Alex. "Some Sociological Observations on Culture and Personality Studies," in C. Kluckhohn, H. Murray and D. Schneider, *Personality in Nature, Society and Culture*. rev. ed. New York: Alfred A. Knopf, 1952. An important critical discussion of the anthropological studies.

Kaplan, Bert (ed.). *Studying Personality Cross-Culturally*. New York: Harper & Row, Publishers, 1961. Like the Hsu volume, a significant collection of advanced papers, largely theoretical.

Kluckhohn, Clyde, Henry Murray, and David Schneider (eds.). *Personality in Nature, Society and Culture*. rev. ed. New York: Alfred A. Knopf, 1952. Probably the most valuable collection of papers of its time, with significant introductory essays by Kluckhohn and by Murray, linking the anthropological and the psychodynamic traditions.

La Barre, Weston. *The Human Animal*. Chicago: University of Chicago Press, 1954. A profound synthesis of evolutionary theory, linguistics, psychoanalysis and analysis of culture. One of the most important contributions of the twentieth century to the understanding of man.

Malinowski, Bronislaw. *Sex and Repression in Savage Society*. London: Routledge & Kegan Paul, 1927.
Malinowski's use of his ethnographic study of the Trobriand Islanders to challenge basic Freudian conceptions of the Oedipus complex ushers in the confrontation of psychoanalysis and anthropology pursued since that time.

Mead, Margaret. *Male and Female*. New York: William Morrow and Company, 1949, and many later paperback editions.
A good example of this prolific anthropologist's work. Combines richness and sensitivity of direct observation in many primitive societies, acuteness of comparative analysis, and demonstration in detail of the psychodynamic view. A significant modification of the stridently cultural-relativistic view on these problems that Mead took in *Sex and Temperament in Three Primitive Societies*. New York: William Morrow & Co., 1935.

————. "Totem and Taboo Reconsidered with Respect," *Bulletin of Menninger Clinic*. Vol. 27, 1963, pp. 185-99.
A thoughtful reappraisal of Freud's "construction" in the light of recent advances in the knowledge of man's evolution.

Parsons, Talcott. *Personality and Social Structure*. New York: Free Press of Glencoe, 1965.
A collection of major theoretical papers relating personality to the social system. See especially papers on the Oedipus complex and social structure, and the incest taboo.

Róheim, Géza. "The Origin and Function of Culture," *Nervous and Mental Disease Monographs*. 1943.
A difficult seminal essay relating the infantilization of man to the development and perpetuation of culture.

————. *Psychoanalysis and Anthropology*. New York: International Universities Press, 1950.
The most thoroughly psychoanalytic analysis of several primitive cultures to be found in the literature. Challenges most of the personality-culture work of anthropologists in this field.

Ross, R. and E. Van den Haag. *The Fabric of Society*. New York: Harcourt, Brace and World, 1957.
Makes suggestive linkages of Freudian psychology and sociological analysis of society.

Sapir, Edward. *Selected Writings of Edward Sapir in Language, Culture and Personality*. Edited by David G. Mandelbaum. Berkeley: University of California Press, 1949.
The papers relating culture and personality, dating from the 1920s, the forerunners of the whole field.

Shibutani, Tamotsu. *Society and Personality: An Interactionist Approach to Social Psychology*. Englewood Cliffs, N.J.: Prentice-Hall, 1961.
A thorough and systematic exploration of relations between personality and society from a viewpoint very different from that of the present volume.

Smelser, Neil and William (eds.). *Personality and Social Systems*. New York: John Wiley & Sons, 1963.
A fine collection of mostly recent papers, representing a variety of theoretical perspectives and a large body of empirical studies.
Spitz, René A. *The First Year of Life*. New York: International Universities Press, 1965.
Documents the critical importance of emotional response and "mothering" during earliest infancy.
Whorf, Benjamin Lee. *Language, Thought, and Reality*: Selected Writings of Benjamin Lee Whorf. Edited by John B. Carroll. New York: John Wiley & Sons, 1956.
Major papers arguing the intrinsic linguistic infra-structure of culture and of different cultures. Relevant to the discussion of relations of personality, language, and culture introduced in this chapter.
Wrong, Dennis. "Human Nature and the Perspective of Sociology," *Social Research*. Vol. 30, No. 3, 1963, pp. 300-18.
An extension of the "oversocialized conception of man" argument.

TWO

Socialization: the family and its alternatives

In this chapter we shall pose some of the fundamental problems of socialization to be found in all societies and then examine some of the manifold ways these problems are handled in different societies, communities, or subcultures.

As Dennis Wrong has pointed out, socialization is used in two different senses, which should not be confused. One is the universal processes by which we become social human beings, functioning members of any human society. The other is culture-specific: the acquisition of the patterns and ways of life of a particular human society in a specific time and place. It is the former set of problems that is our first concern.

1. THE TASKS OF SOCIALIZATION

We can formulate the tasks of socialization in any society as the following: the channeling of libidinal forces, dealing with the unconscious, dealing with anxiety, the handling of aggression, life-cycle progression, learning of social roles, attainment of identity, internalization of values, dealing with play, provision of diversity, and the provision of integration. Let us briefly consider each of these in turn.

Channeling libidinal forces. Socialization must deal with the fundamental libidinal forces at the mainsprings of the human animal.

We have discussed some of the major features of these forces in their evolutionary and persisting elements in Chapter One. Each society must provide some degree of gratification for these drives and at the same time impose some restraints. No social system can handle a complete freedom of the potential polymorphous eroticism of human beings. But neither can it dam up these forces completely without risking destructive consequences. On one side, complete permissiveness of libidinal expression conflicts with any society's need for structured patterns of cooperation and control. On the other, the blocking of these powerful libidinal forces produces aggression with its great potential for either destructive constriction or explosive disruption of social order.

Dealing with the unconscious. Socialization must handle the unconscious forces in man and tie them in with meaningful social experience with cultural validation. It must provide some channeling for the unconscious fantasy life of man that is so crucial and often fateful a part of childhood development. To say that socialization must deal with the unconscious is almost a tautology, for inevitably the socialization process involves unconscious molding, pressuring, and manipulating of the new human animals by the regular agents of socialization—parents, siblings, other kin, teachers, preachers, and the rest. In the earliest stages of socialization unconscious communication of the socializers is an essential part of the whole process. The child learns not only what the socializers say, but also what they communicate non-verbally, by tone, gesture, stance, expression, the whole repertoire of phatic communication, as already discussed. The commonalities among the socialization agents, at this unconscious level, are an important part of the process. There must be, paradoxically, some coherence within this area of irrationality and non-rationality, and between it and the areas of conscious verbalized directions. Where they are at odds, the socialization process needs to provide some kinds of bridges and reconciliations among these conflicting forces.

Dealing with anxiety. Socialization must deal with anxiety. There are universal conditions that create or exacerbate anxiety. These conditions include the inevitable frustration of the human infancy situation, the conflict in infancy between magical omnipotence and almost total helplessness, the ever-present danger of regression; the perpetual danger of breakthrough of forbidden inner strivings, the conflict among the inner, unconscious, or barely conscious drives themselves and between these drives and the outer controls and restrictions; and the uncertainty and ambiguity of that outer world itself. The latter is a problem of perhaps unprecedented complication in the modern industrialized world.

Socialization has to provide for a repertory of mechanisms for handling such anxieties. It must further tie these mechanisms in with the learning and playing of meaningful roles and the acquisition of values at costs that are not too excessive. Psychoanalysis has taught us much about the mechanisms for dealing with anxiety, and it has pointed out the enormous inner costs that these devices and strategies can have. Socialization involves the social and cultural patterning of such mechanisms and their reinforcement by (often unverbalized) cultural validation. Not that the goal is simply "peace of mind." Under certain kinds of social conditions, it may be that the most positive device a socialization system can offer is the sheer capacity to *face* anxiety rather than defending against it by costly unconscious maneuvers.

Handling aggression. Socialization must provide patterned means of dealing with aggression, a universal human force. Whatever its relationship to instinctual forces, *aggressive feeling* is aroused in any human society by the blocking of libidinal expression, by the imposition of outer and inner controls upon behavior, by conflicts and rivalries with others, and generally by the blocking of attainment of any kind of goals human beings may strive for. Some forms and degrees of such frustration are inevitable in any human society. The problem for socialization then is how to deal with and channelize aggressions: when, how, and how much shall be turned back inwardly against the self of the individual personality; when, how, how much, and against what objects shall be turned outward against objects, human and other, in the outside world, at what costs and with what consequences. Here again, socialization must furnish some patterned ways. It cannot leave the channeling to the special vicissitudes of each individual personality. Whatever the patterns, there are inherent difficulties and dilemmas involved.

Life-cycle progression. Socialization must provide some meaningful pattern of movement or progression through the stages of the life cycle. The pattern must take into account universal aspects of the psychobiological changes and crises of the periods of growth, maturity, and decline, and it must consider the special situational and social pressures of the particular time and place. It needs also to allow for idiosyncratic differences among individuals in stage development. It must provide for some patterning of the psychosexual development that deals with inevitable conflicts in this sphere, provide culturally approved ways of dealing with such conflicts, and offer viable means of going on to the next stages. It must deal with the various maturational tasks confronted in the process of growth and provide stable guidelines for developing the relevant capacities and strengths for these tasks. At each stage it must give necessary social supports and permissions. In all of this there is the dilemma of providing stability without rigidity, permissiveness without chaos.

Role learning.   Socialization must provide meaningful *roles* and role learning which brings the child and developing adult into satisfying relationships with his society. This involves orientation to proximate goals that make sense in terms of the economy, history, and current situation of the particular society. It also involves orientation to the future, either assumed as stable continuation of the past or as something expected to be different in certain definable directions. This is not simply the task of preparing the young for the social roles that exist and keep the system going, for such a formulation assumes the integrity of the ongoing society and culture as a "going concern" and implicitly makes a positive value judgment of presently existing social arrangements. Rather we assume that any system, no matter how apparently well worked out and balanced by tradition, is a tentative arrangement, susceptible to change. Therefore, the question of what kind of socialization anticipatory of future adult roles that any particular society needs to have is problematical. This matter is open to evaluation, according to how well any given system reconciles societal or cultural "necessities" with the "necessities" dictated by the nature of the human animal.

Identity.   A related problem is that socialization must provide for some reasonably stable identities for males and for females, at various ages, and must facilitate the psychological mechanisms by which infant, then juvenile, human beings can arrive at such identities. Identity is, of course, a social product, its range of possibilities limited, if not determined, by the social and cultural forces of a particular society. But it is not only that. Identity for the individual means a uniquely personal configuration of his own choices among a range of models provided by the society. Socialization must provide the models, the standards for choosing among them, and the mechanisms for the pursuit of such choices, with all the intrapsychic and interpersonal difficulties involved in these processes. It must provide some coherence between expected or available social roles at different stages for each of the sexes, and the psychological dynamics of the individual personality. The problems involved are variably acute in different civilizations (and there is chorus of consensus that they are especially acute in our own at the present time). The socialization process must provide a repertory of viable solutions.

Internalization of values. Socialization must provide a meaningful system of values and mechanisms for learning these values. Some degree of internalization is necessary for any system, and socialization must supply the psychosocial mechanisms for such internalization.[1] Significant here, is *what* is internalized, and how, and at what psychic and social costs. What is the balance between such costs and the gratifications provided by the system? Internalization involves some kind of superego formation, and this implies some kind of intrapsychic mechanisms for handling aggression, partially at least by turning it against the self. The "social contract" always involves some kind of bargain, the giving up of some kinds of gratification or some times for gratification, in favor of others. But not all bargains are of equal value. A further complication is that much of the process is unconscious, rooted in early life experiences not easily recalled and therefore not easily open to deliberate change.

Play. Another task for socialization is to make room for *play.* This is related to the problem of dealing with unconscious processes, and to the problem of psychosexuality as an aspect of libidinal forces and of life-cycle stages. Man's protracted, indeed perpetual, infantilism includes his potential for play, not only in infancy and childhood, but throughout all of life. This is a basic, though not sufficient, condition for his enormous creativity. Socialization needs to provide for play as both an individual and a social need. Socially, play involves not only recreation—relaxation from required performances—but also the seeds of innovation, essential to keep any system adaptable to changing situations and changing character needs. Personally, play provides for expression of otherwise neglected or suppressed unconscious powers. It is not only a safety valve from the restrictiveness of any socially structured system of constraints, but also a positive creative force that can be channeled culturally into the arts and sciences or the molding of new social forms; or simply, and impor-

---

[1] See the paper by Dennis Wrong reprinted in Chapter One, on some of the theoretical problems involved in this notion.

tantly, give expression to the sheer exuberance of the human animal.

Diversity. Socialization must provide for human diversity. It must be able to take into account the whole range of genetically given temperament variation, innate potentialities, and accidents of individual history that make for variability in the "human material" with which the society is working to mold its role practitioners. This means that there must be enough role variability to match the variability of the actors and sufficient areas of leeway and permissiveness in how, when, on what terms roles are undertaken and played.

It may seem at first glance that most systems do nothing of this kind, but rather seem to try to mold the variable "human material" into a single, narrow pattern, or at most two or three alternative ones. On closer examination, however, even many primitive societies, which by some accounts seem monolithic in structure and to demand only a single social type for all the population, reveal an internal range of diversity in ways of conforming to the social demands or in patterns of feeling about the standard ways. In any case, it needs to be raised as a question: *How much range* does the society give for different kinds of persons to be their different kinds of selves —recognizing the paradoxes and ambiguities of such a question, since both differences and similarities are partially social products, and not merely expressions of inherent genetic potential.

Integration. Lastly, socialization has to provide for integration: of the person within himself, of the person with social forms and necessities, of the person with the convolutions of the culture. The fulfillment of this requirement may work against the fulfillment of some of the other demands, notably the need for recognition of diversity, the need for play, the need for expression of unconscious forces, and, in general, all those demands that bear on the quality of human freedom. Further, there is the inherent difficulty that the integration of some persons deeply into the fabric of the society and culture may have to be achieved at the expense of the integration of others.

With these "tasks of socialization" in mind, then, let us examine several varieties of childhood-socialization systems. About each we can ask how it works to deal with each of the kinds of problems that we have sketched: who are the primary agents of socialization, and how is the socialization process socially structured at each stage? What cultural norms apply to it at various stages and in various situations? And what are the effects, the costs, as well as the positive productivities, of each system in relation to universal human needs?

2. SOCIALIZATION AGENTS: THE FAMILY AND OTHERS

In Chapter One we discussed the universality of the nuclear family as the primary agency for the socialization and personality development of the child. Now important qualifications need to be made. In many societies the nuclear family is by no means the only socialization agency. In some societies extended family members, in some cases part of the same household, are important adjunctive socializers—for example, grandparents on one side or the other, certain aunts and uncles, and their offspring. In an extended matrilocal household, co-resident sisters of the mother may be active as additional "mothers," and all may share the mothering tasks toward the children of all of them, with their respective husbands as corresponding "fathers." In a polygynous household the co-wives may similarly share, to a great extent, each other's mothering tasks. In other systems relatives in a particular unilineal kin line—either the mother's or the father's—may have important particular roles to play, e.g., the maternal uncle as disciplinarian, teacher, and authority for the boy in a matrilineal system such as that of the Trobriand Islanders and many other primitive societies. In still other cases all of the adults of the local community may diffusely but actively participate as "parents" to all of the children, as in the Arapesh tribe of New Guinea,[2] the community called "Barrio Poyal" in Puerto Rico, and in the Kibbutz of Israel.[3] Do such differences in precisely who the socialization agents are, and how that setting is structured, make any important difference in the nature, patterns, and costs of the socialization process and thus for personality development in that society or community?

Also, considering these variations, is not the inevitability and crucial necessity of the nuclear family very much in doubt? One way of posing these questions is presented by the following paper by Barrington Moore, Jr., who challenges whether the nuclear family as

[2] See Margaret Mead, *Sex and Temperament in Three Primitive Societies* (New York: William Morrow, 1937, and many later editions).
[3] On Puerto Rico and on the Kibbutz, see later parts of this chapter.

familiar in Western cultures is really a functional necessity of a technologically advanced society. He points out some of the costs and disadvantages of the family as we know it.

Thoughts on the Future of the Family
BARRINGTON MOORE, JR.

Among social scientists today it is almost axiomatic that the family is a universally necessary social institution and will remain such through any foreseeable future. Changes in its structure, to be sure, receive wide recognition. The major theme, however, in the appraisal American sociologists present is that the family is making up for lost economic functions by providing better emotional service. One work announces as its central thesis that "the family in historical times has been, and at present is, in transition from an institution to a companionship." In the past, the authors explain, the forces holding the family together were external, formal, and authoritarian, such as law, public opinion, and the authority of the father. Now, it is claimed, unity inheres in the mutual affection and comradeship of its members. Another recent work by a leading American sociologist makes a similar point. The trend under industrialism, we are told, does not constitute a decline of the family as such, but mainly a decline of its importance in the performance of economic functions. Meanwhile, the author tells us, the family has become a more specialized agency for the performance of other functions, namely, the socialization of children and the stabilization of adult personalities. For this reason, the author continues, social arrangements corresponding rather closely to the modern family may be expected to remain with us indefinitely.

In reading these and similar statements by American sociologists about other aspects of American society, I have the uncomfortable feeling that the authors, despite all their elaborate theories and technical research devices, are doing little more than projecting certain middleclass hopes and ideals onto a refractory reality. If they just looked a little more carefully at what was going on around them, I think they might come to different conclusions. This is, of course, a very difficult point to prove, though C. Wright Mills, in a brilliant essay, has shown how one area of American sociology, the study of crime, is suffused with such preconceptions. While personal observations have some value, one can always argue that a single observer is biased. Here all I propose to do, therefore, is to raise certain questions about the current sociological as-

Reprinted by permission of the publishers from Barrington Moore, Jr., Political Power and Social Theory: Six Studies, *Cambridge, Mass.: Harvard University Press, Copyright, 1958, by the President and Fellows of Harvard College.*

sessment of the family on the basis of such evidence as has come my way rather casually. In addition, I should like to set this evidence in the framework of an intellectual tradition, represented, so far as the family is concerned, by Bertrand Russell's *Marriage and Morals*, that sees the family in an evolutionary perspective, and raises the possibility that it may be an obsolete institution or become one before long. I would suggest then that conditions have arisen which, in many cases, prevent the family from performing the social and psychological functions ascribed to it by modern sociologists. The same conditions may also make it possible for the advanced industrial societies of the world to do away with the family and substitute other social arrangements that impose fewer unnecessary and painful restrictions on humanity. Whether or not society actually would take advantage of such an opportunity is, of course, another question.

It may be best to begin with one observation that is not in itself conclusive but at least opens the door to considering these possibilities. In discussions of the family, one frequently encounters the argument that Soviet experience demonstrates the necessity of this institution in modern society. The Soviets, so the argument runs, were compelled to adopt the family as a device to carry part of the burden of making Soviet citizens, especially after they perceived the undesirable consequences of savage, homeless children, largely the outcome of the Civil War. This explanation is probably an accurate one as far as it goes. But it needs to be filled out by at least two further considerations that greatly reduce its force as a general argument. In the first place, the Soviets, I think, adopted their conservative policy toward the family *faute de mieux*. That is to say, with their very limited resources, and with other more pressing objectives, they had no genuine alternatives. Steel mills had to be built before crèches, or at least before crèches on a large enough scale to make any real difference in regard to child care. In the meantime the services of the family, and especially of grandma (*babushka*), had to be called upon. In the second place, with the consolidation of the regime in the middle thirties, Soviet totalitarianism may have succeeded in capturing the family and subverting this institution to its own use. At any rate the confidence and vigor with which the regime supported this institution from the early thirties onward suggests such an explanation. Thus the Soviet experience does not constitute by itself very strong evidence in favor of the "functional necessity" of the family.

If the Soviet case does not dispose of the possibility that the family may be obsolete, we may examine other considerations with greater confidence, and begin by widening our historical perspective. By now it is a familiar observation that the stricter Puritan ethics of productive work and productive sex have accomplished their historical purposes in the more advanced sections of the Western world. These developments have rendered other earlier elements of Western culture and society, such as slavery, quite obsolete, and constitute at least prima facie evidence for a similar argument concerning the family. Let us ask then to what extent may we regard the family as a repressive survival under the conditions of an advanced technology? And to what extent does the modern family perform the function of making human beings out of babies and small children either badly or not at all?

One of the most obviously obsolete features of the family is the obligation to give affection as a duty to a particular set of persons on account of the accident of birth. This is a true relic of barbarism. It is a survival from human prehistory, when kinship was the basic form of social organization. In early times it was expedient to organize the division of labor and affection in human society through real or imagined kinship bonds. As civilization became technically more advanced, there has been less and less of a tendency to allocate both labor and affection according to slots in a kinship system, and an increasing tendency to award them on the basis of the actual qualities and capacities that the individual possesses.

Popular consciousness is at least dimly aware of the barbaric nature of the duty of family affection and the pain it produces, as shown by the familiar remark, "You can choose your friends, but you can't choose your relatives." Even if partly concealed by ethical imperatives with the weight of age-old traditions, the strain is nevertheless real and visible. Children are often a burden to their parents. One absolutely un-Bohemian couple I know agreed in the privacy of their own home that if people ever talked to each other openly about the sufferings brought on by raising a family today, the birth rate would drop to zero. It is, of course, legitimate to wonder how widespread such sentiments are. But this couple is in no way "abnormal." Furthermore, a revealing remark like this made to a friend is worth more as evidence than reams of scientific questionnaires subjected to elaborate statistical analysis. Again, how many young couples, harrassed by the problem of getting started in life, have not wished that their parents could be quietly and cheaply taken care of in some institution for the aged? Such facts are readily accessible to anyone who listens to the conversations in his own home or among the neighbors.

The exploitation of socially sanctioned demands for gratitude, when the existing social situation no longer generates any genuine feeling of warmth, is a subtle and heavily tabooed result of this barbaric heritage. It is also one of the most painful. Perhaps no feeling is more excruciating than the feeling that we ought to love a person whom we actually detest. The Greek tragedians knew about the problem, but veiled it under religion and mythology, perhaps because the men and women of that time felt there was no escape. In the nineteenth century the theme again became a dominant one in European literature, but with the clear implication that the situation was unnecessary. Even these authors, Tolstoi, Samuel Butler, Strindberg, and Ibsen, in exposing the horrors and hypocrisies of family life, wove most of their stories around the marital relationship, where there is an element of free choice in the partner selected. Kafka's little gem, *Das Urteil*, is a significant exception. With magnificent insight into the tragedy on both sides, it treats the frustrations of a grown-up son forced to cherish a helpless but domineering father. Henry James's short story, *Europe*, is an effective treatment of the same relationship between a mother and her daughters. Despite some blind spots and limitations, the artists, it appears, have seen vital aspects of the family that have largely escaped the sociologists.

In addition to these obsolete and barbaric features one can point to certain trends in modern society that have sharply reduced rather than increased the effectiveness of the home as an agency for bringing up children. In former times the family was a visibly coherent economic unit, as well as the group that served to produce and raise legitimate children. The father had definite and visible economic tasks, before the household became separated from the place of work. When the children could see what he did, the father had a role to be copied and envied. The source and justification of his authority was clear. Internal conflicts had to be resolved. This is much less the case now.

It is reasonably plain that today's children are much less willing than those of a pre-industrial society to take their parents as models for conduct. Today they take them from the mass media and from gangs. Radio and television heroes, with their copies among neighborhood gangs, now play a vital part in the socialization process. Parents have an uphill and none too successful struggle against these sources. Like adult mobs, children's groups readily adopt the sensational, the cruel, and the most easily understood for their models and standards. These influences then corrupt and lower adult standards, as parents become increasingly afraid to assert their own authority for fear of turning out "maladjusted" children.[4]

The mass media have largely succeeded in battering down the walls of the social cell the family once constituted in the larger structure of society. Privacy has greatly diminished. Newspapers, radios, and television have very largely destroyed the flow of private communications within the family that were once the basis of socialization. Even meals

[4] It is sometimes claimed that the modern family still represents a bulwark against mass and totalitarian pressures. No doubt this is true in the best cases, those few where parents are still able to combine authority and affection. These are, however, mainly a relic of Victorian times. By and large it seems more likely that the family constitutes the "transmission belt" through which totalitarian pressures toward conformity are transmitted to the parents through the influence of the children.

are now much less of a family affair. Small children are frequently plumped down in front of the television set with their supper on a tray before them to keep them quiet. Since the family does less as a unit, genuine emotional ties among its members do not spring up so readily. The advertising campaign for "togetherness" provides rather concrete evidence that family members would rather not be together.

The mother, at least in American society, is generally supposed to be the homemaker and the center of the family. Has she been able to take up the slack produced by the change in the father's role? Is she, perhaps, the happy person whose face smiles at us from every advertisement and whose arts justify the sociologists' case? A more accurate assessment may be that the wife suffers most in the modern middle-class family, because the demands our culture puts upon her are impossible to meet. As indicated by advertisements, fiction, and even the theories of sociologists, the wife is expected to be companion, confidante, and ever youthful mistress of her husband.

If the demands could be met, many wives might feel very happy in this fulfillment of their personality. The actual situation is very different. The father is out of the house all day and therefore can be neither over-lord nor companion. With the father absent, radio and television provide the mother with a watery substitute for adult companionship. A young colleague told me recently that his wife leaves the radio on all day merely to hear the sound of a grown-up voice. The continual chatter of little children can be profoundly irritating, even to a naturally affectionate person. The absence of servants from nearly all American middle-class households brings the wife face to face with the brutalizing features of motherhood and housework. If she had the mentality of a peasant, she might be able to cope with them more easily. Then, however, she could not fulfill the decorative functions her husband expects. As it is now, diapers, dishes, and the state of the baby's bowels absorb the day's quota of energy. There is scarcely any strength left for sharing emotions and experiences with the husband, for which there is often no opportunity until the late hours of the evening. It is hardly a wonder that the psychiatrists' anterooms are crowded, or that both husband and wife seek escapes from psychological and sexual boredom, the cabin fever of the modern family. For the wife, either a job or an affair may serve equally well as a release from domesticity.

A further sign of the modern family's inadequacy in stabilizing the human personality may be seen in the troubled times of adolescence. This stage of growing up has been interpreted as a rejection of adult standards of responsibility and work by youngsters who are about to enter adult life. It seems to me that this period is more significantly one of pseudo-rebellion, when the youngsters copy what they see to be the real values of adult life instead of the professed ones. Even in the more extreme forms of youthful rebellion, relatively rare among respectable middle-class children, such as roaring around in noisy cars to drinking and seduction parties, the adolescents are aping actual adult behavior. Adolescents then do things they know many grown-ups do when the latter think they are escaping the observant eyes of the young. A "hot-rod" is, after all, nothing but an immature Cadillac. Where the Cadillac is the symbol of success, what else could be expected? Adult standards too are made tolerable through commercialized eroticism that lures us on to greater efforts and greater consumption from every billboard and magazine cover. Thus the whole miasma of sexual and psychological boredom in the older generation, pseudo-rebellion and brutality in the younger one, is covered over by a sentimental and suggestive genre art based on commercial sentiment.

No doubt many will think that these lines paint too black a picture. Statistics could perhaps be accumulated to show that families such as the type sketched here are far from a representative cross-section of American middle-class life. Such facts, however, would not be relevant to the argument. As pointed out elsewhere in these essays, the representative character of certain types of social behavior is not necessarily relevant to estimates of current and future trends. This kind of statistical defense of the status quo represents that of a certain maiden's virtue by the claim, "After all, she is only a little bit pregnant."

To refute the appraisal offered in these pages it would be necessary to demonstrate that they misrepresent basic structural trends in the family in advanced industrial countries. The most important argument of this type that I have encountered asserts that the proportion of married people in the population has steadily risen while the proportion of single individuals has steadily dropped. Therefore, people obviously prefer family life to bachelorhood, and the gloomy picture sketched above must be nothing more than vaporings of sour-bellied intellectuals thrown on the dump-heap by the advance of American society.

Before discussing the question further, let us look at some of the relevant facts. Table 2.1 (p. 77) shows changes in the proportions of single, married, and divorced persons in the United States from the age of fourteen onward. The source, an authoritative and very recent statistical survey of the American family, has standardized the proportions for age, using the 1940 age distribution as a standard, in order to eliminate changes due merely to shifts in the age composition of our population, which would merely confuse the issue.

The figures do show a rise in the proportion of married persons and a decline in the proportion of single ones. They also show that the proportion of married persons is overwhelmingly larger than the number of divorced ones. But the biggest change has been in the proportion of divorced people. For men it has risen ninefold since 1890 and for women

Table 2.1

PERCENTAGE DISTRIBUTION OF PERSONS 14 YEARS AND OVER
BY MARITAL STATUS AND SEX IN THE CIVILIAN POPULATION 1890–1954

Year	MALE Single	Married	Divorced	FEMALE Single	Married	Divorced
1954	28.4	66.7	1.8	22	65.8	2.2
1950	29.4	65.5	1.5	22.5	64.8	2.1
1940	34.8	59.7	1.2	27.6	59.5	1.6
1930	34.7	59.1	1.1	26.9	59.7	1.3
1890	36.7	57.9	0.2	27.8	57.7	0.4

more than fivefold. A bigger proportion of people are married now than in 1890, but a much bigger proportion have abandoned the marital state. In the long run, the latter change might turn out to be the more important one.

Even the statistical evidence, in other words, does not uphold in a completely unambiguous manner the sociologists' argument for the family. Sometimes an attempt to save the case is made by interpreting the rise in divorce as something that allows greater freedom for the individual to choose marital partners on the basis of congeniality. Thereby divorce allegedly strengthens the family's function as a source of emotional support. By talking about greater freedom for the individual in this fashion one has already taken a long step toward the opponents' view that marriage as such may be superfluous.

The point cannot be considered merely in the light of the facts as they exist now or have existed in the past. To do this in social questions is basically unscientific. Those who dismiss negative appraisals of the family with the crude observation that they reflect personal bias or mere "European decadence" deserve an equally crude reply: "So what if Americans prefer to get married! That simply shows how stupid they are."

Acrimony here unfortunately conceals a genuine issue. It is perfectly possible that conditions exist, perhaps even now, that permit better institutional arrangements than most people would be willing to accept. The word "better," of course, implies a definite standard of judgment. One can debate such standards endlessly, and perhaps cannot reach agreement without at some point making arbitrary assumptions. I shall not enter this debate here except to say that any social institution is a bad one that imposes more suffering on people than is necessary when they have sufficient material resources and scientific knowledge to do away with this suffering. This standard, anthropologists tell us, is that not only of Western culture, but of all culture.

What then, are the prospects for the future? We need not take a completely deterministic view. Indeed, the perceptions that both plain people and opinion-makers have about the present enter in as a significant component among the forces shaping the future and thereby provide an entering wedge for rational adaptation.

Among those who accept a substantial part of the preceding image of the family as basically correct, one frequently hears the prescription that what American culture really needs is a higher evaluation of the social role of the housewife and of motherhood. The trouble with this prescription, I would suggest, is that it merely increases the element of self-deception already so prevalent in our culture. Under present conditions motherhood *is* frequently a degrading experience. There is nothing to be gained by concealing the facts in the manner of an advertising campaign designed to raise the prestige of a particular occupation. We would not think of trying to eliminate the hazards of coal mining in this way. Why should we try to do it with motherhood? If it is true that under present circumstances the experience of motherhood narrows and cramps the personality rather than promotes the development of its capacities, some other way will have to be found if it is not to be a real solution.

The trend towards a continually more efficient technology and greater specialization, which dominates the rest of our culture, may conceivably provide an answer. In regard to the division of labor it is important to recall one widely known but neglected fact. In the past, whenever human beings have acquired sufficient resources and power, as among aristocracies, they have put the burden of child-rearing on other shoulders. Twenty years ago Ralph Linton pointed out that "aristocrats the world over . . . are reluctant to take care of their own children. Anyone who has had to take care of two or three infants simultaneously will understand why. This arduous business is turned over to slaves or servants . . ."

Since the decline of slavery, a basic trend in European society has been to transfer to machines more and more tasks formerly carried out by slaves. By and large, this change has been accompanied by the growth of large organizations to perform tasks formerly scattered among many small groups. This trend may well affect the family. Specialized human agencies, developing from such contemporary forms as the crèche, play school, and boarding school, might assume a much larger share of the burden of child-rearing, a task that could in any case be greatly lightened by machinery for feeding and the removal of waste products. Can one sensibly argue that the technical ingenuity and resources required to solve this problem are greater than those necessary for nuclear warfare? Are we to regard as permanent and "natural" a civilization that develops its most advanced technology for killing people and leaves their replacement to the methods of the Stone Age?

Against this viewpoint it is usually argued that human infants require some minimum of human affection, even fondling, if they are to survive, and that therefore some form of the family is bound to remain. The premises may be correct, but the conclusion does not follow. A nurse can perform these tasks of giving affection and early socialization just as well as the parents, often better. The argument does not prove anything therefore about the inevitable necessity of the family.

At the same time this point of view does call attention to certain important problems. Industrial society is not likely to produce household nurses, or any form of "servant class" in abundance. On the other hand, as everyone knows who has been in a hospital, nurses in a bureaucratic setting have a strong tendency to treat persons under their care "by the book," without much regard for their individual tasks and requirements. This is a well-known trait of bureaucracy, which tends to treat people and situations alike in order to achieve precision and efficiency. Infants and small children on the contrary require individual attention. For some years they may need to feel that they are the center of the universe. How then can the characteristics of bureaucracy be brought in line with those of maternal affection?

Though this may be the most difficult problem facing any qualitative transformation of the family, it is not necessarily insoluble. In the first place, as Bertrand Russell points out, a good institutional environment may be better for the development of the human personality than a bad family one. In the second place, an increase in the resources allocated to a bureaucratic organization can greatly increase its flexibility and capacity to satisfy variations in individual temperament. Any first-class hotel knows how to cope with this problem. In a few of the best ones in Europe the guest can have privacy and the illusion of being the center of the universe. Finally, one might legitimately expect that the persons who are drawn to serve in any such child-rearing institutions of the future would have more than the average amount of fondness for children, as well as general human warmth and kindliness. Under proper circumstances and management such institutions could give full scope to these benevolent sentiments.

Certain other considerations suggest an alternative that has at least the merit of being much more palatable to the vast majority of people today, since it is more in line with our deep-rooted cultural traditions. These considerations are essentially two. One is the possibility of some innate biological trait roughly resembling the "maternal instinct." The other lies in technological developments that might allow for wider dissemination of machinery to lighten household tasks and to take over the more routine aspects of child rearing. The dish-washing machine, laundromat, and, as a much more extreme device, the "Skinner box" represent prototypes of this technological development that could strengthen decentralized arrangements for rearing children.

I do not know what students of human physiology now believe about the maternal instinct. Common observation is enough to show that it cannot be an instinct like sex or hunger. There are many women who never become fond of children, or who soon cease to be fond of them. For them the institutional outlet just sketched would be the most satisfactory way of providing for their offspring. But for others, possibly the majority, the gestation period with its trials and burdens may be enough to create in the mother a desire to retain the infant under her care, after which she could become reluctant to give it up. If machinery were available to lighten child-rearing and household tasks on a far wider scale than is now the case, mothers might be able to satisfy the more positive desires of motherhood. One that seems to be quite important in the middle class is the desire to mold the child according to some ideal image, though it is now contradicted by fears of damaging the child that derive from superficial popularizations of Freud.

For the home to become again the place where human beings take the first important steps toward realizing their creative potentialities, parents would have to become willing once more to assert their authority. In turn this authority would have to acquire a rational and objective basis, freed of current attempts to revive religious taboos. Thus there would have to be a philosophical as well as a social revolution whose implications we cannot here pursue. One aspect, nevertheless, deserves to be stressed. Rational arguments can be given only to persons competent to understand them. For obvious reasons children are not able to absorb all rational arguments at once, though the present system of education undoubtedly postpones the development of this faculty where it does not destroy it altogether. Therefore parents will have to learn not to be afraid of saying to a child, "You are not old enough yet to understand why you have to do this. But you must do it anyway." The "progressive" family, where every decision turns into an incoherent and rancorous debate, actually contributes to reactionary tendencies in society by failing to equip the next generation with adequate standards of judgment.

There are, however, some grounds for doubting that this conservative solution will eventually prevail as the dominant one. The disappearance of the wider economic functions of the family would make it very difficult, and probably impossible, to restore the emotional atmosphere of a cooperative group in which the father has a respected authority. Furthermore, the bureaucratic division of labor has proved the most effective way of solving recurring and routine problems in other areas of life. Though a considerable part of the task of raising children is not routine, a very great proportion is repetitive. For these reasons one may expect that semi-bureaucratic arrangements will continue to encroach on the traditional structure of the family. No doubt many individual variations, combinations, and compromises will remain for some time to come. Yet one fine day human society may realize that the part-time family, already a prominent part of our social landscape, has undergone a qualitative transformation into a system of mechanized and bureaucratized child-rearing, cleansed of the standardized overtones these words now imply. As already pointed out, an institutional environment can be warm and supporting, often warmer than a family torn by obligations its members resent.

Such a state of affairs, if it comes at all, is well over the visible horizon now. Quite possibly it may never come at all. If it does come, there is not the slightest guarantee that it will solve all personal problems and land us in a state of air-conditioned euphoria. Values that many people hold high today may go by the board, such as the affection older couples show for one another who have shared the same pains in life until they have grown but a single scar. It is also possible that a world of reduced family burdens might be one of shallow and fleeting erotic intrigues, based really on commercial interests. Hollywood could conceivably be the ugly prototype of such a future world, especially in its earlier transitional phases. The most that might be claimed by any future apologist for such institutions, if they ever come to pass, is that they gave greater scope to the development of the creative aspects of the human personality than did the family, which had begun to damage rather than develop this personality under advancing industrialism. And the most that can be claimed for the arguments supporting this possibility is that they correspond to some important trends visible in the family itself as well as in the rest of society. Nevertheless, it would appear that the burden of proof falls on those who maintain that the family is a social institution whose fate will differ in its essentials from that which has befallen all the others.

With Moore's observations in mind, let us look at the actual composition of the family, the related socialization practices, and the kinds of personality patterns that allegedly result. We shall take four different communities for our case studies: three different "subcultures" in Puerto Rico, ranging from an isolated folklike community of small-scale farmers, through a more urbanized community of sugar-cane laborers, who are nevertheless still strongly traditional in their ways, to a highly urbanized segment of the population, the middle class of a small city, and thence to the Kibbutz of Israel. These cases present a range of familial and extra-familial agents of socialization—a range in the intensity and extensity of emotional relationships between the child and the various socialization agents —and a variety of different problems and conflicts (economic, ecological, political, social, and intrapsychic) that bear upon the socialization process and personality development. They show variety in the patterning of sex roles and variation in the extent and kind of inter-generational continuity to be found in each community. The pan-human problems of sex, aggression, fantasy, autonomy, and creativity find different versions, conflicts, and resolutions in the different cases.

3. SOCIALIZATION AND PERSONALITY DEVELOPMENT IN THREE PUERTO RICAN COMMUNITIES

Three communities in Puerto Rico show interesting variations on the common culture patterns of that island. We call them, pseudonymously, Manicaboa, Barrio Poyal, and San José. In socialization practices and personality development they reveal both important divergence and certain common elements within a common traditional culture.

Manicaboa is a community of traditional mountain farmers, living rather far apart on separate family holdings. Barrio Poyal is a community of wage-working sugar-cane laborers and their families, living in close proximity to each other on a narrow strip of land between a main highway and a vast sugar plantation run by an American-owned corporation, for which all the men work harvesting sugar cane five to six months of the year. The third group is the middle class of a rural town, San José, the town center of the county in which Manicaboa is situated.

Manicaboa

Though there are some larger landholdings in the Manicaboa area, the present analysis deals only with the owners of *small* family farms. These Manicaboans work their widely scattered holdings with family labor, supplemented by exchanging labor between neighboring families and on rare occasions with hired help. They grow coffee and tobacco, which they sell in town (San José) for cash to buy

This analysis is based on Kathleen Wolf, "Growing Up and Its Price in Three Puerto Rican Subcultures," Psychiatry, Vol. 15, 1952, pp. 401-33. With permission of the author and The William Alanson White Psychiatric Foundation, I have freely adapted the material of that paper; my interpretations generally follow those of Wolf, but at many points diverge or go beyond them.

their basic foodstuffs. Despite this link to an outside market, however, they lead very isolated, traditional lives. This economically precarious, marginal, family-ownership farming requires a very strict utilization of every family member's labor and frugal control over family consumption patterns. The father is responsible for these tasks. He is unquestioned head of this rather isolated nuclear-family household, with power over his wife and all resident children. The wife is his servant, and children work under his control without remuneration.

The family pattern is set by the combination of traditional Puerto Rican (and by derivation, generally Latin) value on unquestioned paternal authority and the particular economic, technological, and ecological conditions of this type of farming. Ecology favors the isolation of separate families. The technological level of this farming and the economics of raising a limited crop for an outside cash market dictate the rigorous production and consumption controls. These and traditional Latin values combine to make the monopolistic paternal authority especially strong.

In an intensification of general Puerto Rican culture patterns, the differentiation of the sexes in spheres of work and in expected behavior and feelings is particularly strong. Man's sphere is production work, social intercourse, and sharing with neighbors. Woman's sphere is the household and children and serving her husband in any way in dutiful subordination.

The norms for the *man* are the following: Though work is not a value in itself and is not routinized, a man should be a hard worker, skilled in the necessary agricultural techniques and able to work very long hours and with great spurts of energy *when it is necessary*. At other times, relaxation, breaking work to chat with friends, and idleness during the non-work season are all acceptable. In the social intercourse and sharing with neighbors that mark his periods of relaxation, a man should dispense his hospitality carefully, recognizing the guest's status and the probable reciprocal return. He must at all times be aware of his role and the social situation. When drinking, he must not get intoxicated, especially aggressively. He must be able to defend his dignity if offended, at least by threats of aggression within acceptable bounds. If attacked, he must be able to defend himself. He is the more respected if he can resolve a potentially aggressive situation without resort to physical aggression. However, if he is verbally attacked on a point of honor, such as family or politics, *and loses control,* he may aggress against, even kill, his attacker without community condemnation. In such a case, others will not report him to the police, or will refuse to testify against him in court.

For the Manicaboa *woman,* the only socially acceptable role is to be a good wife and mother. She must work hard: child bearing, child rearing, cooking for large numbers, serving her husband, sewing, washing, ironing, all the other work of the household, as well as working in the fields helping the men and boys during tobacco planting and coffee harvest. The criteria by which a man selects a wife are her training for these tasks and her attitudes toward family life, her economic status (any land she may eventually inherit), and lastly, physical attraction. There is no romantic love in a sense familiar to North Americans. Marriages may be by family arrangement or by elopement[5] forcing parental acquiescence.

Frequent child bearing is expected, adding to the eventual economic assets of the family. The first child should be conceived immediately to attest to the man's virility and to validate the marriage. A woman is supposed to show whole-hearted acceptance of bearing and rearing children.

A married woman's social life and self-expression are extremely constricted. The endless round of household chores, the geographic isolation, and the conventional restrictions of Latin tradition ensure this. Neighborliness is her husband's role. Her husband must be present with any male visitor. She may not attend dances, except to sit on the sidelines. She may visit town only for voting or for annual confession. Even errands to stores in town are not for her, but must be made by a male child. She may drink only at ceremonies, and then only a little wine. She may not overdress. She must serve her husband, and any male guests at the table, standing, and then eat with the children and any women visitors in the kitchen. Thus she has no such outlets as ornament, leisure, dancing, or independent remunerative employment. Further, controls on aggression are even tighter on women than on men. She is also not expected to enjoy sex. Trained for her role in life from very early childhood, the Manicaboa woman shows a high degree of personality constriction.

[5] The question has been raised: does elopement not imply romantic love? The answer is: not necessarily. There may be a strong physical attraction to a partner who is not the parents' choice, without the starry-eyed idealization that is typical or expected in North American courtship.

However, the limitations of her life are offset in a number of ways. Gratifications and self-esteem come from her husband's "good treatment" of her (indicated by his spending more than the minimum on the home or on clothing for the children) or from her pride in his land. Personality constriction is partly compensated by the firmness of her feminine identification. This is assured by the rigid distinction of sex roles through all phases of life, from earliest childhood on, and by the simple direct line of her socialization for mastery of adult female tasks begun in early childhood and followed in well-graduated stages into adulthood. Frequent pregnancy also provides narcissistic satisfactions. Having a baby of her own fulfills her girlhood identification with her mother, marks her as an adult woman, and also allows her minor ways of tyrannizing, for example, by insisting on fulfillment of her pregnancy food cravings. Further, she has several indirect outlets for aggression and sexuality, to be discussed presently.

MANICABOA CHILD TRAINING

Pregnancy is casually announced and involves neither change in the mother's work nor many physical symptoms. At labor, female relatives and *comadres* (ritual co-mothers) are called in, and a local midwife delivers the baby in the house. The relatives preferred are the new mother's own mother, sisters, and other female kin, but may include her husband's. These women take over the mother's duties toward husband and child during the confinement. The same mother-surrogates reappear with each new birth or other times of family crisis. Most children witness childbirth openly or surreptitiously early in life.

For only a few days after the birth, the mother is relieved of all tasks and dedicates herself to the new baby. This intimacy, contributing to the baby's security, is however short-lived. Then the mother's other duties are resumed, and baby care is progressively entrusted to older sisters over six. The baby is breast-fed until the next one is on the way. The infant is picked out of his special hammock and given the breast whenever he cries, but as soon as he begins to show gratification, the breast is removed, and he is placed in his hammock. This makes for very frequent feedings of extremely short duration, perhaps only a few minutes. The infant is thus subjected to constant oral frustration and real hunger. However, the child may gratify his *sucking* instincts by homemade pacifiers.

In other aspects baby care is permissive and easygoing. The baby is easily integrated into the household and taken quite for granted. He spends his time in a small hammock over the parents' bed, or at his mother's breast. When he cries, he is rocked in the hammock or held by a woman or girl of the family. Gradually his sisters take over his care, but the mother is always about, watching out for any rough treatment or carelessness. At the age of one year he gets his first solid food, thinned oatmeal. Later he receives rice prechewed by his mother. He is encouraged to eat alone with his fingers as soon as he can. No attention is paid to the mess he makes.

Toilet training is entirely casual. The mother assumes that it takes a long time but that the child will learn by himself. For infants, diapers are used only when visitors are present. Later, in learning toilet habits, the child is expected to be clumsy. He is never reprimanded for soiling himself or the house: his mother or a sister will casually clean up. At the age of two he is taught to use a little chamber pot for bowel movements and is expected to urinate outside. Up to the age of four or five he is washed daily by his mother before the father's return from the fields. Later he is expected to do this with an older sister's help, then finally by himself. The whole toilet and cleanliness training process is casual, permisssive, and timed to the child's own capacities.

The child's motor development and gradual mastery over the environment is encouraged but never forced. In the creeping stage he is given wide latitude within the house. As he learns to walk, he can play outside the house. Mothers take more pride in a baby's early walking than early talking. Meanwhile the child is dependent on his mother's breast and is babied until a new sibling comes. Even then dethronement is gradual. Dethronement frustration is partly compensated by the increasingly active role permitted the child in the family. At four or five the child's independence is fostered, and he must begin to give up the warm affectionate fondling of his father as well as his mother in favor of younger siblings. Still five- and six-year-olds get a lot of attention and affection.

The gradual development of mastery is particularly strong in Manicaboa for both sexes. One of its effects is to mitigate the frustraions of being dethroned by younger siblings and of giving up the erotically tinged dependency on both parents. The Manicaboans actively encourage learning by experimental handling of objects and imitation of parental activities. Prescribed tasks are set at each age level, gradually integrating the child into the economic unit. The fact that the Manicaboan nuclear family household is a production as well as consumption unit, and therefore all children are economic assets from the age of about five or six, is important here. At five or six, both boys and girls fetch water, in pairs, and both help tend babies, though girls more actively. From about the age of six, the sex distinctions in prescribed tasks become increasingly sharp. At about six, girls sweep house and start learning cooking chores. Long before puberty a girl is expert in all aspects of child care. During this period the girl is increasingly confined to the household by her growing share of household tasks. As she approaches puberty, she is scarcely ever let out of sight of the house. Her schooling, if any, ends with the third grade, and she never runs errands. By contrast, the boy from about six years of age runs errands to stores and takes lunch to the men in the fields. At seven or eight, he is out of the house most of the time and inducted gradually into farm work—planting tobacco, picking coffee berries from low boughs, weeding taro patches. By nine or ten, he has his first man-sized job—moving cattle. By now he is a skilled horseman. Errands bring contacts with other boys. They stop or walk together, seriously discussing crops and animals, much like their fathers. More boys go to school than girls, parents recognizing that a man will be less easily swindled by town folk if he can read and write. However, at tobacco-planting and coffee-harvest time, the schoolroom is almost empty. The separation of boys from girls extends to play activities, also, even before the age of six.

Thus the gradual, unhurried, unpressured but very definite acquisition of mastery of sex-linked skills means not only a very strong ego development, but also a strong and unambiguous sexual identity. It also compensates for or mitigates the various frustrations of childhood, including dethronement, sibling rivalries, the constriction of the female's life, and the authoritarian submission of the boy to his father and elder brothers. We may note some of the essential elements in this ego strength through mastery: the tasks expected of the child are clearly and obviously useful to the family as an economic unit; in each case the child has a clear-cut visible model in an adult or older child of the same sex; and while a special level of skill, as in boys' carpentry or girls' sewing, are encouraged and given recognition, no child is pushed to perform beyond his capacities at any given time. Also, while few activities are exclusively play, the acquisition of mastery includes many playlike situations. A little girl is not reprimanded if in fetching water from the spring, she dawdles and plays with the tin can, testing ways of filling it, and pretending it is an iron. A boy moving cattle for the first time (a man's job) is not expected to do it right at once, nor is he punished for mistakes. Thus, the task both lacks the urgency of work and gives the boy more ego gratification than any purely play act could. Even within the careful limits set by the father, boys do have opportunities for ego emancipation through tasks that are both useful and have a play element of skill and daring. For example, boys as young as ten accompany, on foot, visitors who have been loaned horses by the household. When the visitors reach the highroad, the boys race back home down the mountainside on the horses, with great feats of skill and daring. (By contrast, girls rarely if ever have such ego opportunities.)

Mastery, ego-strength, and clear sexual identity are also related to early learning in relation to the body. With the important exception of the early-infancy oral frustration, most of this learning is casual, matter-of-fact, and permissive. Anal training is unhurried and permissive, in the context of a casual matter-of-fact attitude toward dirt, soiling, and messiness generally. This would appear to have a direct connection with the absence of compulsiveness about work in adults. Working hard is important as a necessity, but work is not a value in itself. Manicaboans are not compulsive or routinized about work. Work follows from the necessities of family economics, not from non-rational inner "driven-ness." Relatedly, though the sexual sphere is not without its complications, knowledge about sex and reproduction is casually and matter-of-factly acquired firsthand. Children see pet animals mate and reproduce and inevitably witness parental sexual relations. Most children see their mother bear another child nearly every year. Older daughters may help with the delivery. Girls do not have to be told about menstruation or marriage. And the recognition of physical sex differences is constantly reinforced by the sharp sex distinctions in social and economic roles and expected psychological reactions.

MASTERY AND AUTONOMY

Though mastery is rather strong in Manicaboa, autonomy is not. Most generally the functioning unit is the *whole* family. It is a relatively isolated residential entity and economically both a production and consumption unit. The interests of the family unit as a whole always outweigh those of individual members, a fact learned early in the tasks and chores children must take on. Related to this is the fact that children must learn to accept a long period of dependence on the family group. Growing girls are under the strict control and supervision of mother and older sisters, and periodically of other older female relatives. They are kept within or very close to the physical household itself. And all females, including the mother, are by social definition strictly subordinate to the authoritarian father. Too much formal schooling (meaning anything beyond third grade) for girls is discouraged. One reason for this attitude is that the female schoolteacher (necessarily a town woman, hence a representative of alien values) may come to be a model of aspiration for girls, preventing them from being satisfied with repeating their mothers' patterns in the next generation. The adult woman's area of autonomy is severely limited.

For males, infancy and early childhood mean control by the mother and older sisters. From about five or six on, the boy comes under the stern authority of the father, who in teaching and directing him in his farm chores makes incontestable demands that strongly limit any expression of autonomy by the boy. The father's authority, in contrast to the sadistic and domineering pattern of the classical European authoritarian family, is secure and need not be asserted, since it has a firm base in the direction of family resources and labor. The father need not, and does not, resort to violence. Wife-beating or corporal punishment of children is very rare. Further, the father becomes authoritarian to the child only when the child is old enough to be integrated into the work unit, that is, not before the child is about six. Earlier he is gentle, indulgent, and erotically responsive and presumably gratifying to the child. Nevertheless, for the boy in the post-Oedipal period, any move overstepping the limits set by the father in the mastery development of the child endangers the boy's economic security and his position in the family.

DEVIANT SOCIAL ROLES

For the female, there is no alternative institutionalized role other than that of the good subservient wife and mother of the household. For the male, however, there are two recognized deviant alternatives to the role of the hard-working, controlled, authoritative family head. One is the *guapo*, the other the clown or idiot.

The clown is a "shrewd, crazy man" who uses his talents to amuse people and thus manages to get himself supported economically. Such deviancy is accepted once perceived: "He was always hare-brained, and always will be. He had a fever as a baby." The child is thus not held responsible. Signs of this kind of deviancy appear when the boy's performances on the graduated tests of childhood reveal him to be lacking in the bodily skills and mental capacity needed to make him an able worker. No attempt is made to correct him or fit him into a mold. There are always other children, and they are of course not all alike. The "fool" is therefore assigned tasks within his capacity. His place in the family is secure; he may even get an extra share of babying. The "fool" thus represents Manicaboa's way of recognizing *deficiency* in expected masculine characteristics. Their acceptance of the "fool" reflects their high tolerance and respect for individual differences and lack of "driven-ness" toward work and achievement goals. Early recognition of diagnostic "signs" and tacit encouragement for continuation of the pattern, supported by facile rationalizations such as the early fever, ensure the absence of conflict or identity difficulties in such individuals.

The *guapo* has a more pervasive significance. The word may be translated as gallant, beau, lovemaker; or as brawler or quarrelsome person. Thus the *guapo* epitomizes an intensity of sexuality and aggression, the two basic drives that may be disruptive in any social order. Sexual aggressiveness and interpersonal aggressiveness in self-assertion or violence are also socially defined in Manicaboa (indeed in Puerto Rican culture generally) as especially masculine character-istics. Significantly, however, for the normal Manicaboan male, both of these drives are supposed to be kept under very careful control, the demand being the more compelling because Manicaboans be-lieve that males in general have a harder time controlling their im-pulses than females.

As with the clown, but even more so, the potential future *guapo* is spotted early. A male child of constitutionally or otherwise deter-mined greater aggressivity than average is early recognized as a prob-able *guapo*. It is easy to excuse him because "he can't help it" or "he was born that way." More than merely excusing him, the mother actively encourages his assertiveness. She fosters his omnipotence and megalomania fantasies and also his assertive "getting away with things." To the father, the *guapo* son is a source of pride (though later a potential threat to his authority), for he has not only produced a son, but one whose aggressiveness connotes hyper-masculinity, hence the more conclusively proving the father's virility. Hence, though only up to a point, the father supports the mother's encouragement of the budding *guapo*, probably at the expense of other, less assertive sons who will be all the more strictly dominated by the father as though in compensation.

The adult *guapo* may express his aggression openly and be provocative without reason, but his untamed violence may be expressed only in a neighborhood outside his own. He is viewed with admiration mixed with awe. People lament his actions and show vicarious pleasure in them. They identify with him, though they would tolerate his behavior in no one else. There is usually room for only one really violent *guapo* in a neighborhood. If there are two in one neighborhood, hence likely to feud with each other, they may be controlled by making them *compadres*, a ritual kinship tie of strong mutual obligation which demands an etiquette of courtesy precluding open aggression. Through the group's identification with him, the *guapo* can also channel other people's aggressions against an outgroup. The mountain folk delight in tales of outrageous acts of their local *guapo* against people of neighboring or alien localities, acts of a kind that would be drastically tabooed within their own neighborhood.

The mother is important in the *guapo* phenomenon. A generalized but usually not openly expressed dissatisfaction with her married life would tend to lead her to an early unconscious seduction of the assertive male child. He can be the instrument for gratification of her heavily repressed sexuality. Significantly, Manicaboa women say that a woman who openly says she enjoys sex with her husband, must be suffering from an illness, presumably mental. A *guapo* son, a prospective beau-gallant and wild aggressor, can be a permissible answer. "He can't help it," therefore, implicitly, neither can she, his mother, for encouraging him in his wild ways. The aggression component of the *guapo* is significant for her too. Taboos on physical aggression are even more stringently imposed on women than on men. Through a *guapo* son she may vicariously, and without reproach, express such aggression.

Other women derive gratifications as well. Those who are the objects of his sexual gallantries may derive otherwise tabooed sexual gratification without too heavy a cost of guilt, on the plausible excuse that by definition the *guapo* is sexually irresistible. Still other women may derive vicarious enjoyment by identifying in fantasy with the *guapo's* "victims." In the light of the fact that prevalent women's gossip portrays women as sexually exploited victims, such gratifications would probably have to operate largely at the unconscious level and contain a large measure of masochism.

For men, the *guapo* role is the major aggression safety valve, both for those who are so typed and for others vicariously. Significantly, it is the *guapo* son, rather than the good conforming son, who is more likely to inherit the father's farm, and he thus becomes one of the main male authorities of the next generation. In this way violation, within bounds, of the otherwise strict aggression control is rewarded, by maternal favoring, by later community support, and often by economic success in rivalry with the brothers. It represents, then, a kind of equilibrating mechanism for the problems generated by the whole dominance-submission-aggression complex of this patriarchal system. If sons are ordinarily rigorously trained in submission to the father in childhood and adolescence, how does the community have sufficiently assertive fathers in the next generation? A *guapo* son is a partial answer, though necessarily limited by the norm of one to a neighborhood. Perhaps *guapo*-like tendencies, short of the full social type, appear sufficiently frequently among other young men to supplement this answer. Vicarious identification with other men who are *guapos* probably also suggests reserves of assertiveness in many other males, that can be tapped on accession to the authority role of farm-and-household head. Ego strength through skill mastery would also be a supporting psychological configuration.

The mixture of awe, lament, and respect with which the *guapo* is regarded shows the basic ambivalence of the Manicaboans about aggression. The *guapo* expresses for everyone else what they would like to do and say, if only they dared. He serves the community's inner needs and further serves as the executor of their outgroup aggressions, thus helping keep the lid on potentially very disruptive intra-community aggressions. The *guapo* in vicariously expressing others' sexuality and aggressions is comparable to the figure of the delightful and charming villain or rogue of North European and derived North American cultures, for example the figure of the confidence man, or more broadly the Trickster or *Til Eulenspiegel* figure.[6]

[6] See discussion of play in Chapter Five.

AGGRESSION

Certain features of child rearing and the adult situation make aggression a problem in the Manicaboan subculture, as already suggested in other connections. For both sexes, sources of aggression derive not only from universal dilemmas of growing up in any society, but also from certain features specifically Manicaboan. Among these are the early oral frustration in infancy, dethronement and sibling rivalries, restrictions on sexual expression, and authoritarian submission to the parents, especially the father and to a lesser extent older siblings. For males, there are additionally the constraints on the expression of autonomy in work. For females, there are the constriction of the female role generally, and the greater degree of sexual repression than is true for the males.

Oral frustration. The breast-feeding pattern has already been mentioned. The baby is given the breast for periods so brief that he is only beginning to be gratified when he is put down. He gets just enough nourishment to take the edge off his hunger and to thwart his anger. Emotional frustration and real hunger are both involved here. This cannot but be a major source of aggression. By contrast, the sucking needs of the child are extensively gratified by homemade pacifiers. The combination results in a pervasive *oral fixation,* indicated by a tremendous preoccupation with food and eating that prevails in this subculture. One might argue that such preoccupation could be explained on the basis of real food deprivation that obtains here because of the impoverished marginal farming. But how would we then explain the absence of such preoccupation among the people of Barrio Poyal, who are economically as badly off as the Manicaboans, or the presence of such preoccupations in some populations that have no real food deprivations, such as well-to-do second-generation American Jews? In Manicaboa real food shortages may provide the rationalizations for the food preoccupations and also for the mother's feeding behavior—a "reason" she does actually give—and thus reinforce a pattern that also has deep intrapsychic roots. Support for the "depth" interpretation offered here comes from inconsistencies and other apparent irrationalities in various aspects of related behavior. For example, we can point to the indulgence of pregnancy cravings: in response to his pregnant wife's demands, a man may kill a chicken to give to her, an act which violates the fundamental and pervasive scarcity- and economy-mindedness of these households and one that would not be repeated in other circumstances. Further, the connection of orality with aggression, especially for women, is shown in other ways. The threat of the orally demanding pregnant wife is abortion, an extremely aggressive act in this context. Interestingly, though deliberate attempts at abortion are made by women in this culture, the threat accompanying pregnancy-craving demands is of *spontaneous miscarriage*, thus allowing the woman this aggressive threat while not holding her responsible for the aggression implied in it. This is surely unconscious functioning in almost classic clarity. Since children are economic assets and of special symbolic value to the father ("to validate his virility") even miscarriage, let alone deliberate abortion, is very aggressive against the husband. Further links of orality and aggression are seen in the fact that the method used in deliberate abortions is invariably an oral one, the taking of powerful purgatives. So also is the method used in suicide, which appears to be predominantly if not entirely a female phenomenon here. The lack of discrimination with which such oral purgatives are used in Manicaboa (though they do have some, limited, practical value) indicates some determination by intrapsychic forces. It is evident, then, that the oral frustration pattern experienced by the baby, itself a source of further aggressions, is at least in part derived from the aggressions of the mother. These in turn reflect a pervasive ambivalence about the constrictive feminine role that is her only choice in life. (This role is probably among the most restrictive and suppressive that women have to bear anywhere in the world.)

Dethronement and sibling rivalries.   Since contraceptives are not used, the woman has a new baby almost annually. Dethronement is hence a basic experience for all children but the few who are the last-born of these large families. Though the mother gives a lot of attention to all the children under the age of about five, this attention must be divided among many. Similarly the father's loving fondling of his children in his after-work hours ceases for the child when he is about four or five, and the child must give way to younger siblings. Sibling rivalries among brothers are expressed in fighting. An older sister can express hers toward babies in her charge by aggressive ways of taking care of the child, e.g., rocking the baby violently in his hammock so that he is in danger of falling out. Sisters may express such aggressions against each other by telling tales on each other to the mother. Though not intentionally for this purpose, parents deal with boys' rivalries by pairing them. The two boys nearest in age to each other sleep together, stick together, play together, and are expected to be very close even into adult life. The "reason" given is that they take care of each other, help each other avoid dangers, and save the parents a lot of trouble. Pairing is less common for girls, probably because they remain close within the mother's reach.

Dethronement frustration is compensated by the child's progressive integration into the instrumental aspects of family life through his growing mastery of household or farm skills. For the girls there is the further compensation of taking over the care of younger siblings, with its opportunities for not only mastery, but also various ways of tyrannizing over them.

Boys' rivalries may also be expressed in competitive feats of daring, such as their racing their horses down the mountainside. The pairing of close-in-age brothers parallels other types of pairing of males in this culture. One of these is the *compadre* (ritual cofather) relationship. There, the exaggeration of mutual courtesy, cooperation, and obligation, certainly suggests that it represents, in part, a reaction formation against strong aggressive rivalrous feelings. Significantly the *compadre* relationship is deliberately enjoined upon two neighboring *guapos*, as a control on potential aggressions against each other. Another indication of the close affinity of mutual aggression to the *compadre* relationship is seen in the fact that when young boys play at being *compadres*, they overtly express a great deal of aggression, jokingly hitting and kicking each other. It is clear that the boys are not imitating the overt behavior of adult *compadres*, where such physical aggression is strenuously tabooed. Hence it seems reasonable to conjecture that the boys have picked up the latent, or unconscious, content of the *compadre* relationship. In effect, the boys are saying, "We're doing as you [adult *compadres*] *feel*, not as you say and pretend." Such apparently "uncanny" perceptiveness of adults' subliminal feelings is not at all unusual in very young children in other societies. These games occur primarily in early childhood in the age period from about four to seven, before the boy has much responsibility for farm chores. Later, the boys "know better"—that is, repressions and reaction formations have set in.[7] The fighting that intermittently breaks out among adult male peers is also proba-

[7] Suppose one argues that these are just little boys playing mildly aggressive games, as boys of this age do anywhere, and are just expressing the aggressions they themselves feel and that it is only incidentally called playing *compadres*. Why infer subliminal perception of adults' "real feelings"? The question then is, why is it called "*compadres*" and not something like "two men fighting when drunk" or some other such title reflecting realistic imitation? We do not regard it as accidental if children call a certain game "playing doctor."

bly partially derived from the repressed aggressions of the sibling rivalry situation.

Authoritarian submission. Children of both sexes must submit to the definite and strict authority of the parents—both to the domination of the household by the father, girls to control by the mother in household tasks, and boys to the specific control by the father in learning the farm chores. True, this authority is rooted in economic realities and does not typically involve petty domineering such as would occur in cases like a minor town employee asserting his control over his family in reaction to the control exerted over him by others in his work. True also that the authority is exerted in a context which aids the child of each sex to grow progressively in mastery of the skills appropriate to his sex. Still, the unthinkability of challenging the parent's authority in any of these matters must arouse some aggressive feelings, and these in turn cannot be expressed against the parents.

HANDLING OF AGGRESSION

There are various ways of expressing or dealing with the aggressions we have considered. These include denial that the aggression exists, repression, reaction formations, conversion symptoms, vicarious release, and direct or displaced releases.

One significant way of meeting aggression in the early childhood situation is to deny its existence. A little girl rocks her infant brother in his hammock so violently that he almost falls out before the mother intervenes. The mother does not openly recognize the little girl's aggression and does not express any counteraggression against the child. She merely shows her the "right" way to take care of the baby. The girl is thus given no chance to recognize her own aggression, and she is not allowed to measure her own aggression against reality, as she would if adults counteraggressed. Such a child may come to feel her own aggression as omnipotent, become frightened of it, and be forced to repress it and substitute its opposite. This appears to be the prevalent mechanism for children of both sexes.

For *males*, aggressions aroused by oral frustrations, sibling rivalry, constraints on autonomy, and submission to paternal authority, are handled by repression and a variety of reaction formations, by vicarious gratification through the *guapo*, and by occasional direct physical expression in fighting, especially when drunk.

The reaction formations against aggression are many and varied, probably indicating the intensity and extensity of the aggression that must be controlled. In societies without so much preoccupation with "honor" (such as in North America generally) extreme politeness can be spotted clinically as a sign of an enormous load of repressed aggression expressed in its opposite. (The extreme cases are the "model boys" who suddenly make headlines by killing several members of their families.) When this is related to Manicaboa, we find a culture with an enormous emphasis upon "dignity" and "honor." A man may kill to counter a verbal attack upon his or his family's "honor." Men are supposed to deal with each other by an etiquette which to a North American seems excessively formal and courteous and with verbalisms that seem "high-blown." The other side of this is violence, such as is expressed when men get drunk or otherwise go out of control or is used as a "justifiable" reaction to an attack on their honor. An extreme of courteous respect behavior is demanded of two men linked as *compadres*, as already noted. The mutual aid and cooperation codes among neighbors may also be seen as, in part, reaction formations against aggressions. (They are of course *not only* that.)

Another form of expression of aggression is against the self, in the form of conversion symptoms. Bodily ailments of this kind are less prevalent in men than in women, indicating a lesser masochistic need, and when they do occur, they are attributed to magical practices of others.

The *guapo's* exploits as a vicarious release of aggression for other men have already been discussed. We have indicated that the *guapo* serves other men as the executor of their outgroup aggressions.

For *females*, a different set of patterns relating to aggression is apparent. These relate to the much greater constriction of the female than the male social role and greater repressiveness regarding sexuality. Outlets for girls include rough handling of younger siblings and telling tales against each other. For adult women, there are conversion symptoms, the frustrating pattern of breast-feeding, abortions, and miscarriages or the threat of them, tyrannizing by pregnancy cravings, aggressive gossiping, and sly subversions of the husband's economic controls of the household. The conversion symptoms include various aches and pains which suddenly disappear, dizziness, fainting, partial paralysis, and "attacks." Such symptom formation appears to be related to the powerful inhibition of direct expressions of aggression, which is much greater for women than for men. Symptoms turn aggression both against oneself and partially against others, thus operating as a mechanism of social control. For example, a girl sees her fiancé dancing with another girl. She goes into a faint. (Note that she does not physically attack the other girl or her fiancé: such violence would be unthinkable.)

Aggression against oneself and indirectly against others is also seen in the fact that in the period of a year and a half in which the field work for this study was done, the four suicides that occurred in Manicaboa were all women. The method was poison, taken orally. This recalls the oral method (strong purgatives) used to induce abortion and the almost indiscriminate use of purgatives, representing an aggression outlet against both oneself (discomfort) and the outer world (soiling). Abortion or miscarriage is, of course, a highly aggressive response toward the husband, as already discussed. So also are the pregnancy-craving demands, which often demand real economic sacrifice, and subvert the father's attempts to maintain strict consumption controls in the household. The latter controls are also subverted by the woman in a number of petty, sly, crafty ways. She may secretly sell eggs, tobacco or coffee surreptitiously taken from the family's accumulated stores and spend the slim proceeds on the children, thus mitigating the father's discipline and allying herself with the children against the father's strict economy and consumption limitation.

Another major aggression release available to women—gossip— clearly links aggression with orality. The aggressive comments are an oral attack on other women, on herself, and on men. The gossip is typically malicious against other women and commonly concentrates on sexual themes—stories of rapes, difficult births, miscarriages, difficult relations with the husband, and so on. In these stories women are typically portrayed as the victims of men. The complex of sexuality for women is interesting. On the one hand, the facts of sexual activities are openly available to children's perceptions; older girls may help with their mother's later deliveries, and girls do not have to be told about menstruation or marriage. Menstruation is accepted easily, and marks the casual but clear transition of the girl to adulthood. On the other hand, since girls' learning about sex derives also from adult women's talk and gossip, with its aggressive content and woman-as-victim themes, girls learn primarily painful and fearsome aspects of the sexual relationship, and most brides show fear of marriage and their husbands. The dominant role of the man permits the woman little independent expression in sexuality.

Significantly, a woman who admits enjoying sex is regarded by other women as "sick."

A major mechanism for women's expression of both aggression and sexuality, then, is through the seductive fostering of a *guapo* son, the primary means she has for "breaking out" of the constrictive feminine role that is within the strict traditional cultural limits.

Barrio Poyal

The sugar-cane laborers of Barrio Poyal live in closely contiguous houses on a narrow strip of public land between a main highway and the large sugar plantation of an American-owned corporation. The workers own no land. They work for wages, harvesting sugar cane on the plantation. They have steady work for only five or six months of the year when the cane is harvested. The men can look forward to no other livelihood than this labor. Wages are standardized by law, and it is difficult for any man to earn more. As a result, all members of the community are on a basis of economic equality, and they share a strong feeling of conscious group identity as wage laborers, defined in opposition to the foreign corporate owners of the plantation.

The ecology is an important aspect of the sugar workers' situation. Their geographic concentration facilitates intensive visiting and socializing. One of the by-products of this is that children wander freely into any house in the community sure of a welcome, some food, a friendly response, and even the possibility of being sent on some errand for the neighbor, kinsman, ritual relative, or foster relative. Hence the child is exposed to what can be called a "multiple mothering pattern."

The ecological situation does not just happen, however, nor is it strictly dictated by the particular "proletarian" condition of the workers. With available work only for barely half the year, these people might well have adopted the pattern of migrant workers. Such workers constitute a major part of the agricultural labor force in the continental United States and elsewhere. Since they lack permanent residence anywhere, it is unlikely that they would develop the kind of strong community feeling and group identity the Poyal people have.

The equality condition under which the Poyal people live is economically very poor. As far as local consciousness is concerned, the immediate life conditions that are available to people growing up in this community are extremely limited. Therefore, the community is unlikely to produce aspirations to surpass one's peers in wealth and status. Objectively, it would be impossible to do so in the local community, the income range being so narrow. By education or skill young males from Poyal would scarcely qualify for something economically higher elsewhere. Basically, then, the "opportunity structure" is closed, allowing as alternatives only positions of similar skill and income level. Strong group identity can be seen as an adaptation to this (apparently) "objective" limitation. The lack of the education and skill that could lead to economic improvement or upward mobility is itself a product of local conditions of socialization. No value is placed on formal schooling, and boys are expected to be sugar-cane workers like their fathers or to pursue an occupation on a similar skill-income level. There is no individualistic status striving here. Identification with the whole community is especially strong. This is interrelated with the ecological compactness. This compactness is a product not only of economic circumstances, but also of the group feeling and the strength of a traditional culture more sharply defined because it is at odds, in part, with that represented by the dominating economic force, the corporation. In turn it promotes the great diffusion of socialization agents. Nearly all the adults of the community are parents or parent surrogates to all of the children.

FAMILY NORMS

Men and women, though subject to a definite division of labor by sex, are much more nearly equal in status in Poyal than in Manicaboa. Since no one owns any land in Poyal, it cannot be a basis for a man's assertion of authority nor a criterion in choosing one woman over another for a wife. Rather men and women are seen as each possessing skills which in their union supplement each other. The man's economic role is only as a wage *earner*. He is not responsible for managing income, nor does he have anything at all like the absolute authority the Manicaboa husband-father does. Woman's value lies in her indispensability to do the man's housework and tend his livestock. She can also earn a little money on the side making candy, selling lottery, and taking in laundry. Central to the woman's role, of course, is being a wife and mother of a large family. Though the father is supposed to punish children for major infractions, neither the children nor his wife voice fear of him. He is nominally head of the household, but his real authority is minimal.

Hospitality, amicable relations with his fellows, and, above all, capacity for hard work are the major virtues demanded of a man. He is expected to expend himself to the limit in the five to six months of the cane harvest. Aggression against neighbors or co-workers is extremely taboo. Aggressive hostility can, however, of course, be expressed against the foreign sugar company.

Though there is lip-service to church marriage and bridal virginity, common-law marriage is the dominant and preferred pattern, and marriage *follows* sexual experience. These unions are monogamous, fairly stable, and often lifelong. The community censures the infidelity of either party, but more in the case of the wife. The marriage may be dissolved by common consent, for example, if the man leaves the community to find work elsewhere. Children remain with the mother, who readily finds a new partner. New couples set up a house of their own, often nearer to and with stronger ties to the wife's family. The latter help take care of the children if the father leaves.

CHILD TRAINING

The new couple wants a child right away. While children are not economic assets, a woman must have children to fulfill her role. They say: "Throw away what does not bear." Unlike the Manicaboa women, the women of Poyal give no indication of ambivalence about the feminine role and about bearing children. Childbirth is very casual; there are few preparations. A midwife delivers the baby at home. Rarely is use made of a nearby town clinic unless the infant is ill. The baby is breast-fed without schedule until another is on the way, sometimes longer. Weaning is a long, drawn-out process and may last till the child is as old as three years. Toilet training is just as casual as it is in Manicaboa and is begun somewhat earlier for girls.

All matters oral, anal, and genital are handled very casually and permissively and with respect for the child's individuality and his own rhythms and developmental needs. Take food, for example: the breast-feeding is unscheduled, free and relaxed, and long continued. Solid food is given at about one year, but the child sets his own feeding pace and is never forced. If he is not hungry, he simply does not eat. There is no anxiety by the mother about the baby *not* eating, nor any concern with his overeating. Between-meal nibbling is allowed and common. Sharing food, and everything else, is taught early. Eating has no routine. Children may eat anywhere they like in the kitchen. As in common Puerto Rican patterns, father, however, sits at the table. The relaxed casualness about food and the fact that the baby is essentially well gratified both nutritionally and oral erotically evidently account for the lack of food anxieties and preoccupations, quite in contrast to Manicaboa even though Poyal is economically just as badly off.

The anal discipline, in common with that of Manicaboa, is also relaxed, unhurried, and without anxieties. Correspondingly, the work pattern of Poyal men is very much like that of Manicaboa men: great devotion of energies when necessary, but no anal-compulsiveness about work.

The sexual disciplines are much more permissive in Poyal than in Manicaboa. Masturbation is acceptable in a young child. In fact, adults may manipulate the child's genitals to soothe him. The child is openly seen as a sexual being. A baby boy may be teased by playfully pulling his penis, asking, "What's it for?" Up to the age of five, boys run about with genitals exposed, girls always wear panties. Thus boys' sexuality is overtly emphasized, while girls are given a different kind of overevaluation: they are taught that they have something precious which must be covered and protected. Since the male genital is both highly valued and exhibited, the treatment of girls suggests that this is a way of handling penis envy.

Sex play, which is frequent in young children, ceases abruptly around the age of five. By seven, boys and girls who were earlier playmates are increasingly separated.

The much more open attitude toward sexuality in Poyal than in Manicaboa is reflected in adult sexual attitudes and practices, which are the least repressed or repressive of the three subcultures here considered. Poyal adults are much more open in sexual talk than Manicaboans and in groups with both sexes present. Women's gossip lacks the aggressive quality or emotional charge found in Manicaboa. Premarital sexual experience seems to be casually taken for granted, and sexual relations in marriage seem to be positively toned if not great in emotional depth.

DIFFUSION OF PARENTAL TIES

A major feature of the Poyal situation is the wide diffusion of parental roles. In addition to his mother and his father or stepfather, every child has a large number of surrogate parents in the community: older sisters, grandparents on either or both sides, many aunts and uncles, neighbors and friends of his parents, godparents, and in some instances, foster parents. A child is casually taken care of in any household into which he wanders, and feels at home anywhere in the village. He does, however, have a kind of "home base" in, usually, the household of his mother and siblings and mother's current husband. Since the seasonal work patterns allow fathers to be at home a great deal in Poyal, the multiple parents may to some extent include "fathers" as well as "mothers." Nevertheless for the very young child, probably the multiple mothering is the more significant aspect.

This whole pattern suggests that the casual permissiveness of any of the caretakers of the child, including the mother, is one in which the relationship between mother and child does not reach, or is not allowed to reach, any great level of intensity. This would appear to have been the pattern for at least more than a generation, since the common-law marriages seem to be rather brittle and easily broken without intense feeling, particularly if the man has an economic reason to leave the village.

The multiple-mothering pattern, however, raises difficult questions. Just what *are* its effects on the growing child? There does not appear to be one single answer to that question. It is possible that if the relation to the natural mother were particularly frustrating, then the transfer of love to a surrogate-mother might be very difficult, and the child might get lost in the multiplicity of relationships and develop poor capacity to form any relationship. The implication is, then, that the relationship to the original or primary mother must be basically gratifying for the child to be able to develop other gratifying dependency ties to any of the many surrogate-mothers. Then the dispersion weakens the intensity and exclusiveness of the tie to the one mother and probably should produce a personality pattern with extensive but relatively unintense and easily transferable emotional ties. This seems to be essentially what we find in Poyal.

Correspondingly, the diffuseness of affective relationships is evidently related to the strong group consciousness of this community, which overrides (indeed suppresses) individualistic striving or self-expression.

Some children are passed from hand to hand in their early years, living for long periods with families other than their own. One example of this is the foster-child (*hijo de crianza*) pattern, which is widespread in Puerto Rico. The foster child is "loaned" or "given" to a relative, ritual relative, or friend, ostensibly because of the parents' poverty or to get some advantage such as schooling. Often in reality the child given is a *rejected* child. The foster parents may be a couple, or an unmarried woman, with no children of their own. The adopted children may live near their real parents and visit them and the siblings who have remained home. Such children, though they voice positive feelings for the foster parents, must have deep feelings of rejection: "Why was I given away and not my brother?" Some deep tie to the mother may persist, either negatively formulated or in rejection-denying fantasies, for example, she really wanted to keep me, but was forced by evil persons or hardship to give me up. The child may idealize the real parents and displace the hostility onto the foster parents, sometimes abetted by the latter's showing preference for children of their own.

Another feature of the communal-mindedness of the people of Poyal is the total absence of privacy as a fact or as a value. The child growing up here experiences constant noise and movement, people talking, visitors coming and going all around him. Privacy has no place in any of this. A child is expected to fall asleep through any kind of noise or commotion; his sleep is not sacred. Intervisiting of people of all ages is intense. The whole community thus becomes a huge extended family, a place where the child nowhere feels strange and alone. He thus develops facility in dealing with both adults and contemporaries (in contrast to the "newness-shy" mountain child). To the Poyal child, the community is not a hostile alternative to the home. The extent and intensity of social relations here rob the parent-child relationship of the unique intensity it has in other cultural settings.

FATHER-CHILD RELATIONS

Because of lack of work for much of the year, the Poyal father is home a great deal, assumes much responsibility for the care of the children and spends a great deal of time with them. His attitude is tender and interested. Still, sexual division of labor strictly limits the type of care he gives. For example, he never washes or cleans a child. He may reprimand or punish the child, but this is rarely by corporal means. He may take responsibility for the child's school attendance, walk with the child, rock the child to sleep. His precise authority varies by household. Since children usually stay with the mother when a marriage breaks up, a stepfather is expected to take over the role of the father, earn the children's affection and respect, and show equal affection and indulgence toward his step-children as toward his own. Some households may have a succession of "fathers." Probably such instability of fathers makes for a stronger tie to the mother, who remains a constant. But we must note also that this extension and changeability of fathers occurs in a commu-nity context where nearly all adults are responsive, protective, and affectionate toward nearly all children, whether their own or not. Hence the emotional impact of changing fathers is likely to be much less than it would be where nuclear-family households are more iso-lated and where the parents are a more distinct focus of emotional concentration for the child.

OEDIPAL PROBLEMS

Oedipal conflict in Barrio Poyal could be expected to be quite different from those of continental American culture. The father is less of an authority and less of a menacing, castrating figure. This should result in less repressed hostility, less guilt, and less necessity to internalize what he stands for. Thus, a boy may find it rather easy to transfer his affection to another non-hostile father figure. How-ever, if the father leaves at a crucial stage in the boy's development, this may appear to the boy as a fulfillment of the boy's unconscious wish to do away with him and replace him, which might lead to strong guilt feelings and difficulties in male identification.

For the daughter, the father's departure may arouse hostility against the mother: mother made him leave. Such hostility must be repressed because of the girl's dependency on her mother's love and the cultural taboos on aggression. Further, with a stepfather, incest barriers are lowered. This lowering, combined with repressed hostil-ity against the depriving mother, promotes attraction between step-father and stepdaughter, probably reaching its peak at the time the girl reaches adolescence. In any of these cases, the intensity of the emotional reactions aroused is likely to be mitigated by the general-ized diffuseness of parent-surrogate ties throughout the community.

Nevertheless, there is a definite Oedipal phase, regardless of whether a father or a stepfather is the main male adult present. This is indicated by an abrupt change of response to the boy's sexuality around the age of five. Until then the boy may run about with his genitals uncovered. After that age he does not. There is an abrupt de-emphasis on the boy's sexuality. This seems to be related to the par-ents' near-conscious fear of incest. It is assumed that from five years

on the little boy, like the grown man, will not be able to control his
sexual impulses. (By contrast, the girl is taught early control.)
From five till puberty, boys play in boys' groups, shun girls, and engage in much sexual joking, often homosexual in nature. These
would appear to be almost "classical" post-Oedipal reactions.

The girl's sexuality is not overtly emphasized until she reaches
puberty. Men then remark on her budding womanhood. At this
point her economic contribution to the household reaches its peak,
since by this time she has mastered essentially all of the basic feminine household tasks, and she is essentially ready to assume an adult
woman's role. By contrast, a boy at this age *declines* in economic
value. He has no way to contribute to the household until he is
sixteen and can work in the cane fields. Then he will soon be on a
level of equality with his father and be ready to set up his own
household.

MASTERY AND AUTONOMY

The children of Poyal, though not as clearly economic assets as
those of Manicaboa, are expected to develop early mastery by graded
steps in a trial-and-error learning process. Sex typing here is definite.
Children's jobs are necessary ones, not "made" chores, and have a
definite place in family life. Boys catch crabs and fish, cut tinder and
grass to feed animals, collect coconuts and other fruits, run errands,
put animals to pasture, carry men's lunches to the cane field, shine
shoes, and sell candy. Girls wash and iron by the age of seven, care
for babies, and perform other household chores. Boys' jobs take
them all over the village. Girls' chores center at home, though, unlike the Manicaboan girls, they do go to school and they do visit
freely all over the community.

Thus ego development through mastery of useful sex-linked tasks
is as strong in Poyal as in Manicaboa. Unlike Manicaboa, however,
Poyal encourages a much stronger development of *autonomy* as well.
A condition for this is the less intense and less restrictive relationship
of parents to children. Further, property as a base of paternal power
is not important here, in contrast to its centrality in Manicaboa.
Autonomy in Poyal does not mean individualistic assertiveness,
much less competitiveness with others. The whole pressure toward
communal-mindedness and group identity work against any competitiveness. Aspirations for individualistic success or invidious
status above others are definitely devalued. The good person of
Poyal is cooperative, mutually supportive with others, and uninter-

ested in marking himself off as better than others. His individual autonomy can find expression as long as it does not threaten other members of the group or the group as a whole. The non-competitive personality formation is also related to the fact that sibling rivalries in Poyal are very mild compared to those of most communities, and this in turn depends on the general diffuseness and relative shallowness of affective ties.

AGGRESSION

Perhaps primarily because aggression does not get such a strong start in extreme early oral frustration in Poyal as in Manicaboa, it is not an intensely problematic concern in Poyal. Infantile frustration beyond the universally inevitable, has no one specific focus here. It may be a by-product of the multiple mothering and in many cases of the *hijo-de-crianza* adoption pattern. The circumstances and effects are individually variable. Early body disciplines, oral, anal, and genital, are probably as easygoing and permissive as could be found anywhere in the world. Loss of the father through marital break-up, and his early replacement by a stepfather, appear to be frequent enough to constitute a pattern for a good part of the population. This probably has frustrating effects, though mitigated, as noted, by the general diffuseness of emotional bonds. Crucially timed, however, it could precipitate intense Oedipal problems for either the son or the daughter. Sibling rivalry is probably about the same as would be found in large families anywhere. However, it can be complicated by the appearance of a new stepfather, or by an adoption situation, but it is still alleviated by general emotional diffuseness. Another mitigating factor is the absence in Poyal of a *scarcity* mentality. Though economically as poorly off as the Manicaboans, they do not show, like the latter, a preoccupation with holding on to and conserving food and other good things of everyday life. Rather they give generously to each other and each other's children. A child who gets an easy welcome—and food—in any household in the community is not likely to develop a strong scarcity consciousness. Food anxieties do not appear to be prevalent either. All this is in definite contrast with Manicaboa. Hence, since the economic situation for ready availability of food is if anything worse in Poyal than in Manicaboa, the difference can hardly be attributed to economic realities, and the plausibility for arguing early-derived intrapsychic determinants for such patterns is strengthened.

In infancy there is one pattern source and outlet for aggression for

boys, but not for girls. Boys to the age of three or four are deliberately teased and provoked into temper tantrums. Adults then admir-
ingly comment on their masculinity. By contrast, uncontrolled behavior in the girl is punished quickly and decisively. Thus in a clear
instance of self-fulfilling prophecy[8] adults contrive to produce in boys
evidence of their folk belief that males are intrinsically less capable
of controlling their impulses than females. With this kind of training, girls of course have fewer temper tantrums. Consistently, they
are also given earlier toilet training than boys.

The general picture, then, is this: aggression-generating customs
and institutions in Poyal childhood are relatively slight and mild.
The taboo on directing aggression against the socializing agents
themselves (probably nearly universal), of course, is there. So too is
the taboo against aggressing against siblings and other peers, and
such thwarting can produce further aggressions. On the other hand,
there is no model for violence in the behavior of parents toward
each other nor in parents toward children. In Poyal, in contrast with
many other working-class settings, corporal punishment of children
is extremely rare. The major aggression control, however, is probably
the strong group consciousness and group identity of these people.
Taboos on open aggression within the group—meaning the whole
community—are very strong. Aggression, therefore, must and does
get directed outside the group. The realistic target here is the planta-
tion-owning corporation. Strikes and other forms of labor strife are
common.

Alternatively, the aggression can be turned against the self in disguised and group-sanctioned ways. A group form of this is a Pentecostal sect. The small but growing following, all sugar workers, meet to
pray and sing together with a local lay preacher who is their peer.
Under conditions of group elation, some members publicly confess
and have seizures which are given religious definition. The sect taboos drinking, adultery, dancing, and fighting, but it does tolerate
the customary common-law marriage. The sect asserts the homogeneity and cohesion of the group, while permitting individual autonomy. One person's decision to join does not commit others of his
family, but it does bind him firmly to the sect's commandments.
Seizures that occur in the sect meetings may express thwarted aggres-

[8] Compare Robert K. Merton, "The Self-fulfilling Prophecy," in *Social
Theory and Social Structure* (New York: Free Press of Glencoe, 1949), pp.
179-98.

[9] The reform government of the time (1950) had stopped such group aggressions as strikes and local political action.

sion[9] turned against oneself in a group-sanctioned way. The meetings also create a state of euphoria, denying anger about economic difficulties, and reinforcing reaction formations. In these ways, and in its antilibidinal taboos and channeling of aggression, the sect unwittingly exerts social control and guards the status quo.

Thus a strong sense of identification with the work group, which is also the local community, a minimization of individual competition, and a maximization of mutual aid are achieved by suppression or repression of aggression within the group. Such aggression is then either directed outward, against the dominant outgroup, the sugar corporation, or channelized in a structured way into an emotionally charged, expressive group activity such as the Pentecostal sect. Significantly, wherever aggression does find expression, it is to reinforce the sense of group identity. All of this occurs in a context —in a sense both source and consequence—which can be defined as dispersion of affect.

The Middle Class of San José

In the rural town of San José the middle class is intermediate between an upper class of wealthy landowners and store owners and a lower class of semi-urbanized workers. The middle-class men are government officials, teachers, owners of middle-sized stores, and owners of public conveyances. Many of the women are teachers, secretaries, nurses, or dieticians. The jobs of this class derive from an increase in government positions, diffusion of education, growth of small-scale marketing, and the development of transportation facilities during the American occupation of the island since the turn of the century. Many middle-class persons have risen recently from a lower socio-economic status. They earn a more or less steady income from non-manual labor. Much of their income is spent on conspicuous consumption in competition with their status equals. The parents of this class hope their children will rise to a higher social and economic position.

ADULT NORMS

The San José middle-class family differs markedly from the two others just discussed. The man is *nominally* the head of the family and the authority over it. He is supposed to be the chief source of income, either unearned (preferable, but rare in reality) or gained by non-manual labor. Status derives from the importance and steadiness of his occupation, family connections, unearned income, or a combination of these. *Working hard is no value.* In fact, the ideal is not working at all (in emulation of the wealthy upper class, of mainly Spanish descent). However, middle-class men must work at steady occupations to keep up a standard of living that distinguishes them from manual workers. Thus how they have to live contradicts how they would like to live. A feasible solution is to hold a job but do a minimum of actual work. That brings prestige. People talk of how good it is to get a sinecure, a job with lifetime tenure but with few demands. The ideal is so strong that people who do work very hard pretend they do little on the job. Working should be a casual and effortless situation. A man with a reputation for being a hard worker is laughed at.

By upper-class norms, which are emulated in this middle class, the man's role as chief income source implies nearly complete authority over his family: his wife cannot complain if he neglects her for other women; he is master of his time and money; he may awaken his wife in the early morning to prepare a meal for him after a night out with his friends. The men of San José are adamant about keeping up the appearance of such prerogatives, and they dread anything which might look like domination by the wife. A man must also show his fellows that he is beyond any tie of responsibility, that his wife respects his complete freedom of decision, that he can cut himself free of job and family at a moment's notice or on a dare. Men's drinking bouts produce fantasies of breaking loose, spending weeks away from home in instinctual gratification and free of all everyday necessities. (These fantasies are rarely realized, of course.)

The ideal woman's role is mother and faithful wife, devoted entirely to home and family. At marriage, a girl should be a virgin and know how to keep house and cook, though she will have a servant. She should have a number of children; though by tacit understanding, she may limit that number. The first child should be conceived immediately and should be a boy, to testify to the man's masculinity. The wife should show compliance with her husband's wishes and show verbally that she expects and condones his "flights to freedom."

Reality is far from these ideals. In fact, the very frequency of protestation of male prerogatives suggest that they are challenged by newly emerging real family patterns. Male domination is undermined mainly by women increasingly contributing to family income by working as teachers, secretaries, home economists, nurses, seamstresses, or small business proprietors. They hold such jobs before marriage and even after marriage until the first child is born. Many of them resume working after the child can be cared for by a nursemaid. Men publicly object to this, but they privately welcome the additional income, since conspicuous consumption is so high a value. The working wife gains freedom through her income, often her own to dispose of. Men are thus caught between asserting the traditional authority over the wife and the desire for social standing which forces him to grant her an economic autonomy that contradicts the ideal. The woman, however, can better harmonize ideal and reality. She strives to keep a spotless house, be a good cook, have children well cared for; simultaneously, she can hold down a job because servants are cheap and available. Thus, women are apparently secure in their roles, while men are torn between irreconcilable norms.

Women's conversations show these changes. In mixed groups they pay lip-service to male authority, thus upholding family prestige. Among themselves, however, attitudes vary from contemptuous amusement at men's antics to irritated discussion of how to handle men when they are drunk or enraged. In domestic crises, men with their protestations of masculine assertiveness take the role of rebellious but dependent children, while the wives take the role of irritated yet indulgent and solicitous mothers. The women seem to value men's infantile dependence on them.

To the man, his wife is a double threat. First, her increased autonomy suggests that she may be able to do without him. Second, marriage deprives him of his own autonomy, committing him to the slavery of work. (Men say among themselves, marriage is a contract where he gives up his freedom so his wife will love him.) Many a man claims that he was spiritually lost before marriage and that his wife saved him from the gutter by helping him control his impulses. Part of him feels this rescue should be repaid by hard work and self-control. Another part cannot help feeling hostility against a wife who burdened him with such a debt. Thus relations of spouses are marked by deep ambivalence.

Men, therefore, face their jobs with conflicting attitudes. In the absence of the ideal unearned income, a man must hold a job to earn a living, fulfill his role as head of the household, and keep the respect of family and community. But the job is a burden forced by his marriage, inhibiting the "real man" in him. The split in his masculine ideals is further widened by the *kind* of job he has: he cannot set his work terms, especially if he works for a large company or the government. Either organization encumbers him with impersonal bureaucratic rules and work expectations set by *continental* American culture, a foreign dominating power, often enforced by continental Americans. These standards often conflict with island culture, but are accepted by dint of fifty years of acculturation. They lead the middle-class Puerto Rican to compare himself unfavorably with what Americans supposedly are able to achieve in similar positions. The continental norm of prestige by hard work directly contradicts the island norm of *non*-work. The man consciously rejects the former, but unconsciously it leaves him with a sense of inadequacy. Now he feels that in marriage and in his job he has twice sold his birthright to freedom. And *both* job ideals conflict with his ideal of the carefree, yet dominating male. Thus, his masculine identity is threatened at home and on the job, the two most important areas of his life.

MARRIAGE

Since children are likely to be at least as socially ambitious as parents, marriage choice as a part of the status struggle can usually be left to the free decision of the youngsters themselves, though some arranged marriages do occur.

Qualifications of the partner are supremely important; wealth, "good family" (one meaning is whiteness, but this factor can be outweighed by wealth). "Good family" can make up for character defect, such as drunkenness or job instability.

Marriage is preceded by separate one-sex parties for the bride and for the groom. The groom's is a drinking party where his friends jokingly condole with him about his coming loss of freedom. The bride's party has a special amalgam of sex and aggression themes.

Marriages are celebrated, usually in church with great display. Invitations go to all one's social equals and as many of one's social superiors as will come.

The new couple hope for a child soon after marriage. Contraception, accepted in spite of church prohibitions, is not practiced until after the first child. It is used to space children and to limit the number, usually to four at most.

The bride eagerly awaits symptoms of pregnancy. When she is

certain, and announces her condition, she is the object of attention from the whole female circle: mother, sisters, other female relatives, friends. As her pregnancy progresses, her husband increasingly withdraws and seeks out his male friends. The service of an obstetrician and delivery in an expensive private clinic are the norm for the middle-class San José family. This again is in keeping with the value placed upon conspicuous consumption even though these services often cost much more than the new family can afford. Men express preference for a boy. Women say they prefer a girl: boys are more rowdy (even in the womb it is believed) and more of a nuisance, while a girl has no "vices" and stays with her mother.

CHILD TRAINING

Childbirth brings a great fuss around mother and child. The woman replaces breast-feeding with the bottle after a month or two; some bottle-feed from the start. The baby is taken for regular checkups to a doctor or clinic, even involving trips to the capital. Child-training patterns are contradictory. Recommendations of continental-trained pediatricians often conflict with the older cultural heritage. For example, the doctor advises that the baby lie naked in the sun for short periods; the mother feels this harms the child and his prized whiteness. Traditional beliefs about "hot" and "cold" foods clash with prescribed diets, while mothers worry about caloric intake in modern terms. In accord with "modern" ideas, a baby's lack of hunger is considered a most alarming symptom. Generally relaxed toilet training (traditional) is interrupted by fearful application of "new" theories of North American-trained doctors. Mother and nursemaid both use pacifiers extensively; doctors disapprove.

MASTERY AND AUTONOMY

A significant feature of the whole child-training process, and obviously in contrast with Manicaboa and Poyal, is the great stunting of the development of mastery by the child. Where the American high-chair has been introduced, it is not used to give the baby greater mastery in feeding, but as an item of conspicuous consumption. The child is supposed to be completely passive, being fed by his mother or nurse until about the age of three, very much in contrast to the messy early mastery of babies feeding themselves in Manicaboa and Poyal. Similarly, San José children are never expected to learn to handle tools or help around the house, or in fact do anything for themselves. They are accompanied by nursemaids at all times. Whenever a child shows signs of assuming any independent action, however harmless, he is thwarted by being carried off bodily to another place. If he expresses anger, he is picked up, cuddled, kissed to restore the placidity so valued in children. The nursemaid is supposed to entertain the child at all times, singing songs, cuddling, bouncing, and so on, and to anticipate the child's desires, and to do for him what he would try to do for himself. The children's many bought toys are not used to encourage independent play. They are show objects. The child is praised if his toys remain unsoiled and unbroken. The playpen, now common in these middle-class homes, is rarely used since the child is preferably left with a nursemaid and must not be left alone for a moment, even when in the pen. Thus, he cannot explore for himself even that small area.

Farmers and laborers make derogatory remarks about the dependency and helplessness of these middle-class children, comparing them unfavorably (and accurately) with their own competent young. This helplessness is fostered as a class distinction. Correspondingly, this child learns early that he can order about a number of other people who must minister to his needs. The major weapon of boys and girls up to the age of about four is the temper tantrum. The child discovers early that his prime means of control is a display of mood changes. His relation to servants is the model for later relationships with all people of lower status, though in adulthood the distinction is overlaid by courteous etiquette.

Deliberately keeping children dependent and devoid of mastery, of course, is related to the fact that in the San José middle class children are economically useless. Girls do learn a few skills useful for the household in later childhood, but otherwise children of both sexes develop scarcely any adult-related mastery. Hence the transition to adult skills after years of formal non-utilitarian schooling is abrupt and associated with marriage or getting a job.

A related fact is that children are objects of conspicuous consumption for their parents, with much time and money spent on the rituals of dress display. Until school age, this applies to both sexes, after that only for girls, and to an extent that greatly intensifies female narcissism.

MULTIPLE MOTHERING

The child is typically faced with at least three different and frequently conflicting mothering persons. The natural mother cares for the child herself only during the early stages of infancy. Later a nursemaid takes over, especially the tasks of washing and changing the child (which are frequent due to the great narcissistic value for the mother of the cleanliness and dressiness of the child). If the mother goes back to work, the nursemaid will be responsible for nearly all of the child care. In addition to the nursemaid, female relatives, especially the maternal grandmother, often take care of the child. In contrast to the culturally homogeneous multiple "mothers" a child has in Poyal, the San José child's mother, nursemaid, and grandmother may all differ in their child rearing methods, and the confusion and resulting insecurity are heightened by the child's physical helplessness.

The nursemaid, usually a girl of twelve to sixteen years, of small-farm or town working-class background, may bring standards similar to those of Manicaboa or Poyal, for example, on toilet training, on use of the pacifier, on cleanliness generally, thus conflicting with the mother. She plays a kind of older sister to the child, but with none of the gratifications in achievement and autonomy such a girl would enjoy at home. Instead she is under constant pressure to entertain the child, something unknown in her background, and gets criticism from her employers, themselves ambivalent about what they want for the child.

The grandmother brings standards of an older middle-class tradition, more in line with traditional Puerto Rican culture and less influenced by pediatric notions from mainland America. Mothers think grandmothers "spoil" the children. In fact, the grandmother may be more consistent in child care, because there was less bi-cultural conflict in her youth.

The mother herself is caught in contradictions between the traditional standards under which she herself was raised and the "modern" methods represented by continental-trained doctors. Also her drive for autonomy through her middle-class job conflicts with traditional expectations of the feminine role as centered on child rearing and household. Cheap and available servants enable her to combine the two roles, but then she has to contend with the nursemaid, of different standards, and her mother, who differs in yet other ways.

Thus the baby is confronted with multiple and *conflicting, inconsistent* mothers. He is likely to be both subject and object of a great amount of anxiety, and this is in fact reflected in the overprotective-ness of the middle-class parents, which in turn, fosters his extreme dependency. A further complication is rivalry for the child's allegiance, promoting friction between mother and grandmother and between mother and nursemaid.

The mother-nursemaid dichotomy teaches the child two worlds. In one, being clean, wearing good clothes, rigid control over impulse, and mother's acceptance go together. In the other are soiling, careless appearance, rejection by the mother, indulgence of impulse, and a warm relationship with a female figure of lower status. For the boy, the long-term effects are clear-cut: the nursemaid becomes the prototype for his later relations with women of lower social status, relations that are sexually indulgent and generally permissive toward his impulse life. By contrast, the desired and unattainable mother, with whom he is allowed to be only when immaculately dressed and clean, is the seductive but rejecting female, the kind of woman he will seek as a virgin bride. (This development of a male double standard in sexuality has parallels in higher-status groups in many other societies.)

The effects for the girl are different. The nursemaid gives her one kind of model, the mother another, and the grandmother possibly still another. Girls would also learn to associate freer impulse expression with the nursemaid and may, by identifying with the nursemaid, take over that kind of role toward the father, who encourages it by showering his daughters with affection (in contrast with his more reserved behavior toward young sons). She may thus compete with her more cold and strict mother for the father. From the mother, by contrast, she derives narcissistic gratifications in the elaborate dressing, which emphasizes her solitary pedestal-like position of aloof cool beauty. Her vacillation between the conflicting standards toward impulse (nurse vs. mother) would no doubt enter into her adult relationships with men, particularly her husband, and in her handling of motherhood herself later on. This, in fact, seems to be the case with the present generation of young mothers. For them there is probably not only the external conflict between two cultures, but also an intrapsychic one if they have been themselves raised in this particular multiple-mother pattern. It is probable that the San José girl carries into marriage *both* roles, cold strict mother and warm permissive nursemaid, in varying combinations, expressed in different circumstances toward husband and toward son, perhaps differentiating the two.[10] Certainly some of the behavior of the present younger mothers

10 On this point my interpretation differs from that of Wolf in the original paper. See Wolf, *op. cit.*, p. 430.

toward their sons indicates such ambivalence, since much of it is simultaneously rejecting and seductive (for example, the evening washing of the boy, having him in bed with the mother, and so on).

ROLE OF THE FATHER

The father is supposed to have little to do with bringing up children. He is away from home for long periods, at work or in the company of his male friends. This distant father is ideally an authoritarian figure to be obeyed without demur, and when home, he does assert this authority. He is also to mete out punishment when necessary. On the other hand, he should also at times bring home gifts on which he spends his money freely.

Fatherhood validates his manhood and gives him prestige. He acknowledges his responsibility toward his children and takes pride in their accomplishments. But they also bind him more strongly to home and intensify the pervasive conflict about freedom; consequently, his feelings toward the children are ambivalent.

In turn, the children get contradictory impressions of the father. When he is home, the mother upholds his authority role. But children also know that she often deprecates him when he is away (though rarely in front of them).

MALE SEXUAL DEVELOPMENT

The boy's sexual development involves the dichotomy between mother and nursemaid, already discussed, the contradictory elements in his relationship to his mother, the ambiguity of the father, and the Oedipal conflicts.

The boy's identification with his father is troubled because the father's real strength is so often questioned. Such weakening of the father also increases the boy's ability to compete for the mother. Thus when father *does* assert authority, the boy may feel this as punishment for his incestuous wishes.

The mother's behavior toward the boy is complex and contradictory. In many ways she rejects the boy's sexuality; in other ways she encourages it. Little boys may run about the home uncovered. But a boy's masturbation is noticed by the mother and stopped by scolding or diversion. Yet women sexually tease boys up to the age of three, jocularly kissing or handling their genitals. Parental sex life is carefully guarded from the children. Commonly a boy shares his mother's bed until he is five or six. This is part of a pattern that continues, which may amount to the mother's supporting a boy's unconscious wishes to replace his father, especially if the mother feels unfulfilled in the marriage. The mother, for example, continues to supervise the boy, including washing him, when he goes to bed and may remain with him in his bed till he falls asleep. This may continue until the boy reaches puberty. When he is sick or frightened, she will take him into her bed, thus actually displacing the father. Adolescent boys may walk arm in arm with their mothers in the street, without any self-consciousness. Strong mother-son ties last into adulthood.

Conversely, many boys, by the age of fifteen, have had sexual experience with a prostitute, rarely with a girl of their class. This suggests that the mother-son tie is maintained without threat to the boy by eliminating any conscious sexual element in the relationship. The object of sexuality has been misplaced to women of a different type, modeled on the lower-class nursemaid. In turn, the continued attachment to the mother, desexualized, widens the split in the female image.

The combination of the ambiguously weak yet threatening father and of the contradictory rejecting yet seductive mother makes for Oedipal conflicts that are particularly intense. One resolution of such conflict involves the split between "low" women as pure sex objects and respectable fine women as potential and actual wives. The latter are cool, aloof, subtly controlling, the kind of woman who "saves the man from the gutter" of an impulse life always threatening to get out of control. Courtship customs abet this split. A non-virgin is considered an undesirable bride. Courtship is chaperoned, and body contact is taboo. Since the man is assumed to be less able to control his sexual feelings, the girl is held responsible if premarital intercourse occurs. This parallels a man's not being held responsible if he loses control over aggression when drinking. This suggests that expression of sexual and aggressive impulses are linked.

Another part of the resolution of Oedipal conflicts is the repeated retreat to the all-male group with its latent homosexual camaraderie and fantasies of flight to freedom. The shakiness of the masculine identity is also suggested by the obsessive preoccupation with begetting a child, preferably a boy, as soon as possible after marriage. This concern with validating one's virility in this way is evidently pervasive throughout Puerto Rican culture (and perhaps Latin cultures generally), but in the San José middle class it takes on a particularly conflictful quality due to the ambiguities discussed.

FEMALE SEXUAL DEVELOPMENT

The girl's sexual development involves the conflicting influences of the mother, nursemaid, and often grandmother, the seductiveness of the father, the narcissistic emphasis on dress display, and a variety of contradictions in reference to control of impulse life.

Girls learn early to value and hide their sexuality. From infancy on, they wear panties, in contrast with the boys running about the house uncovered. They are rarely sexually teased as boys are, but the frequent masturbation by little girls is not reprimanded. This appears to be in line with the narcissistic emphasis in female sexuality later on. The conflict between mother and nurse as two different models has already been discussed. The father is openly affectionate to his daughter. The girl very early notes the father's double role (officially the authority of the house, actually frequently demeaned and deprecated by the mother). Her response to his affection is warm and accepting and devoid of criticism. In effect, she is competing with her strict mother for the father's affection and is assuming a role like the nursemaid's to a little boy rejected by his mother. Part of her thus identifies unconsciously with the lower-status woman.

Controls on both sexual expression and aggression are strenuous on the girl. From school age on, girls are restricted to the house, are highly conforming and "goody-goody." Aggression comes out only indirectly, for example, in sibling rivalries and "telling tales." Conscious sex knowledge is minimal. In contrast with Manicaboa and Poyal parental sex relations are here kept secret from the children. Many girls have no adequate sex knowledge until marriage, so that the first sexual contact is often traumatic. Many girls also have no prior knowledge of menstruation (again, sharply in contrast with the situation in Manicaboa or Poyal). By informal custom, a bride on returning from her honeymoon will tell a group of her girl friends, gathered for that purpose, the details of her wedding night. These are usually related in such frightening terms that it hardly alleviates the sexual ignorance of the unmarried and probably increases their fears.

A girl is expected to be virgin at marriage; a non-virgin is considered an undesirable bride. The girl is responsible for making sure that premarital intercourse with her fiancé does not occur. Chaperoning, with strong body contact taboos, helps to insure this.

Both the pre-bridal party and the post-honeymoon party for the all-female group indicate great fear, anxiety, and aggression relating to sex. Sex talk among women and late-adolescent girls is free but highly conspiratorial in quality. In the pre-bridal party this quality is carried to an otherwise unparalleled extreme. The bride-to-be is openly considered the victim of her friends. The party is said to be to "mortify" her. The highlight consists of practical jokes on the bride, always sexual in content. For example, amid much giggling and laughter the guests present the bride with an elaborate gift package containing a crude representation of the male genitalia. The donors remain anonymous. The bride must not become shy and inhibit the others, but rather must show just the right mixture of elation and verbalized shame. The unwrapping then unleashes a stream of openly sexual conversation, often hysterical. Ostensibly, the party is to acquaint the girl with what she will face sexually in her marriage. But the intensity and emotional tone of the older women show it as an outlet for deeper feelings: if they have been mortified by sexuality, they may in turn mortify someone else.

The bride's post-honeymoon recital of her experiences to her unmarried friends, likewise is heavily laden with fright and aggression. There is thus clearly a great deal of fear and anxiety related to sex, which co-exists with the relatively serene acceptance of the feminine role (in contrast to the constantly threatened men). It would be unlikely that men would be so threatened in their sexual identity without its having repercussions on the women. Sexual repression in women is indicated in numerous ways: the great concern to hide the infant girl's sexuality with its overtones of penis-envy, the great protectiveness toward young girls, the premarital chaperoning, the insistence on premarital virginity. These all reflect the other side of the double standard which gives the males so much comparative sexual freedom. Repression has its related outlets in aggression: against men (mainly verbally, in contemptuous indulgence and the rest), against other women (gossip, mortifying the bride) and against themselves (as in the pregnancy symptoms and other conversion symptoms). Getting a job is self-assertive for the woman. In the cultural context it is also aggressive against the husband, in a sly manipulative way, because she knows he cannot afford to object and could not really stop her if he tried.

The prevalence of pregnancy symptoms here (in contrast with both Manicaboa and Poyal) suggests problems about sexual identity, the feminine role, and aggression against men. The bride's great eagerness for signs of pregnancy seems extreme enough (for example, having nausea a few days after she *thinks* conception occurred) to suggest it serves important intrapsychic needs. One of these seems to be a desire to escape sexual relations with her husband by immersion in the prospective mother role. Once the pregnancy is known, she is ensconced in an all-female world from which her husband is by circumstance excluded. That pregnancy revitalizes a woman's infantile relationship to her own mother is of course no news in any culture. This particular subculture seems, however, to have capitalized on psychosocial dimorphism of the sexes to a greater than ordinary degree, in the following way. There seems to be a great need to segregate mother-child sexuality from mate-mate sexuality, and this female world of pregnancy and the early postpartum period is one where women are united in the continuity of mother-to-child-to-grandchild, in which men are only brief incidental necessities. The husband's exclusion leads him to go back to spending more time with his male friends, something the honeymoon presumably interrupted. Probably he now devotes himself sexually less to his wife, and he may turn to lower-class paramours or prostitutes, probably to the pregnant wife's relief. Her pregnancy symptoms are implicitly an aggressive demand for attention from him (and others, like her mother) but in such a form as to preclude or at least discourage, frequent sexual relations with her husband. In effect, she is demanding to be pampered like a sick *child* rather than wooed as a mistress. The gratifications she seeks, and probably gets, seem to be analogous to those of the Manicaboa pregnant woman with her special cravings. Here, however, the symptoms also reflect aggression against *herself* so that along with indulgence she also has suffering. This is probably tied in with the later limitation of family size by contraception, even against the Church's taboo, though such planning has other functions as well.

Other indicators of women's ambivalence to child bearing and to biologically based elements of the feminine role, are seen in the haste to return to a salaried job as soon as the baby can be cared for by a nursemaid. While these women show great competence in meeting the demands of both roles (wage earner and mother) with the aid of a servant, this is still achieved only at a price. Thus, in relation to their husbands, these women express aggressions aroused by the impact of sexuality by casting the husband in the role of rebellious dependent child, while the wife takes the role of irritated yet indulgent mother.

AGGRESSION

Aggression-generating customs and situations are much more abundant in the San José middle class than in either of the other two communities. Many of the sources and discharge channels of aggression have already been mentioned. In infancy there is inconsistent multiple mothering, thwarting of assertiveness, exploration and mastery, mothers' anxieties about the baby's not eating, lack of adaptation to the baby's own needs and rhythms, and the diffuse ambivalence and conflict within the mother. All these conduce to anxieties, frustrations, and aggressive feelings in the baby, never easily discharged against a realistic outside object. The mother is internally conflicted in several ways: between her desire to be a wage earner and the wish for traditional feminine indulgences; between her need for the nurse and grandmother as surrogates and her various disagreements with them; between her need for the prestigious American-trained pediatrician and persisting traditional ideas; and also, in many cases, between earlier lower-class norms from her childhood and her convertlike determination to attach herself to middle-class norms. Status obsessions, the drive for the "best" for her child, demeaning of the grandmother and her "old-fashioned" ways, all conduce to anxiety surrounding the whole mother-child situation. The child, his clothes, his toys, the gadgetry of highchair, playpen and the rest, are all dealt with as tokens in a game of competitive status display, with consequent great thwarting of the child. Children so restricted have one great recourse, the temper tantrum, used as a device to manipulate the adults, or at least the lower-class nursemaid.

Sibling rivalry is another important source of aggression. The birth of a sibling is especially traumatic in San José. The dethroned child has been an object of display and continuous care, and he cannot compensate for the loss by increasing mastery and ego strength. Aggression gets released in violent quarrels with siblings, often over toys, about which strong property feelings are instilled. Rivalries between siblings of opposite sex are intensified by the strong father-daughter and mother-son relationships.

The restraints imposed on the expression of aggression, more intense for girls, are a further source of frustration. In adult life sources of frustration are multiplied: conflict between new middle-class norms and traditional ones, especially on the relations of the sexes; the men's conflicts about their work and about their wives' working; intensive competitive consumption striving; the women's conflicts about sexuality, about child bearing, and about child rearing. And again, controls on expression of aggression are pervasive and intense, as in the elaborate courtesy codes and the great concern that each respect any other's social role, be it ever so humble, with its concomitant of great touchiness about being snubbed. The restraints required by such codes, however, further increase inner aggressions.

Channeling of aggressions in the San José middle class involves repression, reaction formations, displacements of various kinds, and introjection. Reaction formations include the elaborate courtesy codes. Displacement may be against an outgroup, such as the continental Americans, though even that is rare except for situations of loss of self-control, such as drinking for the men. Conversion symptoms are frequent for both sexes, marking an introjection of aggression.

Men's drinking parties show many of the dynamics of their aggressions. They typically go through three phases. In the first there is brotherly euphoria, singing of nationalistic nostalgic, non-activitistic songs; they proclaim they are Puerto Ricans and want independence from the United States (sentiments little expressed when sober, and played down in political life)—thus reflecting displacement of aggression against the outgroup. In the second phase, men play aggressive jokes on each other, start sudden fights which are as quickly ended. Here aggression is turned against each other. Phase three brings feelings of depression and sadness; the man turns aggression against himself, depreciates himself, and tries to drink himself into oblivion.

Since drinking evidently suppresses superego inhibitors, and probably progressively so, the progression in aggression outlets in the three phases is revealing. First, the men stay close to their reaction formations in the form of group solidarity, but they release some of the aggression against a safe object, the United States as outgroup, in the classic manner of reinforcing ingroup identity by outgroup aggression. In the second phase, aggression is released closer to home, against each other. This is a more direct aggression release, but it is not necessarily closer correspondence between the subject that aroused the aggression and the object against which it is now directed. In the third phase, self-aggression by depression and self-depreciation, the man is not objectively getting any nearer the original sources of the aggression, and the self-hatred represents a self-punishment, in effect, for the aggressive releases of the first two phases. In another sense, however, this third-phase aggression is getting closer to the "heart of the matter," for it is *internal* conflict that is wracking the man; he is "his own worst enemy," hence is punishing himself. That drunkenness ultimately produces this self-punitive pattern is testimony to how deeply the curbs on aggression have been internalized in this subculture.

Men's drinking parties also include expression of fantasies of breaking out of all their bonds, to job and family, spending weeks away from home in completely free instinctual gratification. This is not aggression against women generally, but only by implication against the wife (and children) who represent responsibility and the necessity for the job and non-freedom. The gratification fantasied includes free sexual relations with non-demanding (usually lower-status) women available for men's pleasures, women in effect modeled after his childhood nursemaid.

A much more restrained expression of aggression for men is the phenomenon of the *disgusto*, a falling-out between two men over a point of honor. One feels he has been snubbed by the other and silently harbors a long-term resentment. The touchiness involved reflects widespread anxiety about the stability of one's roles and one's adequacy about filling them. In the case of a *disgusto* friends of both parties will try to mediate to bring the parties together again—often successfully. During and after reconciliation the breach or its causes are never mentioned. Mediators have a stake in their success, perhaps because the latent aggression implied in the breach threatens the stability of other relationships based on repression of aggression, for example, the possibility that their own repressed hostilities would break through. Here are again important reaction formations against aggression.

Women express aggressions through gossip, against each other; through "mortifying" a bride or frightening unmarried girls with sexual stories or mothers-to-be with tales of difficult pregnancies, and so on; and against men by manipulative control over them through the weapon of her job; through conversion symptoms, especially in pregnancy, and widespread almost indiscriminate use of purgatives and enemas. Women rarely drink, except at parties; they express fear of the effects of alcohol, and in fact it does quickly make them lose control.

Other aggression releases, for either sex, are the quadrennial elections, in which people voice fear of a great deal of violence (much less actually occurs) and in the secret practice of spiritualism. In the latter, the audience strongly identifies with the medium, who is "seized" by the spirit of the departed, becomes extremely agitated (and often violently aggressive), and may also release gossip about other people.

Comparison of the Three Communities

All three communities share certain attributes pervasive in Puerto Rican culture: strong differentiation between the sexes, in social roles, expected and typical personality characteristics, degrees and kinds of impulse control; great male concern with dignity, honor, and virility; great efforts at aggression control.

Their differences can be examined by placing the three subcultures on a continuum from traditionalism to modernity, with Manicaboa at one extreme and San José at the other, and Poyal somewhere in between. Still, in many aspects of socialization and personality development, Manicaboa and San José are more alike than either is like Poyal. The women of Manicaboa and San José, for example, for all their surface differences, seem more alike than either is like the sexually freer, warmer, more permissive, and more cooperative women of Poyal. Both are more repressive toward the sexuality of females, and in this respect more traditional, than the people of Poyal. Deferment of gratifications is an important value in child training in both these subcultures, while it is of little importance in Poyal. In both, the nuclear family is a more distinct and self-enclosed unit than it is in the more cooperative-collective styled Barrio Poyal.

The men in both Manicaboa and San José show a similar touchiness about honor, dignity, recognition of the status of a man, sensitivity to the proper courtesies, and so on. The more equalitarian and solidary group-minded men of Poyal do not seem to be so obsessed. Interestingly, though the Poyal man's objective material situation is more like that of the Manicaboa man, it is only in Poyal that a father or stepfather spends a great deal of his time nurturantly or playfully with his children. However, in the other two communities it is more "traditional" to emphasize (though not exclusively) the authority element of the father's role. This must be qualified, however, by noting that the Manicaboan father spends much time with his *sons*, teaching and supervising them in farm skills. This is a powerful source of identification denied to the San José boy.

The import of these differences and similarities, then, is that the impact of the forces of urbanization, industrialization, and bureaucratization, the development of cash markets, the growth of a large consumption economy, in short, the imposition of modern "world culture" upon a more traditional society, is quite uneven in its effect on different subcommunities within that society and not in direct relationship to the apparent external look of "modernity."

To round the picture out, there are other aspects in which the Manicaboa and Poyal communities stand together at one pole in these developments, while the San José middle class is at the other. Both of the materially poorer communities are far more effective in providing the growing child with gradual mastery of the environment and useful adult skills that provide a firm development of ego and strong sex identity. San José by contrast systematically blunts this aspect of ego development and provides a confusing and contradictory picture of the adult roles and personalities of the two sexes, making for a range of problems. Both Manicaboa and Poyal are basically permissive toward body disciplines (though Poyal more so regarding sexuality). They lack devices forcing or constricting the child's own paths of development in these areas. Both in particular are without *anal* obsessions and their derivatives, in compulsiveness and related reaction formations. Both emphasize basic equality of members of the community and the need for cooperative sharing as one element in a strong group solidarity (though Poyal is stronger in this respect). This contrasts with San José's driving individualistic competitiveness and general weakness of group feeling.

Also, interestingly, considering that North American concepts usually link individualism with respect for individual differences and idiosyncrasies, it would seem that both Manicaboa and Poyal show greater respect for the diversities of different children than do the driven consumers of San José. The Manicaboans also have room for the deviant *guapo* and idiot types. Both the mountain people and the cane workers respect the truism that "Children are not all alike." They never try to force a child into a mold, and they allow and encourage a child to learn at his own pace and in his own way. Poyal goes further and accepts with equanimity a child's preference for an aunt or godmother over his mother and expects that different chil-

dren will develop different kinds and degrees of affection and loyalty among the range of parents and parent-surrogates. Neither Poyal
nor Manicaboa assumes that individuality, in the sense of the inevitable differences in temperament and personality among different
children and adults, need subtract from a person's group solidarity
ties, nor that it is in conflict with cooperative sharing, nor that it
requires "privacy" in the sense of seclusion from others and their
busy and often noisy round of activities.

These three subcultures, then, show variations of life patterns in
relation to the interplay of traditionalism and "modernity." They
show variations in ways people can be caught or trapped in conflicts
or constrictions that come from tradition, or from the impact of
"modernity," or the clash of the two. They show varied costs, some
of them greater in the more traditional, some in the culture more
under the impact of change. They illustrate how very different even
so "basic" an institution as the family can be under the impact of
different forces, and how different, and differently costly, other institutional arrangements woven around the family can be in their impact on socialization and on personality.

4. THE ISRAELI KIBBUTZ: SOCIAL STRUCTURE AND PERSONALITY DEVELOPMENT

The Kibbutz, or agricultural collective settlement, of Israel represents one of the great deliberate social experiments in community
organization and child rearing of modern times. For the study of
socialization and personality it has the special advantage that since
the late 1940s, it has been under scrutiny by a variety of sophisticated modern social scientists and continues to be the object of attention by scientifically oriented planners of an advanced modern
society. As a source of insights about the possibilities of being
human in the modern technological world, it thus has enormous
advantages over the many non-literate societies whose description
and analysis twentieth-century anthropology brought into the study
of man. The implications of the latter studies of the "primitive"

My sources for this essay are given in the Selected Bibliography at the end of
the essay. The most comprehensive single source is Melford Spiro, Children of
the Kibbutz (Cambridge: Harvard University Press, 1958).

could be resisted by the ethnocentrically modern with the charge that, while fascinating in an Alice-in-Wonderland way, these studies of primitive societies could really not touch the problems of living in the technologically and socially complex modern world precisely because they dealt with qualitatively different kinds of societies.

The Kibbutz has the important distinction from primitive tribes, as well as from folklike communities within modern societies[11] of being a *deliberately anti-traditional society* (if we may stretch the term "society" for the context). The Kibbutz was the intentional creation of a highly self-conscious and "modern" intelligentsia of East European Jews steeped in some of the main currents of "advanced" social thought of the late nineteenth and early twentieth centuries and guided by a particular and explicit sociological world view. This view drew mainly on one of the pillars of modern social science—Karl Marx—and also derived implications from the work of another—Sigmund Freud. In brief, the communal agricultural collective was designed to remedy the plight, not only of urban bourgeois European (and by extension, all Diaspora) Jews, but of modern industrial man in general. The Kibbutz was to do away with the alienation of man traced in Marxian terms to the property institutions of capitalist industrialism and also prevent the psychic ills of modern neurotics, traced in Freudian terms to the unhealthy relationship of adults and children in the institution of the nuclear family. The Kibbutz was to take literally and seriously the Marxian formula for the distribution of labor and rewards: "From each according to his ability, to each according to his needs." Thus the great concern with the twin values of social justice and optimal fulfillment of the potentialities of human nature were explicitly central in the guiding ideas for revolutionary change of man himself by a deliberate and systematic innovation in social organization. One of the cornerstones of the Kibbutz is the deliberate creation and maintenance of a system of socialization designed to carry the new society into succeeding generations. Such experiment is not, of course, unprecedented,[12] but it is unique in its particular configurations. It begins as explicitly anti-traditional and then attempts to provide continuity

[11] Such as two of the three in Puerto Rico discussed in the preceding section.

[12] Compare the (unsuccessful) attempt to establish communal nurseries in the early days of the Soviet revolution, the communes of present-day Communist China, the numerous communal utopian communities especially of the nineteenth century, the religious sectarian communities such as the Hutterites, the Amish, etc. which approximate such communal organization and education, the latter distinct, however, in their *traditional* religious emphasis.

through education of succeeding generations. It is non-religious (even anti-religious). It attempts to fashion policy based on modern social and psychological knowledge, and in the most radical attempt of all such experiments, it tries to abolish the nuclear family.

In this last feature, this thriving experiment[13] is an exciting test for propositions widely entertained by social scientists about the inevitability and indispensability of the human family.

Our concern in this text is with the collective socialization process in the present-day Kibbutz, its relationship to the general social organization of the Kibbutz and its normative ideals, and the personality products of this collective system. To what extent have marriage and the family in fact been abolished in this subsociety, and what can be learned from the Kibbutz about the classic universal problems of the incest taboo and the Oedipus complex?

In 1954, there were 227 different communal agricultural settlements in Israel to which the term Kibbutz could be applied, organized into three major federations and four minor groupings (with important ideological differences among them, although within the general Zionist-Socialist pattern.) Further, local variations and the current state of flux in adaptation to changing conditions and problems, make it very difficult to generalize about all the Kibbutzim. Nevertheless, the advantages in perspective to be gained by attempting some kind of synthesis seem to justify the degree of license necessary to pull together into a composite picture the many accounts which range from the very intensive study of one single Kibbutz by Melford and Audrey Spiro (see Bibliography at end of essay), to specialized comparisons of selected samples from many different Kibbutzim (as in the work of Rabin), to illuminating comments made on the basis of unsystematic and non-random exposures, and then to important secondary interpretations (such as Bettelheim). My guideline is to emphasize those features that distinguish all the Kibbutzim from the patterns of other modern Western societies, including non-Kibbutz agricultural settlements in Israel itself,[14] and to de-emphasize internal differences within the Kibbutz movement.

[13] Unlike most of its predecessors, the Kibbutz has not died out; it now has a second and third generation, and continues to recruit additionally by bringing in new adolescent or young adult members through the youth movements in the cities of Israel and abroad.

[14] My account does, however, draw more heavily on the *radical-socialist* federations in contrast with those who have modified "back" to conditions more like "bourgeois" family life and individualism; on the non-religious or atheist Kibbutzim, in contrast to those who maintain Judaism.

SOCIAL ORGANIZATION OF THE KIBBUTZ

The Kibbutz is an agricultural commune consisting of a few hundred people (the range is anywhere from forty to as many as a thousand) living together with complete collective ownership of property, collective production (agriculture, animal husbandry, and in many cases light industry) and collective child rearing and education from earliest infancy. There is no private property even of such items as personal clothing, let alone of food, houses, furniture, appliances, or vehicles. The only thing approximating a "private" domicile is the room assigned to a man and woman who announce that they want to live together as a "couple" (words for marriage, married couple, husband, wife, do not exist in the vocabulary) and establish a relatively permanent sexual relationship including the subsequent decision to have children. (Because of the extraneous pressure of the larger Israeli polity, most such couples subsequently go through a formal—therefore, in Israel, religious—marriage ceremony, but this is a concession to Israeli law, which otherwise stigmatizes offspring of such unions as illegitimate, therefore deprived of certain civic rights. In atheist Kibbutzim, the religious ceremony is regarded as hypocritical—a "farce"—by most couples.) Aside from the common domicile and the concentration of sex and other intimacy in each other, the Kibbutz couple do not constitute a marriage in any of the economic or other senses familiar to most other societies. They are neither a producing nor a consuming unit, and their offspring do not share a common domicile with them. By the same token, the *family, as known in other societies,* does not exist. The offspring, from birth, live in communal nurseries, later in communal children's houses, later still in the high school dormitories. They are spoken of as the "children *of the Kibbutz,"* though their biological parenthood is recognized, and they do have some important relationships to their parents.

The economy of the Kibbutz is based on agricultural production and animal husbandry, partly for its own food supply and partly for market, in some cases supplemented by small-scale industry for an outside market. In the ideal-type Kibbutz, labor of all kinds is performed entirely by the adults who are members of the Kibbutz and by the older children growing up on the Kibbutz[15] under centralized control, and, of course, without wages or salaries, but "naturally" as

[15] They are not technically "members" till they have qualified after high school graduation and a period of work or army service away from the Kibbutz.

fulfillment of communal obligation to the Kibbutz. This communal production and distribution of labor is paralleled by communal consumption. The Kibbutz provides for the needs of all of its members and children—food, clothing, shelter, health care, education, and any other needs recognized as legitimate by the entire collective through its democratic assembly of all adult members or its various administrative committees.

The Marxian formula "from each according to his ability, to each according to his needs" is the touchstone for the distribution of work and products of the society. Since "ability," and even more so "needs," are subject to a variety of interpretations, the application of the formula to specific instances always has to be decided in reference to a given actual situation. For example, does a woman "need" a new, pretty, and stylish dress for a visit to the city? The general tendency of the Kibbutz is to interpret "according to need" in a radically equalitarian way rather than on some principle of equity that might emphasize individual differences, as in talents that might justify special training or appurtenances such as oil paints or a violin. Generally, the more stark and rudimentary the economic situation (as in older Kibbutzim in their struggling formative years, or newer ones today) the more likely will "needs" be defined in strictly equalitarian terms, and often the whole formula, on both sides, is taken to mean strict equality, of both work and rewards. The system is designed to prevent any exploitation of man by man. It is also intended to provide exactly the same dignity and rewards and security to women as to men and to demand from them fully equal participation in work and decisions of the community.[16] Full equality of the sexes in child rearing and education is correspondingly also the ideal, and to a great extent the practice, in the Kibbutz. In fact, the more radical socialist Kibbutzim, such as those of the Federation called Hashomer Hatzair, practice a degree of sexual non-segregation probably unparalleled anywhere in the world, including coeducational dormitories and (until recently) showers in the high school.

The whole community is run as a single economic unit, like a

[16] In fact, this last is very far from realized. Economically better-off, larger, and more "developed" Kibbutzim tend to develop rather sharp lines of sexual division of labor, quite different patterns of *actual* communal participation, and rather different emotional involvements of women than of men—in some cases, a source of deep dissatisfaction to the women. See Eva Rosenfeld, "Social Stratification in a Classless Society," *American Sociological Review*, Vol. 16, 1952, pp. 766-74.

single household. All adults eat together in a communal dining hall, the food being prepared and served by members, usually women, who have that particular job at that time. Children eat in separate children's dining rooms or at a different time.

All the income of the Kibbutz goes into a common treasury and is dispensed according to the decisions of the appropriate committees. They in turn are responsible to the assembly of all adult members. Individual members thus have all their "needs" satisfied by communal institutions and receive only a small cash allowance for "personal needs," allotted according to strict equality.

Members are assigned to their jobs by standards that attempt to combine appropriateness of talent, strength, and so on ("ability") with equality of effort or sacrifice. But there is also a rotation principle, intended to insure that no persons or group be *permanently* placed in the most menial or unpleasant or onerous jobs while others maintain a long-term hold on more prestigious, more pleasant, more "fulfilling" types of work positions.[17]

In all Kibbutzim there is the distinction between the "production" (agricultural) branch and the "service" branches of the economy. (In larger wealthier ones, further differentiation appears.) "Service" branches include child care, education, clerical work, sewing, care and distribution of clothing, and food preparation. Generally, a sexual division of labor is followed: men are more concentrated in production, women more in services.

CHILD REARING AND EDUCATION

The crux of this social experiment, and the key to its success and continuity, is the raising of new generations born into this new culture. This is done according to a carefully determined plan of action in the collective child care and educational institutions. The development of the infant into a *Sabra*[18] takes the child through a series of carefully planned socialization stages:

[17] Inevitably, in larger, older, richer collectives greater differentiation *has* set in, with considerable departure from these standards, especially by long-term continuation of particular persons, mostly men, in executive-managerial posts, and some *women* maintained for relatively long periods either in relatively menial jobs, or in positions of recognized value—e.g., baby nurses—for which they however have personal distaste. See Rosenfeld, *op. cit.*

[18] In Israel generally, a *Sabra* is a native-born Israeli. In the Kibbutz the term is used in a more restricted sense to mean a member of the Kibbutz born and raised there, as distinguished from the "first generation" born elsewhere, who joined the Kibbutz as adults. The distinction is enormously significant in nearly all important social, ideological, and psychological dimensions.

1. Earliest Infancy: the first six months. Infants live in the nursery (Infants' House) all of the time, cared for by nurses; parents visit them there; mothers breast-feed their own infants there.

2. Infancy: six months to one year. Infants continue to live in the nursery, cared for by nurses, and visited by parents; but parents now take the infant to their own room for a daily evening period.

3. Toddlers: one year to about four years. Infants are moved into the Toddlers' House, form a group (*kevutza*) which will remain together for the rest of their childhood; they are cared for by a nurse later supplemented by a nursery teacher. Visits to the parents' room continue.

4. Kindergarten: four to seven years. At age four, two toddlers' groups of eight each are united to form a kindergarten group; moved to a Kindergarten House, in the care of one nurse and one nursery teacher. At age six this group begins formal schooling (Grade 1) but remains that year in the Kindergarten House. Evening visits to parents.

5. Grammar School: seven to twelve years (Grades 2-6). Each kindergarten *kevutza* of sixteen is moved to a Grammer School House (a combination school and dormitory), in the care of a new nurse and a grammar school teacher (both female). Each *kevutza* remains intact, but contacts widen to include the whole grade school population. Evening visits to parents.

6. High School (*Mosad*): twelve to eighteen years (Grades 7-12). This is a major move. The youngsters go to a different building that is a combination school and dormitory for all the high school children and physically somewhat apart from the rest of the Kibbutz. Male teachers are encountered for the first time, and more teachers are brought in from outside the Kibbutz. The program includes not only formal school studies, but an increasing amount of work on the Kibbutz. Visits to parents decline.

7. Graduation from high school. This is a major transition from childhood to adulthood.

8. A year (or more) of required work in a city or some other non-Kibbutz environment, or of army service, so that the subse-

quent choice (if made) to stay in the Kibbutz will be based on a comparison with alternative possibilities.

9. (If the *Sabra* so chooses) Return to the Kibbutz; application for membership in the Kibbutz.

10. (If accepted) Adult membership in the Kibbutz. Formation of couples ("marriage") usually occurs at this time (though it can be earlier): assignment to a couple's room.

The socialization agents are:

1. Nursery teachers, grammar school teachers: all female
2. High school teachers: male and female
3. The peer group (*kevutza*); almost exact age-mates, of both sexes, remaining a constant group all through childhood
4. The parents: only as loving nurturant friends, never disciplinarians
5. The whole Kibbutz adult community

The first six months. Immediately upon the mother's return from the hospital, the infant is placed in the Infants' House, where it remains in the care of nurses—ideally, women especially trained and suited for this job.

During the first six months of his life the infant stays in the Infants' House, along with three to seven other infants[19] of almost exactly the same age, cared for by the nurse or relief nurse and visited at regular intervals during the day and night by the mother, and after work by the father as well. The mother usually breast-feeds her own infant. In most Kibbutzim this is on a strict four-hour schedule and with all mothers breast-feeding their infants at the same time and in the same place, the Infants' House (not in the couples' rooms). This makes the feeding time, an emotionally and erotically charged session of free play with the infant which may be prolonged at the mother's discretion, also a *social* rather than private occasion. The mother has her regular work in the Kibbutz as well, but her work schedule is reduced to allow for feeding her baby.

Some Kibbutzim have more recently changed to a demand-feed-

[19] The number of babies in an infant peer group may be as few as four, or as many as eight, depending on the nurse labor resources available in the Kibbutz, the number of children born at that particular time, etc. In the Kibbutz most intensively studied, that reported on by Spiro, the number was typically eight. Other Kibbutzim, and the "expert" advisers on child rearing for the Federations, generally consider that too many for a nurse to take care of at once.

ing system, as opposed to rigidly scheduled feedings: in these cases, the particular mother is summoned by hoisting a flag of a particular color. It seems that this change was made on the insistence of some of the mothers, who objected to the group nursing situation, and was backed by child-care "experts" in line with "modern" ideas that demand feeding is more satisfying and less frustrating to the infant. This is a significant departure pushed for two quite different reasons, of the mother and the "experts," for demand feeding automatically staggers the feeding time and breaks up the group structure, ensuring greater privacy to the mother, and probably accordingly intensifies the affective erotic qualities of the mother-child situation at that time. For infants beyond the earliest infancy it also has another implication: it reduces the amount of time the whole group *of infants* are together as a group, and thus shifts the balance of the three different care-and-socializing forces which the child encounters at this age, that is, the mother, the nurse, and *the peer group*.[20]

During this period, then, the infant has only one home—the Infants' House—the professional care of a responsive and usually well-qualified, but necessarily emotionally neutral nurse, whom he shares with the four to seven other infants, and the special, intense but necessarily intermittent relationship with the breast-feeding mother. Bettelheim[21] makes the point that breast-feeding is the norm, the actual prevailing pattern, and something most Kibbutz mothers want and enjoy—in contrast to the bottle-feeding norm of most American mothers, who may be with or near their babies more of the time, but much of that time is not in such warm and loving contact as the time typically spent by the Kibbutz mother with her child. The Kibbutz mother is relieved of all other tasks and responsibilities at these times, and automatically the communal system does away with elaborate chores of private housekeeping. (Depending on the resources of the Kibbutz, however, a lot of housekeeping chores may devolve upon the nurse, thus seriously reducing the time and attention she can give to the babies, attention which must already be divided among the six or eight that she has.)

During these first six months the mother never takes the infant

[20] Rivkah Bar-Yoseph (an Israeli sociologist, who for a time was herself an infant-nurse in a Kibbutz) notes that the interaction influence of the group of infants can be discerned as early as three months. See "Patterns of Early Socialization in Collective Settlements of Israel," *Human Relations,* Vol. 12, 1959, pp. 345-60.

[21] Bruno Bettelheim, "Does Communal Education Work?" *Commentary,* Vol. 33, 1962, pp. 117-26.

away from the Infants' House, but she does spend more or less prolonged periods with him there and she does put the infant to bed. Breast-feeding is supplemented by the bottle, from about the age of three months, according to the idiosyncrasies of the child and feelings of the mother. From then on, the nurse takes an increasing role in the feeding of the child. By the time the gradual weaning is complete, the nurse has the feeding role exclusively. In the process of weaning the period between breast-feedings is gradually increased so that the mother gradually spends less time with the infant during the day.

The first six months set a very important pattern in the relationship of the child to the different agents of socialization: in this period there are two central socializing agents, the nurse and the mother. They differ greatly in their functions for the child, in their emotional tone toward the child, and in the times that they spend with the child. The kinds of patterns of gratification which the child has with each also differ markedly. The mother provides gratifications of intense oral-erotic and affective quality for the infant, in a situation where the infant is basically passive, and there is a wide range of gratifications in restricted time periods. With the nurse, the range of gratifications is more restricted, but there is very little restriction in time. It is a relationship which necessarily lacks great personalization because the nurse is an occupational functionary and also must divide her attentions among all of the children. The nurse does, however, provide continuing security: she is *there*, the infant can see her at any time, and if he cries, she comes and helps him. And the relationship to the nurse is such that the child is encouraged to take an active role in eliciting gratifications from her.

By contrast, however, the nurse can be, and often is, replaced. Her position is an occupational *role*, whereas the mother is, and always is, the child's mother. Thus, though the nurse does carry on many of the tasks done by mothers in nuclear-family societies, and is thus a "surrogate-mother," still the child learns to differentiate her from the mother, in time very clearly. (That this differentiation is not complete is shown in those children who call their nurses "mother." [22]) The differentiation is somewhat like distinguishing a nursery school teacher from the mother in our society, with the exception that in the Kibbutz the child has a nurse around (not always the same one) nearly all of the time from his earliest infancy while

[22] Spiro, *op. cit.*, p. 72.

there is the intense, diffuse affective relationship to the mother only at very limited times.

Six months to one year. When the infant reaches the age of six months, the parents may then take the child to their own room for a daily period after their work in the early evening, but they must return the infant to the nursery at night. The parents put the infant to sleep, but in the nursery, never in their room. (Thus, never in the ordinary experiences in his lifetime does the child sleep in the parents' domicile.)

The evening visit to the parents, begun at six months and continuing all through childhood, now serves to differentiate the relationship to nurses and later to teachers, on the one hand, and to parents, on the other, in terms of place as well as time and circumstance. This differentiation is sharp, and its implications are pervasive throughout Kibbutz life. When a young child says "my room," he means his *parents'* room, as distinguished from "our house" which means the house where *he and his peer group* live. By the age of one year, the baby will have learned to recognize three different foci of his life—the nurse, his mother and father, and his peer group. And these three are important in quite different ways in his development and personality.

Toddlers. At the age of about one year, babies are moved in groups of four or five to a different house, the Toddlers' House, sometimes getting a new nurse as well at this time. (This periodic changing of nurses, added to the usual short-term shiftings involved in days off, vacations, and illnesses, make for an important and evidently disturbing discontinuity, in the care experienced by the child. This, in turn, heightens the significance of the relative constancy of the mother and father.) In the Kibbutz which Spiro studied other babies are added as they reached the age of one year until the group numbers eight. Such a group, now constituting a *kevutza*, is supposed to stay together in the Toddlers' House until kindergarten, (age about four) and is supposed to have the same nurse or pair of nurses through this whole period, though this is often not the case. At about three years, this group also acquires, in addition to the nurse (or in replacement of one of the nurses) a nursery *teacher*—another new authority figure, also female.

Feeding is now done entirely by the nurse, until the child can master feeding by himself. Once that is accomplished, eating is something done by the whole group of toddlers together (under supervision of the nurse), as it will be for the *kevutza* for all the rest of their childhood.

Toilet training is instituted around the age of two, but very variably and permissively, with the group as a major agent helping in this learning process. The toddlers all being put on little potties together at the same time, in an atmosphere of free-and-easy group play, is an important feature of this learning process. (*Sabras* later indicate their solidarity with co-members of their own *kevutza* by saying "We sat on the potty together." [23])

The peer group is also an important factor in the development of *mastery* generally in this period (in fact in all phases of childhood). In such a peer atmosphere a child tends to push himself to his maximal maturational level. This is partly an effect of trying to keep up with the others of the group, and partly of the partial neglect of the nurses, inevitable where a nurse has eight children of the same age to take care of all at once and cannot possibly attend to the problems of each one of them at the exact moment that he would like. Some observers have emphasized the frustrating aspects of such experience for the child.[24] But we must note also that these circumstances frequently push a child to learn to do something for himself faster than he might otherwise, as contrasted with a situation presented in its extreme by the Puerto Rican middle class in San José where a mother or nursemaid, in avid concentration on one child, rushes to do everything for him as soon as a need arises and also anticipates his needs, enormously increasing his dependency. The Kibbutz situation is at the opposite pole, with the added positive element that the learning goes on in a group situation where the child is rewarded not only by the satisfaction of his own sense of mastery, but also by the approval or implied approval of the whole peer group. (The other side of the coin, of course, is that a child whose maturation is slower than his age-mates', or who is enough younger than they that he is at an earlier maturational stage, is especially handicapped in such a group situation, and his psychological frustration may be intense. However, an insightful and patient nurse

[23] This is also a referent in their way of explaining their own spontaneously developed incest taboo: "How can you fall in love with a girl you sat on the potty with?" See Yonina Talmon, "Mate Selection in Collective Settlements," *American Sociological Review*, Vol. 29, 1964, pp. 491-508.

[24] See Spiro, *op. cit.*, and Elizabeth Irvine, "Observations on the Aims and Methods of Child Rearing in Communal Settlements in Israel," *Human Relations*, Vol. 5, 1952, pp. 247-75.

and mother can mitigate such effects.) Thus, in this stage autonomy and mastery are maximized, at the cost of having to learn to tolerate delays and other frustrations.

The group structure, however, also limits the mastery demands to, at most, the maturational level of the most "advanced" infant in the group, and since rates of maturation in different respects may differ significantly in the same child, no one child is likely to be consistently either first or last in any particular developmental task. Further, the daily visits to the parents have two contradictory kinds of influences on the child in these respects which tend toward some kind of equilibrium: first, they make a great fuss over the child's new achievements in movement, coordination, talking, and the like; and, second, in their extreme permissiveness, and total dedication to this one child's needs at this time, they allow him expression of feelings that may be more infantile than those demanded or tolerated in his group, and they are also likely to anticipate his needs, in a manner analogous to anxious middle-class parents in North America. They also very rarely rebuke the child and never punish him. He also has in his parents' room toys that are exclusively his own (his only private property, all toys in the Toddlers' House being communal), and aside from possibly one older sibling (at this age he is unlikely yet to have a younger one) his parents are exclusively his, in contrast to the nurse who must be shared with the seven other children. Therefore, his parents' room and the Toddlers' House represent complementary worlds, which together strike an important balance in the dependency-autonomy struggles of this stage. While the group pushes his mastery and frustration tolerance, his parents allow him to be more babyish and to experience times when there is no time gap between impulse or need and gratification. Though probably not all these consequences were intended in the planning of communal nurseries in the first place, the system, with its counterbalancing visits, does show a very great social and psychological wisdom.

The fact that these loving, nurturant, warm, permissive, and protective nurses are frequently *replaced*, in the experience of the child, is of course a disturbing and frustrating experience, as Spiro and Irvine emphasize. But two further points need to be made about this constellation: the *form* the disturbance most frequently takes and the compensating features. The common symptoms of such disturbance that have been noted are thumb-sucking and (in children who had already learned urinary continence) enuresis. Thumb-sucking is significant: it has been noted by practically all observers in children of all ages and evidently is present to a wider extent in Kibbutz children generally than in comparable Western populations. But thumb-sucking, rather than being regarded merely as a pathological symptom, must be seen in the context of early breast-feeding gratifications and of the *general* permissiveness toward any kind of auto-erotic gratifications, which is the deliberate child-rearing policy of the Kibbutz. Thumb-sucking can be seen as the recovery, in auto-erotic form, of the erotic gratification of the infant at the mother's breast. In earliest infancy this breast-feeding is the great compensation for the necessary delays in gratification from the busy nurse, and it is the prototype for finding further such gratifications in the mother-child situation, which is *the* highly eroticized relationship in the child's life. In the absence of the mother thumb-sucking provides a viable substitute and consolation whenever absence or change of nurse frustrates the child. In the body-permissive atmosphere of the Kibbutz nursery such a consolation is not laden with guilt reactions (as it commonly is in middle-class Western societies). Hence, it is probably *not* an indicator of pathology.

The possible gratificatory significance of enuresis, however, is more complex. In the Kibbutz context it represents a regressive device more relevant to the achievement-mastery norms of the peer group. It can be seen as aggressive to both the child himself and toward his caretakers (though this element is probably less extreme in the Kibbutz than elsewhere, considering the general permissiveness that touches on all body control tasks). It may also be seen as more distinctively attention-seeking than the thumb-sucking behavior. It is evidently a plea for less stringent maturational demands and more infantile treatment, implying that peer-group and nurses' performance expectations can be considered legitimate only if the nurse provides the security of the same continuing, affectional response. The compensating factors mitigate the severity of such disturbance: the continuing constancy of the parents as permissive, nurturing buffers; and *probably* a secondary development of a kind of *coping-toughness*, when the child discovers that the previously adored nurse *can* be replaced, that he can get comparable satisfactions from the new nurse, and that there are compensations in the *group*. In their differing ways the peer group and the parents provide the basic constancy and continuity in his life, and while each is limited—the parents by time, the peer group by their similar state of helpless dependency, so that neither can quite replace a very good nurse—together they provide a certain ongoing security in the child's world.

Nurses do show very loving affection toward the children, and they welcome reciprocating displays from them—but only to a point. They are not mothers. If we view the whole Kibbutz social structure as a totality, there are good reasons why they should not be[25] (that is, mothers, in the Kibbutz sense of adult women who devote a certain time to total nurturance of and permissiveness toward one particular child). Since the nurse must divide her giving among the eight children, she cannot give exclusive loving toward any one; and she must also resist any one child's attempt to eroticize the relationship toward her, beyond a certain mild point. Spiro, documenting how demonstrative the children are of their affection for their nurse, presents this revealing footnote:[26]

> In general, the nurses accept and return this voluntary affection. Sometimes, however, if the acts become too pronounced, a nurse may insist that they cease. Ron (four years), for example, had a tendency to smother his nurses with affection. He would crawl all over the nurses when they were sitting down, and the nurse's response in one instance was typical: "Ron, I don't consent"; "Ron, I don't want to"; "Ron, that's enough."

The nurse here sounds like a woman who has discovered she has let herself go too far toward a seduction that she did not intend. It is also interesting that Spiro gives no indication of a *mother* putting such a limit on erotic encounter. This contrast must be further indication to the child of the differences between nurse and mother. The child, then, is learning very important boundaries.[27] In these terms, the nurse's imposed limitations are very important for the psychological health of the child. Conversely, the rather intense eroticism of parents toward their children in the Kibbutz probably does

[25] Note the important Kibbutz policy that no woman should be a nurse to a *kevutza* that includes her own child. Here the Kibbutz explicitly recognizes the conflict of roles and enforces their segregation.

[26] Spiro, *op. cit.*, p. 73, fn. 2.

[27] Let us note at this point that recent studies in our society show schizophrenia invariably linked with early childhood incest problems, toward which seductiveness by mother to son can strongly contribute—with the interpretation that the schizophrenic suffers from lack of effective *affective* boundaries. See Gregory Bateson, *et al.*, "Toward a Theory of Schizophrenia," *Behavioral Science*, Vol. 1, 1956, pp. 251-64. See also, for a cross cultural analysis of early-puberty extrusion customs, in similar terms, Yehudi Cohen, *The Transition from Childhood to Adolescence* (Chicago: Aldine Press, 1964).

not have the kind of damaging consequences this might have in a nuclear-family system, precisely because it is limited by the highly segregated (though important) role the parents have in the children's lives. (We shall return to this theme in discussion of the Oedipus complex and psychosexual development.)

In the three Kibbutzim studied by Spiro (one) and Irvine (two), respectively (representing two different federations, differing somewhat ideologically), another problem appears for children at this age level. For considerable periods of the day the toddlers are left unsupervised to play by themselves, e. g., in very large playpens outside. Both Spiro and Irvine noted that the children seemed relatively *neglected*, that they tended to be rather apathetic and listless, and that they showed a great deal of unorganized aggression against each other, for which there was no recourse in adult authority, because the nurse was not present, usually being very busy with household chores. This situation was probably the result of a current womanpower shortage in the Kibbutzim concerned rather than official Kibbutz policy. (However, the line between permissiveness and neglect is sometimes hard to draw, and the official policies of permissiveness and letting the group develop its own social control norms could be interpreted to support this kind of unsupervised group play.) The notion that a group of very young children, if left to their own group processes, will develop their own aggression controls is certainly not supported by the data here. In fact, what these children crucially lack in this situation is protection by an adult authority capable of enforcing aggression-control norms (which, once enunciated, could be reinforced by *group* pressures, where the group, as a solidarity, wants to maintain adult approval). The Kibbutz ideologists, in their extreme permissiveness toward aggression and fear of imposing adult authority (another strong reaction formation against the domination in the patriarchal family) have neglected some very important aspects of aggression control: first, that the weakest and most timid necessarily suffer and are victimized in a situation of free-for-all peer group aggressions; and, second, probably more important, that the aggressors also suffer, from the lack of boundaries on their aggressions (which the peer group, unaided, cannot here provide), and this is likely to produce illusions of omnipotence in their aggression, hence a frightening inability to control them oneself. To expect this much ego development in children this young is, of course, expecting too much. Another ideological illusion which may be operating here is the notion that a group of three-year-olds, left unsuper-vised, would spontaneously improvise their own creative play, without interference from adults. The cases presented by Spiro and Irvine would seem to refute this notion. These three-year-olds, in spite of an atmosphere that is otherwise very responsive and welcom-ing to creative efforts (for example, making things out of mud or sand), do *not* so improvise when left to themselves for protracted periods, but rather appear "apathetic and listless."

Kindergarten age (age four–seven). The age of four marks an-other important transition in the child's life. His toddlers' *kevutza* of eight children is merged with another such group of similar age, to form a kindergarten group of sixteen children. There is a shift of supervisory personnel here, too: of the one nurse and one nursery teacher each of these octets had as toddlers, only the nurse from one group and the nursery teacher of the other are retained in the new expanded kindergarten group. Thus, each of the children loses either a nurse or a nursery teacher. Initially, each of the subgroups com-petes with the other for the attention of their "own" respective nurse or nursery teacher. (The retention of one of each at least miti-gates this nurse-change situation. The plan is deliberate for this rea-son, but the transition difficulties are there, nevertheless.) The nurse change is accompanied by a residence change as well, the new group moving into a Kindergarten House. Here at six their primary school-ing will formally begin, giving them a year remaining in the same *residence* at least to make this next transition.

This is the age at which in nuclear-family societies Oedipal prob-lems are said to reach their crisis, with resolution by renunciation of the sexuality of the opposite-sex parent and of the parenticidal im-pulse toward the same-sex parent and their resolution by repression, reaction formation, identification, and sublimation. Because of the social-structural differences, the psychosexual patterns in the Kib-butz are bound to be different. We shall discuss these separately in a later section.

In this phase, the peer group is consolidated in the size and per-sonnel that it will have through the rest of the group's childhood, and this is no doubt a crucial factor in the handling of sexual feel-ings. This is a period of continuing bisexual infantile play, and great openness of sexual play among all the children of the peer group.

Middle childhood: the peer group. The group now stays to-gether continuously for the rest of their childhood: they will live together, eat together, sleep together, bathe together, play together, study together. This continuous peer group is a major socializing force for all the children. The children learn from each other, soothe and comfort each other (especially, when, as inevitably happens, the nurse or nursery teacher is not available at the moment), confide in each other, learn the give-and-take of aggression and counterattack, compete with each other for the nurse's attentions and help. As one young adult *Sabra* said of his *kevutza*, "We know each other inside out." These children go through all their developmental stages and crises together, get all their basic disciplines together. This total sharing is completely coeducational. Kibbutz ideology explicitly is determined to eliminate sexual shame or embarrassment about the body and the differences of the sexes. Any *kevutza* is composed of children of both sexes, preferably in equal numbers, but not necessarily always so. From infancy they bathe together, undress (or are undressed) in front of each other, may freely engage in sexual play and exploration, and so on, in a completely matter-of-fact manner. Even in the high school a typical dormitory room will have two boys and two girls, and until recently both sexes had showers together. (Protests, mostly by the girls, led to the abolition of that custom in many Kibbutzim).

The peer group is thus *the* great source of continuity and of security for the child growing up in the Kibbutz—in contrast to the repeatedly changing adult socializers, the nurses, nursery teachers, and teachers. There is also the continuity of the parents. However, quantitatively the child is not with them very much, and, qualitatively, their emotional importance to him definitely declines in later childhood so that by the time the children are adolescents, the typical parental complaint is that their children are strangers to them. As Bettelheim puts it,[28] the parents (if they were original founders), determined to spare their children the intense dependency-hostility ties they had toward their parents, which led to their rebellion in the form of the Kibbutz movement, now get more than they bargained for. For the child here really is independent of his parents. What the founders sought to abolish—their notion of the European patriarchal family, built around private property power—they have in fact abolished, and very effectively. The children are indeed "children of the Kibbutz"—not only are they collectively the responsibility of *all* the Kibbutz, but they also feel themselves to belong, not to

[28] Bettelheim, *op. cit.*, p. 124.

individual families, but to the whole community, and most intensely *to their own group.*

PARENTS AND CHILDREN

The family, to be sure, has not been totally abolished, but its functions are radically reduced compared to the nuclear family in any other modern society, or any society for that matter. The parents are not personally the source of support, care, feeding, clothing, or medical care for the child: all of these are provided by the Kibbutz as a communal entity. Nor does the child ever live with the parents. The parents are part of the total community of adults who provide for, care about, love, teach, and imbue ideals in all of the children.

The children visit the parents daily, on the Sabbath, and on special holidays. In addition, they see their parents frequently during the day. Whenever a mother or father has occasion during his own work to be near the children's house or where they are playing, the parent will typically stop to greet the child and if possible spend some time with him. Similarly, a child will frequently encounter his father or mother when his group is engaged in a guided exploration of the Kibbutz, observing the various kinds of work going on; then there will always be a greeting and some brief loving attention to the child. (An incidental effect here is that the Kibbutz child will typically know a great deal more concretely about the work of both of his parents than the average child of most urban Western communities, and especially be a lot more familiar with the work of the *father.*) The intensity of these incidental contacts, however, is mitigated by the fact that in such encounters all of the working adults will show an interest in all of the children in the group, thus emphasizing the communal tie, implying (often stating) that all of the adults are the parents of all the children—in contrast to the exclusive parent-child relationship.

The visits of the child to the parents' room are by contrast an exclusive relationship. The setting here is radically segregated in time, place, and emotional and social atmosphere from everything else in the child's life. In the little time that the child is with the parents, they devote all of their attention to him. They are not at work, they have no household chores (or only very minimal ones, since a couple's room is typically rather small and bare), and the time is definitely set aside for the children. This is also the only time

when biological siblings are together, all relating to the same affectively important adult at the same time. There is scarcely any exercising of authority over the child during this period. Rather it is a
time of play, relaxation, and emotional contact. Both parents share
this. In line with the general (deliberate) sexual equalitarianism of
the Kibbutz, fathers and mothers are very much alike in their affective reponses to the children. Fathers have some edge in the children's affections, possibly because a child could have had some frustrating experiences with the mother in the early-infancy feeding,
whereas he has not (ordinarily) had such experiences with the father. Another possible basis for children's slight preference for the
father is that he is the only male adult with whom they have important contact (especially in the earliest years) and he is totally a nurturant figure. By contrast, female adults who are important to the
child are several in number (nurses, nursery teachers, and mother)
and are partly nurturant and partly disciplinary and punitive toward
the child (while mother is almost wholly nurturant, nurses and
teachers are partly both). Hence, it is possible that ambivalence toward the nurse generalizes somewhat to the mother as an adult figure of the same sex.[29]

The parents, then, are basically warm, loving, indulgent, responsive playful adults to the child, with the father more clearly seen in
that role.

Interestingly, then, here in a society which sets out to all but abolish the family, the ties of children to their parents are, in fact, rather
intense.While on the Moral Ideology Test the children of the Kibbutz Spiro studied[30] name both nurses and teachers and parents
equally as the ones who would praise them for good deeds, they only
rarely name the parents as persons who would criticize them for bad
deeds (nurses and teachers three times as frequently). Parents are
the source of indulgence and undelayed gratification and scarcely the
source of discipline or negative sanctioning of any kind. On the
Emotional Response Test, parents are never mentioned as a source
of anger, fear, shame or sadness in the child—only the *absence* of
parents is a source of sadness or seen as one of the worst things that
can happen.[31] In fact, the children show rather extreme emotional
reactions to the absence of either of the parents, and even more, of

[29] Spiro, *op. cit.*, p. 232, fn. 3.
[30] *Ibid.*, p. 81.
[31] *Ibid.*, p. 82.

both at once. Disturbed children Spiro observed were invariably children whose mother or father, or both, were away on a trip (such as for advanced training or a vacation) or for army service, or ill, or were divorced, with the consequence of one of them leaving the Kibbutz, or worse still, were dead. Spiro also attributes the tremendous commotion that accompanies the children's evening meals to their being keyed up in anticipation of the evening visit with the parents. While Spiro's account also gives much evidence of strong emotional attachments of children, especially very young ones, to their nurses, and of suffering in response to the inevitable changings of nurses and teachers, or even to a very temporary absence of a nurse (as on her day off), the balance is certainly in the direction of the parents' being more centrally, because more constantly, the great emotional tie for the child.

The parents have this importance because, while nurses and teachers dispense both affection and discipline, security and punishment, the parents give only love. The extreme segregation of this love relationship also probably contributes to its intensification. From the evidence in Spiro's and others' accounts of the lavishing quality of this parental affection and indulgence, there is probably something compensatory and guilt-ridden about it—probably primarily for first-generation parents and less for parents who are themselves *Sabras*. A comment by Elizabeth Irvine[32] is relevant in this context:

> It is apt to be difficult for the rebellious child confidently to assume the responsibilities of parenthood, since this involves identification with the rejected parent; so the delegation of parental function is a natural and welcome solution of a dilemma. By vesting authority in professionals, parents are relieved of the necessity of asserting it themselves, and of the fear that by doing so they would alienate the children as their parents alienated them.

The rebellious founders of the Kibbutz were in effect rejecting the intense love-hate-dependency atmosphere of the typical Jewish families in which they grew up. Kibbutz ideology crystallizes their desire not to have their own children growing up in such a family atmosphere. Communal nurseries are the answer. However, the ambivalence of such parents persists, and it is unlikely that any Kibbutz mother is unconflicted about handing over "her" baby to be cared

[32] Irvine, *op. cit.*, p. 250.

for and raised primarily by the communal nursery. Irvine was impressed by the indications of conflict between the mother and the nurse, particularly in the earliest infancy of the child. Spiro's account gives many examples of this also. Since the nurse must inevitably divide her attentions among seven or eight babies (and often household chores too), the mother feels that often a baby does not get as immediate or adequate attention as the mother would like and thinks she herself would provide the child. In addition, there are frequently differences in feeling about child-care policy between mother and nurse, made the more frustrating to the mother because official policy of the movement presupposes that the nurse, as a professionally trained functionary, "knows better" (often as not untrue). Many mothers (including, interestingly, some of the *Sabras*) report feeling frustrated in the expression of their "maternal instincts" by the child-care system.[33] I surmise from the various reports, then, that this ambivalence toward parenthood and toward delegation of most of its tasks to communal agents is general for both men and women (probably more for women) of the first generation. This sets the stage for the intensity of the parent-child relationship in the visiting hours. This intensity seems to indicate a yearning by these parents to re-establish at least the positive aspects of their own relations with their parents and to fulfill some of the promise of their own lives that derives from their having grown up in a certain kind of emotionally intense Western Jewish family.

The prevalent tone of disappointment of these parents in their children when the latter have reached adolescence is poignantly revealing. Among many other things it suggests that they had hoped, with their lavishing of love and attention on the children in the evening visits, to bind these children to them emotionally for life, somewhat as they feel their parents did to them. (Though at a manifest level they have rebelled and rejected their own parental past, at deeper emotional levels this rebellion-rejection is evidently far from complete.[34]) Note that their complaint is not that the adolescents are *rebelling* against them or the ideology of the Kibbutz (they are not) but rather that the youngsters seem *indifferent* to the parents. It looks almost as though the parents are complaining that the adolescents *do not* rebel—for rebellion, as these erstwhile rebels must

[33] Leading, in some Kibbutzim, recently, to a shift (or "regression" ideologically) to something more like conventional Western mothering.
[34] For further elaboration of this theme, see Stanley Diamond, "Kibbutz and Shtetl," *Social Problems*, Vol. 5, Fall 1957, pp. 167-77.

know in their own depths, comes out of profound feelings of both love and hate, whereas indifference signifies the absence of both.

All this suggests that there is something strongly overdetermined (in Freud's sense) about the intense lavishing of love, indulgence, attention, and affection upon the children by the parents in the visiting periods. Partly it may be a reaction to guilt feelings for having "abandoned" their children to the communal functionaries for the main portion of their time. This I would suspect is stronger in the mothers than in the fathers; therefore, ambivalence is stronger there, with the consequence that the father's attentions and indulgences to the child are less alloyed with such negative feelings, and hence freer and more spontaneous. This surmise is consistent with the commonly reported fact that, if anything, Kibbutz children are more fondly attached to their fathers than to their mothers. Another element in this overdetermination of parental lavishing and indulgence is that this is the main occasion for the parents to express otherwise frustrated maternal and paternal feelings. Many parents explicitly state this.[35] Many, especially mothers, feel deprived that they cannot carry on the various care-taking functions for their children that the system of communal rearing was explicitly designed to relieve them of. Spiro also suggests fear of losing the children as another basis for the intensity of love lavishment on the children during the evening visits. The parents evidently perceive that under the communal system this love is the only hold that they have on their children, since all other aspects of the children's dependency—security, support, feeding, housing, medical care—are fulfilled by the commune in general, and not by the parents personally. The parents are thus caught in the paradox of consequences of their own ideological devotion and sacrifice. Ambivalence to and rebellion against their own parents led them to the communal system, which now frustrates their own ambivalent parent-child feelings in relation to the other role—a poignant commentary, since in most parts of the world a major part of life's drama is the resolution of childhood's pains and terrors by being able to reverse the parent-child roles in the next generation, a resolution painfully denied these parents.

Kibbutz parents also show, in their "children's hour" lavishment, their own latent unwillingness or inability to let go completely of their own parental-family past. A touching illustration of this is given in an excerpt from Spiro's field notes:[36]

[35] Spiro, *op. cit.*, p. 61.
[36] *Ibid.*, p. 59. (Italics added.)

> *At dinner,* CHAVIVA *sits and slices olive after olive to spread on bread. I ask her, "How do you have the patience to do this?" and she answers that it is not for her, but for her children, who had asked for an olive sandwich.* LEAH, *also sitting there, says* "for the children, there's always patience; for yourself, never."

To anyone who knows Jewish culture, the familiarity of tone and content of that last sentence suggests that these revolutionary women are daughters of the *Shtetl* through it all. The scene could be transposed out of an Israeli communal dining hall and repeated, with scarcely a changed word, in almost any Jewish family in the Diaspora.[37]

One further feature of the "children's hour":[38]

> . . . *not only that the parent sets aside these hours to be devoted to his child, but that he spends these hours as the child wishes. If the child wishes to take a walk, the parents take a walk; if the child wishes to visit a friend, they visit a friend; if the child wishes to hear a story, they tell him a story. In short, the child controls the situation.*

This illustrates the absence of control or domination of authority in the parents' relationship to the child. It shows that the relationship is one of almost total indulgence of the child's wishes and unconditional giving by the parent to the child. It is hardly surprising, then, to learn that the children, as they grow up, feel no need to rebel against their parents.

THE SIGNIFICANCE OF FOOD

As part of the general ideology and feelings of the Kibbutz adults, the children are regarded as the focal point of existence for the whole Kibbutz, for they are the future, the continuity of the Kibbutz way of life. In keeping with this, food is available for the children in lavish quantities and variety, sometimes very much out of line with the general economic situation of the Kibbutz, so that adults may eat sparely, even ascetically.[39] There is another difference: the communal dining hall for adults represents an important reac-

---

[37] Lest I be misunderstood: I, of course, do not mean that only Jews lavish love and attention on their children, nor that only they do so with such concentration on food-giving, but only to show that these first-generation Kibbutz mothers, revolutionary communalists though they are, show a profound continuity with their own Jewish family origins.

[38] Spiro, *op. cit.*, p. 58.

[39] This contrast pervades the Kibbutz. In any economically struggling Kibbutz, housing, shower and toilet facilities, clothing, and all consumption goods are much more sparse and rudimentary for the adults than for the children.

tion formation against both the gustatory and emotional-social richness and complexity of family dining in the *Shtetl* or derived Jewish cultures of the antecedents of the Kibbutzniks in Europe and America.[40] Food-sharing was a major focal point of family structure and cultural tradition of the *Shtetl*. To the Kibbutz founders, traditional eating patterns represented the "pathology" of Jewish familial emotional ties and the "abnormal" masochistic position of the Jews in the Diaspora. The communal dining hall is an attempt to erase such traditions by separating the family not only from food production, but also from food consumption, and also by almost totally de-emotionalizing and de-socializing the consumption of food. The adult Kibbutzniks eat *communally*, but not *socially*: it is not an occasion for stretching out a meal in pleasant social conversation. Rather they eat quickly, even in haste, and in a peremptory, businesslike manner. This in turn is consonant with the basically ascetic style of at least the older *chaverim*. By interesting contrast, however, the children's communal dining is marked not only by more lavish and varied food, but also by a constant turmoil of "social" activity, singing songs, shouting, and the like, typically producing an uproar of noise.[41] Thus the *regular* eating of adults and children in the Kibbutz represents two different eating social patterns, both marked by communality of peers, but one by spareness, speed, and asceticism, the other by lavishness, variety, and social-emotional turbulence.

But there is still a very significant third eating pattern, and that is eating in the parents' room. By Kibbutz norms, it is taboo for people to eat their regular meals in their own rooms—that would encourage "bourgeois" privatization that is absolutely opposed by Kibbutz ideology. However, it is permissible to brew some tea and have tidbits or snacks, especially if it is the "children's hour" and the parent wishes to serve some special little treat like a cookie, cake, or piece of fruit. This is the significance of Chaviva's olive sandwiches for her children. They may be well fed in the regular dining hall, but that is part of the general taken-for-granted security of the Kibbutz. Food

[40] See Diamond, *op. cit.*, for a perceptive analysis of this point.

[41] Bettelheim, *op. cit.*, remarks on this, seeing in it a sign of fine emotional health on the part of the children, and praising the social wisdom of an institution which not only precludes the eating emotional problems of the "eat-eat-my-child" parent-child encounter, but also spares the parents the wear and tear of such turbulent children's eating. He notes that many of the severely disturbed children he has treated at his unique Orthogenic School in Chicago, very rapidly "get over" their eating disturbances when they have to eat with a whole gang of children in exactly such a turbulent noisy setting as is found in the children's dining halls in the Kibbutz.

in the parents' room, by contrast, has the special quality of a love gift, and of something where the child's special whims (if possible) will be gratified. Thus the parents have managed, in this small way, to perpetuate some of the emotional quality of food-sharing of their ancestral Jewish families.[42]

SIBLINGS

Generally the relation of parents to children is a positive one of unconditional love, unalloyed with elements of domination or authority. The one possibly negative note, however, is in the area of siblings. By deliberate plan children are rather widely spaced within a family.[43]

By the use of contraception births are spaced at least two years apart. It is common for the older sibling to be four or five before the next one is born. The evening visits are automatically the primary situation in which sibling rivalries will appear, and they commonly do; usually with the older (dethroned) sibling feeling this toward the new baby, and not the other way around. In this intensely child-centered society, the newest arrivals receive considerably more attention than older children. A sibling of age four or five is likely to feel such dethronement all the more intensely because he has monopolized all of his parents' loving attention for such a long period. Some older siblings feel this so intensely that they refuse to visit the parental room at all while the baby is there.[44]

Sibling rivalry is greatly mitigated, however, by the social structure

[42] Another indication of such persistence, in spite of revolutionary rebellion, is in the parents' use of pet names for their small children: "Almost all [such] names are both Yiddish-ized and diminutized after the Yiddish. Chana becomes Chaneleh; Yitzhak becomes Itzik; Yaakov becomes Yankele." Spiro, *op. cit.*, p. 59, footnote 11.

In view of the Kibbutz, and general Israeli antagonism to Yiddish as the language of Diaspora Jewry—hence symbol of the degraded masochistic position of the Jews—this persistence is especially striking in that it occurs in the most intense, personalized, and eroticized relationship of adults to children that exists in the Kibbutz. We may well consider this a case of the "return of the repressed," showing that in the most intimate relations pervaded by unconscious survivals, some of the deepest levels of these parents' own familial past are preserved and repeated.

[43] In some Kibbutzim a couple must even present their plan to have a child for approval to the assembly of the commune, so much is this considered a communal responsibility. This was or is more true in new and economically struggling Kibbutzim, where resources to care for babies have to be carefully rationed and the womanpower of the prospective mother herself may be considered indispensable in some currently more crucial area, such as food production.

[44] Spiro, *op. cit.*, p. 92 ff.

of the Kibbutz. This situation is well summarized by Rivkah Bar-Yoseph:[45]

> The sibling relationship is less competitive than it is in the modern nuclear family. The atmosphere of the home is one of general affection for everyone. The older child, even if he is jealous of the baby and would like to act like a baby, is checked by the approval or disapproval of his peer group. Having siblings is very important for the child, because "everybody" has siblings, and they bring prestige in the peer group. Conflict situations between the siblings are minimized by segregation and the differentiation of the activities of children within different age groups. Older children take some responsibility for their younger siblings, but mostly as a favour to their parents and not as a duty. It is not customary to compel them to do so. For a smaller child, a bigger one is a mixture of the parental and the peer-group figure. His world is an intermediate world between the small child's world and the adult world, without being too different from the child's own experience. In the main siblings are somewhat like peers, only they are more affectionate and less menacing.

The psychologist A. I. Rabin presents definite evidence that sibling rivalry is less intense for Kibbutz children than for contemporary Israeli children raised in "the traditional patriarchal family setting." He compared responses of twenty-seven ten-year-old Kibbutz boys, with those of twenty-seven ten-year-old boys from non-Kibbutz Israeli agricultural villages (with the traditional family system), on the "Blacky" test.[46] His findings show that the Kibbutz boys, while showing some sibling rivalry, show significantly less of it than the control group, as indicated by much less likelihood of responding to parental attention to the sibling by aggression or attack, and less likelihood of expressing the anger against the sibling, rather than the parents.[47]

---

[45] Bar-Yoseph, op. cit., p. 357.

[46] A projective test, using cartoons of a family of dogs, Mama, Papa, Blacky (the son, and central character), and a younger brother Tippy. The relevant picture for sibling rivalry shows parents showering attention on Tippy, Blacky watching. Subject is asked to tell a story; then specific questions are asked: 1. What does Blacky feel like doing now? 2. Does Blacky think Tippy deserves the praise? . . . 5. If Blacky is angry, at whom most: Mama, or Papa, or Tippy? Rabin found that questions 1 and 5 proved statistically significant differences between the Kibbutz and non-Kibbutz boys: the latter more likely to express aggression or attack and to direct the anger at the sibling rather than the parents. Both groups overwhelmingly thought Tippy did not deserve the praise. Note, however, that the Kibbutz boys do show some sibling rivalry, though less than those raised in traditional families.

[47] A. I. Rabin, "Some Psychosexual Differences Between Kibbutz and Non-

The two groups of boys, however, did not differ in the proportion feeling that the sibling did not deserve the praise or attention. In fact, slightly more of the Kibbutz boys (23 out of 27) thought this than of the non-Kibbutz boys (21 out of 27). These findings, however, deserve some comment. That both groups overwhelmingly thought that the sibling did not deserve the praise indicates the presence of sibling rivalry in both. The Kibbutz boys, however, express anger about equally toward the parents (14 cases) as toward the sibling (13), while for the family-raised boys the figures are 8 and 19, respectively. But this can be interpreted to mean, simply, that, given a situation of sibling rivalry, Kibbutz boys are more likely to feel anger toward the parents, and not necessarily that they feel less rivalry with the sibling. All the features of Kibbutz social structure and child rearing would conduce toward this result: since the parents are not dominating and hence threatening authorities for the Kibbutz child, he can more easily recognize and express anger against them. Relevant to this, Spiro notes the freedom with which Kibbutz children in general express anger or aggression against adults, a not surprising result of the extremely anti-authoritarian upbringing of these children. However, Rabin's finding that only four out of the twenty-seven Kibbutz boys respond to the Blacky picture by expressions of aggression or attack (toward any object) does seem to confirm that the sibling rivalry situation is felt less intensely, and as less of a frustration, for the Kibbutz boys than for the others. The general picture, then, is that for the Kibbutz child (at least for the boy) sibling rivalry does appear, but it is less intense than for non-Kibbutz children, and the feelings it engenders are directed as much at the parents as at the sibling.[48]

THE ADULTS IN THE CHILD'S LIFE

Through the grammar school years the *kevutza* continues to have a nurse and a schoolteacher, both female. They are typically replaced at periodic intervals. Thus the pattern prevails, from the nurseries into the school years, of discontinuity of the specific adult

---

Kibbutz Israeli Boys," *Journal of Projective Techniques*, Vol. 22, 1958, pp. 330-31.

[48] One could guess that the child raised in the conventional family *feels* such reactions to the parents as well, but is much more inhibited from *expressing* them toward the parent, whereas the sibling as a contemporary is a much safer object for such aggression. For the Kibbutz child, the extremely permissive and non-authoritarian quality of the parents eliminates this danger differential.

persons who are the major socializers of the child. By school age, then, the child will have learned to expect that the nurse and the teachers he has one year may or will be replaced by someone else in the following year (and at various other times and occasions). Bettelheim has an interesting comment on this problem.[49]

> . . . *much of the American discussion of Kibbutz education sees replacements in the staff of the communal school as the central weakness of the system, a factor which necessarily causes emotional disturbances in the children. But if child-care workers remained the same during most of the children's infancy and childhood, they would simply have turned out to be parents by another name. By entrusting the child's total education to workers who are replaced —though not too often—the Kibbutz system prevents him from forming either positive or negative identifications with the whims, idiosyncrasies, or emotional constellation of one or two particular adults. Instead, it forces him to organize his life along the consistent patterns and values of the community, held in common by all the adults: the ones who take care of him and the others living around him.*

The point about identifications is essentially important. The removal of the child from economic and other dependencies on his natural parents, and hence the avoidance of the child's being too intensely influenced by the special personality quirks and problems of these two individuals, is a cardinal point in official Kibbutz ideology. The Kibbutz child evidently develops a kind of composite adult image, based on relationships to this whole succession of caretakers as well as to the parents—but the parents' place in this composite is drastically reduced compared to their role in such identifications in the nuclear family. Hence, the special kinds of pathologies common to nuclear-family societies—a compound of guilts, anxieties, dependencies, and frustrated quests for autonomy from specific emotionally tyrannical adults—are absent or rare in the Kibbutz child. The relationship to the parents is a strong one, affectively. However, since it is so partial in the child's life and decreases in immediate practical relevance as the child grows older—and, most important, because it does not include the crucial element of near total dependency of the child on the parent—identifications based on this relationship are not an important part of the experience of the child. Where any such dependencies and identifications are incipient in any Kibbutz child, they are strongly counteracted by the influence of the caretak-

[49] Bettelheim, *op. cit.*, p. 123.

ers and probably, even more importantly, of the peers, both of which tend toward identification with the community in general rather than with any specific adults. The possibility of any parent, or of any nurse or teacher, by their special idiosyncrasies, offering a strong role model for the child, in any direction deviant from the general community norms, is readily counteracted by the influence of the peer group, and of other adults generally in the Kibbutz. It seems that for the Kibbutz child, the parents are somewhat analogous to a doting and indulgent uncle, aunt, or grandparent for a child in our society, a relative whom one sees occasionally, or even frequently, and then always in some pleasant gratifying context, but a relative upon whom one has no regular dependency and who is not in any sense an authority or wielder of discipline over the child. Such relatives may be important in certain childhood phases as buffers for the child against those adults who are both objects of dependency and wielders of authority; and they may contribute something to the complex of identifications of the child—perhaps conflict, perhaps confusion, perhaps enrichment. Another analogy is certain types of relatives, in many primitive societies, who are neither food and protection providers nor agents of learning and discipline, but people with whom one can be relaxed, spontaneous, and playful, or more infantile, or salaciously sexual. In some such societies these relationships may be rigidly designated as proper in certain particular kinship roles—and these have been called by anthropologists "joking relationships"—for example, the Hopi boy toward his father's sister. Typically, these have been analyzed as "tension-release mechanisms." [50]

What is interesting, however, in carrying this analogy further to the Kibbutz, is that while the relationship to the parents in early childhood appears to be a mild joking relationship, by adolescence it has become what to anthropologists is its opposite—an avoidance relationship—though not by any formal norms. As noted before, Kibbutz parents complain that their adolescent children are "strangers" to them, have no time or are "too busy" to visit them, do not confide their troubles in them, and so on. The adolescents in reply find such excuses as their busy round of activities or the distance from the Mosad (high school) to the rest of the Kibbutz. Also, when they are with their parents, they are generally uncommunica-

[50] See Fred Eggan (ed.), *Social Anthropology of North American Tribes* (Chicago: University of Chicago Press, 1937), especially pp. 75-81.

tive with them. This seems to be a spontaneous development of an "avoidance relationship" that has as yet no normative backing but stems from common intrapsychic dynamics of all the children, and it parallels the spontaneous development of an "incest taboo" among these same children of the Kibbutz.[51] How is this shift from an earlier free-and-easy loving relationship (somewhat like a joking relationship) to the later avoidance relationship of reticence and "strangeness" to be explained?

The early relationship to the parents is infantile and totally in the private sphere. It is infantile in the sense of providing unqualified and unconditional indulgence and undelayed gratifications for the child. The child's almost total control of the situation (parents do what *he* wants) is almost a model of infantile omnipotence fantasies. But everything else in the child's socialization pushes him to outgrow and reject infantilism. Secondly, it is in the *private sphere.* Kibbutz social structure has produced (unintentionally) a radical split between the public or collective sphere of life (almost everything in the Kibbutznik's experience) and the private sphere, which is limited to those very few relationships: child to parents, and later, husband to wife. The latter sphere, according to the general ideological push (a determined one) of the Kibbutz, is kept as limited as possible. In a sense it is only tolerated as a kind of concession to some persistent quirks in human nature which the collectivist revolution has been unable to abolish. Therefore in this second respect also, the early relationship to the parents goes against the rest of the child's socialization. By middle childhood, school learning is full of ideological messages supporting the collectivist ideals (injected, in fact, into every conceivable extraneous subject matter). The peer group, with its fiercely communal or collective values, is a constant force against private attachments and interests and provides its own strong gratifications that are not merely compensations for having so little (relatively) of the joys of parental indulgence. And there are absolutely no other ties to the parents as specific individual persons to support and sustain those joys. The pressure and desire to grow up—presumably universal in children—work against sustaining the relationship to the parents, with its infantilism and privacy, at the

[51] The quotation marks are to indicate that in terms of culture and social structure, these patterns of behavior and feeling are not the *same* as what are called "avoidance relationships" and "incest taboo" in other societies, because there is no socially sanctioned norm that says this is the way these youngsters are supposed to behave, according to community values.

earlier childhood level. What seems to be functioning here is the particular Kibbutz version of the *latency phase*, different in the details of its dynamics from that found in nuclear-family societies such as our own. What needs to be repressed in the Kibbutz is not so much the dependency (which was never exclusively or even primarily on the parents in the first place), but the infantilism and privacy of the parent-child erotic attachments. This repression is aided by all the institutions of Kibbutz life. The most important mechanism by which this is accomplished is the generalization of identifications to the whole adult community and to the total peer group (as opposed to its individualization). The Kibbutz child during this phase seems to develop a hard protective armor against any single relationship becoming overwhelmingly important to him. The collective way of life provides him with social and cultural support for such armor. Hence, there is a gradual diminution of the value to him of the parental visits. He does not yet become quite "strange" to his parents, however, since some infantile needs persist, or are strong at certain times, and their indulgence produces no special conflict when satisfied in that segregated context and relationship, and because sexuality is not of central importance during this phase.[52]

In adolescence, however, the picture changes. With the onset of puberty, infantile sexuality is revived, and now the infantile element of parental indulgence becomes a major threat. Therefore, the estrangement from the parents at this stage constitutes a genuine reaction formation. If it is reaction formation, then, why does it not go all the way, to felt *hatred* toward the parents and *rebellion* against them—the way in which these parents reacted to their parents at that age? The answer is simple: hatred and rebellion are reactions against the complex of love with *domination-dependency* and the identifications based on this syndrome. But domination has no part in the parents' relationships to Kibbutz children. Nor does any intense identification. Hatred-rebellion can also be crystallized by adopting a system of values opposed to those of the parents, especially if these values expose those of the parents as hollow, hypocritical, or unjust. (Again that was the model of the Kibbutz founders' rebellion against their parents.) The opposed values would have to

---

[52] I postulate that di-phasic onset of sexuality is universal in human beings (see Chapter One) and hence true of Kibbutz-reared children too. The whole evidence of contrasts between middle childhood and adolescent relations with the parents is consistent with this postulate.

come from some alternative facets of socialization available to the adolescent, as was true of Zionist Socialism in the urban centers of Europe. But the Kibbutz child has no conflict of values with his parents; everything he has learned to cherish, they cherish, and they are part of the adult world to which he (almost willy-nilly) aspires. Thus there is neither social nor psychodynamic basis for *rebellion*. But there is both for *estrangement*, in the sense of withdrawal of intense, erotic, infantile, private attachments. Since the Kibbutz child was never bound to the parents by domination, there are no chains to break. But what does need to be transcended is the infantile sexuality implied in the hot lavishment of love of parents upon their young children, the privacy and intimacy of that relationship (therefore no more confiding one's private woes to the parents), and the particularization of feelings toward certain members of the older generation. The "estrangement" represents a self-imposed generation taboo: the bond between the generations (for the adolescent at least) must be the diffuse collective one generated by all the institutions of Kibbutz child training—loyalty to the Kibbutz ideals and the community, not to specific persons of the older generation. This feeling reverberates in the constant reference to the children being the children of all the adults in the Kibbutz, and the adults being parents to all of the children.[53]

"Estrangement," of course, has also to do with adolescent quest for identity. That quest inevitably takes different forms in the Kibbutz from those of nuclear-family societies. Bettelheim remarks of the middle-class American adolescent, that he "feels the need to fight free of dependence on his parents by developing a unique personality that is different from theirs. . . ."[54] Bettelheim then argues, "Kibbutz-educated children feel no such defensive need to develop a unique personality."[55] It is probably true that the Kibbutz child does not have this particular defensive need, but he does have a need to establish his own identity, which is not the same as "unique personality." It is not enough that he is, as Bettelheim says, "safe from

[53] One of the authors consulted even reported an incident where a couple who had recently had a child (of course cared for in the communal nursery) decided to leave the Kibbutz. The assembly devoted a long discussion to the question of whether the couple were entitled to take their baby with them—inasmuch as the baby is a "child of the Kibbutz." "Bourgeois sentiment" prevailed, and the couple did take the baby, but not without ideological grumblings among the collectivist purists.

[54] Bettelheim, *op. cit.*, p. 123.

[55] *Ibid.*

anonymity because he is well known to all who count in his human surroundings," [56] for this is a rather negative concept of identity: he can be "known" to everyone in the community, and yet hardly at all *know himself*. There is evidence however that this *is* a problem with Kibbutz adolescents, and not merely a pathological peculiarity of the anonymous Western urban world. Yonina Talmon, in a brilliant paper on mate selection among Kibbutz *Sabras*, indicates that many of them seek lovers, and eventually mates, from *outside* the Kibbutz, as a process of *self-discovery*:

> "*We are all cut from the same mold. We take each other and ourselves for granted. Reaching-out to an outsider has made me conscious of myself. I know now more clearly what I am and what I stand for.*" The search for self-awareness and genuine intimacy as distinct from mere familiarity is an insistent and recurrent theme in many interviews.[57]

The quote is from a young *Sabra* a few years beyond the period of adolescent "estrangement" from the parents. It shows that the identity quest is not satisfied by having one's assured and known place in a particular *kevutza* and hence being known ("identified") by all other persons in the Kibbutz. That is a *status* and not an identity. True, the Kibbutz adolescent does not have to fight his way out of a conflict-ridden dependency on the *parents* to become his adult self. But evidently he must find a new diadic relationship of intense intimacy that has some similarities to his early-childhood relationship to his parents, but transcends the infantilism of that relationship, and to find it he has to go some place that is structurally outside the collective sphere which has been and is the dominant area of his life, that is, the whole Kibbutz, its schools, work groups, etc. In order to transcend the infantilism of the child-parent relationship, he must first give up these objects and find a new object at a psychosexually more mature level. And *that is precisely the problem of growing up in any society: the quest for new objects.* I would say that the adolescent estrangement from the parents constitutes the Kibbutznik's *puberty ceremony*: he goes away, then later returns in a new form (the later love affairs and marriage, which re-create the *private sphere* and channelize sexuality, at his own generation level, but are

[56] *Ibid.*
[57] Talmon, *op. cit.*, p. 504. The interviews referred to are with young *Sabras* who have formed liaisons or marriages with persons from outside their own Kibbutz.

outside the context of his childhood collective, the *kevutza,* or even his whole generation of *this* Kibbutz).[58]

PSYCHOSEXUAL DEVELOPMENT

From this discussion, we can now recapitulate the psychosexual development of Kibbutz-reared boys and girls as I reconstruct it from the various accounts of Kibbutz life and childhood.

Both boys and girls establish a strong erotic bond to the mother in the early-infancy breast-feeding experience. This mothering is intermittent, and segregated from the other mothering-care functions (which are carried out by a succession of nurses), but it is strong and unconditional and full of great erotic affect when it occurs. Further, the mother is a constant gratifying adult female, even though the infant's time with her is limited. From almost as early in infancy, the father appears, again similarly for children of both sexes, as another part of the combined indulgent nurturant parent figure. While the mother *may* sometimes be a source of frustration in feeding, the father never is. He is a totally positive erotic figure for the children of both sexes from early infancy on. He is not experienced as a frustrating or dominating or rule-imposing figure (with the exception that either parent may be felt as frustrating by their absence at any time and later by their attentions to a younger sibling). Erotic ties to nurses are there, but they are diffused by the periodic replacement of nurses and the necessity to share the nurse with all the other children of the *kevutza.* These ties are not individualized as are the ties toward the mother and the father.

All body disciplines are permissive in infancy, and children live in a bisexual world of polymorphous sexual play, with scarcely any differentiation between the sexes. Children of both sexes sleep in the same room, shower together, play and run around in the nude, and there is a great deal of wrestling, tickling, exploring, soothing, caressing, and other body contact among them. Sexual differentiation between fathers and mothers is similarly minimized by the social structural situation of their both playing almost identical roles for the child. Sexual feelings toward both parents develop, with encouragement by parental "seductive" behavior toward the children, somewhat more developed by each parent toward the child of the opposite sex. Sexual anatomy of peers is open knowledge from earliest infancy, and there is no strangeness or morbid curiosity in that area.

[58] See Talmon, *op. cit.,* for details of the actual marriage choices.

However, knowledge about adults is much more limited, and the residence arrangements preclude the child witnessing parental (or any other adult) intercourse.

We can surmise that preschool children have some sense that the parents possess each other sexually, and there *are* indications of desires by children to monopolize the erotic attentions of the parent of the opposite sex. (It seems that with the Kibbutz's extreme de-differentiation of the sexes in child rearing, especially in the preschool age, and the absence of differentiation of the parents in affective attention to the children, whatever *heterosexual* emphasis such monopoly desires on the part of children may have is largely a product of the heterosexual emphasis in the parent's seductiveness toward the child.) Preschool age children show abundance of identifications (as indicated in fantasy play) with the parents of both sexes, though girls identify more with the mother, and boys, interestingly, identify most either with the mother or with *animals* (presumptively male peer figures). Early school years show an abundance of both heterosexual and homosexual play. The former declines in later prepuberty childhood. The homosexual play of that stage is part of a general constellation of self-segregation of boys and girls (in spite of totally coeducational schoolrooms, dormitories, showers, etc.)[59] to the point where, as one nurse put it, "They absolutely hate each other at this stage." (Note this is almost a classic Western "latency" phenomenon.)

Oedipus complex. Do the Kibbutz children develop the Oedipus complex? Perhaps it would be better to put the question: *to what extent* do they do so, especially as compared to children in nuclear-family settings? The answer is not entirely clear. If the Oedipus complex is the result of the combination of intense sexual feelings and a situation of paternal domination, one would expect it either not to appear at all in the Kibbutz or to be greatly modified, since paternal domination simply does not exist. The evidence is

[59] This statement applies, at least, to the Kibbutz studied by Spiro, *op. cit.* Talmon, *op. cit.*, however, points out that Spiro's case is of a Kibbutz belonging to a federation that follows a more extreme policy of sexual desegregation than any of the others. At the opposite pole, the *religious* Kibbutzim have extensive sexual segregation. Talmon's study covers a wide range of types of Kibbutzim, and her statement about dormitories and bathing at this age is as follows: "Gradually, a sense of sexual shame emerges, and a growing distance between the sexes. Showers are taken separately. Sleeping arrangements are reshuffled; from the fourth grade on, room occupancy is unisexual. All group activities remain bisexual but friendship becomes unisexual." *Idem.*, p. 502.

rather fragmentary, and as interpreted in previous writings, not very satisfactory. Spiro (whose data are the most profuse of any study yet published) finds indications in *some* boys of the wish to get rid of the father and monopolize the mother, but for other children the data are sparse (not negative, however). Boys pointing out that a girl has no penis may possibly be taken as some kind of evidence of castration anxiety, as do some other play situations Spiro reports.[60] Rabin's study[61] does show that ten-year-old Kibbutz boys (compared with age-mates of non-Kibbutz agricultural settlements with traditional family structure) show *less* "Oedipal intensity," on one of four criteria. They were judged by responses to the Blacky Oedipal picture (Mama, Papa making love, Blacky standing on the side watching). More *non*-Kibbutz boys said it would be better if Blacky were with Mama, and Papa aside. (However, on the other three measures of Oedipal intensity—does Blacky express jealousy, does he anticipate rejection for looking from Papa or Mama, respectively— there are no differences at all between the Kibbutz and non-Kibbutz boys.) A related finding of Rabin's in this study was that to the question (about a different Blacky picture) "Which one would Blacky rather be like—Mama, Papa, or Tippy?" significantly more of the non-Kibbutz boys indicated Papa; while on the question "Whom is Blacky most likely to obey—Mama, Papa, or Tippy?" again more of the non-Kibbutz boys said Papa (21 to 6 as contrasted with 15 to 12 for the Kibbutz boys). The last question, of course, reflects the fact that neither parent is especially expected to be obeyed by the Kibbutz child. Therefore, the mother-father choices could be expected to be random; while for the non-Kibbutz boys, the results show clearly the norm of the father-dominated household. (Probably for the Kibbutz child this question is not a good indicator of positive identification with the parent of either sex.)

The upshot of these fragmentary pieces of evidence is that Kibbutz life, not having eliminated the role of the parents in socialization entirely, but having in fact accentuated certain erotic features of parent-child relationships, has not eliminated Oedipal problems entirely. However, it does seem to have greatly reduced great fear of the father as a threatening authority, as a major element in the psychosexual development.

Hetero- and homo-sexual relationships.   Spiro hypothesizes the

---

[60] Spiro, *op. cit.*, p. 235.
[61] Rabin, *op. cit.*

following path of psychosexual development. Both boys and girls develop a strong attachment to the totally nurturant father, and ambivalence toward the mother (on the basis partly of earliest infancy frustrations, and partly by generalization from the nurse element in the mother image). Hence for girls the path to adult heterosexuality is a continuous one from this early-childhood base. For boys, however, the problem is to switch the attachment from the male parent to the female, and therefore probably more boys than girls would remain fixated at a passive homosexual level of psychosexual development. Rabin's data on the Blacky responses would seem to offer some support for this hypothesis: seventeen of the twenty-seven Kibbutz boys say it would be better if Blacky were with Papa, and Mama apart; while for the non-Kibbutz boys the figures are reversed: seventeen prefer to be with Mama. Whether this really *does* indicate being "fixated at a passive-homosexual level" is a moot question, and one would wonder about the choice of *ten-year-olds* (classically, in the midst of the latency period) as an age at which to test such hypotheses. We may note, however, that homosexual play among peers is strong in the Kibbutz at this age (we have no way of knowing whether it is more prevalent than in nuclear families; but probably, from sheer opportunity, it is). But this may be no more than a reflection of the general permissiveness toward sexual play of any kind in the Kibbutz. In any case, there is no indication whatever that latency-phase passive homosexuality in boys carries over into overt homosexuality in adolescence or adulthood. In fact, from all reports there is *no* evidence of any overt homosexuality in either sex. Thus the relatively minimal affective differentiation of the sexes, and of erotic responses of adults toward children that prevails in the Kibbutz does not seem to interfere with the development of adult heterosexuality later on.

The child seems to move from a polymorphous infancy and early childhood where any peers of either sex and parent of either sex (and to a milder degree nurses) are all permissible objects for erotic gratification to a later childhood where opposite sex peers decline, then drop out as possible erotic objects, and parents also decline, producing an almost classic latency homosexual phase. Then at puberty, direct erotic gratification from another person's body seems to cease almost completely. Affectionate contact with parents declines, even disappears. Homosexual play ceases. And between the sexes, there is a great increase in sexual shame and development of great hostility. Girls take pains to hide their nudity. In classrooms boys and girls sit separately; so also at assemblies and parties. They say they detest each other. There are many petty quarrels. An important aspect is that within the same *kevutza*, where the co-members are necessarily the same age chronologically, the girls are usually more sexually mature than the boys. The girls then regard the age-mate boys as immature and uncouth and treat them with disdain.[62] Boys react by teasing and annoying the girls and poking fun at them. This hostility goes on until the ages of fourteen or fifteen, then recedes as the boys "catch up." From then on, concealment of nudity continues, but it is done in a more matter-of-fact way, less charged with the tension of the twelve-to-fourteen-year-olds. Peer group unity is restored, relations become easy, unconstrained, and friendly, but *totally nonerotic*: they treat each other as asexual peers rather than as potential sex objects.

Adolescence. Norms of this period are anti-sexual. Seductiveness, coquetry, flirtatiousness are entirely discouraged. Girls wear no make-up; nor do they dress in sexually stimulating ways. All social activity is in groups rather than in couples. Dating is totally out, by Kibbutz ideology. A boy and a girl who are age-mates, especially if in the same *kevutza*, would consider it unthinkable to be sexually interested in each other, let alone have intercourse. And in instances of sexual interest between a younger girl and an older boy (say fifteen and eighteen) if they are both in the high school, teachers and other students alike strongly disapprove of their seeing much of each other privately, even more of their becoming sexually involved. Sex relations between high school students are considered as "undesirable" (not the same as the general Western puritanical taboos) because they distract the students from their serious business of study, work, and *group activities and loyalties.*[63]

The adolescent disinterest in sex, and general paucity of preoccupation with sexual themes, is well documented in Rabin's interesting comparative researches, where Kibbutz youngsters of various ages are compared with a "control" group of children from non-collectiv-

---

[62] Phenomena to be found also in family-organized societies such as our own, especially around the age of thirteen. Teachers of junior high schools in our society report this to be a characteristic problem that affects discipline in the classroom.

[63] A clear case of what Slater calls opposition to "diadic withdrawal." See Philip Slater, "On Social Regression," *American Sociological Review*, Vol. 28, No. 3, 1963, pp. 339-64.

ist agricultural villages in Israel. In one paper Rabin specifically compares adolescents who are seventeen years of age,[64] drawing upon the results of three projective techniques, the Rorschach, the TAT, and the Sentence Completion Test. In completing a sentence with the stub: "If I had sexual relations . . ." the vast majority of the Kibbutz youngsters rejected the notion categorically, for example, "I would discontinue," or "not at my age," whereas only about a third of the non-Kibbutz agricultural adolescents gave such responses. Then at a deeper level: To a TAT picture (card 4) that typically elicits stories involving some kind of sexual relationship between the man and the woman in the foreground, or other sexual themes, far fewer of the Kibbutz than of the non-Kibbutz adolescents saw the man and woman as husband and wife or as lovers (70 percent as compared to 95 percent), nearly a third defining them simply as "a fellow and a girl." Thematically, infidelity (involving the "other woman" in the background of the picture) appears in over half of the non-Kibbutz stories, but in only 10 percent of the Kibbutz, but "rejection of love" themes appear in 30 percent of the Kibbutz stories while only in 5 percent of the others. Then very significantly, some kind of *aggression* appears in 50 percent of the Kibbutz stories, but in only 11 percent of the non-Kibbutz. Similarly, in the action elements, prevention of separation predominates in the non-Kibbutz stories, while prevention of aggression appears more frequently in the Kibbutz stories. The TAT fantasies of the Kibbutz youth show much less sexual curiosity than those of the non-Kibbutz. Sex has less potency for them as a theme; hence they use more aggression themes, with the woman as peacemaker. A Rorschach finding is also significant: in the types of content of human movement responses, Kibbutz youngsters use significantly more *play* themes than the other youth (69 percent vs. 32 percent), and somewhat more themes of *orality* (18 percent vs. 5 percent) and *less* aggression (15 percent vs. 32 percent). (Sexuality was not one of the categories.)

Let us go beyond Rabin's interpretations. Together these different findings seem to indicate a definite constellation: where eroticism in the forms of play or orality are strong, aggression is relatively weak; where sexual stimuli (adult heterosexual) must be strongly rejected, aggression is strong. Though Rabin's paper does not indicate the types of play involved in these responses, one would expect, from

[64] A. I. Rabin, "Kibbutz Adolescents," *American Journal of Orthopsychiatry,* Vol. 31, 1961, pp. 493-501.

knowledge of Kibbutz conditions, that this is strongly group-oriented. The element of *orality* is interesting, also, as it suggests persistence or return to erotic gratification forms from earliest infancy. The total picture shows a massive denial of contemporary sexual need, producing an undercurrent of aggression and alternative release through pregenital modes, some of these sublimated as in group play. (Note, however, that all of this is in a context where the Kibbutz adolescents reveal themselves, in these tests, as more *spontaneous and productive* than their contemporaries from conventional families, as more sophisticated in intellectual attainment, and as at least as "well-adjusted"—in terms of typical psychologist's measurements—as their non-Kibbutz peers.) The combination of greater play and orality themes, and the generally greater spontaneity, productivity, and lesser anxiety, of the Kibbutzniks is impressive indication that whatever else the postponement of adult sexuality means for these youngsters, it does not produce a generalized constriction of the personality.

Thus, we have an apparently paradoxical situation: an otherwise sexually permissive society fosters an almost total suppression (or repression) of sexual expression just at the time when (in glandular terms at least) sexual impulses could be expected to be strongest. And the adolescents, far from rebelling against this, support these norms and seem generally satisfied to devote their great energies to non-sexual pursuits at this time.

They themselves say that the bodies of both sexes are so entirely familiar to them from earliest childhood experiences on through the present, that sex has no mystery to them. (To which the skeptic may answer that seeing is not copulating!) We may note also that the Kibbutz environment is also totally lacking in the vast paraphernalia stimulating sexual feelings and interests that are so ubiquitous in our society: the constant use of sexual stimuli in advertisements, popular music, modes of attire, etc., and the complete absence of dating or *any* kind of social gathering where boy-girl couples are the unit: in the Kibbutz all activities are *group* activities.[65] Note also that the disapproval of sexual intercourse during the high school years does not apply to single adults beyond the high school years, where there is complete freedom to form sexual liaisons, the major norm being,

[65] A by-product is that no adolescent boy or girl need ever agonize over not having a partner to go to a party or dance with, "popularity" in such terms is unheard of and no one is ever excluded from group activities.

however, that liaisons be serious love relationships and not frivolous promiscuity.

The fact is that the very permissiveness about body exposure and the code of total sharing and non-segregation of the sexes throughout the formative years, including the bisexual dormitories of the high school, seem to conduce to the special kind of "adolescent puritanism" we find here. The lifelong bisexual group solidarity of the *kevutza* is precisely what makes sexual intercourse between two of its members impossible. Structurally, this can be described as the opposition of the group to diadic withdrawal. Dynamically, it is analogous to the psychics of the incest taboo, that is, those with whom you have shared intense protracted socialization experiences cannot be the objects for intense diadic erotic relations (the earlier sex play tends to be indiscriminate rather than diadic). The youngsters say it their way: "We know each other inside out," or "How can you fall in love with a girl you sat on the potty with?" In effect, the youth have instituted their own incest taboo. But this taboo gets generalized beyond one's own *kevutza* to include the whole high school, in effect. Here, from the community's point of view, it is not exactly a taboo, since the community does not consider it categorically wrong for a high school boy and girl to have sexual intercourse—only if it interferes with their studies and group participation. Here however the youngsters' own motivations are even stronger than community opinion, and for many Kibbutzim it is reported that the observer knows of *no* instance of intercourse between two students both in the high school at the time.

What seems to have happened is that collective education has really "paid off." It has produced a group solidarity so strong that it is a major instrument of sublimation during a potentially turbulent period. Here, perhaps, is another clue to the "estrangement" of adolescent children to their parents during this phase: perhaps they are saying, in effect: "Don't rock the boat." That is, do not introduce personalized eroticism again into my life, at a time when I am struggling to keep erotic impulses under control and the school and the *kevutza* are helping me do so.

The group solidarity of this age also extends to aggressiveness toward teachers—not limited to the high school years, but probably more developed and more skillfully used at this age. Teachers—especially those from outside the Kibbutz—complain of the "fresh" attitude of the students, their *chutzpah* (insolence). Some outside teachers cannot take it and resign. (Respect for authority has no place in Kibbutz values, so it is not surprising students feel no compunctions about these matters. What is of interest here is the *group* function of such behavior.) The aggressions are probably more intense at this age because they represent outlets for unacknowledged sexual frustration.[66] Their form accentuates the solidarity of the peer group against the teacher (not as a threatening authority, of course, but simply as a member of an outgroup, by virtue of being of a different generation and often, as well, coming from outside the Kibbutz).[67] Parents, in effect, fall into that category also.

Thus the high-school period is marked by a massive sublimation maintained by the extraordinary strength of the comrade bonds that have been created by the communal child rearing. It is only after high school graduation—when the group structures are broken up by the assignment of the graduates to various city jobs or their being called up into army service—that the burgeoning sexuality can be freely recognized and felt and expressed. Then the object choice is almost invariably someone from *outside* the Kibbutz, or at least someone not of one's own generation within the Kibbutz (that is, they could be near in age, but they have not *grown up* together in the Kibbutz; they have only recently arrived as young adults) and absolutely not someone of the same *kevutza*.

The high school years might, therefore, be considered a kind of psycho*sexual* moratorium. By this I mean that during this period the youngster is provided with a highly structured *delay* in dealing with the sexual impulses. The moratorium is part of a general puberty ceremony process[68] constituting the *departure* phase, as suggested above in relation to parent-child eroticism. This delay, lasting two to five years depending on the sexual maturity of the child, makes possible the withdrawal of Eros from the parents, consolidates its withdrawal from the sociological siblings (co-members of the *kevutza*) and facilitates the sublimating development of consolidation of the collective ethos as a way of life and group solidarity as the social-

[66] See Rabin, "Kibbutz Adolescents," *op. cit.*

[67] Other outgroup antagonisms are abundant also: against Jews (that is, as distinct from Israelis); against the Oriental Jews; against people from the cities; against ideologically different other federations, etc. See Spiro, pp. 319-20; 386-87, 418.

[68] Compare Chapter Four in this book. See also Erik Erikson on the psychosocial moratorium in "The Problem of Ego Identity," *Identity and the Life Cycle, Psychological Issues,* Vol. 1, 1959, pp. 110-12.

psychological structure for carrying it out. There is very little conflict about choice of a way of life; most want to stay on the Kibbutz—or *a* Kibbutz, since there are pioneering opportunities in developing new Kibbutzim. No conflicts occur between their values and those of the older generation; there is no domination of the elders to be overthrown. A year or two after graduation from high school each *Sabra* can expect to be admitted to full adult membership in the Kibbutz, giving him or her a place of equality in the communal assembly with any of the other adult members and a role in sharing the Kibbutz work, the models (and most of the concrete details) of which he has already well learned through eighteen years of communal education. The Kibbutznik adolescent has no specific dependency on, or indebtedness to, or conflicted guilt feeling toward any particular adults of the community. There is only a feeling of generalized solidarity and a sense of responsibility to the whole community, whose child he is. Hence, a whole host of problems that beset, for example, an American middle-class adolescent are totally absent for the Kibbutz high school student. He does not so desperately need to "try his wings" sexually to prove his manhood or adulthood. He has a firm status and role which lead by certain steps into a secure adulthood. Nobody and no social practice have kept him childlike (the only ones who could—his parents—are overwhelmingly counteracted, and they have no weapons to use) so that he has no need stridently to assert a level of adulthood beyond what he "naturally" has. In this complex of circumstances, then, perhaps sublimation is not at all a difficult task.

The one area where the young Kibbutznik may feel some tension or disagreement with the older generation may be in subtleties of perspective on the collective values. If the older generation are not *Sabras*, but founders or people who joined the Kibbutz in their adulthood, their sense of fulfillment of the Kibbutz will necessarily be quite different from the adolescent's: it is viewed by them in the light of their own rebellious youthful aspirations of yesteryear, and the whole complex relationship of that rebellion to the conditions of Jewish life in Diaspora Europe or America. In short, they are complicated, and emotionally involved in this great revolutionary experiment, and experience in a thousand ways its wrench from the past. For the *Sabra*, no such complexities exist. This is the good life he has known all through his life; it has given him great satisfactions, security, freedom from anxiety all through his childhood, and (though he knows intellectually of alternatives) it is the only way of life. It holds no problems or ambiguities for him. He has also learned, by the very education his elders have devised for him, to have contempt for "the Jew" and things "Jewish," for the superstitions called "religion" that include the (to him) fantastic and irrational ritualism of Judaism, and particularly, for the wallowing in suffering that the two-thousand years of the Jewish Diaspora represent.[69]

Hence the adolescent is relatively simple-minded, uncomplex about the Kibbutz and its way of life. His view of the older generation may verge on barely amused tolerance, for the latter are "the generation of the desert" and cannot know the securities of the Kibbutz in their very blood and bones, as he does. He is also basically unemotional about the whole thing, very much in contrast to the older generation.

To the adults then, the *Sabra*, who is the fulfillment of what they sought to build in their hard-won utopia, is an object of conflicted feelings of admiration and disappointment. He is so simple, direct, sunny, and free; he has no emotional problems; and he is bland, without depth, flat, unconvoluted—in short, he is not a tortured Jewish intellectual. And he is just what they set out to create in a new conflict-free generation. Among themselves many of the parents refer to the *Sabras* as "the Goyim." This is a term suffused with tragic irony: it is a term meaning to the Zionist-Socialist rebel a "normal," "adjusted," "emotionally healthy" man, a man of the soil, a realist, a tough-minded anti-sentimentalist—and also *a man without a soul*. (Weber's word: "unmusical" comes to mind.) The parental generation set out to de-mystify, to de-mythologize the world for the next generation. Having largely succeeded in doing so, they now look at the product—and feel a mixture of pride, horror, and awe.

[69] See Spiro, *op. cit.*, Chapter 14 for elaboration. See also Spiro's paper, "The Sabras and Zionism: A Study in Personality and Ideology," *Social Problems*, Vol. 5, Fall 1957, pp. 100-09. Note that the high school students consider all Jewish history between the Old Testament period and the founding of modern Israel "boring." Old Testament stories are interesting, for they are full of heroic fighting back against terrible odds, by contrast the whole two millennia of the Diaspora represent contemptible suffering of persecution without resistance, and by strict Marxian-Zionist chant, the "abnormalization" of the Jew by removal from the land and productive labor. The term "boring" quite evidently covers an intense ambivalence, for their own parental generation, founders of the Kibbutz, came out of that world these students scorn. So we have a phenomenon not dissimilar to that of low-status immigrants to America from Southern or Eastern Europe, as opposed to their second-generation American-born children.

Of course, the *Sabras*, for all their doctrinaire atheism, are not without religion. For they are an almost literal embodiment of the sociologist Émile Durkheim's conclusion about the ultimate meaning of religious practice and belief: God is—*society itself*. The ultimate value for the *Sabras* is their own form of society—the group, the collective, the community. *This* replaces all the "superstitious nonsense" or belief in deities and saints and miracles and such.

YOUNG ADULTHOOD

Graduation from high school concludes the *Sabra's* formal communal education. To the Kibbutz, the *Sabra* is almost ready to embark on adulthood. At this point the movement deliberately imposes a formal transition process, involving departure and later return, which also provides a new and different kind of moratorium. According to Kibbutz ideology, the youngster's decision to remain in the Kibbutz and devote his adult life to it should be based upon some opportunity to consider alternative possibilities. The young graduate is, therefore, required to spend a year (or more) away from the Kibbutz in a different kind of social environment, such as working in the city. (Now, army service usually takes this function.) This is not only an "educational" experience for the *Sabra*, but also a kind of test of the communal educational system: if it was effective, the *Sabras* should want to come back to the Kibbutz. And most of them do, or they join in the establishment of some new Kibbutz. Either way, it is a decision to perpetuate the Kibbutz way of life into another generation.

At this point sexuality is no longer taboo, and *Sabras* are free to establish love affairs including full sexual relations with no opposition from the Kibbutz. How they proceed to do so is tremendously significant. We now have one careful report on this[70] which, though concentrating on marriage choices also provides illuminating information about premarital affairs. The only community norm about sex in such affairs is that sex belongs in a *serious* relationship, of intense interpersonal intimacy, and should not be carried on for simply frivolous pleasure-seeking.[71]

[70] Talmon, *op. cit.*

[71] Thus even in permissiveness, the Kibbutz is basically *ascetic* in perspective. Sex should be only one part—in effect an instrument—of something more important: the deep meaningfulness of two persons to each other. It should not be of value in itself or sheer *play*. No one should imagine that this "utopia" is in any sense a fulfillment of a notion of a non-repressive society, open to polymorphous eroticism, such as envisioned by Norman Brown or Herbert Marcuse.

Where and how do the *Sabras* find their love partners? First, be it noted that the older generation does not by any means taboo the choice of other members of one's own generation within the same *Kibbutz*—in fact, there is some preference on their part that their respective children should choose each other. But typically they *do not*. The vast majority of marriages, and evidently also of love affairs, involve a *Sabra* who has grown up in "this" Kibbutz and an outsider: someone from another Kibbutz, or a new member of this Kibbutz who was socialized outside the Kibbutz movement, or a city person now working (for example, as a teacher or nurse) in this Kibbutz, and in some cases, though not many, someone totally outside the Kibbutz movement (for example, someone met while the *Sabra* is in army service). Basically, where the relationship involves marriage, Talmon refers to this as "exogamy"—that is, marriage outside the group. (The quotation marks indicate that it is by personal predispositions rather than by a community rule—that these are the marriage choices made.)

The choice of a lover who is in some degree an outsider is highly significant. A love affair (for many *Sabras* the first one is also their very first experience of intercourse) involves an intense personal intimacy, something totally *private* to the persons involved. Contrary to Bettelheim's extrapolations from a reading of some of the literature,[72] these youngsters *are* concerned with privacy—and very intensely so. Many of them say about such affairs: "Everything else I've had in life, I've had to share with the group; but this is *mine*— not *ours*—something very personally and intimately for *myself*." If such an affair should start while the girl is still in high school, there will be extraordinary precautions to maintain its secrecy, to keep it safe from ubiquitous (and in this instance destructive) group sharing of the peers. Even if it is a post-high school affair on both sides, some of this concern for secrecy persists. There are no structured situations for such a pair to co-participate casually, since dating is non-existent, in fact taboo, and all social activities are by groups, not lover-couples. Thus the radical social structural separation of the collective from the private spheres of life conduces to pushing the love affair entirely into the private, even secret, sphere. Because of that, it conduces to the choice of a partner who is outside the focus of solidarity of the collective sphere, that is, one's peers. Co-members of the same *kevutza* who have grown up together are sociological siblings—even more than siblings of a nuclear family—and thus spon-

[72] See Bettelheim, *op. cit.*

taneously taboo to each other. This "taboo" generalizes to one's whole generation who have co-experienced the communal education.

There is yet another meaning to "exogamy." Since the *Sabra's* early experiences have been very different from his parents', the parents are in many ways strangers and outsiders to him. (There is abundant evidence of conflicting or divergent views between the first, or founding, generation, and the second.) Yet, *these* strangers were earlier of great erotic significance for the child. Are not, then, the outsiders who are chosen as lovers, then as mates, re-creations of the parents, in this way?

Talmon repeatedly uses such terms as the "same generation" or "different generation." They are not used in a chronological sense. For Talmon the "same generation" means those brought up together in a particular *Kibbutz*. New joiners of this Kibbutz, even though chronologically contemporary with these *Sabras*, are *not* referred to by Talmon as of the "same generation." Talmon has unwittingly, by this terminology, hit upon an essential similarity between an age-mate outsider and the chronologically different generation of the parents, who are outsiders in a different sense, to the child. Talmon's findings that most mating choices are of outsiders who still are not too far outside (they are rarely from outside the movement entirely) fits this analogy. They are like the parents, who are outsiders not of the same generation, and not raised in the Kibbutz but also *not* outsiders (they are after all the makers of the Kibbutz and part of that general adult community who gave the young their values). The choice of *such* strangers for lovers or mates thus resolves the "strangeness" adolescents feel toward their parents, and allows a symbolic *inter*generational incest, while forcefully upholding the *intra*generational incest taboo. The combination of strangeness and intimacy has a quality of the uncanny, and this, in turn, derives from return of unconscious memories, the object of which are the parents—or more technically, the parental *imagos* (which include unconscious distillations of experiences with the *nurse* as well). Thus the contemporary stranger condenses features of the (sexually taboo) peers—age—and features of the (differently tabooed) parents. Hence the stranger presents to the Kibbutznik possibilities of sharing feelings at deep unconscious levels that are different from the collective experiences with one's own solidarity group.

Another important feature is the quest for *identity*. Generally the Kibbutz culture and social structure tends to delay this quest until after high school. Sexual encounter then plays an important part in this process of self-exploration, and this can be most effective if the partner is *different*. Note that this is the first serious chance the Kibbutznik has had in his life to differentiate himself and discover his own unique self. Diamond argues that his Rorschach findings indicate that Kibbutz youngsters display something very close to a genuine "modal personality," that is, they all are, at deep levels, very much more like each other than any comparable group of modern urbanite contemporaries, and that this is one of the (perhaps even intended?) consequences of communal education and the radical sharing of experiences it involves. Without the supporting data, it is difficult to evaluate this conclusion. However, the other reports do not seem to agree with this. Spiro's *Children of the Kibbutz* is replete with indications of individual personality differences among the children, and Talmon's report on mate selection suggests that at this stage, at least, strong individuation among the *Sabras* is evident. It is precisely the discovery and fostering of such individuality that activates the quest for outsider love objects.[73]

The great preoccupation with developing the private sphere not only results in "exogamous" love affairs and marriages, it also shows the *Sabras* in an important reaction formation against the extreme collectivism of their childhood. They do not typically rebel to the point of rejecting the Kibbutz way of life (most of them do return); rather they take the communal values for granted and are casual and non-militant about these values—in contrast to their parents at that age, where militancy was a highly determined part of their rebellion and functioned also to still doubts about the validity of the collectivist ideals. In effect, the second generation does not have to *prove* collective life can work: they know it in all their experience. But they *do* need to assert *other* psychosocial needs that collectivism subordinates or suppresses, precisely those of the private sphere. We now find the young married *Sabras*, or those engrossed in love affairs, spending a lot more time to themselves in their leisure hours and a lot less time in communal activities, such as the assembly and

---

[73] It is also difficult to reconcile Diamond's assertion with the high degree of spontaneity and productivity of the Kibbutzniks on Rabin's Rorschach tests—see above, p. 167. Would not such extreme sameness militate against such access to inner resources?

various committees, as the ideology expects. Some of them even say bluntly, "We've had enough of collective activity all through our childhood; now we want some privacy and the chance to be ourselves, and to be alone." The other side of what concerns Bettelheim —the problem of anonymity in mass society—and the fact that it simply does not exist in the Kibbutz, is this: The avoidance of anonymity by all the members of a small communal society acting together, known to each other, in communal activities, also has its *price*, and that is the suppression of those personal qualities and idiosyncrasies that cannot be organized toward group goals. The Kibbutz-reared child does not suffer from loneliness, true. But he may suffer from a monopolization of his life by the collective sphere. It is this, or the possibility of it, that young *Sabras* are seeking to transcend in the formation of intense private ties with *partial outsiders*—a compromise formation, as Talmon shows, that reconciles the conflicting needs of continuity with a fresh start and the conflicting drives of preserving the securities of communalism that are the heritage of the childhood experiences and of striking out toward new experience. Thus the private sphere of love affairs and later marriage are a bulwark against the sea of collectivism. This fact makes it less likely than ever that marriage and the family will be eliminated from Kibbutz institutions: the balancing need for them is all the stronger where communal education has become consolidated, entrenched, and basically successful in its goals. What the Kibbutz has done, in effect, is to radically segregate the two spheres, the collective and the private, and to allow marriage and the family their area of expression, carefully circumscribed, as a counterbalance to the strong collectivist forces. The Kibbutz leadership (correctly) perceives expansions of the scope of private life (for example, by more privately owned consumer goods such as radios, tea kettles, etc.) as a threat to the collective ideals of the society.

THE PERSONALITY PRODUCT OF THE KIBBUTZ

To summarize a description of the personalities who are the products of this unique communal educational system, we can first point out what they are *not*. Essentially absent from the picture of the young *Sabras* are most of the pathologies, symptomatologies, and sufferings prevalent among youth in most parts of modern urbanized industrialized societies—that is, juvenile delinquency and crime, homosexuality, promiscuity, narcotization by spectator entertainment, guilt-ridden lascivious preoccupations with sexuality, destructively driving personal ambitions, a relentless and never-fulfilled craving for consumer possessions, conflicts about aggressivity, dominance, and submission, the cult of popularity, frenetic quests for never-satisfying Dionysian experiences, guilt-ridden flights from parental domination, narcotics addiction, and the great variety of neurotic and character disorders that fill the offices of our psychotherapists with ever-renewed cases. What *Sabras* display instead is a particular kind of maturity, a direct and naturalistic openness toward the world, a conviction in a clear-cut and (to them) unambiguous system of values, a dedication to their community ideals, a solidarity with their comrades so ingrained that it need scarcely be mentioned, and an impatience with complexity and ambiguity. Emotionally they are comparatively well-integrated, their channelizations of sex and aggression narrow but firm and basically unconflicted, their spontaneity and productivity strong but not defensively harnessed to any individualistic need to escape authoritarian domination. Emotionally they are relatively uncomplicated. They do not show the kind of personality convolution and ambiguity displayed or valued by their own progenitors or by *their* counterparts among agonized or tortured intellectuals, artists, and doubters in the wider turbulent modern world. Because of this, to many they present an appearance of flatness and limited sensitivity. These are not agonizing doubters, or psychically driven rebels, but people with a strong dedication to preserve and extend the particular good kind of world that has given them security, warmth, protection, comradeship, basic equalitarian dignity, work, love, and a full sense of meaningfulness in life.

SELECTED BIBLIOGRAPHY: THE ISRAELI KIBBUTZ

Bar-Yoseph, Rivka. "Patterns of Early Socialization in Collective Settlements of Israel," *Human Relations.* Vol. 12, 1959, pp. 345-60.

Bettelheim, Bruno. "Does Communal Education Work?" *Commentary.* Vol. 33, 1962, pp. 117-26.

Diamond, Stanley. "Kibbutz and Shtetl," *Social Problems.* Vol. 5, Fall 1957, pp. 71-99.

Golan, Shmuel. "Collective Education in the Kibbutz," *Psychiatry.* Vol. 22, 1959, pp. 167-77.

Irvine, Elizabeth. "Observations on the Aims and Methods of Child Rearing in Communal Settlements in Israel," *Human Relations.* Vol. 5, 1952, pp. 247-75.

Luft, Gerda. "The Kibbutz in Crisis," *Commentary.* Vol. 32, 1961, pp. 334-40.

Rabin, A. I. "Attitudes of Kibbutz Children Toward Family and Parents," *American Journal of Orthopsychiatry.* Vol. 29, 1959, pp. 172-79.

————. "Infants and Children Under Conditions of Intermittent Mothering in the Kibbutz," *American Journal of Orthopsychiatry.* Vol. 28, 1958, pp. 577-86.

————. "Kibbutz Adolescents," *American Journal of Orthopsychiatry.* Vol. 31, 1961, pp. 493-504.

————. "Personality Maturity of Kibbutz and Non-Kibbutz Israeli Boys," *Journal of Projective Techniques.* Vol. 21, 1957, pp. 148-53.

————. "Some Psychosexual Differences Between Kibbutz and Non-Kibbutz Israeli Boys," *Journal of Projective Techniques.* Vol. 22, 1958, pp. 328-32.

Rapaport, David. "Behavior Research in Collective Settlements in Israel," *American Journal of Orthopsychiatry.* Vol. 28, 1958, pp. 587-97.

Rosenfeld, Eva. "Institutional Change in the Kibbutz," *Social Problems.* Vol. 5, Fall 1957, 110-36.

————. "Social Stratification in a 'Classless' Society," *American Sociological Review.* Vol. 16, 1952, pp. 766-74.

Schwartz, Richard. "Democracy and Collectivism in the Kibbutz," *Social Problems.* Vol. 5, Fall 1957, pp. 137-46.

Spiro, Melford. *Children of the Kibbutz.* Cambridge: Harvard University Press, 1958. Paperback edition, New York: Schocken Books, 1965.

————. "Education in a Communal Village in Israel," *American Journal of Orthopsychiatry.* Vol. 25, 1955, pp. 283-93.

————. "Is the Family Universal?" *American Anthropologist.* Vol. 56, 1954, pp. 839-46 and Addendum, 1958, in Norman W. Bell and Ezra F. Vogel (eds.), *A Modern Introduction to the Family.* New York: Free Press of Glencoe, 1960.

————. *Kibbutz: Venture in Utopia.* Cambridge: Harvard University Press, 1956. Paperback edition, New York: Schocken Books, 1963.

————. "The Sabras and Zionism: A Study in Personality and Ideology," *Social Problems.* Vol. 5, Fall 1957, pp. 100-09.

Talmon, Yonina. "Mate Selection in Collective Settlements," *American Sociological Review.* Vol. 29, 1964, pp. 491-508.

————. "Social Differentiation in Cooperative Communities," *British Journal of Sociology.* Vol. 3, 1952, pp. 339-57.

5. CONCLUSION

In this chapter we have begun the exploration of socialization and personality development in the context of comparative analyses of social and cultural arrangements of different communities. We have tried to sketch the main tasks of socialization, seeing it as a process responsive to the "requirements" of social structure and culture, on the one hand, and the "demands" of the human animal, on the other. We then presented Barrington Moore's discussion questioning the essentiality of the family as we know it for the socialization of the child in modern technologized society. From there we moved to intensive case studies of the whole patterning and context of socialization of four quite different contemporary communities—three revealingly different though similar subcultures in Puerto Rico and the significant social experiment of the Israeli Kibbutz. In these case studies part of the focus is on variations from and alternatives to the nuclear family as the primary context for the early socialization of the child. But in each we are also concerned with how the familial and auxiliary or alternative agencies of socialization are imbedded in the connected social structures of the community. In each we tried to trace the connections among ecological and economic bases, cultural traditions, marriage and family patterns, other social structures, and socialization and personality development. Confronting us were the variability of socialization *agents* possible in different versions of a modern society, differences in socialization *procedures* and *conditions*, and presumably connected differences in *personality results*.

Without implying any subscription to an equilibrium theory of societal functioning, we find that each community or subculture has its own unique combination of strengths and weaknesses in different aspects of the socialization tasks, its own blend of "costs" and what might be called "pay-offs" in personality results, its own kind of balance between private and public or collective spheres and their respective impacts on personality, its own kind of interplay between social constraints and liberation of personality potentials. Where the Manicaboans are repressed and narrow in perspective but strong on mastery and sexual identity and capacity for useful, productive and non-compulsive work, the working people of Poyal are diffuse and rather shallow in emotional attachments, free in sexuality, and enjoy a strong group identity in cooperative mutual aid at the expense of individualized ambition. The more highly individualized middle class of San José, in turn, shows both costs and benefits of its ambiguous participation in North American modernity, in dilemmas over work and sexual identity, in multiple contradictory socialization exposures, and in the psychic effects of the undermining of formally persistent familial roles. The *Sabras* of the Israeli Kibbutz, by further contrast, reveal some of the paradoxical personality results of a deliberately revolutionary socialization which destroys old nuclear-family structures while retaining in a transformed and partly intensified version, the critical nuclear-family emotional attachments; show new variations on Oedipal involvements, the incest taboo, and the vicissitudes of sexual development; and an ironic blend of excessive fulfillment of their parents' intentions and disappointment of their parents' unconscious expectations deriving from a very different childhood world. The *Sabras'* clarity and relative lack of psychic turmoil impress their elders and yet offend the progenitors' persisting taste for convoluted ambiguity.

With this we leave the detailed exploration of personality, socialization, and social structure in specific and reasonably definable communities and turn in the next chapter to a consideration of a variety of different problems involved in socialization in a large-scale modern society, approached from a number of different viewpoints. Many of the questions raised in relation to the Kibbutz or one of the Puerto Rican communities will appear again in different contexts as they are encountered in large-scale mass societies. Still others will recur as specific topical concerns in the later chapters: the problem of transitions in the life cycle with special emphasis on puberty (Chapter Four), the cross-cutting forces of work and play in the human personality (Chapter Five), man in extreme situations (Chapter Six), and the ambiguities and perplexities of the nature of "normality" (Chapter Seven).

SELECTED BIBLIOGRAPHY

Family and Socialization: General References

Parsons, Talcott and Robert F. Bales. *Family, Socialization and Interaction Process.* New York: Free Press of Glencoe, 1955.
Working theoretical papers linking small-group dynamics with analyses of family and socialization patterns.

Sears, Robert R., Eleanor Maccoby, and Henry Levin. *Patterns of Child Rearing.* New York: Harper & Row, Publishers, 1957.
Detailed analysis of American patterns.

Whiting, John and Irwin Child. *Child Training and Personality: A Cross Cultural Survey.* New Haven: Yale University Press, 1953.
Pioneering systematic cross-cultural studies of child rearing, using the Yale Human Relations Area Files.

Socialization Studies of Particular Tribes or Communities

The following are among the more important "case studies" of culture, socialization, and personality development in particular tribal cultures or communities within large-scale societies.

Bateson, Gregory and Margaret Mead. *Balinese Character: A Photographic Analysis.* New York: The New York Academy of Sciences, 1942.
Imaginative presentation of the feel and look of Balinese experience by the synthesis of photographs and verbal analysis.

Cohen, Yehudi A. "Structure and Function: Family Organization and Socialization in a Jamaican Community," *American Anthropologist.* Vol. 58, 1956, pp. 664-86.
Interesting for comparison with the Puerto Rican studies, involving a different Caribbean folklike community within modern society. Sophisticated treatment of family patterns in relation to wider aspects of social structure.

Dennis, Wayne. *The Hopi Child.* New York: Appleton-Century-Crofts, 1940.

Du Bois, Cora. *The People of Alor: A Socio-Psychological Study of an East Indian Island.* Minneapolis: University of Minnesota Press, 1944.
One of the pioneering culture-personality studies to use the Rorschach for "modal personality" analysis.

Erikson, Erik. *Childhood and Society.* New York: W. W. Norton & Co., 1950.
The case studies of the Yurok and Sioux Indian tribes are particularly interesting.

Gladwin, Thomas and Seymour Sarason. *Truk: Man in Paradise.* New York: Viking Fund Publication in Anthropology, 1953.

Goldfrank, Esther. "Socialization, Personality, and the Structure of Pueblo Society (with Particular Reference to Hopi and Zuni)," in

Douglas Haring (ed.), *Personal Character and Cultural Milieu*. 3rd edition. Syracuse: Syracuse University Press, 1956.

Havighurst, Robert J. and Bernice L. Neugarten. *American Indian and White Children: A Socio-Psychological Investigation*. Chicago: University of Chicago Press, 1954.

Henry, Jules. *Jungle People: The Kaingang Tribe of the Highlands of Brazil*. New York: Augustin, 1941.

Kaplan, Bert and Thomas S. A. Plaut. *Personality in a Communal Society: An Analysis of the Mental Health of the Hutterites*. Lawrence: University of Kansas Social Science Studies, 1956.
Very valuable for comparison with the Kibbutz: how does a very different kind of communally organized society deal with socialization and with what personality effects?

Kardiner, Abram, with the collaboration of Ralph Linton. *The Individual and His Society*. New York: Columbia University Press, 1939.
Neo-Freudian analysis of the "societal personality structure" of the Marquesan Islanders of Polynesia and the Tanala people of Madagascar.

———— and collaborators. *The Psychological Frontiers of Society*. New York: Columbia University Press, 1945.
With the help of anthropologists Ralph Linton, Cora DuBois, and James West, Kardiner analyzes the "basic personality structure" of the Comanche Indians, the Alorese of Indonesia and the people of "Plainville, U.S.A."

Landes, Ruth. "The Personality of the Ojibwa," *Character and Personality*. Vol. 6, 1937, pp. 51-60. (The journal is now called *Journal of Personality*.)

Landy, David. *Tropical Childhood*. Chapel Hill: University of North Carolina Press, 1959; New York: Harper Torchbooks, 1965.
A detailed ethnographic study of a cane workers' community in Puerto Rico that resembles in some ways both the Manicaboa and the Barrio Poyal people of Wolf's study.

Leighton, Dorothea and Clyde Kluckhohn. *Children of the People: The Navaho Individual and His Development*. Cambridge: Harvard University Press, 1947.

Lewis, Claudia. *Children of the Cumberland*. New York: Columbia University Press, 1946.
A sensitive study by a woman who is not a professional anthropologist, bringing the kind of sensitivity and artistic acuity of perception that characterizes the best work of such anthropologists as Margaret Mead.

Macgregor, Gordon. *Warriors Without Weapons: A Study of the Society and Personality of the Pine Ridge Sioux*. Chicago: University of Chicago Press, 1946.

Mead, Margaret. *Coming of Age in Samoa*. New York: William Morrow and Company, 1928, and later paperback editions.

————. *Growing Up in New Guinea*. New York: William Morrow and Company, 1930, and later paperback editions.
Leaving aside the now outgrown polemical thrust, these early impres-

sionistic, novelistically written studies of Mead's are the "classic" fore-runners of the whole field.

————. *Sex and Temperament in Three Primitive Societies.* New York: William Morrow and Company, 1935, and later editions.
Of the three New Guinea tribes studied (Arapesh, Mundugumor, and Tchambuli), the analysis of the Arapesh the most complete in reference to socialization and personality development.

———— and Martha Wolfenstein (eds.). *Childhood in Contemporary Cultures.* Chicago: University of Chicago Press, 1955.
Application of the Mead methods and insights to a number of modern societies.

Montague, Ashley. *Coming Into Being Among the Australian Aborigines.* London: Routledge & Kegan Paul, 1937.

Read, Margaret. *Children of Their Fathers: Growing Up Among the Ngoni of Nyasaland.* New Haven: Yale University Press, 1960.

Whiting, Beatrice (ed.). *Six Cultures: Studies in Child Rearing.* New York: John Wiley & Sons, 1963.
Systematic cross-cultural data on child rearing in six cultures. Includes the following studies, each of which has also been republished in 1966 as a separate paperback volume:
Fischer, John and Ann. *The New Englanders of Orchard Town.*
LeVine, Robert and Barbara. *Nyansongo: A Gusii Community of Kenya.*
Maretzki, Thomas and Hatsumi. *Taira: An Okinawan Village.*
Minturn, Leigh and John Hitchcock. *The Rājpūts of Khalapur, India.*
Nydegger, William and Corinne. *Tarong: An Ilocos Barrio of the Philippines.*
Romney, Kimball and Romaine. *The Mixtecans of Juxtlahuaca, Mexico.*

Whiting, John W. M. *Becoming a Kwoma: Teaching and Learning in a New Guinea Tribe.* New Haven: Yale University Press, 1941.

THREE

Socialization: some problems in large-scale societies

In the previous chapter we concentrated on detailed "case studies" of four different and relatively circumscribed communities. To varying degrees, to be sure, each could be treated in some sense as a microcosm, where one could relate the adult situation and personality with the socialization practices and these in turn to the personality development of the emerging generation and trace some of the stresses and dilemmas of that generation into their own adult lives. The degree of continuity differs, of course, ranging from very great in Manicaboa, to less so in Poyal, to still less in San José, and in turn to an almost radical generational gap between the founders and the *Sabras* of the Kibbutz. Similarly, the four communities range in roughly the same order, in degree of contact and interconnectedness with the wider populations of the modern urban industrial world. Still each community studied was something of a manageable entity. How, by contrast, can we say something manageable, useful, and meaningful about the common or general trends of socialization and personality development for a whole large-scale modern society? If the variations among three communities in so relatively small an island society as Puerto Rico are as great as the preceding case studies have revealed, is it not a hopelessly gigantic task to attempt such a characterization for a whole modern nation such as the Soviet Union or the United States or even one like France or Japan?

Our approach shall be drastically selective. We have chosen to present, discuss, and reflect upon three very different kinds of report.

One is a thoughtful essay (frankly labeled "speculative") attempting to marshall and interpret a great number of specific empirical studies carried out over the past few decades on socialization practices in the United States and the presumably related personality traits of the emerging younger generation. This is Urie Bronfenbrenner's paper, "The Changing American Child," which attempts to juggle variations over time (about thirty years) and variations by class, by sex of parent, and by sex of child to arrive at some very broad and necessarily tentative generalizations of trends in this sprawling complex society. The trends concern a variety of specific and more general socialization procedures and their agents and recipients. The resultant picture, inevitably simplified, suggests the presence of a much broader uniformity than one might have expected if one had concentrated mainly on the variety and pluralism of this society.

The second paper boldly tackles a different huge modern industrialized society, but with a somewhat different objective and with different tools and strategies. This is the paper by Alex Inkeles, Eugenia Hanfmann, and Helen Beier on "Modal Personality and Adjustment to the Soviet Socio-Political System." Here by a skillful and imaginative use of data on a very small number of individuals the authors find the means to sketch a broad yet subtly detailed picture of the Great Russian personality. They present an arresting and illuminating comparison of that "national character" with the corresponding trends of the people of the United States.

The third paper comes to socialization and the broad trends of a whole society from still another angle, with a different kind of empirical data and a different extrapolative strategy. This report deals with Germany of the early nineteenth century and approaches the relationship between socialization and society through a very special agency: the modern published fairy tale. The original paper by Henry Carsch, "Fairy Tales and Socialization: The Fairy in Grimms' Tales" applies a special kind of interpretive analysis to the body of children's literature known as *The Fairy Tales of the Brothers Grimm*. It is an especially illuminating analysis, since the Grimms' tales represent one of the first deliberate attempts to utilize the "mass medium" of the printed page as a consciously intended socialization device to apply to masses of children throughout a whole society.

Each of these papers has its special contribution as well as, of course, its weaknesses and limitations. We have attempted in the interstitial commentaries on the papers to make some of the connecting links that will heighten their cumulative value in shedding light on the complexities of socialization for a mass modern society.

1. NORTH AMERICA: UNIFORMITIES AND VARIATIONS BY CLASS AND TIME[1]

It is an understatement to say that it is difficult to generalize about America. Yet we shall try to do so nonetheless. How does one find useful things to say about socialization and personality development that would be reasonably valid for a whole sprawling heterogeneous population of close to 200 million persons, whose differences can be abundantly documented in reference to socio-economic class; rural, urban, and suburban settings; ethnic, racial, and religious affiliations; regional and linguistic variations; generations from original immigrants, and so on? And if we are to include Canada as well, are the difficulties not further compounded when we have to consider the substantial minority of French Canadians?

Still, we can talk about some broad uniformities, in two major ways: (1) by contrasting North America with other whole societies; and (2) by focusing attention on broad *homogenizing* forces at work in modern America, which are perceptibly reducing internal differences within the society. In reference to the former, class, regional, ethnic, and other differences can be put in the background if we concentrate on how the North American societies differ from the whole gamut of folk and primitive societies about which modern anthropology has taught us so much. They also differ importantly from such entities as the Kibbutz of Israel and other communal-collectivist communities or enclaves, such as the religious sects like the Hutterites, wherever they may live. They differ importantly also

[1] I am using "North America" here to refer to a *cultural* unit, i.e. the United States and Canada, rather than a geographic one, which would of course include in the term "North America" all of Mexico and Central America as well. Unfortunately there is no simple term in common use to refer to "the United States and Canada"—one could coin a term such as "Americanada," or "the Americanadians"—for the purpose, but it too would have to be explained. There are many good reasons for referring to North America in this sense. Most of what one could say in a generalizing sense about the culture of the United States applies also to Canada, so that the two nations can be considered—for *this* purpose—as but minor regional variations on a common culture.

from such other modern industrial societies as the Soviet Union, Japan, and (though less so) the countries of Western Europe. They can also be contrasted in important respects with societies currently undergoing rapid revolutionary transformation, such as most of the new nations of Africa and Asia, Castro's Cuba, and so on.

The second perspective, the emphasis on homogenizing forces, leads us to pay attention to a number of significant phenomena about modern America: the narrowing in class differences (see the Bronfenbrenner paper, following); the influence of mass media of communication (television, radio, movies, popular magazines); the growing commonalities in the *secondary agencies* of socialization, especially the schools, in offsetting differential family influences on the child; and the substantial narrowing of the range of influences of the family itself upon the child. Further in this vein we can point to the influence of common outside forces upon the family as a socialization setting as well as upon other socialization agencies. These forces include the disappearance of the family as a production unit, now with limited exceptions almost a universal feature of this modern society; the fact that increasingly this is an employee society, even at high socio-economic levels, rather than one of farming or craft or business entrepreneurs or of rentiers; the essential isolation of the nuclear family as the primary situation of affectional intimacy, a society-wide trend accentuated by the whole industrialization process.

By emphasizing such trends as these, and ignoring for the moment the many differences we know exist, we can present one kind of picture of modern America as it applies to socialization and personality development. We can speak of a kind of "core culture" often referred to as a basically "middle-class culture," based on the absence of any hereditary nobility, and of any *structurally distinct* class demarcations.[2] Mass industrialism creates common experiential

---

[2] Of course, I do *not* mean that there are no glaring inequalities in income, power, and prestige or gross differences in life styles, but rather that these differences appear in a kind of fluid continuum rather than being marked off into structurally fixed strata. Witness the great difficulties all sociologists of class in America have in "deciding" how many classes there are, where their demarcation lines are to be drawn, and how different and inconsistent are the various pictures of "America's class structure" drawn by different "expert" observers, the disagreements on what criteria to consider most important, and so on. A rewarding confrontation with these problems is to be found in Dennis Wrong, "Social Inequality Without Social Stratification," *The Canadian Review of Sociology and Anthropology*, Vol. 1, No. 1, February 1964, pp. 5-16. Witness also the

situations for all, the media communicate mass values, the schools proclaim the same life goals for all, culture products are commonly dispensed to the whole population. Future-orientation is a broadly respected value, there is a generalized rejection of the past as out of date, a generally anti-traditional bias. The nuclear family is basically isolated, particularly from ancestral generations, and this means that its socialization tasks must be confronted by each generation *de novo* without reliance on (or even with outright rejection of) the "wisdom" of earlier generations. The small size of the family, an increasingly homogeneous feature with the widespread dissemination of contraceptives to all income levels, also makes for commonalities in the socialization setting. Increasingly, the producing and rearing of chilren is a deliberate *project* of the family, with increasingly widespread attention to the *problematics* of the task and concern for the consequences of particular socialization techniques. Self-consciousness and anxiety on the part of the parents, the turning to homogenized mass media sources for guidance in the task, these are further features that tend to override differences in ancestral background among succeeding parental generations, reinforce the general future-orientation, and give an aura of tense uncertainty and expectancy to the whole socialization situation.

This "core culture" can be described as being basically derived from Anglo-Saxon Protestant backgrounds with a strong Puritan streak, even though large portions of the population have not had that specific ancestral cultural background. (Note for example the commonplace that American Catholics seem much more "puritanical" or "protestant" than their co-religionists in Europe or Latin America and that Reform Jews are scarcely distinguishable from communicants of the more "enlightened" Protestant denominations.) The Anglo-Saxon Protestantism is, in turn, modified as a cultural influence by the developments in the economy and the occupational structure and the influence of the mass media, which in effect distill universalizing influences from a great variety of ethnic and religious differences.

The values of this "core culture" emphasize individualism, achievement, universalism, and mobility. These values are commu-

---

ideological acrobatics of doctrinaire Marxists when confronted with the "bourgeois" identifications, interests, consumption patterns, etc., of the American "working classes" and the frequent welfare-statist sympathies of comfortable "upper-middle-class" professionals.

nicated by the universalizing mechanisms of the mass media, the schools, and major religious institutions so that they reach and influence (though not equally)lower income elements of the population and the various ethnic minority groups by the pressure of their prestige value and by their "success" value. The emphasis on achievement is particularly important, for it is always phrased in terms of *individual* endeavor and success, and it is constantly tied in with the major ideological affirmations of the society as "the land of opportunity," abetted by constant efforts of activitists and reformers to make "equality of opportunity (according to ability)" a reality. Though there are some counterforces to this individualism-achievement complex at work in this society (as explored in the following paper by Bronfenbrenner), it is still a dominant motif, which stands out in higher relief when we compare this society with the values and socialization of the Kibbutz or with those of either Manicaboa or Poyal in Puerto Rico, as explored in the preceding chapter. Achievement-orientation in the Kibbutz is always *collective*-oriented rather than individualistic. In Manicaboa its sights tend to be limited to improvement within the narrow confines of individual-family farming, and there in the context of the family rather than of *individual* affirmation. In Poyal achievement aspirations are but slightly developed, if at all, and group solidarity is a far more important value. But in America, for all the cooperative counterelements, individual achievement is still a cornerstone. It seems unlikely to diminish in a future marked by further technological development, hence competition for advantageous placement in the industrial complex.

Within this broadly uniform picture, let us consider some of the variations in socialization by class differences, and by changes through time, as explored in the following paper by Urie Bronfenbrenner.

The Changing American Child—A Speculative Analysis[3]
URIE BRONFENBRENNER

A QUESTION OF MOMENT

It is now a matter of scientific record that patterns of child rearing in the United States have changed appreciably over the past twenty-five

Reprinted with permission, from Journal of Social Issues, Vol. 17, No. 1, 1961, pp. 6-18.
[3] This paper draws heavily on results from a program of research being con-

years (Bronfenbrenner, 1958). Middle class parents especially have moved away from the more rigid and strict styles of care and discipline advocated in the early Twenties and Thirties toward modes of response involving greater tolerance of the child's impulses and desires, freer expression of affection, and increased reliance on "psychological" methods of discipline, such as reasoning and appeals to guilt, as distinguished from more direct techniques like physical punishment. At the same time, the gap between the social classes in their goals and methods of child rearing appears to be narrowing, with working class parents beginning to adopt both the values and techniques of the middle class. Finally, there is dramatic correspondence between these observed shifts in parental values and behavior and the changing character of the attitudes and practices advocated in successive editions of such widely read manuals as the Children's Bureau bulletin on *Infant Care* and Spock's *Baby and Child Care*. Such correspondence should not be taken to mean that the expert has now become the principal instigator and instrument of social change, since the ideas of scientists and professional workers themselves reflect in part the operation of deep-rooted cultural processes. Nevertheless, the fact remains that changes in values and practices advocated by prestigeful professional figures can be substantially accelerated by rapid and widespread dissemination through the press, mass media of communication, and public discussion.

Given these facts, it becomes especially important to gauge the effect of the changes that are advocated and adopted. Nowhere is this issue more significant, both scientifically and socially, than in the sphere of familial values and behavior. It is certainly no trivial matter to ask whether the changes that have occurred in the attitudes and actions of parents over the past twenty-five years have been such as to affect the personality development of their children, so that the boys and girls of today are somewhat different in character structure from those of a decade or more ago. Or, to put the question more succinctly: has the changing American parent produced a changing American child?

A STRATEGY OF INFERENCE

Do we have any basis for answering this intriguing question? To begin with, do we have any evidence of changes in the behavior of children in successive decades analogous to those we have already been able to find for parents? If so, we could take an important first step toward a solution

---

ducted by the author in collaboration with Edward C. Devereux and George J. Suci. The contribution of these colleagues to facts and ideas presented in this paper is gratefully acknowledged. The research program is supported in part with grants from the National Science Foundation and the National Institutes of Health.

of the problem. Unfortunately, in contrast to his gratifying experience in seeking and finding appropriate data on parents, the present writer has, to date, been unable to locate enough instances in which comparable methods of behavioral assessment have been employed with different groups of children of similar ages over an extended period of time. Although the absence of such material precludes any direct and unequivocal approach to the question at hand, it is nevertheless possible, through a series of inferences from facts already known, to arrive at some estimate of what the answer might be. Specifically, although as yet we have no comparable data on the relation between parental and child behavior for different families at successive points in time, we do have facts on the influence of parental treatment on child behavior at a given point in time; that is, we know that certain variations in parental behavior tend to be accompanied by systematic differences in the personality characteristics of children. If we are willing to assume that these same relationships obtained not only at a given moment but across different points in time, we are in a position to infer the possible effects on children of changing patterns of child rearing over the years. It is this strategy that we propose to follow.

THE CHANGING AMERICAN PARENT

We have already noted the major changes in parental behavior discerned in a recent analysis of data reported over a twenty-five year period. These secular trends may be summarized as follows:

1. Greater permissiveness toward the child's spontaneous desires
2. Freer expression of affection
3. Increased reliance on indirect "psychological" techniques of discipline (such as reasoning or appeals to guilt) vs. direct methods (like physical punishment, scolding, or threats)
4. In consequence of the above shifts in the direction of what are predominantly middle class values and techniques, a narrowing of the gap between social classes in their patterns of child rearing.

Since the above analysis was published, a new study has documented an additional trend. Bronson, Katten, and Livson (1959) have compared patterns of paternal and maternal authority and affection in two generations of families from the California Guidance Study. Unfortunately, the time span surveyed overlaps only partially with the twenty-five year period covered in our own analysis, the first California generation having been raised in the early 1900's and the second in the late Twenties and early Thirties. Accordingly, if we are to consider the California results along with the others cited above, we must make the somewhat risky assumption that a trend discerned in the first three decades of the century has continued in the same direction through the early 1950's. With this important qualification, an examination of the data cited by Bronson, *et al.* (1959) points to still another, secular trend—a shift over the years in the pattern of parental role differentiation within the family. Specifically:

5. In succeeding generations the relative position of the father vis-à-vis the mother is shifting with the former becoming increasingly more affectionate and less authoritarian, and the latter becoming relatively more important as the agent of discipline, especially for boys.

"PSYCHOLOGICAL" TECHNIQUES OF DISCIPLINE AND THEIR EFFECTS

In pursuing our analytic strategy, we next seek evidence of the effects on the behavior of children of variations in parental treatment of the type noted in our inventory. We may begin by noting that the variables involved in the first three secular trends constitute a complex that has received considerable attention in recent research in parent-child relationships. Within the last three years, two sets of investigators, working independently, have called attention to the greater efficacy of "love-oriented" or "psychological" techniques in bringing about desired behavior in the child (Sears, Maccoby, and Levin, 1957; Miller and Swanson, 1958, 1960). The present writer, noting that such methods are especially favored by middle class parents, offered the following analysis of the nature of these techniques and the reasons for their effectiveness.

Such parents are, in the first place, more likely to overlook offenses, and when they do punish, they are less likely to ridicule or inflict physical pain. Instead, they reason with the youngster, isolate him, appeal to guilt, show disappointment—in short, convey in a variety of ways, on the one hand, the kind of behavior that is expected of the child; on the other, the realization that transgression means the interruption of a mutually valued relationship. . . .

These findings (of greater efficacy) mean that middle class parents, though in one sense more lenient in their discipline techniques, are using methods that are actually more compelling. Moreover, the compelling power of these practices is probably enhanced by the more permissive treatment accorded to middle class children in the early years of life. The successful use of withdrawal of love as a discipline technique implies the prior existence of a gratifying relationship; the more love present in the first instance, the greater the threat implied in its withdrawal (Bronfenbrenner, 1958).

It is now a well-established fact that children from middle class families tend to excel those from lower class in many characteristics ordinarily regarded as desirable, such as self-control, achievement, responsibility, leadership, popularity, and adjustment in general.[4] If, as seems plausible, such differences in behavior are attributable at least in part to class-linked variations in parental treatment, the strategy of inference we have adopted would appear on first blush to lead to a rather optimistic conclusion. Since, over the years, increasing numbers of parents have been adopting the more effective socialization techniques typically employed by the middle class, does it not follow that successive generations of children should show gains in the development of effective behavior and desirable personality characteristics?

Unfortunately, this welcome conclusion, however logical, is premature, for it fails to take into account all of the available facts.

SEX, SOCIALIZATION, AND SOCIAL CLASS

To begin with, the parental behaviors we have been discussing are differentially distributed not only by socio-economic status but also by sex. As we have pointed out elsewhere (Bronfenbrenner, 1961), girls are exposed to more affection and less punishment than boys, but at the same time are more likely to be subjected to "love-oriented" discipline of the type which encourages the development of internalized controls. And, consistent with our line of reasoning, girls are found repeatedly to be "more obedient, cooperative, and in general better socialized than boys at comparable age levels." But this is not the whole story.

. . . At the same time, the research results indicate that girls tend to be more anxious, timid, dependent, and sensitive to rejection. If these differences are a function of differential treatment by parents, then it would seem that the more "efficient" methods of child rearing employed with girls involve some risk of what might be called "over-socialization" (Bronfenbrenner, 1961).

One could argue, of course, that the contrasting behaviors of boys and girls have less to do with differential parental treatment than with genetically based maturational influences. Nevertheless, two independent lines of evidence suggest that socialization techniques do contribute to individual differences, *within the same sex*, precisely in the types of personality characteristics noted above. In the first place, variations in child behavior and parental treatment strikingly similar to those we have cited for the two sexes are reported in a recent comprehensive study of differences between first and later born children (Schachter, 1959). Like girls, first children receive more attention, are more likely to be exposed to "psychological" discipline, and end up more anxious and dependent, whereas later children, like boys, are more aggressive and self-confident.

---

[4] For a summary of findings on social class differences in children's behavior and personality characteristics, see P. H. Mussen and J. J. Conger, *Child Development and Personality* (New York: Harper & Row, Publishers, 1956).

A second line of evidence comes from our own current research. We have been concerned with the role of parents in the development of such "constructive" personality characteristics as responsibility and leadership among adolescent boys and girls. Our findings reveal not only the usual differences in adolescents and parents' behaviors associated with the sex of the child, but also a striking contrast in the relationship between parental and child behaviors for the two sexes. To start on firm and familiar ground, girls are rated by their teachers as more responsive than boys, whereas the latter obtain higher scores on leadership. Expected differences similarly appear in the realm of parental behavior: girls receive more affection, praise, and companionship; boys are subjected to more physical punishment and achievement demands. Quite unanticipated, however, at least by us, was the finding that both parental affection and discipline appeared to facilitate effective psychological functioning in boys, but to impede the development of such constructive behavior in girls. Closer examination of our data indicated that both extremes of either affection or discipline were deleterious for all children, but that the process of socialization entailed somewhat different risks for the two sexes. Girls were especially susceptible to the detrimental influence of overprotection; boys to the ill effects of insufficient parental discipline and support. Or, to put it in more colloquial terms: boys suffered more often from too little taming, girls from too much.

In an attempt to account for this contrasting pattern of relationships, we proposed the notion of differential optimal levels of affection and authority for the two sexes.

The qualities of independence, initiative, and self-sufficiency, which are especially valued for boys in our culture, apparently require for their development a somewhat different balance of authority and affection than is found in the "love-oriented" strategy characteristically applied with girls. While an affectional context is important for the socialization of boys, it must evidently be accompanied by and be compatible with a strong component of parental discipline. Otherwise, the boy finds himself in the same situation as the girl, who, having received greater affection, is more sensitive to its withdrawal, with the result that a little discipline goes a long way and strong authority is constricting rather than constructive (Bronfenbrenner, 1960).

What is more, available data suggest that this very process may already be operating for boys from upper middle class homes. To begin with, differential treatment of the sexes is at a minimum for these families. Contrasting parental attitudes and behaviors toward boys and girls are pronounced only at lower class levels, and decrease as one moves up the socio-economic scale (Kohn, 1959; Bronfenbrenner, 1960). Thus our own results show that it is primarily at lower middle class levels that boys get more punishment than girls, and the latter receive greater warmth and attention. With an increase in the family's social position, direct discipline drops off, especially for boys, and indulgence and protectiveness decrease for girls. As a result, patterns of parental treatment for the two sexes begin to converge. In like manner, we find that the differential effects of parental behavior on the two sexes are marked only in the lower middle class. It is here that girls especially risk being overprotected and boys not receiving sufficient discipline and support. In the upper middle class the picture changes. Girls are not as readily debilitated by parental affection and power; nor is parental discipline as effective in fostering the development of responsibility and leadership in boys.

All these trends point to the conclusion that the "risks" experienced by each sex during the process of socialization tend to be somewhat different at different social class levels. Thus the danger of overprotection for girls is especially great in lower class families, but lower in upper middle class because of the decreased likelihood of overprotection. Analogously, boys are in greater danger of suffering from inadequate discipline and support in lower middle than in upper middle class. But the upper middle class boy, unlike the girl, exchanges one hazard for another. Since at this upper level the more potent "psychological" techniques of discipline are likely to be employed with both sexes, the boy presumably now too runs the risk of being "oversocialized," of losing some of his capacity for independent aggressive accomplishment.

Accordingly, if our line of reasoning is correct, we should expect a changing pattern of sex differences at successive socio-economic levels. Specifically, aspects of effective psychological functioning favoring girls should be most pronounced in the upper middle class; those favoring boys in the lower middle. A recent analysis of some of our data bears out this expectation. Girls excel boys on such variables as *responsibility* and *social acceptance* primarily at the higher socio-economic levels. In contrast, boys surpass girls on such traits as *leadership, level of aspiration, and competitiveness,* almost exclusively in lower middle class. Indeed, with a rise in a family's social position, the differences tend to reverse themselves with girls now excelling boys.[5]

TRENDS IN PERSONALITY DEVELOPMENT: A FIRST APPROXIMATION

The implications for our original line of inquiry are clear. We are suggesting that the "love-oriented" socialization techniques, which over the past twenty-five years have been employed in increasing degree by American middle class families, may have negative as well as constructive aspects. While fostering the internalization of adult standards and the development of socialized behavior, they may also have the effect of undermining capacities for initiative and independence, particularly in

[5] These shifts in sex differences with a rise in class status are significant at the 5 percent level of confidence (one-tailed test).

boys. Males exposed to this "modern" pattern of child rearing might be expected to differ from their counterparts of a quarter century ago in being somewhat more conforming and anxious, less enterprising and self-sufficient, and, in general, possessing more of the virtues and liabilities commonly associated with feminine character structure.[6]

At long last, then, our strategy of inference has led us to a first major conclusion. The term "major" is appropriate since the conclusion takes as its points of departure and return four of the secular trends which served as the impetus for our inquiry. Specifically, through a series of empirical links and theoretical extrapolations, we have arrived at an estimate of the effects on children of the tendency of successive generations of parents to become progressively more permissive, to express affection more freely, to utilize "psychological" techniques of discipline, and, by moving in these directions to narrow the gap between the social classes in their patterns of child rearing.

FAMILY STRUCTURE AND PERSONALITY DEVELOPMENT

But one other secular trend remains to be considered: what of the changing pattern of parental role differentiation during the first three decades of the century? If our extrapolation is correct, the balance of power within the family has continued to shift with fathers yielding parental authority to mothers and taking on some of the nurturant and affectional functions traditionally associated with the maternal role. Again we have no direct evidence of the effects of such secular changes on successive generations of children, and must look for leads to analogous data on contemporaneous relationships.

We may begin by considering the contribution of each parent to the socialization processes we have examined thus far. Our data indicate that it is primarily mothers who tend to employ "love-oriented" techniques of discipline and fathers who rely on more direct methods like physical punishment. The above statement must be qualified, however, by reference to the sex of the child, for it is only in relation to boys that fathers use direct punishment more than mothers. More generally, . . . the results reveal a tendency for each parent to be somewhat more active, firm, and demanding with a child of the same sex, more lenient and indulgent with a child of the opposite sex. . . . The reversal is most complete with respect to discipline, with fathers being stricter with boys, mothers with girls. In the spheres of affection and protectiveness, there is no

[6] Strikingly similar conclusions were reached almost fifteen years ago in a provocative essay by Arnold Green, "The Middle Class Male Child and Neurosis," *American Sociological Review*, Vol. 11, 1946, pp. 31-41. With little to go on beyond scattered clinical observations and impressions, Green was able to detect many of the same trends which we have begun to discern in more recent systematic empirical data.

actual shift in preference, but the tendency to be especially warm and solicitous with girls is much more pronounced among fathers than among mothers. In fact, generally speaking, it is the father who is more likely to treat children of the two sexes differently (Bronfenbrenner, 1960).

Consistent with this pattern of results, it is primarily the behavior of fathers that accounts for the differential effects of parental behavior on the two sexes and for the individual differences within each sex. In other words, it is parental authority and affection that tend especially to be salutary for sons but detrimental for daughters. But as might be anticipated from what we already know, these trends are pronounced only in the lower middle class; with a rise in the family's social status, both parents tend to have similar effects on their children, both within and across sexes. Such a trend is entirely to be expected since parental role differentiation tends to decrease markedly as one ascends the socioeconomic ladder. It is almost exclusively in lower middle class homes that fathers are more strict with boys and mothers with girls. To the extent that direct discipline is employed in upper middle class families, it tends to be exercised by both parents equally. Here again we see a parallelism between shifts in parental behavior across time and social class in the direction of forms (in this instance of family structure) favored by the upper middle class group.

What kinds of children, then, can we expect to develop in families in which the father plays a predominantly affectionate role, and a relatively low level of discipline is exercised equally by both parents? A tentative answer to this question is supplied by a preliminary analysis of our data in which the relation between parental role structure and adolescent behavior was examined with controls for the family's social class position. The results of this analysis are summarized as follows: . . . Both responsibility and leadership are fostered by the relatively greater salience of the parent of the same sex . . . Boys tend to be more responsible when the father rather than the mother is the principal disciplinarian; girls are more dependable when the mother is the major authority figure. . . . In short, boys thrive in a patriarchal context, girls in a matriarchal. . . . The most dependent and least dependable adolescents describe family arrangements that are neither patriarchal nor matriarchal, but equalitarian. To state the issue in more provocative form, our data suggest that the democratic family, which for so many years has been held up and aspired to as a model by professionals and enlightened laymen, tends to produce young people who "do not take initiative," "look to others for direction and decision," and "cannot be counted on to fulfill obligations" (Bronfenbrenner, 1960).

In the wake of so sweeping a conclusion, it is important to call attention to the tentative, if not tenuous, character of our findings. The results were based on a single study employing crude questionnaire methods and rating scales. Also, our interpretation is limited by the somewhat "attenuated" character of most of the families classified as patriarchal or matriarchal in our sample. Extreme concentrations of power in one or another parent were comparatively rare. Had they been more frequent, we suspect the data would have shown that such extreme asymmetrical patterns of authority were detrimental rather than salutary for effective psychological development, perhaps even more disorganizing than equalitarian forms.

Nevertheless, our findings do find some peripheral support in the work of others. A number of investigations, for example, point to the special importance of the father in the socialization of boys (Bandura and Walters, 1959; Mussen and Distler, 1959). Further corroborative evidence appears in the growing series of studies of effects of paternal absence (Back, 1946, Sears, Pintler and Sears, 1946; Lynn and Sawrey, 1959; Tiller, 1958). The absence of the father apparently not only affects the behavior of the child directly but also influences the mother in the direction of greater overprotectiveness. The effect of both these tendencies is especially critical for male children; boys from father-absent homes tend to be markedly more submissive and dependent. Studies dealing explicitly with the influence of parental role structure in intact families are few and far between. Papanek (1957), in an unpublished doctoral dissertation, reports greater sex-role differentiation among children from homes in which the parental roles were differentiated. And in a carefully controlled study, Kohn and Clausen (1956) find that "schizophrenic patients more frequently than normal persons report that their mothers played a very strong authority role and the father a very weak authority role." Finally, what might best be called complementary evidence for our inferences regarding trends in family structure and their effects comes from the work of Miller, Swanson, and their associates (1958; 1960) on the differing patterns of behavior exhibited by families from *bureaucratic* and *entrepreneurial* work settings. These investigators argue that the entrepreneurial-bureaucratic dichotomy represents a new cleavage in American social structure that cuts across and overrides social class influences and carries with it its own characteristic patterns of family structure and socialization. Thus one investigation (Gold and Slater, 1958) contrasts the exercise of power in families of husbands employed in two kinds of job situations: (a) those working in large organizations with three or more levels of supervision; (b) those self-employed or working in small organizations with few levels of supervision. With appropriate controls for social class, equalitarian families were found more frequently in the bureaucratic groups; patriarchal and, to a lesser extent, matriarchal in the entrepreneurial setting. Another study (Miller and Swanson, 1958) shows that, in line with Miller and Swanson's hypotheses, parents from these same two groups tend to favor rather different ends and means of socialization, with entrepreneurial families putting considerably more emphasis on the development of independence and mastery and on the use of "psychological" techniques of discipline. These differences appear at both upper and lower middle class levels but are less pronounced in higher socio-economic strata. It is Miller and Swanson's belief however, that the trend is toward the bureaucratic way of life, with its less structured patterns of family organization and child rearing. The evidence we have cited on secular changes in family structure and the inferences we have drawn regarding their possible effects on personality development are on the whole consistent with their views.

LOOKING FORWARD

If Miller and Swanson are correct in the prediction that America is moving toward a bureaucratic society that emphasizes, to put it colloquially, "getting along" rather than "getting ahead," then presumably we can look forward to ever increasing numbers of equalitarian families who, in turn, will produce successive generations of ever more adaptable but unaggressive "organization men." But recent signs do not all point in this direction. In our review of secular trends in child rearing practices we detected in the data from the more recent studies a slowing up in the headlong rush toward greater permissiveness and toward reliance on indirect methods of discipline. We pointed out also that if the most recent editions of well-thumbed guidebooks on child care are as reliable harbingers of the future as they have been in the past, we can anticipate something of a return to the more explicit discipline techniques of an earlier era. Perhaps the most important forces, however, acting to redirect both the aims and methods of child rearing in America emanate from behind the Iron Curtain. With the firing of the first Sputnik, Achievement began to replace Adjustment as the highest goal of the American way of life. We have become concerned—perhaps even obsessed—with "education for excellence" and the maximal utilization of our intellectual resources. Already, ability grouping, and the guidance counsellor who is its prophet, have moved down from the junior high to the elementary school, and parents can be counted on to do their part in preparing their youngsters for survival in the new competitive world of applications and achievement tests.

But if a new trend in parental behavior is to develop, it must do so in the context of changes already under way. And if the focus of parental authority is shifting from husband to wife, then perhaps we should anticipate that pressures for achievement will be imposed primarily by mothers rather than fathers. Moreover, the mother's continuing strong emotional investment in the child should provide her with a powerful lever for evoking desired performance. It is noteworthy in this connection that recent studies of the familial origins of need-achievement point to the matriarchy as the optimal context for development of the motive to excel (Strodtbeck, 1958; Rosen and D'Andrade, 1959).

The prospect of a society in which socialization techniques are directed toward maximizing achievement drive is not altogether a pleasant one. As a number of investigators have shown (Baldwin, Kalhorn and Breese, 1945; Baldwin, 1948; Haggard, 1957; Winterbottom, 1958; Rosen and D'Andrade, 1959), high achievement motivation appears to flourish in a family atmosphere of "cold democracy" in which initial high levels of maternal involvement are followed by pressures for independence and accomplishment.[7] Nor does the product of this process give ground for reassurance. True, children from achievement-oriented homes excel in planfulness and performance, but they are also more aggressive, tense, domineering, and cruel (Baldwin, Kalhorn and Breese, 1945; Baldwin, 1948; Haggard, 1957), It would appear that education for excellence if pursued single-mindedly may entail some sobering social costs.

But by now we are in danger of having stretched our chain of inference beyond the strength of its weakest link. Our speculative analysis has become far more speculative than analytic and to pursue it further would bring us past the bounds of science into the realms of science fiction. In concluding our discussion, we would re-emphasize that speculations should, by their very nature, be held suspect. It is for good reason that, like "damn Yankees" they too carry their almost inseparable sobriquets: speculations are either "idle" or "wild." Given the scientific and social importance of the issues we have raised, we would dismiss the first of these labels out of hand, but the second cannot be disposed of so easily. Like the impetuous child, the "wild" speculation responds best to the sobering influence of friendly but firm discipline, in this instance from the hand of the behavioral scientist. As we look ahead to the next twenty-five years of human socialization, let us hope that the "optimal levels" of involvement and discipline can be achieved not only by the parent who is unavoidably engaged in the process, but also by the scientist who attempts to understand its working, and who—also unavoidably—contributes to shaping its course.

[7] Cold democracy under female administration appears to foster the development of achievement not only in the home but in the classroom as well. In a review of research on teaching effectiveness, Ackerman reports that teachers most successful in bringing about gains in achievement scores for their pupils were judged "least considerate," while those thought friendly and congenial were least effective. (W. I. Ackerman, "Teacher Competence and Pupil Change," *Harvard Educational Review*, Vol. 24, 1954, pp. 273-89.)

REFERENCES

1. Back, G. R., "Father-Fantasies and Father-Typing in Father-Separated Children," *Child Development*, 1946, 17, 63-79.
2. Baldwin, A. L., Kalhorn, J., and Breese, F. H., "The Appraisal of Parent Behavior," *Psychological Monographs*, 1945, 58, No. 3 (Whole No. 268).
3. Baldwin, A. L., "Socialization and the Parent-Child Relationship," *Child Development*, 1948, 19, 127-36.
4. Bandura, A., and Walters, R. H., *Adolescent Aggression*. New York: Ronald Press, 1959.
5. Bronfenbrenner, U., "Socialization and Social Class Through Time and Space," in Maccoby, E., Newcomb, T. M., and Hartley, E. L., *Readings in Social Psychology*. New York: Holt, 1958, pp. 400-25.
6. Bronfenbrenner, U., "Some Familial Antecedents of Responsibility and Leadership in Adolescents," in Petrullo, L., and Bass, B. M. *Leadership and Interpersonal Behavior*. New York: Holt, Rinehart and Winston, 1961.
7. Bronson, W. C., Katten, E. S., and Livson, N., "Patterns of Authority and Affection in Two Generations," *Journal of Abnormal and Social Psychology*, 1959, 58, pp. 143-52.
8. Gold, M., and Slater, C., "Office, Factory, Store—and Family: A Study of Integration Setting," *American Sociological Review*, 1959, 23, 64-74.
9. Haggard, E. A., "Socialization, Personality, and Academic Achievement in Gifted Children," *The School Review*, 1957, 65, 388-414.
10. Kohn, M. L., and Claussen, J. A., "Parental Authority Behavior and Schizophrenia," *American Journal of Orthopsychiatry*, 1956, 26, 297-313.
11. Kohn, M. L., "Social Class and Parental Values," *American Journal of Sociology*, 1959, 44, 337-51.
12. Lynn, D. B., and Sawrey, W. L., "The Effects of Father-Absence on Norwegian Boys and Girls," *Journal of Abnormal and Social Psychology*, 1959, 59, 258-62.
13. Miller, D. R., and Swanson, G. E., *The Changing American Parent*. New York: John Wiley & Sons, 1958.
14. Miller, D. R., and Swanson, G. E., *Inner Conflict and Defense*. New York: Holt, Rinehart and Winston, 1960.
15. Mussen, P., and Distler, L., "Masculinity Identification, and Father-Son Relationships," *Journal of Abnormal and Social Psychology*, 1959, 350-56.
16. Papanek, M., *Authority and Interpersonal Relations in the Family*. Unpublished doctoral dissertation on file at the Radcliffe College Library, 1957.
17. Rosen, B. L., and D'Andrade, R., "The Psychosocial Origins of Achievement Motivation," *Sociometry*, 1959, 22, 185-217.
18. Schachter, S., *The Psychology of Affiliation*. Stanford, Calif.: Stanford University Press, 1959.
19. Sears, R. R., Pintler, M. H., and Sears, P. S., "Effects of Father-Separation on Preschool Children's Doll Play Aggression," *Child Development*, 1946, 17, 219-43.
20. Sears, R. R., Maccoby, Eleanor, and Levin, M., *Patterns of Child Rearing*. Evanston, Ill.: Row, Peterson & Company, 1957.
21. Strodtbeck, F. L., "Family Interaction, Values, and Achievement," in McClelland, D. C., Baldwin, A. L., Bronfenbrenner, U., and Strodtbeck, F. L., *Talent and Society*. Princeton, N.J.: D. Van Nostrand Company, 1958, pp. 135-94.
22. Tiller, P. O., "Father-Absence and Personality Development of Children in Sailor Families," *Nordisk Psykologis Monograph Series*, 1958, 9.

23. Winterbottom, M. R., "The Relation of Need Achievement to Learning Experiences in Independence and Mastery," in Atkinson, J. W., *Motives in Fantasy, Action, and Society.* Princeton, N.J.: D. Van Nostrand & Company, 1958, pp. 453-94.

Reflections

In cross-cultural perspective, there is a significant unstated assumption in the foregoing paper by Bronfenbrenner, as in almost all of the studies of socialization and the family made by sociologists or social psychologists working only within the American setting. That is, the nuclear family and, therefore, its adults—the mother and father—are the crucial if not the sole socializers of the child. Supplementary or counterinfluences of peer groups, of other adults (whether extended relatives such as grandparents, aunts, etc., or teachers or other authorities), and of mass media are not taken into serious consideration—and with some considerable justification if one follows the essentially Freudian line of analysis we have been pursuing in this book, according to which the influences of earliest childhood are of critical, though not exclusive, importance in determining the path of personality development. Note, however, that much of the socialization procedure, e.g., in reference to discipline, that Bronfenbrenner deals with refers importantly to *later* childhood as well as to earlier childhood, and there one must surely ask whether influences of other authority figures such as teachers, and of peers and mass media, do in any significant ways counteract or reinforce those of the parents themselves. Clearly, in comparison with the radical case of the Kibbutz, the role of peers and of non-familial authorities, such as teachers, is drastically less important in modern America. Much of the frustration of educational reformers, whether working within the classroom or in over-all structural features as in attempts at school pairings, etc., seems to derive from the all-pervasive fact in America that the *family* sets patterns and limitations which it is extremely difficult to undo, short of near-total separation of the child from the family in full-time boarding schools. The latter is an institution, very interestingly, used in America almost exclusively by the very rich.

Bronfenbrenner's paper points to some findings which have an intriguing relevance when one compares America with the Israeli Kibbutz. The founders of the Kibbutz were intent upon abolishing the patriarchal family as they saw it through their special ideological lenses, drawing on their own experiences with their parental families in Eastern Europe, and reinforced by certain social theories and by the writings of Freud. The posited family structure they set out to destroy included rigid authoritarian control by parents over children and clear-cut dominance of the *father*. But if the findings cited by Bronfenbrenner and the casual or impressionistic observations of hundreds of other observers are right, that kind of family is rapidly disappearing in America and probably also in most of Europe. This is being accomplished without formal abolition, but by the diffuse cumulative impact of internal changes deriving from several different sources in the social structure, and crystallized in the influential work of the child-rearing "experts" and journalistic proponents of the equalitarian family. The result is that in *affectional* aspects the relations of modern American parents toward their children have become very similar to what we find in the Israeli Kibbutz, that is, that both parents have come to be about equally responsive and giving of affection toward the child, and in very similar ways. This means that the position of the *father* vis-à-vis the child has significantly *changed*. Bronfenbrenner, challenging the easy optimism of the proponents of the equalitarian family, points up some of the disturbing implications of this change. These implications are important for a society like America in a way that they are not for one like the Kibbutz. In the latter the forces of discipline and control are clearly allocated to the non-familial authorities (until high school years, exclusively female) who are clearly not part of the private sphere, while in modern industrial societies like America which have retained the nuclear-family structure, the problems of balance between positive emotional support and affection on the one side and discipline and control on the other remain to be handled in this private sphere of the nuclear family. That balance has been disturbingly upset by the near disappearance of disciplining functions in the *father* and the uneasy and ambiguous shifting of the greatest weight of such functions to the mother, at the same time that the pressures toward "enlightened" child rearing have shifted the mother's behavior toward greater indulgence and made the whole area of discipline more ambiguous and in many cases guilt-laden. The dominant keynote in this whole situation seems to be *confusion*. Certainly reports and impressions of psychiatrists and psychoanalysts dealing with the psychic disturbances of youth who have grown up in such families point to the near disappearance of "classic" neurotic syndromes of the kind that spurred Freud's early brilliant formulations and their replacement by a congeries of more vague and more pervasive disturbances, ambiguously lumped together under such a term as "character disorders," or "identity confusions" or a generalized diffuseness and ambiguity of direction.

The lack of clear-cut disciplining, the confusion and ambiguity of controls, the decline or disappearance of singular or sharply defined life goals, all these have been reported and commented on from a number of different angles by social-psychological and psychiatric observers. Riesman in his imaginative *The Lonely Crowd* [8]—which, significantly, had a popular success that astounded his original publishers—tried to pull together a whole range of different concurrent trends in the society in the concept of a shift from "inner-direction" to "other-direction," a stimulating simplification which gave a relatively educated public a new set of polarities to supplant clichés of vulgarized Marxism and Freudianism which had come to be felt as increasingly inadequate and anachronistic to deal with the modern malaise. Erik Erikson touched sore spots of a similar, perhaps somewhat more educated public with his explorations of the "identity crisis" of adolescence which may be protracted through much of chronologically adult life.

Bruno Bettelheim approves[9] the clarity and directness of the educational *goals* of the Israeli Kibbutz, in his eloquent defense of the "success" of the Kibbutz system *on its own terms*, contrasting it with the great confusion and ambiguity of our own educational goals. Here he has put his finger on a crucial aspect of the socialization situation in modern America—one that is shared to greater or lesser degree by all modern industrialized societies. We are not quite sure what socialization should be *for*, what kind of society we want our children in their formative years to be prepared for—except perhaps in the purely negative phrasing that it is *not* to be a *traditional* society, that it is not to be the same as their parents and grandparents have known. Bettelheim, of course, has no "solution" to this problem—no one has. Despite his enthusiasm for the Kibbutz as he (somewhat too rosily) sees it, he does *not* propose that we should

[8] David Riesman, Nathan Glazer, and Reuel Denney, *The Lonely Crowd* (New Haven: Yale University Press, 1950).

[9] Bruno Bettelheim, "Does Communal Education Work?," *Commentary*, Vol. 33, 1962, pp. 117-26.

adopt its values and its methods (a scarcely feasible project, to say the least). Bronfenbrenner notes that in the pendulum swings of the child-care advisers' enthusiasms, the naive overemphasis on "permissiveness" has in recent years given way to two related trends, a kind of return to discipline and firmness and a revitalized concern with "achievement"—not that either of these had ever entirely disappeared from either preachings or practice. It is evident that there is still a great concern for (necessarily, in this society, *competitive*) achievement. At more comfortable income levels this is seen in pressures on the child for formal competitive performance on the (arbitrary) school tests for placement, for college entrance, going on to graduate school, and so on, which continues unabated the basic motif of *striving for the future* that has long been a central value of this society. (Significantly, the *content* of that "future" is vague and ill-defined so that there is all the more furious concentration on the immediate means or proximate goals.) For the more "deprived" segments of the population, enlightened reform endeavors concentrate on such things as "higher horizons," getting the scions of the Lumpen-proletariat onto the ladder of individualistic success-achievement struggle, in effect trying to "normalize" them into scrubbed acceptable protagonists of the universal drama of individualistic straining-striving. (Note that this emphasis ignores completely alternative goal possibilities, such as the strong group solidarity with limited achievement demands, as found in certain *stable* working-class communities.[10] The assumption is that "democracy" and "equality" of "opportunity" require that everyone in the society should be pursuing the same kinds of goals, and individualistic ones at that. To state this in another way, the middle-class reformers are insisting that the "underprivileged" should have it good—*our* way. Thus the possibilities of pluralistic variety of communities are denied or undermined.)

There are powerful structural features of a modern industrialized society which conduce to this achievement emphasis, which I would argue has not been lost and then only recently (with Sputnik) rediscovered (as Bronfenbrenner's analysis suggests) but has rather been a persistent and continuing feature of the society. The constantly

[10] See Herbert Gans, *The Urban Villagers* (New York: Free Press of Glencoe, 1962), for an American urban example, and Michael Young and Peter Willmott, *Family and Kinship in East London* (Harmondsworth, Eng.: Pelican Books, 1962), for an English case.

changing talent-resource demands of dynamic industrialism have persistently put a premium upon ease of placement of *individuals* into occupational niches according to their capacities to mold and direct innate potentialities into talents and abilities as required by the immediate current scene. This requires and continues to require *mobility* as a general social process and adaptability in striving as the individual personal embodiment. If the only thing one can be sure of is change—in the specific technology, though not in basic institutions—then *adaptability* is a crucial aspect of the striving process. Consequently, consistently, the content of achievement drives *must* remain fluid. Too specific a commitment to a special set of skills can lead to the cul-de-sac of technological unemployment of the kind now becoming increasingly widespread under the impact of "automation." However adaptability is at odds with *specialization*, another significant demand of a complex technological order where the "division of labor" has reached a profusion unprecedented in history. Small wonder that the goals of our educational (more broadly, our whole socialization) system are confused, unclear, internally conflicted. A reflection on the Kibbutz is again illuminating: the "crisis of the Kibbutz" today can be seen as the threat to its self-containment brought by the combination of its economic prosperity and the related increased contacts with and inroads from the broader Israeli society, which is but another version of a dynamic urban industrialized and cosmopolitan society, structurally not much different from those of Western Europe or even America. In such a situation, can it remain so dedicated to such a limited set of community goals, and hence to so elegantly simple a set of socialization objectives? A Kibbutz with an increasingly diversified economy (the earlier opposition to adding factories was prescient), hence increased specialization of labor, and increasingly cosmopolitan contacts with the wider society, becomes much more like a "small town in mass society" [11] and less and less an isolated sectarian enclave. Hence an increasing diversification of socialization goals for such a community seems to me inevitable, in spite of the persistence of certain central ideological perspectives, such as the basic norms of collectivism.

The idea that reformers are trying to remake the children of the

[11] Compare Arthur Vidich and Joseph Bensman's illuminating analysis of a small upstate New York community, under that title (Princeton: Princeton University Press, 1958). See discussion of it in Chapter Seven of this book, pp. 559-62.

poor into a middle-class image, implies however that there is *not enough* diversity in socialization goals in our society. By contrast the present discussion seems to point to a great deal of diversity, even too much, based on the conflicting demands of adaptability and specialization in an industrial order. Both these apparently contradictory trends are true. The achievement-drive emphasis is so exclusively *individualistic* in our society, that more communal- or collectivist-minded alternatives, such as found in the earlier Kibbutz and in stable working-class neighborhoods, are ruled out of the officially acceptable range of goals. Still such alternatives find themselves extremely unstable and vulnerable in an industrialized system, the Kibbutz for the reasons indicated (as long as it is anti-traditional), the working-class neighborhoods because their subsistence base depends on employment in the technological economy subject to all the horrible vicissitudes of technological change, relieved by no basis for modifying or mitigating the direction of that change. (Witness the destruction of the neighborhood community Gans studied [12] by the "progress" of urban renewal. In other instances, we find the destruction of the self-respect of the working-class men of such neighborhoods when they become technologically unemployed by the automation of the factories.) Therefore, *these kinds* of mitigations of the merciless costs of the achievement drive can be but temporary refuge at best. Toward what kinds of goals can such adults reasonably orient their children for the future? And what kind of viable amalgam of love and authority can they provide these children?

More generally, in the institutions of this society, the achievement drives are countered and mitigated by the norms of "getting along" and a special version of "cooperativeness" in the socialization of the child, primarily in the secondary agencies of socialization (the school and the variety of adult-directed activities like camps, settlement houses, "community centers," and so on). Riesman sees "other-directedness" in these trends and suggests a new cooperative ethic is supplanting the competitive (or Protestant) ethic of the past. A different look, such as that provided by Jules Henry in his acid portrayal of *Culture Against Man*,[13] suggests that the cooperativeness and groupiness of such formations is spurious at best, a deceitful (but to the child not deceiving) cover for persisting individual com-

[12] Gans, *op. cit.*
[13] New York: Random House, 1963.

petitiveness. The children still have to achieve by (largely) individual effort, and getting grades is still the primary mechanism of reward for individual performance according to adult-set standards and of movement through the minutely graded system. However, to the skills of mobilizing abilities in directed tasks are now added the myriad and more complex skills of "getting along," "working with the group," "cooperating,"—in short, the whole repertoire of tactics of social manipulation and self-manipulation by which one pushes to personal success while appearing at least to remain a "good guy," vitally interested in the group. There is a fake collectivism here since the goals are not the collective prosperity of the group. The *means* of getting ahead have become more complex and subtle, but getting ahead—for oneself, for one's family at most—is still the objective. And getting ahead—success, whether based on substantive achievement or not—is still seen as the touchstone of personal identity in a society where such identity is never assured and where the very process of mobility (ideologically, "equality of opportunity") demanded and fostered by the industrial system, promotes a constant process of self-evaluation and self-doubt and constant invidious comparison of oneself and the co-runners of the race.

In fact, schools which promote a subtle combination of competitive and cooperative drives of the kind just discussed can be seen as socializing *well* for the kind of adult society these children's parents now live in. If these trends continue, these children as adults should be well adapted to the peculiar kind of status struggle involved. Such adaptation, of course, has its price, the signal one being the pervasive *status anxiety*. Anxiety is expectable from the ambiguities of the meaning of achievement or success, the ambiguities and insecurities of possible reward for the efforts and manipulations demanded, and the inherent instability of *any* status in a fluid "open-class" society. The anxiety may be further compounded by the fact that the values toward which the massive status striving is directed are hollow and empty of any obvious moral worth, in contrast with the simplicity and solidity of the values of a community like the Kibbutz or a religious sect. (Bettelheim points out that a term such as "happiness" does not occur in statements of the goals of life made by members of the Kibbutz—but rather is *assumed* to be a natural by-product of productive work, comradeship, and the sharing of collective ideals.) In its crudest versions, most widespread, "success" in America means material possessions. These bring zeal and gusto in their pursuit, and hollowness and emptiness in their attainment. Strident and anxious efforts to formulate meaningful "goals for Americans" (and failure to arrive at any) precisely at a time when most of the population is at its materially most prosperous level ever are a commentary on the hollowness of values of the society.

As mentioned, it is assumed that for America, socialization is a product of what the adults, especially the parents, do with and for the children. The peer groups of children themselves receive only secondary attention. Commonly we find them increasingly manipulated by (presumably well-meaning) adults, as in the pathetic phenomenon of the Little League baseball teams. This contrasts significantly with the large (perhaps even oppressive) role of the group of contemporaries in the Kibbutz. Significantly, there are some situations in modern America where the peer group seems to have an overriding importance in the socialization of the child—and that is in the delinquent gang. We may interpret this as meaning that the peer group is especially important only where the parents (and other adults) *fail* the child, providing neither viable authority and guidance, nor love, affection, emotional support, nor even (in the lower-class cases) elementary protection or material security. Though admirable in its refusal to believe the lies of the conventional agencies such as school and settlement house, and in its ruthless adoption of the real *operating* norms of the society (as against the sentimental *verbal* norms of democracy, fair play, and respect for the personality), the gang is, nonetheless, a recourse of desperation and futility. It is incapable, in the immaturity, shapelessness, and ego-weakness of its personnel, of constructing any viable counterculture to the chaotic environing world. (A significant phenomenon is their fawning on youth-board workers assigned to some such gangs, in pathetic expectations of his giving them meaning and strength in dealing with the world—while they are either individually unamenable to the striving-conforming demands the worker may make upon them, or if amenable, find themselves multiply blocked from "making it" in the world he beckons them to.)

There are a host of other problems in American socialization and personality development that have not been touched on at all as yet. Many of these will be dealt with as special topics in later portions of this book. At this point, however, it will be useful to look at another comparative case study from a different society, which has value in itself in relating personality to the patterns of a whole complex society and also comparatively to set off American socialization and personality. We turn then to one interesting study of personality in the contemporary Soviet Union.

2. THE SOVIET UNION: MODAL PERSONALITY TRENDS

In this part, we take a different tack. We introduce a study that is not concerned with socialization directly at all, but rather with *adult personality* patterns as these show certain commonalities in a selected group of a whole national population, commonalities seen as "modal personality trends." The paper deals with Great Russians of the Soviet Union and compares their "modal personality trends" with those of a matched selection of Americans.

Modal Personality and Adjustment to the Soviet Socio-political System[14]

ALEX INKELES, EUGENIA HANFMANN, AND HELEN BEIER

Two main elements are encompassed in the study of national character.[15] The first step is to determine what modal personality patterns, if any, are to be found in a particular national population or in its major subgroups. In so far as such modes exist one can go on to the second stage, studying the interrelations between the personality modes and various aspects of the social system. Even if the state of our theory warranted the drafting of an "ideal" research design for studies in this field, they would require staggering sums and would probably be beyond our current methodological resources. We can, however, hope to make progress

Thanks are due to the publishers of Human Relations *and Alex Inkeles, Eugenia Hanfmann, and Helen Beier for permission to reprint their article,* "Modal Personality and Adjustment to the Soviet Socio-Political System," *from Vol. 11 (1958).*

[14] Revised and expanded version of a paper read at the American Psychological Association Meetings in San Francisco, Sept. 1955. Daniel Miller read this early version and made many useful comments. The authors wish to express their warm appreciation for the prolonged support of the Russian Research Center at Harvard. Revisions were made by the senior author while he was a Fellow of the Center for Advanced Study in the Behavioral Sciences, for whose support he wishes to make grateful acknowledgment.

[15] For a discussion of the basic issues and a review of research in this field see Alex Inkeles and Daniel J. Levinson (17).

through more restricted efforts. In the investigation we report on here we studied a highly selected group from the population of the Soviet Union, namely, former citizens of Great Russian nationality who "defected" during or after World War II. We deal, furthermore, mainly with only one aspect of the complex interrelations between system and personality, our subjects' participation in an adjustment to their Communist socio-political order.[16] We find that certain personality modes are outstanding in the group, and believe that we can trace their significance for our subjects' adjustment to Soviet society.

SAMPLE AND METHOD

An intensive program of clinical psychological research was conducted as part of the work of the Harvard Project on the Soviet Social System.[17] The Project explored the attitudes and life experiences of former Soviet citizens who were displaced during World War II and its aftermath and then decided not to return to the U.S.S.R. Almost 3,000 completed a long written questionnaire, and 329 undertook a detailed general life history interview. The individuals studied clinically were selected from the latter group. Criteria of selection were that the interviewee seemed a normal, reasonably adjusted individual who was relatively young, had lived most of his life under Soviet conditions, and was willing to undertake further intensive interviewing and psychological testing.

The group studied clinically included 51 cases, 41 of whom were men. With the exception of a few Ukrainians, all were Great Russians. Almost half were under 30, and only 8 were 40 or older at the time of interview in 1950, which meant that the overwhelming majority grew up mainly under Soviet conditions and were educated in Soviet schools. Eleven had had a minimum education of four years or less, 22 between four and eight years, and 18 advanced secondary or college training. In residence the group was predominantly urban but if those who had moved from the countryside to the city were included with the rural, then approximately half fell in each category. As might be expected from the education data, the group included a rather large proportion of those in high-status occupations, with 11 professionals and members of the intelligentsia, 7 regular army officers, and 9 white-collar workers. Sixteen were

[16] For analysis of another aspect of the psychological properties of this group, see Eugenia Hanfmann (12).

[17] The research was carried out by the Russian Research Center under contract AF No. 33(038)12909 with the former Human Resources Research Institute, Maxwell Air Force Base, Alabama. For a general account of the purposes and design of the study see: R. Bauer, A. Inkeles, and C. Kluckhohn (2). The clinical study was conducted by E. Hanfmann and H. Beier. A detailed presentation is given in the unpublished report of the Project by E. Hanfmann and H. Beier (13).

rank-and-file industrial and agricultural workers, and 5 rank-and-file army men. In keeping with the occupational pattern but running counter to popular expectations about Soviet refugees, a rather high proportion were in the Party (6) or the Young Communist League (13). Again running counter to popular expectations about refugees, the group was not characterized by a markedly high incidence of disadvantaged family background as reflected either in material deprivation, the experience of political arrest, or other forms of repression at the hands of the regime. Ten were classified as having been extremely disadvantaged, and 15 as having suffered minor disadvantage.

All of the Soviet refugees have in common their "disaffection" with Soviet society. The clinical group included mainly the more "active" defectors who left Soviet control on their own initiative, rather than the "passive" who were removed by force of circumstance. Thirty-four had deserted from the military[18] or voluntarily departed with the retreating German occupation armies. In general, however, the clinical group was not more vigorously anti-Communist than the other refugees. They overwhelmingly supported the principles of the welfare state, including government ownership and state planning, and credited the regime with great achievements in foreign affairs and economic and cultural development. They refused to return for much the same reasons given by other refugees: fear of reprisal at the hands of the secret police, because of former oppression, opposition to institutions like the collective farm, or resentment of the low standard of living and the absence of political freedom. In psychological adjustment, finally, they seemed to reflect fairly well the tendency toward adequate adjustment which characterized the refugees as a whole.

With regard to the parent refugee population, then, the clinical group was disproportionately male, young, well-educated, well-placed occupationally and politically, and "active" in defecting.[19] In its internal composition, the sample was also unbalanced in being predominantly male, but otherwise gave about equal weight to those over and under 35, in manual vs. white-collar occupations, from urban or rural backgrounds, with education above or below the advanced secondary level.

Each respondent was interviewed with regard to his childhood experi-

---

18 This was in part a result of our selection procedure. The larger project was particularly interested in post-war defectors, almost all of whom came from the Soviet military occupation forces in Germany. Half of the men fell in that category.

19 The young post-war defectors on the whole did prove to be less stable and more poorly adjusted. Apart from this issue of adjustment or "integration," however, they shared with the rest of the sample much the same range of outstanding personality traits. Therefore, no further distinctions between that group and the rest are discussed in this paper. See E. Hanfmann and H. Beier (13).

ence, some aspects of his adult life, and his adjustment to conditions in a displaced persons' camp. Each took a battery of tests which included the Rorschach, TAT, a sentence-completion test of 60 items, a "projective questions" test including eight of the questions utilized in the authoritarian personality study, and a specially constructed "episodes" or problem-situations test. We regard the use of this battery of tests as a matter of special note, since most attempts to assess modal tendencies in small-scale societies have relied upon a single instrument, particularly the Rorschach. The various tests differ in their sensitivity to particular dimensions or levels of personality, and differentially reflect the impact of the immediate emotional state and environmental situation of the subject. By utilizing a series of tests, therefore, we hope that we have in significant degree reduced the chances that any particular finding mainly peculiar to the special combination of instrument, subject, and situation will have been mistakenly interpreted as distinctively Russian. In addition the use of this battery enables us to test our assumptions in some depth, by checking for consistency on several tests.

Each test was independently analyzed according to fairly standard scoring methods, and the results were reported separately.[20] In reporting their results, however, each set of analysts made some observations on the character traits which seemed generally important to the group as a whole. Further, in drawing these conclusions the analysts made use of a criterion group of Americans matched with the Russian sample on age, sex, occupation, and education. The availability of such test results posed a challenge as to whether or not these general observations, when collated and analysed, would yield any consistent patterns for the group as a whole.

To make this assessment we selected the eight major headings used below as an organizing framework. We believe that they permit a fairly full description of the various dimensions and processes of the human personality, and at the same time facilitate making connections with aspects of the social system. These categories were, however, not part of the design of the original clinical research program,[21] and were not used by the analysts of the individual instruments. While this circumstance

[20] On the "Episodes Test" a detailed report has been published, see Eugenia Hanfmann and J. G. Getzels (14). A brief account of results on the Projective Questions has also been published in Helen Beier and Eugenia Hanfmann (4). The other results were described in the following as yet unpublished reports of the Project, which may be examined at the Russian Research Center: Beier (3), Rosenblatt et al. (21), Fried (10), Fried and Held (11), Roseborough and Phillips (20).

[21] The basic categories were suggested to A. Inkeles by D. J. Levinson in the course of a seminar on national character, and are in part discussed in Inkeles and Levinson (17). They were somewhat modified for the purposes of this presentation.

made for lesser comparability between the tests, it acted to forestall the slanting of conclusions to fit the analytic scheme. The statements in the conclusions drawn by the analysts of each instrument were written on duplicate cards, sorted, and grouped under all the categories to which they seemed relevant. The evidence with regard to each category was then sifted and weighed, and where there were ambiguous findings the original tables were re-examined for clarification. Relevant impressions based on the interviews were also drawn on. Similarities and differences between those in our sample and the matching Americans aided in grasping the distinctive features of the Russian pattern. On this basis a characterization of the group was developed under each heading of the analytic scheme.

It should be clear that the sketch of modal personality characteristics presented below is not a simple and direct translation of particular test scores into personality traits. Rather, it is an evaluative, summary statement, following from the collation and interpretation of conclusions drawn from each test, conclusions which were in turn based both on test scores and on supplementary qualitative material. The word modal should not be taken too literally in this context. We have relied on some test scores when only a small proportion of the sample manifested the given response or pattern of responses, if this fits with other evidence in developing a larger picture. In stating our findings we have been freer with the evidence than some would permit, more strict than others would require. We attempted to keep to the canons of the exact method, without neglecting the clinical interpretations and insights. In this way we hoped to arrive at a rich and meaningful picture of the people studied, a picture that would provide an adequate basis for an analysis of their adjustment to the socio-political system.

BRIEF SKETCH OF RUSSIAN MODAL PERSONALITY CHARACTERISTICS

1. *Central needs.*[22] Since all human beings manifest the same basic needs, we cannot assert that some need is unique to a given national population. Among these universal needs, however, some may achieve greater strength or central importance in the organization of the personality, and in this sense be typical of the majority of a given group.

Probably the strongest and most pervasive quality of the Russian personality that emerged from our data was a need for *affiliation*. By this we mean a need for intensive interaction with other people in immediate, direct, face-to-face relationships, coupled with a great capacity for having this need fulfilled through the establishment of warm and personal contact with others. Our subjects seemed to welcome others into their lives as an indispensable condition of their own existence, and generally felt neither isolated nor estranged from them. In contrast to the

[22] See H. Murray (18). We do not strictly follow Murray in our use of the "need" terminology.

American subjects, the Russians were not too anxiously concerned about others' opinion of them and did not feel compelled to cling to a relationship or to defend themselves against it. Rather, they manifest a profound acceptance of group membership and relatedness. These orientations were especially prevalent in test situations dealing with relations between the individual and small face-to-face groups, such as the family, the work team, and the friendship circle.

Closely linked with the need for affiliation is a need for *dependence* very much like what Dicks (5) spoke of as the Russians' "strong positive drive for enjoying loving protection and security," care and affection. This need shows not only in orientation toward parents and peers, but also in the relations with formal authority figures. We did not, however, find a strong need for submission linked with the need for dependence, although Dicks asserts it to be present. In addition there is substantial evidence for the relatively greater strength of *oral* needs, reflected in preoccupation with getting and consuming food and drink, in great volubility, and in emphasis on singing. These features are especially conspicuous by contrast with the relative weakness of the more typically compulsive puritanical concern for order, regularity, and self-control. However, our data do not permit us to stress this oral component as heavily as does Dicks, who regards it as "typical" for the culture as a whole.

Several needs rather prominent in the records of the American control group did not appear to be of outstanding importance in the personality structure of the Russians. Most notable, the great emphasis on *achievement* found in the American records was absent from the Russian ones. Within the area of interpersonal relations our data lead us to posit a fairly sharp Russian-American contrast. Whereas the American records indicate great strength of need for *approval* and need for *autonomy*, those needs were rather weakly manifested by the Russians. In approaching interpersonal relations our American subjects seemed to fear too close or intimate association with other individuals and groups. They often perceived such relations as potentially limiting freedom of individual action, and therefore inclined above all to insure their independence from or autonomy within the group. At the same time the Americans revealed a strong desire for recognition and at least formal acceptance or approval from the group. They are very eager to be "liked," to be regarded as an "all right" guy, and greatly fear isolation from the group. Finally we note that certain needs important in other national character studies were apparently not central in either the American or the Russian groups. Neither showed much need for dominance, for securing positions of superordination, or for controlling or manipulating others and enforcing authority over them. Nor did they seem markedly distinguished in the strength of hostile impulses, of desires to hurt, punish, or destroy.

2. *Modes of impulse control.* On the whole the Russians have rela-

tively *high awareness* of their impulses or basic dispositions—such as for oral gratification, sex, aggression, or dependence—and, rather, *freely accept* them as something normal or "natural" rather than as bad or offensive.[23] The Russians show evidence, furthermore, of *giving in* to these impulses quite readily and frequently, and of *living them out*. Although they tended afterward to be penitent and admit that they should not have "lived out" so freely, they were not really punitive toward themselves or others for failure to control impulses. Of course, this does not mean complete absence of impulse control, a condition that would render social life patently impossible. Indeed, the Russians viewed their own impulses and desires as forces that needed watching, and often professed the belief that the control of impulses was necessary and beneficial. The critical point is that the Russians seemed to rely much less than the Americans on impulse control to be generated and handled from within. Rather, they appear to feel a need for aid from without in the form of guidance and pressure exerted by higher authority and by the group to assist them in controlling their impulses. This is what Dicks referred to as the Russians' desire to have a "moral corset" put on his impulses. The Americans, on the other hand, vigorously affirm their ability for *self-control*, and seem to assume that the possession of such ability and its exercise legitimates their desire to be free from the overt control of authority and the group.

In this connection we may note that the review of individual cases revealed a relative lack of well-developed *defensive structures* in many of the Russian subjects. Mechanisms that serve to counteract and to modify threatening feelings and impulses—including isolation, intellectualization, and reaction formation—seem to figure much less prominently among them than among the Americans. The Russians had fewer defenses of this type and those they had were less well established.

3. *Typical polarities and dilemmas.* Within certain areas of feelings and motives individuals may typically display attitudes and behavior that belong to one or the opposite poles of the given variable, or else display a preoccupation with the choice of alternatives posed by these poles. Such preoccupation may be taken to define the areas of typical dilemmas or conflicts, similar to the polarized issues, such as "identity vs. role diffusion" and "intimacy vs. isolation," which Erikson (6) found so important in different stages of psychological maturation.

In our Russian subjects we found a conscious preoccupation with the problem of *trust vs. mistrust* in relation to others. They worried about the intentions of the other, expressing apprehension that people may not really be as they seem on the surface. There was always the danger that

[23] Such a statement must, of course, always be one of degree. We do not mean to say that such threatening impulses as those toward incest are present in the awareness of Russians or are accepted by them more than by Americans.

someone might entice you into revealing yourself, only then to turn around and punish you for what you have revealed. Another typical polarity of the Russians' behavior is that of *optimism vs. pessimism*, or of faith vs. despair. One of our projective test items posited the situation that tools and materials necessary for doing a job fail to arrive. In responding to this item our Russian subjects tended to focus on whether the outcome of the situation will be good or bad for the actor, while the Americans at once sprang into a plan of action for resolving the situation. Finally, we may include under the typical polarities of the Russians' attitude that of *activity vs. passivity*, although in the case of this variable we found little indication of a sense of a conscious conflict. However, the subjects' choice of alternatives in the projective tests tended to be distributed between the active and the passive ones, while the Americans' preference for the active instrumental response was as clear-cut and strong as was their generally optimistic orientation.

The pronounced polarities of the Russians' orientation lend support to Dick's assertion that "the outstanding trait of the Russian personality is its contradictoriness—its ambivalence" (5). Two qualifications, however, must be kept in mind. First, the strength of our Russian subjects' dilemmas may have been greatly enhanced by the conditions of their lives, both in the Soviet Union and abroad. Second, the American subjects also show some involvement in problematic issues, though they were different from the Russian ones. Thus the problem of "intimacy vs. isolation" or "autonomy vs. belongingness," to which we have already alluded, seemed a major dilemma for Americans whereas it was not such an issue for the Russians.

4. *Achieving and maintaining self-esteem.*   In their orientations toward the self, the Russians displayed rather low and *unintense self-awareness* and little painful self-consciousness. They showed rather high and *secure self-esteem*, and were little given to self-examination and doubt of their inner selves. At the same time they were not made anxious by examination of their own motivation or that of others, but rather showed readiness to gain insight into psychological mechanisms. The American pattern reveals some contrasts here, with evidence of acute self-awareness, substantial self-examination, and doubting of one's inner qualities.

We were not able to discern any differences between Americans and Russians in the relative importance of *guilt* versus *shame* as sanctions. There were, however, some suggestive differences in what seemed to induce both guilt and shame. The Americans were more likely to feel guilty or ashamed if they failed to live up to clear-cut "public" norms, as in matters of etiquette. They were also upset by any hint that they were inept, incompetent, or unable to meet production, sports, or similar performance standards. The Russians did not seem to be equally disturbed by such failures, and felt relatively more guilty or ashamed when they assumed that they had fallen behind with regard to moral or interpersonal behavior norms, as in matters involving personal honesty, sincerity, trust, or loyalty to a friend. These latter qualities they value most highly and they demand them from their friends.

5. *Relation to authority.*[24]   Our clinical instruments presented the subjects with only a limited range of situations involving relations with authority. These did not show pronounced differences in basic attitudes between Russians and Americans, except that Russians appeared to have more fear of and much less optimistic expectations about authority figures. Both of these manifestations might, of course, have been mainly a reflection of their recent experiences rather than of deeper-lying dispositions. Fortunately, we can supplement the clinical materials by the life history interviews which dealt extensively with the individual's relations with authority. A definite picture emerges from these data. Above all else the Russians want their leaders—whether boss, district political hack, or national ruler—to be warm, nurturant, considerate, and interested in the individuals' problems and welfare. The authority is also expected to be the main source of initiative in the inauguration of general plans and programs and in the provision of guidance and organization for their attainment. The Russians do not seem to expect initiative, directedness, and organizedness from an average individual. They, therefore, expect that the authority will of necessity give detailed orders, demand obedience, keep checking up on performance, and use persuasion and coercion intensively to insure steady performance. A further major expectation with regard to the "legitimate" authority is that it will institute and enforce sanctions designed to curb or control bad impulses in individuals, improper moral practices, heathen religious ideas, perverted political procedures, and extreme personal injustice. It is, then, the government that should provide that "external moral corset" which Dicks says the Russian seeks.

An authority that meets these qualifications is "good," and it does what it does with "right." Such an authority should be loved, honored, respected, and obeyed. Our Russian subjects seemed, however, to expect that authority figures would in fact frequently be stern, demanding, even scolding and nagging. This was not in and of itself viewed as bad or improper. Authority may be, perhaps ought to be, autocratic, so long as it is not harshly authoritarian and not totally demanding. Indeed, it is not a bad thing if such an authority makes one rather strongly afraid, makes one "quake" in expectation of punishment for trespassing or

---

[24] Relations to authority may be thought of as simply one aspect of a broader category—"conceptions of major figures"—which includes parents, friends, etc. We have included some comments on the Russians' perceptions of others under "cognitive modes" below.

wrongdoing. Such an authority should not, however, be arbitrary, aloof, and unjust. It should not be unfeeling in the face of an open acknowledgment of one's guilt and of consequent self-castigation. Indeed, many of our subjects assumed that authority can in fact be manipulated through humbling the self and depicting oneself as a weak, helpless person who needs supportive guidance rather than harsh punishment. They also assumed that authority may be manipulated by praise or fawning, and seduced through the sharing of gratificatory experiences provided by the supplicant—as through the offer of a bottle of liquor and the subsequent sharing of some drinks. Russians also favor meeting the pressure of authority by evasive tactics, including such devices as apparently well-intentioned failure to comprehend and departures from the scene of action.

Throughout their discussions of authority our respondents showed little concern for the preservation of precise forms, rules, regulations, exactly defined rights, regularity of procedure, formal and explicit limitation of powers, or the other aspects of the traditional constitutional Anglo-Saxon approach to law and government. For the Russians a government that has the characteristics of good government listed above justifies its right to rule by virtue of that performance. In that case, one need not fuss too much about the fine points of law. By contrast, if government is harsh, arbitrary, disinterested in public welfare—which it is apparently expected to be more often than not—then it loses its right to govern no matter how legal its position and no matter how close its observance of the letter of the law.

6. *Modes of affective functioning.* One of the most salient characteristics of the Russian personality was the high degree of their *expressiveness* and emotional aliveness. On most test items the Russian responses had a stronger emotional coloring, and they covered a wider range of emotions, than did the American responses. Their feelings were easily brought into play, and they showed them openly and freely both in speech and in facial expression, without much suppression or disguise. In particular they showed a noticeably greater *freedom and spontaneity in criticism* and in the expression of hostile feelings than was true for the Americans. There were, further, two emotions which the Russians showed with a frequency far exceeding that found in the Americans— *fear*, and *depression* or despair. Many of the ambiguous situations posited in the tests were viewed by them in terms of danger and threat, on the one hand, and of privation and loss, on the other. Undoubtedly this was in good part a reflection of the tense social situation which they had experienced in the Soviet Union, and of their depressed status as refugees, but we believe that in addition deeper-lying trends were here being tapped. These data provide some evidence in support of the oft-noted prevalence of depressive trends among the Russians.

7. *Modes of cognitive functioning.* In this area we include characteristic patterns of perception, memory, thought, and imagination, and the processes involved in forming and manipulating ideas about the world around one. Of all the modes of personality organization it is perhaps the most subtle, and certainly in the present state of theory and testing one of the most difficult to formulate. Our clinical materials do, however, permit a few comments.

In discussing people, the Russians show a keen *awareness of the "other"* as a distinct entity as well as a rich and diversified recognition of his special characteristics. Other people are usually perceived by them not as social types but as concrete individuals with a variety of attributes distinctly their own. The Russians think of people and evaluate them for what they are rather than in terms of how they evaluate ego, the latter being a more typically American approach. The Russians also paid more attention to the "others' " basic underlying attributes and attitudes than to their behavior as such or their performance on standards of achievement and accomplishment in the instrumental realm.

Similar patterns were evident in their perception of interpersonal situations. In reacting to the interpersonal relations "problems" presented by one of the psychological tests they more fully elaborated the situation, cited more relevant incidents from folklore or their own experience, and offered many more illustrations of a point. In contrast, the Americans tended more to describe the formal, external characteristics of people, apparently being less perceptive of the individual's motivational characteristics. The Americans also tended to discuss interpersonal problems on a rather generalized and abstract level. With regard to most other types of situation, however, especially problems involving social organization, the pattern was somewhat reversed. Russians tended to take a rather broad, sweeping view of the situation, *generalizing* at the expense of detail, about which they were often extremely vague and poorly informed. They seemed to feel their way through such situations rather than rigorously to think them through, tending to get into a spirit of grandiose planning but without attention to necessary details.

8. *Modes of conative functioning.* By conative functioning we mean the patterns, the particular behavioral forms, of the striving for any valued goals, including the rhythm or pace at which these goals are pursued and the way in which that rhythm is regulated. In this area our clinical data are not very rich. Nevertheless, we have the strong impression that the Russians do not match the Americans in the vigor of their striving to master all situations or problems put before them, and to do so primarily through adaptive instrumental orientations. Although by no means listless, they seem much more *passively accommodative* to the apparent hard facts of situations. In addition, they appeared less apt to persevere systematically in the adaptive courses of action they did under-

take, tending to backslide into passive accommodation when the going proved rough. At the same time, the Russians do seem capable of great bursts of activity, which suggests the bi-modality of an *assertive-passive pattern* of strivings in contrast to the steadier, more even, and consistent pattern of strivings among the Americans.

To sum up, one of the most salient characteristics of the personality of our Russian subjects was their emotional aliveness and expressiveness. They felt their emotions keenly, and did not tend to disguise or to deny them to themselves, nor to suppress their outward expression to the same extent as the Americans. The Russians criticized themselves and others with greater freedom and spontaneity. Relatively more aware and tolerantly accepting of impulses for gratification in themselves and others, they relied less than the Americans on self-control from within and more on external socially imposed controls applied by the peer group or authority. A second outstanding characteristic of the Russians was their strong need for intensive interaction with others, coupled with a strong and secure feeling of relatedness to them, high positive evaluation of such belongingness, and great capacity to enjoy such relationships. The image of the "good" authority was of a warm, nurturant, supportive figure. Yet our subjects seemed to assume that this paternalism might and indeed should include superordinate planning and firm guidance, as well as control or supervision of public and personal morality, and if necessary, of thought and belief. It is notable, in this connection, that in the realm of conative and cognitive functioning orderliness, precision of planning, and persistence in striving were not outstandingly present. Such qualities were rather overshadowed by tendencies toward overgeneralizing, vagueness, imprecision, and passive accommodation. Countering the image of the good authority, there was an expectation that those with power would in fact often be harsh, aloof, and authoritarian. The effect of such behavior by authority is alienation of loyalty. This fits rather well with the finding that the main polarized issues or dilemmas were those of "trust vs. mistrust" in relations with others, "optimism vs. pessimism," and "activity vs. passivity," whereas the more typically American dilemma of "intimacy vs. isolation" was not a problem for many Russians. Though strongly motivated by needs for affiliation and dependence and wishes for oral gratification—in contrast to greater strength of needs for achievement, autonomy, and approval among the Americans—our Russian subjects seemed to have a characteristically sturdy ego. They were rather secure in their self-estimation, and unafraid to face up to their own motivation and that of others. In contrast to the Americans, the Russians seemed to feel shame and guilt for defects of "character" in interpersonal relations rather than for failure to meet formal rules of etiquette or instrumental production norms. Compared with the Americans, however, they seemed relatively lacking in well-developed and stabilized defenses with which to counteract and modify threatening impulses and feelings. The organization of their personality depended for its coherence much more heavily on their intimate relatedness to those around them, their capacity to use others' support and to share with them their emotions.

RELATIONS OF MODAL PERSONALITY AND THE
SOCIO-POLITICAL SYSTEM

In the following comments we are interpreting "political participation" rather broadly, to cover the whole range of the individual's role as the citizen of a large-scale national state. We, therefore, include his major economic and social as well as his specifically political roles. This may extend the concept of political participation too far for most national states, but for the Soviet Union, where all aspects of social life have been politicized, it is the only meaningful approach. Specifically, the questions to which we address ourselves are as follows:

Assuming that the traits cited above were widespread among the group of Great Russians studied by our project, what implications would this have for their adjustment to the role demands made on them by the social system in which they participated? To what extent can the typical complaints of refugees against the system, and the typical complaints of the regime against its own people, be traced to the elements of non-congruence between these personality modes and Soviet social structure?

A full answer to these questions would involve us in a much more extensive presentation and a more complex analysis than is possible here. We wish to stress that our analysis is limited to the Soviet socio-political system as it typically functioned under Stalin's leadership (see Bauer *et al.*, 2, and Fainsod, 7), since this was the form of the system in which our respondents lived and to which they had to adjust. To avoid any ambiguity on this score we have fairly consistently used the past tense. We sincerely hope that this will not lead to the mistaken assumption that we regard the post-Stalin era as massively discontinuous with the earlier system. However, to specify in any detail the elements of stability and change in post-Stalin Russia, and to indicate the probable effects of such changes on the adjustment of Soviet citizens to the system, is beyond the scope of this paper. As for the personality dimensions, we will discuss each in its relations to system participation separately, rather than in the complex combinations in which they operate in reality. Only those of the personality traits cited above are discussed that clearly have relevance for the individual's participation in the socio-political system.

Need affiliation.   Virtually all aspects of the Soviet regime's pattern of operation seem calculated to interfere with the satisfaction of the Russians' need for affiliation. The regime has placed great strains on friendship relations by its persistent programs of political surveillance, its encouragement and elaboration of the process of denunciation, and its assignment of mutual or "collective" responsibility for the failings of particular individuals. The problem was further aggravated by the regime's insistence that its élite should maintain a substantial social distance between itself and the rank-and-file. In addition, the regime developed an institutional system that affected the individual's relations with others in a way that ran strongly counter to the basic propensities of the Russians as represented in our sample. The desire for involvement in the group, and the insistence on loyalty, sincerity, and general responsiveness from others, received but little opportunity for expression and gratification in the tightly controlled Soviet atmosphere. Many of the primary face-to-face organizations most important to the individual were infiltrated, attacked, or even destroyed by the regime. The break-up of the old village community and its replacement by the more formal, bureaucratic, and impersonal collective farm is perhaps the most outstanding example, but it is only one of many. The disruption and subordination to the state of the traditional family group, the Church, the independent professional associations, and the trade unions are other cases in point. The regime greatly feared the development of local autonomous centers of power. Every small group was seen as a potential conspiracy against the regime or its policies. The system of control required that each and all should constantly watch and report on each other. The top hierarchy conducted a constant war on what it scornfully called "local patriotism," "back-scratching" and "mutual security associations," even though in reality it was attacking little more than the usual personalizing tendencies incidental to effective business and political management. The people strove hard to maintain their small group structures, and the regime persistently fought this trend through its war against "familyness" and associated evils. At the same time it must be recognized that by its emphasis on broad group loyalties, the regime probably captured and harnessed somewhat the propensities of many Russians to give themselves up wholly to a group membership and to group activity and goals. This is most marked in the Young Communist League and in parts of the Party.

Need orality. The scarcity element that predominated in Soviet society, the strict rationed economy of materials, men, and the physical requirements of daily life seem to have aroused intense anxieties about further oral deprivation that served greatly to increase the impact of the real shortages that have been chronic to the system. Indeed, the image of the system held by most in our sample is very much that of an orally depriving, niggardly, non-nurturant leadership. On the other hand, the regime can hope to find a quick road to better relations with the population by strategic dumping or glutting with goods, which was to some extent attempted during the period of Malenkov's ascendancy, although perhaps more in promise than reality.

Need dependence. The regime took pride in following Lenin in "pushing" the masses. It demanded that individuals be responsible and carry on "on their own" with whatever resources were at hand, and clamored for will and self-determination (see Bauer, 1). Clearly, this was not very congruent with the felt need for dependent relations. At the same time the regime had certain strengths relative to the need for dependence. The popular image of the regime as one possessed of a strong sense of direction fits in with this need. Similarly it gained support for its emphasis on a massive formal program of social-welfare measures, even if they were not too fully implemented. This directedness has a bearing also on the problem of submission. Although the regime had the quality of a firm authority able to give needed direction, it did not gain as much as it might because it was viewed as interested in the maximation of power *per se*. This appears to alienate the Russian as he is represented in our sample.

The trust-mistrust dilemma.   Everything we know about Soviet society makes it clear that it was extremely difficult for a Soviet citizen to be at all sure about the good intentions of his government leaders and his immediate supervisors. They seemed always to talk support and yet to mete out harsh treatment. This divided behavior pattern of the leadership seemed to aggravate the apparent Russian tendency to see the intentions of others as problematical and to intensify the dilemma of trust-mistrust. On the basis of our interviews one might describe this dilemma of whether or not to grant trust as very nearly *the* central problem in the relations of former Soviet citizens to their regime. The dilemma of optimism vs. pessimism, of whether outcomes will be favorable or unfavorable, presents a very similar situation.

The handling of shame.   The regime tried exceedingly hard to utilize public shame to force or cajole Soviet citizens into greater production and strict observance of the established rules and regulations. Most of our available public documentary evidence indicates that the regime was not outstandingly successful in this respect. Our clinical findings throw some light on the reason. The regime tried to focus shame on non-performance, on failures to meet production obligations or to observe formal bureaucratic rules. To judge by the clinical sample, however, the Russian is little shamed by these kinds of performance failures, and is more likely to feel shame in the case of moral failures. Thus, the Soviet Russian might be expected to be fairly immune to the shaming pressures of the regime. Indeed, the reactions of those in our sample suggest the tables often get turned around, with the citizen concluding that it is the regime which should be ashamed because it has fallen down in these important moral qualities.

Affective functioning.   The general expansiveness of the Russians in our sample, their easily expressed feelings, the giving in to impulse, and the free expression of criticism, were likely to meet only the coldest reception from the regime. It emphasized and rewarded control, formality, and lack of feeling in relations. Discipline, orderliness, and strict observance of rules are what it expects. Thus, our Russian subjects could hope for little official reward in response to their normal modes of expression. In fact, they could be expected to run into trouble with the regime as a result of their proclivities in this regard. Their expansiveness and tendency freely to express their feelings, including hostile feelings, exposed them to retaliation from the punitive police organs of the state. And in so far as they did exercise the necessary control and avoided open expression of hostile feelings, they experienced a sense of uneasiness and resentment because of this unwarranted imposition, which did much to color their attitude to the regime.

Conative functioning. The non-striving quality of our Russian subjects ties in with the previously mentioned characteristics of dependence and non-instrumentality. The regime, of course, constantly demanded greater effort and insisted on a more instrumental approach to problems. It emphasized long-range planning and deferred gratification. There was a continual call for efforts to "storm bastions," to "breach walls," "to strive mightily." With the Russian as he is represented in our sample, it does not appear likely that the regime could hope to meet too positive a response here; in fact it encountered a substantial amount of rejection for its insistence on modes of striving not particularly congenial to a substantial segment of the population. Indeed, the main influence may have been exerted by the people on the system, rather than by the system on them. Soviet official sources have for many years constantly complained of the uneven pace at which work proceeds, with the usual slack pace making it necessary to have great, often frenzied, bursts of activity to complete some part of the Plan on schedule, followed again by a slack period. It may well be that this pattern results not only from economic factors such as the uneven flow of raw material supplies, but that it also reflects the Russian tendency to work in spurts.

Relations to authority. In many ways the difficulties of adjustment to the Soviet system experienced by our subjects revolved around the gap between what they *hoped* a "good" government would be and what they *perceived* to be the behavior of the regime. Our respondents freely acknowledged that the Soviet leaders gave the country guidance and firm direction, which in some ways advanced the long-range power and prestige of the nation. They granted that the regime well understood the principles of the welfare state, and cited as evidence its provision of free education and health services. The general necessity of planning was also allowed, indeed often affirmed, and the regime was praised for taking into its own hands the regulation of public morality and the conscious task of "raising the cultural level" through support of the arts and the encouragement of folk culture.

SOCIALIZATION: SOME PROBLEMS IN LARGE-SCALE SOCIETIES 226

Despite these virtues, however, the whole psychological style of ruling and of administration adopted by the Bolsheviks seems to have had the effect of profoundly estranging our respondents. A great gulf seemed to separate the rulers and the ruled, reflected in our respondents' persistent use of a fundamental "we"-"they" dichotomy. "They" were the ones in power who do bad things to us, and "we" were the poor, ordinary, suffering people who, despite internal differences in status or income, share the misfortune of being oppressed by "them." Most did not know that Stalin had once asserted that the Bolsheviks could not be a "true" ruling party if they limited themselves "to a mere registration of the sufferings and thoughts of the proletarian masses" (23). Yet our respondents sensed this dictum behind the style of Soviet rule. They reacted to it in charging the leaders with being uninterested in individual welfare and with extraordinary callousness about the amount of human suffering they engender in carrying out their plans. Our subjects saw the regime as harsh and arbitrary. The leaders were characterized as cold, aloof, "deaf" and unyielding to popular pleas, impersonal and distant from the people's problems and desires. The regime was seen not as firmly guiding but as coercive, not as paternally stern but as harshly demanding, not as nurturant and supportive but as autocratic and rapaciously demanding, not as chastening and then forgiving but as nagging and unyieldingly punitive.

The rejection of the regime was however by no means total, and the Bolshevik pattern of leadership was in many respects seen not as totally alien but rather as native yet unfortunately exaggerated. This "acceptance" did not extend to the coldness, aloofness, formality, and maintenance of social distance, which were usually rejected. It did, however, apply to the pressures exerted by the regime, which were felt to be proper but excessive. Coercion by government was understandable, but that applied by the regime was not legitimate because it was so harsh. The scolding about backsliding was recognized as necessary, but resented for being naggingly persistent and caustic. And the surveillance was expected, but condemned for being so pervasive, extending as it did even into the privacy of one's friendship and home relations, so that a man could not even hope to live "peacefully" and "quietly." The elements of acceptance within this broader pattern of rejection have important implications for the future of the post-Stalin leadership. They suggest that the regime may win more positive support by changing the mode of application of many of its authoritarian and totalitarian policies without necessarily abandoning these policies and institutions as such. Indeed in watching the public behavior of men like Khrushchev and Bulganin one cannot help but feel that their style of leadership behavior is much more congenial to Russians than was that of Stalin.

The preceding discussion strongly suggests that there was a high de-

gree of incongruence between the central personality modes and dispositions of many Russians and some essential aspects of the structure of
Soviet society, in particular the behavior of the regime. Most of the
popular grievances were clearly based on real deprivations and frustrations, but the dissatisfactions appear to be even more intensified and
given a more emotional tone because they were based also on the poor
"fit" between the personality patterns of many Soviet citizens and the
"personality" of the leaders as it expressed itself in the institutions they
created, in their conduct of those institutions and the system at large,
and in the resultant social climate in the U.S.S.R.

SOCIAL CLASS DIFFERENTIATION

Since personality traits found in the Russian sample are merely modal
rather than common to the group at large, it follows that sub-groups can
meaningfully be differentiated by the choice of appropriate cutting
points on the relevant continua. As a way of placing the individuals in
our sample on a common scale, three elements from the total range of
characteristics previously described were selected. They were chosen on
the grounds that they were most important in distinguishing the Russians as a group from the Americans, and also because they seemed
meaningfully related to each other as elements in a personality syndrome. The three characteristics were: great strength of the drive for
social relatedness, marked emotional aliveness, and general lack of well-
developed, complex, and pervasive defenses. The two clinicians rated all
cases for a combination of these traits on a three-point scale. Cases
judged on the basis of a review of both interview and test material to
have these characteristics *in a marked degree* were placed in a group
designated as the "primary set." Individuals in whom these characteristics were clearly evident, but less strongly pronounced, were designated
as belonging to a "variant" set. The "primary" and "variant" sets together constitute a relatively homogeneous group of cases who clearly
revealed the characteristics that we have described as "modal." All the
remaining cases were placed in a "residual" category, characterized by
markedly stronger development of defenses, and in most instances also
by lesser emotional expressiveness and lesser social relatedness. This group
was relatively the least homogeneous of the three because its members
tended to make use of rather different combinations of defenses without
any typical pattern for the set as a whole. Subjects placed in the "residual" group appeared to differ more from those in the "variant" set than
the "primary" and the "variant" sets differed from each other. However,
even the "residual" pattern was not separated from the others by a very
sharp break: emotional aliveness and relatedness to people were present
also in some members of this group. Each of our 51 cases was assigned to
one of four social-status categories on the basis of occupation and educa-

tion. All those in group A were professionals and higher administrative personnel most of whom had university training, and all those in the D group were either peasants, or unskilled or semi-skilled workers with no more than five years of education. Placement in the two intermediary categories was also determined by the balance of occupation and education, group B consisting largely of white-collar workers and semi-professional and middle supervisory personnel, and group C of more skilled workers with better education.

Table 3.1 gives the distribution of cases among the three personality types within each of the four status groups. It is evident that the primary pattern has its greatest strength in the lower classes, becomes relatively less dominant in the middle layers, and plays virtually no role at all in the top group. The "residual" pattern predominates at the top level and is very rare among peasants and ordinary workers.[25]

Table 3.1

STATUS DISTRIBUTION OF PERSONALITY TYPES
AMONG FORMER SOVIET CITIZENS

Status	Primary	PERSONALITY TYPE Variant	Residual	Total
A	—	1	12	13
B	2	8	6	16
C	3	4	2	9
D	8	3	2	13
TOTAL	13	16	22	51

Since the distinctive patterns of adjustment to the Soviet system by the various socio-economic groups will be the basis of extensive publications now in progress, we restrict ourselves here to a few general observations. First, we wish to stress that, as our interviews indicate, both the more favored and the rank-and-file share substantially the same range of complaints against the regime, find the same broad institutional features such as the political terror and the collective farm objectionable, and view the same welfare features such as the system of education and free medical care as desirable. In spite of these common attitudes our data suggest that personality may play a massive role with regard to some aspects of participation in and adjustment to the socio-political system.

[25] The method of assigning the cases to the three psychological groups was holistic and impressionistic. It is of interest to note, therefore, that when more exact and objective techniques were used on the Sentence Completion Test to rate a similar but larger sample of refugees on some differently defined personality variables, the relationship between occupation and education and the personality measures was quite marked in three out of five variables. See M. Fried (10).

The educational-occupational level attained and/or maintained by an individual in an open-class society is one of the major dimensions of such participation. This is particularly the case in the Soviet Union, where professional and higher administrative personnel are inevitably more deeply implicated in the purposes and plans of the regime, are politically more active and involved, and are subjected to greater control and surveillance. It seems plausible that persons in whom the affiliative need was particularly strong, expressiveness marked and impulse control weak, and the defensive structures not well developed or well organized would be handicapped in competition for professional and administrative posts in any society; they certainly could not be expected to strive for or to hold on to positions of responsibility in the Soviet system.

The pattern of marked association between certain traits of personality and educational-occupational level clearly invites a question as to whether the personality really affected the level attained and held, or whether the appropriate personality traits were merely acquired along with the status. This question raises complex issues which we cannot enter into here. We do wish to point out, however, that the characteristics on which our psychological grouping was based belong to those that are usually formed at an early age and are relatively long enduring and resistant to change. At first glance this affirmation of the early origins of the patterns described seems to be inconsistent with their observed association with educational-occupational level. However, the contradiction exists only if one assumes that obtaining a higher education and a superior occupation in Soviet society is a matter either of pure chance or exclusively of ability, unrelated to family background and the person's own attitudes and strivings. The data on stratification and mobility in Soviet society show, however, that persons born into families of higher social and educational level have a much better chance than do others to obtain a higher education and professional training (Feldmesser, 8; see also Inkeles, 15). Consequently, many people of the professional and administrative class grew up in families of similar status, and in those families were apparently reared in a way different from that typical of the peasant and worker families.[26] Presumably this produced enduring effects on their personality formation, which were important prior to exposure to common educational experience.

In addition, mobility out of the lower classes may have been mainly by individuals whose personality was different, for whatever reason, from that of the majority of their class of origin. Such differences can easily express themselves in a stronger drive for education and for a position of status. We must also allow for the role played by the regime's deliberate selection of certain types as candidates for positions of responsibility.

[26] For a detailed discussion of *class differences* in the child-rearing values of pre-Soviet and Soviet parents see Alice Rossi (22).

Finally, there is the less conscious "natural selection" process based on the affinity between certain personality types and the opportunities offered by membership in the élite and near-élite categories. In this connection we are struck by the relative distinctness of the highest status level in our sample, since only one person with either of the two variants of the modal personality of the rank-and-file shows up among them. These results bear out the impression, reported by Dicks, of radical personality differences and resultant basic incompatibilities between the ruled population and the rulers. The latter, we assume, are still further removed from the "modal pattern" than are our subjects in the élite group.

We have yet to deal with the question of how far our observations concerning a group of refugees can be generalized to the Soviet population and *its* adjustment to the Soviet system? The answer to this question depends in good part on whether personality was an important selective factor in determining propensity to defect among those in the larger group who had the opportunity to do so.[27] It is our impression that personality was not a prime determinant of the decision not to return to Soviet control after World War II. Rather, accidents of the individual's life history such as past experience with the regime's instruments of political repression, or fear of future repression because of acts which might be interpreted as colloboration with the Germans, seem to have been the prime selective factors. Furthermore, such experiences and fears, though they affected the loyalty of the Soviet citizen, were not prime determinants of his pattern of achievement or adjustment in the Soviet sociopolitical system.[28] The refugee population is not a collection of misfits or historical "leftovers." It includes representatives from all walks of life and actually seemed to have a disproportionately large number of the mobile and successful.

Though we are acutely aware of the smallness of our sample, we incline to assume that the personality modes found in it would be found within the Soviet Union in groups comparable in nationality and occupation. We are strengthened in this assumption by several considerations. First, the picture of Russian modal personality patterns which emerges from our study is highly congruent with the traditional or classic picture of the Russian character reported in history, literature, and cur-

[27] It is impossible to estimate accurately how many former Soviet citizens had a real chance to choose not to remain under Soviet authority. The best available estimates suggest that at the close of hostilities in Europe in 1945 there were between two and a half and five million former Soviet citizens in territories outside Soviet control or occupation, and of these between 250,000 and 500,000 decided and managed to remain in the West. See G. Fischer (9).

[28] Evidence in support of these contentions is currently being prepared for publication. A preliminary unpublished statement may be consulted at the Russian Research Center: A. Inkeles and R. Bauer (16).

rent travellers' accounts.[29] Second, much of the criticism directed by the regime against the failings of the population strongly suggests that some of the traits we found modal to our sample and a source of strain in its adjustment to the system are widespread in the population and pose an obstacle to the attainment of the regime's purposes *within* the U.S.S.R. Third, the differences in personality between occupational levels are consistent with what we know both of the general selective processes in industrial occupational systems and of the deliberate selective procedures adopted by the Soviet regime. Because of the methodological limitations of our study, the generalization of our findings to the Soviet population must be considered as purely conjectural. Unfortunately we will be obliged to remain on this level of conjecture as long as Soviet citizens within the U.S.S.R. are not accessible to study under conditions of relative freedom. We feel, however, that, with all their limitations, the findings we have reported can be of essential aid in furthering our understanding of the adjustment of a large segment of the Soviet citizens to their socio-political system and of the policies adopted by the regime in response to the disposition of the population.

REFERENCES

1. Bauer, R. *The New Man in Soviet Psychology.* Cambridge, Mass.: Harvard University Press, 1952.
2. Bauer, R., Inkeles, A., and Kluckhohn, C. *How the Soviet System Works.* Cambridge, Mass.: Harvard University Press, 1956.
3. Beier, Helen. "The Responses to the Rorschach Test of the Former Soviet Citizens." Unpublished Report of the Project. Russian Research Center, March 1954.
4. Beier, Helen, and Hanfmann, Eugenia. "Emotional Attitudes of Former Soviet Citizens as Studied by the Technique of Projective Questions." *J. abnorm. soc. Psychol.,* Vol. 53, pp. 143-53, 1956.
5. Dicks, Henry V. "Observations on Contemporary Russian Behaviour." *Hum. Relat.,* Vol. V, pp. 111-74, 1952.
6. Erikson, Erik. *Childhood and Society.* New York: Norton, 1950.
7. Fainsod, Merle. *How Russia is Ruled.* Cambridge, Mass.: Harvard University Press, 1953.
8. Feldmesser, R. "The Persistence of Status Advantages in Soviet Russia." *Amer. J. Sociol.,* Vol. 59, pp. 19-27, July 1953.
9. Fischer, G. *Soviet Opposition to Stalin.* Cambridge, Mass.: Harvard University Press, 1952.
10. Fried, Marc. "Some Systematic Patterns of Relationship between Personality and Attitudes among Soviet Displaced Persons." Unpublished Report of the Project. Russian Research Center, October 1954.
11. Fried, Marc, and Held, Doris. "Relationships between Personality and At-

[29] After this article was completed we discovered a report based almost entirely on participant observation which yielded conclusions about modal personality patterns among Soviet Russians extraordinarily similar to those developed on the basis of our tests and interviews. See: Maria Pfister-Ammende (19).

titudes among Soviet Displaced Persons: A Technical Memorandum on the Derivation of Personality Variables from a Sentence Completion Test." Unpublished Report of the Project. Russian Research Center, August 1953.

12. Hanfmann, Eugenia. "Social Perception in Russian Displaced Persons and an American Comparison Group." *Psychiatry*, Vol. XX, May 1957.

13. Hanfmann, Eugenia, and Beier, Helen. "Psychological Patterns of Soviet Citizens." Unpublished Report of the Project. Russian Research Center, August 1954.

14. Hanfmann, Eugenia, and Getzels, J. G. *Interpersonal Attitudes of Former Soviet Citizens as Studied by a Semi-Projective Method. Psychol. Monogr.,* Vol. 69, No. 4, whole number 389, 1955.

15. Inkeles, A. "Stratification and Social Mobility in the Soviet Union: 1940-1950." *Amer. sociol. Rev.,* Vol. 15, pp. 465-79, August 1950.

16. Inkeles, A., and Bauer, R. "Patterns of Life Experiences and Attitudes under the Soviet System." Russian Research Center, October 1954.

17. Inkeles, A., and Levinson, Daniel J. "National Character: The Study of Modal Personality and Sociocultural Systems." In G. Lindzey (ed.), *Handbook of Social Psychology,* Vol. II, pp. 977-1020. Cambridge, Mass.: Addison-Wesley, 1954.

18. Murray, H. *Explorations in Personality.* New York: Oxford University Press, 1938.

19. Pfister-Ammende, Maria. "Psychologische Erfahrungen mit sowetrussischen Fluchtlingen in der Schweiz." In M. Pfister-Ammende (ed.), *Die Psychohygiene: Grundlagen und Ziele.* Bern: Hans Huber, 1949.

20. Roseborough, H. E., and Phillips, H. P. "A Comparative Analysis of the Responses to a Sentence Completion Test of a Matched Sample of Americans and Former Russian Subjects." Unpublished Report of the Project. Russian Research Center, April 1953.

21. Rosenblatt, Daniel, Slaiman, Mortimer, and Hanfmann, Eugenia. "Responses of Former Soviet Citizens to the Thematic Apperception Test (TAT): An Analysis Based upon Comparison with an American Control Group." Unpublished Report of the Project. Russian Research Center, August 1953.

22. Rossi, Alice. "Generational Differences among Former Soviet Citizens." Unpublished Ph.D. thesis in sociology, Columbia University, 1954.

23. Stalin, J. *Leninism.* New York: Modern Books. Vol. I, pp. 95-6, 1933.

Discussion: Russians and Americans

The paper just presented is a bold attempt to make generalizations about personality development in a whole national society on the basis of a limited number of cases intensively studied, with a "control group" similarly studied from a different national society. Though it must be admitted that the fact that twenty-two of the fifty-one persons studied (about 43 percent) differed importantly from the "modal type" considerably vitiates the notion that there can be one standard or dominant personality trend for the whole society, still the fact that the *range* for the Russians was substantially different than the range for the matched American group, does seem to be an important first step in making broad comparisons and contrasts in something that may loosely be called "national character"—as long as we keep in mind the qualifications that have to be made to allow for the differences within each of the national groups.

The findings on the Russians are intriguing in relation to questions about socialization. Since the pressures of the Stalin-period Soviet regime were in many respects pointedly in opposition to many of the "modal" personality trends depicted, and since these pressures would be stronger on adults than on juveniles, the authors seem to have a good case to argue that the personality trends depicted—the emotional aliveness, the great need for interpersonal warmth and affiliation, the need for a strong, nurturing, and demanding authority—are in fact "deep-seated," that is, based upon early and crucial socialization experiences. Since communal nurseries did not play more than a brief and limited experimental role in Soviet child rearing, the crucial socializers must have been members of the *family*. Though the data given do not reveal its prevalence for the persons intensively studied in this case, one role that has been widespread in Soviet child rearing has been that of the *grandmother*. She has a major part in the early infant care and training, with the mother actively engaged in the formal occupational structure. This would be consistent with the indication given in the paper that the "modal" type represents the *older* Russian character structure as can be interpreted from pre-Bolshevik Russian literature. The persistence of these trends in the face of the revolutionary changes brought by the Revolution, especially the *deliberate* efforts of the regime to create a "new Soviet man," would be the more easily understandable if grandmothers have in fact been among the important (if not crucial) early socialization agents, for they could clearly provide more continuity with traditional Russian ways than the younger generation of mothers. However, this would still not have to be a major part of the picture. The parents of these subjects would certainly have been raised under the pre-Soviet traditional Russian standards, and more important than that, the features explored in this paper concern the deepest (and possibly least changeable) aspects of personality functioning. Such depth trends would presumably reflect the influence of strong *unconscious* forces of the parental (and grandparental) personalities, as communicated phatically to the infant and young child. The centrality of oral needs in the "modal personality" picture is consistent with these assumptions.

Interestingly, the grossly uneven representation of the different class levels as between modal and non-modal types, rather than challenging the validity of the modal analysis, if anything strengthens it. For the "residuals" do not fall into any one single personality pattern, but vary among themselves in the ways in which they differ from the modal types. In consequence there is stronger homogeneity among the approximately 57 percent who do fit, at least rather closely, the modal patterns. This seems to support the authors' implication that there is one modal trend, which is a traditional Russian character, but that variations from it are appearing. Evidently this is occurring because of the regime's deliberate efforts, but not according to any one single pattern that fits congruently with the regime's image of the ideal Soviet man.

These findings underline the general line of analysis we have been following, especially what we have drawn from Dennis Wrong's paper: that socialization is never complete and total, never totally congruent with the demands of the society—and we may now add, may even be significantly out of line with the "requirements" of the particular society. Inkeles, Hanfmann, and Beier show us some of the *costs* for the persons involved and for the society (in this case the regime) of such incongruence.

RUSSIAN CHILD-REARING VALUES

The results of another study by Inkeles drawing on the same research, provide some interesting side commentaries.[30] Inkeles compared the values governing child rearing of the Tsarist period parents with those of the post-Revolutionary period parents by coding what Soviet refugees who were over forty-five years of age in 1950 (who, therefore, were born before 1905 and were young adults during the Revolution) said about *their* parents' ways of raising them and *their* ways of raising their own children in the post-Revolutionary period. The values inferred were classified into six categories: Tradition (emphasis on religion or strong family ties); Adjustment (getting along, staying out of trouble); Achievement (attainments, industriousness, mobility, material rewards); Personalistic (honesty, sincerity, justice, mercy); Intellectuality (learning, knowledge, as ends); Political (values dealing with the government). His findings are set forth in Table 3.2.

The findings show both persistence and change: persistence in that,

[30] Alex Inkeles, "Social Change and Social Character: the Role of Parental Mediation," *Journal of Social Issues*, Vol. II, No. 2, 1955, pp. 12-23.

Table 3.2

CHILD-REARING VALUES OF PARENTS IN RUSSIAN
PRE-REVOLUTIONARY AND POST-REVOLUTIONARY TIMES

Values	Emphasis in Tsarist Period	Post-Revolution
Tradition	75 percent[n]	44 percent
Achievement	60	52
Personalistic	32	44
Adjustment	16	21
Intellectuality	12	22
Politics	12	20

[n] This means 75 percent of the respondents mention this theme as applying to the values of the parent generation indicated.

with one major and one minor exception, the rank *ordering* of the six values is much the same in each generation. Changes are the sharp decline in the importance of family tradition and religion, and the increased emphasis on learning (intellectuality) and on positive personal qualities as ends in themselves. Though achievement has the top rank order for the later generation, in absolute weight it *declined* from the Tsarist generation—contrary to Inkeles' original expectations (perhaps attributable to the refugee nature of the sample population).

These data do not say much about specific socialization techniques and emotional settings, but they do document that while a general hierarchy of values persists from one generation to the next (despite almost cataclysmic changes in social structure), the new adult generation of the immediate post-Revolutionary period did not duplicate their parents' socialization emphases completely. These did shift in directions consonant with the social-political changes brought by the new regime. Another part of Inkeles' findings shows that the criteria of parental pressures on the child's *occupational* choice also shifted, away from family tradition to greater emphasis on self-expression of free job choice, a shift consistent with the decline of tradition and the rise of "personalistic" orientations in the general value picture given above.

AMERICANS SEEN IN THE LIGHT OF THE RUSSIANS

The modal personality paper provides a basis for elaboration of the picture of socialization and personality which we began to draw earlier in this chapter. The indications are that the Inkeles group used a selection of Americans matched in age, education, and occupation to the Russian refugee group; hence we assume roughly 57 percent of the group were "middle class" (professionals, supervisors, white collar) and 43 percent working class. From the data offered, we do not discover whether the trends where the Americans differ importantly from the Russians are more true of the middle class than of the working class. It seems safe to assume (on the basis of all the other sources of knowledge about class differences in the United States) that the picture *does* better represent the middle class than the working class. But if we ignore that question, the fact that the Americans *generally* are systematically different from the Russians in these respects is certainly significant. Let us recapitulate the major differences the Inkeles group found, in the form of a characterization of the Americans.

The Americans show strong needs for achievement, approval, and recognition from others and for autonomy. In line with the achievement need, they show great concern about meeting *performance* standards and less concern with how they shape up in terms of moral character. They seem to fear too close or intimate association with other individuals and groups.[31] They emphasize control of impulses from *within*. They proudly affirm this self-control and assume it justifies their freedom from overt control by an authority or a group. Faced by threatening feelings and impulses, Americans use defenses such as isolation, intellectualization, and reaction formation. Their most strongly felt dilemmas are between intimacy and isolation and between autonomy and belongingness. They have an acute self-awareness and are much given to self-examination and self-doubt. They deal with others in terms of how the others seem to evaluate them (rather than on the basis of the intrinsic qualities of the others), and they tend to describe others in terms of formal characteristics, such as status, occupation, age, rather than in terms of inner qualities. They strive to master all situations and problems put before them; they do so by adaptive instrumental orientations. In Americans, guilt or shame is evoked by failures in formal rules of behavior, such as etiquette, or in formal production norms.

[31] Compare the common Latin American observation that North Americans always back away when you get very close to them (physically) or touch them when conversing with them. Since Latin Americans (evidently in common with Russians) want and enjoy such closeness, a conversation between a Latin and a North American becomes a kind of comic dance, with the Latin constantly trying to come closer, the North American constantly backing away.

This whole picture is remarkably consistent with observations from other sources and elaborates what we have discussed earlier (see part 1 of this chapter) in the direction of the inner dynamics. What we have here is a very strong ego set to self-driving and -striving, intense individualization and self-scrutiny, and the whole individualistic mastery-activism complex. The superego formation is basically repressive: intense impulse control from within and denial of Eros wherever it might be expressed in terms of intense interpersonal relatedness. The costs of this personality formation are shallowness and constriction in relationships with others, defensive backing away from any close relationships, and loneliness marked with longing for (but inability to achieve) intimacy with others. This person wants desperately to be liked, to be approved, and to be recognized. He reacts strongly to such reactions (or their negatives) from others he deals with. He is capable of shallow friendliness to large numbers of others, but scarcely of any intimacy with any. Hence the *stereotyping* of relations to the others, as reflected in concentrating on their *formal* (hence external or extrinsic) characteristics.

The picture we have here combines the features of both the inner-directed and the other-directed character of Riesman's types (suggesting that an amalgam of both—dynamically related as indicated just above—is the persistent American character trend, rather than one giving way historically to the other as Riesman suggests). If these are the features of people aged twenty to forty-five in 1950, hence born between 1905 and 1930, is this then a picture soon to be outdated with the coming to maturity of the next generation, which presumably (according to Bronfenbrenner's findings) has undergone a much more permissive socialization, especially in reference to impulse expression, and less obsessive emphasis upon the achievement drives? It would be of great interest to see some kind of replication of the Inkeles study with young adults in the late 1960s. Failing such information, do we have any indications? It does seem likely that the proportion of the Soviet population who would be classified as "residuals" in Inkeles' categories, would increase over time, if successive post-Stalin regimes (as seems likely) are able to provide enough reward gratifications for personality trends moving away from the traditional "modal" Russian type. At the same time, it also seems likely that the American patterns are moving in the opposite direction, away—though perhaps not drastically—from the character pattern just described. Thus the two populations may be becoming less distinguishable in the *ranges* of their personality types, though the ranges would be quite large in each case. Still it is difficult to see any trends in American social structure that would favor anything close to the traditional "modal" Russian personality type appearing here, since the whole industrialization process in the Anglo-Protestant West seems to have obliterated or at least strongly discouraged anything like the Russian trends which may have existed in some portions of the American population, notably in immigrants from Eastern or Southern Europe.

3. SPECIAL AGENCIES OF SOCIALIZATION: FAIRY TALES IN A MODERN SOCIETY

In all societies one of the major ways of inducting the young into the moral values and prevailing ideas of the culture is by telling stories. Between the folk tales characteristic of all primitive societies and their analogues in stories told by the mass media in modern societies stands the special kind of story called the "fairy tale." The fairy tale develops materials from preliterate origins, through a medieval setting, into a more or less standardized form in published literature (but also perpetuated orally) into modern times. In the early nineteenth century the Brothers Grimm as a deliberate socialization device published a collection of fairy tales. Sociologist Henry Carsch in the following paper has attempted to analyze their efforts.

Fairy Tales and Socialization: the Fairy in Grimms' Tales
HENRY CARSCH

L'absurde c'est la raison lucide qui constate ses limites.

CAMUS

I

This paper constitutes a part of a comprehensive report dealing with the Grimm Brothers' *Fairy Tales*.[32] The Grimm Brothers had begun to collect these tales from a number of informants and literary sources in

Original paper published here for the first time. Henry Carsch is Associate Professor in the Department of Sociology and Anthropology at Carleton College, Northfield, Minnesota.
[32] Grimm (Brüder), *Die Kinder und Hausmärchen* (Reutlingen: R. Bardtenschlager Verlag, 1956), is the source referred to in the present analysis. Specific tales are referred to by the designation KHM and a number, as they appear in the indicated edition.

1805 when Napoleon invaded Germany and when, as a result, a good many Germans had become concerned with problems of national as well as cultural autonomy. It was the explicit intention of the authors to save from extinction something which they thought to be quintessentially German and which they hoped to forge into an instrument of socialization. The patriotism which they wished to promulgate would achieve the preservation of a valuable cultural heritage, and also specific national purposes. In this, they were undoubtedly guided by the platonic notion that those political myths, fables, and legends which were calculated to create a distinctive cosmology in the minds of the citizenry would serve to induce the appropriate conduct.[33] ". . . the times of national decline . . . ," wrote Hermann Grimm, ". . . would have been impossible, had German historical presence and Germanic thinking been made the basis of our popular education." [34]

Such a stance would appear to approximate closely established positions in the social sciences: Folk tales, the orally transmitted precursors of Fairy Tales, are reported to be present in every known society. Testimony to some of the importance which is attached to such folk tales derives from the ritualistic, if not ceremonial, manner which characterizes their presentation in a wide variety of societies. Thus, tales are told by specially selected raconteurs, at particular times and in specified settings.[35]

The characteristically European folk tale, however, seems to have been more of a family affair, flourishing in cottages on long winter evenings when there was little work to be done. Eventually, it was the invention of the printing press which made possible the systematic collection and distribution of folk tales, and with this begins the history of what is now known as fairy tales.[36]

One of the earliest anthologies of fairy tales was Giovan Francesco Strapola's Le piacevolli notti (Venice, 1550) which was followed by Basile's Pentamerone in 1635 and by Charles Perrault's Contes des Fées in 1696, which started a veritable flood of "fairy tales" composed by a plethora of French ladies, who were as much impressed by Perrault's

---

[33] Plato, The Republic (Cleveland: The World Publishing Co., 1946), p. 69; Andrew Hacker, Political Theory (New York: The Macmillan Company, 1961), p. 44; R. M. MacIver, The Web of Government (New York: The Macmillan Company, 1947), pp. 39-54.

[34] J. Grimm, Deutsche Sagen (München: Winkler Verlag, 1865), p. 27.

[35] For a detailed discussion of the anthropology and history of folk tales and fairy tales, see Henry Carsch, Dimensions of Meaning and Value in a Sample of Fairy Tales. Unpublished Ph.D. dissertation, Department of Sociology, Princeton University, 1965.

[36] The earliest written antecedents of fairy tales, the Sumerian Gilgamesh date to about 2000 B.C. There also exist a series of Egyptian papyri dating to about 1200 B.C. and the Indian Pancantantra dating to A.D. 750. Diverse Arabic manuscripts containing fairy tales are of as yet undetermined antiquity.

success as with his characteristic idiom. Perhaps the most notable of these was one Madame de Murat, author of *Le Cabinet des Fées*, which expanded from eight volumes on first publication in 1749 to forty-one volumes in its 1785 edition; Raspe's German amplification, *Das Cabinett der Feen* (1761); and finally F. J. Bertuch's own fairy tales, *Die Blaue Bibliothek aller Nationen* in eleven volumes (1790). Many of the tales of these earlier collections remain either intact or slightly modified in the Grimms' anthologies. Their first edition, product of the brothers' combined efforts, was published in 1813 and 1815. The brothers differed on the nature and scope of the editing to be undertaken. The older, Jacob, tended to reject all modifications, while the younger, Wilhelm, wanted to render the tales more "fairy-tale-like" and to fashion them into an *Erziehungsbuch*, a book by means of which to bring up children.[37]

Significant modifications of content (revealed by a close comparison of the two editions) involved many changes in the status of *dramatis personae*, especially of authority figures. Mothers were changed to stepmothers (as in Snow White), and princesses became millers' daughters. In addition, thirty-three tales were excluded altogether, being replaced by others. Significantly, of the excluded tales, three involved princesses who bore illegitimate children, one was entitled "the Mother-in-Law," two were versions of "Blue Beard," and one, entitled "How Children Played at Being Butchers," violated all sentiments but the expectations suggested by the title.

That Wilhelm Grimm introduced such modifications reflects his deliberate socialization intentions, and is consistent with Riesman's statement that even in preliterate societies, "the stories are modulated for and built into the web of values which obtain in a society at a given time." [38] The preliterate society "depends for conformity on its oral traditions, its myths, legends and songs." However, when they are put into printed form the efficiency of such forms of socialization increases. The number of "story tellers" is reduced,[39] the message becomes consequently more uniform, and to the extent that the children may read themselves, the attention of the audience is guaranteed.

II

An analysis of the fairies in relation to the other *dramatis personae* in Grimm's stories has significant implications with respect to socialization and the conscious *Erziehungsbuch*-intentions of Wilhelm Grimm.[40]

---

[37] As he put it in his postscript to the Second edition, 1819. See Carsch, *op. cit.* for fuller discussion and citation of sources.

[38] Riesman *et al. op. cit.*, p. 87.

[39] *Ibid.*, p. 93f.

[40] The present analysis is but a small part of a systematic research treating the

WHO AND WHAT ARE THE FAIRIES?

The concept of "Fairy" is an old one, deriving either from Old French *faerie* (related to Anglo-Saxon *aelf* and Old High German *alp*)[41] or from Old French *vair*[42] but probably did not gain literary currency until Perrault's publication *Les Contes des Fées* in 1696. While the elf image (probably an early formulation) has survived changes which the word has undergone, elves do not occur in the Grimms' tales. However, these tales do show a close connection between Fairies and Witches, who owe their existence in the popular rhetoric to their salient role in pre-Christian fertility cults distributed widely in Europe. Witches' magic was believed to influence events in both nature and society: by incantations they were believed to be capable of ruining an entire harvest; and by means of philters or potions they were held to be able either to inhibit or to consummate sexual desire. Remarkably, the nature of witchcraft and the role of witches seemed to have remained largely unchanged from Roman times until about 1750, when after over 500 years of progressive persecution the Church seems finally to have repressed the practice. However, while in Roman and medieval belief, any witch may perform both beneficial and malevolent acts, in the Grimms' tales we find a split between benevolent and sagacious old women on the one hand and malevolent and shrewd old women on the other. Yet in one guise or another, the old fertility function of these women has persisted: in each of the fifteen tales in which fairies occur, their primary purpose is to in-

---

whole corpus of the Grimms' tales sociologically, as though they constituted an autonomous community. For full details, see Carsch, *op. cit.*

The basic methodological procedures are as follows: The study begins with a complete "census" in which each person, animal and object was carefully observed and registered in terms of the relationships in which he, she, or it were found. The "population" was divided into status categories, e.g. king, fisherman, cat, shoes, etc. I then analyzed the interaction of each occupant of such a category with each of his alters, in terms of conventional categories of age, sex, and socio-economic position. From this analysis could be determined the degree to which the roles associated with a given position varied systematically, as distinct from being assigned arbitrarily. Careful comparison of the social interaction of each of the relevant episodes, and of the context of each such interaction, made it possible to establish that the roles assigned to the person or objects of the appropriate status did in fact display that measure of organic unity which would justify our treating these tales as if they were an independent social collectivity. In fact, the analysis does show that kind of consistency and organic unity, as the present phase of the analysis will indicate.

41 Hence the Alps, i.e., land of the fairies, a sort of glacial counterpart to the mermaids. The German word *Fee* was in fact not used by the Grimms, probably because of its French origin (fée), but the German word "Märchen" is translated as "fairy tale."

42 ". . . *Cinderalle portait une pantouffle de vair* . . ." homophonous also with *verre* = glass, hence glass slipper. The two possible etymologies are given in J. T. Shipley, *A Dictionary of Word Origins* (New York: The Philosophical Library, 1945), pp. 189-90.

crease eligibility for or facilitate advantageous marriages of their protégés.[43]

THE ROLE OF THE FAIRIES IN GRIMMS' TALES

Old women with magical powers and insight into the problems and aims of their protégés occur in fifteen out of the two-hundred of the Grimms' tales. Their purposes would appear to be of a compensatory nature, and in this role they are mostly rewarding (but also punitive in four instances). Characteristically, they appear without warning when needed (that is, when the protégé has been deprived in some way), bestow a gift, and disappear as quickly when their services have been completed, without incurring obligation on the part of their protégés. There are altogether twenty-seven fairies[44] interacting with a total of thirty-one protégés. There are slightly more tales where fairies interact with female protégées than tales where they deal with male protégés (10:8). In six tales, the protégés are adults. How the fairies interact with their protégés varies systematically according to the age and sex status of the latter. Age and sex determine the vulnerability to the particular form of deprivation to which Fairies address themselves in these tales, and which in turn determines the nature of the magic gift bestowed by the Fairy.

The stories can be classified on the basis of the type of deprivation incurred by the protégé.

Deprivation of Paternal Support and Protection: Three tales are involved,[45] in each the protégée is a young girl, but accessory protégés, all males, occur in one of these.[46]

Deprivation of Maternal Support and Protection: Six tales are involved.[47] In four of these the protégée is a young girl, while in the remaining two tales there are both boys and girls presented as protégés.[48] Mothers are absent, and children are left to the tender mercies of stepmothers.

Miscellaneous Malfaisance: In five of these six tales[49] the protégé is a male, in only one a female; but each of the protégés is an adult. In

[43] Actually, this becomes apparent in four of these tales in which the old women occupy a position intermediate between fairy and witch. *Cf.* KHM Nos. 29, 50, 93, and 135. Moreover one of the tales goes to the trouble to point out that the fairy is not in fact a witch. *Cf.* KHM 178.

[44] This constitutes approximately 2.6 percent of the total "human" population of these tales.

[45] KHM 9, 50, 178.

[46] KHM 9.

[47] KHM 24, 95, 128, 139, 185, 187.

[48] KHM 95, 139.

[49] KHM 29, 89, (93), 120, 131, (135).

addition, all of the tales in which the "Fairy" is intermediate in status between Fairy and Witch are in this category.[50] The forms of victimization include theft, financial exploitation, interference in love and marriage, attempts at usurpation of status, and attempted murder.

Let me now select for detailed analysis one story from each of these categories:[51]

Deprivation of Paternal Support and Protection: KHM 178. "The Goose-Girl at the Well."

Summary

A king wishes to know which of his three daughters loves him most so that he can leave her his kingdom. The first two daughters flatter him while the third tells him that the best food does not taste well in the absence of salt. She loves him like she loves salt. The king is furious and has her led into a forest with a sack of salt tied to her back. She encounters an old woman (Fairy) who gives her a mask which makes her look old and haggard, provides food and shelter in return for the girl's herding geese. The Fairy encounters a young count hiking through the forest who offers to help her carry firewood to her cottage. The Fairy accepts the offer, leads him to the cottage where he encounters the "goose girl," and gives him a box containing a precious gem as a reward for his trouble. The count leaves and after three days arrives at the court of the king. He presents the queen with the Fairy's gift. The queen faints and subsequently explains that her youngest daughter used to cry "perles" just like the one in the box. The decision is made to find the girl. En route, the count finds the girl washing in a brook in the moonlight and without the mask. He falls in love with her. A reunion is effected, the king deplores having given his kingdom away, but the Fairy informs him that the tears his daughter cried for her parents are worth more anyway. They turn into "perles," the Fairy disappears, the cottage turns into a castle, and the young couple marry.

Structure

Analysis of the relevant episodes of the tale reveals the following structure: The king rejects his youngest daughter in favor of the two older ones on the false premise that she does not love him as much as they do. He soon regrets his rash decision to have forced her to leave her home. As the consequence of her father's rejection, the girl is now without home and protection and faces serious dangers to her health and future. She has not resolved her ties with her parents (cries "perles"). The Fairy appears and provides a substitute home, protection (including a com-

---

[50] The parentheses of KHM numbers indicate such intermediate status.
[51] Selections were made on the basis of simplicity of plot.

plete disguise), a husband, and finally effects the reunion between the girl and her parents.

Deprivation of Maternal Support and Protection: KHM 24: "Mrs. Holle."

Summary

A widow has an ugly and lazy daughter and a beautiful and diligent stepdaughter. She accords preferential treatment to the real daughter while the stepdaughter is forced to do all of the work and must weave by the well in the street. Finally, hard work causes the stepdaughter's fingers to bleed, the blood soiling the spool which she drops into the well accidentally on trying to clean it. The stepmother is furious at this and commands the girl to retrieve the spool. In desperation, the girl jumps into the well and loses consciousness. When she regains consciousness, she finds herself lying on a meadow near an oven filled with bread and close to an apple tree full of ripe apples. On request of the Fairy who appears, the girl pulls the bread out of the oven and shakes the tree, gathering up the apples and stacking them in neat piles. The girl wanders through the meadow and finally arrives at a cottage, whose occupant, an old woman with large teeth, invites her to stay in return for doing domestic work. The girl consents and remains for a time working well until she feels homesick. She then asks the Fairy (the old woman) to let her go back up to join her people. The Fairy grants her request and leads her to a gate from which falls a rain of gold, some of which sticks to the girl as she passes through it. This is the reward for your diligence, says the Fairy, giving her the spool at the same time. When she returns to her home with her wealth, the Mother [sic] wants to procure the same riches for the other daughter who, on instructions, promptly jumps down the well also. The same events are repeated, but the stepsister refuses to pull the bread from the oven or to shake the apples from the tree, or to work properly for the Fairy. The latter soon dismisses her, and when she passes through the gate on her way home, she is covered with tar which cannot be removed.

Structure

This story has the following structure: The stepmother loves her real daughter and not her stepdaughter, whom she mercilessly exploits. She values the spool more than her stepdaughter. For fear of further denigration and punishment or perhaps in the hope of receiving a modicum of love, the stepdaughter jumps down the well. The Fairy appears providing a substitute home, food, and, finally, great wealth as a reward for the stepdaughter's diligence, orderliness, and miscellaneous domestic skills. When the stepdaughter returns home wealthy, her stepmother gives her a warm welcome. The real daughter, having demonstrated her lack of diligence and capacity for domestic work, returns home permanently unattractive.

Miscellaneous Malfaisance: KHM 131.
  "The Shoes That Were Danced to Pieces."

Summary

All of a king's twelve daughters sleep together in a room. The king himself locks the door at night. However, each morning when he unlocks the door, he finds that his daughters' shoes are worn out from dancing. The king announces that whoever finds out where his daughters spend their nights could marry one of them and assume the throne after his death. But only three nights are allotted for the task, and unsuccessful candidates are to be decapitated. A number of princes attempt to solve the mystery, but they all fall asleep at the crucial time and pay with their lives. A poor, wounded ex-soldier is en route to the town when he meets an old woman who asks him what he is about. He informs her that he is not quite sure but adds half in jest that he would not mind finding out where the twelve princesses dance at night. The Fairy replies that that would not be difficult and that he must not drink any wine that he will be offered. She gives him a cloak which will render him invisible so that he can follow the girls. With that, the soldier makes up his mind and goes to the castle.

He is well received and given a room adjoining the princesses'. He pretends to drink the wine offered him by the oldest princess and soon pretends to be fast asleep. In the meantime the girls dress for the dance and descend, beds and all, into the bowels of the earth. (Hell?) There they find themselves in an alley lined with trees which bear leaves of silver, gold, and diamonds. They go down the alley and finally come to a big "water" (Styx?) where twelve princes with little boats await their arrival. Each prince takes a princess into his little boat and rows her across the lake to a castle where an orchestra composed of drums and trumpets has already begun to play. The soldier has followed them in his cloak and sees all of this. The next day he reports these events to the king, showing him branches of the subterranean trees that he brought back for this purpose. He marries the oldest princess, but the princes, whose subterranean existence is due to a spell, must continue under that spell for as many more days as they spent nights dancing with the princesses.

Structure

Here the relevant episodes have the following structure: The king has lost control over his children. Other members of the nobility are unable to restore order. A military man is interested in the situation but lacks courage to intervene. A Fairy gives him strategic advice, the necessary implements, and confidence. He successfully investigates the problems at court and is instrumental to the king's being able to restore order. He is rewarded by marriage to one of the princesses and by the promise of the throne.

III

The question arises how such literature may be seen as an "agent of socialization." In this connection we shall ask two questions: 1. What are the meanings attributable to these tales? 2. In what manner are such meanings communicated to the audience? To guard against undisciplined speculation, in each endeavor we rely on theoretical formulations that are supported by the body of the data.

DELINEATION OF RELEVANT THEORETICAL FORMULATIONS

A first point of departure may be called Resolution of Ambiguity and the Establishment and Maintenance of Shared Perspectives in Society. Thus in their analysis of the Navaho, Kluckhohn and Leighton[52] write:

> . . . adjustments and adaptations [of societies] are always selective. Almost always more than one solution is objectively possible. The choices which a people make, and the emphasis which they give to one problem at the expense of another, bear a relationship to the things they regard as especially important . . . each different way of life makes assumptions about the ends and purposes of human existence, about what human beings have a right to expect from one another and from the gods . . .

The implications would appear to be as follows:

(1) Societies are faced with a series of ambiguities which need to be resolved in order to promote and perpetuate collective action. Such resolution is possible if the relevant selectivities are subject to consensus. "Solutions" of ambiguities must be collective ones, and, being related to the ends and purposes of human life as conceived in a given society, reflect the *logos* (the ideational basis) of that society.[53] (2) Men have reciprocal obligations with one another and the supernatural. Reciprocal normative expectations involve "exchanges" in which "input" is balanced by "return" which may ultimately lead to the establishment of an equilibrium. (3) *What* is being exchanged in such mutual expectations,

---

[52] C. Kluckhohn and D. Leighton, *The Navaho* (Cambridge: Harvard University Press, 1946), p. 216.

[53] See G. Bateson, *Naven* (Stanford, Calif.: The University Press, 1958), Chapters 14 and 15, for detailed discussion.

varies from one society to another: quantitatively (that is, in measurable units of objects) and qualitatively, including the affective dimension of behavior. Thus we deal with the culturally patterned assignment of meanings and values to objects and object relationships. Dimensions for such analysis include: (a) the *equilibrium* or *discord* of the situation; (b) *homeomorphic* exchanges (elements exchanged are similar in quality, as in *lex talionis*) as distinct from *heteromorphic* exchanges (the elements are dissimilar, as in "love" for "protection");[54] and (c) symmetrical exchanges (participants in egalitarian relationships) as distinct from *complementary* exchanges (one participant superordinate to the other).[55]

APPLICATION OF SUCH THEORETICAL FORMULATIONS

We may now apply these formulations to a further analysis of the tales introduced.

The first tale deals with the ambiguities of love between a father and his daughter. The king's problem is this: To which of his three daughters should he leave his kingdom? His solution: to the one who loves him the most. We may presume that until he raised this question harmony prevailed in the family, but this is strained as the king tries to measure his "input" (love, protection, nurturance, etc.) against his "returns" of love and obedience. Precisely this attempt brings the project to grief: the older girls reply in superficial and conventionalized terms of limited value, while the youngest, resorting to a more original and thoughtful idiom, is not understood at first. That is, the king is unaware that she is actually saying just what he wants to hear.

The father's rejection and abandonment of his part of the exchange puts the girl into great difficulty. She is prepared only to relate reciprocally with another person, but not to enter a series of exchanges with the anonymous outer world. She has not resolved her ties with her parents, but continues to love and cry ("perles") for them while carrying on her back the bag of salt as testimony to her continuing obedience. It is the Fairy who restores the equilibrium by standing in *loco parentis*, providing food, shelter, protection (the disguise), considerable wealth, a husband, a reunion with her parents, and eventually a castle. In return, the girl works for her, herding geese and keeping house. Significantly, however, the Fairy, once her task is accomplished, disappears again, leaving her protégée without any further obligation.

The second tale deals with the ambiguity of the consequences of the absence of a mother. Instead there is a stepmother who forces the step-daughter into maximizing her "input" in exchange for minimal "re-

[54] See A. W. Gouldner, "The Norm of Reciprocity," *American Sociological Review*, Vol. 25, No. 2, April 1960, pp. 172f.

[55] Margaret Mead, *Male and Female*. New York: William Morrow, (1949), pp. 63-65.

turns." Worse still, the reverse is true between stepmother and her "real" daughter, whose "input" is minimal and whose "returns" are maximal. With the Fairy, both girls are given the opportunity to partici- pate in a harmonious form of reciprocity: the real daughter's "input" falls short, and she is given a just "return" by the premature termination of the relationship, and by being rendered permanently unattractive (tarring). The stepdaughter's "input" is more than satisfactory, and her "return" is permanent attractiveness and wealth. The Fairy also com- pensates the stepmother for the financial strain of the stepchild by pro- viding the latter with wealth, thereby apparently facilitating the harmo- nious relationship which ensues.

The third tale deals with ambiguities on two levels: disobedience on the part of the princesses vis-à-vis their father; and irresponsibility on the part of the king vis-à-vis the wounded ex-soldier, unable to find employ- ment and discharged without compensation. The reciprocities which are violated are those of the princesses who owe obedience to their father and those of the king who should have compensated the soldier on his dis- charge. The princesses, however, do not seem to be held responsible for their "underground" ventures. Rather it is the princes who must expiate the nights they have spent "dancing" with the girls, for their spell is prolonged by an equivalent period. The soldier, on the other hand, re- ceives advice and aid from the Fairy which enables him ultimately to marry one of the princesses, with the consequent prospect of the throne.

Thus the ambiguities here discussed involve the mutual expectations of persons toward each other and the consequences of the violation of the relevant expectations, as exemplified by reciprocal exchanges.

MAINTENANCE AND PERPETUATION OF CONSENSUS

The selective attribution of specific meanings and values determines the norms governing the nature of interpersonal relationships. Such shar- ing of meanings and values determines normative expectations and facili- tates concerted action by members of the society vis-à-vis the relevant goals. Yet the promotion of the appropriate degree of consensus is a difficult process: not only must members of the society be persuaded to accept such meanings and to resist the temptation of appealing alterna- tives, but also the meanings must be kept alive in memory and attitude.[56] To accomplish all of this, the meanings and values so attributed must be: (1) *simple* enough to be amenable to the widest possible diffusion; (2) *attractive*, that is, defensible against alternative formulations; (3) *dangerous to violate*; and (4) *interesting*, that is, amenable to repeated presentation. These criteria are closely interrelated.

[56] E. Durkheim, *Les formes élémentaires de la vie religieuse*. Paris: Alcan, 1912, pp. 246ff.

Simplicity.   The apparently simple notion that a daughter should be obedient and affectionate to her father in return for love, nurturance, and protection is met by the multiplicity of other "love" relationships in which the girl is involved—mother, sisters, future boy friends, lovers, husband, children—requiring her to discriminate quantities and qualities of "input" in each of these. Social systems tend to integrate such congeries of attributed meanings and values into systems of belief—"ideologies" or "myths." [57] However designated, it is the knitting together of selectively resolved ambiguities into more or less self-sustaining systems of belief, amenable to a simplified formulation, which greatly facilitates their diffusion.

Attractiveness.   The relative attractiveness of a belief system may be demonstrated in the manner and degree to which it guarantees desirable returns to those involved. Relevant practices may be invested with the halo of proven precedent and tradition, suggesting that doing things as they have always been done is to be in harmony with the ontogenetic dimension of society and perhaps with one's deceased ancestors.[58] Attractiveness is enhanced by delineating palpable rewards for abiding by the belief systems, such as positive sanctions by social or supernatural agencies, or generally, predictable continuities. Connections between agents of the supernatural and notions of the traditional are significant here.

Dangers of violation.   The implicit notion here is that a measure of threat may be needed to reinforce the message. The important mechanisms are again: investing relevant behavior with the halo of precedent and tradition, hence violation of the beliefs may result in unknown and potentially undesirable consequences (that is, give rise to the initial ambiguities); and delineation of the undesirable effects of violation in concrete terms, such as negative sanctions by social or supernatural agencies.

Interest.   Repeated articulation of belief systems and their component parts as such risks boredom in the audience. This can be avoided by presenting the beliefs in idiomatic contexts and devices. The most important of these, for our purposes, are *dramatization* and *overdetermination*. Dramatization of a belief system means presenting it in terms of violent contrasts, converting the abstract into concrete forms, and presenting putative cause-and-effect relationships in highly exaggerated

[57] See T. Parsons, *The Social System* (New York: Free Press of Glencoe, 1951), pp. 349, 351, 352 for the former formulation. For the latter, see Durkheim, *op. cit.* (New York: Free Press of Glencoe, 1950), pp. 101, 418, 421, 428-29; B. Malinowski, *Sex and Repression in Savage Society* (New York: Meridian Books, 1955), p. 101; and R. MacIver, *op. cit.*, p. 4f. The relative merits of these different formulations are outside our present concern.

[58] See Bateson, *op. cit.*, p. 250; B. Malinowski, *Magic, Science and Religion* (New York: Doubleday & Company, 1954), p. 108; and F. Hsu, *Clan, Caste and Club* (Princeton: Van Nostrand, 1963) for its specific application to classical China where this idea is fostered at a high level of articulate awareness.

terms. Closely related is overdetermination: the combination of different components in a condensed form amenable to interpretation on a variety of levels of analysis.

Let us examine how these four criteria are at work in the three tales selected for analysis: The reciprocities, already examined, in these tales, provide very *simplified* formulations. In addition, the Grimms' *Fairy Tales*, taken as a total body of literature, are mutually sustaining in terms of the meanings and values they provide.[59] In the tales we have discussed, the fairies are "interchangeable" from one story to the next, and the kings who appear in two of these tales could also be one and the same person, when considered in terms of the values and meanings attributed to them.[60]

These tales emphasize both the past (tradition) and the positive sanctions for conduct consonant with the beliefs. They even suggest that things were better in the *remote* past, implying the desirability (*attractiveness*) of similar circumstances being brought about. The Fairy provides positive sanctions by supernatural forces: she not only compensates the banished princess for rejection by her father, but rewards the girl's loyalty and love by effecting a family reunion which in turn gives the girl her father's support in her wedding to the count. The Fairy gives the stepdaughter a substitute home, and also rewards her diligence and orderliness with a great supply of wealth. Finally the Fairy's advice and implements yield for the brave and disciplined ex-soldier a princess and the prospect of the throne. The underlying idea is that those who display the appropriate conduct may be unfortunate for a time, but ultimately will be rewarded for their virtues.

Conversely, the *dangers of violation* are similarly spelled out in these tales: a father loses his daughter, twelve princes must continue to live under a spell to expiate their sins, and the ugly and lazy daughter returns home from a trip down the well, even uglier than before in her new coat of tar.

An obvious question arises: who is to undertake the rewarding? In each instance, when the victim has exhausted his or her last resource, the Fairy, representing the supernatural, appears and re-establishes an equilibrium. The Fairy is thus a *dramatic representation* of precisely those forces which the belief system requires in order to establish its intrinsic merit.

Dramatic also are the contrasts and drastic changes of status occurring in each of these tales: the youngest daughter's response to the king con-

[59] See Carsch, *op. cit.*, for detailed documentation.

[60] This, in fact, can be said of each of the kings who appear in stories in which Fairies occur (KHM 9, 50, 178). The same holds true for stepmothers (KHM 24, 139, 185), mothers (KHM 89, 135), and siblings (KHM 9, 24, 95, 138, 139, 178, 185).

trasted with those of her two older sisters; the contrasting life styles of the princess before and after her banishment and again after her marriage to the count; the contrast implicit between the wealthy powerful king and the apparently impoverished Fairy, living in her cottage in the forest, carrying firewood, seemingly grateful to have the young princess herd her geese for her. The tale about the stepdaughter is replete with dramatic contrasts: between the two daughters as treated by the (step) mother; between the two as treated by the Fairy; and the contrast between the mother and the Fairy in their treatment of the two girls; and finally the one girl returning covered with gold, the other with tar. In the tale of the dancing princesses, all the royal characters contrast dramatically with the impoverished ex-soldier, whose changing fortunes in turn mark a great contrast to his previous denigration. Clearly, such differences again point up and dramatically display the behavior which is being rewarded or punished.

Overdetermination is repeatedly displayed in these tales. In the banished princess story much is made of "carrying" things. Expelled from her home, the young girl must carry a bag of salt strapped to her back. This is to provide "substance" for her tears. Symbolically, the king is telling her to be unhappy, it is as if he said, "Cry, and here is something for you to cry *with!*" Again, encountering the carefree young count, the old fairy wants him to carry baskets full of apples, pears, and hay up the hill to her cottage. She says she must carry all of this while rich people's children never do; amongst the peasants the saying goes that "They should not turn around lest they see that their backs are crooked." The count obliges, but just as he begins to feel the full weight of his load, the Fairy jumps on top so that he must carry her also. Thus before meeting the disguised princess, the count is tested for his ability to carry his burden, that is, whether he is capable of supporting a wife. Finally, the count (seemingly of his own volition) carries the "perle" back to the queen, affecting the reunion of parents and daughter. The "perle" of course, is the distilled remnant of the girl's tears, of her grief, which the prince is now unloading on her parents who caused it, and this burden is too much, for the queen faints at the sight of it.

Such meanings are not, of course, merely "read into" the tale, but constitute part of it and are subject to derivation on the basis of consistent and self-sustaining symbolism systematically congruent with their referents.[61]

[61] Note Freud's definition of the relationship between a symbol and its referent as a common quality shared between the symbol and its object. Freud was fully aware, of course, that all sorts of things share common qualities with all sorts of other things without the one being symbolic of the other. He, therefore, cautioned against loose interpretations and suggested that consistency of usage and the context in which such usage occurs be taken into consideration. Durkheim's relevant formulations in which it is suggested that anything can be learned

In the second tale the stepdaughter jumps down the well to retrieve the spool covered with blood. After a temporary loss of consciousness, she then walks about a meadow, first pulling loaves of bread—fully baked— out of an oven, then shaking apples off a tree and stacking these most neatly, and finally arriving at the cottage of the Fairy where she remains for a time until she feels compelled to return to earth. The Fairy, although delighted to have had the girl, is in full support of her returning to earth. She takes her up to the big gate underneath which the girl is covered with gold prior to going home.

We suggest that the above sequence is fully congruent with the processes of conception (girl jumps down the "well," fully "baked loaves of bread" in "oven," "apples"), gestation (stay in "cottage"), and parturition (the Fairy takes the girl to the "gate" and locks it after her). What seems in fact to be happening is that the girl is "reborn," or, to put it more accurately, that she dies only to be reconceived and to be born a second time for a more fortunate existence.

The third of these tales on analysis reveals both sexual and political symbolism. Despite all of his efforts, the old king cannot keep order among his children, and other princes (i.e. the nobility) are unable to help him, losing their lives in the attempt. It is only the brave and well-disciplined ex-soldier who refuses to accept the wine from the oldest princess and who does not fall asleep at the critical moment. He is able to cope with the situation, find out where the princesses are "dancing," and is thus promised the kingdom. The political implication is that the nobility, if unable to keep order among themselves, may have to be replaced by the military.

In the meantime, the events underground from which the twelve princesses return with worn-out shoes are highly suggestive. It is their beds which "lower" them to the mysterious alley-ways in which grow trees the branches of which are so very precious. They then come to a lake where they find waiting for them twelve princes, each with "his little boat" in which to row them to a well "lit" castle where the band, composed of "drums" and "trumpets" is already playing. The nature of the "dance" cannot, therefore, be said to be altogether obscure.

Most probably the function and merit of such overdetermination, quite apart from its aesthetic dimension, is to elicit further interest, specifically the interest of those unhappy adults whose task it may be to read the fairy tales to their children.

---

to symbolize anything else does not necessarily contradict the Freudian system as it addresses itself to a different type of symbolism, namely signs, the meanings of which must be shared to be taught once they are understood. In this sense his perspectives come close also to those of G. H. Mead. The difference is that of affective compared with cognitive symbolism.

IV

At this point the question may be raised, what are the functions of these fairies? Most strikingly, perhaps, these revolve about their role of *deus ex machina* of supernatural derivation facilitating the perpetuation of a system of justice, or more specifically, the amelioration of social inequality on both intrafamilial and societal levels.[62]

On the intrafamilial level, as has been shown, fairies stand in *loco parentis*, acting the role of father or mother vis-à-vis their protégés. In fact, even in those tales in which the protégés continue to live with their parents, the fairies' role was, nevertheless, congruent with that of the mother. In one of these tales the fairy actually was the mother of the protégée.[63] In another tale she is the godmother,[64] in a third she is the wetnurse.[65] Moreover, when the fairies bestow feminine personality attributes on their protégées as magical gifts, these involve qualities which may be in one way or another "inherited" or otherwise derived from one's mother, for example, beauty, virtue, piety, wealth.[66] By contrast, masculine qualities, such as aggressiveness, adventurousness, and courage, are not bestowed by fairies. Rather they are rewarded and encouraged if present in the male protégés.[67] Most importantly perhaps, fairies may provide a home, food, and shelter if the protégé's relationship with his or her family make it necessary for him to leave.[68] Of considerable importance also is what may be referred to as a "rebirth" sequence, in which the protégé goes underground, as it were, for a time, only to appear appropriately modified (for example wealthy) and thus be in a position to contract a hypergamous marriage. This, of course, occurs in two of the tales discussed in this paper,[69] as well as in ten additional tales.[70] In these tales the fairy would seem to function as a "mother" facilitating the appropriate "rebirth."

On the societal level the amelioration of social inequality is implemented by the fairies' facilitation of hypergamous marriages (that is, of commoners with royalty). It is important to note, however, that in addition to being the innocent victim of depriving circumstances, to qualify

---

[62] One must, of course, bear in mind the medieval setting which provides the context of most of these tales. For detailed descriptions of the relevant inequalities, see J. Huizinga, *The Waning of the Middle Ages* (New York: Doubleday & Company, 1954), Chap. III; M. de Montaigne, *Essays*, J. M. Cohen, tr. (Harmondsworth, Eng.: Penguin Books, 1958), pp. 137-41.

[63] KHM 89.

[64] KHM 135.

[65] KHM 187.

[66] KHM 139.

[67] KHM 120.

[68] KHM 24.

[69] KHM 24, 131.

[70] KHM Nos. 9, 29, 50, 89, 95, 128, 135, 139, 178, 185.

for such a sequence the protégé must display a series of qualities, "rewardable" in terms of the prevailing value system.[71] The Fairy compensates for the deprivations suffered and further implements the "due" rewards, thereby inducing a measure of optimistic trust in the validity of the prevailing value structure.

A third major function of these Fairies is that of being models for the projection of hopes and as a means of giving such hopes the requisite normative directions, and this would apply particularly to children and those in whom the relevant hopes stand close to the centers of conscious awareness. They serve further as models for identification and guidance, particularly for parents and others who stand in relationship of authority vis-à-vis children.[72]

In this connection it is noteworthy that on one level of analysis Fairies are essentially mythological constructs who as agents of compelling extrahuman forces seem dedicated to the perpetuation of justice. On another level, however, they may be conceived as normative forces in personified form. It is in this capacity that they serve the additional function of simplifying to a considerable extent complexities of the prevailing value system, which, in their abstract form, would not be amenable to popular diffusion while the knowledge and memory of them may, nevertheless, be necessary for the cohesion of society in terms of prerequisite consensus.

Finally, as has been shown in a preceding section, these Fairies function as resolvants of ambiguities. Thus they provide answers to such questions as what would life be like without a father, a mother, or a stepmother; what happens when people die (prematurely); or again, what happens when the children of the powerful (i.e. kings) are not subject to parental control? Ultimately, of course, these questions address themselves to the causes and agents of human suffering and implicitly respond to (the basically theological) question regarding the reasons for human suffering and their possible forms of amelioration.

The implications then are essentially conservative, in the sense that they obviate any thought about the desirability of change, and optimistic, in the sense that they imply the existence of a self-correcting mechanism of supernatural derivation which functions to correct imbalances in the social system. The resultant perspectives may, therefore, be delineated as follows: First, they involve a relatively precise conceptualization

[71] These are: good looks, courage, abstemiousness, discipline and obedience for men; and beauty, diligence, orderliness, submissiveness and love of parents for girls.

[72] The reverse of the above processes, of course, holds with respect to the Fairies' protégés: the latter would serve as models for identification for those in relatively powerless positions and as objects of projection for those in more powerful positions.

of the forms and contents of "good behavior," stressing the relevant cardinal virtues; second, they provide a guide of how to come to terms with suffering and hope; and third, they set the stage for trust in vague, mysterious, and cosmic forces which remain perhaps long after Fairies and their associates have been relegated to the reservoir of disbelief.

4. CONCLUSION

Each of the papers presented in this chapter has been concerned, in a different way, with social change and problems of personality or socialization in connection with change. Bronfenbrenner deals explicitly with changes over time (roughly a generation) in prevalent socialization practices in a particular large-scale society. His analysis points to some of the ambiguous and contradictory implications and consequences of the progressive narrowing of the gap between middle and lower classes and between the sexes, both of the parents and of the children, in socialization measures, and the spread of more permissive and love-oriented child-rearing and child-disciplining practices. While the sources of these shifts can be identified in a general way, the consequences, in terms of adaptation of the younger generation to the complex and ambiguous changing world, are problematical to say the least.

The paper on Soviet modal personality trends even more sharply refers to the problematics of social change in reference to culturally standardized personality trends. There the demands of the revolutionary regime, in its commitment to rapid transformation of the society, clash significantly with "deeper" personality trends of those socialized under older but persistent socialization patterns.

Lastly, though it is not directly concerned with this theme, the analysis of Grimms' *Fairy Tales* points some indications of how these special socialization agents may act as a brake on the impact of social change on a society and how they may serve to preserve elements of older cultural tradition in this special almost subterranean manner. As Carsch's analysis shows or implies, the fairy tales are a strongly conservative cultural force in numerous ways. The antiquity of the tales themselves (or their forerunners) and their medieval setting maintains the linkage of new generations of listeners or readers with older cultural traditions. They teach (through the expressive indirection of art, entertainment and fantasy full of out-of-this-world magical interventions) the conservative traditional virtues of obedience, duty, industry, piety, and courage. Significantly, they perpetuate certain conceptions of a system of justice, dealing compensatorily with injustices and inequalities parallel, in their aesthetic transformation, to stresses of that kind experienced in the actual world. They implicitly reassure the listening child of the justice of the world through the resolution of ambiguities and the erasure of existential inequalities by the devices of magical intervention, supervision, and ultimate just reward. In providing "a guide in how to come to terms with suffering and hope" and "setting the stage for trust in vague, mysterious, and cosmic forces," they present and prescribe a view of the world fundamentally resistant to activist change. We can here only scratch the surface of the implications of these fascinating socialization measures. Their realm of magic, mystery and metanatural connections and sequences points clearly to the dark, convoluted, and non-logical domain of the unconscious. Here we find its forces selected, directed, controlled, and transformed. What we witness is perpetutation not merely of overt tradition, but also of its unconscious substructure from past generations, guided and channelized (only in part by the conscious intent of the collector-editors) along certain lines. The immense detour of indirection involved in the distancing of time and space and situation, as well as the qualitative leap to the world of magic, provides in fact the short way home to the critical unconscious conflicts and dilemmas. We can safely assume that many aspects of these reflect universal human problems and perplexities, especially of childhood with its closeness to the paradoxical juxtaposition of omnipotence fantasy and helplessly dependent reality. Other themes probably reflect perpetuation of difficulties indicative of particular earlier generations, for example, those of the European medieval period so frequently represented in these stories. Still others may indicate the selectivity of the particular editors, namely the Grimms, of a specific time and place, Germany of the early 1800's. How roundly or richly these tales resonated with the unconscious and conscious personality themes of the audiences of that time or since we have no reliable way of gauging. We certainly have indications of their persisting appeal to ever-new generations down to the present day, though further studies may reveal a decline in their appeal, over time, and a quite variable distribution of this appeal through different parts of modern populations. The persistence suggests some universal elements. However, perhaps part of it is accountable by a posited continuation, especially at the subterranean level, of some elements of specifically Western culture over long historical periods.

Both the modal personality trends of the Great Russians, as revealed in the Inkeles study, and the patterns that we can more speculatively and less reliably intuit from the fairy tales, suggest persistences in aspects of personality functioning (especially at the unconscious or less than fully conscious, level) that even far-reaching changes brought by the world-wide sweep of the forces of industrialization have not fully (or even partially) subdued.

There are paradoxes in both cases. While the compilation and dissemination of these fairy tales was intended as a deliberate socialization device by the Grimms, the nature of the material, even after careful selection and considerable rewriting to their special social slant, is far too inchoate, polymorphous, and polyvalent to be confined in its effects to one specific place and age. Hence, the material, connecting with a multiplicity of unconscious forces, may simultaneously arouse countertrends to those the editors intended and even facilitate a breakthrough out of the authors' intended molds, with the potential of transformation of society. The multiple valences of the tales as a total collection may also provide material for a later generation to put to uses very different from the Grimms' ideological intentions.

Correspondingly, in the Soviet case, there is a persistent tension between the Great Russian modal personality trends and the changes being attempted by the regime, such that where the actions of the ruling group may give gratification to some modal psychic needs (for example, the need to be taken care of by a controlling and nurturant authority), this very gratification itself may stand in the way of the development of other psychological characteristics the regime is trying to foster, such as a more routinized, hence compulsive, approach to work.

In this chapter we have ventured into a number of rather centrifugal explorations, all bearing, but very dissimilarly, on the question of the relation of socialization to personality development, and of both of these to wider social structural forces. Each of the papers leads into a host of additional questions, in quite variant directions, suggesting the never-ending ramifications of problems in this area.

The problems become almost infinitely complex when one attempts to deal meaningfully with large-scale, complicated, heterogeneous modern societies, with their great variety of styles of life and socialization settings, and with their wide pluralism of personality configurations. A further dimension of complexity is introduced when we move from the merely interpersonal socialization of parents, teachers, and other elders with children, to the impersonal but deeply cutting (and all but totally immeasurable) influences of media of mass communication.

What common strands can we bring together here? What centripetal pull against the flying in all directions of the three studies presented? One is a kind of truism, yet one that needs to be repeated in the face of the various deterministic schemes for conceiving socialization, personality, and society. That is that socialization is never complete. Neither is the child ever fully socialized in perfect accordance with the personality demands on adults of his society, nor is the socialization process for any particular child ever in full accord with the social-structural or cultural strains and pushes and necessities. And this is to say there is present both freedom and the potential of conflict, and even of chaos. The following chapters will pursue special aspects of these themes.

SELECTED BIBLIOGRAPHY

Class and Race Differences in Socialization

Aberle, David F. and Kasper D. Naegele. "Middle-class Fathers' Occupational Role and Attitudes Toward Children," *American Journal of Orthopsychiatry.* Vol. 22, 1952, pp. 366-78.
Careful exploration showing how pervasively middle-class occupational status unconsciously influences American fathers' differential socialization of sons and daughters.

Bronfenbrenner, Urie. "Socialization and Social Class Through Time and Space," in E. Maccoby, T. M. Newcomb, and E. L. Hartley (eds.), *Readings in Social Psychology.* 3rd edition. New York: Holt, Rinehart and Winston, 1958.
A masterful brief overview of changes in American socialization patterns from the 1920s through the 1950s.

Davis, Allison. "American Status Systems and the Socialization of the Child," *American Sociological Review.* Vol. 6, 1941, pp. 345-54. Reprinted in C. Kluckhohn, H. Murray, and D. Schneider (eds.), *Personality in Nature, Society and Culture.* New York: Alfred A. Knopf, 1955.
An influential early paper analyzing the mutual involvement of socialization and class status in America.

———— and John Dollard. *Children of Bondage.* Washington, D.C.: American Council on Education, 1940.
A pioneering study of personality patterns of Negro youth of different social classes in the South of the late 1930s. Compare Rohrer-Edmonson for later follow-up.

———— and Robert J. Havighurst. "Social Class and Color Differences in Child-Rearing," *American Sociological Review.* Vol. 11, 1946, pp. 698-710. Reprinted widely, as in C. Kluckhohn, H. Murray, and D. Schneider (eds.). *Personality in Nature, Society and Culture.* New York: Alfred A. Knopf, 1955.
"Classic" analysis of class and race differences in socialization in America of that time. Compare Bronfenbrenner and Miller and Swanson for changes since that time.

Kardiner, Abram and Lionel Ovesey. *The Mark of Oppression: A Psychosocial Study of the American Negro.* New York. W. W. Norton & Co., 1951.
Explores some of the psychic costs of being black in America.

Kohn, Melvin. "Social Class and the Exercise of Parental Authority," *American Sociological Review.* Vol. 24, 1959, pp. 325-66.

Miller, Daniel R. and Guy E. Swanson. *The Changing American Parent: A Study in the Detroit Area.* New York: John Wiley & Sons, 1958.
Suggests that class differences are becoming less relevant in socializa-

tion than differences between "entrepreneurial" and "bureaucratic" orientations.

Rohrer, John H. and Munro S. Edmonson, *et al. The Eighth Generation.* New York: Harper & Row, Publishers, 1960.
A follow-up of the "Children of Bondage" (see Davis and Dollard) in the 1950s.

Cross-Cultural and "National Character"
Studies in Large-scale Societies

Bauer, Raymond. *The New Man in Soviet Psychology.* Cambridge: Harvard University Press, 1962.
The Soviet Union's attempt to produce a new form of social character. Significant in relation to the Inkeles studies.
————. *Nine Soviet Portraits.* Cambridge, Mass.: The M.I.T. Press, 1955.
These semi-fictionalized composite case studies give a vivid sense of personality in the context of social milieu in the Soviet Union shortly after World War II.
————, Alex Inkeles, and Clyde Kluckhohn. *How the Soviet System Works: Cultural, Psychological, and Social Themes.* Cambridge: Harvard University Press, 1956.
A broad general statement. Provides the context of the more specialized studies such as the Inkeles-Hanfmann-Beier report.
Benedict, Ruth. *The Chrysanthemum and the Sword.* Boston: Houghton Mifflin, 1946.
A study "at a distance" of Japanese character. Challenged by much of the later research, e.g. Stoetzel (see below).
Gorer, Geoffrey. *The American People.* New York: W. W. Norton & Co., 1948.
A speculative study of the "national character" of Americans by an imaginative British anthropologist.
Hanfmann, Eugenia. "Social Perception in Russian Displaced Persons and an American Comparison," *Psychiatry.* Vol. 20, No. 2, May 1957, pp. 131-49.
Valuable additional material to the Inkeles-Hanfmann-Beier study.
Henry, Jules. *Culture Against Man.* New York: Random House, 1963.
An analytically oriented anthropologist's impassioned indictment of many trends in American socialization, based on a variety of studies of families and schools.
Inkeles, Alex. "Social Change and Social Character: The Role of Parental Mediation," *Journal of Social Issues.* Vol. 11, 1955, pp. 12-32.
Shows how parental socialization practices can operate to change rather than (or as well as) perpetuate social and cultural patterns, with special reference to Soviet practices.
———— and Daniel J. Levinson. "National Character: The Study of Modal Personality and Sociocultural Systems," in G. Lindzey (ed.), *Handbook of Social Psychology.* Reading, Mass.: Addison-Wesley Publishing Co., 1954.
Critical review of literature and problems.

Mead, Margaret. "National Character," in A. L. Kroeber (ed.), *Anthropology Today: An Encyclopedic Inventory*. Chicago: University of Chicago Press, 1952.

Two systematic essays surveying the literature and problems.

Riesman, David, Nathan Glazer, and Reuel Denney. *The Lonely Crowd*. New Haven: Yale University Press, 1950.

The changing "social character" of Americans.

Stoetzel, Jean. *Without the Chrysanthemum and the Sword*. New York: Columbia University Press, 1955.

While not a "national character" study, this analysis of attitudes of postwar youth in Japan is a critical challenge to Benedict's study.

Wolfenstein, Martha and Nathan Leites. *Movies: A Psychological Study*. New York: Free Press of Glencoe, 1950.

An imaginative probing of "national character" differences among America, Britain, and France through thematic analysis of their films.

FOUR

Transitions:
rites de passage

Universals of mankind refer to his biology, his prototypical human social relationships, and the uniformities of culture. They can also be seen in terms of the temporal progression of life, the "life cycle." Here again we have a biological base, certain prototypical social involvements, and the impress of patterns of culture, some universal, others culturally diverse.

We are all begot by man in the body of woman, nourished and grown in the womb, cast out by the trauma of birth or else "untimely ripped," facing a strange new world, helpless infants, less helpless and growing children, pubescent fledglings, young adults, adults in prime, adults in decline, then aging, then aged, losing teeth and hair and energy, increasingly infirm, then dying, and finally dead. The "ages of man" have been sung in story and song by poets known and anonymous for many centuries. We know that the biologically given milestones, like puberty and menopause, may or may not have the impress of special cultural recognition and patterning and may, in timing at least, be virtually ignored. Yet all cultures distinguish in some way infant and child, child and adult, young adult and old, and recognize that we can be very *differently* human at different stages. The facts of process and development and change, of movement away and also of return, are part of the universals of mankind. The coordinate is *time:* in one sense, continuous uni-directional movement and in another, *rhythm.* Human life follows both patterns—a constant progression toward death and a constant rhythmical fluctuation. Again there seems to be a duality of press. One is toward the persistence and maintenance of forms and patterns learned and maintained throughout life—the great determinism of the earliest years. The other is toward change as an expression of growth and enhancement and the possible abandonment of earlier, no longer adaptive forms—in short, the emergence of untapped powers and the possibility of creative leaps beyond the apparently given. Change may also be seen as *cyclical* (as implied in the very term "life cycle"): as movement away from, then back around and return to the earliest forms. This cycle is illustrated in such notions as the greater closeness of both the very young and the very old to the supernatural, in contrast to the more mundane, even "polluted" nature of the prime years of life. The notion that certain broad ranges of roles are appropriate for particular stages in life, as in the greater permission of "un-seriousness" in both the very young and the very old, also seems to be a recurrent theme, if not a universal, of culture. The "return" of more infantile modes and responses often noted in old age, appears also to have some universal substructure.[1]

There is much to be said that is universal about life-cycle stages despite the great cultural variations. Though susceptible of some modification by cultural factors such as nutrition, the sheer physiology of different ages—in terms of endocrine balance, energy output, fatigability, capacity for energy bursts, and the like—points to some pan-human problems of personality in connection with the life cycle. Here again we note the enormous infantilization of man as compared with other animals. This suggests that the persistence of infantile kinds of response patterns into adulthood and continuing (not returning) into old age operates in antagonism to the processes of change and differentiation. The universal human problem is that we are doing both—both aging and maturing, on the one hand, and holding on to infancy, on the other. We can see the massive tenacity of infantile patterns revealed in psychodynamic analysis of personality. It is also likely that the most complex and "advanced" individuals (by intellectual endowment, creativity, or whatever other such criterion one may wish to propose) manifest this antagonism of growing up and staying young in more acute forms than more ordinary people. One such creative type is the artist. In the Western

[1] Compare Philip Slater, "On Social Regression," *American Sociological Review*, Vol. 28, No. 3, June 1963, pp. 339-63.

tradition, at least, he is traditionally and typically depicted as being, and having a right to be, more infantile than other people. In other words, in positive terms, he is expected to be more spontaneous, more open to genuine feeling, more guilelessly expressive, and more capable of *play*; in negative terms, to be less amenable to demands of respectable social responsibility, to routinization accepted by the more "average" as necessary conditions of life, less "dependable" emotionally, financially, and otherwise, and less comfortable for conventional people to deal with or live with. It is, therefore, no surprise that the artist is both admired and rebuked for his "infantilism." [2]

All cultures are faced with the problem of defining the stages of the life cycle and providing for standard ways of moving from one stage to the next, providing some kind of balance between persistence from past stages and change to the new. That is, provision must be made for some balance (some dynamic in fact) between continuity and discontinuity in the life cycle.

1. CONTINUITY OR DISCONTINUITY?

The late Ruth Benedict, in a now classic paper, "Continuities and Discontinuities in Cultural Conditioning" set forth some of the main problems for all the ensuing anthropological discussion. In a frankly value-laden discussion of some of the difficulties of growing up in our own culture at the time of writing (1938), she shows how contrasting are those primitive societies (her examples are largely from American Indian tribes) where the child's learnings are continuous into adult roles. The instances of *dis*continuity she discusses, from the primitive world, are interestingly all cases where the break from childhood learning is made with the aid of ritualization, sometimes with distinctive age grading so that youth gets the support of the whole age group in making the sometimes drastic transition to the next stage roles. By implication, Benedict seems to be arguing that continuity of conditioning is the norm, or at least the desideratum—thus indicting our culture for its deviation in this respect—and that discontinuity, therefore, calls for special cultural arrange-

[2] Compare the discussion of the psychodynamics of the creative artist, Chapter Five.

ments to enable individuals of the society to make the transition without the excessive cost of such phenomena as the *Sturm und Drang* so characteristic of adolescence in our society.

The problem is taken up again, with a very different emphasis, by C. W. M. Hart in his paper, "Contrasts Between Prepubertal and Postpubertal Education." Hart's basic premise appears to be the exact opposite of Benedict's. Hart's theme is that *discontinuity*—at least from late childhood to postpuberty—is to be assumed as the norm and something not at all to be deplored, at least if the culture provides adequate ways of standardizing, stabilizing, and resolving the transition. Where Benedict implies that a culture makes difficulties if the child learns things he has to unlearn later, Hart's analysis suggests that *inevitably*—according to social role demands, if not by any biological necessity—the prepubertal child is conditioned to behavior and attitudes which he must *perforce* unlearn in the postpubertal period. (Interestingly, his primary examples come from Australia—his own study of the Tiwi—and Melanesian and African tribal societies and not from American Indians as in Benedict's case for continuity.)

Hart is interested in those societies where a sharp and clear-cut transition is made from the prepubertal to the postpubertal period by the institution of "puberty ceremonies" or "initiation ceremonies." He considers these rites primarily in their relationship to the *institutionalized roles* assigned to youngsters at different ages rather than in terms of psychobiological universals of the stages in question. His analysis also shows how the discontinuity from childhood to postpuberty also contributes to the continuity of both of these (in different ways) to the adult roles to be played in the society: for while later childhood (in those tribes) contributes technical mastery of the *secular* crafts of livelihood that adults need in the society in question, the pubertal education of protracted initiation ceremonies contributes the mastery of the "cultural" world and its "sacred" lore and values, making the man not only a producer and provider, but more importantly, a citizen and perpetuator of his culture. While Hart eschews probing into psychodynamic meanings of the ritualized pubertal transitions, their analysis is in no way precluded by or inimical to his interpretation in terms of social roles and cultural necessities. It is to these that we shall turn after presentation of the Benedict and Hart papers.

Continuities and Discontinuities in Cultural Conditioning
RUTH BENEDICT

All cultures must deal in one way or another with the cycle of growth from infancy to adulthood. Nature has posed the situation dramatically: on the one hand, the new born baby, physiologically vulnerable, unable to fend for itself, or to participate of its own initiative in the life of the group, and, on the other, the adult man or woman. Every man who rounds out his human potentialities must have been a son first and father later and the two roles are physiologically in great contrast; he must first have been dependent upon others for his very existence and later he must provide such security for others. This discontinuity in the life cycle is a fact of nature and is inescapable. Facts of nature, however, in any discussion of human problems, are ordinarily read off not at their bare minimal but surrounded by all the local accretions of behavior to which the student of human affairs has become accustomed in his own culture. For that reason it is illuminating to examine comparative material from other societies in order to get a wider perspective on our own special accretions. The anthropologist's role is not to question the facts of nature, but to insist upon the interposition of a middle term between "nature" and "human behavior"; his role is to analyze that term, to document local manmade doctorings of nature and to insist that these doctorings should not be read off in any one culture as nature itself. Although it is a fact of nature that the child becomes a man, the way in which this transition is effected varies from one society to another, and no one of these particular cultural bridges should be regarded as the "natural" path to maturity.

From a comparative point of view our culture goes to great extremes in emphasizing contrasts between the child and the adult. The child is sexless, the adult estimates his virility by his sexual activities; the child must be protected from the ugly facts of life, the adult must meet them without psychic catastrophe; the child must obey, the adult must command this obedience. These are all dogmas of our culture, dogmas which in spite of the facts of nature, other cultures commonly do not share. In spite of the physiological contrasts between child and adult these are cultural accretions.

It will make the point clearer if we consider one habit in our own culture in regard to which there is not this discontinuity of conditioning. With the greatest clarity of purpose and economy of training, we achieve

Reprinted by special permission of The William Alanson White Psychiatric Foundation, Inc. and of the estate of the late Ruth Benedict, from Ruth Benedict, "Continuities and Discontinuities in Cultural Conditioning," Psychiatry, Vol. 1, May 1938, pp. 161-67. Copyright held by The William Alanson White Psychiatric Foundation, Inc.

our goal of conditioning everyone to eat three meals a day. The baby's training in regular food periods begins at birth and no crying of the child and no inconvenience to the mother is allowed to interfere. We gauge the child's physiological make-up and at first allow it food oftener than adults, but, because our goal is firmly set and our training consistent, before the child is two years old it has achieved the adult schedule. From the point of view of other cultures this is as startling as the fact of three-year-old babies perfectly at home in deep water is to us. Modesty is another sphere in which our child training is consistent and economical; we waste no time in clothing the baby and in contrast to many societies where the child runs naked till it is ceremonially given its skirt or its pubic sheath at adolescence, the child's training fits it precisely for adult conventions.

In neither of these aspects of behavior is there need for an individual in our culture to embark before puberty, at puberty, or at some later date upon a course of action which all his previous training has tabooed. He is spared the unsureness inevitable in such a transition.

The illustration I have chosen may appear trivial, but in larger and more important aspects of behavior, our methods are obviously different. Because of the great variety of child training in different families in our society, I might illustrate continuity of conditioning from individual life histories in our culture, but even these, from a comparative point of view, stop far short of consistency and I shall therefore confine myself to describing arrangements in other cultures in which training which with us is idiosyncratic, is accepted and traditional and does not therefore involve the same possibility of conflict. I shall choose childhood rather than infant and nursing situations not because the latter do not vary strikingly in different cultures but because they are nevertheless more circumscribed by the baby's physiological needs than is its later training. Childhood situations provide an excellent field in which to illustrate the range of cultural adjustments which are possible within a universally given, but not so drastic, set of physiological facts.

The major discontinuty in the life cycle is of course that the child who is at one point a son must later be a father. These roles in our society are strongly differentiated; a good son is tractable, and does not assume adult responsibilities; a good father provides for his children and should not allow his authority to be flouted. In addition, the child must be sexless so far as his family is concerned, whereas the father's sexual role is primary in the family. The individual in one role must revise his behavior from almost all points of view when he assumes the second role.

I shall select for discussion three such contrasts that occur in our culture between the individual's role as child and as father: 1. responsible—non-responsible status role. 2. dominance—submission. 3. contrasted sexual role. It is largely upon our cultural commitments to these three contrasts that the discontinuity in the life cycle of an individual in our culture depends.

RESPONSIBLE—NON-RESPONSIBLE STATUS ROLE

The techniques adopted by societies which achieve continuity during the life cycle in this sphere in no way differ from those we employ in our uniform conditioning to three meals a day. They are merely applied to other areas of life. We think of the child as wanting to play and the adult as having to work, but in many societies the mother takes the baby daily in her shawl or carrying net to the garden or to gather roots, and adult labor is seen even in infancy from the pleasant security of its position in close contact with its mother. When the child can run about, it accompanies its parents still, doing tasks which are essential and yet suited to its powers, and its dichotomy between work and play is not different from that its parents recognize, namely the distinction between the busy day and the free evening. The tasks it is asked to perform are graded to its powers and its elders wait quietly by, not offering to do the task in the child's place. Everyone who is familiar with such societies has been struck by the contrast with our child training. Dr. Ruth Underhill tells me of sitting with a group of Papago elders in Arizona when the man of the house turned to his little three-year-old granddaughter and asked her to close the door. The door was heavy and hard to shut. The child tried, but it did not move. Serveral times the grandfather repeated, "Yes, close the door." No one jumped to the child's assistance. No one took the responsibility away from her. On the other hand, there was no impatience, for after all the child was small. They sat gravely waiting till the child succeeded and her grandfather gravely thanked her. It was assumed that the task would not be asked of her unless she could perform it, and having been asked, the responsibility was hers alone just as if she were a grown woman.

The essential point of such child training is that the child is from infancy continuously conditioned to responsible social participation while at the same time the tasks that are expected of it are adapted to its capacity. The contrast with our society is very great. A child does not make any labor contribution to our industrial society except as it competes with an adult; its work is not measured against its own strength and skill but against high-geared industrial requirements. Even when we praise a child's achievement in the home, we are outraged if such praise is interpreted as being of the same order as praise of adults. The child is praised because the parent feels well disposed, regardless of whether the task is well done by adult standards, and the child acquires no sensible standard by which to measure its achievement. The gravity of a Cheyenne Indian family ceremoniously making a feast out of the little boy's first snowbird is the furthest removed from our behavior. At birth the little boy was presented with a toy bow, and from the time he could run about serviceable bows suited to his stature were specially made for him by the man of the family. Animals and birds were taught him in a graded series, beginning with those most easily taken, and as he brought in his first of each species, his family duly made a feast of it, accepting his contribution as gravely as the buffalo his father brought. When he finally killed a buffalo, it was only the final step of his childhood conditioning, not a new adult role with which his childhood experience had been at variance.

The Canadian Ojibwa show clearly what results can be achieved. This tribe gains its livelihood by winter trapping and the small family of father, mother, and children live during the long winter alone on their great frozen hunting grounds. The boy accompanies his father and brings in his catch to his sister as his father does to his mother; the girl prepares the meat and skins for him just as his mother does for her husband. By the time the boy is 12, he may have set his own line of traps on a hunting territory of his own and return to his parents' house only once in several months—still bringing the meat and skins to his sister. The young child is taught consistently that it has only itself to rely upon in life, and this is as true in the dealings it will have with the supernatural as in the business of getting a livelihood. This attitude he will accept as a successful adult just as he accepted it as a child.[3]

DOMINANCE—SUBMISSION

Dominance—submission is the most striking of those categories of behavior where like does not respond to like but where one type of behavior stimulates the opposite response. It is one of the most prominent ways in which behavior is patterned in our culture. When it obtains between classes, it may be nourished by continuous experience; the difficulty in its use between children and adults lies in the fact that an individual conditioned to one set of behavior in childhood must adopt the opposite as an adult. Its opposite is a pattern of approximately identical reciprocal behavior, and societies which rely upon continuous conditioning characteristically invoke this pattern. In some primitive cultures the very terminology of address between father and son, and more commonly, between grandchild and grandson or uncle and nephew, reflects this attitude. In such kinship terminologies one reciprocal expresses each of these relationships so that son and father, for instance, exchange the same term with one another, just as we exchange the same term with a cousin. The child later will exchange it with his son. "Father—son," therefore, is a continuous relationship he enjoys throughout life. The same continuity, backed up by verbal reciprocity, occurs far oftener in

[3] Ruth Landes, *The Ojibwa Woman*, Part 1, Youth—Columbia University Contributions to Anthropology, Volume XXXI.

the grandchild-grandson relationship or that of mother's brother—sister's son. When these are "joking" relationships, as they often are, travelers report wonderingly upon the liberties and pretensions of tiny toddlers in their dealings with these family elders. In place of our dogma of respect to elders such societies employ in these cases a reciprocity as nearly identical as may be. The teasing and practical joking the grandfather visits upon his grandchild, the grandchild returns in like coin; he would be led to believe that he failed in propriety if he did not give like for like. If the sister's son has right of access without leave to his mother's brother's possessions, the mother's brother has such rights also to the child's possessions. They share reciprocal privileges and obligations which in our society can develop only between age mates.

From the point of view of our present discussion, such kinship conventions allow the child to put in practice from infancy the same forms of behavior which it will rely upon as an adult; behavior is not polarized into a general requirement of submission for the child and dominance for the adult.

It is clear from the techniques described above by which the child is conditioned to a responsible status role that these depend chiefly upon arousing in the child the desire to share responsibility in adult life. To achieve this little stress is laid upon obedience but much stress upon approval and praise. Punishment is very commonly regarded as quite outside the realm of possibility, and natives in many parts of the world have drawn the conclusion from our usual disciplinary methods that white parents do not love their children. If the child is not required to be submissive however, many occasions for punishment melt away; a variety of situations which call for it do not occur. Many American Indian tribes are especially explicit in rejecting the ideal of a child's submissive or obedient behavior. Prince Maximilian von Wied, who visited the Crow Indians over a hundred years ago, describes a father's boasting about his young son's intractability even when it was the father himself who was flouted; "He will be a man," his father said. He would have been baffled at the idea that his child should show behavior which would obviously make him appear a poor creature in the eyes of his fellows if he used it as an adult. Dr. George Devereux tells me of a special case of such an attitude among the Mohave at the present time. The child's mother was white and protested to its father that he must take action when the child disobeyed and struck him. "But why?" the father said, "he is little. He cannot possibly injure me." He did not know of any dichotomy according to which an adult expects obedience and a child must accord it. If his child had been docile, he would simply have judged that it would become a docile adult—an eventuality of which he would not have approved.

Child training which brings about the same result is common also in other areas of life than that of reciprocal kinship obligations between child and adult. There is a tendency in our culture to regard every situation as having in it the seeds of a dominance—submission relationship. Even where dominance—submission is patently irrelevant, we read in the dichotomy, assuming that in every situation there must be one person dominating another. On the other hand some cultures, even when the situation calls for leadership do not see it in terms of dominance—submission. To do justice to this attitude it would be necessary to describe their political and especially their economic arrangements, for such an attitude to persist must certainly be supported by economic mechanisms that are congruent with it. But it must also be supported by—or what comes to the same thing, express itself in—child training and familial situations.

CONTRASTED SEXUAL ROLE

Continuity of conditioning in training the child to assume responsibility and to behave no more submissively than adults is quite possible in terms of the child's physiological endowment if his participation is suited to his strength. Because of the late development of the child's reproductive organs, continuity of conditioning in sex experience presents a difficult problem. So far as their belief that the child is anything but a sexless being is concerned, they are probably more nearly right than we are with an opposite dogma. But the great break is presented by the universally sterile unions before puberty and the presumably fertile ones after maturation. This physiological fact no amount of cultural manipulation can minimize or alter, and societies therefore which stress continuous conditioning most strongly sometimes do not expect children to be interested in sex experience until they have matured physically. This is striking among American Indian tribes like the Dakota; adults observe great privacy in sex acts and in no way stimulate children's sexual activity. There need be no discontinuity, in the sense in which I have used the term, in such a program if the child is taught nothing it does not have to unlearn later. In such cultures adults view children's experimentation as in no way wicked or dangerous but merely as innocuous play which can have no serious consequences. In some societies such play is minimal and the children manifest little interest in it. But the same attitude may be taken by adults in societies where such play is encouraged and forms a major activity among small children. This is true among most of the Melanesian cultures of Southeast New Guinea; adults go as far as to laugh off sexual affairs within the prohibited class if the children are not mature, saying that since they cannot marry there can be no harm done.

It is this physiological fact of the difference between children's sterile unions and adults' presumably fertile sex relations which must be kept in mind in order to understand the different mores which almost always govern sex expression in children and in adults in the same culture. A great many cultures with preadolescent sexual license require marital fidelity and a great many which value premarital virginity in either male or female arrange their marital life with great license. Continuity in sex experience is complicated by factors which it was unnecessary to consider in the problems previously discussed. The essential problem is not whether or not the child's sexuality is consistently exploited—for even where such exploitation is favored, in the majority of cases the child must seriously modify his behavior at puberty or at marriage. Continuity in sex expression means rather that the child is taught nothing it must unlearn later. If the cultural emphasis is upon sexual pleasure, the child who is continuously conditioned will be encouraged to experiment freely and pleasurably, as among the Marquesans;[4] if emphasis is upon reproduction, as among the Zuñi of New Mexico, childish sex proclivities will not be exploited for the only important use which sex is thought to serve in his culture is not yet possible to him. The important contrast with our child training is that although a Zuñi child is impressed with the wickedness of premature sex experimentation, he does not run the risk as in our culture of associating this wickedness with sex itself rather than with sex at his age. The adult in our culture has often failed to unlearn the wickedness or the dangerousness of sex, a lesson which was impressed upon him strongly in his most formative years.

DISCONTINUITY IN CONDITIONING

Even from this very summary statement of continuous conditioning the economy of such mores is evident. In spite of the obvious advantages, however, there are difficulties in its way. Many primitive societies expect as different behavior from an individual as child and as adult as we do, and such discontinuity involves a presumption of strain.

Many societies of this type, however, minimize strain by the techniques they employ, and some techniques are more successful than others in ensuring the individual's functioning without conflict. It is from this point of view that age-graded societies reveal their fundamental significance. Age-graded cultures characteristically demand different behavior of the individual at different times of his life and persons of a like age-grade are grouped into a society whose activities are all oriented toward the behavior desired at that age. Individuals "graduate" publicly and with honor from one of these groups to another. Where age society members are enjoined to loyalty and mutual support, and are drawn not only from the local group but from the whole tribe as among the Arapaho, or even from other tribes as among the Wagawaga of Southeast New Guinea, such an institution has many advantages in eliminating conflicts among local groups and fostering intratribal peace. This seems

4 Ralph Linton, class notes on the Marquesans.

to be also a factor in the tribal military solidarity of the similarly organized Masai of East Africa. The point that is of chief interest for our present discussion, however, is that by this means an individual who at any time takes on a new set of duties and virtues is supported not only by a solid phalanx of age mates but by the traditional prestige of the organized "secret" society into which he has now graduated. Fortified in this way, individuals in such cultures often swing between remarkable extremes of opposite behavior without apparent psychic threat. For example, the great majority exhibit prideful and nonconflicted behavior at each stage in the life cycle even when a prime of life devoted to passionate and aggressive head hunting must be followed by a later life dedicated to ritual and to mild and peacable civic virtues.[5]

Our chief interest here, however, is in discontinuity which primarily affects the child. In many primitive societies such discontinuity has been fostered not because of economic or political necessity or because such discontinuity provides for a socially valuable division of labor, but because of some conceptual dogma. The most striking of these are the Australian and Papuan cultures where the ceremony of the "Making of Man" flourishes. In such societies it is believed that men and women have opposite and conflicting powers, and male children, who are of undefined status, must be initiated into the male role. In Central Australia the boy child is of the woman's side and women are taboo in the final adult stages of tribal ritual. The elaborate and protracted initiation ceremonies of the Arunta, therefore, snatch the boy from the mother, dramatize his gradual repudiation of her. In a final ceremony he is reborn as a man out of the men's ceremonial "baby pouch." The men's ceremonies are ritual statements of a masculine solidarity, carried out by fondling one another's *churingas*, the material symbol of each man's life, and by letting out over one another blood drawn from their veins. After this warm bond among men has been established through the ceremonies, the boy joins the men in the men's house and participates in tribal rites.[6] The enjoined discontinuity has been tribally bridged.

West of the Fly River in southern New Guinea there is a striking development of this Making of Men cult which involves a childhood period of passive homosexuality. Among the Keraki[7] it is thought that no boy can grow to full stature without playing the role for some years. Men slightly older take the active role, and the older man is a jealous partner. The life cycle of the Keraki Papuans includes, therefore, in suc-

---

[5] Henry Elkin, manuscript on the Arapaho.
[6] B. Spencer, and F. J. Gillen, *The Arunta*; N.Y., Macmillan, 1927 (2 vols.). Géza Róheim, Psycho-Analysis of Primitive Cultural Types. *Internat. J. Psychoanal.* (1932) 13:1-224—in particular, Chapter III, on the Aranda, The Children of the Desert.
[7] Francis E. Williams, *Papuans of the Trans-Fly*; Oxford, 1936.

cession, passive homosexuality, active homosexuality, and heterosexuality. The Keraki believe that pregnancy will result from postpubertal passive homosexuality and see evidences of such practices in any fat man whom even as an old man, they may kill or drive out of the tribe because of their fear. The ceremony that is of interest in connection with the present discussion takes place at the end of the period of passive homosexuality. This ceremony consists in burning out the possibility of pregnancy from the boy by pouring lye down his throat, after which he has no further protection if he gives way to the practice. There is no technique for ending active homosexuality, but this is not explicitly taboo for older men; heterosexuality and children, however, are highly valued. Unlike the neighboring Marindanim who share their homosexual practices, Keraki husband and wife share the same house and work together in the gardens.

I have chosen illustrations of discontinuous conditioning where it is not too much to say that the cultural institutions furnish adequate support to the individual as he progresses from role to role or interdicts the previous behavior in a summary fashion. The contrast with arrangements in our culture is very striking, and against this background of social arrangements in other cultures the adolescent period of *Sturm und Drang* with which we are so familiar becomes intelligible in terms of our discontinuous cultural institutions and dogmas rather than in terms of physiological necessity. It is even more pertinent to consider these comparative facts in relation to maladjusted persons in our culture who are said to be fixated at one or another preadult level. It is clear that if we were to look at our social arrangements as an outsider, we should infer directly from our family institutions and habits of child training that many individuals would not "put off childish things"; we should have to say that our adult activity demands traits that are interdicted in children, and that far from redoubling efforts to help children bridge this gap, adults in our culture put all the blame on the child when he fails to manifest spontaneously the new behavior or, overstepping the mark, manifests it with untoward belligerence. It is not surprising that in such a society many individuals fear to use behavior which has up to that time been under a ban and trust instead, though at great psychic cost, to attitudes that have been exercised with approval during their formative years. Insofar as we invoke a physiological scheme to account for these neurotic adjustments, we are led to overlook the possibility of developing social institutions which would lessen the social cost we now pay; instead we elaborate a set of dogmas which prove inapplicable under other social conditions.

Constrasts Between Prepubertal and Postpubertal Education
C. W. M. HART

. . . My starting point is a distinction that is made by Herskovits. In his chapter on education in the book called *Man and His Works* (1948) he finds it necessary to stress that the training of the young in the simpler societies of the world is carried on through two different vehicles. The child learns a lot of things knocking around underfoot in the home, in the village street, with his brothers and sisters, and in similar environments, and he learns a lot of other things in the rather formidable apparatus of . . . the initiation ceremonies or the initiation schools.

Herskovits stresses that initiation education takes place outside the home and is worthy to be called schooling, contrasts it with the education the child receives knocking around the household and the village long before the initiation period begins, and decides that the main feature of the latter is that it is within the home, and that it should therefore be called education as contrasted with schooling. There he, and many other writers on the subject, tend to leave the matter.

This tendency, to leave the problem at that point, is rather a pity. Further exploration of these two contrasting vehicles for training of the young will pay rich dividends, and it is to such further exploration that the bulk of this paper is devoted. Before going further certain unsatisfactory features of Herskovits' treatment must be mentioned. To suggest, as he does, that preinitiation education is "within the home" is misleading to people unacquainted with the character of primitive society. While initiation education is very definitely outside the home and . . . this remoteness . . . is a very essential feature of it, it does not follow that the other has to be, or even is likely to be, "within the home." The home in most primitive societies is very different indeed from the connotation of "home" in America, and the type of education to which Herskovits refers takes place in every conceivable type of primary group. The young child in primitive society may be subjected to the learning process in his early years in his household (Eskimo), or in a medley of dozens of households (Samoa); his parents may ignore him and leave him to drag himself up as best he can (Mundugumor); he may be corrected or scolded by any passer-by (Zuñi); his male mentor may not be his father at all but his mother's brother (many Melanesian societies); and so on.

I do not intend to explore the social-psychological results of this variety of primary-group situations; all I mention them for here is to demonstrate how misleading it is to lump them all together as comprising "ed-

Reprinted, slightly abridged, from Education and Anthropology, *edited by George D. Spindler, with the permission of the publishers, Stanford University Press. Copyright 1955, by the Board of Trustees of the Leland Stanford Junior University.*

ucation within the home." About the only things they have in common are that they all take place in the earlier years of life and they don't take place within the formal framework of initiation ceremonies. I propose therefore to call all this type of education by the title "preinitiation" or "prepuberty" education (since most initiation ceremonial begins at puberty or later), and the problem I am mainly concerned with is the set of contrasts . . . between what societies do with their children in the preinitiation period and what is done with them in the postinitiation period. In other words Herskovits' distinction between education and schooling becomes clearer and more useful if they are simply called prepuberty education and postpuberty education.

PREPUBERTAL AND POSTPUBERTAL EDUCATION—HOW DO THEY DIFFER?

If attention is directed to the ways education is carried on in the prepuberty and postpuberty periods in a large number of simple societies —viz., those "with initiation ceremonies"—some very impressive contrasts begin to appear. They can be dealt with under four heads—(1) Regulation, (2) Personnel, (3) Atmosphere, (4) Curriculum; but the nature of the data will require us to jump back and forth between these four divisions, since they are all interwoven.

1. *Regulation.* Postpuberty education, in such societies, does not begin until at least the age of twelve or thirteen, and in many cases several years later than that. By that age of course, the child has already acquired a great deal of what we call his culture. How has he acquired the things he knows at the age of twelve or thirteen? The traditional anthropological monographs are said to tell us little or nothing about "early education." I suggest that the reason the older literature tells us so little that is definite about the early prepubertal training of the children is basically for the same reason that we know so little about preschool education in our own culture, or did know so little before Gesell. Until the appearance of *The Child from Five to Ten* (Gesell and Ilg, 1946), the information on the preschool "enculturation" of the American child was just as barren as the anthropological literature. Whether Gesell has really answered the question for the American child and whether a Gesell-like job has been done or can be done for a primitive society are questions which need not concern us here except to point up the real question: Why is it so rare to find clear information as to what goes on in the learning process during the preschool years, in any culture?

One possible answer is that preschool education is rarely if ever standardized, rarely if ever regulated around known and visible social norms.*

* *Editor's note* (G. S.): Nonanthropologist readers should be aware of the fact that Dr. Hart's statements concerning the lack of uniformity in prepubertal child training would be contested by many anthropologists, though the same

It is an area of cultural laissez faire, within very wide limits of tolerance, and society at large does not lay down any firm blueprint which all personnel engaged in "raising the young" must follow. If, instead of asking for a "pattern" or "norm," we ask the simpler question, "What happens?" it seems to me that the literature is not nearly so barren of information as has been argued. It tends to suggest that anything and everything happens in the same society. For instance Schapera's account of childhood among the Bakgatla is pretty clear: "The Bakgatla say that thrashing makes a child wise. But they also say a growing child is like a little dog and though it may annoy grown-ups, it must be taught proper conduct with patience and forbearance" (Schapera, 1940). As Herskovits has pointed out, this mixture of strict and permissive techniques is also reported for Lesu in Melanesia by Powdermaker, for the Apache by Opler, and for the Kwoma by Whiting (Herskovits, *op. cit.*). This list can readily be added to.

There is no point in counting how many cultures use severe punishment and how many do not. The explicit statements of the fieldworkers just cited are at least implicit in dozens of others. Do the natives beat their children? Yes. Do they fondle and make a fuss over their children? Yes. Do they correct them? Yes. Do they let them get away with murder? Also yes. All this in the same culture. I repeat that it is pretty clear what happens in the prepuberty years in the simpler societies. Anything and everything from extreme punishment to extreme permissiveness may occur and does occur in the same culture.

The fieldworkers do not tell us what the pattern of early education is because there is rarely any one clear-cut pattern. What each individual child learns or is taught . . . is determined pretty much by a number of individual variables. A few such variables are: interest or lack of interest of individual parents in teaching their children, size of family and each sibling's position in it, whether the next house or camp is close by or far away, whether the neighbors have children of the same age, the amount of interaction and type of interaction of the particular "peer groups" of any given child. The number of variables of this type is almost infinite; the child is simply dumped in the midst of them to sink or swim, and as a result no two children in the same culture learn the same things in the same way. One, for example, may learn about sex by spying upon his parents, a second by spying upon a couple of comparative strangers, a third by getting some explicit instruction from his father or his mother (or his elder brother or his mother's brother), a fourth by listening to sniggering gossip in the play group, and a fifth by observing a pair of

---

ones might accept his basic position that in comparison to pubertal and postpubertal training the earlier years of experience are *relatively* less structured and less subject to the pressure of public opinion. (See discussion following Hart's paper, in Spindler volume.)

dogs in the sexual act. Which of these ways of learning is the norm? Obviously none of them is, at least not in the same sense as that in which we say that it is the norm for a person to inherit the property of his mother's brother, or to use an intermediary in courtship, or to learn certain important myths at Stage 6B of the initiation ceremonies.

In asking for a uniform cultural pattern in such a laissez-faire, any-thing-goes area, we are asking for the inherently impossible, or at least for the nonexistent. There are, of course, some cultural limits set in each society to this near anarchy: there will, for example, be general outrage and widespread social disapproval if one family shamefully neglects its children or some child goes to what is by general consensus regarded as "too far," but such limits of toleration are very wide indeed in every society. The household is almost sovereign in its rights to do as much or as little as it likes—that is, to do what it likes about its offspring in the *preschool* years. The rest of society is extraordinarily reluctant every-where to interfere with a household's sovereign right to bring up its pre-school children as it wishes. And most primitive parents, being busy with other matters and having numerous children anyway, leave the kids to bring each other up or to just grow like Topsy.

There are other strong lines of evidence supporting this judgment that prepuberty education in the simpler societies is relatively so variable as to be virtually normless. One is the self-evident fact which anybody can verify by reading the monographs, that no fieldworker, not even among those who have specifically investigated the matter of child practices, has ever found a tribe where several reliable informants could give him a rounded and unified account of the preschool educational practices of their tribe comparable to the rounded and generalized picture they can give him, readily and easily, of the local religion, or the folklore, or the moral code for the adults, or the local way of getting married, or the right way to build a canoe or plant a garden. This difference can best be conveyed to an anthropologist audience, perhaps, by contrasting the sort of answer fieldworkers get to such questions as "Tell me some of your myths," or "How do you make silver ornaments?" or "How do you treat your mother-in-law?" with the answer they get to a question like "How do you bring up children?" To the former type of question (not asked as crudely as that, of course) the answers will come (usually) in the form of norms—stereotyped and generalized statements that don't differ a great deal from one informant to the next, or, if they do so differ, will always be referred to a "right" way or a "proper" way: the "right" way to build a canoe, the "proper" way to treat one's mother-in-law, the "correct" form of a myth or a ceremony, and so on. Even in the type of sentence structure the answers come in, they will have this official char-acter—"We do it this way" or "It is our custom here to do thus and so"—and often in case of conflicting versions an argument will develop, not over what the informant himself does but over whether what he says is "right" or socially sanctioned as "the right way."

But given the opportunity to perform a similar generalized descriptive job upon "how children are or should be brought up," informants fail dismally to produce anything of this kind. They either look blank and say little or nothing, or come up with a set of empty platitudes—"All boys should be brought up good boys," "They should all respect their elders," etc.—which clearly have no relation to the facts of life going on all around the speaker; or (most common of all) they fall back onto their own life history and do a Sun Chief or Crashing Thunder sort of job. That is, they give in endless and boring detail an account of how they individually were brought up, or how they bring up their own children, but they clearly have no idea of whether their case is typical or atypical of the tribe at large. And the anthropologist equally has no idea of how representative or unrepresentative this case is. This happens so constantly that we are left with only one conclusion, namely, that if there is a cultural tradition for preschool education (comparable to the cultural tradition for religion or for taboo-observance or for technology), then the average native in a simple society is completely unaware of what it is.

This same conclusion is also supported by another line of evidence, namely, the complete change that comes over the picture when we move from prepuberty education to postpuberty education. Postpuberty education is marked in the simpler societies by the utmost degree of standardization and correctness. At puberty the initiation rituals begin, and perhaps the most universal thing about these is their meticulously patterned character. Every line painted on a boy's body, every movement of a performer, every word or phrase uttered, the right person to make every move, is rigidly prescribed as having to be done in one way only—the right way. A wrongly drawn line, a misplaced phrase, an unsanctioned movement, or the right movement made by the wrong person or at the wrong time, and the whole ritual is ruined. They belong to the same general type of social phenomena as the English Coronation ceremony or the Catholic sacrifice of the Mass; there is only one way of doing them, regardless of the individuals involved, namely the "right" way. By contrast that meticulously patterned feature throws into sharp relief the haphazard, permissive, and unstandardized character of the education that *precedes* the time of puberty.

2. *Personnel.* So far, then, our stress has been on the unregulated character of primitive preschool education. Certain further things become clearer if at this point we switch our attention . . . to the focus of personnel—i.e., from the question of whether the education is controlled and standardized to the question of who imparts the education. Anthropologists are coming more and more to realize the importance of

the "Who does what?" type of question in field work, and perhaps nowhere is it so important to know who does what than in the area we are discussing. From whom does the child learn in the simpler societies? As far as the preinitiation years are concerned the answer is obvious: He learns from his intimates, whether they be intimates of a senior generation like his parents or intimates of his own generation like his siblings, cousins, playmates, etc. In the preinitiation years he learns nothing or next to nothing from strangers or near-strangers. Strangers and near-strangers are people he rarely sees and even more rarely converses with; and, since learning necessarily involves interaction, it is from the people he interacts with most that he learns most, and from the people he interacts with least that he learns least.

This is so obvious that it needs little comment. But one important point about intimates must be made. In all culture it appears as if this "learning from intimates" takes two forms. The child learns from his parents or other senior members of his family, and he also learns from his play groups. And the interaction processes in these two situations are different in several important respects. The parents are intimates and so are the members of the play group, but there is the important difference that parents, to some extent at least, represent the official culture (are the surrogates of society, in Dollard's phrase), while the play groups do not. All the work upon play groups in Western society has tended to stress what autonomous little subcultures they are, each with its own social organization, its own values. The family is a primary group, but one which is tied into the total formal structure of the society and therefore subject to at least some over-all social control. The play group is an autonomous little world of its own, whose rules may be, and often are, directly at variance with the rules of the home or of the wider society.

If, then, as suggested above, it is true that in most societies—simple or modern—each household is allowed a great deal of freedom to bring up its children pretty much as it chooses, and if this wide degree of tolerance leads in turn to a wide variation in the ways in which the culture is presented to different children, then obviously such variation is enormously increased by the role of the play group. Even if we were told of a culture in which all households rigidly standardized their child-training practices, it would still fall far short of being convincing evidence of a standardized child-training situation because of the great amount of knowledge which children in all cultures acquire without the household or at least the parents being involved in the transmission process, namely the knowledge which the child "picks up somewhere."

Once we recognize the influence of this second group of intimates on how the child acquires certain aspects of his culture, the case for wide variation in early child training is greatly strengthened. There seems to be no evidence that would suggest that the play group in simple societies functions in any notably different way from the way it functions in modern societies, but unfortunately we have few studies of the "subcultures" of the playworld in other than Western cultures. Among child psychologists dealing with Western cultures, Piaget in particular has some findings that are relevant to the present discussion (Piaget, 1929, 1932). These findings tend to show that at least by the age of ten or eleven the child has become empirical and secular in his attitudes toward rules and norms of play behavior, partly because he has learned by that time that each primary group has its own rules, so that there is no "right" way, no overall norm—at least for children's games such as marbles—for all play groups to conform to. Piaget, of course, is describing European children, but primitive children spend at least as much time in unsupervised play groups as European or American children, and since their preschool period is certainly many years more prolonged, there is no apparent reason why this conclusion of Piaget should not have cross-cultural validity.

However, I am not trying to develop a theory but merely to follow through some of the difficulties that are hidden in the simple statement above that preschool learning is between intimates. There are different sorts of intimacy because of the child's dual relation to his home and to his playmates, and some of his culture is mediated to him by each. We don't know nearly enough about degrees of intimacy, and we may be forced by further research to start making classifications and subdivisions between the different sorts of intimate relationships (different "levels" of primary groups?) to which the child in any culture is exposed in his preschool years. Even if we do, however, the fact still remains that in his preinitiation years the child in primitive society learns nothing from strangers or near-strangers. And this leads to the second comment under the head of Personnel, which is that in his *postpuberty* education in contrast to that of *prepuberty* he *has to* learn from strangers or near-strangers and cannot possibly learn from anybody else. When puberty arrives and the boy is, therefore, ready for initiation (or the girl for marriage), his family, his siblings, his gangs, his village, all the intimates to whom his training or learning has been left up to now, are roughly pushed aside and a whole new personnel take over his training. Who these new teachers are varies from culture to culture, but a very common feature is that they be nonintimates of the boy, semistrangers drawn from other sections of the tribe (opposite moieties, different districts or villages, hostile or semihostile clans, different age groups, and so on), people with whom he is not at all intimate. Who they are and what they represent is made painfully clear in the ritual. An actual case will help to make clear the nature of the transition.

Among the Tiwi of North Australia, one can see the traumatic nature of the initiation period in very clear form, and part of the trauma lies in the sudden switch of personnel with whom the youth has to associate. A boy reaches thirteen or fourteen or so, and the physiological signs of puberty begin to appear. Nothing happens, possibly for many months. Then suddenly one day, toward evening when the people are gathering around their campfires for the main meal of the day after coming in from their day's hunting and food-gathering, a group of three or four heavily armed and taciturn strangers appear in camp. In full war regalia they walk in silence to the camp of the boy and say curtly to the household: "We have come for So-and-So." Immediately pandemonium breaks loose. The mother and the rest of the older women begin to howl and wail. The father rushes for his spears. The boy himself, panic-stricken, tries to hide, the younger children begin to cry, and the household dogs begin to bark. It is all terribly similar to the reaction which is provoked by the arrival of the police at an American home to pick up a juvenile delinquent. This similarity extends to the behavior of the neighbors. These carefully abstain from identifying with either the strangers or the stricken household. They watch curiously the goings-on but make no move that can be identified as supporting either side. This is particularly notable in view of the fact that the strangers are strangers to all of them, too, that is, they are men from outside the encampment, or outside the band, who, under any other circumstances, would be greeted by a shower of spears. But not under these circumstances.

In fact, when we know our way around the culture, we realize that the arrival of the strangers is not as unexpected as it appears. The father of the boy and the other adult men of the camp not only knew they were coming but have even agreed with them on a suitable day for them to come. The father's rush for his spears to protect his son and to preserve the sanctity of his household is make-believe. If he puts on too good an act, the older men will intervene and restrain him from interfering with the purposes of the strangers. With the father immobilized the child clings to his mother, but the inexorable strangers soon tear him (literally) from his mother's arms and from the bosom of his bereaved family and, still as grimly as they came, bear him off into the night. No society could symbolize more dramatically that initiation necessitates the forcible taking away of the boy from the bosom of his family, his neighbors, his intimates, his friends. And who are these strangers who forcibly drag the terrified boy off to he knows not what? In Tiwi they are a selected group of his senior male cross-cousins. To people who understand primitive social organization that should convey most of what I want to convey. They are "from the other side of the tribe," men with whom the boy has had little to do and whom he may have never seen before. They belong to the group of men who have married or will marry his sisters, and marriage, it is well to remember, in primitive society is a semihostile act. As cross-cousins, these men cannot possibly belong to the same clan as the boy, or to the same territorial group, and since only senior and already fully initiated men are eligible for the job they will be men in their thirties or forties, twenty or more years older than he.

By selecting senior cross-cousins to conduct the forcible separation of the boy from the home and thus project him into the postpuberty proceedings, the Tiwi have selected men who are as remote from the boy as possible. The only thing they and he have in common is that they are all members of the same tribe—nothing else. If, then, we have stressed that all training of the child in the prepuberty period is carried on by intimates, we have to stress equally the fact that the postpuberty training has to be in the hands of nonintimates. Anybody who is in any way close to the boy—by blood, by residence, by age, or by any other form of affiliation or association—is *ipso facto* ineligible to have a hand in his postpuberty training.

I selected the Tiwi as my example because the case happens to be rather spectacular in the clarity of its symbolism, but if one examines the literature, one finds everywhere or almost everywhere the same emphasis. Those who prefer Freudian symbolism I refer to the initiation ceremonies of the Kiwai Papuans (Landtmann, 1927), where during initiation the boy is required to actually step on his mother's stomach; when Landtmann asked the significance of this he was told that it meant that the boy was now "finished with the place where he came from" (i. e., his mother's womb). Van Gennep has collected all the older cases in his classic *Rites de passage* (Van Gennep, 1909), and no new ones which invalidate his generalizations have been reported since his time.

I therefore suggest two reasonably safe generalizations about initiation rituals: (a) The rituals themselves are designed to emphasize in very clear terms that initiation ceremonies represent a clear break with all home, household, home-town, and friendship-group ties; and (b) as a very basic part of such emphasis the complete handling of all initiation proceedings, and initiation instruction, from their inception at puberty to their final conclusion often more than a decade later, is made the responsibility of men who are comparative strangers to the boy and who are thus as different as possible in their social relationships to him from the teachers, guiders, instructors, and associates he has had up to that time.

3. *Atmosphere.* It should now be clear what is meant by the third head, Atmosphere. The arrival of the strangers to drag the yelling boy out of his mother's arms is just the spectacular beginning of a long period during which the separation of the boy from everything that has gone before is emphasized in every possible way at every minute of the day and night. So far his life has been easy; now it is hard. Up to now he has never necessarily experienced any great pain, but in the initiation period in many tribes pain, sometimes horrible, intense pain, is an obligatory feature. The boy of twelve or thirteen, used to noisy, boisterous,

irresponsible play, is expected and required to sit still for hours and days at a time saying nothing whatever but concentrating upon and endeavoring to understand long intricate instructions and "lectures" given him by his hostile and forbidding preceptors (who are, of course, the men who carried him off to initiation, the "strangers" of the previous section). Life has suddenly become real and earnest, and the initiate is required literally to "put away the things of a child," even the demeanor. The number of taboos and unnatural behaviors enjoined upon the initiate is endless. He mustn't speak unless he is spoken to; he must eat only certain foods, and often only in certain ways, at fixed times, and in certain fixed positions. All contact with females, even speech with them, is rigidly forbidden, and this includes mother and sisters. He cannot even scratch his head with his own hand, but must do it with a special stick and so on, through a long catalogue of special, unnatural, but obligatory behaviors covering practically every daily activity and every hour of the day and night. And during this time he doesn't go home at night or for the week end or on a forty-eight-hour pass, but remains secluded in the bush, almost literally the prisoner of his preceptors, for months and even years at a time. If he is allowed home at rare intervals, he has to carry all his taboos with him, and nothing is more astonishing in Australia than to see some youth who the year before was a noisy, brash, boisterous thirteen-year-old, sitting the following year, after his initiation has begun, in the midst of his family, with downcast head and subdued air, not daring even to smile, still less to speak. He is "home on leave," but he must just as well have stayed in camp for all the freedom from discipline his spell at home is giving him.

The preoccupations of anthropologists with other interests (that of the earlier fieldworkers with the pain-inflicting aspects of the initiations, and the recent preoccupation with early physiological experiences) have directed attention away from what may well be the most important aspect of education in the simpler societies, namely the possibly traumatic aspect of the initiation ceremonies. From whatever aspect we view them their whole tenor is to produce shock, disruption, a sharp break with the past, a violent projection out of the known into the unknown. Perhaps the boys are old enough to take it in their stride and the experience is not really traumatic. If so, it would seem that primitive society goes to an awful lot of trouble and wastes an awful lot of man-hours needlessly. Actually we don't know what the psychological effects of initiation upon the initiates are. All that can be said safely is that judged by the elaboration and the minuteness of detail in the shocking and disruptive features of initiation rituals, they certainly appear to be designed to produce the maximum amount of shock possible for the society to achieve.

This may suggest that our own exaggerated concern with protecting our own adolescents from disturbing experiences is quite unnecessary. If the grueling ordeal of subincision, with all its accompanying disruptive devices, leaves the young Australian psychologically unscathed, we needn't worry that Universal Military Training, for instance, will seriously upset the young American. But perhaps something in the prepuberty training prepares the young Australian and makes him capable of standing the trauma of the initiation period.

4. *Curriculum.* What is the purpose of all this elaboration of shock ritual? Ask the natives themselves and they will answer vaguely, "to make a child into a man." Occasionally a more specific verb is used and the answer becomes, "to teach a boy to become a man." What is supposed to be learned and what do the preceptors teach in the initiation schools? Perhaps the most surprising thing is what is not taught. It is hard to find in the literature any case where the initiation curriculum contains what might be called "practical subjects," or how to make a basic living. (There appear to be certain exceptions to this generalization, but they are more apparent than real.) The basic food-getting skills of the simpler peoples are never imparted in the initiation schools. Where practical subjects are included (as in Polynesia or in the Poro schools of Liberia and Sierra Leone), they are specialized crafts, not basic food-getting skills. Hunting, gardening, cattle-tending, fishing, are not taught the boy at initiation; he has already learned the rudiments of these at home in his intimate groups before his initiation starts. This is a surprising finding because of the well-known fact that many of these people live pretty close to the starvation point, and none of them manage to extract much more than subsistence from their environment. But despite this, the cultures in question are blissfully oblivious of economic determinism, and blandly leave instruction in basic food production to the laissez-faire, casual, hit-or-miss teaching of parents, friends, play groups, etc. When society itself forcibly takes over the boy in order to make him into a man and teach him the things a man should know, it is not concerned with teaching him to be a better hunter or gardener or tender of cattle or fisherman, even though the economic survival of the tribe clearly depends on all the adult men being good at one or another of these occupations. The initiation curricula cover instead quite a different series of subjects, which I am tempted to call "cultural subjects"—in either sense of the word "culture."

Of course, there is much variation here from tribe to tribe and region to region, but the imparting of religious knowledge always occupies a prominent place. This (in different cultures) includes such things as the learning of the myths, the tribal accounts of the tribe's own origin and history, and the performance, the meaning, and the sacred connections and connotations of the ceremonials. In brief, novices are taught theology, which in primitive society is inextricably mixed up with astronomy, geology, geography, biology (the mysteries of birth and sex), philosophy, art, and music—in short, the whole cultural heritage of the tribe. . . . As Pettit has pointed out, the instruction in the initiation schools is "a constant challenge to the elders to review, analyze, dramatize, and defend their cultural heritage" (Pettit, 1946). That sentence . . . is very striking, because you can apply it equally aptly to a group of naked old men in Central Australia sitting talking to a novice in the middle of a treeless desert, and to most lectures in a college of liberal arts in the United States. It serves to draw attention to the fact that, in the simpler societies, the schools run and manned and controlled and financed by the society at large are designed not to make better economic men of the novices, or better food producers, but to produce better citizens, better carriers of the culture through the generations, people better informed about the world they live in and the tribe they belong to. It is here finally, through this sort of curriculum, that each adolescent becomes "enculturated," no matter how haphazard and individualized his learning and his growth may have been up to now. It is through the rigidly disciplined instruction of a common and rigidly prescribed curriculum that he assumes, with all his fellow tribesmen, a common culture. This is where standardization occurs in the educational process of the simpler societies. Everybody who goes through the initiation schools, generation after generation, is presented with the same material, organized and taught in the same way, with no allowances made for individual taste or choice or proclivity, and no substitutions or electives allowed. When we realize how standardized and rigid and uniform this curriculum is, it should help us to realize how variable, how un-uniform, how dictated by chance, accident, and the personal whims of individual parents, individual adult relatives, and the variation in peer and play groups is the "curriculum" on or in which the individual child is trained during the long impressionable period that precedes puberty.

GENERAL CONCLUSION

1. There are typically (though not universally) in primitive societies two sharply contrasting educational vehicles, the preschool process, lasting from birth to puberty, and the initiation procedures, beginning around puberty or a little later and lasting from six months to fifteen years. These two educational vehicles show some highly significant contrasts.

2. From the point of view of regulation, the preschool period is characterized by its loose, vague, unsystematic character. Few primitive societies follow any set standards or rules on how children shall be brought up. . . . This is not, of course, to deny that there are differences from culture to culture in the degree to which children are loved and fussed over or treated as nuisances or joys. I am not questioning the fact, for

example, that the Arapesh love children, whereas the Mundugumor resent them. . . . (But) there is still . . . wide variation in conditioning and learning between one Mundugumor child and the next.

3. If this view is correct, it raises certain interesting possibilities for theory. Because of the heavy Freudian emphasis in the literature on child training in recent years, there exists a strong and unfortunate tendency to talk of child training as if it were co-terminous with swaddling, suckling, weaning, and toilet-training practices. But these "physiological" areas or "bodily functions" areas are only a small part of the preschool education of the primitive child. Even if in primitive cultures the physiological areas of child training are relatively standardized (and this is by no means certain), there is no evidence that the nonphysiological areas are. On the contrary, the evidence points in the other direction. Among adult members of the same society there may be, for example, great variation in apparent strength of the sex drive, or in the overt expression of aggressive or passive personality traits (Hart, 1954). Where does such "personality variation" come from? From childhood experiences, say the Freudians. I agree. But in order to demonstrate that personality variation in adult life has its roots in early childhood experiences, it is necessary to show not that childhood experiences are highly standardized in early life and that child training is uniform, but that they are highly variable. How can we account for the self-evident fact of adult personality variation by stressing the uniformity of standardization of childhood training? Surely the more valid hypothesis or the more likely lead is to be found in those aspects of child training which are not uniform and not standardized.

4. So much for the preschool training. But there is also the other vehicle of education and youth training in primitive society, the initiation rituals. The initiation period demonstrates to us what standardization and uniformity . . . really mean. When we grasp the meaning of this demonstration we can only conclude that compared with the rigidities of the initiation period, the prepuberty period is a loose, lax period. Social scientists who find it necessary for their theories to stress uniformity and pressures toward conformity in simple societies are badly advised to take the prepuberty period for their examples. The natives themselves know better than this. When they are adults, it is to the happy, unregulated, care-free days of prepuberty that they look back. "Then my initiation began," says the informant, and immediately a grim, guarded "old-man" expression comes over his face, "and I was taken off by the old men." The same old men (and women) who sit around and indulgently watch the vagaries and idiosyncrasies of the children without correction become the grim, vigilant, reproving watchers of the initiates, and any departure or attempted departure from tradition is immediately reprimanded.

5. Who are the agents of this discipline? Primitive societies answer in

loud and unmistakable tones that discipline cannot be imposed by members of the primary group, that it has to be imposed by "outsiders." The widespread nature of this feature of initiation is, to my mind, very impressive. Making a boy into a man is rarely, anywhere, left to the family, the household, the village, to which he belongs and where he is on intimate terms with people.[8] The initiation schools are directed at imparting instruction that cannot be given in the home, under conditions as unlike home conditions as possible, by teachers who are the antithesis of the home teachers the boy has hitherto had. The symbolisms involved in the forcible removal from the home atmosphere; the long list of taboos upon homelike acts, homelike speech, homelike demeanor, homelike habits; the selection of the initiators (i.e., the teachers or preceptors) from the semihostile sections of the tribe—all tell the same story, that the turning of boys into men can only be achieved by making everything about the proceedings as different from the home and the prepuberty situation as possible. Everything that happens to the initiate during initiation has to be as different as it can be made by human ingenuity from the things that happened to him before initiation.

6. . . . what is actually . . . taught in the initiation schools is the whole value system of the culture, its myths, its religion, its philosophy, its justification of its own entity as a culture. Primitive society clearly values these things, values them so much that it cannot leave them to individual families to pass on to the young. It is willing to trust the haphazard, individually varied teaching methods of families and households and peer groups and gossip to teach children to walk and talk, about sex, how to get along with people, or how to be a good boy; it is even willing to leave to the individual families the teaching of how to hunt or to garden or to fish or to tend cattle; but the tribal philosophy, the religion, the citizenship knowledge, too important to leave to such haphazard methods, must be taught by society at large through its appointed and responsible representatives.

In doing this, society is asserting and underlining its rights in the child. The . . . [Australian cross-cousins, etc., who seize the child] . . . are the representatives of society at large, the native equivalents of the truant officer, the policeman, and the draft board, asserting the priority of society's rights over the family's rights in the child. Clearly, in every society there is always a family and there is always a state, and equally clearly both have rights in every child born into the society. And

[8] In the original draft of this paper I mentioned the Arapesh as one of the few exceptions. At the Stanford conference, however, Dr. Margaret Mead pointed out that while it is true that initiation in Arapesh is carried out by intimates, they wear masks. To me this correction of my original remark dramatically emphasizes the main point. The Arapesh social structure is such that there are no "strangers" to use for initiation; therefore they invent them by masking some intimates.

no society yet—Western or non-Western—has found any perfect way or equal way of adjudicating or harmonizing public rights and private rights. The state's rights must have priority when matters of citizenship are involved, but the assertion of the state's rights is always greeted with wails of anguish from the family. "I didn't raise my boy to go off and get subincised," wails the Australian mother, but he is carried off and subincised just the same. "I didn't raise my boy for the draft board or the school board," says the American mother, but her protests are of no avail either. It is an inevitable conflict, because it arises from the very structure of society, as long as society is an organization of family units, which it is universally. The only solution is to abolish the family or abolish the state, and no human group has been able to do either.

7. The boy is not ruined for life or a mental cripple as a result of the harrowing initiation experience, but is a social being *in a way he never was before*. He has been made aware of his wider social responsibilities and his wider membership in the total society, but more important in the present context, he has been exposed to a series of social situations in which friendship counts for naught, crying or whining gets one no place, whimsy or charm or boyish attractiveness pays no dividends, and friends, pull, and influence are without effect. The tribal tradition, the culture, treats all individuals alike, and skills and wiles that were so valuable during childhood in gaining preferential treatment or in winning approval or avoiding disapproval are all to no avail. He goes into the initiation period a child, which is a social animal of one sort, but he comes out a responsible enculturated citizen, which is a social animal of a different sort.

8. Primitive societies, then, devote a great deal of time and care to training for citizenship. They make no attempt to even start such training until the boy has reached puberty. But once they start, they do it thoroughly. Citizenship training in these societies means a great deal more than knowing the words of "The Star-Spangled Banner" and memorizing the Bill of Rights. It means exposing the boy under particularly stirring and impressive conditions to the continuity of the cultural tradition, to the awe and majesty of the society itself, emphasizing the subordination of the individual to the group at large and hence the mysteriousness, wonder, and sacredness of the whole individual-society relationship. In Australia, the most sacred part of the whole initiation ritual is when the boys are shown the *churinga*, which are at the same time their own souls and the souls of the tribe which came into existence at the creation of the world. Citizenship, being an awesome and mysterious business in any culture, cannot be imparted or taught or instilled in a secular atmosphere; it must be imparted in an atmosphere replete with symbolism and mystery. Whether it can be taught at all without heavy emphasis on its otherworldliness, without heavy sacred emphasis,

whether the teaching of citizenship can ever be a warm, friendly, loving, cozy, and undisturbing process, is a question I leave to the educators. Primitive societies obviously do not believe it can be taught that way, as is proved by the fact that they never try.

9. One last point, implied in much of the above but worth special mention, is the rather surprising fact that technological training, training in "getting a living," is absent from the initiation curricula, despite its obvious vital importance to the survival of the individual, of the household, and of the tribe or society. . . . The reason for this omission . . . is, I think, pretty clear. In the simpler societies there is nothing particularly mysterious, nothing spiritual or otherworldly about getting a living, or hunting or gardening or cattle-herding. It is true that there is apt to be a lot of magical practice mixed up with these things, but even this heavy magical element is conceived in very secular and individualistic terms. That is, it either works or doesn't work in particular cases, and each man or each household or clan has its own garden magic or cattle magic or hunting magic which differs from the next man's [etc.]. Dobu, for instance, is . . . riddled with garden magic; so is . . . Trobriand, but each group's magic is individually owned and comparisons of magic are even made between group and group. For this reason, garden skills or hunting skills, even though they include magical elements, can still safely be left by society to the private level of transmission and teaching. Public control, public supervision is minimal.

This leads to two further conclusions, or at least suggestions. (1) On this line of analysis, we can conclude the primitive societies, despite their marginal subsistence and the fact that they are frequently close to the starvation point, devote more care and attention, *as societies*, to the production of good citizens, than to the production of good technicians, and therefore they can be said to value good citizenship more highly than they value the production of good food producers. Can this be said for modern societies, including our own? (2) This relative lack of interest in standardizing subsistence training, while insisting on standardizing training in the ideological aspects of culture, may go a long way toward enabling us to explain the old sociological problem called cultural lag . . . technology is easier to change, this change takes place with less resistance than change in nontechnological or ideological fields. [The present discussion is helpful by pointing to the laissez-faire attitude toward prepubertal training, including training in food getting and other technology; therefore] the attitude toward these techniques that the child develops is a secular one. . . . Hence variations and alternatives . . . are not resisted with anything like the intensity of feeling [given] . . . variations or alternatives [in ideology]. . . . [Hence white man's gun or spade may be accepted matter of factly while ideological elements are strongly resisted, because they involve elements learned] . . . in the

awesome sacred atmosphere of the initiation schools, wherein no individual variation is allowed and the very notion of alternatives is anathema. [The apparent exception of specialized technical training imparted in Polynesia and in Poro schools in Africa, do not involve the ordinary food-getting techniques, but special crafts regarded as "mysteries," just as crafts were still called in England under Henry VIII.]
. . . . To conclude . . . one final summary. In primitive society there are two vehicles of education, the prepuberty process and the postpuberty process. No Western writer has succeeded in contrasting them as much as they need to be contrasted, because they are in every possible respect the Alpha and Omega of each other. In time of onset, atmosphere, personnel, techniques of instruction, location, curriculum, the two vehicles represent opposite poles. . . . Standardization of experience and uniformity of training is markedly present in postinitiation experiences: it is markedly absent in the prepuberty experience of the growing child. . . . [This] has a very important implication for the whole field of personality studies, especially for those studies which seem to claim that personality is very homogeneous in the simpler societies and for those allied studies which allege that child training and growing up in primitive society are very different from their equivalents in modern Western cultures. It [suggests] a base for answering [the question], "Why do individuals in simple cultures differ from each other so markedly in personality traits, despite common cultural conditioning?" [also relevant for problems of linkage between personality formation and cultural change]. . . . [A single linking thread is this:] . . . that childhood experience is part of the secular world, postpuberty experience part of the sacred world. What is learned in the secular world is learned haphazardly, and varies greatly from individual to individual. Therefore, no society can standardize that part of the child's learning which is acquired under secular circumstances. . . .

REFERENCES

Gesell, Arnold, and Frances L. Ilg. 1946. The Child from Five to Ten. New York: Harper & Brothers.
Hart, C. W. M. 1954. "The Sons of Turimpi," American Anthropologist, LVI, 242-61.
Herskovits, Melville J. 1948. Man and His Works. New York: Alfred A. Knopf, Inc.
Landtmann, Gunnar. 1927. The Kiwai Papuans of British New Guinea. London: The Macmillan Company.
Pettit, George A. 1946. "Primitive Education in North America," University of California Publications in American Archaeology and Ethnology, XLIII, 182.
Piaget, Jean. 1929. The Child's Conception of the World. New York: Harcourt, Brace and Company.
——. 1932. The Moral Judgment of the Child. London: Kegan Paul.

Schapera, I. 1940. *Married Life in an African Tribe.* London: Sheridan House.
Van Gennep, Arnold. 1909. *Les rites de passage.* Paris: E. Nourry.

Comment on Hart's paper

While the universality of the contrasts Hart presents is probably overdrawn in his presentation, it is useful to take his picture as a provisional view of some universal problems of growing up and link his interpretation to the *psychodynamic* problems we are concerned with in this book. As noted, while Hart is skeptical toward interpretations of puberty ceremonies that emphasize psychosexual aspects, e.g., genital operations, themes of death and rebirth, etc., there is nothing in psychodynamic analysis that is incompatible with the interpretations on which he focuses. If one accepts provisionally Hart's characterization of the later-childhood prepuberty period as involving laissez-faire secular training, one can legitimately ask what common psychosexual problems—*in addition to* the adulthood-preparation problems—are posed by this stage, which is precisely the Freudian *latency* period. And conversely, what problems are raised by the pubertal period.

The answers, in line with the themes developed in the earlier chapters of this book, seem to me to be clear: man evolved as an infantilized ape with a di-phasic onset of sexuality (infantile and pubertal). The latency period represents a delay between the maturation of *germa* at roughly the age of five years, and the maturation of *soma* (the body) several years later.[9] This time of delay provides an opportunity for the child to acquire an essential part of that learning transmitted by any human culture, without which he cannot become a fully participating member of a human society. The *kind* of learning characteristic of this phase is congruent with the psychosexual nature of latency: that is, the forces of sexuality, while not completely subdued are *relatively* in abeyance. Hence attention is released for the basically *objective*—i.e., secular—learning tasks. In "simpler" cultures these include practically all the basic technological skills. Boys learn hunting and fishing and all their ancillary arts, while girls learn wild-plant gathering or horticulture, food and clothing preparation, and child care. In modern societies this is the age when schools provide the ABC's or the "three R's," i.e. at least the

[9] Compare the passage from Róheim and related discussion in Chapter One.

rudiments necessary for getting along in a literate culture with a money economy—in contrast to the mythological learning such as "history" and cultural (useless) learning such as the fine arts at the high school level.

By contrast, the nonutilitarian, more sacred, and more formal learning of the postpubertal period suggests not only the necessity to acquire the "secrets" of the culture as preparation for citizenship rather than mere livelihood—for we could ask why at that stage, why couldn't those things also be learned at the prepubertal level? I think the answer must be sought on the psychodynamic plane. Puberty reintroduces infantile sexuality into the life of the child-becoming-adult, after the several years of moratorium from its pressures that he has enjoyed in later childhood. Sex with all its mysteries and anxieties has returned in full force, and a casual, laissez-faire, secular approach to this powerful force is simply not adequate to the psychosocial demands of this phase. The changes in the body, the rearousal of feelings reminiscent of a much earlier period the child seemed to have long since outgrown, are all mysterious and potentially terrifying experiences. The anxieties cry for some binding and containing. The potential chaos of sexuality calls for both recognition and regulation, and casual permissiveness would seem to be the last thing in the world the child needs at this stage. We have already noted some types of "solutions," for example, the fierce collectivist puritanism of the Kibbutz *Sabras* during this phase, where largely lacking authoritarian controls from adults, they have instituted such regulation themselves. (See Chaper Two.) In our own society, where laissez-faire policies are followed, out of neglect or out of misguided psychologism, and/or where the curricular emphasis is utilitarian, we have plenty of evidence of great unrest and dissatisfaction among the adolescents, frequently expressed in some form of "delinquency" outbursts signaling a cry for help. In effect they are crying for more restrictive boundaries—even where the youngsters *appear* to be crying for license to do whatever lustful mischief they please. Note the phenomenon in our present-day society where parents are baffled to find their permissiveness toward their adolescent children met with the latter's great preoccupation with parental or dorm-parents' rules and regulations. The youngsters' attitudes are not only negativistic toward the rules, but rather basically *ambivalent* (otherwise would they be so shrill?). The authorities are accused of being too restrictive and simultaneously of being too uncaring, too indifferent, or too confused and inconsistent, so that the adolescents do not know *what* to expect from them. (Rather than taking these charges at face value, we do better to take them as reflections of the unbalance and conflict felt by the adolescents *themselves* in reaction to their own ill-understood internal and external pressures.) It would be useful to consider the adolescent reactions as a cry for something functionally equivalent to the highly restrictive, conventionalized, and ritualized postpubertal education Hart is describing for (certain) primitive tribes, an education both authoritarian in method and highly sacred in content.

2. MEANINGS AND DETERMINANTS OF PUBERTY CEREMONIES

Neither Benedict nor Hart raises the following question: If some societies are marked by great continuity from childhood to postpuberty, and others by great discontinuity, dealt with by dramatic ritualization of puberty or initiation ceremonies, why is this so? What distinguishes those that have more continuity, those that have less? Why do some societies have elaborate puberty ceremonies, others not? The question can be further elaborated by the distinction between ceremonies for males and those for females: Which have such rituals only for males, which only for females, and which for both?

If puberty is a crisis with a biological base, why is it psychologically and culturally so different in different societies? The following papers and discussion examine this question.

The Function of Male Initiation Ceremonies at Puberty
JOHN W. M. WHITING, RICHARD KLUCKHOHN, AND ALBERT ANTHONY

Our society gives little formal recognition of the physiological and social changes a boy undergoes at puberty. He may be teased a little when his voice changes or when he shaves for the first time. Changes in his social status from childhood to adulthood are marked by a number of minor events rather than by any single dramatic ceremonial observance. Gradu-

Reprinted by permission, from Readings in Social Psychology, *Third Edition, edited by E. Maccoby, T. Newcomb, and E. Hartley, copyright © 1958 by Holt, Rinehart and Winston, Inc.*

ation from grammar school and subsequently from high school are steps to adulthood, but neither can be considered as a *rite de passage*. Nor may the accomplishment of having obtained a driver's license, which for many boys is the most important indication of having grown up, be classed as one. Legally the twenty-first birthday is the time at which a boy becomes a man; but, except for a somewhat more elaborate birthday party this occasion is not ceremonially marked and, therefore, cannot be thought of as a *rite de passage*. Neither physiologically, socially, nor legally is there a clear demarcation between boyhood and manhood in our society.

Such a gradual transition from boyhood to manhood is by no means universal. Among the Thonga, a tribe in South Africa, every boy must go through a very elaborate ceremony in order to become a man.[10] When a boy is somewhere between ten and sixteen years of age, he is sent by his parents to a "circumcision school." Here in company with his age-mates he undergoes severe hazing by the adult males of the society. The initiation begins when each boy runs the gauntlet between two rows of men who beat him with clubs. At the end of this experience he is stripped of his clothes and his hair is cut. He is next met by a man covered with lion manes and is seated upon a stone facing this "lion man." Someone then strikes him from behind, and when he turns his head to see who has struck him, his foreskin is seized and in two movements cut off by the "lion man." Afterward he is secluded for three months in the "yards of mysteries," where he can be seen only by the initiated. It is especially taboo for a woman to approach these boys during their seclusion, and if a woman should glance at the leaves with which the circumcised covers his wound and which form his only clothing, she must be killed.

During the course of his initiation, the boy undergoes six major trials: beatings, exposure to cold, thirst, eating of unsavory foods, punishment, and the threat of death. On the slightest pretext he may be severely beaten by one of the newly initiated men who is assigned to the task by the older men of the tribe. He sleeps without covering and suffers bitterly from the winter cold. He is forbidden to drink a drop of water during the whole three months. Meals are often made nauseating by the half-digested grass from the stomach of an antelope which is poured over his food. If he is caught breaking any important rule governing the ceremony, he is severely punished. For example, in one of these punishments, sticks are placed between the fingers of the offender, then a strong man closes his hand around that of the novice practically crushing his fingers. He is frightened into submission by being told that in former times boys who had tried to escape or who revealed the secrets to women or to the uninitiated were hanged and their bodies burnt to ashes.

[10] The following account is taken from Henri A. Junod, *The Life of A South African Tribe* (London: Macmillan & Co., Ltd., 1927), pp. 74-95.

Although the Thonga are extreme in the severity of this sort of initiation, many other societies have rites which have one or more of the main features of the Thonga ceremony. Of a sample of 55 societies[11] chosen for this study, 18 have one or more of the four salient features of the Thonga ceremony, e. g., painful hazing by adult males, genital operations, seclusion from women, and tests of endurance and manliness; the remaining 37 societies either have no ceremony at all or one which does not have any of the above features.[12]

HYPOTHESES

It is the purpose of this paper to develop a set of hypotheses concerning the function of male initiation rites which accounts for the presence of these rites in some societies and the absence of them in others. The theory that we have chosen to test has been suggested by previous explanations for the rites, particularly those of psychoanalytic origin.[13] These explanations were modified to fit the problem of this research in two respects. First, certain of the concepts and hypotheses were restated or redefined so as to be coherent with the growing general behavioral theory of personality development,[14] and second, they were restated in such a way as to be amenable to cross-cultural test, i.e., cultural indices were specified for each variable.

We assume that boys tend to be initiated at puberty in those societies in which they are particularly hostile toward their fathers and dependent upon their mothers. The hazing of the candidates, as well as the genital operations, suggests that one function of the rites is to prevent open and violent revolt against parental authority at a time when physical maturity would make such revolt dangerous and socially disruptive. Isolation

---

[11] The method of sample selection is discussed below.

[12] Seven of these societies have a minor ceremony which generally takes place during adolescence. In these societies the boy's change in status is announced by investing him with some symbol of manhood such as donning of long pants which played such a role in our society in former years. Specifically, these are tattooing—Maori and Ontong Javanese; tooth filing—Alorese, Balinese, and Lakher; donning the "sacred thread"—Hindu (Khalapur Rajput). The Kwakuitl fall in a similar category. Their ceremony consists of a potlach given for the boy by his father. The ceremonies in these societies are so different in sociopsychological import from those to be described below that they will be classed hereafter with those societies which lack puberty ceremonies.

[13] See, e.g., Sigmund Freud, *Moses and Monotheism* (New York: Alfred A. Knopf, Inc., 1939); Bruno Bettelheim, *Symbolic Wounds* (Glencoe, Ill.: Free Press, 1954); Margaret Mead, *Male and Female* (New York: William Morrow & Co., Inc., 1949).

[14] See, e.g., J. W. M. Whiting and Irwin L. Child, *Child Training and Personality* (New Haven: Yale University Press, 1953); Robert R. Sears, Eleanor E. Maccoby, and Harry Levin, *Patterns of Child Rearing* (Evanston, Ill.: Row, Peterson & Co., 1957); and John Dollard and Neal E. Miller, *Personality and Psychotherapy* (New York: McGraw-Hill Book Co., 1950).

from women and tests of manliness suggest that another function of the rites is to break an excessively strong dependence upon the mother and to ensure identification with adult males and acceptance of the male role.

It is to be noted here that the educational and disciplinary functions of the initiation are not limited in time to the actual period of initiation. The boy knows all during childhood and latency about the initiation which he will face at puberty. While he is overtly not supposed to know any of the secrets of the rite, he actually knows almost everything that will happen to him. He is both afraid of what he knows will happen and also envious of the kudos and added status which his older friends have acquired through having successfully gone through this rite. Thus, through the boy's whole life the initiation ceremony serves as a conditioner of his behavior and his attitudes toward male authority, while at the same time emphasizing the advantages of becoming a member of the male group through initiation.

We assume that a long and exclusive relationship between mother and son provides the conditions which should lead to an exceptionally strong dependence upon the mother. Also, we assume that if the father terminates this relationship and replaces his son, there should be strong envy and hostility engendered in the boy which, although held in check during childhood, may dangerously manifest itself with the onset of puberty, unless measures are taken to prevent it.

As we indicated above, the hypothesis is derived from psychoanalytic theory. However, it should be noted that there are some modifications which may be important. First, no assumption is being made that the envy is exclusively sexual in character. We are making the more general assumption that if the mother for a prolonged period devotes herself to the satisfaction of all the child's needs—including hunger, warmth, safety, freedom from pain, as well as sex—he will become strongly dependent upon her. In accordance with this we believe rivalry may be based upon a competition for the fulfillment of any of these needs. Second, we do not propose, as most psychoanalysts do, that Oepidal rivalry is a universal, but rather we claim it is a variable which may be strong or weak depending upon specific relationships between father, mother, and son. Thus, we assume father-son rivalry may range from a value of zero to such high intensities that the whole society may be required to adjust to it.

An illustration of cultural conditions which should intensify the dependency of a boy on his mother and rivalry with his father is found in the following case.

Kwoma dependency. The Kwoma,[15] a tribe living about 200 miles

[15] For a description of the Kwoma child-rearing reported here see J. W. M. Whiting, *Becoming a Kwoma* (New Haven: Yale University Press, 1941), pp. 24-64.

up the Sepik River in New Guinea, have initiation rites similar to those of the Thonga. Examination of the differences in the relationship of a mother to her infant during the first years of his life reveals some strong contrasts between the Kwoma and our own society. While in our society an infant sleeps in his own crib and the mother shares her bed with the father, the Kwoma infant sleeps cuddled in his mother's arms until he is old enough to be weaned, which is generally when he is two or three years old. The father, in the meantime, sleeps apart on his own bark slab bed. Furthermore during this period, the Kwoma mother abstains from sexual intercourse with her husband in order to avoid having to care for two dependent children at the same time. Since the Kwoma are polygynous and discreet extramarital philandering is permitted, this taboo is not too hard on the husband. In addition, it is possible that the mother obtains some substitute sexual gratification from nursing and caring for her infant.[16] If this be the case, it is not unlikely that she should show more warmth and affection toward her infant than if she were obtaining sexual gratification from her husband. Whether or not the custom can be attributed to this sex taboo, the Kwoma mother, while her co-wife does the housework, not only sleeps with her infant all night but holds it in her lap all day without apparent frustration. Such a close relationship between a mother and child in our society would seem not only unbearably difficult to the mother, but also somewhat improper.

When the Kwoma child is weaned, a number of drastic things happen all at once. He is suddenly moved from his mother's bed to one of his own. His father resumes sexual relations with his mother. Although the couple wait until their children are asleep, the intercourse takes place in the same room. Thus, the child may truly become aware of his replacement. He is now told that he can no longer have his mother's milk because some supernatural being needs it. This is vividly communicated to him by his mother when she puts a slug on her breasts and daubs the blood-colored sap of the breadfruit tree over her nipples. Finally he is no longer permitted to sit on his mother's lap. She resumes her work and goes to the garden to weed or to the swamp to gather sago flour leaving him behind for the first time in his life. That these events are traumatic to the child is not surprising. He varies between sadness and anger, weeping and violent temper tantrums.

It is our hypothesis that it is this series of events that makes it neces-

---

[16] This is, of course, difficult to determine and is a presumption based upon the following factors: (1) Kwoma informants reported that mothers had no desire for sexual intercourse as long as they were nursing the infant and (2) clinical evidence from women in our own society suggests that nursing is sexually gratifying to some women at least. See Therese Benedek, "Mother-Child, the Primary Psychomatic Unit," *Am. J. Ortho-Psychiatry*, 1949, XIX; Helene Deutsch, *The Psychology of Women* (New York: Grune & Stratton, Inc.,. 1944-45), Vols. I and II; Sears, Maccoby, and Levin, *op. cit.*

sary, when the boy reaches adolescence, for the society to have an initiation rite of the type we have already described. It is necessary to put a
final stop to (1) his wish to return to his mother's arms and lap, (2) to
prevent an open revolt against his father who has displaced him from his
mother's bed, and (3) to ensure identification with the adult males of
the society. In other words, Kwoma infancy so magnifies the conditions
which should produce Oedipus rivalry that the special cultural adjustment of ceremonial hazing, isolation from women, and symbolic castration, etc., must be made to resolve it.

TESTING THE HYPOTHESIS

To test this hypothesis a sample of 56 societies was selected. First, the
ethnographic material on more than 150 societies was checked to determine whether or not there was an adequate description of our variables,
e.g., sleeping arrangements, postpartum sex taboo, and initiation rites at
puberty. Only half of the societies reviewed fulfilled these conditions.
Although we had initially endeavored to select our cases so as to have
maximum distribution throughout the world, we found that some areas
were represented by several societies, while others were not represented
by any. To correct for any bias that might result from this sample, we
made a further search of the ethnographic literature in order to fill in
the gaps, and we thereby added several societies from areas previously not
represented. Finally, to maximize diversity and to minimize duplication
through selection of closely related societies, whenever there were two or
more societies from any one culture area which had the same values on
all our variables, we chose only one of them. Using these criteria, our
final sample consisted of 56 societies representing 45 of the 60 culture
areas designated by Murdock.[17]

The societies comprising our final sample range in size and type from
small, simple, tribal groups to segments of large, complex civilizations
such as the United States or Japan. In the latter case, our information
has been drawn from ethnographic reports on a single delineated community.

When this sample had finally been chosen, the material relevant to
our variables was first abstracted, and then judgments were made for
each society as to the nature of the transition from boyhood to manhood, the sleeping arrangements, and the duration of the postpartum sex
taboo. To prevent contamination, the judgments on each variable were
made at different times and the name of the society disguised by a code.
All judgments were made by at least two persons and in every case where
there was a disagreement (less than 15 percent of the cases for any given
variable), the data were checked by one of the authors, whose judgment

[17] G. P. Murdock, "World Ethnographic Sample," *Am. Anthropol.*, 1957,
LIX, 664-87.

was accepted as final. Our findings with respect to initiation rites have been tabulated in Table 4.1 below.

We discovered that only five societies out of the total number had sleeping arrangements similar to our own, that is, where the father and mother share a bed and the baby sleeps alone. In only three societies did the mother, the father, and the baby each have his or her own bed. In the remaining 48, the baby slept with his mother until he was at least a year old and generally until he was weaned. In 24 of the latter, however, the father also shared the bed, the baby generally sleeping between the mother and father. The remaining 24 societies had sleeping arrangements like the Kwoma in which the mother and child sleep in one bed and the father in another. Often the father's bed was not even in the same house. He either slept in a men's club house or in the hut of one of his other wives, leaving mother and infant not only alone in the same bed but alone in the sleeping room.

Similarly, the societies of our sample were split on the rules regulating the resumption of sexual intercourse following parturition. Twenty-nine,

Table 4.1

THE RELATIONSHIP BETWEEN EXCLUSIVE MOTHER-SON SLEEPING ARRANGEMENTS AND A POSTPARTUM SEX TABOO* AND THE OCCURRENCE OF INITIATION CEREMONIES AT PUBERTY

Customs in infancy		Customs at adolescent initiation ceremonies		
Exclusive mother-son sleeping arrangements	Postpartum sex taboo	Absent	Present	
Long	Long		Azande	hgs †
			Camayura	hs
			Chagga	hgs
			Cheyenne	ht
			Chiricahua	ht
			Dahomeans	hgs
			Fijians	gs
			Jivaro	ht
		Ganda	Kwoma	hgs
		Khalapur (Rajput)	Lesu	gs
		Nyakyusa	Nuer	hs
		Tepoztlan	Samoans	g
		Trobrianders	Thonga	hgs
		Yapese	Tiv	hgs
	Short	Ashanti		
		Malaita	Cagaba	ht
		Siriono		

Table 4.1 continued

Customs in infancy		Customs at adolescent initiation ceremonies		
Exclusive mother-son sleeping arrangements	Postpartum sex taboo	Absent	Present	
Short	Long	Araucanians Pilaga Pondo Tallensi	Kwakiutl Ojibwa Ooldea	s t hgs
	Short	Alorese Balinese Druz Egyptians (Silwa) Eskimos (Copper) French Igorot (Bontoc) Japanese (Suye Mura) Koryak (Maritime) Lakher Lamba Lapps Lepcha Maori Mixtecans Navaho Ontong Javanese Papago Serbs Tanala (Menabe) Trukese United States (Homestead) Yagua	Hopi Timbira	hs hst

* Both of a year or more duration.
† The letters following the tribal designations in the right-hand column indicate the nature of the ceremony—h = painful hazing, g = genital operations, s = seclusion from women, and t = tests of manliness.

like our own, have a brief taboo of a few weeks to permit the mother to recover from her delivery. In the remaining 27, the mother did not resume sexual intercourse for at least nine months after the birth of her child, and in one instance, the Cheyenne, the ideal period adhered to was reported as ten years. The duration of the taboo generally corresponded to the nursing period and in many cases was reinforced by the belief that sexual intercourse curdles or sours the mother's milk, thus making it harmful for the infant. In other societies, like the Kwoma, the taboo is explicitly for the purpose of ensuring a desired interval between children where adequate means of contraception are lacking. In these societies the taboo is terminated when the infant reaches some maturational stage, e.g., "until the child can crawl," "until the child can walk," or "until he can take care of himself." For the 27 societies that have this taboo, more than a few weeks long, the average duration is slightly more than two years.

RESULTS AT THE CULTURAL LEVEL

Our hypothesis may now be restated in cultural terms as follows: *Societies which have sleeping arrangements in which the mother and baby share the same bed for at least a year to the exclusion of the father and societies which have a taboo restricting the mother's sexual behavior for at least a year after childbirth will be more likely to have a ceremony of transition from boyhood to manhood than those societies where these conditons do not occur (or occur for briefer periods).* For the purposes of this hypothesis, transition ceremonies include only those ceremonies characterized by at least one of the following events: painful hazing of the initiates, isolation from females, tests of manliness, and genital operations.

The test of this hypothesis is presented in Table 4.1. It will be observed from this table that of the 20 societies where both antecedent variables are present, 14 have initiation ceremonies and only six do not. Where both antecedent variables are absent only two of the 25 societies have the ceremonies. Thus, over 80 percent of the 45 pure cases correspond with the prediction.[18] Though our hypothesis was not designed for predicting the mixed cases, that is, where only one of the antecedent variables is present, it seems that they tended not to have the transition ceremonies.

Although the eight cases which are exceptional to our theory, the six in the upper left-hand column and the two in the lower right-hand column may be simply misclassified through error of measurement, reexamination uncovers some other unanticipated factor which may account for their placement.[19] This analysis turns out to be enlightening.

Reviewing, first the six cases in the upper left-hand column, that is, the societies which have both exclusive mother-son sleeping arrangements

[18] Even though we made every effort to ensure at least a reasonable degree of independence for our cases, there are many instances of known historical connections among them. A statistical test of significance is therefore difficult to interpret. If the cases were independent, the probabilities are less than one in one thousand that this relationship could be obtained by chance $(\chi^2 > 18)$.

[19] This procedure was suggested by G. G. Homans and D. M. Schneider, *Marriage, Authority, and Final Causes; A Study of Unilateral Cross-Cousin Marriage,* (Glencoe, Ill.: Free Press, 1955). It was used most effectively in their cross-cultural study of authority patterns and cross-cousin marriage.

and a postpartum sex taboo but no initiation, we found that four of them (Khalapur, Trobrianders, Nyakusa, and Yapese) have an adjustment at adolescence which may serve as a psychological substitute for the initiation ceremony. The boys at this time leave the parental home and move to a men's house or a boys' village where they live until they are married. Malinowski[20] observed this type of adjustment amongst the Trobrianders in 1927. He wrote:

> But the most important change, and the one which interests us most is the partial break-up of the family at the time when the adolescent boys and girls cease to be permanent inmates of the parental home . . . a special institution . . . special houses inhabited by groups of adolescent boys and girls. A boy as he reaches puberty will join such a house. . . . Thus the parent home is drained completely of its adolescent males, though until the boy's marriage he will always come back for food, and will also continue to work for his household to some extent. . . .[21]
>
> At this stage, however, when the adolescent has to learn his duties, to be instructed in traditions, and to study his magic, his arts and crafts, his interest in his mother's brother, who is his teacher and tutor, is greatest and their relations are at their best.[22]

This account suggests that this change of residence serves the same functions that we have posited for initiation ceremonies, for example, by establishing male authority, breaking the bond with the mother, and ensuring acceptance of the male role. It is important for our hypothesis, also, that there are only two other societies in our sample where such a change of residence occurs. One of these is the Malaita, which has one but not both of our antecedent variables; the other is the Ashanti, where the boy may move to the village of his mother's brother at or before puberty, but this is not mandatory and only half the boys do so. Thus, if we were to revise our hypothesis such that a change of residence was considered to be equivalent to initiation, the four societies mentioned should be moved over to the right-hand column and the exceptional cases would be reduced from eight to four.

Some comment should be made on the two remaining cases in the upper left-hand column. The Ganda are reported to have an interesting method of child rearing which may or may not be relevant to our theory. For the first three years of his life, a Ganda child sleeps exclusively with his mother and she is subject to a sexual taboo. At this point the boy is reported to be weaned and transferred to the household of his father's brother by whom he is brought up from then on. It might be assumed

---

[20] B. Malinowski, *Sex and Repression in Savage Society* (New York: Harcourt, Brace & Co., 1927).

[21] *Ibid.*, p. 67.

[22] *Ibid.*, p. 69.

that this event would obviate the need for later ceremonial initiation into manhood. Since several other societies that do have initiation also have a change of residence at weaning, however, this simple explanation cannot be accepted and the Ganda must remain an unexplained exception. Finally Lewis[23] reports for the Tepoztlan that there was some disagreement among his informants as to the length of the taboo and exclusive sleeping arrangements. Since again there were other equally equivocal cases, we shall have to accept the verdict of our judges and let this case also remain an exception.

A reconsideration of the two exceptions in the lower right-hand column, the Hopi and the Timbira, which have the type of initiation into manhood required by our theory but have neither exclusive sleeping arrangements nor a prolonged postpartum sex taboo, also turns out to be fruitful. In neither of these societies does the father have authority over the children.[24] This is vested in the mother's brother who lives in another household.[25] That these societies should have an initiation rite, again, does not seem to contradict our general theory, even though it does contradict our specific hypothesis. From clinical studies in our own society it is clear that even with the lack of exclusive sleeping arrangements and a minimal postpartum sex taboo, an appreciable degree of dependence upon the mother and rivalry with the father is generated. The cases here suggest that, although these motives are not strong enough to require ceremonial initiation into manhood if the father is present in the household and has authority over the child, this may be required if he lacks such authority.

But what of the cases which have but one of the antecedent variables? Taking into account the societies with exclusive sleeping arrangements but no postpartum sex taboo, our theory predicts that these conditions should produce dependency and rivalry. However, since the mother is receiving sexual satisfaction from her husband, she has less need to obtain substitute gratification from nurturing her infant, so that the dependency she produces in her child would be less intense and the need for initiation should be attenuated. Three of the four cases with exclusive sleeping arrangements but no taboo appear to fulfill these conditions. As we have reported above, the Ashanti and the Malaita practice a change of residence which, it could be argued, is somewhat less drastic than initiation. In any case this is permissive and not required for the Ashanti. When the Cagaba boy reaches adolescence, he is given instruc-

[23] O. Lewis, *Life in a Mexican Village: Tepoztlan Restudied* (Urbana: University of Illinois Press, 1951).

[24] A consideration of the influence of authority patterns was suggested by the work of Homans and Schneider, *op. cit.*

[25] This is also true of the Trobrianders discussed above, but of no other society in our sample about which we have information on authority patterns.

tion in sexual intercourse by a priest and then sent to practice these instructions with a widow who lives with him temporarily in a specially built small hut. The boy is not allowed to leave this hut until he succeeds in having sexual intercourse with her. This trial is reported to be terrifying to the boy and it is often several days before he does succeed. This type of initiation, however, does not seem to compare with other societies which like the Thonga have a fullfledged ceremony. The Siriono, on the other hand, do not have any ceremonial recognition of the shift from boyhood to manhood, and they must be regarded as an exception to our theory.

The final group of cases to consider are those that have a long postpartum sex taboo but not exclusive mother-son sleeping arrangements. For these, our theory would also predict an attenuated need for initiation ceremonies. Although the mothers of this group are presumed to gain substitute sexual gratification from being especially nurturant and loving toward their infants, they have less opportunity to do so than with those of societies where there are also exclusive sleeping arrangements.

As in the previous group of societies, the ceremonies are, except for the Ooldea which will be discussed below, mild. The Kwakiutl have a ceremony which consists of a potlach given by the father for the son. There the boys undergo no hazing or genital operations but are secluded and expected to perform a dance. For the Ojibwa, the boy is expected to obtain a guardian spirit in a vision before he reaches maturity. Thus, generally when he is 11 or 12 years old, he goes alone into the forest where he stays often for several days without food, water, and generally without sleep until he either has a vision or returns home to recuperate before trying again. Again neither hazing nor genital operations are involved.

The Ooldea, a tribe situated in southwestern Australia do, however, have a fullfledged initiation rite with hazing, isolation, and a very painful genital operation. This apparently runs counter to our assumption that the rites should be mild if only one determinant is present.

Radcliffe-Brown, however, reports that in many Australian tribes

> . . . the discipline of very young children is left to the mother and the other women of the horde. A father does not punish and may not even scold his infant children, but if they misbehave, he will scold the mother and perhaps give her a blow with a stick. He regards the mother as responsible for misbehavior by very young children. When they are a little older, the father undertakes the education of the boys but leaves the education of the girls to the mother and the women of the horde. But the father behaves affectionately and is very little of a disciplinarian. Discipline for a boy begins when he approaches puberty and is exercised by the men of the horde. The big chance comes with the initiation ceremonies when,

in some tribes, the father, by a ceremonial (symbolic) action, hands over his son to the men who will carry out the initiation rites. During the initiation period of several years the boy is subjected to rigid and frequently painful discipline by men other than his father.[26]

If the Ooldea be one of those Australian tribes described above, they fall, along with the Trobrianders, Hopi, and Timbira, into the class of societies where the function of initiation is to make up for the lack of discipline exercised by a father over the boy during childhood.

A study of those societies without exclusive sleeping arrangements and with a long postpartum sex taboo which do not have the rites is interesting. In the first place both the Pondo and the Araucanians are reported to have had initiation ceremonies in the recent past, indicating that they are perhaps near the threshold of needing them. The Tallensi also are interesting. An observer notes that the Tallensi should have invented the Oedipus-conflict theory since they are quite open and conscious of the strong rivalry and hostility between father and son, a conflict which remains strong and dangerous, guarded only by ritualized forms of etiquette, until the father dies and the son takes his place. Furthermore, family fissions are reported to occur frequently, and the oldest son often leaves the family to establish a new lineage of his own.

Thus, the presence of a postpartum sex taboo alone seems to produce tension, which these societies commonly seek to resolve through initiation ceremonies. Societies in this group which do not have ceremonies either had them recently or show evidence of unresolved tension.

Summary. The cross-cultural evidence indicates that:

1. A close relationship is established between mother and son during infancy as a consequence of either (a) their sleeping together for at least a year to the exclusion of the father, or (b) the mother being prohibited from sexual intercourse for at least a year after the birth of her child, or (c) both of these together have measurable consequences which are manifested in cultural adjustments at adolescence.

2. The cultural adjustments to the presence of the above factors are made when the boy approaches or reaches sexual maturity. These adjustments are either (a) a ceremony of initiation into manhood involving at least one and generally several of the following factors; painful *hazing* by the adult males of the society, tests of endurance and manliness, seclusion from women, and genital operations, or (b) a change of residence which involved separation of the boy from his mother and sisters and may also include some formal means

[26] Cited from a letter by A. R. Radcliffe-Brown to these authors in Homans and Schneider, *op. cit.*, p. 41.

for establishing male authority such as receiving instructions from and being required to be respectful to the mother's brother or the members of the men's house.

3. If both the factors specified in (1) are present, the consequences at adolescence tend to be more elaborate and severe than if only one is present.

4. The cultural adjustments specified in (2) also occur in societies where the father does not have the right to discipline his son, whether or not the conditions specified in (1) are present.

The evidence for these statements is summarized in Table 4.2

Table 4.2

THE RELATIONSHIP OF INFANCY FACTORS TO CULTURAL ADJUSTMENTS AT ADOLESCENCE

Customs in infancy and childhood			Cultural adjustment at adolescence		
Authority of father over son	Exclusive mother-son sleeping arrangement	Postpartum sex taboo	None	Change of residence	Initiation ceremony
Present	Long	Long	2	3	14
		Short	1	2	1
	Short	Long	4	0	2
		Short	23	0	0
Absent			0	1	3

THE SOCIOPSYCHOLOGICAL IMPLICATIONS

So much for the manifest results at the cultural level. But what is the most reasonable sociopsychological interpretation of these relationships? What are the psychodynamics involved? We are not concerned with the bizarre rites of the Thonga or the peculiar life of a Kwoma infant, for their own sakes, but rather in discovering some general truths about human nature. We, therefore, wish to state what we believe to be the underlying processes that are involved. These are processes that we have not directly observed and which must be accepted or rejected on the grounds of their plausibility or, more important, on the basis of further research implied by our theory.

We believe that six sociopsychological assumptions are supported by our findings:

1. The more exclusive the relationship between a son and his mother during the first years of his life, the greater will be his emotional dependence upon her.

2. The more intensely a mother nurtures (loves) an infant during the early years of his life, the more emotionally dependent he will be upon her.

3. The greater the emotional dependence of a child upon a mother, the more hostile and envious he will be toward anyone whom he perceives as replacing him in her affection.[27]

4. If a child develops a strong emotional dependence upon his mother during infancy, and hostility toward and envy of his father in early childhood at the time of weaning and the onset of independence training, these feelings (although latent during childhood) will manifest themselves when he reaches physiological maturity in (a) open rivalry with his father and (b) incestuous approaches to his mother, unless measures are taken to prevent such manifestations.

5. Painful hazing, enforced isolation from women, trials of endurance or manliness, genital operations, and change of residence are effective means for preventing the dangerous manifestation of rivalry and incest.

6. Even a moderate or weak amount of emotional dependence upon the mother and rivalry with the father will be dangerous at adolescence if the father has no right to (or does not in fact) exercise authority over his son during childhood.

If these sociopsychological hypotheses are true, they have some interesting implications for individual differences in our own society.[28] It has long been known that there is an association between certain types of juvenile delinquency and broken homes.[29] We would predict that the

[27] If, however, the mother herself is perceived by the child as the one responsible for terminating the early intense relationship, this should lead the boy to both envy her and identify with her. This should produce conflict, with respect to his sex role identity, which initiation rites would serve to resolve.

[28] In a study of infant training William Sewell reports that "the children who slept with their mothers during infancy made significantly poorer showings on the self-adjustment, personal freedom, and family relations components of the California Test of Personality and suffered more sleep disturbances than did those who slept alone." W. H. Sewell, "Infant Training and the Personality of the Child," *American Journal of Sociology*, 1953, LVIII, 157.

[29] *Cf.* for example, E. Glueck and S. Glueck, *Unravelling Juvenile Delinquency* (New York: Commonwealth Fund, 1950); W. W. Wattenberg and J. J. Balistrieri, "Gang Membership and Juvenile Misconduct," *American Sociological Review*, December 1950, XV, 744-52.

probability of a boy becoming delinquent in such instances would be highest where the separation of the mother and father occurred during the early infancy of the boy and where she remarried when he was two or three years old.

We would further predict that insofar as there has been an increase in juvenile delinquency in our society, it probably has been accompanied by an increase in the exclusiveness of mother-child relationships and/or a decrease in the authority of the father. It is not unreasonable that industrialization and urbanization have done just this, but, of course, this matter should be investigated before such an interpretation is accepted.

Finally, if further research shows that juvenile delinquency in our society is in part a function of the early-childhood factors that have been described in this paper, then it can be countered either by decreasing the exclusiveness of the early mother-child relationship, increasing the authority of the father during childhood, or instituting a formal means of coping with adolescent boys functionally equivalent to those described in this paper. Change of residence would seem more compatible with the values of our society than an initiation ceremony. The Civilian Conservation Corps camps of the 1930s were an experiment which should provide useful data in this regard. The present institution of selective service would perhaps serve this purpose were the boys to be drafted at an earlier age and exposed to the authority of responsible adult males.

Puberty ceremonies: variant interpretations

The Whiting group's cross-cultural study interprets the male initiation ceremonies as resolving incestuous feeling toward the mother and rivalry-hatred toward the father, in a variant of the Freudian Oedipal syndrome. In a slightly later paper, however, in collaboration with a different colleague, Whiting modified that interpretation of the initiation ceremonies.[30] The later paper sees initiation ceremonies as an institution which resolves a *cross-sex identification*. It argues that the infancy situation of exclusive-mother-son sleeping arrangements and postpartum taboo, followed by mother's resumption of sexual relations with the father and simultaneous emotional abandonment of the son, leads the son to envy the status of the mother as resource-giver and hence to identify with her. It is this identification that needs to be broken if the boy is to attain the

[30] Roger V. Burton and John W. M. Whiting, "The Absent Father: Effects on the Developing Child," Paper read at the 1960 meeting of the American Psychological Association.

status of adult masculinity. The initiation ceremonies, therefore, are seen as making this break complete.

Frank W. Young,[31] however, challenges both of the Whiting group interpretations. He sets out, using the same data, to test an alternative hypothesis. Young finds that a much better case can be made for relating the presence of initiation ceremonies to the existence of exclusive male organizations, indicating a high degree of male solidarity. He demonstrates that, with the presence or absence of exclusive male organizations held constant, the relationship between the cultural practices of mother-son sleeping arrangements and postpartum sex taboo, on the one hand, and initiation ceremonies, on the other, is greatly reduced compared to what Whiting and his colleagues found. On this basis, he rejects the Whiting interpretations and argues that the initiation ceremonies are exclusively a matter of dramatization of the male sex role, "at a time when it is particularly problematical, although not in the manner suggested by Whiting." [32] What is problematical, according to Young, is not any earlier cross-sex identification, or dependency on the mother, or rivalry toward the father, but rather that the uninitiated boy simply does not have identification with the male solidarity *group,* where "identification" (for Young) means taking as one's own the cluster of social meanings held by the cohesive group of adult males, which the uninitiated in the nature of the case cannot know, much less accept.

In keeping with this reinterpretation of the meaning of the initiation ceremonies, Young also proceeds to "explain away" any relationship still remaining between the constellation of mother-son sleeping arrangements and postnatal taboo and the existence of initiation ceremonies. He argues that the combination of these first two elements (now called "the absent-father pattern") is simply, and *only,* a manifestation of *polygyny* combined with exclusive male organizations.

Whiting responded to this interpretation[33] by arguing that *both* male solidarity and male initiation rites are a consequence of conflict in sex identity engendered in infancy and early childhood, by the

[31] Frank W. Young, "The Function of Male Initiation Ceremonies: A Cross-Cultural Test of an Alternative Hypothesis," *American Journal of Sociology,* Vol. LXVII, 1962, pp. 379-96.

[32] *Ibid.,* p. 381.

[33] John W. M. Whiting: "Comment." Following the Young article, *op. cit.,* pp. 391-94.

absent-father constellation, which in turn would be a product of polygyny.

Here then are alternative hypotheses. Young says that the function of the initiation rites is to dramatize and make explicit the male sex role, maintaining the solidarity of the male organizations. Whiting and his colleagues argue that it is to resolve conflicts of cross-sex identity, or to resolve the Oedipal constellation. But these hypotheses are not really mutually exclusive "explanations" of the rites. Something as complex as a ritual ceremony involving genital operations, hazing, exclusion from women, and tests of manliness—to name only the four elements that Whiting considered crucial and Young accepted for the sake of argument—must surely not have been determined by only *one* "functional need." Here the Whiting works, while derived from a version of Freudian ideas, appear to be insufficiently insistent on maintaining a psychoanalytic perspective (especially when Whiting rather hastily abandoned the Oedipal-conflict theme as central to his interpretation). The Freudian concept of *overdetermination* may help us here. In reference to individual pathology a neurotic symptom is seen as "overdetermined" in that not merely one, possibly traumatic, event or condition produces the symptom, but rather a whole constellation of different or related antecedent events and the intricate network of the person's responses to and defenses against these events. The symptom serves to accomplish many different things simultaneously, and condenses within itself a whole range of different elements, whose coming together gives the symptom its special binding force and its intractability to common-sense "treatments." We may fruitfully apply a similar approach, here, to a "cultural symptom," in this case puberty ceremonies for males.

Young argues that:[34]

> The [initiation] rituals themselves only remind him [the newly initiated] of what it means to be a man in his society; in themselves they contain no meaning. On this view circumcision is not different in kind from a gift, a new name, a dance, etc. It differs in degree only insofar as its acquisition has a more dramatic and emotional context. Thus almost anything can figure in the initiation ceremony. The sound of the bullroarer or some test of endurance have an intrinsic dramatic quality . . . empirical work on ritual must allow for a wide variety of symbolic contents; it may not be limited to particular customs.

[34] Young, *op. cit.*, p. 391.

This statement provides a good point of departure for the confrontation of the Whiting and the Young interpretations. The initiation ceremonies no doubt in fact do many things, but we do need to look at the actual content of any particular ceremony to see what sorts of things it does accomplish, and what strands among dozens of possible ones, in the earlier biography of the initiate, it pulls together, weaves into a pattern, resolves, or suppresses. In this connection, the difference between circumcision and a gift may be a very striking one indeed, even if both do, as Young contends, serve the same function of reminding the boy that he is now a man. To argue that the "rituals in themselves contain no meaning"—that is, in their content—is to make an arbitrary absurdity of practically all of human experience. Circumcision *is* very different from a gift. It involves suffering, regardless of cross-cultural variations in tolerance or stoicism toward such pain.[35] Mr. Young's analysis seems to have lost touch with the fact that these are real live human beings undergoing these experiences. Circumcision, quite unlike receiving a gift, involves *giving up* (not receiving) a part of one's body. What body organ, for a male, could be more emotionally charged or more linked with his sense of sexual identity?[36] Clearly, one of the questions we have to ask is: Why do the initiation rituals include circumcision in some societies, and something else in others? The favorite notion of "functional equivalence" can easily be misused: two alternative customs may be functionally equivalent only in some very restricted way, and otherwise have extremely different functions and meanings. *Which* symbolic contents of the "wide variety of symbolic contents" in rituals that Young refers to, may make an enormous difference.

OTHER FORMULATIONS: BRUNO BETTELHEIM

In *Symbolic Wounds*[37] Bruno Bettelheim is concerned directly with the *content* of male initiation ceremonies, particularly those of the Australian aborigines (which seem always to have most attracted the attention of psychoanalytic observers). He singles out the geni-

[35] In a rare and illuminating autobiography by a literate tribalist, Camara Laye gives a poignant description of his own circumcision, and his feelings about it. See Camara Laye, *The Dark Child*, trans. by J. Kirkup, E. Jones and E. Gottlieb (New York: The Noonday Press, 1954), Chapter 8. Originally written in French.

[36] To quote a colleague: "A penis is not just a phallic symbol." Jule Nydes, in ex tempore comments at meetings of the Council of Psychoanalytic Psychotherapists, New York City, February, 1966.

[37] Bettelheim, *op. cit.*

tal operations, circumcision and subincision, the special position of the women vis-à-vis the ceremonies, the use of fire in the ceremonies, the great urgency to keep the rituals secret from the women, and the myths connected with the ceremonies. Here again we encounter the problem that no one inventory of features of the initiation rites of a particular tribe is necessarily shared by many, let alone all, initiatory tribes, even if the features be phrased in such broad terms as Whiting's (see above). Bettelheim's whole analysis, based as it largely is on the tribes having the features indicated, and especially on those Australian tribes where these characteristics are generally found in the combination shown, is probably too special to serve as an interpretation of *all* initiation ceremonies. But the analysis does suggest what may be *some* of the most important functions of puberty rites for males. (Bettelheim does not raise the question of why these functions should be more urgently in need of satisfaction in some societies than in others, since his interest is in the *universal* intrapsychic problems which could give rise to initiation rites as one possible way of resolving them.)

Though the genital operation of circumcision is far from universal as a feature of initiation ceremonies (see Table 4.1), and subincision even less so, Bettelheim singles out these operations as being, in effect, at the core of the psychology of initiation. He observed in four disturbed youngsters in present-day Chicago what seemed to him a dramatic parallel to primitive initiation ceremonies. Spontaneously four borderline schizophrenic children—two boys and two girls—at the Orthogenic School, invented a secret ritual: Each month the boys would "cut themselves in a secret place," and the four youngsters—all at or near puberty—would mix their blood. The magical effect of the ritual would ensure their all becoming rich and famous in the entertainment world and living a life of great sexual pleasure. Bettelheim saw the proposed ritual as an attempt by both the boys and the girls to come to terms with great ambivalence toward their own sex as well as the opposite sex. To make males bleed monthly like females, for the girls reduces the strangeness and terror of males, and for the boys it gives them an analogue of female functioning. He noted that the ritual was first proposed by one of the girls, who had just begun menstruating. He noted also the secrecy of the rite and the willingness of the children to suffer pain as a price of entry into an adulthood of supposed success and sexual freedom. Since these were schizophrenic or pre-schizophrenic children, Bettelheim argued that their freedom of expression of unconscious content should give us a clue to common universal problems of puberty. Hence the drive to examine the anthropological literature on puberty ceremonies and understand their import.

Bettelheim suggests that puberty rituals are not only imposed on children by the adults, but also supported by the deeper psychic motivations of the children themselves—on the analogy of his four spontaneous puberty-rite inventors. Such rites may represent efforts of the youngsters themselves to "resolve the conflict between their pre-genital desires and identifications, and the biological and social role of their sex according to nature and the mores of the society," [38] . . . more broadly, "to resolve the antithesis between child and adult, between male and female, and between polymorphous-perverse and genital tendencies." [39] The argument is that mere submission to custom, the authority of the elders and so on, would not account for the willingness, even eagerness, to undergo the ordeals of initiation on the part of the young in those primitive tribes. Further, it is not only expression of id drives, but also *integrative* tendencies of the children, that feed their resolve to undergo the ceremonies. Bettelheim suggests that the uniform development of adolescents in undergoing puberty rites, indicates that the adolescents are not merely having something imposed upon them unwillingly by powerful adults, but that they are reacting spontaneously, autonomously, and as a group to problems of finding instinctual satisfaction. (By contrast, individuals, he argues, develop dissimilarly in regard to outside imposed control or modification of instinctual tendencies, for example, toilet training.)

Bettelheim then proposes the following combination of functions for the initiation rites for boys, and finds plausible documentation for this analysis at least in the well-studied cases of puberty ceremonies of the Australian aborigines:

1. Initiation rites are part of fertility rites: circumcision produces a "reborn" penis, with the glans freed.
2. Initiation rites promote and symbolize full acceptance of the socially prescribed sexual role.
3. These rites may assert that men, too, can bear children. "Only women can have babies, but only men can make men." The idea of death and rebirth as part of the ritual is widespread. Envy of

[38] *Ibid.*, p. 42.
[39] *Ibid.*, p. 45.

women's child-bearing function would lie behind this complex of feelings and practices, especially in tribes like the Australian aborigines who do not understand the male's actual biological role in procreation.

4. Through subincision men may try to acquire the sexual apparatus and functions of women. Subincision creates a genital with both male and female features. Spurting of blood from the subincision wound is analogous to menstrual flow. These symbolic connections are richly and repeatedly documented. Subincision requires the man to squat while urinating, like a female. The subincision wound is voluntarily at intervals reopened, producing more bleeding and pain, again in unmistakable analogy to menstruation; the voluntary element shows the men's own strivings at work, rather than imposition of authority from above. Subincision thus appears as an extreme form of ritualization of men's envy of and preoccupation with female sex functions, and it fits with the need to prove men are as good at procreating as are women—in fact they are better, since subincised they have the genitals and powers of both sexes.

5. Circumcision may be a male substitute for the first menstruation of the girl, the male's attempt to have a definite mark of sexual maturity, parallel to the first menses of the girl. Or it may have originally been imposed on males by women, as the mythology of some tribes suggests. If so, some aspects of circumcision may be associated with castration anxiety, the threatening castrator being the mother rather than the father.

6. The great secrecy of the male rites may disguise the fact that the desired goal has not been reached. That the men do not in fact acquire female procreative powers by the rituals, must, of course, be denied, and the obsessive secrecy maintained about the rituals in many tribes to prevent their being known to women and uninitiated boys may divert attention from the fact that the ceremonies have not in fact changed reality. This would be related to official ignorance of the male role in procreation (in some tribes). Here the genital operations, the attendant ceremonies, and the secrecy about them may represent a desperate measure by males to reassure themselves of creative powers equal to, in fact superior to, those of women.

The special merits of Bettelheim's formulations lie, first, in his broadening of the Freudian emphasis on penis envy in females and castration anxiety in males to a perspective which sees each sex as having envy of the special anatomy and functions and presumed powers of the other. Second, there is his insistence that emotionally powerful ceremonies such as the initiation rites could not be maintained and continued from one generation to another *only* by the force of authority of the elders of the community, but must include an important element of motivation on the part of the young themselves not only to submit to but actively to desire the ceremonies and their attendant ordeals. Bettelheim contributes another significant insight: such ceremonies may be much more critical in the growing up of males than of females because in any social structure with official social dominance of males overt expression of envy of the social roles of the opposite sex may be permissible for females, but for males it must be expressed in the much more disguised and roundabout manner of formalized, and protesting, rituals. This point connects with Margaret Mead's insight that growing up for girls is in a sense much less complicated than for boys: the girl has only to wait for something inside herself to develop and unfold; she does not have actively to *do* something to demonstrate her achievement of adulthood, while the male does have to demonstrate and prove his manhood. Related to this is the need of the male to have some unmistakable sign of having reached sexual maturity, comparable to, and to compensate for, the obvious sign in the female, first menstruation.[40]

GÉZA RÓHEIM

In *Psychoanalysis and Anthropology*[41] Géza Róheim deals at length with the initiation ceremonies of the tribes of central Australia which he had studied firsthand, as well as those reported by other anthropologists such as Lloyd Warner on the Murngin. Róheim sees in the ceremonies a range of functions even broader and more comprehensive than those suggested by Bettelheim. From his complex and convoluted analysis, we may extract the following as salient points:[42]

Initiation in Central Australia and in Australia in general, shows certain *typical features*. These are:

[40] Margaret Mead, *Male and Female* (New York: New American Library, Mentor Edition, 1955), Chapter VII and p. 136.
[41] Géza Róheim, *Psychoanalysis and Anthropology* (New York: International Universities Press, 1950), pp. 74-97, and generally in Chapter 2.
[42] *Ibid.*, p. 74.

(a) The boy has to undergo suffering;

(b) The separation from the mother is emphasized;

(c) He is shown certain things which he was previously not allowed to see;

(d) He has to accept restrictions and taboos;

(e) He receives certain objects of a symbolic (magical) value;

(f) Rites of reintegration are carried out, and the seclusion ends (*rite d'agrégation*);

(g) He receives a wife; his sexual life is officially recognized.

Róheim sees the suffering the boys have to undergo as serving multiple functions. There is a basically ambivalent relationship between the old men and the young: identification and hostility combined. That the circumcizer is at one level in fact making a hostile attack upon the boy is indicated by the ferocious, beard-in-mouth expression of the old man while carrying out this operation. Thus in contrast to Bettelheim, and in line with Freud, Róheim does not hesitate to include the element of symbolic (or mitigated) castration as *one* of the meanings of circumcision, and it *is* a symbolic castration by older males, that is, by fathers. But it is not only that. Crucial is the great ambivalence and duplicity of the rituals on the part of both the old men and the boys. The suffering is far from arbitrary, and certainly not exclusively punitive. Rather the ritual is suffused with compensatory elements: one thing is given, another taken away. Circumcision is balanced by the giving of the *churinga*;[43] the food taboos by the showing of totemic secrets.

The separation of the boy from the mother points not only to social attainment of male adulthood (the removal of the boy from the category of women-and-children into the category of adult men), but also to the connection of the rites to the infantile situation of mother and infant son.

Being shown things which the boy was previously not allowed to see is part of the general process of acquisition of esoteric lore that is a prominent feature of the Australian initiation ceremonies. The functions here are manifold: compensation for the suffering undergone and for the various taboos and restrictions; attainment of the symbols of male adulthood; and intellectualization, one of the important mechanisms for dealing with id impulses in the adolescent

---

[43] A somewhat phallic-shaped object of wood or stone, to which are attached intense and multiple symbolic values; one of the most sacred objects in Australian cultures.

period. This is the "going-to-college" element in adolescent education that Hart points to in his paper (see above). It is significant that learning of such esoteric lore is not only a chore imposed on the boys by the elders, but an activity avidly sought out by the boys themselves. (Compare Bettelheim's insistence on the youngsters' own motivations as indispensable for the puberty ceremonies.)

The acceptance of a great variety of taboos and restrictions marks the ascetic aspect of adolescent reaction to id impulses. It shows the *superego formation* function of the initiatory rites. The churinga can be seen as symbolic representation of the superego. Examples of the taboos imposed are the following:[44]

> *Don't shout! Always sit down in the dark! Don't stand up or you will be seen! Don't cut wood for your fire, but you may pick it up when you find it. Don't eat or drink anything hot, it will give you a pain in your penis. Don't eat tjilkamata (porcupine), it will make the penis get stiff. Don't eat the wallaby when it is just taken from the pouch, your forehead will get rough, hair will grow on it. Don't eat black iguana. If you do, your fire will go out. Walk on all fours so that women and children will not see you.*

Other formulations are explicitly moral in content. Among the Murngin the old men command the initiates to respect their father and mother, never to tell lies, not to run after women who do not belong to them, and to live up to the tribal code.[45] The fact that the big churinga, the symbol of the protecting genius and ancestor, is given to the boy after the circumcision and, at the same time, he is told what *not* to do while simultaneously he introjects (drinks) the blood of the old men, shows that the period of separation is the period of superego formation. The ceremonies, in fact, abound in dramatizations of superego formation in a variety of symbolisms, relating, for example, the two churingas as representations of the primal scene, food taboos, and renunciation identification. Other features that support the interpretatation that the rites involve dramatization of superego development are the drinking of the blood of the old men (introjection rites), the castration symbolism implicit in circumcision and subincision, the emphasis on suffering in general (operations, deprivations), and the endowment of the boy with a magical object that represents the superego (the churinga).

[44] Róheim, *op. cit.*, p. 85.
[45] *Ibid.*, p. 86.

OVERVIEW

We have considered several approaches to or interpretations of initiation ceremonies, with special reference to those for males. For Benedict, such ceremonies are ways of bridging discontinuities between early-childhood conditioning and very different adult expectations, and they are necessary only where there are such pronounced discontinuities. For Hart, discontinuity of some degree and kind is to be assumed in most societies, but the distinguishing element of "postpubertal education"—of which the puberty ceremonies are a special case—consists in removal from the arena of intimacy, sudden imposition of discipline, change from secular to sacred content, and change from utilitarian learning to "useless" citizenship learning. Consistent with Young's emphasis, strong initiation ceremonies here would *dramatize* the processes Hart is defining. Whiting and his colleagues find male initiation ceremonies more likely wherever there is an "absent-father syndrome" consisting of exclusive mother-son sleeping arrangements and parental postpartum sex taboo (or where there is a "functional equivalent" of this pattern, though mitigated, in weakness of authority of father over son in early childhood). The Whiting group explains this relationship as involving either (1) excessive dependency on the mother, desire to maintain her possession, and rivalry and hostility to the father; or (2) the boy's developing cross-sex identification based on this early experience. In either case, the initiation ceremony is "necessary" to counteract these tendencies and to assure development of an adequate adult male sex role. Young is also concerned with the male sex role, but he sees its necessity only in terms of the adult male solidarity group, considering early-childhood determinants as unnecessary and unfounded. Bettelheim sees the ceremonies not only as asserting the male sex role, but also as simultaneously asserting, symbolically, an equality or superiority to women in female functions as well (menstruation, child bearing) and ritualized expression of the need to disguise the failure of the rites to bring about the desired effects (hence the great secrecy). To him these rites are also the expression not only of adult-imposed demands, but of deep intrapsychic needs of the initiates themselves. Róheim adduces ambivalence between identification and hostility, between the young men and the old; symbolic castration by the threatened rivalrous older men; separation of the boy from the mother, and from the category of women and children; asceticism in various forms of suffering serving superego-formation needs; internalization of moral commands and eso-teric lore acquisition as well as many other modes of dramatizing the superego development.

Is it possible to reconcile the variety and apparent contradictions among the several interpretations of the male puberty ceremonies? Perhaps the question is impossible to answer. We may question whether it is helpful at all to regard different interpretations as mu-tually exclusive. And since among different tribes the phenomena we are dealing with as "male initiation ceremonies" may be quite varia-ble in content, with no one set combination of elements invariably appearing in all tribes having such ceremonies, one interpretation may be especially apposite for certain of the tribes and a different one for others. Further, several different interpretations may be si-multaneously valid, at different levels, for the rituals of any one tribe. The concept of multidetermination is necessary here. The complexity of the ceremonies for any particular tribe is instructive. That they typically occur at a critical psychosexual stage, that they frequently involve modifications of precisely that part of the male anatomy most affect laden and most obviously tied to male identity, tell us clearly enough of the weight of significance of such customs. They suggest also that patterns so involved, so deeply and complexly textured in the culture of their participants, so closely related to bio-logical sexual processes, and so persistent in cultural traditions, must surely be *multiply* determined by a complex of psychic, cultural, and social forces, no single one of which is likely to be *the* key to their understanding.

The variety of forms of these initiatory rites may or may not, in any specific instance, include genital operations, hazing and suffer-ing, separation from women, or mothers specifically, powerful con-trols by older males, complex learning of esoteric lore and taboos, significant use of blood, tests of manliness. This variety suggests that no one theory or set of related theories will necessarily apply to all of the kinds of initiation customs to be found in the world. However, we can suggest at this point a summary list of all of the possible meanings or functions of such ceremonies, any of which may be more applicable to some particular tribal instances than to others:

1. Introduction into adult male status in the tribe.
2. Maintenance of the solidarity of the adult male organization of the tribe.
3. Resolution of infantile or childhood conflict about sexual iden-

tity, induced by particular child-rearing practices (e.g., those involved in the "absent-father pattern") or induced by the general phenomenon of all children, male and female, being categorized with the adult females of the tribe in opposition to the adult males.

4. The power of the old men of the tribe over the young, and the dramatic demonstration of this power at precisely the time the young males become a conspicuous potential threat to the older men.

5. Acquisition of significant tribal lore, particularly of a nonutilitarian variety, emphasizing strong induction of the young males into the critical symbol systems of the culture.

6. The learning of tribal lore as a process of intellectualization, serving as one means of dealing with threatening id impulses that are stronger precisely at the pubertal stage.

7. Suffering, deprivation, and asceticism as an additional or alternative mode of dealing with id impulses.

8. The learning of moral codes and taboos as a consolidation and reinforcement of the basic values of the culture, and incidentally as a control on deviant potentialities.

9. The expression and partial resolution of profoundly felt ambivalence in relation to both fathers (by extension all older men) and mothers (by extension all older women).

10. Symbolic death and resurrection or rebirth, dramatizing the irreversibility of the status change.

11. Connected with this, the symbolic affirmation of special creative powers in men that are as good as, in fact better than, the natural reproductive powers of women, as epitomized in the phrase, "Only women can make babies, but only men can make men."

12. Symbolic castration, in any of the following complexes: as a punishment for real or fantasied sexual transgressions or wishes; as service to a divinity, especially a female divinity; as an Oedipal response of the fathers to the potentially rivalrous sons; as a process of making males into females, emulatively or self-abasingly, or both.

13. Symbolic "male protest," expressing envy of female functions, especially the reproductive functions and anything connected with them: strikingly apparent in subincision where the male genital becomes simultaneously a kind of female genital and bleeds in imitation of menstruation.

14. A complex exchange process where the initiate gives up in order to receive in return: gives up some of his masculinity in order to gain adulthood and an "improved" maleness; gives up the foreskin to receive in return the churinga as symbol of magical male power; gives up certain foods to receive in return totemic and other secrets; gives up autonomy by submission to the adult males, to receive in return his adult sexual status and finally sexual gratification with females.

15. A resolution of conflicts and anxieties about the primal scene and the secret of the origin of life.

3. THE MILITARY AS A *RITE DE PASSAGE*

If we look for analogues of the male initiation ceremonies of primitive societies, we are hard put to find directly comparable institutional arrangements in large-scale modern societies—except for one, wartime conscription into military service. Social psychological studies of the American military during World War II[46] provide a wealth of material from which it is possible to make a *post-facto* analysis of the *rite de passage* process. Authur J. Vidich and Maurice Stein present an analysis of the psychological adaptations of the draftee soldier, under the title of "The Dissolved Identity in Military Life." [47] Vidich and Stein view the process of becoming a soldier or marine as a "dissolution" of prior civilian identity and the acquisition of a military identity. This is a difficult and painful process, and one that is typically *imposed* on the draftee against his will. The political legitimation of universal military conscription by America's entry into the war did not legitimate the individual soldier's participation to himself. A major finding of the Stouffer group's studies was that in general the American soldier had neither strong beliefs about national war aims nor any strong personal commitment to the war effort. Lack of ideological commitment to the war was com-

[46] Samuel Stouffer, *et al.*, *The American Soldier*, 4 Vols. (Princeton: Princeton University Press, 1959). See also critical commentaries on these studies, in: Robert K. Merton and Paul Lazarsfeld (eds.) *Continuities in Social Research* (New York: Free Press of Glencoe, 1956). Novels about World War II experience, notably those of Norman Mailer and James Jones, are also of obvious value in giving a descriptive picture of the experiences and reactions of the draftee soldier.

[47] In A. J. Vidich, M. R. Stein, and D. M. White (eds.), *Identity and Anxiety* (New York: Free Press of Glencoe, 1960), pp. 493-506.

pounded by widespread resentments about inequality of sacrifice, the "relative deprivation" felt by many inductees when comparing themselves with others of similar civilian situation who got deferments or other preferential treatment, or with others of dissimilar civilian situation who were in the same military position.

The military *rite de passage* process involves:

1. Separation from the prior civilian situation, its roles, involvements, commitments, supports, and psychic integrations.
2. Dramatized induction into the new, military situation, its roles and statuses, etc.
3. Sustained inculcation of the norms, values, symbols of the new roles and statuses; intensively enforced learning of the behavior, especially the interpersonal behavior, demanded by the new organizational setting; persistent attack upon prior conceptions of self and any of their psychological supports, buttresses, and mechanisms; and the systematic building of motivations to play the new role and to find self-involvement and gratification in it, and hence to become the new kind of person demanded by the organization. This whole part of the process takes place in a setting recognized by all involved as "abnormal" or "emergency" and apart from the ordinary contexts and places of everyday "normal" life—i.e., in a "world apart."
4. Consolidation of the new identity in special conditions that test its viability and resilience, i.e., its basic value—in this case, war combat as the ultimate "scene" for the expression of the transformed personality.

It is interesting, and probably significant, that in the military *rite de passage*, the tripartite pattern Arnold Van Gennep[48] indicated for typical *rites de passage* is not strictly followed through. That pattern involves separation, inculcation, and then return in the new role to the normal community. The basic discrepancy in the military—especially for the draftee soldier—is that the return to the normal community is *not* in the new, military, role, but rather poses instead a whole new set of *re*adjustments, according to which the military identity, to the extent it has been achieved, must be again discarded or at least very drastically modified.

[48] Arnold Van Gennep, *The Rites of Passage*, trans. by Monika B. Vizedom and Gabrielle L. Caffee (Chicago: University of Chicago Press, 1960).

Vidich and Stein vividly describe the processes of separation and dramatic induction as follows:[49]

> *The Marine Corps, because it is an extreme case, can be used as a particularly apt illustration of the psychic impact of indoctrination. Here, the recruit was symbolically separated from society, by removing him to an offshore island which precluded all contact with conventional social symbols and relationships. Immediately upon arrival, the recruit was propelled through the training center rite de passage which forced him into a common mold. His civilian clothing was removed; his hair was shorn to baldness; and he was conducted naked through a delousing chamber, at the opposite end of which he was given "shots" and an issue of clothing. Upon regrouping, the training platoon had already lost its previous quality of disparate individuality.*

Here the recruit has been literally "stripped of all his civilian ego-supports—property, clothing, family, friends." The removal to a special isolated *place* is also exactly parallel to what is typically done in the initiation ceremonies of primitive societies. Other details are also closely parallel: the shaving of the head, the delousing of the naked body, and the "shots"—apart from their utilitarian functions—are reminiscent of the physical transformations of the boy novices of the African, Oceanic, and Australian tribes. Here too we find the *collectiveness* of the transforming experience, just as critical here as among the aborigines. Being conducted bald and naked through the delousing chamber and emerging from it a new person, could hardly be a more graphic symbolizing of a rebirth experience. "Only men can make men," say the aborigines. The Marines emphatically agree.

The "standard uniform with matching dog-tags . . . provided impartially for all" again emphasizes both the new, transformed status and the collective equality of all the novices in this status. It recalls precisely the donning of strange and identical special costumes by the initiates of the West African Malinke tribe as described by Laye in *The Dark Child* [50] and parallel practices involving either clothing or decoration to be found in practically all tribes practicing male initiation ceremonies.

To follow Vidich and Stein's account through the next stage:[51]

---

[49] Vidich and Stein, *op. cit.*, p. 498. This passage and the subsequent quotations are reprinted here with permission of The Free Press. Copyright © 1960 by The Free Press, a Corporation.

[50] Laye, *op. cit.*, pp. 113 ff.

[51] Vidich and Stein, *op. cit.*, p. 499.

In the next stage, the second rite in the passage, each man was given a full issue of equipment, including rifle, with which he would live for the duration. Carrying this equipment over their shoulders in a sack, the training platoon was then hazed by the drill instructor who conducted it through a senseless and interminably long and circuitous march to quarters, which turned out finally to be only several hundred yards from the beginning point of the march. The recruits were stunned and confused, but out of this common experience had been formed a group that was psychologically held together by the symbols of the common uniform and haircut, by the delousing purification and by the new equality of hazing. The drill instructor had become the focal point of authority and resentment, and immediately began to serve as a substitute for the unpatterned resentments and authoritative centers of the recruits' civilian selves. . . .

To be a Marine was to be a man, and to be a Marine-man, it was necessary to have had the combat experience. The combat role was held up as the major area of self-fulfillment. In line with this, training included the inculcation of new definitions of masculinity, a feature perhaps more necessary in Marine training, since the recruit tended to bring with him a conventional civilian conception of himself as a strong he-man type; many were athletes and some were top collegiate athletes. The civilian self-conception of he-man and athlete was broken down in training by the techniques of physical hazing and rifle calisthenics, wherein the recruit had to accept the hazing mutely and without self-defense and allow himself to be physically taxed in ways to which he was unaccustomed. Frequently the heroic athlete was selected as the specific object of hazing to the point of collapse, thereby standing as an example to all others of the inadequacy of civilian forms of manliness.

The valued form of manliness found a focus in adeptness in the use of the rifle. A small man with supple muscles could frequently sustain 500 rifle push-ups better than the muscle-bound athlete. In such instances, he would be held up as an example of physical virtuosity. Dropping a rifle or having a dirty one was cause for punishment and humiliation. Disciplinary action, in cases of breach of respect for, or lack of proper care of, the rifle, took the form of requiring the offender to sleep with his "piece," the other term by which the weapon is known in military terminology. In Marine Corps culture, the "piece" was the pre-eminent symbol of masculinity; having to sleep with it introduced a confusion of symbols and cast aspersion on the masculine identity of the degraded victim.

Hazing and tests of manliness, familiar elements in primitive initiation ceremonies, are here evident in dramatic form. The "senselessness" of such disciplines as enforced circuitous marches, and the anti-utilitarian elements in much of the physical training, ostensibly intended to produce combat fitness, all serve to underline the *cultural-transformative* functions of these transition rites. The symbolic significance of the rifle is also revealing, for here the rifle emerges as a direct counterpart of the Australian aboriginals' churinga, toward which an absolutely sacred attitude is required. This sacred function does not preclude the purely utilitarian importance of the rifle, but the obsessiveness and nonutilitarian extremes of the rules for the rifle's care do indicate this sacred element. The rifle as "pre-eminent symbol of masculinity" is also directly parallel to the churinga as a penis symbol, as a sacred object to be seen and handled only by males. The punishment of sleeping with this male sexual symbol is thereby significant at many levels. "Piece" is one of those multiply-resonant bits of American slang, which can refer to the male genital and also to a sexually available female, or specifically to her sexual organs, as in the phrase "piece of tail." Sleeping with the rifle thus introduces an ambiguously homosexual implication that must be particularly disturbing in the all-male world of the military, particularly in that branch of it, the Marines, that most graphically demonstrates reaction formations against any underlying elements of feminine identification in any of its members. At the same time the Marines impose on the trainee a totally passive acceptance of severe domination by powerful males, which in turn is bound to awaken elements of ("feminine") submissiveness, leading to renewed and ever more urgent demonstrations of the required signs of masculinity. In the midst of this we can observe the strong homoerotic implications of the theme that "only men can make men" and of the intense emotional solidarity of the all-male group of comrades who have been through the communal ordeal first of hazing and training and later of combat. Other observers have pointed out that the intensity of affective involvement of wartime military buddies, especially of those who have gone through combat together, is seldom carried over into friendship in postwar civilian life, where it is evidently a threat to civilian heterosexuality as expressed in marriage and family life.[52]

The goal of the transition into the military role is ultimately the identity of the *combat* soldier. Conditions for this transition include very prominently the acceptance of the "caste system" of the military, a system grossly at odds with the democratic values of civilian life.

[52] *Cf.* Geoffrey Gorer, *The American People* (New York: W. W. Norton, 1948), p. 128.

*The image of combat experience that had been built up em-
phasized the theme that hated caste etiquette was dropped in favor
of front-line comradeship. In combat, moreover, the soldier could
affirm a self-respecting masculinity. Combat men were looked up to
by all, especially in the training camp itself where they were accorded special deference well beyond their nominal rank. In combat,
the restoration of self-esteem could be found and a manly self acted
out. . . .*

*The enlisted man, then, accepts caste and chicken because that's
the way the "social system" works, and the officer enjoys his caste
privileges without pangs of conscience. At this stage, both the officer
and the enlisted man resolve caste tension by ignoring social reality,
through the technique of conceiving their combat-selves to be their
true selves. This dynamic was so compelling that it frequently led
the soldier to exaggerate his combat experience, and, in some cases,
to falsely claim combat experience.*

*The capacity to achieve an identity rested on the ability to ignore
immediate experience and to construct, each according to his situation, a self-image sufficiently serviceable that it would sustain the
motivation to act his part. The civilian self was dissolved, at least
for the duration, and in its place was substituted a highly plastic
military identity that in some way enabled the soldiers to think of
themselves as soldiers and to fight. The soldier seems to develop a
capacity to dissolve himself in a situation and then to find a self
consistent with it. . . .*

*The major mechanism of self-defense for the soldier is to enter-
tain those preferred self-images that allow him to act, irrespective of
the consistency, or lack of it, between reality and the preferred image sustained by illusion. Since there seems to be no one self-image
that can consistently integrate immediate experience, the soldier's
self exists in shifting and disparate layers of consciousness, which
parallel similar dynamics in the community as a whole. The civilian
past, the defeated self of the training period, the magnified or falsi-
fied self of combat, and above all, the future-civilian self all combine
in various ways to produce a workable self-mechanism. The capacity
to live with self depends upon capacity to live in a world of multiple
realities and multiple self-consciousness. The consciousness that falls
victim to each new situation constitutes the dissolution of identity
in the military community.*[53]

Significant in this analysis is its indication of the nonviability of
the combat soldier identity even during the wartime military experience, let alone in postwar civilian life, for which the military man
must undergo a whole new series of transitions and transformations.
True it is not totally discontinuous, since as Vidich and Stein point
out, the imagined postwar civilian identity is an ever-present part of
the reality perception and self-image for the wartime soldier.

[53] Vidich and Stein, *op. cit.*, pp. 504-6.

Other dimensions of the significance of the combat-soldier identity can be pointed out. The role of combat as direct expression of aggression is obvious. Its relationship to dissolution of the usual military caste restrictions thus gets further illumination. That the aggression expressed in combat has been at least in part generated by hated caste regulations can hardly be doubted. It also seems unlikely that all of it was successfully redirected against enemy troops. Reports have been many of combat soldiers taking advantage of the confusion of battle to shoot at some of their own hated officers. The dissolution, in combat, of caste barriers between officers and enlisted men, would thus appear to be all the more necessary to obviate more of that kind of killing occurring.

That combat experience is the ultimate affirmation of military masculinity can be seen also in relation to two other dynamic aspects of military *rite de passage:* separation anxiety and the homoerotic potential of the all-male military world. Induction into the military, with its enforced separation from any significant females in the man's life—wife, girlfriend, and mother—must, in exact parallel with the puberty ceremonies of primitive societies, involve *separation* anxiety, the prototype of which would be the intense feelings evoked in the young boy by separations of any kind from the mother. The solidarities of the all-male military world, and especially the highly intensified solidarity of men who have been through the ordeal of combat together, are one kind of answer to that anxiety. (It is parenthetically significant that armies, from ancient times, have been understandably suspicious of arrangements for on-base housing with wives and children, as threatening a man's commitment to the military as his primary identity, and one theory of the bases for decline of Roman imperial power points to demoralization of Roman armies occupying outlying areas attributed to their acquiring and living with wives from the local population, and the children thus produced, thus greatly weakening the intensity of all-male military solidarity. The difficulty of sustaining such solidarity at all in periods without active warfare is repeatedly pointed out in studies of armies.) Combat provides solutions for separation anxiety by the heightened comradeship developed in the experience, a comradeship which in the extremity of the situation allows expression of highly nurturant and succurant kinds of behavior both ordinarily associated with *feminine* roles—the nurturance of mother or nurse, the succurant behavior of the passive-dependent mistress or wife. Combat is thus a situation combining extreme "masculine" violence and aggression and depths of tender "feminine" compassion usually strongly denied in the "tough masculine" military identity.

This ties in with the other major dynamic theme of military life: homoeroticism. Combat aggression provides reaction formation against homoerotic feelings engendered in the military male solidarity, reassuring the man of his ultimate masculinity through the extremity of battle. At the same time homoerotic attachment may be *heightened* by the general intensification of affective involvement of the battle comrades. It is significant that the ordinary American limitations on males' physical expression of affection for each other (barriers that are extreme when viewed in cross-cultural perspective) are greatly reduced, even dissolved, in the crisis experience of wartime combat. (One is reminded of an agonizingly tender combat scene in *Home of the Brave* involving a Negro and a white American soldier, with its explicit message of interracial love exploding the surface of hate, and *implicit* affirmation of polymorphous human love.) This element is probably another reason for the difficulty of reestablishing the relationships of the combat scene, in postcombat circumstances even within the wartime military setting, let alone in postwar civilian situations.

Universal military conscription, in its fullest form limited to the wartime situation, provides essentially the only analogue in modern society of the male initiation ceremonies of primitive societies that has anything approaching *universal* application. True, rituals of initiation occur in many subsystems of modern society, for example, the socialization into such roles as medical student or of novice in many other occupations, hazing in initiation into college fraternities, and so on, but none of these represents a common experience for all, or anywhere nearly all, young males in the society. The other significant fact about the military *rite de passage* is that the new roles and statuses acquired are not, except for career army men, roles and statuses which are to be maintained throughout the rest of adult life. For a boy in primitive society the initiation ceremonies lead him into the role of manhood which he will continue to maintain throughout his life in that tribe. By contrast, the military experience in modern society, though it does "make a man out of the boy" who undergoes that training at a late-adolescent age, does so in such a way as to require him to make yet another transition after he leaves military life in order to acquire a civilian manhood—and *that* transition does *not* involve the ritualization and collectivity of experience that mark military induction as a true initiation ceremony.

4. ADOLESCENCE AND ADDICTION

The lack of any significant universal rites of initiation into manhood in our society is a point of reference of the following analysis of some of the pathologies of adolescence for males in this society. Victor Gioscia, in the following paper, presents an analysis of the significance of narcotic drugs for male American adolescents, in terms of basic socialization difficulties of this society and in terms of a phenomenon to which Gioscia is (to our knowledge) the first to give systematic attention, and a name, in sociological literature, the phenomenon of *achrony*.

Adolescence, Addiction, and Achrony

VICTOR J. GIOSCIA

Narcotics addiction raises a number of questions about the problem of growing up in America today. Narcotics addiction or use appears to be spreading among adolescents at all class levels in the United States. Use of drugs—not all of them narcotic—to produce altered states of consciousness and feeling is an important element of a significant deviant subculture: that of the Beat. In Beat culture, drug-taking is part of an apparently paradoxical amalgam of Western jazz and oriental mysticism. In an earlier study[54] we attempted to show the relationship of drugs, Zen, and jazz in the Beat configuration. The connections provide points of departure for understanding the relationship of drug-taking and adolescence in our society generally, and the relationship of both of these to processes in the experience of time. These are the tasks of the present paper.

As William James had known many decades ago, the ingestion of certain chemical substances induces states of consciousness which are, to the participant, indistinguishable from classical mysticism. The experience James called an "Anaesthetic Revelation." [55] In our own study we

An *original paper published here for the first time. Victor J. Gioscia is Associate Professor of Sociology at Adelphi University and Director of Sociological Research at Jewish Family Service, New York.*

[54] *The Beats* (unpublished).

[55] William James, *The Varieties of Religious Experience* (New York: Mod-

also found that the contents of a paragraph or a poem written by one of the great mystics resembled to the point of near-identity the contents of a paragraph or a poem written by the ingestors of certain drugs. The traditional ordeals to which the religious mystics of antiquity had subjected themselves (fasting, flagellation, fire)[56] had brought about a condition which the Beats could bring about by chemical agents. It was this same mystical experience that the Beats seek in poetry, Zen, and jazz. There are further similarities. The classical mystic seeks eternity, a timeless realm above and beyond the travail of a faltering and imperfect civilization.[57] Comparably, the Beats are convinced that Spengler's dire prophecies are about to come true. The Beat conviction that the original meaning of "Beat" derives from *beatus* (Latin, holy)[58] also links the Beats to the religious task of classical mystics to preach to their doomed brothers of salvation. The Beats emerge as a new set of articulators of the classical mystic's sense of cultural alienation. They do so with certain major departures in mystical repertoire and in sociological setting: fire and fasting are replaced by jazz and drugs; and the monk's solitary cell is replaced by a cultic group setting, distinct from both mystical isolation and the formal organizations of Western religions. The Beats, we hypothesized, are engaged in an attempt to banish the corrosive alienation of their generation by "turning on" quasi-mystical experiences.

The importance of drugs in the culture of the Beats provides clues to an understanding of the phenomenon of addiction generally, and especially to addiction in adolescents.

First, to clarify the phenomena we are dealing with: We are *not* concerned with habitual users of marijuana,[59] nor with habitués of L.S.D. or other "psychedelic" or "mind-expanding" drugs.[60] We are dealing with users of narcotic drugs, i.e., drugs that have the properties of inducing: (1) *tolerance* (an increasing dosage must be taken to produce an equiva-

---

ern Library, 1936), pp. 294-98; and *The Will to Believe and Other Essays in Popular Philosophy* (New York: Dover Books, 1956).

[56] *Cf.* Theodore Reik, *Masochism in Modern Man* (New York: Farrar, Straus & Company, 1949). See his interesting account of the Monk Basilius' practices.

[57] St. Augustine's two cities were a terrestrial and a heavenly pair. For the pharmacological equivalent, see Aldous Huxley, *Heaven and Hell* (New York: Harper Colophon, 1963).

[58] *Cf.* Lawrence Lipton, *The Holy Barbarians* (New York: Julian Messner, Inc., 1959).

[59] Which is neither a narcotic, nor addicting, but may be habit-forming. See Howard Becker, "Becoming a Marijuana User," *American Journal of Sociology,* Vol. LIX, November 1953, p. 3, and his *Outsiders* (New York: Free Press of Glencoe, 1964). See also D. Wakefield, "The Prodigal Powers of Pot," *Playboy,* August 1962.

[60] *Cf. Psychedelic Review,* 1:104 (1963-64). See also Sherwood, *et al.,* "The Psychedelic Experience, A New Concept in Psychotherapy," *Journal of Neuropsychiatry,* Vol. IV, December 1962, pp. 69-80.

lent experience); (2) *withdrawal syndrome* (termination of dosage induces a sickness whose symptoms include severe pain and dysphoria);[61]
and (3) *euphoria* (an extreme, unrealistic experience of happiness, feelings of well-being, and absence of anxiety). These are the psychophysiological aspects of the addiction syndrome. Second, we note the incidence
of this syndrome in the American population: all available evidence indicates that narcotics addiction is a phenomenon overwhelmingly of young
adult and late adolescent *males*.[62] Third, addiction occurs in certain patterns of *social interaction*, about which we at present have insufficient
systematic knowledge. However, available observational or impressionistic accounts indicate that addicts form near-group[63] or gang-group clus-
ters, since, not surprisingly, addicts seek out the company of other addicts. Through such organization they pool information, communicate
patterned evasions of law enforcement, make and share patterns of contact with the hierarchy of illegitimate sources of drug supply, and after
the drug experience indulge in collective reminiscence in which they accord to each other various statuses and rewards based on how "high"
each was and provide collective catharsis of the negative status they have
incurred by becoming addicted. Thus addict sociation makes possible a
viable way in a society whose hostility toward the addicts is symbolized
in its negative norms toward them and is concretized in the negative
action of policing agencies. But the sociation occurs *before* and *after* the
actual ingestion of drugs and the experience it brings, which is an *isolat-
ing* experience. The sociation pattern is thus a strange one where addicts
organize for an experience which temporarily disintegrates the organization.

The fourth significant aspect of addiction is the extent to which it
constitutes a subculture. The sharing of common or similar experiences,
and of a common perspective on the world, need not depend on actual
physical presence in visible group array. The existence of subculture sharing is indicated by the fact of a junkie argot that is largely identical on a
nation-wide basis. An addict going from New York to San Francisco, for
example, can with this vocabulary secure instant recognition from other
addicts. Two addicts who are otherwise complete strangers feel themselves in instant primary communication, recognizing in each other common, even identical, feelings. Addicts are also generally aware of the

61 *Cf.* D. Asubel, *Drug Addiction: Physiological, Psychological and Sociological Aspects* (New York: Random House, 1958) for a more detailed
account.

62 *Cf.* J. Clausen, "Drug Addiction" Ch. 4 in R. Merton and R. Nisbet, eds.,
Contemporary Social Problems (New York: Harcourt Brace and World, 1966,
second edition), pp. 193-235; and Isidor Chein, Donald S. Gerard, Robert S.
Lee and Eva Rosenfeld, *The Road to H* (New York: Basic Books, 1964).

63 *Cf.* Lewis Yablonsky, *The Violent Gang* (New York: The Macmillan Co.,
1962).

great number of others who share their patterns, and they derive rebellious sustenance from this knowledge. Tell-tale signs of addict behavior, often subliminally communicated, will also readily draw two junkies to each other.

A brief account of the subculture language of junkies is the following: The addict who injects heroin into his veins refers to taking a "fix" or a "shot." He "shoots up." If his needle ("spike," "nail") enters a vein, he achieves a "hit." The preparation of heroin powder dissolved in water and then heated is called "cooking" or "cooking up" in his "works" (equipment), consisting usually of a bottle top held with a bobby pin, a hypodermic needle, an eye dropper, and two matches. If he "hits," he then "turns on" or "gets high," i.e., begins his euphoric experience. The heroin powder comes in a cellophane "bag," and is variously called "H," "horse," "shit," "schmeck," or "stuff." The fix produces a "high," a "flight," during which the addict is "high," "flying," "out of it," "gone," or "stoned." The "high" wears off (proportional to dosage, individual metabolism, and tolerance) but leaves a semi-euphoric state during which the addict "goofs" or "nods" (goes in and out of a sleep-like state) or "nods out" (goes to sleep entirely or becomes unconscious). After several hours (depending on dosage, tolerance, the "size" of his "habit") he may "get sick" (i.e., experience withdrawal symptoms) and begin to need another "shot," "fix," "bag," etc.

He must then seek his "connection," "dealer," "pusher," or "mother" for a fresh supply. He tries to "cop" or "connect" so that he can "score" (renew his supply). If he has insufficient funds, he may try to "beat" or "con" (i.e., persuade) someone to give him the required amount. He may attempt to accumulate the purchase price by cajoling his fellow addicts, whom he variously calls "man," "daddy," "lover," "sweetheart," or a number of other nicknames. While "looking to score" he must beware of the police ("fuzz") or agents ("narcos") of the special narcotic agencies and departments empowered to apprehend him. "The Man" may appear from anywhere, at any time, to arrest ("bust") him. He has to avoid "getting busted" because while incarcerated he will be forced to "kick" (break the addiction cycle) "cold turkey" (without drugs). If he does "score," he must try to avoid a lethal overdose ("O.D."). (We offer some interpretation of these terms later in the text.)

Thus, narcotics addiction has a wide incidence among late-adolescent or young adult males in this society. It involves certain patterned psychophysiological experiences, notably temporary states of euphoria taking the participant totally "out of" the contexts and pressures of everyday life, certain distinctive forms of sociation, and a subculture signalized by a shared specialized lingo and common understandings. We can raise these questions: What needs does addiction satisfy for the individual participants, particularly what needs that are common to the whole range of the addicted population? How are these needs derived from commonly experienced trends in the wider culture and social structure of the society?

Observations and analyses from a variety of perspectives—chemico-physiological, psychological, sociological, and anthropologial—can be integrated to help us find answers to these questions.

There is evidence to indicate that narcotic drugs have a physiological effect similar to that of a pre-frontal lobotomy.[64] Referring to the accompanying schematic diagram: the frontal lobes of the brain are frequently

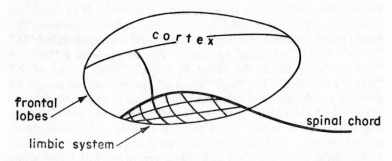

referred to as the "association" or "silent" areas, and sometimes as the seat of social learning. Here are said to be "localized" the memories of learned values, norms, and expectations, i.e., the social conscience.[65] Fibers from the cortex (the area of consciousness) pass through the association areas on their way to the limbic system (the area of primitive feeling and emotion, part of the old brain). Fibers from the limbic system also pass through the association areas on their way to the cortex. It is as if the silent areas were a filter for cortico-limbal and limbo-cortical fibers. Psychoanalytically, cortex can be seen as ego, the limbic system as id, and the association areas as superego. A pre-frontal lobotomy is held to release cortico-limbic and limbo-cortical fibers from associative modulation. That is, consciousness of primitive emotion is released from social definition by parenthesizing the inhibitory role of the silent areas. The effect on social behavior of lobotomy can be illustrated in the following case of an accidental lobotomy. A sober, responsible, quiet, and dutiful miner one day suffered the accidental passage of a crowbar up through the socket of his eye, on through the frontal lobes of the brain and out

[64] I. Wechsler, A *Textbook of Clinical Neurology*, 5th edition (Philadelphia: Saunders, 1943).

[65] Of course association areas are not exclusively localized in the frontal lobes, since there are also disinhibitory effects brought about by the analgesic drugs in the *cortical* area, as indicated by the occasional appearance of distorted perceptions, illusions and hallucinations under the influence of such drugs.

the top of his skull. Miraculously he survived, but on recuperation he abandoned his family, job, and former responsible roles to become the town drunk and "skirt-chaser." In effect, he had experienced an accidental pre-frontal lobotomy. Having severed his pre-frontal lobes from effective participation in cerebral events, he drastically altered his style of life.

Using narcotics evidently produces a similar, though temporary, effect. In effect, then, the addict is turning *off*, not "turning on." But since he is turning off an inhibitory process, the *net perceived result* is an increase in felt well-being, a release from feelings of guilt and anxiety which presumably result from repressive socialization of feeling and awareness. In psychoanalytic terms, the superego is being put to sleep, and the feelings of guilt, shame, and moral anxiety which are the results of its impact on the ego are pushed below the threshold of perception. Whether this is an act of repression, in which anxieties are allayed by an almost automatic defensive reaction, or an act of suppression, in which a conscious decision is made deliberately to exclude painful contents from consciousness, remains to be seen. But our question here is to account for the origin and content of the feelings of moral anxiety, guilt, and depression that are turned off by the narcotic experience[66] and ask what common experiences have been undergone by these adolescent males, leading to such feelings and the need to "turn them off," which can be related to general trends in the social structure of contemporary society.

Studies attempting a theory of delinquency are of some help here. By the fact that narcotics use brings them into conflict with the law, adolescent addicts are defined as "delinquents." Some of them, in fact, have "graduated" to drug use, in group formation, from other forms of delinquency, such as "bopping" gangs. Though theories of delinquency in general must be too broad to explain specifically the drug-using form, they do provide some clues.

Albert Cohen in *Delinquent Boys*[67] combines social structural and psychoanalytic insights in a theory of the genesis of the "delinquent subculture." The delinquent subculture is seen as a patterned response of adolescent males all facing similar or common psychological conflicts. Working-class and lower-class boys, to the extent that they have been socialized to middle-class values of status striving, are faced with the improbability of achieving adult male status according to those values. They also spend more time in peer-group relations than do middle-class boys, and hence they are more dependent on peer-group definitions of masculinity. These definitions tend to conflict with middle-class values,

[66] A parenthetical question is this: Is the addict trying to perform a chemical lobotomy on himself to relieve unbearable tensions, or is he primarily seeking an euphoric experience, and willingly paying the price of loss of social memory?

[67] Albert Cohen, *Delinquent Boys* (New York: Free Press of Glencoe, 1955).

and behavior in terms of them also tends to make the achievement of middle-class values improbable. Still middle-class values, being pervasive in the society, have been at least partially internalized by working-class boys. Delinquency then represents a reaction formation, repudiating the manifest cause of the status problem while its content goes underground, unacknowledged, yet lingering. This accounts for the delinquent's "irrational, malicious, and unaccountable" hostility to the enemy, the norms of the respectable middle-class society. The essential point, for our present discussion, is the conflicting, hence impaired, socialization of the adolescent male. Two questions need to be raised to link Cohen's analysis to our attempt to understand adolescent addiction: (1) Why do some of the participants in the "delinquent subculture" Cohen alludes to, turn to drugs from or instead of other delinquent activity, such as stealing or fighting? [68] (2) Do some of the socialization dilemmas that Cohen sees in the working-class boys also apply to many middle-class boys so that they are relevant for understanding the addicted adolescent males, whose class distribution is in fact much broader than that of the "delinquent subculture" Cohen describes?

The first question is given a partial answer in the work of Cloward and Ohlin in *Delinquency and Opportunity*.[69] They find delinquency partly traceable to the rather severe limitations which adolescents find on legitimate opportunities for mobility and success. Some of those who have found no available legitimate opportunities attempt to use illegitimate opportunity structures, e.g., stealing and rackets. Some, however, fail in that attempt as well, and these "double failures" are likely to turn to drugs. This theoretical proposition is a promising line of approach. However, in our own observations[70] some of the young men observed are addicts but not "double failures" [71] and some are "double failures" but not addicts.[72]

The theories of Cohen and of Cloward-Ohlin have in common the observation that male adolescents are confronted by deficits in their social worlds, deficits, familial and/or communal, which leave the adolescent less adequately socialized than he might be.

The nature of such deficits that seems most directly relevant to adolescent drug addiction is suggested by the work of Chein and his cowork-

[68] Commonly "bopping" gangs that turn to drugs stop "bopping."

[69] Richard Cloward and Lloyd Ohlin, *Delinquency and Opportunity* (New York: Free Press of Glencoe, 1960).

[70] The observations were made during a two-year participant-observation study of "Junkville," a high-delinquency area of New York City with a large incidence of drug addiction in late-adolescent males. Some observations on particular cases are given at a later point in the text.

[71] For example, one of the boys studied in Junkville, Billy A.

[72] For example, another of the Junkville boys, Joey R., who is one of the two of the ten cited who are *not* addicted.

ers.[73] In their exhaustive study of thirty adolescent drug users, they find that those male adolescents who experienced a graver difficulty than their siblings in achieving a viable relationship with their male parent or male parent surrogates, appear more frequently in the addict population. Especially significant for our purposes is their finding that those adolescent addicts who experienced difficulty in father-identification and in "healthy" superego formation were also observed to have a strong distrust of major social institutions, so that, in addition to their faulty socialization, they were less attitudinally amenable to resocialization by interested agencies of the community.

Rado[74] describes certain features of the addict personality from a classical psychoanalytic orientation. He argues that the lack of masculinization frequently observed in the addict is only one side of the coin. The other side is a continuing dependency on the mother-figure and a residue of psychic fixation which is commonly termed oral-infantilism. Chein and Rosenfeld's findings reinforce this interpretation since their subjects also reported feelings of dependency toward their mothers.

Another study puts the problem of deficits in socialization into a cross-cultural perspective. Bloch and Niederhoffer[75] contrast the situation of male adolescents of our society with that of their counterparts in many primitive societies, specifically those that engage in initiation ceremonies. In the latter cases, successful negotiation of the puberty rites, involving various ordeals and special training, confers some of the status privileges of masculine adulthood, epecially rights to property and to adult modes of sexual experience. The absence of significant initiations of adolescents into adult sex and property roles in our society, by contrast, has motivated some of these adolescents to attempt an initiation of themselves into maturity. But since they have neither the requisite community power, nor access to property and/or women, nor the social wisdom which age is alleged to confer, they do not actually accomplish their purpose. Their attempt to confer sociological maturity on themselves is aborted. The resultant sociation is the gang, a form of social group marked by cohesive and mutually dependent feeling and behavior. While Bloch and Niederhoffer's analysis refers to delinquency in general, the significance of their concern with the lack of initiation rituals in modern society can be applied specifically to the problem of male adolescent drug addicts.

Bloch and Niederhoffer's frequent reference to Bruno Bettelheim's

[73] Cf. Chein et al., op. cit.

[74] Sandor Rado, "The Psychoanalysis of Pharmacothymia," Psychoanalytic Quarterly, Vol. II, 1933, 1-23.

[75] Herbert Bloch and Arthur Niederhoffer, The Gang (New York: Philosophical Library, 1958).

Symbolic Wounds[76] provides connecting links. Bettelheim's main insight into the nature of male puberty rites is to show how these rites reveal male envy of the apparently greater fertility of females. Puberty rites are thus not only efforts to achieve both maturation and masculinization, but also, in apparent opposition, to ritualize a desire to obliterate the differences between male and female and to return to a common ground of simple undifferentiated being, prior to the first, the sexual, division of labor. In the light of this formulation, addict sociation in our society can be seen as an aborted puberty ritual which also expresses a wish for the intra-uterine simplicity of the prenatal stage of human life, a stage of abject dependency *in* the mother. Details of the content of the addict subculture, as will be seen, are entirely consonant with this view.

In the absence of such publicly institutionalized puberty rituals to provide for maturation and masculinization, adolescents may remain bound in the swaddling stages of their childhood or feel impelled to institute their own "functional equivalents" in forms expressing their own particular conflicts and ambivalences. In the absence of means of achieving maturation and masculinization in line with institutionalized values of the society, the forms by which adolescent males will devise their own equivalent rites, will necessarily be deviant from the prevailing culture. Adolescent male addiction can be seen as one such form. It remains to interpret the details of the addiction complex—its psychology, its forms of sociation, and its culture—in terms of the converging lines of analysis we have been describing.

SOME OBSERVATIONAL DATA

It is of interest to report here some observations made over a two-year period at a social service center in New York City in an area we call "Junkville." Some of the youngsters in Junkville are addicted to heroin. Some of these "junkies" show up somewhat regularly at the center run for them by an agglomeration of social and religious agencies. Most but not all of the people who come to the center are male adolescent addicts. No pretense is made of systematic sampling of any kind; however, a selection of ten boys aged eighteen to twenty-three who come to the center may be instructive in relation to the ideas developed in this paper. All live in an area and in milieux where addicting drugs are readily available and the rate of drug use is high. The "clientele" of the social center does consist largely of addicts, but not all of these boys are addicted. Five of them are, and three others are intermittently, but two are not at all, though one of those has been a "dealer" in drugs. These boys are from roughly similar backgrounds, lower class or near lower class, Roman

[76] See discussion of this work in the earlier part of this chapter of this volume, pp. 312-16. See also Bettelheim's *Truants from Life* (New York: Free Press of Glencoe, 1955).

Catholic, and most of them Italian. Superficially, it would seem to be difficult to predict which of them are addicted, which are not. The five who are addicted have in common the fact that none of them has achieved a successful identification with his father or father-surrogate. One is illegitimate and never knew his father; in all four other cases the father deserted or was "thrown out" before or during the boy's adolescent years. In these cases the mother is the central parental figure. The three who are only intermittently addicted are instructive. Each of these boys may go for as long as three months at a time without taking drugs, but each invariably returns to the "habit." Each seems to hover between part-successful and part-unsuccessful identification with the father. The two boys of these ten who have made successful identifications with the father have both escaped the addiction syndrome. In one case the father is a family man who devotes time to his son and motivates him to be mobile. In the other both the father, a gangster, and an older brother have exerted strong moralistic guidance and discipline, and though he has rejected them, the boy feels strongly masculine. Thus the extent and success of father-identification seems to be the critical differentiating factor among these similarly situated young men.

IMPLICATIONS OF JUNKIE LANGUAGE

A careful consideration of junkie argot sheds light on the peculiar psychological world of the addict and helps elucidate the problems we have been discussing. *Ambivalence* is probably the single most striking feature of the addict's approach to the world. Unsuccessful strivings for masculinization and perpetuated infantile dependency on the mother are one part of this ambivalence. Note the set of opposing terms the addict uses for the act of injection. He calls this action both a "shot" as in "shot down" or feeling "shot" (as if someone or something had shot him) and "fix" as if he is in need of repair. This masochistic allusion is carried through in the name of the mechanism of repair, the needle, which he calls a "nail" or a "spike"; and it is neatly counterbalanced by referring to the head of the eyedropper as a "nipple," the source of his reparative nourishment. Although he is thus taking in food, finding a vein is called a "hit," a strange denotation suggesting a shooting gallery, which in fact is what the police usually call a "pad" where many junkies "shoot up." The masochistic implications reflect the addict's coupling of his broken and estranged feelings with a need for punishment for his felt inadequacy.

Paradox is further evident in other parts of addict lingo. Heroin, the addict's emotional food, is called either "shit" (suggesting coprophilia) or "schmeck," which is near Yiddish for taste, hence a specifically oral term. A favorable proportion of heroin to the material used to cut it, is referred to as "tasty," confirming the oral implication. The combination of these terms is consonant with the affective patterns of the obsessive-compulsive. Another term for heroin, "horse," suggests that heroin magically enables the adolescent to mount his own Pegasus, on which he makes his high "flight." Flying so high, he is "out of it" and "gone"—but then he is also referred to as "stoned," another indication of the intense ambivalence the addict feels. In addition, during his euphoric "flight" the junkie also "goofs" and "nods"—a peculiar phasing in and out of his special euphoric sleep, indicating the bipolar nature of the addict's syndrome.

In a similar vein, we may observe that the "pusher" (power is clearly implied here) is, nevertheless, also called "mother"—the giver of nutritional and emotional food. The addict's occasional rage, consequent upon frustration by such a maternal figure, motivates him on occasion to "beat" someone for the purchase price of his specific emotional milk. In doing so, he calls his fellow addict "baby," "daddy," "man," "lover," or "sweetheart." "Baby" reinforces the interpretation of the addict's infantile feelings, here perceived in the peers. "Man" and "daddy" as alternates for "baby" reflect again the bipolar identity. What then shall we make of "lover" and "sweetheart"? The hypothesis of latent homosexuality, which is in any case easily confirmed, is part of the picture. But it is the *confluence* of infantile daddy-seeking and latent homosexual themes on which we wish to focus attention. By viewing these themes together, we gain some insight into the special heterosexual (mother)-homosexual (father) flavor of the addict's bipolar nature. The addict is rather automatically hostile to authority, and yet he devotes enormous quantities of his energy to behaving in terms of authority. This helps us to understand how the blind hatred of narcotics agents can convert itself with dramatic suddenness into a warm and total acceptance of an "understanding" and permissive narcotics officer. It is provocative to speculate whether this bipolarity permits us to interpret getting "busted" (arrested) as both getting broken and "getting breasted."

(Parenthetically, the addict's ambivalence is met by the ambivalence of the social-control institutions, in the dual character of penal-therapeutic concern for the addict population. It must come as no surprise and indeed probably confirms the addict's vision of the world to learn that recent legislation constructs a route through officialdom in which he may "choose" between being sentenced to jail and being sentenced to a therapeutic program. One may predict that this kind of enforced therapeutic program will serve rather to intensify the ambivalence the addict already has.)

It might well be argued that a social structure which simultaneously demands and prevents the adoption of highly cathected adult statuses is inflicting an unbearably burdensome set of conflicting demands on the adolescent, and that this dislocation in the social structure of his self, deriving from dark powers over which he feels he can exert no ameliorative influence, can be avoided in no quicker or better way than by chemical ingestion, the normative guidance for which is set in the aspirin and cigarette fetishes so prevalent in our national culture.[77]

ADDICTION AND ACHRONY

Another observation about addiction is important to round out this analysis. Clausen says, "Perhaps the most striking effect [of drug addiction] . . . is that one's perception of time is markedly affected." [78] In our own study, among the hundreds of addicts we have interviewed, we have encountered not one who did not spontaneously offer a similar observation.[79] In one way or another, adolescent addicts have told us that their enjoyment of narcotics was directly proportional to the extent to which drugs transported them from the realm of inexorable time to some ecstatic eternity. Once one conceives that the addict's apperception of the flow of time lies at the bottom of his feelings of depression, it is not difficult to infer that heaven, eternity, nirvana, ecstasis, and so on, all represent illusory releases from the psychic prisons erected by oppressive social processes.[80] Recalling the Zen frame of reference into which the Beats had cast their narcotic experiences helps us to perceive that the high which heroin seems to deliver also makes the shores of the "oceanic feeling" seem less remote. The waves of euphoria which wash over the addict also become far less allegorical in this light. It is not without

[77] In this connection, it is pertinent to question the validity of regarding drug addicts as "retreatists" according to the now classical paradigm for analysis of deviant social roles provided by Robert Merton in his paper, "Social Structure and Anomie," in *Social Theory and Social Structure* (New York: Free Press of Glencoe, 1957). Cloward and Ohlin (*op. cit.*) apply the Merton scheme and find drug addicts "retreatists" in that they presumably reject both the culturally prescribed goals (success) and the institutionally indicated means (hard, respectable work). However, if we took, instead of occupational success, the equally institutionalized goal called "the pursuit of happiness" and considered as an acceptable, indeed widely utilized means, that of instantaneous chemical ingestion, as indicated in aspirins and cigarettes, then drug addicts score a plus on both goals and means, and hence can be regarded as supreme "conformists" for this culture. Perhaps it is precisely because they are conformists to these hedonistic values, without tempering them by the countering ascetic norms, that addicts are so disturbing to the nonaddict population.

[78] J. Clausen, *op. cit.*, p. 198.

[79] Firsthand accounts supporting the proposition that drug experience alters the apperception of time, are found in the excellent anthology compiled by D. Ebin, *The Drug Experience* (New York: Orion Press, 1961), especially the section entitled "Opiates, Addicts, and Cures." See also Norman Taylor, *Narcotics* (New York: Delta Publications, 1963).

[80] For classic accounts of the use of religion to allay anxiety, see Sigmund Freud, *The Future of an Illusion*, in the Standard Edition, Vol. XXI, *op. cit.*, and B. Nelson, "The Future of Illusions," in *Psychoanalysis*, Vol. II, Spring-Summer 1954, p. 54, of which a condensed version appears in this volume.

significance that the classical psychoanalytic perspective predicts a high coincidence of father-alienation and mystical longing.

We deduce that these adolescent addicts find the flow of time pathogenic, that their flight "out of time" indicates that they otherwise feel themselves in a state to which we give the term *achrony*.[81] Briefly, a state of achrony means feeling "out of step" with the culturally accepted definitions of the "normal" flow of time. To discuss this, we need to clarify the notion of time itself. Many approaches are open to us, but we shall restrict our attention to two.

First, we may inquire whether there resides within us a sense of the *rate of attainment of ideals*, so that it is not nonsense to speak of "going somewhere," "getting ahead," and other folklore expressions of the mobility ethos of our culture. Such expressions imply a back-drop of temporality in actions and strivings.

Second, time may be defined as the emotional interval between impulse and gratification. That is, time is *felt* as the *waiting* which ensues consequent to the onset of a stimulus and prior to the initiation of a reward. Waiting too long often leads to feelings of frustration. The application to delinquency is obvious: when waiting for a chance to lead a satisfying life seems useless, why wait? *Carpe diem:* seize the day, lest tomorrow we fail.

The superego (alternatively, the normative organization of a social system) is essentially a timing device which defines how long instinctive gratifications are to be postponed while sublimations are being erected (alternatively, how long prepubescent roles must be maintained while adult roles are being sought). Those adolescents who are made to wait too long for the onset of sociological maturity will, at some time, begin to feel frustration and will, in the absence of viable opportunity structures, indulge in behavior which calls forth the observation, "There is a child acting out his conception of a man."

The conception of the superego as a temporal filter helps us to ac-

---

[81] Space precludes adequate development of this concept here. It is developed in other writings of this author. See V. Gioscia, "On Social Time" (mimeographed report on file at Jewish Family Service, New York). For related discussion on the concepts of time see the following: V. Gioscia, "Plato's Image of Time: An Essay in Philosophical Sociology" (Fordham University, 1962, unpublished Ph.D. dissertation); G. J. Whitrow, *The Natural Philosophy of Time* (New York: Harper Torchbooks, 1961); Robert MacIver, *The Challenge of the Passing Years: My Encounter with Time* (New York: Simon and Shuster, 1962); Georges Gurvitch, *The Spectrum of Social Time* (Stuttgart: Reidel Co., 1963); Lewis A. Coser and Rose L. Coser, "Time Perspective and Social Structure," in A. Gouldner and H. Gouldner, *Modern Society* (New York: Harcourt, Brace & World, 1963), pp. 638-46; H. Meyerhoff, *Time in Literature* (Berkeley: University of California Press, 1955); Edmund Husserl *The Phenomenology of Internal Time-Consciousness*, trans. J. Churchill (The Hague: Martinus Nijhoff, 1964).

count for the selection of narcotics as the form of deviation many adolescents "choose." Drugs "turn off" the association areas of the brain, the "seat" of the superego. It is the extent to which this "watch" of the personality measures evaluatively the performance of behavior, which heroin quickly, almost instantaneously, puts to sleep. In the absence, or the oppressive presence, of this social clock, the ego may attempt to retire, to allow the twin horses of the id to gallop at will once the floodgates of fantasy have been released. In addition, the conception of superego as clock brings us closer to the peculiarly modern character of adolescent drug addiction. Has not this age invented the phrase "Time is money?"

We suggest that modern urban culture, that culture whose pathologies have been variously diagnosed by the assorted brilliance of Marx's concept of alienation, Durkheim's concept of anomie, and Freud's concept of anxiety, has erected so complex a normative organization that the pace of social gratification is slowing down. That is, the number of normatively defined behaviors is increasing so rapidly that the number of spontaneously defined behaviors is decreasing with proportional and alarming rapidity. It is not only that urban life is complex, it is increasing in its *rate* of complexification. In such circumstances it is probable that the socialization of the new norms will lag behind the emergence of new norms and that some will be handed an obsolete set of standards for their behavior. There will ensue a kind of social anachronism in which old norms will be unduly stretched to fit new situations. More specifically, we hypothesize that those adolescents in our culture who have not been given a set of norms which will synchronize them with the pace of contemporary urban culture will be subjected to the condition of achrony.

Achrony, then, refers to any situation in which there is a felt discrepancy between the rate of behavior and the rate of fulfillment of expectations, and thus it represents a generalization of the concept of frustration. Since all men are born, pass through stages, and die, we may say that relating to the process of time is a cross-cultural necessity and that every culture organizes this passage in some way.

Narcotic drugs specifically alleviate *feelings* of achrony by producing the illusion of timelessness, spinning a cocoon of euphoric dissociation from the hurtling inexorability of social process. Those for whom the process of socialization has not devised synchronous roles and expectations will find that such drugs provide surcease. Instead of hurrying up, and "rushing against time" in the mode of the middle-class conformist, and instead of posing (temporizing) as mature and masculine adults (as in the violent gang), some adolescents attempt to evade the process of maturation itself by *rising above it* into an illusory realm of eternity, a temporal defense we call *epichrony*.

Epichronic stances are characterized by a feeling that a zero speed of time is immensely comfortable. The ideal typical epichronic stance is perfectly timeless: within it one can believe that the social organization of experience is not subject to the ravages of temporal change. Marijuana use produces a feeling that time has "slowed down" so that a few moments "seem like an eternity." This property also characterizes the so-called hallucinogenic drugs, i.e., mescalin, L.S.D., peyote, and psilocybin. It is important to note that this alteration of the time sense is common to the addicting as well as the nonaddicting drugs. Thus the pattern common to drug addicts of switching from addictogenic to hallucinogenic substances is not necessarily a step out of character. When we focus on this common property, we begin to account for the variety of drugs the expert drug user enjoys. This variety of epichronic experiences supports our hypothesis that *drugs are taken* specifically *to alleviate feelings of achrony*, since any of these drugs will bring about a feeling that eternal laws have been fashioned which are binding for all time, or the feeling that the normative regulation of pace is completely absent, as in the transtemporal Buddhahood of the Beats. Each of these drugs may be said to comprise the structural material of an epichronic hiding place from inexorability.

With these insights, we may return to certain features of addict sociation and addict subculture. The epichronic flight of the narcotic "high" state brings relief, we have suggested, from oppressive feelings of achrony, or, otherwise stated, from oppressive aspects of social process. Indeed, the addict's, like the mystic's, view of eternity or nirvana carries the implication that *all* regular social processes are oppressive. Hence, the peculiar, aborted kind of "social organization" of the junkies: a momentary experience of organization followed by its fragmentation into individual euphorias, followed by further momentary organization in the reminiscent glow. It is as if the drug groups reached briefly for a moment of genuine social process, only to return to the sea of their despair on the ebb tide of social disorganization. But "genuine social process" is precisely what the individuals who need to turn to narcotics cannot achieve, for the reasons we have analyzed.

The kind of sharing of addict subculture can now also be better understood. In contrast to the enormous complexity of the urban culture, and its increasing rate of development of new norms, the subculture of addiction has a congenial simplicity: the norms are few and rudimentary and make only minimal demands. Further, since the taking of drugs inhibits both sexual and aggressive drives, two basic sources of disruptive and conflictful social processes, the addict's relationship to his world has undergone an enormous simplification.

Having perceived, accurately, that the courses of their lives might not be steered toward the achievement of social promise, addicts fly up into the arms of a serene eternity in which they are not only the sole inhabitants, but also the sole government. As on all islands of paradise, ethnocentrism is achieved, but at the usual terrible cost of restricted participation in the affairs of the world at large. To be above time is to be "out of it." This posture brings with it the illusion of escape, but, so posturing, the addict renders himself sociologically impotent, i.e., he can do nothing to alter the events which have plagued him by reason of his self-styled removal from them. It would seem that addict subculture seeks removal from the sphere of sex-aggressive behavior by perpetuating a condition of physiological as well as sociological dependency.

We have seen that delinquent addicts share their unaddicted brothers' pessimism with respect to legitimate mobility, and that addicts, like delinquents, do not feel themselves to have been initiated into the ways and paths of adult masculinity. And we have seen that the narcotic experience turns off that depression which results from the simultaneous adoption of a high set of expectations coupled with a perception of their unattainability. But we feel closer to the data when we say that the chemically induced epichronicity which the addict brings about almost instantly is, in fact, exactly what the addict seeks.

Thus, when Freud states that there is "no time in the id," we might add that perhaps, for some, there is too much time in the superego. That is, when the process of becoming human is perceived to take too long or to proceed too slowly, men, as ever, devise forms of illusory attainment of harmony with their era. It does not seem to us that addicts are especially deviant in this effort. Our age seems otherwise willing to speed headlong toward the fulfillment of its cherished ambitions, anachronizing massive portions of its self in the process. Yet it condemns the dramatic efficiency with which the addict relieves his achronistic feelings, heaping criminal statuses upon his head because he seeks an analgesic revelation. Do we demean Icarus for his wings of wax or for his attempted flight?

5. CONCLUSION

Gioscia's paper brings us full circle from the exotics and mysteries of primitive culture, radically epitomized in the initiation ceremonies, to the corresponding cultural phenomena of modern society as seen in the "pathology" of drug addiction, viewed as an attempted and aborted initiation ceremony of the pathogenically socialized and socially dispossessed. Gioscia's paper echoes elements of all the others presented or discussed in this chapter. The reference point of *time* is essential to Benedict's, to Hart's, or to any other anthropologist's discussion of "continuities" or "discontinuities" in culture or conditioning or socialization. The term "life cycle" is of course meaningless without a temporal dimension. By using "cycle" instead of something like "line," this term also implies a rejection of a linear conception of time provided by the mechanistic view of the universe, reverting instead to biological and psychological reference points—to either the "timeless id" or to repetitious rhythms with movements from and back to points of origin, evoking the favorite wheel imagery of oriental world views. In all of these papers we find a recurrent tension between continuity and discontinuity, a peculiarly acute problem of the adolescent phase of development with its re-evocation, hence continuity, of infantile sexuality and dependency and its drive to new adult status and feeling and relationship, hence discontinuity. The papers and our own discussion have concentrated particularly on the transition problems of males since these seem almost invariably to be more acute than those for females, regardless of great variations of culture and social structure. Evidently, as Margaret Mead argues, there is a basic biological substratum for this sex difference, epitomized in the fact that the little girl has only to wait for something inside herself to unfold and develop to become a woman, while the boy has to *do* something, be assertive and active, achieve some mastery, to prove his adult masculinity. The wide-ranging cross-cultural examples from many primitive societies indicate that the difficulties are by no means exclusive to hectic, "disorganized" or "alienated" modern populations. The latter, however, significantly lack any standardized initiation rituals applying to all the young males in the society. This lack, in turn, can be seen as filled by such approximate "functional equivalents" as the way in which the young man is initiated into the military corps or the ways in which various kinds of delinquents initiate themselves, in effect, including the special initiation into the world of drug use. Such initiation into drugs may, as Gioscia suggests, represent rejection of the conventional world—into which certain segments of youth can find no satisfying initiation or prospect of future satisfying life—and the substitution of something out and beyond, above and out of it. To which we can add: with all the attendant, sometimes horrifying, costs.[82]

[82] Some related themes are explored in "Play Elements in Delinquency" presented in Chapter Five.

Selected Bibliography

Bateson, Gregory. *Naven.* 2nd edition. Stanford, Calif.: Stanford University Press, 1958. (Original publication, 1936.)
Detailed analysis of a puberty ritual in the Iatmul of New Guinea, from several perspectives.

Berndt, Ronald M. *Excess and Restraint: Social Control Among a New Guinea Mountain People.* Chicago: University of Chicago Press, 1962.
Contains excellent data on puberty rites and initiations.

Bettelheim, Bruno. *Symbolic Wounds: Puberty Rites and the Envious Male.* New York: Free Press of Glencoe, 1954.

Bloch, H. and A. Niederhoffer. *The Gang.* New York: Philosophical Library, 1958.
Interesting analysis of delinquent gangs in modern society in relationship to initiation ceremonies of primitive societies.

Brown, Judith K. "A Cross-Cultural Study of Female Initiation Rites," *American Anthropologist.* Vol. 65, 1963, pp. 837-53.

Cohen, Yehudi A. "The Establishment of Identity in a Social Nexus: The Special Case of Initiation Ceremonies and Their Relation to Value and Legal Systems," *American Anthropologist.* Vol. 66, 1964, pp. 529-52.
See next item.

————. *The Transition From Childhood to Adolescence.* Chicago: Aldine Publishing Co., 1964.
Significant cross-cultural analysis of the two pubertal transitions, distinguishing a "first stage of puberty" (at age 8-11) which some societies demarcate by extrusion or brother-sister avoidance, from the "second stage" (the usual "puberty" stage).

Dornbusch, Sanford M. "The Military Academy as an Assimilating Institution," *Social Forces.* Vol. 33, May 1955, pp. 316-21.
Though not explicitly analyzed in terms of transition rituals, the data show such features clearly.

Eliade, Mircea. *Birth and Rebirth.* New York: Harper & Row, Publishers, 1958.
Initiation ceremonies seen as symbolic death and rebirth and related to other religious traditions.

Erikson, Erik. "The Problem of Ego Identity," in: *Identity and the Life Cycle: Selected Papers. Psychological Issues.* Vol. 1, No. 1, Monograph No. 1. New York: International Publishers Press, 1959.
One of the most profound recent formulations of the psychosocial "tasks" of adolescence.

———— (ed). *Youth: Change and Challenge.* New York: Basic Books, 1963.
Symposium of insightful papers by a variety of social science professionals.

Friedenberg, Edgar Z. *Coming of Age in America: Growth and Acqui-escence.* New York: Random House, 1965.
A powerful analysis of the value constrictions inculcated in American adolescents through the schools. See also the author's earlier *The Van-ishing Adolescent.* New York: Dell Publishing Co., 1962.

Goodman, Paul. *Growing Up Absurd.* New York: Random House, 1960. The dilemmas and alternatives open to youth in the "organized society," as seen by a major humanist critic.

Laye, Camara. *The Dark Child.* Translated by J. Kirkup, E. Jones, and E. Gottlieb. New York: The Noonday Press, 1954.
An absorbing autobiography of a Malinké (West Africa) boy with a vivid account of his puberty ceremonies.

Mead, Margaret. *Male and Female.* New York: William Morrow and Company, 1949, and many later paperback editions.
Illuminating discussion of puberty ceremonies.

Richards, Audrey. *Chisungu: A Girl's Initiation Ceremony Among the Bemba of Northern Rhodesia.* New York: Humanities Press, 1956.
A fine ethnographic case study, a multifaceted analysis.

Rigney, Francis and Douglas Smith. *The Real Bohemia.* New York: Basic Books, 1960.
It would be fruitful to subject these authors' analysis to "transition-ceremony" analysis.

Stephens, William N. *The Oedipus Complex: A Cross-Cultural Study.* New York: Free Press of Glencoe, 1962.
By the use of Human Relations Area Files data on a large number of cultures, documents the variable appearance of presumed manifesta-tions of the Oedipus complex (indicators of castration anxiety, sexual fears, avoidances, etc.) and their higher correlation with cultures prac-ticing mother-child sleeping arrangements and postpartum sex taboos. Relates to the Whiting, *et al.* studies.

Van Gennep, Arnold. *The Rites of Passage.* Translated by Monika B. Vizedom and Gabrielle L. Caffee. Chicago: University of Chicago Press, 1960. (Original publication in French, Paris: E. Nourry, 1909.)
A "classic" formulation of the sociological nature of transition rituals.

Vidich, Arthur J. and Maurice R. Stein. "The Dissolved Identity in Mil-itary Life," in M. Stein, A. Vidich, and D. White (eds.). *Identity and Anxiety.* New York: Free Press of Glencoe, 1960.

Young, Frank W. "The Function of Male Initiation Ceremonies: A Cross-Cultural Test of an Alernative Hypothesis," *American Journal of Sociology.* Vol. LXVII, No. 4, 1962, pp. 379-96.

Young, Frank W. *Initiation Ceremonies: A Cross-Cultural Study of Status Dramatization.* Indianapolis: Bobbs-Merrill, 1965.
This much fuller development of the earlier article makes a stronger case for status dramatization, in relation to solidarity groups, as the key to male initiation ceremonies, rejecting "personality-culture" in-terpretations of the Whiting variety. It also thoughtfully integrates analyses of female initiation rites and parenthood rituals, including "couvade."

FIVE

Personality: work and play

In this chapter we turn to the psychodynamics of work and play. How is personality related to the kinds of work we do and the ways we play? Are doctors more like each other than like truck drivers? Does it take a certain kind of personality to become a salesman, a policeman, a nurse, a professional thief? Or do the adult practitioners of a particular craft become more alike in personality once in the trade? Or do both of these processes—selective recruitment of certain personality types, and occupational transformation of the personality to fit the psychic demands of the kind of work—both come into play (or work)? Or is there perhaps really no intrinsic pattern, but instead different kinds of work merely represent different masks to be donned for certain times and places and tasks only to be dropped again in other times and climes? Are these masks that almost anyone can wear, with many different personalities "underneath"? And what is the psychic link between work and play? If we "play a role" at work, what do we do at play? Is work itself suffused with play, or only for some, or only some kinds of work? Can we distinguish the two?

These are some of the questions we want to raise, and they are all questions for which the students of man are far from having answers.

We can start by setting forth some general sociological considerations. The great single fact of developed societies is their complex division (more accurately, specialization) of labor, the elaborate subdivision of the tasks to be carried out in the society into a host of specialized more-or-less full-time occupations. These occupations differ greatly in their demands of physical, intellectual, and social skill and presumably accordingly, in their demands of *psychic* orientation: obvious cases that come to mind are the methodical precision of the accountant, the devotion, even slavishness to rules, of the petty bureaucrat, the mercurial versatility of the confidence man, the hyper-sociability of the salesman, the reveling in feats of stamina of the stevedore, the unctuous oiliness of the funeral director. (Whether these are genuine "personality" differences, will concern us anon.) Secondly, the more technologically advanced societies are increasingly *employee* societies—i.e., the means of livelihood for most, if not all, of the population consists of regular work for salary or wages in a consistent, and necessarily specialized, occupation. This applies to practically all of the adult males of the society and for a varying and increasing portion of the adult females as well. Thus, work is a major and a compelling, constraining, and facilitating part of life, in which the personality must needs be involved. We know, of course, that even where an absolute economic necessity, work is not always or necessarily *felt* as the central activity of one's life. This suggests that we should not expect some over-all commonality of personality configuration among *all* those doing the same kind of work. But we can raise the question of whether in *some* occupations more than in others, work is *a*, if not *the*, central organizing force of the adult personality to such an extent that there are in fact strong, even deep, similarities in total personality structure among all the practitioners of that line of endeavor. Even where it is not central, however, its demands in psychic orientations may be sufficiently compelling that only by some combination of selective recruitment and subsequent selective socialization for the salience of certain psychological characteristics, can these demands be even minimally fulfilled so that we find similar kinds of people similarly *un*committed or *un*engaged in their daily work.

At the same time, modern specialization of labor is accompanied by the phenomenon of a rather compelling separation between work and play spheres, at least at the institutional level. At that level, work is "serious," it has consequences, it "matters," while play is seen as that arena of activity that "doesn't count," an arena where one can do what one pleases and need not take responsibility for the sequels of one's acts. (But this simple formulation, as we shall see, misses the complexity of the actual concatenation of sentiments and commitments involved in any of the activities formally labeled either "work" or "play.") Still we can say that the elaboration of work tasks in an at least formally rationalized modern economy does officially mark off "work" in distinct time-space contexts, with all else by residual deduction being consigned to the area of "play."

While it is questionable whether any particular occupation requires one particular personality type and that type only, it is certainly demonstrable that particular occupations require, or at least put a premium on, certain psychological "predispositions," whether these be organized into one total personality pattern or can be achieved within the context of many different total personality syndromes. A starting point for this kind of analysis is the now classic paper by Robert K. Merton, "Bureaucratic Structure and Personality." [1] Merton, taking off from a sociological analysis of the characteristics of bureaucratic organization (à la Max Weber), proceeds to discuss its "dysfunctions" (rigidity, overconformity resulting in failure to accomplish its substantive goals because of overconcentration on means, rules and regulations). Merton shows that a psychological prerequisite of bureaucratic functioning is a mental set of discipline, of sentiments supporting the rightness of the bureaucratic authority structure and all its rules and regulations. ". . . in order to ensure discipline (the necessary reliability of response), these sentiments are often more intense than is technically necessary." [2] The rules, in fact, become symbolic in cast rather than strictly utilitarian, resulting in a fetishism of the regulations. Merton emphasizes the many and powerful *social-structural* sources of such "overconformity" (the graded career line within the bureaucracy, the sense of common destiny among the bureaucrats, reducing ingroup aggression and encouraging its displacement onto clientele, the emphasis on impersonal secondary-group relations in conflict with clients' wishes for primary-group treatment, and so on). Merton then raises a number of substantive problems for research: [3]

> To what extent are particular personality types selected and modified by the various bureaucracies (private enterprise, public service, the quasi-legal political machine, religious orders)? Inasmuch as ascendancy and submission are held to be traits of personality . . . do

[1] Robert K. Merton, "Bureaucratic Structure and Personality," *Social Forces*, Vol. 18, 1940, pp. 560-68, reprinted in Merton, *Social Theory and Social Structure* (New York: Free Press of Glencoe, 1949), pp. 151-60 and 382-84.
[2] *Ibid.*, p. 563.
[3] *Ibid.*, p. 568.

*bureaucracies select personalities of particularly submissive or as-
cendant tendencies? . . . does participation in bureaucratic office
tend to increase ascendant tendencies? Do various systems of recruitment . . . select different personality types?*

In this chapter we shall examine the results of one study that
provides partial answers to some of these questions, William E.
Henry's study of the psychodynamics of the business executive, that
is, a high-level functionary in private business bureaucracy. We shall
then extrapolate some cross-national evidence on the psychology of
the executive elite of another modern society, the Soviet Union, derived from Raymond Bauer's study of three "case histories" of Soviet
middle elite of the same period (late 1940s). Then we turn to a
series of work roles that are rather ambiguously related to bureaucratic structures, though quite different from strictly bureaucratic
positions of the kind Merton had in mind, that is, the work roles of
scientists, both physical and social. In these occupations, the "separation of the worker from the tools of his work" is almost complete
in the sense that it is almost impossible for any physicist, chemist,
biologist, psychologist, anthropologist, sociologist, or any other kind
of scientist to work in a private-property entrepreneurial context;
rather each is dependent on having a position in a formal organization such as a university, a research laboratory or a foundation-
supported research team in order to carry on his work. In the context,
tension develops between bureaucratic features of such formal organization—authority structure, discipline to the organization (as
distinct from the craft and ultimate values of the science), and rules
and regulations pertaining to both of these, on the one side, and the
need for circumstances maximizing freedom of inquiry, on the
other. What are the psychological characteristics of persons recruited into such work, and how do they differ from one type of
scientist to another? We present excerpts from the unique researches of Anne Roe on eminent scientists of four kinds: for the
natural scientists, physicists and biologists; for the social sciences,
psychologists and anthropologists. Next we consider the creative artist, who in the ideal case works entirely alone and out of his own
inner resources. The artist, the ultimate in human creative freedom,
in turn is reminiscent in many ways of that great first profession of
primitive societies: the shaman, who in a sense is scientist, artist,
doctor, and priest all rolled into one. Artist and shaman are both
characterized by a combination of extraordinary contact with their

own unconscious (especially those features of it that resonate strongly with the unconscious of others of their society) and extraordinary capacity to contain, balance, control, and transform those powerful and terrifying inner forces. Both also show enormous discipline without the constraints of organizational control. The shaman takes us into the world of the sacred (from another view, the deepest reaches of the unconscious), and correspondingly into that arena farthest removed from required, constrained, routinized work—in other words, into the world of *play*. The connections are further explored when one looks at the comic entertainer with these perspectives in view, and we present an essay on a great and disturbing contemporary comic, the late Lenny Bruce, as seen by the writer Albert Goldman. Some further manifestations of the world of play are explored in Endleman's paper on "Play Elements in Delinquency."

1. EXECUTIVES

In America, the successful businessman has long been a major social cynosure, that is a model for aspiration crystallizing important values regarding ways of acting and being in society. The transformation from small-scale private-owner capitalism to large-scale corporate capitalism has shifted this cynosure role from the individualistic owner-manager of his own business to the corporate executive of a complex business hierarchy. The latter role is pervaded by a tension between the values of independence and decisive judgment possible and necessary for the owner-manager entrepreneur and those of bureaucratic accommodation necessary for the executive of the large and complex corporate organization. What are the personality dynamics of men who fill such roles? The psychologist William E. Henry explores this question in the article that follows.

Following the Henry paper, we shall attempt to extend his discussion by bringing in relevant findings from one study of the incumbents of the analogous positions in a different modern industrialized society embodying an explicitly opposing ideology, namely the managerial "middle-elite" of the contemporary Soviet Union.

The Business Executive: the Psychodynamics
of a Social Role

WILLIAM E. HENRY

The business executive is a central figure in the economic and social life of the United States. His direction of business enterprise and his participation in informal social groupings give him a significant place in community life. In both its economic and its social aspects the role of the business executive is sociologically a highly visible one. It has clearly definable limits and characteristics known to the general public. These characteristics indicate the function of the business executive in the social structure, define the behavior expected of the individual executive, and serve as a guide to the selection of the novice.

Social pressure plus the constant demands of the business organization of which he is a part direct the behavior of the executive into the mold appropriate to the defined role. "Success" is the name applied to the wholehearted adoption of the role. The individual behaves in the manner dictated by the society, and society rewards the individual with "success" if his behavior conforms to the role. It would punish him with "failure" should he deviate from it.

Participation in this role, however, is not a thing apart from the personality of the individual. It is not a game that the person is playing; it is the way of behaving and thinking that he knows best, that he finds rewarding, and in which he believes. Thus the role as socially defined has its counterpart in personality structure. To some extent, too, the personality structure is reshaped to be in harmony with the social role. The extent to which such reshaping of the adult personality is possible, however, seems limited. An initial selection process occurs which reduces the amount of time involved in teaching the appropriate behavior. Persons whose personality structure is most readily adaptable to this particular role tend to be selected, whereas those whose personality is not already partially akin are rejected.

This paper describes the personality communalities of a group of successful business executives. The research upon which it is based explored the general importance of personality structure in the selection of executive personnel. Many aptitude tests have been employed in industry to decrease the risk involved in the hiring of untried personnel and to assist in their placement. These tests have been far less effective in the selection of high-level executive personnel than in the selection of clerical and other nonadministrating persons. Many business executives have found

Reprinted from William E. Henry, "The Business Executive: The Psychodynamics of a Social Role," American Journal of Sociology, Vol. 54, 1949, pp. 286-91, by permission of The University of Chicago Press. Copyright 1949 by the University of Chicago.

that persons of unquestioned high intelligence often turn out to be in-effective when placed in positions of increased responsibility. The reasons for their failure lie in their social relationships. No really effective means has yet been found to clarify and predict this area of executive function-ing. It is to this problem that our research[4] was directed.

From the research it became clear that the "successful"[5] business executives studied had many personality characteristics in common. (It was equally clear that an absence of these characteristics was coincident with "failure" within the organization.) This personality constellation might be thought of as the minimal requirement for "success" within our present business system and as the psychodynamic motivation of persons in this occupation. Individual uniqueness in personality was clearly present; but, despite these unique aspects, all executives had in common this personality pattern.

ACHIEVEMENT DESIRES

Successful executives show high drive and achievement desire. They conceive of themselves as hard-working and achieving persons who must

---

[4] The research undertaken will be described in its entirety in a subsequent report. In summary, it involved the study of over one hundred business execu-tives in various types of business houses. The techniques employed were the Thematic Apperception Test, a short undirected interview, and a projective analysis of a number of traditional personality tests. The validity of our analyses, which were done "blind," rested upon the coincidence of identical conclusions from separately analyzed instruments, upon surveys of past job performance, and upon the anecdotal summary of present job behavior by the executive's superiors and associates. The writer wishes to express his thanks to these executives; to Dr. Burleigh Gardner, of Social Research, Inc., under whose auspices the study was made; and to Carson McGuire, Robert F. Peck, Norman Martin, and Harriet Bruce Moore, of the University of Chicago, for their assistance in the collection and analysis of data and the clarification of conclusions.

[5] Success and failure as here used refer to the combined societal and business definitions. All our "successful" executives have a history of continuous pro-motion, are thought to be still "promotable" within the organization, are now in positions of major administrative responsibility, and are earning salaries within the upper ranges of current business salaries. Men in lower supervisory positions, men who are considered "failures" in executive positions and men in clerical and laboring jobs show clear deviations from this pattern. This suggests, of course, that this pattern is specific for the successful business executive and that it serves to differentiate him from other groupings in industry.

The majority of these executives come from distributive (rather than manu-facturing) businesses of moderately loose organizational structure in which co-operation and team work are valued and in which relative independence of action is stressed within the framework of a clearly defined over-all company policy. In organizations in which far greater rigidity of structure is present or in which outstanding independence of action is required, it is possible that there will be significant variations from the personality pattern presented here. We are cur-rently extending our data in these directions.

accomplish in order to be happy. The areas in which they do their work are clearly different, but each feels this drive for accomplishment. This should be distinguished from a type of pseudo-achievement drive in which the glory of the end product alone is stressed. The person with this latter type of drive, seldom found in the successful executives, looks to the future in terms of the glory it will provide him and of the projects that he will have completed—as opposed to the achievement drive of the successful executive, which looks more toward the sheer accomplishment of the work itself. The successful business leader gets much satisfaction from doing rather than from merely contemplating the completed product. To some extent this is the difference between the dreamer and the doer. It is not that the successful executives do not have an over-all goal in mind or that they do not derive satisfaction from the contemplation of future ease or that they do not gain pleasure from prestige. Far more real to them, however, is the continual stimulation that derives from the pleasure of immediate accomplishment.

MOBILITY DRIVE

All successful executives have strong mobility drives. They feel the necessity of moving continually upward and of accumulating the rewards of increased accomplishment. For some the sense of successful mobility comes through the achievement of competence on the job. These men struggle for increased responsibility and derive a strong feeling of satisfaction from the completion of a task. Finished work and newly gained competence provide them with their sense of continued mobility.

A second group relies more upon the social prestige of increased status in their home communities or within the organizational hierarchy. Competence in work is of value and at times crucial. But the satisfactions of the second group come from the social reputation, not from the personal feeling that necessary work has been well done. Both types of mobility drive are highly motivating. The zeal and energy put into the job is equal in both instances. The distinction appears in the kinds of work which the men find interesting. For the first group the primary factor is the nature of the work itself—is it challenging, is it necessary, is it interesting? For the second group the crucial factor is its relation to their goals of status mobility—is it a step in the direction of increased prestige, is it appropriate to their present position, what would other people think of them if they did it?

THE IDEA OF AUTHORITY

The successful executive posits authority as a controlling but helpful relationship to superiors. He looks to his superiors as persons of more advanced training and experience, whom he can consult on special problems and who issue to him certain guiding directives. He does not see the authorities in his environment as destructive or prohibiting forces.

Those executives who view authority as a prohibiting and destructive force have difficulty relating themselves to superiors and resent their authority over them. They are either unable to work smoothly with superiors or indirectly and unconsciously do things to obstruct the work of their bosses or to assert their independence unnecessarily.

It is of interest that to these men the dominant crystallization of attitudes about authority is toward superiors and toward subordinates, rather than toward self. This implies that most crucial in their concept of authority is the view of being a part of a wider and more final authority system. In contrast, a few executives of the "self-made," driving-type characteristic of the past of business enterprise maintain a specific concept of authority with regard to self. They are the men who almost always forge their own frontiers, who are unable to operate within anyone else's framework, and to whom cooperation and team work are foreign concepts. To these men the ultimate authority is in themselves, and their image does not include the surrounding area of shared or delegated power.

ORGANIZATION AND ITS IMPLICATIONS

While executives who are successful vary considerably in their intelligence-test ratings, all of them have a high degree of ability to organize unstructured situations and to see the implications of their organization. This implies that they have the ability to take several seemingly isolated events or facts and to see relationships that exist between them. Further, they are interested in looking into the future and are concerned with predicting the outcome of their decisions and actions.

This ability to organize often results in a forced organization, however. Even though some situations arise with which they feel unfamiliar and are unable to cope, they still force an organization upon it. Thus they bring it into the sphere of familiarity. This tendency operates partially as a mold, as a pattern into which new or unfamiliar experiences are fit. This means, of course, that there is a strong tendency to rely upon techniques that they know will work and to resist situations which do not readily fit this mold.

DECISIVENESS

Decisiveness is a further trait of this group. This does not imply the popular idea of the executive making quick and final decisions in rapid-fire succession, although this seems to be true of some of the executives. More crucial, however, is an ability to come to a decision among several alternative courses of action—whether it be done on the spot or after detailed consideration. Very seldom does this ability fail. While less competent and well-organized individuals may become flustered and operate inefficiently in certain spots, most of these men force their way to a conclusion. Nothing is too difficult for them to tackle and at least try to solve. When poorly directed and not modified by proper judgment, this attitude may be more a handicap than a help. That is to say, this trait remains in operation and results in decision-making action regardless of the reasonableness of the decision or its reality in terms of related facts. The loss of this trait (usually found only in cases in which some more profound personality change has also occurred) is one of the most disastrous for the executive: his superiors become apprehensive about him. This suggests an interesting relationship to the total executive constellation. The role demands conviction and certainty. Whenever a junior executive loses this quality of decisiveness, he seems to pass out of the socially defined role. The weakening of other aspects of the ideal executive constellation can be readily reintegrated into the total constellation. The questioning of the individual's certainty and decisiveness, however, results in a weakening of the entire constellation and tends to be punished by superiors.

STRONG SELF-STRUCTURE

One way of differentiating between people is in the relative strength or weakness of their notions of self-identity, their self-structure. Some persons lack definiteness and are easily influenced by outside pressures. Some such as these executives, are firm and well-defined in their sense of self-identity. They know what they are and what they want and have well-developed techniques for getting what they want. The things they want and the techniques for getting them are, of course, quite different for each individual, but this strength and firmness is a common and necessary characteristic. It is, of course, true that too great a sense of self-identity leads to rigidity and inflexibility; and, while some of these executives could genuinely be accused of this, in general they maintain considerable flexibility and adaptability within the framework of their desires and within the often rather narrow possibilities of their own business organization.

ACTIVITY AND AGGRESSION

The executive is essentially an active, striving, aggressive person. His underlying motivations are active and aggressive—not necessarily is he aggressive and hostile overtly in his dealings with other people. This activity and aggressiveness are always well channeled into work or struggles for status and prestige—which implies a constant need to keep moving, to do something, to be active. This does not mean that they are always in bodily movement and moving physically from place to place (though this is often true) but rather that they are mentally and emotionally alert and active. This constant motivator unfortunately cannot be shut off. It may be part of the reason why so many executives find themselves unable to take vacations at leisure or to stop worrying about already solved problems.

APPREHENSION AND THE FEAR OF FAILURE

If one is continually active and always trying to solve problems and arrive at decisions, any inability to do so successfully may well result in feelings of frustration. This seems to be true of the executives. In spite of their firmness of character and their drive to activity, they also harbor a rather pervasive feeling that they may not really succeed and be able to do the things they want to do. It is not implied that this sense of frustration comes only from their immediate business experience. It seems far more likely to be a feeling of long standing within them and to be only accentuated and reinforced by their present business experience.

This sense of the perpetually unattained is an integral part of this constellation and is part of its dilemma. It means that there is always some place to go, but no defined point at which to stop. The executive is "self-propelled" and needs to keep moving always and to see another goal ever ahead, which also suggests that cessation of mobility and of struggling for new achievements will be accompanied by an inversion of this constant energy. The person whose mobility is blocked, either by his own limitations or by those of the social system, finds this energy diverted into other channels. Psychosomatic symptoms, the enlargement of interpersonal dissatisfactions, and the development of rationalized compulsive and/or paranoid-like defenses may reflect the redirection of this potent energy demand.

STRONG REALITY ORIENTATION

Successful executives are strongly oriented to immediate realities and their implications. They are directly interested in the practical, the immediate, and the direct. This is, of course, generally good for the immediate business situation, though the executive with an overdeveloped sense of reality may cease to be a man of vision; for a man of vision must get above reality to plan and even dream about future possibilities. In addition, a too strong sense of reality, when the realities are not in tune with ambitions, may well lead to a conviction that reality is frustrating and unpleasant. This happens to many executives who find progress and promotion too slow for their drives. The result is often a restlessness rather than an activity, a fidgetiness rather than a well-channeled aggression, and a lack of ease that may well disrupt many of their usual interpersonal relations.

THE NATURE OF THEIR INTERPERSONAL RELATIONS

In general the mobile and successful executive looks to his superiors with a feeling of personal attachment and tends to identify himself with them. His superior represents for him a symbol of his own achievement and desires, and he tends to identify himself with these traits in those who have achieved more. He is very responsive to his superiors—the nature of this responsiveness, of course, depends on his other feelings, his idea of authority, and the extent to which he feels frustrated.

On the other hand, he looks to his subordinates in a detached and impersonal way, seeing them as "doers of work" rather than as people. He treats them impersonally, with no real feeling of being akin to them or of having deep interest in them as persons. It is as though he viewed his subordinates as representatives of things he has left behind, both factually and emotionally. Still uncertain of his next forward step, he cannot afford to become personally identified or emotionally involved with the past. The only direction of his emotional energy that is real to him is upward and toward the symbols of that upward interest, his superiors.

This does not mean that he is cold and that he treats all subordinates casually. In fact, he tends to be generally sympathetic with many of them. This element of sympathy with subordinates is most apparent when the subordinate shows personality traits that are most like those of the superior. Thus the superior is able to take pride in certain successful young persons without at the same time feeling an equal interest in all subordinates.

THE ATTITUDE TOWARD HIS OWN PARENTS

In a sense the successful executive is a "man who has left home." He feels and acts as though he were on his own, as though his emotional ties and obligations to his parents were severed. It seems to be most crucial that he has not retained resentment of his parents, but has rather simply broken their emotional hold on him and been left psychologically free to make his own decisions. We have found those who have not broken this tie to be either too dependent upon their superiors in the work situation or to be resentful of their supervision (depending, of course, upon whether they are still bound to their parents or are still actively fighting against them).

In general we find the relationship to the mother to have been the most clearly broken tie. The tie to the father remains positive in the sense that he views the father as a helpful but not restraining figure. Those men who still feel a strong emotional tie to the mother have systematically had difficulty in the business situation. This residual emotional tie seems contradictory to the necessary attitude of activity, progress, and channeled aggression. The tie to the father, however, must remain positive—as the emotional counterpart of the admired and more successful male figure. Without this image, struggle for success seems difficult.

THE NATURE OF DEPENDENCY FEELINGS AND CONCENTRATION UPON SELF

A special problem in differentiating the type of generally successful executive is the nature of his dependency feelings. It was pointed out above that the dependency upon the mother-image must be eliminated. For those executives who work within the framework of a large organization in which cooperation and group-and-company loyalty are necessities, there must remain feelings of dependency upon the father-image and a need to operate within an established framework. This does not mean that the activity-aggression need cannot operate or that the individual is not decisive and self-directional. It means only that he is so within the framework of an already established set of over-all goals. For most executives this over-all framework provides a needed guidance and allows them to concentrate upon their achievement and work demands with only minimal concern for the policy-making of the entire organization. For those executives who prefer complete independence and who are unable to work within a framework established by somebody else, the element of narcissism is much higher and their feelings of loyalty are only to themselves rather than to a father-image or its impersonal counterpart in company policy. These feelings differentiate the executives who can cooperate with others and who can promote the over-all policy of a company from those who must be the whole show themselves. Clearly there are situations in which the person highly concentrated upon self and with little feeling of dependency loyalty is of great value. But he should be distinguished in advance and be placed in only situations in which these traits are useful.

The successful executive represents a crystallization of many of the attitudes and values generally accepted by middle-class American society. The value of accumulation and achievement, of self-directedness and independent thought and their rewards in prestige and status and property, are found in this group. But they also pay the price of holding these values and of profiting from them. Uncertainty, constant activity, the continual fear of losing ground, the inability to be introspectively leisurely, the ever present fear of failure, and the artificial limitations put upon their emotionalized interpersonal relations—these are some of the costs of this role.

Discussion

Henry's study is one of the most precise psychodynamic delineations of an occupation that has been made for a modern society. In relation to the question we raised at the beginning of this chapter, it is evident that selective recruitment of certain personality types is part of the process. Whatever the greatly differential opportunities for recruitment into the business elite, according to ascribed status at birth and differential earlier education (sociogenic factors amply documented in the abundant literature on social stratification in

America) even from among those who "objectively" have such an opportunity open to them, only certain men, with the kind of early parent-child experiences and resulting personality trends, are likely in fact to reach the higher echelons of business leadership. Specifically, they are men who have successfully and without guilt broken ties of dependency on the mother (or never had such ties intensely) and men who have resolved the relationship with the father by a strong identification with a positive and strong father image. They are men who have internalized profoundly intense achievement drives, accompanied by some compulsion mechanism which drives them toward ever-renewed manifestations of their adequacy. They are men who have suppressed any capacities for introspective imaginative thought and feeling and have oriented themselves strictly to the immediate external material "reality," men of the kind of "ego-strength" which gives them a constant strong self-directedness. Though these characteristics would no doubt be reinforced by these men's actual experiences in their executive work, it seems safe to suppose that the characteristics were there *before* being consolidated in their lifework, and hence were in fact a selective recruitment factor. (Henry does state, in fact, that men who lacked some of these crucial features—such as freedom from emotional ties to the mother —typically did have difficulties in the business situation which blocked their further advancement in executive position.) The picture can be restated slightly as a grim and humorless concentration on the work situation, which is of utmost centrality to the life of such a man (note inability to enjoy vacations and horror of retirement), ruling out introspection, artistic appreciation, or in fact anything in the realm of play, except perhaps a certain enjoyment of gamelike challenge in the work itself, which must, however, never be recognized as play. These features suggest some of the psychic *costs* of the successful executive's "success." Another cost is suggested by the element of "constant uncertainty" about one's continued achievements which Henry notes but does not further explore. This uncertainty certainly suggests that the successful executive's great satisfactions—the satisfaction of achievement itself, that is, getting things done, which is an aspect of "pride of craft," and of the rewards for such achievement, in power, prestige, and wealth and the things it can buy—are not unalloyed but in fact are felt as ever *contingent*. One may wonder why so much uncertainty in the fact of high achievement and success. There is no indication of any access of conscious guilt feelings about the highly unequal rewards of power, prestige, and wealth the top business executive derives. (At the manifest level at least, he appears to accept the idea that he *deserves* them, and he is supported by the whole ideology of business and the widely accepted notion of the business executive as one of the primary cynosures of the society.) But the constant uncertainty suggests a compulsiveness in the activity drive and, behind that, great anxiety. Does denial of helpless dependence on the nurturant mother cover a deeper persistence of such dependency which must be constantly disproved by the decisive marks of manly independent adulthood? Is the almost total lack of empathy or emotional identification with subordinates a compelling buttress for denial of such weakness in oneself? And what is the significance of the great *masculinity* emphasis of the business executive—as revealed, for example, in the great pride in "hard-headedness," as opposed to the "soft-headedness" attributed to such "dreamers" as artists, writers, and professors, all of whom in the public imagery long prevalent (though now declining) in America, are portrayed as less masculine types? It seems likely that the successful businessman has become so by suppressing, even repressing, major parts of his self, or at least his potential self, and that at some level it is these that he is constantly battling against, and never quite sure he can "make it." Hence the draining uncertainty and ever-renewed efforts to overcome them.

We recall that in the Great Russian "modal personality" type passive-dependent feelings are rather close to the surface, in men as well as women, and interfere with the development of the kind of self-directed striving the Soviet regime has tried to institutionalize as a part of its attempted social transformation. The successful American business executive illustrates how far such passive dependent needs can be suppressed—and also the psychic costs of doing so. We shall pursue this matter further in looking at the new Soviet middle elite.

In relation to Merton's discussion of the psychic demands of bureaucracy, the business leaders studied by Henry appear to be interestingly poised between adherence to bureaucratic ritualism and the exercise of free independent judgment. Situationally how much of the latter they can realistically exercise depends, of course, on how high up in an organizational hierarchy the executive is placed and also on the degree of spread and complexity of that hierarchy, with constraints being more numerous, more varied, and more complex in the larger organization. An extreme of "sanctification of the rules" would, of course, incapacitate a higher-level executive and interfere drastically with that decisiveness which Henry found to be so central a value in the executive's performance and in his self-image. Still, the executive imbedded in a large complex organization cannot possibly be an individualistic free-wheeler; "There must remain feelings of dependency on the father-image and a need to operate within an established framework." That is, he gets guidance from the corporate or organizational "father" (not a particular person, but the hierarchy as a whole), and *within* that framework he is free to act and achieve. (Some—probably a declining minority, given the course of corporate development—must "be the whole show themselves." In other words, they are old-fashioned entrepreneurial types, necessarily disappearing today. These men are at odds with bureaucratic details and must be at or near the top of the structure to be able to function well.) The "constant uncertainty" that Henry refers to may, therefore, be seen as in part *situationally* produced (though this does not preclude its also having "deeper" intrapsychic sources). That is, it can be seen as deriving from the strain between conforming to bureaucratic subordination and the simultaneous need to exercise individualistic decisiveness and activity appropriate to immediate situational demands.

Comparisons with the Soviet elite

We have available only very limited studies of the psychology of the Soviet elite. The most revealing study is provided by Raymond Bauer's researches in connection with the same project that produced the Inkeles, *et al.*, work on modal personality presented earlier in this volume. Bauer, in a paper entitled, "The Psychology of the Soviet Middle Elite: Two Case Studies" [6] presents two contrasting types of middle-level elite and briefly characterizes a third type. One type is the idealistic Communist Party member, who shows these characteristics: a well worked-out and highly integrated system of humane values; a strong emotional tie to the mother; a seeking out of an ideal father image in the image of the ideal party member; intense self-discipline and capacity and liking for hard work, even to the extent of compulsiveness toward work; a high evaluation of "ob-

[6] In C. Kluckhohn, H. Murray and D. Schneider (eds.), *Personality in Nature, Society and Culture*, rev. ed., (New York: Alfred Knopf, 1952), pp. 633-50.

jectivity" and intellectual analysis of social-political situations. The self-discipline of the individual entails control on hedonistic pursuits and acceptance of the responsibilities attendant on party membership and on the person's specific organizational administrative position. The orientation to discipline, hard work, and responsibility mark a definite departure from the typical Great Russian psychology of the period. The idealistic value system, accompanied by a strong concern for intellectual analysis, makes this type of elite member a constant potential threat to the regime (the man Bauer discusses defected) through disaffection by recognition of the disparities between their value system and the actual conditions of Soviet life. Such types also, being highly capable and highly motivated, tend to rise disproportionately fast in the system.

The second type can be described as an authoritarian conformist. This type of individual has no central inner core of values; he can be loyal to any system that gives him recognition and support, regardless of its values or ideological content. This type thrives on rigidly hierarchical relationships and is close in these respects to the classic "authoritarian personality" dissected by Adorno and his colleagues.[7] Bauer describes this Soviet type as follows:

> His underlying impulses are repressed and subject to very rigid and presumably brittle external controls. He lacks a unified sense of values and needs to find a definition of himself in his relationship to the external world. He is a man of little flexibility and adaptability, but one who had found a niche in Soviet society in which he could operate very effectively. . . .
>
> [He] . . . approves of the regime's methods and the authoritarian nature of the Soviet order [as of the Stalin era], is indifferent to its social goals, and might even be characterized as antagonistic to its humanitarian pronouncements. . . .
>
> His hyperactivity and militant masculinity seem quite clearly . . . to be reaction formations against an underlying passivity and feminine identification. . . . [Similarly] apparently in reaction against underlying . . . dependency, he vigorously asserts his independence . . . and [as a result is] unable to establish successful warm relationships with other persons.[8]

Correspondingly, this type sees society as having the task of keeping its members under firm disciplined control, just as he keeps his own

[7] T. W. Adorno, et al., The Authoritarian Personality (New York: Harper & Row, Publishers, 1950).

[8] Raymond A. Bauer, in Kluckhohn, Murray, and Schneider, op. cit., pp. 634-36.

impulses and inner life in general. Rigidly hierarchical relationships —ideally met in the military—are his ideal social milieu. The military provides the nearest thing to a value system for such a man: an officer's code that has the quality of externality, a code that is not a part of, and does not define, an inner "self" but rather provides a set of imperatives for conduct to which one must rigidly conform regardless of consequences.

A third type, probably encouraged in greater numbers by more recent developments in the Soviet system, is the opportunistic careerist. Like the conformist, he is not deeply committed to the humane ideological values of the system. He dresses himself in the trappings of allegiance to the regime in order to gain the material advantages and prestige that come from advancing in the system. This type is evidently scarcely distinguishable from careerists in business or professional bureaucracies in America or other Western countries: he is disciplined, capable of hard work, pays a great deal of attention to the "right" cues from the "right" persons higher up, has his eye on the main chance. In the Soviet Union, "Such a person is primarily loyal to his own interests, but in practice this is usually identical with primary loyalty to the system, as long as the system remains stable, since it is only through the system that his goals are served." [9] (Unfortunately, Bauer does not provide us with any case histories of careerists by which we might make valuable comparisons with the psychodynamic portrait of the American business executive given by Henry. It would be particularly instructive to know whether the careerist, unlike the idealistic party member described but like the authoritarian conformist and like the American business executive, is a man who has broken ties of dependency and close emotional relationship with the mother, while maintaining a strong identification with the father. The careerist of Bauer's brief description does however seem sufficiently similar to Riesman's "other-directed character" [10] to lead us to wonder whether this type maintains any strong identifications with either mother or father, in contrast to a generalized orientation to all of the "others"—i.e., collectively, or as a system.)

What all of these have in common—the American business executive and each of the three types of Soviet elite—are a high degree

[9] Bauer, *op. cit.*, p. 647.

[10] See David Riesman, Nathan Glazer, and Reuel Denney, *The Lonely Crowd* (New Haven: Yale University Press, 1950).

of self-discipline and self-directedness, control over impulses, and strong achievement drive—in effect, variations, within different personality syndromes, of Weber's "Protestant ethic."

2. SCIENTISTS

The modern transformation of business entrepreneurs into organizational executives and of governmental leaders into administrative bureaucrats is paralleled by the modern transformation of the role of the scientist from lone-wolf ("entrepreneurial") discoverer to the at least somewhat bureaucratized member of a research "team" or university faculty or both. The "separation of the [scientific] worker from [private property in] the tools of his work [research]" has already been noted. The bureaucratization is, of course, in many ways different in quality from and never as complete as that of the organizational man in public or private business, government, or services. The life center of the scientist's work lies in pursuit of transcendental goals beyond the immediate concerns of whatever organization he is attached to—most broadly and idealistically stated as "the pursuit of truth." Normatively this goal supersedes any immediate organizational purpose or individual ambition of the scientist. Normatively, here dedication of one's life to a "calling" is at its highest and "purest" pitch. What kind of men and women are these? How are they different from business executives and government bureaucrats? What distinct types of personality, the product of what distinctive socialization experiences, are recruited into their ranks? Some partial answers are provided by the unique psychological research of Anne Roe, the major findings of which are abstracted in the following selection.

A caution should be noted in advance that the subjects of Roe's study, being men of the highest eminence in their respective scientific fields, are probably the *least* bureaucratized scientists, and those freest to pursue their own lines of "pure" research; even the larger sample of scientists to whom Roe gave the Rorschach for comparison with the eminent, are all working in university settings. We have no way of knowing how these may differ from the large numbers of scientists, particularly chemists and physicists, working not in the universities but in industry in various capacities, men for whom the scientific ethos is in variable ways countered by the organizational demands of the industries which employ them.[11]

Personalities of Eminent Scientists

ANNE ROE

This study investigated relationships between life history, intellectual functions, personality characteristics, and the selection of and eminence in a particular science as a profession. Its subjects are 64 men who were selected for their eminence in research, as judged by their peers: 22 physicists, 20 biologists, 14 psychologists, and 8 anthropologists. The data comprise life histories, discussion of their work, and the results of three tests: a Verbal-Spatial-Mathematical Test, the Thematic Apperception Test, and the Rorschach. In addition, group Rorschachs were given to 288 other university professors in these fields, for comparison with the eminent: 65 physicists, 94 biologists, 104 psychologists, and 25 anthropologists.

The life history interviews were little structured. The subject was asked at the outset for information on general family background, early family and school life, and everything that related to his choice of vocation. Later he was asked specifically for information on health, religion, present leisure interests, and use of imagery. Projective material suggested some leads for later interviews, but deep probing was not attempted. The combination of projective material and verbatim life histories offered excellent cross checks.

[11] See Simon Marcson, *The Scientist in American Industry* (New York: Harper & Row, Publishers, 1960), William Kornhauser, *Scientists in Industry: Conflict and Accommodation* (Berkeley: University of California Press, 1962), and Anselm Strauss and Lee Rainwater, *The Professional Scientist: A Study of American Chemists* (Chicago: Aldine Publishing Co., 1962); and a comparative review of these works, Norman Kaplan, "Professional Scientists in Industry: An Essay Review," *Social Problems*, Vol. 13, No. 1, Summer 1965, pp. 88-97.

Adapted and abstracted from Anne Roe, "A Psychological Study of Eminent Psychologists and Anthropologists, and a Comparison with Biological and Physical Scientists," Psychological Monographs, Vol. 67, No. 2, 1953, pp. 1-55; incorporating portions of Anne Roe, "A Psychological Study of Eminent Biologists," Psychological Monographs, Vol. 65, No. 14, 1951, pp. 1-68; and Anne Roe, "A Psychological Study of Physical Scientists," Genetic Psychology Monographs, Vol. 43, Second Half, 1951, pp. 121-235. Adaptation by Robert Endleman.

Printed here with the permission of the author, of the American Psychological Association (for Psychological Monographs) and of Genetic Psychology Monographs.

SOCIAL CHARACTERISTICS

Age.   Average age is: physicists, 44.7 years; biologists, 51.2; psychologists, 46.7, anthropologists, 49.4.

Socio-economic background.   The 64 scientists studied are by no means randomly selected from the population at large: 54 percent had fathers who were professionals. (By contrast, census reports for 1910 show only 3 percent of the gainfully employed men in the country were professionals.)[12] Of another 31 percent, the fathers were in business, many of them owning their own. Thus fully 85 percent of these scientists came from families of professional or business background. One-eighth came from farm homes; only two fathers (3 percent) were skilled laborers; and none were unskilled. The incidence of professional fathers varies by type of scientists: 73 percent for physicists (84 percent for theorists, 50 percent for experimentalists); 45 percent for biologists; 50 percent for psychologists; and 38 percent for anthropologists. Though none of the 64 scientists came from families of great wealth, seven of the eight anthropologists came from well-to-do homes, as contrasted with much smaller percentages for the other specialties. Generally, then, the scientists tend to come from at least middle to upper middle class backgrounds.

Marital status.   All of these men are married, and most have children. Average age at marriage for all the groups is rather late (around 27 years), doubtless connected with long educational histories. Permanence of marriage varies notably, however, by type of scientists: only one of the physicists has been divorced (5 percent); three biologists (15 percent); but five psychologists (36 percent) and four anthropologists (50 percent) have been divorced, and of these, several more than once.

Religion.   Not one of the 64 eminent scientists is Catholic by family background or present belief and practice. Five come from Jewish homes (two social scientists, three natural scientists), the rest Protestant, including two Mormons and two Quakers. Generally in all groups the level of religious participation and concern in both the parental family and in the scientist himself today is very low; a few are militantly agnostic, but most are just not interested. There are no differences among the types of scientist, in this regard.

Birth order.   In all of these groups, the incidence of first-born is significantly greater than chance (*p.* 01). (This accords with Cattell and Brimhall's findings for a group of 855 scientists.[13]) In addition, of the 25 scientists who were not first-born, 5 are oldest sons, two of the second-

[12] Compare Cattell and Brimhall's finding in 1921 that 51 percent of the 66 leading scientists they studied had professional fathers. J. M. Cattell and D. R. Brimhall, *American Men of Science*, 3rd ed. (Garrison, N.Y.: Science Press, 1921).

[13] Cattell and Brimhall, *op. cit.*

born were effectively the oldest due to early-infancy death of the older sib. I have no explanation for this finding.

Early social attitudes. Among the biologists and physicists I encountered no direct expression of feelings of personal or parental family superiority, and there were few by inference. Awareness of intellectual superiority seems not to have been translated into social terms. By contrast, in at least half of the psychologists, and in most of the anthropologists, a feeling of social superiority has definitely played a role in their development. In some instances this feeling is a product of the family's, or particularly the mother's, strivings (or a paternal grandmother's). Among the psychologists, though the class backgrounds ranged from lower to upper middle, more than half had some definite sense of personal or family superiority, and family concern with social status in one way or another. Among the anthropologists, the average economic level of the parental family is higher than that of the other groups (7 of the 8 were well-to-do), and concern with the social status of the family, or a firm conviction of the social superiority of the family is evident in all but one instance, not necessarily manifest in socially snobbish attitudes. Six of the eight went to private schools, likely to encourage superiority feelings.

Childhood health. Special problems relating to health or to constitutional factors seem to have played a part for a large proportion of the anthropologists and of the theoretical physicists. Difficulties such as being undersized, underweight, suffering from many allergies, serious illnesses, being oversized, being always the tallest in his age group, being considered generally sickly, appeared in the life stories of five of the anthropologists; and severe childhood illness was frequent among the theoretical physicists. The contribution of such factors to personal isolation was probably significant in the subsequent career selection in most of these cases.

Familial loss. Loss of one or both parents by death, or divorce of the parents, appears in a large but variable number of instances: Physicists: five (23 percent) lost a parent by death (at ages 5, 6, 9, 15, and 17, respectively) and the parents of one were divorced. Biologists: five (25 percent) lost father or mother before the age of 10; the parents of two others were divorced (subjects age 9, and 16); the parent of one other was incapacitated by serious illness during the boy's early childhood. Psychologists: four (29 percent) lost their fathers by death (at ages 8, 12, 14, and 17) and one also his mother at 17. Anthropologists: the only case is one where the mother died at his birth.

In the case of the biologists and physicists where the losses occurred very early, it seemed possibly to be a factor in the acceptance of isolation by the subjects. For the psychologists and at least one of the physicists, whose losses were later, the effect seems to have been more one of increasing the problems of adolescent reaction to authority, an effect evidently greater for the psychologists who have been more concerned with personal relations from the start.

Early interests. The spontaneous childhood interests of the different types of scientist differ significantly. The physicists nearly all showed early interest in mathematics, chemistry, physics, or gadgeteering, rarely in literature or the humanities. The biologists' early interests were in natural history, in literature, and in chemistry or physics, although the latter usually because these were the only sciences available to them in high school. The interest patterns of the future psychologists and anthropologists were quite different: literature and the classics, and less frequently social welfare interests; and some natural history, particularly among the anthropologists. In the histories of the social scientists and of the biologists, the importance of the discovery of the possibility of doing research is highlighted, and this was often the factor that fixed their choice of vocation. This aspect did not appear among the physicists, probably because the difference between gadgeteering and experimental work is really a matter of degree and emphasis; the possibility of doing things yourself is obvious, whereas in the other fields it is not.

Intrafamily relations. The data here are more complete for the social scientists than for the others, due partly to professional awareness, partly to their greater freedom in discussing such matters. (The social scientists provide a notably greater amount of life history material *generally.*) Additional evidence from the TAT, however, bear out the differences found: the physicists and biologists early developed ways of life which involved very much less personal interaction, and neither show anything like the extent of rebelliousness and family difficulty that the psychologists and anthropologists show. For the latter, patterns involving overprotection and firm, if not overt, control, are very common; more frequent among the psychologists, but in the anthropologists there is more overprotection and more open hostility. Over half of the social scientists reacted with more rebelliousness than common, and some of these are still angry, rejecting, or disrespectful toward one or both parents.

In the physicists, by contrast, there is neither very great closeness nor serious disagreement with either parent during childhood, nor evidence of any present problems here. A general attitude of respect for the father, even among those who went through a transitory rebellious period, is characteristic. The biologists, also, show lack of warmth in the childhood relationship to the parents.

Peer and heterosexual relationships. Both the physicists and the biologists tend to show a picture of a boy who is shy, overintellectualized (sometimes clearly as a defense), not a member of any neighborhood gang, although often with one or two close male friends like him; not dating any girls until late undergraduate or graduate school years, and then only shyly; and in many instances, never dating any other girl but the one he married; and maintaining only a very limited social life to the present day. The early sexual development of the social scientists was quite different: dating was earlier and more varied, and shyness rarely more than a transient adolescent problem. In the theoretical physicists, early isolation was associated with physical illness or disability of some kind, in several instances; in the biologists, it may have been associated with early loss of a parent, 40 percent of them having experienced such before the age of 10. Intellectualization of interests seems to be clearly related to the generally asocial pattern.

TAT findings. Analysis of the content of the TAT protocols shows striking differences among the scientist groups. For the biologists and physicists, the TAT stories confirm the life history picture of relative lack of concern with personal relationships; they show disinterest, or lack of ease in such relations, often dealing with them in distance-getting ways. The *biologists* show independence of their parents, along with considerable interest in playing the parental role toward their own children, with whom they appear to have the warmest and most satisfying of any of their interpersonal relationships. Most have strong convictions about personal responsibility, particularly paternal duties, seeing the paternal role as sympathetic and strongly supporting. Otherwise they generally tend to avoid emotional situations, dealing with them, if they must, by recourse to banality or to overdramatization. Their protocols reveal men who have come to satisfactory terms with life.

The *physicists* show similar independence of parents, and a striking lack of guilt over this; a similar independence of personal relations generally, though with evident effort in some, e.g., sexual, situations, to maintain distance. They are freer than the biologists in expression of aggression. While like the biologists tending to stick to the concrete-factual level in their stories, they were less insistently so, and showed more interest in the thoughts and feelings of their protagonists. Their stories are longer, have more narration and less description, and more frequently give a full time sequence (past, present, future). They give more stories involving unresolved tension or defeat, and at the same time, the tone of their stories is more frequently cheerful or serene, while that of the biologists is more frequently unhappy, tense, or anxious, or one that is melodramatic or sardonic, than is true for the physicists. The physicists' greater tolerance of irresolution, and their more cheerful tone, suggests they have found it easier to accept the fact of difficulties in life, and are less inclined to gloss them over or put distance between themselves and the problem. Still they are men in whom anxiety is easily mobilized.

The *social scientists*, by contrast, are much more interested in interpersonal relations generally. Many of them are uneasy about such relationships, but out of concern rather than dislike of them. Toward the parental figures in their stories, they show very dependent attitudes, and a great deal of rebelliousness, accompanied frequently by guilt feelings. Attitudes of helplessness are much more common here than among the natural scientists. They are also freer than both the other groups in expression of aggression.

A striking feature of all the TAT protocols is that they rarely give indication that the subject is a man of considerable attainments. No large amount of drive is evident in the stories, nor of any other clue to what made these scientists' conspicuous achievements possible.

Rorschach findings. In each of the groups of scientists studied, the Rorschachs show strong individual differences in personality structure. However, there are some general trends in each of the types, which appear with a fair amount of consistency, and which would not characterize a group of adults picked at random.

The *biologists* show a slightly greater than average use of whole responses (using the whole blot as a unit) and a notable use of unusual details; they are somewhat restricted in the use of human movement responses, but not in use of movement responses generally. The percentage of their responses using only the form of the blot, ignoring color and shading, etc., is not especially high, but responses in which form was not the primary determinant are extremely rare. Shading shock (reaction time or quality disturbances in response to tonal qualities of the blot, e.g., texture, vista) is prevalent, from mild to severe in degree, but recovery from such shock is generally good.

By the usual Rorschach interpretations, these trends characterize the eminent biologists as men who have a greater than average tendency to see things as a whole and to generalize, but not to a degree that obliterates attention to details; more important, their attention to *rare* details indicates sensitivity to aspects of a situation not usually noticed. Their dominance of form indicates good control of discrimination and judgment and a tendency to be more objective than most. Other aspects of their protocols show them as men who are not personally aggressive, but stubborn and persistent, not easily pushed around; having little need to dominate others, but clearly not subservient either; not very "outgoing" in a social sense, and not rating very high in "masculinity" (confirming the delayed sexual development shown in the life histories). The anxiety evidenced in shading shock is rather well structured and offset by their relying heavily and effectively on intellectual control of behavior.

The *physicists* are like the biologists in underproduction of human movement responses, only slightly greater than average use of whole responses, notable use of rare detail, and in prevalence of shading shock along with fairly good recovery from it. They differ from the biologists in giving many more responses, and (relatedly) using more determinants (form, color, shading, white space) and in several important aspects of shading, color, and movement. Responses using shading as a three-dimensional effect (vista) are unusually high, presumably indicating anxiety which is very prevalent and unstructured. Color responses differ markedly from the biologists'. The total number of color responses is high, and larger than the number of movement responses. Also, in over half of the physicists, CF responses (color dominates over form as a determinant) outnumber FC (form dominates color). The total pattern indicates greater responsiveness to environmental than to internal stimulation (color over movement) and a tendency toward impulsiveness, to emotional responsiveness where logical considerations are not effective, and to poor tolerance of delay in reaching satisfactions (color over form). The physicists give a higher than usual number of *inanimate* movement responses, partly reflecting vocational concerns, but also suggesting lack of ease with instinctual drives. (This is more true of the theorists than the experimentalists and ties in with greater awareness of conflict.) The *theoretical* physicists (but not the experimentalists) also tend to use an excessive number of anatomy and sex responses; and to show concept domination (the same response given to at least three cards) suggesting that the subject is relatively little constrained by external reality. The general picture for the physicists is one of great and often not too well-controlled intellectual and emotional energy, a great deal of relatively unstructured anxiety, and generally poor social adjustment, sometimes due to considerable impulsiveness and egocentricity, sometimes to general apathy toward social relationships. They also express more aggression than the biologists.

The *social scientists* show no consistent differences between the psychologists and the anthropologists; hence the two are taken together as one group for comparison with the biologists and the physicists. They are like all of the latter in a strong use of unusual details and in the prevalence of shading shock. Thus all of the types of eminent scientist show unusual capacity to see things in ways that are out of the ordinary and share a considerable load of anxiety, probably reflecting underlying insecurities which are presumably connected with their drive toward unusual achievement and the strength and persistence of their immersion in their work. Beyond this, the social scientists' picture departs significantly. They are notably more productive and varied in their responses generally. They produce an absolutely large, but relatively small, number of whole responses, i.e., they can generalize adequately, if sometimes sweepingly. They are quite casual and unsystematic, often to the point of disorganization, in their approach to the cards. (Biologists are least like this, but the theoretical physicists are somewhat similar.) In content, the social scientists give an unusual number of anatomy and sex responses (in half of them, to an excessive extent)—here again most unlike the biologists, but more like the theoretical physicists. They give many original responses, often uncritical ones. Their range of responses is curious: both very broad in number of categories and stereotyped and restricted in some way, e.g., by individual perseveration of themes, or excessive use of animal and human responses. The wide range, associated with general productivity, suggests general receptivity; the restrictiveness imposed obviates the danger of undesirable diffusion. In contrast with the other scientists, the social scientists show frequent human responses, and human movement responses, indicating consistent interest in persons and responsiveness to inner as opposed to environmental stimuli. Probably both vocational interests and deeper personality trends are reflected here.

In contrast with the biologists, the social scientists' form quality is not high (true of half of the group) suggesting problems in contact with reality. The point may be the nature of the "reality," psychologists being more concerned with inner than outer reality, and often drawn to disregard apparent reality to search further. (Is this rationalization?) This may be less true for anthropologists.

An interesting pattern appears in some of the anthropologists, and less frequently in the psychologists: the subject starts a response with free action and then tones the action down so that it becomes very restricted. This suggests a need to repress too direct an interest in persons. Anthropology would be a good vocation for those who feel this way, since the interest in persons can be followed in a somewhat depersonalized way; this is also partly true of experimental psychology. The strong use of human movement in these subjects—definitely in contrast to its underutilization by the biologists and physicists—would indicate consistent interest in persons, but it is an interest that is sometimes restricted in some way, and sometimes carried to extremes.

The social scientists' protocols also reveal a very great sensitivity, and it usually implies a great awareness of other persons, which may sometimes result in an easy irritability. Most show fairly free aggression, clearer and stronger in the anthropologists, more obviously oral in the psychologists. The aggression shown is greater than that shown by the physicists, and very much greater than that shown by the biologists.

Some of the social scientists show a strong consciousness of hidden things, not always accompanied by anxiety. Most of them are fairly warm persons. Conflict over dominance and authority is common. Some, particularly among the psychologists, show a need to hold and feel nurturant attitudes.

Rorschach comparison of eminent and other scientists. Comparing the Rorschach protocols obtained by the group administration method from 288 other scientists, members of university faculties, with the protocols of the eminent in each field:

Social scientists. The eminent group, in addition to its greater productivity, used fewer whole and more unusual detail responses, including more anatomy and sex responses and more concept-dominated responses, and tended to proportionately more color than movement responses. These can be subsumed under the general attitude of greater productivity and reactivity, more originality, and less control.

Biologists. The eminent have protocols which show more balanced rational control, if somewhat greater restriction, than do their more ordinary colleagues—a difference almost exactly the reverse of that found for the social scientists. Compared to the eminent ones, the other biologists show either less rational control (more impulsiveness) or an excess of control, i.e., a tendency toward rigid overintellectualization and a pedantic approach to life. They also show indications of greater free anxiety, and of poorer general adjustment.

Physicists. These show no important differences whatever between the eminent and the larger group.

All scientists. Comparing the 64 eminent scientists taken as one group, with the 288 other scientists taken as a group, the only important differences are these: the eminent make greater use of unusual blot areas, of anatomy and sex responses, and of perseverating responses.

DISCUSSION

Though the 64 eminent scientists studied came very disproportionately from families with professional fathers, compared to the general population, class background per se seems less important than the fact that in practically all of these homes, whatever the occupation of the father, learning was valued for its own sake. Its concomitants in income or social position were not scorned, but rarely were these the most important factor. The value placed on learning certainly was a major facilitation for intellectualization of interests. In my opinion, this, rather than the possibly associated intellectual levels, is the important aspect here. "Overintellectualization" may be a middle class characteristic, and it may interfere with libidinal development in other spheres, as some psychoanalytic writers have pointed out. But can one develop the sort of intense personal involvement characteristic of these scientists, without some degree of this, if channeling of energy in one direction means lessening of it in others? Though intellectualization may be a technique for escaping interpersonal emotional problems, it need not be. I believe concentrated intellectual activity does not *require* a sterile emotional life, but our educational techniques have not fostered this.

The data show the basic importance of the need for independence which is so well met by a career in research. Note that there are no Catholics in the group, that all but three of the subjects have dismissed organized religion as a guide to life (usually by late adolescence), thus asserting independence. As boys, most of these men pursued rather independent paths, with one or a few close friends, following their own interests with great intensity, the interests more often intellectual than not. (True, high intelligence itself would have some of these effects.[14])

There is no one pattern by which they approached science as a career. The modal age of the decision was during the last two undergraduate years, but the range is from early childhood to second year of graduate work. The introduction may have been through natural history interests, through gadgeteering, through interest in high school laboratory science courses, or, for the social scientists, through dissatisfaction with literature as a means of studying the behavior of people, or through a service motivation. When the decisive point can be determined, it was usually the discovery of the possibility of doing research, of finding out things for oneself. For some this was understood very early—as with those experimental physicists who spent much of their childhood playing with erector sets, radios, and all the other equipment that permit manipulation and construction. For others, it came as a revelation of unique moment. Once it was understood that personal research was possible, once some research had actually been accomplished, there was never any question. This was it. The educational implications are obvious enough. There has been no question since. From then on, absorption in the vocation was so complete as seriously to limit all other activities. In the case of the social scientists, at least for those for whom people themselves provide the data, this did not limit social participation; for the others it intensified an already present disinterest. Although a few of them have cut down somewhat on their hours of work as they have grown older, it is still the common pattern for them to work nights, Sundays, holidays, as they always have.

Most of them are happiest when they are working—some only when they are working. In all of these instances, other aspects—economic return, social and professional status—are of secondary importance.

Being curious plays a major role—a trait which many aspects of our educational practice tend to discourage. It is of crucial importance that these men set their own problems and investigate what interests them. No one tells them what to think about, or when, or how. Here they have almost perfect freedom. Their limitations are only those of equipment and time, and the limitations of their own understanding. Certainly this is one vocation in which man can most nearly approach what he can be, and one that satisfies both autonomous and homonomous drives.[15]

[14] However, that intelligence itself is not a decisive factor in these careers is suggested by the pattern of scores on the Verbal-Spatial-Mathematical tests: a striking feature is the very wide range of scores on each of the tests, within each of the scientists' categories, and the unexpectedly low scores that marked the lower limits of these ranges.

[15] *Autonomous* drives are those toward mastery of the environment, imposing oneself upon the world and events; *homonomous* drives are those toward putting

The position these men have reached has not been reached easily, and one must ask why this particular group has made so great an effort. It must be noted that this effort has usually been directed quite specifically toward the immediate problem, rather than to a long-term goal of eminence. There is some evidence that a basic insecurity of perhaps more than the usual proportions is present in many, if not most, of this group, but the causes for this insecurity appear varied. (This would tend to support the hypothesis that the need for independence in this group is generally compensatory.) That intellectual channels were sought to alleviate it must be in large part because of the family background, but there is no question that the research aspect is of more importance than the general intellectualization.

Why the choice of the particular field of science? One often overlooked factor is necessary contact with the field. Coping with early affectional loss has also been mentioned. Some, especially experimental physicists, seem early to have formed direct relationships with objects rather than people, not compensatorily. In others, a generalized anxiety, of unknown cause, possibly only an exacerbation of normal anxiety, is alleviated by a concentration on a particular field.

The social scientists stand apart, being concerned at an earlier age about personal relations (or being willing to tolerate this concern as such, without translation). This may reflect unconscious uncertainty over the consciously felt superiority reported by half the psychologists and most of the anthropologists. It also relates to their difficulties in freeing themselves from their parents. The other scientists seem to have been able, fairly early, to work out an adaptation not nearly so dependent on personal relationships, but rather strikingly independent of them.

Certainly psychology to some extent, particularly social psychology, and anthropology to a large extent, particularly cultural anthropology, offer an ideal vocation to the person whose conviction of personal superiority is not accompanied by asocial characteristics; they permit a somewhat Jovian survey of their own society as well as others and maintain the social scientist in a state of superiority just because he is able to make the survey. (This accounts nicely for the observation that some rather paranoid indications in the test material are not accompanied by forms of paranoid behavior, except perhaps as regards their own colleagues.) The experimental psychologists are generally less concerned with people as people, although this is by no means true of all of them. The further observations that a conflict over dominance and authority is common in the group, and that in a number of their homes the mother was domi-

or fitting oneself into superindividual structures like the family, world order, the realm of ideas, etc. The distinction comes from Andras Angyal, *Foundations for a Science of Personality* (New York: The Commonwealth Fund, 1941).

nant, indicate the possibility of difficulties in achieving masculine identification. The greater divorce frequency of the social scientists is certainly relevant here.

It would seem very probable that the physicists, particularly the experimentalists, were able to identify more easily with their fathers than the other groups and hence to follow comfortably in a science which has rather more of a "masculine" tinge in our culture than the others do.

The kind of person who has gone into social sciences—one acutely and early concerned with human relationships—may have had a biasing effect on their theories of the desirable or mature personality, which place heavy emphasis on richness of personal relations as a basis for "adjustment." The data of this study show conclusively, however, that a more than adequate "adjustment" in the sense of combining a socially extremely useful life with one that is personally deeply satisfying is not only possible, but probably quite common, with little of the sort of personal relations many psychologists consider essential. Many of the biological and physical scientists are very little concerned with personal relations, and this is not only entirely satisfactory to them, but it cannot be shown always to be a compensatory mechanism. It can also be satisfactory to others who are closely associated with them. Here is another possible basis for the lower divorce frequency of these scientists, compared to the social scientists: less attention and emotion are invested, lesser and less specific demands are made of marriage, and hence failure less common.

Another finding is the differences in imagery of the different types of scientist: biologists and experimental physicists tend strongly to *visual* imagery in their thinking; theoretical physicists and social scientists, to dependence on verbalization or similar symbolization in theirs. Lacking data precisely on this, we speculate that these modes were developed early (they are associated with father's occupation) and played a part in choice of science. In accord with these differences are the domination of the formal qualities of the blots in the biologists' Rorschachs (in contrast to the others) and the general more fluid verbalization of the social scientists. Doubtless intellectual factors enter. Theoretical physicists surpass all other types of scientist in both verbal and spatial tests; experimental physicists are high on spatial, low on verbal; psychologists at about the mean on verbal, spatial, and mathematical; anthropologists are high on verbal, lowest on both the others. These differences probably affect selection of vocation, especially for the anthropologists and the experimental physicists.

Discussion

There are a number of significant elements in the foregoing findings. First is the centrality of the independence drive in all of these scientists, which links with their being in their work lives among the occupationally freest men of our time. Connected with this is the fact that for most of these men the boundary line between work and play is practically nonexistent:

> As one of them [the eminent biologists studied by Anne Roe] put it: "My real recreation is doing what I want to do, my work." Another said, "There is nothing I'd rather do [i.e., than work]. In fact my boy says that I am paid for playing. He's right. In other words if I had an income, I'd do just what I'm doing now. I'm one of the people that has found what he wanted to do. At night when you can't sleep you think about your problems. You work at it on holidays and Sundays. It's fun. Research is fun. By and large it's a very pleasant existence.[16]

These men are marked by a total involvement in their intellectual and research pursuits which reduces any other kind of play to a very insignificant role in their lives. Note that "most of them are happiest when they are working—some only when they are working." While the latter instances certainly suggest a compulsive or compensatory component in the psychology of their work, the former at least, when seen in the light of the great emphasis on (and reality of) *freedom* in the choice and direction of their pursuits, suggest a significant coalescence of work and play at the highest creative levels, impressively at variance with the general trends of rationalized and bureaucratized civilization. For them work is not an irksome burden routinized by extraneous dictates and to be escaped after a minimal number of working hours into a round of pleasure-seeking "leisure." Nor is it basically an instrumentality for the compulsive pursuit of material gains to be translated into symbols of an ever-precarious status struggle, nor for the pursuit of prestige, "success," or eminence for their own sake. Probably because the men selected for Roe's study are the most eminent in their fields, there is little indication in their discussions of their work and lives of the process of bureaucratization of scientific work we referred to in our preamble to Roe's report: for them this is probably no problem, or at least

[16] Anne Roe, "A Psychological Study of Eminent Biologists," *Psychological Monographs*, Vol. 65, No. 14, 1951, p. 31.

much less than for the larger ranks of the less successful in their respective fields.

Second, the major differences between the social scientists and the natural scientists are particularly striking and significant in relation to the problems of family relationships in the early life of business and other executives discussed in the earlier part of this chapter. Compared with the other types, the social scientists show very early in their lives a much more intense involvement with personal relations, more conflict and tension with parental authorities, more hostility and guilt in response to such conflict, a greater likelihood of maternal domination in the family, and hence greater difficulties with masculine identification. On the latter point, particularly, they are strikingly in contrast with both the physical scientists and with the various types of executives in both the United States and the Soviet Union as studied by Henry and Bauer (with the notable exception of the idealistic party loyalist of Bauer's study). It is an interesting question to raise, whether if Roe's study had included *sociologists* as well as psychologists and anthropologists, this last finding would have been even more intensively documented.

The role of early isolation, often produced or intensified by loss of one of the parents, is of particular interest in the developmental history of the physical and biological scientists. So too, relatedly, the early development of strong and evidently stabilizing cathexis to objects rather than persons, in the life pattern of the physical scientists, coalescing into a pattern of "normality" and creativity for them that is quite distinct from the models posed by much of current psychological science.

Another point is that Roe is unable to tell us from her exhaustive and intricate studies whether the personality trends she finds to characterize a particular kind of scientist and to differentiate them from other types, are preconditions or determinants for their entrance into and success in that vocation, on the one hand, or the *effects* of successful work in that vocation, on the other—or perhaps some combination of both of these. Clearly, it is impossible to answer this question definitively by a study only of the men who have arrived and at a time when they are at the height of their achievement. Roe's discussion suggests that it is either the first or the third of these possibilities. That is, that personality trends have selected these men, under such favorable circumstances as parental homes valuing learning for itself, for these scientific careers, but also that the satisfaction of and achievement in this work has intensified or consolidated some of these trends, such as the great reliance on intellectualization in all of them and the preference for a relatively nonsocial pattern of living, for the natural scientists at least.

3. THE CREATIVE ARTIST

How does the artist compare with the scientist? What are the psychological trends that select for a vocation in creative art and attend the productive work of the novelist, poet, dramatist, painter, sculptor, or composer?

Of the sparse empirical studies into the psychological and social origins of artists, we may refer briefly to another, earlier, study by Anne Roe. In the early 1940s, Roe studied twenty male American painters of the top rank, representative of most of the major trends in painting of that day. Their average age was fifty-one at the time of the study, thus closely comparable to the scientists reported on in the preceding paper. While like the scientists they were found to be individually distinctive in personality patterns, certain general trends obtained. Their Rorschachs showed unusually great use of whole responses, marked prevalence of color and shading shock, and overproduction of sexual and anatomical content. The shading shock, presumably indicative of anxiety, is reminiscent of all of the scientist groups; and the sexual and anatomical content recalls the theoretical physicists and the social scientists. A significant difference is their great use of whole constructions of the blot, usually interpreted as generalizing ability, which notably enough was not strikingly characteristic of the eminent scientists in any of the fields studied. This could be interpreted here as strictly vocational, since fine painting so obviously demands construction of a meaningful whole, and precisely in the kind of bounded two-dimentional space such as given in an ink-blot card. As a group, Roe found these artists to have a characteristic emotional adaptation which is nonaggressive and rather passive in nature, and somewhat more "feminine" than "masculine" by our cultural stereotypes. Interestingly, though these were all men selected according to critical acclaim as "top rank," Roe found to her astonishment that about half of them did not give any of what have been taken as Rorschach indicators of creative ability; but those who did give such indications (for example, human movement responses) tended to be painters regarded as more original in their work.

More recently, some clues to the definitive early life experiences of the most productive artists are to be found in the study by Bernard Rosenberg and Norris Fliegel (*The Vanguard Artist* [Chicago: Quadrangle Books, 1965]), who with great imaginative skill interviewed twenty-nine of the leading New York painters and sculptors of the early 1960s. They found the social backgrounds of these artists remarkably similar to those of the artists studied by Roe in the 1940s —a wide class range, but none from either the very poor or the very rich; great diversity of parental occupations, formal educational and "cultural" exposures. But they did find common to all of these artists, four definitive conditions during childhood and adolescence, which they postulate as the necessary and sufficient conditions for "the public emergence of inborn talent:" (1) the artist as a child enjoyed a strong, warm, and unambivalent love and acceptance from his mother in his earliest years, and differentiated acceptance from both parents, of himself and of his very early displayed artistic talent; (2) some significant figure, usually a male, appeared in the early life of the child and acted as a catalyst for the expression of his artistic talent, and became a major object of identification; (3) this internalized model then took on an abstract and idealized form, which the artist ever after attempted to express through his work; and (4) in the fourth stage, "the artist offers his perfected—but never perfect—work to the world, which has the unconscious meaning of attempting to attain a specific position vis à vis the symbolized parental image" (pp. 138–39).

Pivotal in the life-view of all of these artists is a very profound quest for, and considerable realization of, autonomy, and a substantial alienation from the conventional values of middle-class life. This is usually effectuated early in youth by an easy and unconflicted break from the family of origin and achieved with a minimum of turmoil or reactive hostility. Such relative assurance and calm recalls the comparative lack of deep emotional involvement with parents or parental imagos that Anne Roe found in many of the eminent physical scientists.

Such studies take us some part of the way into the study of the creative process as a way of life. Let us consider some further perspectives.

The common ground of artists and scientists is the touchstone of individual freedom so characteristically at odds with the powerful prevailing social pressures of the modern world. Distinguishing both the scientist and the artist is a measure of autonomy scarcely even approached in other fields of work; an obliteration of the boundaries between work and play ordinarily imposed and accepted (even embraced) by most persons in the modern industrialized world; and a liberation of the constraints of *instrumentalism* that attach to nearly all other kinds of work. (Though in popular thinking science is perceived as the handmaiden of technological mastery over the world, and hence distinctly *instrumental* in its nature, "pure scientists" reject this linkage as not only unnecessary but even pernicious to the pursuit of "knowledge for its own sake" and thus align themselves with the artist as *expressive* creators rather than as useful gadgeteers. The relationship, however, is far more complex than this simplified statement can suggest, but its further exploration would carry us too far afield for our present purposes.)

In a crude way, one may contrast the work of the scientist and that of the artist as follows: the scientist seeks through freedom to *discover* the order and hence the constraints of the real existing world in all its manifestations; the artist seeks through freedom to *create* a world that soars above the constraints and limitations of the externally "real" world, thus exhibiting the freedom and transcendence of man. This, however, is in part a factitious distinction. In important ways the scientist is not only discovering but *creating* a world, while the artist, to create, must discover the inner forces of humanity and bring them forth in illuminating transformation. Internally, the world of science is variably close to or related to the world of art. It ranges from the extreme of external-object orientation of experimental physicists to the human orientation of psychologists and anthropologists, with their correlates of childhood interests in gadgetry and literature respectively, as revealed in Roe's studies. Interestingly, the field considered by many the pinnacle of "pure science"—theoretical physics—is, with its great concentration on symbolization, closer to the world of art than either its apparent sibling, experimental physics, or the apparently more distantly related science of experimental psychology.

From one psychoanalytic point of view, all art and all science are engaged in the pursuit of the solution to the riddle of the Sphinx. The psychoanalyst Daniel E. Schneider writes:[17]

[17] Daniel E. Schneider, *The Psychoanalyst and the Artist* (New York: Inter-

> To solve the riddle in terms of inanimate forces—chemistry, physiology, physics, mathematics—and not to go beyond into a pleasurable participation in the womb whence we came—these are the lofty exact sciences, where the laws of motion are paramount, and where emotion is, ideally, repressed.

Schneider cites Eugene Delacroix' remark that there is no difference, essentially, between true art and true science, though there is, of course, a difference of endowment, interest, and activity between artist and scientist, and he relates the difference to the distinction between *motion* and *emotion*.[18]

> . . . science is the study and creative theory of the motion and energy exchange of objects in the physical universe. . . . if we might stretch the term "e-motion" to mean expressive motion, we might say that true creative scientists (e.g., Newton, Freud, Galileo, Copernicus, and Einstein) discover and portray the objective "emotion" (motion expressive) of the universe, in relation to the dynamic but human observer.
>
> The true creative artist, contrariwise, discovers and portrays in various media, the subjective emotion of the individual in relation to the dynamic but unobserving universe. . . . Human consciousness is then a resultant of the subjective emotion and the objective motion of the universal or narrower environment.

We may profitably pursue Schneider's study, *The Psychoanalyst and the Artist*, for an analysis of the psychodynamic process of artistic creation. The study concentrates on the "true creative artist" as distinguished from the host of lesser figures. In Schneider's distinction, the former can be characterized as artists who *consistently* create with full artistic *result*, as contrasted with the latter who produce *occasionally*, with artistic *intent*. Though critics and interpreters may quarrel endlessly over whom to include among the truly great artists, certain towering figures stand out as having an indisputable claim: Sophocles, Shakespeare, Goethe, Beethoven, and Dostoevski. (Their counterparts in science would be Galileo, Newton, Copernicus, Einstein, and Freud.) Schneider categorically rejects the view of great creative art as mere sublimation, or reaction formation against unconscious neurotic conflicts. As Freud himself recognized, a study of the psychosexual history of Leonardo da Vinci or of psychodynamic implications in the sculpture of Michelangelo cannot reveal

---

national Universities Press, 1950, Mentor Edition, New York: New American Library, 1962), p. 33. (The page references are to the Mentor edition.)
   [18] *Ibid.*, p. 47. footnote.

to us the psychology of their genius. But psychoanalysis need not, with Freud, despair of ever being able to "explain" artistic genius. Rather, analytic study of men like da Vinci can reveal clues to the incomplete fulfillment of creative endowment, and study of the man and his work, in the cases of more complete fulfillment—such as Goethe and Shakespeare—*can* lead us to the roots of truly great art. Schneider makes the following formulations:

Truly great art comes out of an extremely rare relationship of unconscious and conscious forces. It results from a combination of great "creative thrust"—from the powerful and inexhaustible resources of the unconscious—and great "creative mastery," the product of a powerful conscious ego mustering capacities derived from lifelong arduous acquisition of technical skills relevant to the chosen medium, developed first in imitation of pre-existing work in that medium, then in original production exercising great mastery of form. Both elements are essential: an unusual access to the great fountainhead of unconscious forces and enormous conscious transformational power. The unconscious forces provide the intuition which is essential to any artistic grasping of the world; the conscious provides the cognition, the ordering, and most important, the transforming, the executive mastery without which the intuitive powers of the unconscious remain a mere chaos of sensation and impulse. Artistic creativity means transcending the boundaries of "objective" space-time, the world of "reality" given by the routine of everyday life, and reaching into and utilizing the resources of that other time-space world, the unconscious, in a creatively transforming manner. The artist is open to the world of his dreams without being inundated and overwhelmed by these powerful and unordered forces. He has a rare capacity to move backward and forward through a kind of "corridor of transformation" between the creative thrust of the unconscious and the creative mastery of the conscious, between intuition and cognition, in a manner never attained by more ordinary people, who are either too rigorously repressed to be able to tap the unconscious forces within themselves, or too impulsively open to the unconscious forces to be able to give them any coherent order.

The transformational capacity of the true artist is thus of the same order as that of the truly creative scientist, who is distinguished from lesser workers in that vineyard, by his transcendence of routine and formalism in the scientific pursuit, his rare capacity to combine intuitive leaps (products of access to the dream world of the unconscious) with cognitive rigor and economy and elegance of formal expression. Seen in this light, the "elegance" so prized in great and forward-moving scientific advances, is no mere incidental embroidery, but rather it is directly analogous to the mastery of *form* essential to any great work of art. And aptness of form to content, the unity of form and content, is utterly essential to any truly creative work of art: the sense it gives that this is the true, and the only true, form that can be given to this particular content. This, in turn, is the product of the most creative integration of unconscious thrust and conscious mastery of reality and technique.

From dreams, Schneider tells us, we know the nature of this transforming mechanism which is so powerful and revealing in the work of the true artist: this mechanism is what Freud called the "preconscious"—lying between the conscious and the unconscious, partaking of the qualities of both, capable of becoming conscious though not ordinarily so. This preconscious has direct connections with the sense organs, with inherent aptitudes and sensitivities of these organs; it uses free, mobile psychosexual energy rather than those energies (bound, immobile) of the unconscious repressed; its powers are accessible to the ego; and it is part of the special qualities of man that mark his evolutionary advance over his forebears—his larger frontal lobes, his speech, his handedness, and his erect posture.

The transformational process involved in artistic work is neither an *automatic* linking of unconscious and conscious through the corridor of the preconscious, nor a voluntary act based on sublimated neurotic compulsions. Rather it is *work* that is both masochistic in being a difficult and grueling task and at the same time liberating: widening and deepening psychic conception and producing pleasure through the integration of unconscious thrust and the mastery of painstakingly acquired technical skill. Genius is neither wild intuitive leaps alone, nor alone the infinite capacity for taking pains, but rather the creative fusion of both of these. Reflections of great artists like Goethe on the very processes of their own creative work, reveal some of the elements involved: openness of contact with his own dreams, reflection upon and rehearsing of relevant details of one's everyday experiences in the world of "reality," disciplined selection of the intrinsic, the relevant, the crucial features of these experiences, and a deliberate and painstaking exclusion of distracting and irrelevant influences, contacts, relationships. Goethe's self-analytic comments on his composition of *The Sorrows of Young Werther* show these elements, and his intense self-dedication to the task of creating a "poetic oneness"—with conscious rejection of the blindness of the idiot public ("that herd of swine") wallowing in its morass of routine. He reveals too how the creation of a work of art serves as an integrating act of self-analysis and therapeutic self-liberation for the artist, which, in turn, links him powerfully to mankind through the *universalization* of private experience by the interweaving of powerfully felt reality with the "plastic shape" of dreams. "The consistent artist (like the creative scientist)"—Schneider writes—"*is driven by a vision of the possibility of newer and greater formal interpretation* of things from which he (in himself and as a representative of his time) suffers and by which he is stimulated. . . . to be an artist . . . *is to be compelled.*" [19] The artist thus possesses his vision and is by his vision possessed. He both drives and is driven to bring his vision to masterful expression and has, in turn, the capacious and elastic transforming mechanism to accomplish this.

Artistic talent can thus be described as "a gift, an inherent endowment of compelling visionary sensitivity, permitting the transformation of unconscious . . . and conscious . . . into new and greater possibilities of formal interpretation, scientifically explicit, artistically implicit." The transformational mechanism works best in a setting of real love, security, and full adult (genital) development. Where these conditions are not present, such a transforming power may remain bound to neurotic drives of a sadistic or masochistic nature, and they run the danger of "blocking" creative work, or more seriously, "breakdown" in psychotic disaster. In the healthy conditions of love, security, and genitality, this transforming capacity is an enduring force which never leaves the artist, cannot be abolished or abridged by psychoanalytic treatment, and more than that, has its own inherent development, which can be likened to being analyzed and continuing to be analyzed throughout life. Schneider cites Goethe, Shakespeare, and Freud as the three great exemplars of this lifelong development of transformative creativity, which explains how they "saw so deeply" and have so profoundly engaged the imagination of man. In other media Beethoven and Dostoevski can be added to the list of giants who combined "iron cognitive analytical control over the most violent creative thrust from the near world of passion and dreams."

[19] Schneider, *op. cit.*, p. 85.

One can explore the nature of the powerful element of intuition in great art through clues provided in the lives of great artists. Repeatedly we find a passion for self-observation and self-interpretation, a recognition of a kind of "other self" observing and interpreting even as one experiences profoundly felt events. This "other self" is a kind of identification not only with both the mother and the father (in the young child's curiosity about sexual reproduction), but also with something else beyond—"the unseen, unfelt, but inevitable act and process of creation." The "third element" is a kind of special further identification (often expressed as a kind of tongue-in-cheek identification with God) that encompasses human bisexuality and transcends identification with the actual mother and father—a creator identification combining feminine sensitivity to content and masculine drive toward form, in a fusion transcending specific masculine and feminine objects in the gifted child's world. It is just such an enormous breadth and bisexual extensity of identifications that marks the work of the truly creative artist in literature, drama, and poetry. Identification with a transcendent creative force (the act of sexual creation itself) amounts in fact to a solution of the riddle of the Sphinx—here, at the highest level of creative art. This third element unites the ego, but there is also the danger that it can divide or split the ego, if the process of thinking and artistically creating itself becomes endowed with an overload of sexual tension and leads to an avoidance of loving in reality. In such resulting "breakdowns" the unconscious creative thrust overwhelms the creative mastery capacities of the ego and victoriously invades consciousness in delusion and hallucination.

In the optimal state, by contrast, the balance between creative thrust and creative mastery maintains a *flexibility of repression*, one of the most significantly distinguishing features of the artist from the ordinary man, whose repressions are rigid unless untied by the "third ego" of the analyst. The great artist appears to have a quantitatively greater capacity for multiple identifications, by which he "analyzes" and "synthesizes" a much vaster range of experience than the ordinary mind can find empathic response to, much less capacity to give formal expression.

The psychic economy of those with artistic gifts has qualities which impel it to the mastery of form; the artist has distinctively greater psychic capacities for identification, apparently based on innate endowment; and the endowment becomes developed, in the true artist, first through imitation in the acquisition of technical skills related to a particular art form, later in the form of original production, capable of increasingly higher integrations of unconscious intuitive forces and conscious cognitive and formal mastery. The artist's self-analyzing proclivity enables him to release energy bound in repressions and thus provide material for the exercise of his talent, which in mature integrations involve interpretation of, rather than reacting to, the experiences and stresses of inner and outer reality. The faculty, however, has its own inherent dangers, some of which no creative artist has entirely escaped, and in which a host of lesser artists have been sadly if not tragically bogged down—the danger of blocking, of inhibition of mastery of form, indicative of unresolved Oedipal aggressions and the unconscious reactions to them in frustrating self-punishments, which thus separate creative thrust from creative mastery; and the danger of defensive narcissism, the resistance against giving up self-love. When the latter is present, the creative works become more like symptoms or reaction formations, symbolic restorations of love objects in unconscious fantasy destroyed, expressions of guilt and atonement rather than joyful creative interpretation.

Schneider's postulation of a third, creatorlike identification, in the great artist, illuminates empirical findings such as Roe's that the notable male painters tend to have what in our culture we would consider a rather "feminine" orientation to the world. With Schneider we would probably be more accurate to define these men as going beyond purely masculine and purely feminine identifications to include an identification that partakes of both—feminine intuition and masculine mastery, feminine content and masculine form—and transcends both in a creative synthesis. Schneider sees this synthesis as identification with the process of creation itself, the model for which is, of course, sexual reproduction. This postulation also illuminates the greater similarity of the artists with either theoretical physicists or social scientists—as distinguished from experimental physicists or experimental psychologists (or "hard-nosed" scientists in general). The former camp is frequently seen (or accused) as being more "soft" or more "feminine," the latter as more in line with "hard" "masculine" pursuits, such as business and industry, in our culture. It also suggests some clues to the rarity of women among either great scientists or great artists. Their obvious direct biological creativity would appear to produce much less need to draw upon such a third, creatorlike identification than would impel a similarly gifted male.

4. THE PRIMITIVE SHAMAN

The scientist and the artist each in his own way shows a distinctive welding of unconscious and conscious powers into a central life activity of great creative force, at once compelling and liberating to the practitioner, and of great significance for the life of his society. A different yet related life-encompassing occupation that draws in a gifted creative way upon the "inexhaustible forces of the unconscious" is that of the medicine-man or *shaman* of primitive societies. The shaman in many ways can be seen as artist, scientist, and all-around professional practitioner all rolled into one. He is the exemplar, par excellence, of the way in which a pre-scientific society recognizes in an individual special quantities and qualities of access to great mysterious forces—forces which in modern psychoanalytic terms we see as the forces of the unconscious potentially available to all humanity, and which are seen in pre-scientific cultures as those of the powerful and mysterious world of the supernatural. The shaman is both special and apart, and at the same time (in fact, by his very specialness) the channel and articulator of universal experiences of us all. He is at one and the same time "crazy" and more in touch with reality—the inner reality—of the life of members of his tribe, thus apart from and indispensable to all of them.

First, then, we present an analysis of the psychology of the shaman, and his relationship to the collective psychopathology of his own society, as presented by the provocative psychoanalytic anthropologist, Géza Róheim.

The Role of the Shaman in Primitive Culture

GÉZA RÓHEIM

One way to arrive at an understanding of the nature of a primitive culture is by aiming at the individual who is in the hub of the whole system.

Reprinted, with permission, from Géza Róheim, The Origin and Function of Culture (New York: Nervous and Mental Disease Monographs, 1943), from Chapter One, pp. 3-8, and Chapter Two, pp. 43-51. Copyright © 1943, The Williams & Wilkins Co., Baltimore, Md. 21202 U.S.A.

The typical representative of a Siberian tribe and the leader of the community is the shaman.

Shirokogoroff in his very thorough investigation of Tungus shamanism, tells us that:

> Since the shaman functions as a safety valve and as a regulator of the psychic life of the clan he lives under the permanent feeling of bearing a great responsibility. . . . From the analysis of the relations between the shaman and his spirits, his own spirits and those of other shamans also his spirits and the complex of other spirits, we can see a great number of various prohibitions, avoidances, taboos, binding every step of the shaman. Even in his family, the shaman must be careful not to harm his wife if he is a male shaman, or her husband if she is a female, not to speak of the children. . . . The shaman's spirits which he carries with him may always become involved with other spirits and a continuous trouble may originate from their conflict. Owing to this the shaman is always careful when finding himself with other people. . . . The reaction of other people to the shaman responds to his cautious behavior, so that very often the shaman becomes more or less isolated. . . . Finally there is a special condition more which deprives the shaman of the usual cheerfulness of the Tungus, viz. the worry about the soul.
>
> The shaman being the safety valve of the clan and a clan officer cannot refuse to assist his clansmen.[20]
>
> The inner force in the make up of the shaman which takes him to the heights of Heaven and the depths of Hell, naturally takes something away from this earth.
>
> Owing to the psychomental character of shamanism, most of the shamans are put in an exceptional position in reference to the chief industrial activity of the Tungus: hunting. In fact in Transbaikalia I have met with a shaman who could not kill big animals, such as the elk and therefore was chiefly hunting roe deer. On his part it was a case of self-suggestion. Some shamans cannot hunt tigers and bears for these are animals whose forms may be assumed by other shamans. As the shamans are economically and physically in an inferior position, they live with other people who take care of them as if they were invalids. Other people do the hunting for them, look after the domesticated animals and take care of the shamans.[21]

The influence of the shaman is clearly defined by the transference situation. "The person attended by a shaman must not seek assistance from other shamans unless the shaman recommends it himself. So that the shaman gradually forms around himself a group of permanent clients. Naturally the more numerous are his permanent clients from their

[20] S. M. Shirokogoroff, *Psychomental Complex of the Tungus*, 1935, 380.
[21] *Idem, l. c.,* 379.

childhood, the more influential is the shaman." There can be no doubt
about the neurotic or psychotic character of shamans. We quote Bogoras
on the Chukchee:

> The shamanistic call begins to manifest itself at an early age, in
> many cases during the critical period of transition from childhood
> to youth. It is the period of rapid and intense growth; and it is well
> known that many persons of both sexes manifest during this time
> increased sensitiveness and that the mind often becomes unbal-
> anced. . . . Nervous and highly excitable temperaments are most
> susceptible to the shamanistic call. . . . The shamans among the
> Chukchee with whom I conversed were as a rule extremely excit-
> able, almost hysterical and not a few of them were half crazy. Their
> cunning in the use of deceit in their art closely resembled the cun-
> ning of a lunatic.[22]

The next quotation shows the conflict and the struggle of the healthy
part of the personality against the shamanistic "call."

> Young people as a rule are exceedingly reluctant to obey the call
> especially if it involves the adoption of some characteristic device in
> clothing or in the mode of life.[23]
> The process of gathering inspiration is so painful to young sha-
> mans because of their mental struggle against the call, that they are
> sometimes said to sweat blood on the forehead and temples. . . .
> Afterwards every preparation of a shaman for a performance is con-
> sidered a sort of repetition of the initiative process: hence it is said
> that the Chukchee shamans during that time are easily susceptible
> to hemorrhage and even to bloody sweat. . . . The preparatory
> period is compared by the Chukchee to a long severe illness; and
> the acquirement of inspiration, to a recovery. To people of mature
> age the shamanistic call may come after some great misfortune or
> loss or illness indeed if somebody recovers after such a loss or illness
> he is regarded as having within himself the possibilities of a
> shaman.[24]

The shaman is certainly the representative of one type of civilization,
and there can be no doubt about the fact that he differs from ordinary
men by being a neurotic of some sort. According to Czaplicka:

> Although hysteria lies at the bottom of the shaman's vocation,
> yet at the same time the shaman differs from an ordinary patient
> suffering from this illness in possessing an extremely great power of
> mastering himself in the periods between the actual fits, which
> occur during the ceremonies. A good shaman ought to possess many

[22] W. Bogoras, The Chukchee, Jessup North Pacific Expedition, VII, 1907,
415.
[23] W. Bogoras, l. c., 418, 419.
[24] W. Bogoras, l. c., 421.

unusual qualities but the chief is the power, acquired by tact and knowledge, to influence the people around him.[25]

Siberian culture is a very typical case for here the neurotic nature of the Leader of the cultural area is evident.

It is not so in every culture area. In Central Australia nobody would regard the average "ngankara man" as a morbid person. Obviously this cannot be so because all the middle aged, all the important members of the tribe would be more or less introverts or neurotics as they are all medicine men. On the contrary they are usually capable and healthy men, skillful hunters and leaders in warfare. However further enquiry reveals other facts. This is the initiation dream of Wapiti, an old man of the Ngatatara tribe. He is a pleasant, gentlemanly sort of old man and nobody who knew him would call him a neurotic. Let us hear what he has to say about his own initiation:

> *The altjira Wapiti came to me in his dream and he held a yam in his hand. He thrust the yam into my nail and the nankara stone went right in from there. It spread right through my flesh and came out through the nails of the other hand.*

He had to prepare for this dream by eating the yam (wapiti), that is, his own totem. Every time he ate it he felt a stitch inside till finally he was "made" by the altjira in the dream. When he woke up after this dream, he was deranged and continually talking. He saw a stump and taking it to be a man, he said:

Warkinji	wanka	kunjanga.
Scolding	talk	bad word!

Which means that the imaginary person is saying something bad about him and he protests against this. "Bad words" means Central Australian swearing which usually contains some references to incest or the genital organs. One man was actually standing there but he saw two and said:

Nana	paluna	wanti
That	him (*i.e., the bad words*)	leave it.

After this he understood the words of the animals and knew what babies were laughing at when they play. He can see right through people even if they are standing in a crowd, and he pulls the little bone or stick out and removes the disease.

Now the state in which we find him after the dream amounts to what might be called a transitory paranoia. But first we must understand his dream. In the conception dream of his mother it was the mythological

[25] M. A. Czaplicka, *Aboriginal Siberia*, 1914, 169.

Wapiti who penetrated into her womb in the shape of a tjurunga in order to reappear on earth as a new Wapiti. The would-be medicine man commences by eating his totem, that is, by the oral introjection of the father. In the case of the mother the tjurunga ancestor penetrates *via* the cult symbol in the womb, in the case of the son he goes in in his eatable totemic form through the mouth. The dream itself is very similar to the conception dreams of women. We may therefore suspect a female attitude with regard to the father as latent in the mental make-up of the medicine man. The initiator is a supernatural father and double of Wapiti. When I asked him about the man whom he saw in two shapes in the delirium, he told me it was his own father. Spencer and Gillen recount a similar case among the Warramunga. The future medicine man sees two spirits and when he has his spear poised and is ready to throw it, they say: "Don't kill us, we are your father and brother." [26]

I have analyzed the conception dreams of women in this area and shown that the latent content of these dreams is coitus with the father. This would fit in very well with the latent homosexual content of paranoia. Moreover, if we remember that a Central Australian medicine man is continually seeing the phallic demons, regards himself as being persecuted by them or by other sorcerers, struggles with them and masters them by projecting (the characteristic mechanism of paranoia) invisible stones into the demons, sorcerers, or patients, we must regard these people as dissimulating paranoiacs or as people with whom the paranoiac mechanisms have not resulted in breaking off relations with their environment. Only one of the many nankara men I knew in Central Australia was what might be termed peculiar or a paranoid character. My wife never quite lost her fear of Pukuti-wara because of his peculiar bearing, his fixed stare, and none too friendly manner. When we met him, he had fled from the Pitchentara country with his followers because he had killed a man in a blood-feud. He was the only native I knew who showed anxiety in broad daylight. He used to stop short in the middle of a sentence and cry out "They are coming!" which meant either the *wanapa* (man on a blood-feud expedition) or the *mamu* (demons). His tribes-fellows regarded him as different from other sorcerers; he was not merely a nankara-man but half a *mamu* (demon) himself. If we look at this statement more closely, it is equivalent to saying that he was half mad. Sometimes they would tell me about old women who had spoken incoherently in their death agony and this was called mamuringu (to become a devil).[27] The difference between the dreams of Pukuti-wara and others was the unveiled symbolism in the former. While it is only ana-

---

[26] B. Spencer and F. J. Gillen, *Northern Tribes of Central Australia*, 1904, 482.

[27] G. Róheim, "Women and Their Life in Central Australia," *Journ. Roy. Anthr. Inst.*, LXIII, 1933, 63, 242.

lytic interpretation which can reveal the castration content in the dreams of other medicine men, he has really undergone the excision of one testicle at initiation.[28] We see, therefore, that Pukuti-wara, the most renowned of all the shamans, is really on the verge of normalcy while the others, less famous men, behave like all other people but make extensive use of psychotic mechanisms in their calling of medicine men. We know that among these tribes all adults are more or less medicine men. . . . What we wish to show is that primitive civilizations are societies led by medicine men, and that the medicine man is a neurotic who has succeeded in converting his neurosis into an activity in harmony with his interests. . . .

THE MEDICINE MAN AS THE FIRST PROFESSION

Apart from the "professions" of hunter, fisherman, and gatherer of fruit or edible roots the first profession in human evolution is that of the medicine man. The basic theory is that disease is caused by a foreign substance which has been "shot" into the body of the patient by another medicine man or spirit and which the medicine man has to remove by the aid of suction. Professor Seligman writes on these "sendings" among the Southern Massim:

> Disease is caused by means of a "sending" projected from the body of a sorcerer or witch; particular interest is attached to the "sending" because it is thought of as leading a separate life after the death of the individuals in whom it is normally immanent. The "sending" is most commonly projected from the body of a woman and after her death may pass to her daughter, or with her spirit or shade pass to the other world.
>
> In Gelaria the "sending" was called labuni. Labuni exist within women and can be commanded by any woman who has had children. . . . It was said that the labuni existed in or was derived from, an organ called ipona, situated in the flank and literally meaning egg or eggs. The labuni was said actually to leave the body and afterwards to re-enter it per rectum. Although labuni resemble shadows they wear a petticoat which is shorter than that worn by the women in this part of the country. Labuni produce disease by means of a sliver of bone, or fragment of stone or coral, called gidana, which they insert into their victim's body. A fragment of human bone or a man's tooth is a specially potent gidana. The labuni is said to throw the gidana at the individual to be injured from a distance of about 60 yards. The gidana was then removed by the medicine man by massage and suction.[29]

In Northern California disease is caused by an invisible supernatural object sharp at both ends and clear as ice which they call a "pain." A

[28] Cf. G. Róheim, The Riddle of the Sphinx, 1934, 69.
[29] C. G. Seligman, The Melanesians of British New Guinea, 1910, 640-42.

"pain" possesses the power of moving even after it has been extracted and flies through the air to the intended victim at the command of the person who sends it. The medicine man after extracting the disease object or pain almost always exhibited it. In Northwestern California the medicine man would swallow this pain and the degree of his power depended upon the number of pains he kept in his body. The rattlesnake was thought to inject a material animate object into its victim which the rattlesnake shaman must extract.[30] The Takelma regarded disease as directly caused by a disease-spirit or "pain." The shaman, always feared and always suspected of being responsible for whatever ill might befall the individual or the village community, was said when bent upon the death of some one "to go out of his house with a disease spirit" and to "shoot people with it." [31] The Achomawi believe that a "pain" grows in size and strength by killing people. If a shaman does not catch the "pain" when it returns to him after killing the person it has been shot into, he loses all control over it and it goes about killing people of its own initiative. This is the cause of epidemics. The only way to put an end to it is to kill the shaman to whom such a pain belongs, for at the death of a shaman all his pains die also.[32] Brett mentions a case in Guinea where owing to the idea of these disease-causing substances in the body a woman inflicted on herself a mortal wound with a razor in the attempt to cut out the imaginary cause of the pain.[33]

Regarding the Indians of the Issá-Japurá District (South America, Rio Negro) we are told that "much of the medicine man's ceremonial healing consists of blowing and breathing over the patient, as well as the usual sucking out of the poison, the evil spirit that, in the guise of stick, stone, thorn, etc., lurks in the flesh of the sufferer." Old women breathe over forbidden food to remove the poison and make it permissible to eat, or they will breathe over a delicate child to improve its health.[34]

In some Western Australian dialects the medicine man is called a boylya or more precisely a boylya-gadak, i.e., owner of a boylya.[35] But the medicine man himself is also called a boyla. These boylas of hostile

[30] A. L. Kroeber, The Religion of the Indians of California, University of California Publications in American Archeology and Ethnology, Vol. 4, No. 6, 1907, 333.

[31] E. Sapir, "Religious Ideas of the Takelma Indians," Journal of Am. F. L., 1907, 41.

[32] R. B. Dixon, "Notes on the Achomawi and Atsugewi Indians," Am. Anthr., 1908, 218.

[33] W. H. Brett, The Indian Tribes of Guiana, 1868, 366.

[34] T. W. Wiffen, "A Short Account of the Indians of the Issá-Japurá District," Journal of Am. F. L., 1913, 59, 60.

[35] G. F. Moore, Diary of an Early Settler in West Australia, 1830-41 and also a Vocabulary of the Language of the Aborigines, 1884, 13. Bilyi-navel. Bilyi-gadal-navel-possessor, ibid., 9. Cf. G. Grey, A Vocabulary of the Dialects of South Western Australia, 1841, 17, 18, 40. I. Brady, Descriptive Vocabulary of the Native Language of West Australia, 1845, 16.

tribes eat the flesh of the sleeper and thus cause his death. They travel through the air unseen, eat the flesh of human beings and enter the body in the shape of a quartz crystal.[36] The "boglia" extracts a stone called boglia by sucking it out of the patient's body. The quartz crystal is in the stomach of the "boglia" and this crystal is the seat of his power. He sends these boglias into those whom he wishes to make sick. When he dies, this "*ente malefico*" passes into his sons stomach.[37] There seems to be no other source of this Boollia than the human body, and one of the favorite localities from which it is obtained is the anus.[38]

In Central Australia the objects extracted by the nankara-men from the patient's body are nankara-stones and pointing bones. Naturally both are extracted from the body of the patient after having been projected into the same by another medicine man. The pointing bone or stick is held as if it were taken from the part of the sorcerer's body which lies behind the penis. The characteristic way of holding the bone shows that it is a symbolic penis. The victim must be asleep. The sorcerer takes semen from his penis and excrement from his anus, and by throwing them in the direction of his enemy forms a cloud behind which he hides. An object which is projected from the body of the sorcerer into the body of the victim which is held like a penis and emerges from behind the penis, which is accompanied by semen and excrements is obviously an "anal sadistic" phallos. As for the invisible nankara-stones their significance is made quite clear by Pukuti-waras dreams.

> *My soul flew westward in the form of a* wamulu.[39] *The wind blew the feather; it rolled about and disappeared in the sand. Then I (the soul) flew up to the Milky Way where there was a black mountain to which the souls always fly. Two rocks which looked like fire rolled down; I flew towards the north. Two unborn children (iti-iti) were there in a hollow tree. They were twins and their mother was standing beside the tree.[40] I killed both with my penis. First I stood in front of them as if I were going to throw my testicles and these became nankara stones—and then I killed them with my penis. I roasted them using my forehead as a spit and I will eat them to night (viz., in his dream).[41]*

[36] G. Grey, *Journals of Two Expeditions to North West and Western Australia*, 1841, II, 321-25.

[37] Monsig. D. Rudesindo Salvado, *Memorie storiche dell' Australia particolarmente di Nuova Norcia*, 1851, 299, 354, 358.

[38] A. Oldfield, "The Aborgines of Australia," *Transactions of the Ethnological Society*, III, 235.

[39] Eagle down used at ceremonies. Penis symbol.

[40] The twins in the hollow tree—in the mother. Mother stands beside the tree. (Symbol is duplicated.)

[41] *Cf.* Róheim, *The Riddle of the Sphinx*, 1934, 71.

This dream gives us the clue to the profession of the medicine man. For Pukuti-wara is trying to kill (and eat) two children (the associations show that they are his own children) by breaking a fundamental coitus taboo of all Central Australian societies; he penetrates into the body of a pregnant woman with his penis. Now we can not fail to see that the activity of the medicine man is the equivalent of the infantile body destruction phantasy (M. Klein) with the conscious aim of life instead of death, with restoration instead of destruction. For what is the unconscious meaning of the substances which the medicine man sucks or rubs out of the patient's body? In New Guinea only women who have given birth to children can project a *labuni* and the *labuni* goes back into the body per rectum—a symbol of the child and the feces. The Californian idea of personifying these "pains" points to an underlying child or penis (moving = erection) concept. In Western Australia we found clear evidence for the anal significance of the quartz crystal, while our Luritja and Pitchentara data prove that the projectiles are penis, testicle, and child symbols.

Pukuti-wara the "half-devil" as his friends called him was continually eating demon children in his dreams. We know that, following tribal custom, he has actually killed three or four of his own children and given them to their mother and brothers to eat. Once, he tells us, as he was sleeping beside the fire, a devil child came out of his calf and jumped about on the heads of the men sleeping in the camp. It cut off one testicle from each of them just as his own testicle had been cut off at initiation.[42] From these the child devil formed a supply of kukurpas or nankara-stones which were stored up in Pukuti-wara. This demon is called Tjitjingangarpa (mad child). It urinates on its master's face and is thus the cause, as Pukuti-wara proudly explained, of his fine long beard.[43]

The "mad child" is in Pukuti-wara, he himself is the mad child with the aggression primarily directed against the mother's body and with the phantasy of tearing the father's penis ("combined parent" concept or primal scene) or her children or feces out of the mother's body. He becomes a medicine man in the first instance by a phantasy compensation of the retribution anxiety connected with body destruction ideas. This is the initiation of the shaman.

> *Within the cave the iruntarinia* [44] *(spirit) removes all the internal organs and provides the man with a completely new set. In addition to providing the young medicine man with a new set of internal organs, the iruntarinia is supposed to implant in his body a supply*

[42] The latter is a fact.
[43] G. Róheim, *The Riddle of the Sphinx*, 1934, 38.
[44] Explanation of the name as given to me at Hermannsburg by old Moses (one of Strehlow's informants, head of the Christian Aranda): Erunta-rinja— those belonging to the cold, i.e., the doubles who live under the earth.

of magic Atnongara stones which he is able to project into the body of a patient and so to combat the evil influences at work within. So long as these stones remain in his body he is capable of performing the work of a medicine man.[45]

According to an account given by a Warramunga medicine man, the spirits cut him open, took all his insides out and provided him with a new set. Finally they put a little snake in his body, which endowed him with the powers of a medicine man. A Binbinga medicine man told Spencer that the spirit cut him open right down the middle line, took out all of his insides and exchanged them for those of himself which he placed in the body of the mortal.[46] Two of Pukuti-wara's dreams refer to his initiation. In one of these the spines of the porcupine (Echidna) stick out of the earth and penetrate into his body. A kurunpa (soul) in the shape of an eagle-hawk eats his soul. The real initiation dream is a full version of the same theme.

> *The soul of a man came in the shape of an eagle-hawk. It had wings but also a human penis. It caught my soul with this penis and dragged it out by the hair. My soul hung down from the penis and the eagle-hawk flew about with me, first to the west and then to the east. It was dawn and the eagle-hawk-man made a great fire into which he threw my soul. My penis became quite hot and he pulled the skin down. He took me out of the fire and carried me to the camp. Many nankara-people (medicine men) were there in a group; they were only skeletons with no flesh. Their bones were like the spines of a porcupine. The eagle-hawk threw me on these bones and they went into my body. We went to the west and the eagle-hawk-man opened me. He took out my lungs and liver only leaving my heart. We flew to the west, where there was a small devil child. I saw the child and raised my hand to throw the nankara-stones. My testicles hung down and flew off like nankara-stones. A man came out of one of the testicles and stood beside me. He had a very long penis and with this he killed the devil child. He gave it to me and I ate it. Then both souls (viz., the child and the phallic person) went into my body.*[47]

In the book from which I quote this text I have already interpreted the dream on the phallic, castration anxiety and primal scene level. We know that the dream is the dream version of a real event, for Pukuti-wara really lost one testicle when he was initiated. We now see that from the point of view of the body destruction phantasies the testicle torn out of the scrotum represents also the phantasy child in the body and in general

[45] B. Spencer and F. J. Gillen, *The Arunta*, 1927, II, 392, 393.
[46] B. Spencer and F. J. Gillen, *The Northern Tribes of Central Australia*, 1904, 484-87.
[47] G. Róheim, *The Riddle of the Sphinx*, 75, 76.

valuable body contents. Both the penis as the means by which he as aggressive father penetrates into the mother's body and the child whom he would tear out of the mother's body are in him. The child within is like the nankara-stones or other "internalized" objects, a kind of reassurance against talion anxiety. "It is not true that I shall be torn to pieces because I wished to tear the penis, the child (etc.) out of my mother, on the contrary, I am full of valuable and indestructible magical objects." When he becomes initiated he has already undergone what he is afraid of, viz., being eaten by the mother,[48] or having his intestines removed. The versions in which the removal of the intestines is represented as an exchange of intestines between the shaman and the supernatural clearly prove the talion nature of the removal phantasy. In the Kabi tribe:

> A man's occult art would appear to be proportioned to his vitality, and the degree of vitality which he possessed depended upon the number of sacred pebbles and the quantity of yurru (rope) which he carried within him. One kind of sacred pebble was named "kundir" and the man who had abundance of them was called "kundir bonggan" (pebbles many) and was a doctor of the lower degree. The "manngur" was a step in advance. He had been a party to a barter with "dhakkan" the rainbow and the latter had given him much rope for a number of pebbles which he had taken from the man in exchange. This transaction would take place while the black was in a deep sleep. He would be lying on the brink of a water-hole—the rainbow's abode. The rainbow would drag him under, effect the exchange, and deposit the man, now a "manngur manngur" on the bank again.[49]

A peculiarly Australian form of death anxiety is evidently based on the body destruction phantasy.

> The fat-taking practice of the Wurunjerri Wirrarap or medicine man has been fully described to me (Howitt). It was called Burring and was carried out by means of an instrument made of the sinews of a kangaroo's tail and the fibula of its leg which had the same name. Armed with this the medicine man would sneak up to the camp during a man's first sleep. . . . If the time was propitious, the cord was passed lightly round the sleeper's neck and the bone being threaded through the loop was pulled tight. Another Burring was then passed round his feet and the victim carried off into the bush, where he was cut open and the fat extracted. The opening was

[48] Cf. The Riddle of the Sphinx, 65. Cf. the initiation dream of Urantukutu, ibid., 78, where a child (the dreamer) is eaten and vomited by the initiating demon.

[49] J. Mathew, Eaglehawk and Crow, 1899, 143. The stones are both "good" and "bad" introjects. Cf. J. Mathew, Two Representative Tribes of Queensland, 1910, 172. For another case of exchange, (Binbinga) see above.

*magically closed up, and the victim left to come to himself with
the belief that he had had a bad dream. If the fat thus extracted was
heated over a fire, the man died in a day or two, but otherwise he
would linger for some time.*[50]

We can now attempt to show how the profession of primitive medicine man, this nucleus of all primitive societies, originates. It is evolved
on the basis of the infantile body destruction phantasies, by means of a
series of defense mechanisms. The first formula is abreaction in phantasy
(my inside has already been destroyed) followed by reaction formation
(my inside is not something corruptible and full of feces, but incorrupti-
ble, full of quartz crystals). The second is projection: "It is not I who
am trying to penetrate into the body but foreign sorcerers who shoot
disease substances (penis, feces, child symbols) into people." The third
formula is restitution "I am not trying to destroy people's insides, I am
healing them." At the same time however the original phantasy element
of the valuable body contents torn out of the mother returns in the
healing technique; to suck, to pull, to rub something out of the patient.
The phantasy element of "good" body contents or internalized objects is
also evolved on basis of the restitution tendency. Being shot by shells
means being initiated into the Ojibwa "Mide" society and the shells
symbolize life.[51] The object which the child is trying to tear out of the
mothers body may be the other child who has entered by means of the
father's penis, and the foreign sorcerer or spirit may represent the father
in the primal scene. By healing the patient the medicine man annuls
parental coitus while by "shooting" the patient he identifies himself with
the father in the primal scene. He can do this because he has internalized the parents as "good objects." Pukuti-wara's magic power is based
on three "good objects" in his body. The magic bone, the stone, and the
snake and they can all be used either for killing or healing purposes.
Pukuti-wara called the snake in his body the "mother of the nankara-
stones." Among the Pindupi the snake in the medicine man's body is
both "father and mother" of the medicine man.[52]

Now we may ask: what is the difference between a medicine man and
other individuals in the same society? A hunter lives like a beast of prey,
by his strength and skill in killing animals—but a medicine man lives by
his infantile complexes. The first "profession" is evolved on the basis of

[50] A. W. Howitt, *The Native Tribes of South East Australia*, 1904, 375. *Cf.*
for further data on these phantasies and practices G. Róheim, "Das Selbst,"
Imago, VII, 20. G. Róheim, "The Pointing Bone," *Journ. Roy. Anthr. Inst.*,
LV, 1925.
[51] W. J. Hoffman, *The Midewiwin of the Ojibwa* (Bureau of American
Ethnology, VII,) 1891, 168, 170, 212. *Cf.* P. Radin, "The Winnebago Medicine Dance," *Journ. of Am. F. L.*, 1911, 149-209.
[52] G. Róheim, *The Riddle of the Sphinx*, 1934, 64.

the infantile situation. I assume that, for instance, all the members of the Pitchentara tribe have evolved this system of body destruction phantasies and anxieties. Some of them are more infantile than others, i.e., the libido charge of these phantasy systems is larger than with others. If these individuals manage to find substitutes for the mother's body not in their own body, but in others, they will become medicine men. They are now playing their infantile game based on the system of body-destruction phantasies with others who have the same phantasies only not in the same degree. They are the leaders in this game and the lightning conductors of common anxiety. They fight the demons so that others can hunt the prey and in general fight reality.[53] We can now take leave of our friend the medicine man with a quotation from Melanie Klein:

> We assume therefore that the reaction formations of order, disgust, and cleanliness must originate in anxieties based on the earliest danger situations. When . . . object relations set in, the reaction formation of sympathy becomes stronger. The happiness . . . of the object becomes a proof of one's own security, a protection against destruction from within and without. The integrity of one's own body now depends on the restoration of the object.[54]

Discussion

Anthropologists will, of course, quarrel with much of Róheim's formulation of the role and function of the shaman. Many would question whether his characterization could be similarly applied to the great variety of medico-religious practitioners to be found in the many different primitive societies, who have been more or less conveniently lumped together under the Siberian title, *shaman*. But such questions are peripheral to our present concern. What does concern us here is the way in which a complex of enduring conscious and unconscious forces is channelized, crystallized, and give integrated psychosocial expression in the persistent performance of a specialized occupational role.

A corollary of Róheim's formulation of the shaman as the "first profession"—a judgment confirmed by archaeological studies—is that this is the *only* differentiated full-time profession in societies at

[53] I have repeatedly discussed the problem of the medicine man. Cf. Róheim, A varázserö fogalmának eredete, 1914, 40-68. Idem, "Nach dem Tode des Urvaters," Imago, IX, 1923, 83. Idem, The Riddle of the Sphinx, 1934, 57. Idem, "The Evolution of Culture," Int. Journ. of Psa., XV.

[54] M. Klein, Die Psychoanalyse des Kindes, 1932, 175.

the simplest technological levels (such as the aborigines of Siberia or Australia described) and secondly that there is nothing quite like it in technologically advanced societies. If we look in the modern world for professions that parallel in function that of the primitive shaman, we find there is no single profession that combines together all of the kinds of things the shaman does for the members of his tribe. What the division of labor has done, among other things, is to effect a radical separation of dealing with the supernatural and dealing with the natural world; a separation of religion from science; and a separation of religion from curing, even, to a great extent, in the world of scientific ascendancy, of religion from the curing of souls. Perhaps the nearest analogue to the shaman today is the psychoanalyst (the terms "witch-doctor" and "head-shrinker" clearly reflect this), or perhaps better still, pastoral psychiatry. However, the differences are significant. The psychoanalyst, even where medically trained initially, basically renounces any attempt to deal with what are still regarded as the illnesses of the body, referring these to various somatic specialists on disorders of the soma, thus denying the unity of the person which he may rhetorically aver. Individual psychoanalysis also still works basically with the individual in a kind of vacuum, i.e., in separation from the collective involvements of even the "patient" let alone the community around him.[55] The psychoanalyst or psychotherapist works with individuals or small groups at best, and however prestigious he may be in the eyes of some portions of the modern population, he scarcely enjoys the kind of collective validation so central to the shaman's practice. Whatever marvels of "cure" he may in fact produce, he does not serve as a focus for the kind of "collective catharsis" that a shaman, in his best performances, can effect.

[55] I am aware that this is an extreme characterization, and that consideration of the whole spectrum of different kinds of psycho- and socio-therapies now going on, including the multiple variants of "group therapy," would require considerable modification of these statements. Still in all of these variations there is nothing like the collective involvement of the whole community in the shaman's work, nor even anything approaching the kind of collective community validation of the shaman to be found in primitive tribes.

5. THE COMIC

For a modern parallel to the "collective catharsis" produced by the performances of the shaman in a primitive tribe, we must look in directions other than that of the psychoanalyst. The direction in which we must seek is indicated by the word "performance," which immediately suggests the charisma of an evangelical religious leader, or of a political virtuoso, or of a performer in the entertainment world. It is to a special example of the last of these that we now turn. Not all entertainers, in fact very few, are likely to have anything like the impact on their audiences that a really virtuoso shaman can have. When one such does appear, the excitement generated is likely to be intense—and to include extremely strong and irrational negative responses as well as a special kind of adulation that takes the "entertainment" out of the common run and marks it off as having touched some extremely sensitive points of common but otherwise not formally recognized experience. Such is the case of the late comic Lenny Bruce who died in 1966 at the age of not quite forty, under circumstances suggesting that his death was the consequence of intolerable burdens intimately tied to the kind of "far-out" genius that made him for a brief period a kind of shaman for modern American urbanities. This analogy is explored in the following paper by Albert Goldman, written a few years before Bruce's death.

The Comedy of Lenny Bruce

ALBERT GOLDMAN

> *Since the* Shaman *functions as a safety valve, and as a regulator of the psychic life of the clan, he lives under the permanent feeling of bearing a great responsibility. . . . Sometimes, if he loses control of the spirits, he must be killed.*
>
> —S. M. SHIROKOGOROFF

Several months ago in Chicago, the comedian Lenny Bruce was convicted of obscenity and sentenced to one year in jail and a $1,000 fine. Shortly afterward, he was also convicted by a Los Angeles court of narcotics possession. These convictions, currently being appealed, are by no means the only run-ins Bruce has had with the authorities. Since return-

Reprinted, with permission, from Albert Goldman, "The Comedy of Lenny Bruce," Commentary, October 1963, pp. 312-17. Copyright 1963 by the American Jewish Committee.

ing from his world tour last year, Bruce has been arrested seven times in all: twice in Los Angeles on suspicion of narcotics possession; four times for obscenity (he was acquitted in San Francisco and Philadelphia); and once for assault in Van Nuys, California. Earlier, he had been twice barred from entering England; on the first occasion, he was turned back within an hour at the airport, when authorities simply denied him a work permit. The second time, entering England via Ireland, and bearing with him affidavits attesting to his probity, sobriety, and general moral earnestness, Bruce was allowed to stay the night, only to become on the following day the subject of emergency intervention by the Home Secretary, who declared his presence not to be "in the public interest." On these occasions, as in previous encounters with the agencies of law enforcement, Bruce showed himself courteous, even disarmingly so, to his antagonists and a trifle bewildered, it seemed, at the havoc he could create merely by turning up. He boarded a plane and went back home.

Bruce has been called "blasphemous," "obscene," and "sick"—and not only in the expected quarters (Walter Winchell, Robert Ruark, assorted Variety pundits, etc.) but by critics like Benjamin DeMott and Kenneth Alcott. On the other hand, of course, there are equally sophisticated critics like Robert Brustein and Kenneth Tynan who have arrived at opposite conclusions, finding Bruce not only essentially "healthy," but the physician, as it were, for the illness from which all of us are suffering. While certain spokesmen for an American "underground" have claimed him for their own, Bruce has also earned a vast popular following, far exceeding the limits of any coterie. Long before his present notoriety, indeed, he was one of the most successful nightclub performers in the country, earning on the average of $5,000 a week and with his record-album sales totaling well over 100,000. Fellow comics are among Bruce's keenest admirers, and, if not always admitting their debt to him publicly, frequently reveal it by imitation. Among his most articulate disciples are the British social satirists of groups like "The Establishment" and "Beyond the Fringe," who have been more unstinting than the Americans in acknowledging both his fascination and his influence.

What, then, explains Bruce's unique effect? Certainly, his impact cannot be attributed to his material alone. By now, so completely have the so-called "sick" comics caught on—and so quickly has the authentic radical satire of a few years ago been rendered innocuous by sheer acceptance and then imitation—that it no longer requires daring, originality, or courage to attack sacred cows like integration, Mother's Day, the Flag. Such things are done, albeit in diluted form, virtually on every network. Yet Bruce seems immune from that permissiveness that is in the end perhaps more subversive of true protest than censorship. Uniquely among members of his profession (and matched in others perhaps only among jazz musicians), Bruce continues to shock, to infuriate,

to be the subject on the one hand of a passionate and almost unprecedented advocacy, and on the other of a constant surveillance amounting
to persecution, so that today, at the height of his drawing power, it is
doubtful whether a club in New York would dare to book him.

Bruce slouches on stage in a crumpled black raincoat ("dressed for the
bust," as he confidingly informs the audience, in anticipation of arrest),
pale, unshaven, with long black sideburns—beat, raffish, satanic. Ordering the lights up, he surveys the house: "Yeah. You're good-looking.
You got lotsa bread." He pauses. "Good-looking chicks always got lotsa
bread. That's a hooker syllogism." Having opened on this amiable note,
he abruptly switches his tone and manner to lull the audience into temporary security, then launches into an apparently off-the-cuff discourse
on themes of the moment:

> You know? Liberals will buy anything a bigot writes. They really
> support it. George Lincoln Rockwell's probably just a very knowl-
> edgeable businessman with no political convictions whatsoever. He
> gets three bucks a head working mass rallies of nothing but angry
> Jews, shaking their fists and wondering why there are so many Jews
> there.

Even in this relatively minor bit, the distinctive qualities of Bruce's
satire are in evidence—it is authentically shocking and nihilistic to a
degree that is not altogether apparent at first. To make fun of liberals
these days is an act of conventional daring; to make fun of George Lincoln Rockwell these days is an act of slightly less conventional daring;
but to make fun of a "proper" moral response to George Lincoln Rockwell constitutes the violation of a taboo. What Bruce is doing by finding
in George Lincoln Rockwell an ordinary businessman out for the main
chance, goes far beyond the modish cliché of "the guilt we all share"—it
amounts to an implication of normality itself in the monstrous. Perhaps
this accounts for the slightly hysterical quality of the laughter that his
performances usually elicit. It is helplessness in the face of a truly nihilistic fury that makes the parody currently fashionable in the nightclubs
and the off-Broadway theaters seem safe and cautious.

Bruce's vision forbids the smallest hint of self-congratulation, allows
no comfortable perch from which the audience can look complacently
down on the thing satirized. Even his "conventional" routines take a
bizarre and violent course which transforms them into something quite
different from mere parody. There is one, for instance, in which an "ordinary white American" tries to put a Negro he has met at a party at
ease. The predictable blunders with their underlying viciousness ("That
Joe Louis was a hell of a fighter. . . . Did you eat yet? I'll see if there's
any watermelon left. . . .") are within the range of any gifted satirist
with his heart in the right place; but Bruce gives the screw an added turn

by making the protagonist, besotted with temporary virtue, a forthright and entirely ingenuous Jew-hater as well—sincerely making common cause with the Negro. This is closer to surrealism than to simple farce, a fantasy on the subject of bigotry far more startling than a merely perfect sociological rendition of the accents of race hatred would have been. And as the routine proceeds, the fantasy gets wilder and wilder, with the white man becoming more and more insinuatingly confidential in his friendliness ("What is it with you guys? Why do you always want to ————everybody's sister? . . . You really got a big————on you, huh? Hey, could I see it?") and the Negro becoming progressively stiffer and more bewildered.

Similarly, Bruce has a fairly conventional routine that might have been dreamed up in its general outline fifteen years ago by a stand-up comedian, from the lower East Side, but that he pushes to what would have been unthinkable lengths fifteen years ago. The performer, in the guise of himself, encounters a "typical" Jewish couple while on a Midwestern tour; they are at first shy and admiring, until the inevitable question is asked and the discovery is made—Bruce is Jewish; then their respect and timidity give way first to a slightly insulting familiarity and finally to overt, violent aggression. The routine which, again, would once have been played for folksiness, becomes bizarre and disturbing when Bruce uses it to expose within the couple depths of prurient malevolence far in excess of their apparent "human" failings. The climax is an orgy of vituperation in the familial mode that becomes a glaring and devastating comment on Jewish life in America.

Until a few years ago, this kind of humor had never been seen in a nightclub or theater. It appeared to be completely original, yet obviously it mined a rich, seemingly inexhaustible vein and was, moreover, enforced by a highly finished technique. Critics responded to Bruce at first as though he were *sui generis*, a self-created eccentric of genius without discernible origins. Yet nothing could be further from the truth. What Lenny Bruce is doing today in public had been done for years in private, not only by him, but by dozens of amateurs all over New York City—at private parties, on street corners, in candy stores. His originality consists in his having been the first to use this private urban language in public, and his genius lies in his ability to express the ethos out of which he comes in unadulterated form.

He is, in other words, a genuine folk artist who stands in a relation to the lower-middle-class adolescent Jewish life of New York not unlike that of Charlie Parker to the Negroes of Harlem. And like Parker, he derives his strength from having totally available to himself—and then being able to articulate—attitudes, ideas, images, fragments of experience so endemic to a culture that they scarcely ever come to conscious awareness. Thus for many people the shock of watching Bruce perform is primarily the shock of recognition.

Bruce—who grew up in Brooklyn, the son of an "exotic dancer" who now runs a school for strippers and coaches comics—grew up as part of the adolescent "underground" that exists beneath the lower-middle-class gentility of such Brooklyn neighborhoods as Bensonhurst, Borough Park, and Brighton Beach. Adolescent defiance is scarcely unique, but the group of which Bruce was a part acted out its anger not only by rubbing shoulders with the socially outlawed (pushers, prostitutes, loafers, show-business types, Negro jazzmen) but also through staging sessions of ritualistic parody in which they vented their contempt for the life around them. On Saturday nights, for instance, they would get together, and everyone would have his turn "onstage" to review the events of the week —each performer egging himself on to greater heights of exaggeration, outrage, and sheer fantasy in describing things that had happened in the family, in the neighborhood, and in the dark sexual corners of their world. It was in this "home-cooking" school that Bruce learned how to free-associate on his feet, and it was here also that he trained himself in the technique of the "spritz"—the spontaneous satire that gathers momentum and energy as it goes along, spiraling finally into the exhilarating anarchy of total freedom from inhibition.

The psychological mechanism of this kind of comedy is well enough known by now: it is a means of expressing hatred and contempt and still escaping punishment. But the matter is complicated by the fact that the comic's sensitivity to imperfection and ugliness is heightened by a conviction of his own inadequacy, vulgarity, and hypocrisy, leading him to become doubly intolerant of these faults in others. They haunt him; they are demons which he seeks to exorcise by comic confrontation. The psychological source of such satire is, thus, a persistent, ineradicable hatred of the self, and this is particularly striking in the case of Bruce, whose sense of moral outrage is intimately connected with an awareness of his own corruption. ("I can't get worked up about politics. I grew up in New York, and I was hip as a kid that I was corrupt and that the mayor was corrupt. I have no illusions.") If the practitioner of this kind of comedy is in any way morally superior to his audience, it is only because he is *honest*, and willing to face himself, while they, the audience, are blind enough to think *they* are pure.

From Brooklyn, Bruce went into the Navy, was discharged at the end of the war, and after serving a hitch in the Merchant Marine, returned to New York where he submerged himself in the show-business jungle of Times Square. For several years he moved around digging other comics, haunting their hangouts, trying to work out an act of his own. Finally, in 1951, he appeared on the Arthur Godfrey Talent Show and won. Soon he was doing a conventional "single" at the Strand and other burlesque houses, but he loathed "the business" as much as he despised the Brooklyn of his youth, and for many of the same reasons.

The decisive moment for his career came in 1958 while Bruce was working on the West Coast as a screen writer and nightclub emcee. At about this time Mort Sahl, also on the Coast, was becoming famous. ("I was just a product of my time," Sahl has said. "This license was lying around waiting for someone to pick it up.") Nevertheless, the novelty of Sahl's act undoubtedly stimulated Bruce's own breakthrough and there was an audience ready to respond to Bruce's first original creation—a series of satirical bits based on a potent symbol evolved in the early "home-cooking" days—the shingle man.

A type of "con" man prevalent in the 1940s, the shingle man spent much of his time on the road, usually traveling in groups, doing comic routines, smoking marijuana, taking time off now and then to talk gullible slum residents into buying new roofing. Though strictly a small-time operator, the ruthlessly manipulating shingle man came, in Bruce's universe, to represent any and all wielders of power and authority—up to and including the most grandiose. The great world, in short—all political, social, or religious activity—is nothing but a gigantic racket run by shingle men. In a Bruce routine called "Religion, Inc.," for example, organized religion was reduced to a three-way phone conversation between the Pope, Billy Graham, and Oral Roberts making plans in hipster jargon ("Hey, John! What's shaking, Baby?") for a world-wide religious revival complete with giveaway items (a cigarette lighter in the form of a cross and cocktail napkins bearing the imprint, "Another martini for Mother Cabrini").

Similarly, in another routine of this period, Bruce portrays Hitler as the brainstorm of a couple of shrewd theatrical agents, who discover the new "star" while he is painting their office and set him up with costumes (an armband with the four "7s"), music, routines—in short, an act. Lavishly applying the metaphor of the shingle man to every social institution in the book, Bruce embarked upon a career whose underlying intention has remained constant, though his style has gone through many changes; to set up a remorselessly unqualified identification of power and respectability with corruption.

It is a mistake to regard Bruce simply as a social satirist, for he has long since transcended the limitations of that role, just as he has long since gone beyond mere irreverence in his routines. Indeed, for the most apposite metaphor describing what Bruce does, one must turn from show business to the seemingly remote domain of cultural anthropology. Géza Róheim's description of the *shaman*, exorciser of public demons, sharply reveals the true character of Lenny Bruce's present "act." "In every primitive tribe we find the *shaman* in the center of society, and it is easy to show that he is either a neurotic or a psychotic, or at least that his art is based on the same mechanisms as a neurosis or psychosis. The *shaman* makes both visible and public the systems of symbolic fantasy that are present in the psyche of every adult member of society. They are the leaders in an infantile game and the lightning conductors of common anxiety. They fight the demons so that others can hunt the prey and in general fight reality."

Although "sick" humor appears to be a remarkably unfeeling reaction to misery, particularly to physical deformity, it actually is an oblique protest against the enforced repression of those instinctive emotions of revulsion, anxiety, and guilt evoked by deformity. It represents a distorted rebellion against the piety that demands automatic sympathy for literally every form of human limitation. Though neither Mort Sahl nor Bruce can be wholly identified with "sick" comedy, the shock techniques used by both gave them something in common with the outrageous jokes that were spreading through the country during the mid and late 1950s. (With Sahl, also, Bruce shares other things—the technique of the encyclopedic monologue, the courage to deal in forbidden subjects, the use of hipster language, and an obvious identification with the jazz world.) For a time Bruce's act was sprinkled with "sick" jokes, but they never constituted more than a small portion of his verbal arsenal.

Unlike Sahl, however, whose speciality is political satire, Bruce has never had much to say about politics, the abuse is too obvious. There is a further difference: Sahl is primarily a wit and a social commentator; while Bruce's imagination is a more creative one, which has enabled him to produce a remarkable variety of characters, situations, and lines of comic action. The next stage in Bruce's development saw the shingle man superseded by a richer, more personal metaphor—show business itself. Balancing his own profound self-contempt against his loathing for the "business," Bruce created his most complex parable, a routine called "The Palladium." A cocksure little nightclub comic, crude, untalented, but "on the make" for success, is disgusted with working the "toilets" (second-rate clubs) and determines to take a crack at the big-time. Booked into the London Palladium, he is slated to follow "Georgia Gibbs," a performer who knows exactly what the public wants and "puts them away" every time. His vulgar, corny gags fail to get a laugh and he "dies." Desperate to succeed, he begs for another chance, but is swamped in the wake of the singer, who caps her cunningly contrived performance with a lachrymose tribute to "the boys who died over there."

The little comic lacks the wit to change even a single line of his mechanical act, and again he is about to "die" when, confronting disaster, he blindly ad libs a line: "Hey folks, How 'bout this one—screw the Irish!" This puerile bid for attention instantly transforms the somnolent audience into a raging mob who sweep the comic off the stage and wreck the theater.

Clearly, show business for Bruce stands for American society itself— and indeed, in no other country have entertainers come to be more profoundly symbolic of national values than here. The anxiety to please which takes the form of tear-jerking sentimentality and fake humanitarianism in "Georgia Gibbs" is no less ruthlessly dramatized in the portrait of the brash little comedian, whom we can take as a comic degradation of Bruce himself, and whose story is a reflection of Bruce's own development. Not only does he expose the agonies that assault the performer whose very life depends on his success with the audience; he also satirizes one of the most remarkable features of his own present role as *shaman*— the direct, brutal onslaught on the passions and prejudices of his audience that stems from desperation in the face of failure and that sets off an appalling explosion of primitive hatred.

While he lacks the dramatic gifts of Elaine May, Sid Caesar, or Jonathan Winters—with their actors' techniques of mimicry, foreign accents, and sound effects—Bruce is nevertheless at his best in personal narratives put across with just a suggestion of the dramatic. His work, in fact, is intensely personal and provides an obvious outlet for his private rage; nevertheless, there is a part of Bruce that is utterly disinterested. Like any satirist, he knows that the only effective way to attack corruption is to expose and destroy it symbolically; that the more elaborately and vividly this destruction is imagined, the greater will be his own satisfaction, and the more profound the cathartic effect on the audience. Thus, gradually moving from a wholly conventional act through a series of increasingly wild and outspoken routines, Bruce has indeed become the *shaman*: he has taken on himself the role of exorcising the private fears and submerged fantasies of the public by articulating in comic form the rage and nihilistic savagery hidden beneath the lid of social inhibition.

In one of his recent routines Bruce orders the house lights out and then announces: "Now, you know what's going to happen? I'm going to p—— on the audience. The clapping is from those who had it before and enjoyed it." This promise of outrage is not kept, but is followed rather by Bruce's version of how the audience had reacted. "What did he say?" Bruce asks, taking the part of a male patron, "Did he say he gonna 'S' on us?" Now he mimics a woman's voice: "Oh, shut up, Harry! He does it real cute."

This routine vividly illustrates Bruce's attitude toward his audience; he regards it as an object of sadistic lust, he hates and loves it; it is the enticing enemy, and he attacks it repeatedly. In the past his aggression was masked, but now it is naked. He may pick up a chair and menace a patron; if the audience laughs, he will observe soberly that he might have killed the man and that if he had, everyone would have accepted the murder as part of the act. Here he demonstrates, almost in the manner of a classroom exercise, the repressed violence of modern society. By making the audience *laugh* at incipient murder, he has tricked them into exposing their own savage instincts. The implication is that given the slightest excuse for condoning a killing, even the absurd rationale of its being part of a nightclub act, society would join eagerly in the violence it so conscientiously deplores.

This public display of the ugly, the twisted, the perverse—offensive though it is at times—nevertheless, serves a vital function, for it gives the audience a profound sense, not only of release, but of self-acceptance. Again and again, Bruce violates social taboos—and he does not die! Like the witch doctor or the analyst, he brings the unconscious to light, and thereby lightens the burden of shame and guilt. By its very nature his material cannot come out clear, decorous, and beautifully detached; it must be, and is, charged with self-pity, self-hatred, fear, horror, crudity, grotesquerie.

What is unsatisfactory in Bruce's work is his frequent failure to transmute his rage into real comedy. Sometimes he has nothing more to offer than an attitude. ("Everything is rotten. Mother is rotten. The flag is rotten. God is rotten.") At other times, what starts with a promise of rounded development will flatten out into a direct and insulting statement. A sophisticated listener forgives the comic these lapses, understanding that the ad-lib approach and the often intractable material are apt to betray the performer into mere obscenity; but people with no natural sympathy for this approach are shocked and offended—there has never been a lack of people in the audience to walk out during Bruce's act.

The reason for these occasional lapses into crudity is the almost total lack of "art" in Bruce's present act; he deliberately destroys the aesthetic distance which is a convention of the theater, established by tacit agreement between audience and performer that what is happening on the stage is an illusion of life, rather than life itself. Like other performers who deal in direct communication, Bruce has always tried to *reduce* the barrier between the stage and reality. He has never wanted to appear as an entertainer doing an act, but rather as himself, no different on stage from off, not really a performer, but a man who performs in order to share with others his most secret thoughts and imaginings. The desire, however, to eradicate the distinction between art and reality has at this stage almost completely destroyed the artistry with which Bruce formerly presented his material. Gone, now, are the metaphors of the shingle man and the show-business manipulators; gone, too, are the story-telling devices of the personal narrative and the dramatic impersonations. All that remains are sketchy, often underdeveloped, sometimes incoherent, scraps of former routines.

The new material consists of deep, psychologically primitive fantasies, hurled at a defenseless audience without the mitigating intervention of art. Frequently, Bruce assaults his listeners with scatological outbursts consisting of the crudest and most obvious anal and oral sadistic fantasies, undisguised. There is currently a comic picture book in circulation (*Stamp Help Out*) with a photograph of Bruce on the cover, stripped to the waist like a heroic frontiersman, engaged in shattering a toilet bowl with an axe—Bruce's comment on the surgically white "powder room" of our culture.

Much of his current material is in fact unquotable—not so much because of the language but because its comic effect depends on nonverbal associations and is thereby scarcely intelligible in the reading. In one bit, for instance, he tells how, when the Avon representative called at his house, he drugged her, stripped her, decked her out with galoshes and moustache, raped her, and then wrote on her belly, "You were balled."

In another long and complicated routine, which changes from one performance to another, he explains that the Lone Ranger's bullets are really pellets of Ehrlich's 606 ("That's why he keeps his mouth tightly shut") and that the Lone Ranger is a homosexual ("Bring Tonto here. I wish to commit an unnatural act. Wait a minute. Bring the horse too!") (This deliberate perpetration of outrage on the persons of the most innocuous figures of American folklore—the Lone Ranger, the Avon representative—is, of course, one of the leitmotifs of the recent "sick" humor. The same thing was once done in a grimier way in those pornographic comic books that showed the heroes of the comic strip—familiar to every American child—in complicated sexual situations.)

As his material has become more direct, Bruce has tended more and more to *be* the act. Because the imaginative impulse is naked, unsublimated, Bruce's intention is less and less communicated by what he says, and depends now, to a great extent, on affective devices—his manner, his tone, especially his physical appearance. Whereas in the past Bruce would walk briskly out on the floor, good-looking, impeccably groomed, wearing a chic Italian suit, now he comes on stiff-legged and stooped, wearing shabby clothes, his face a pale mask of dissipation. Having discarded the civilized mask that people wear in public to protect themselves, Bruce comes before his audience as a mythic figure—beat, accused junkie, "underground" man—who has suffered in acting out their own forbidden desires. Where they are cautious, he is self-destructive, alternately terrifying the audience (the very fact that *he doesn't care* is awesome) and arousing their sympathy and concern. (He now regularly opens his act by enacting and commenting on his recent arrests.) Merely looking at Bruce these days is a disturbing experience.

Finally, Bruce is dramatizing his role as shaman by embellishing his act for the first time with consciously contrived bits of hocus-pocus. He turns the lights on and off, strikes drums and cymbals, swings into crude chants. He prowls about the stage, sometimes exposing himself to the audience, at other times crouching in the darkness and hiding from it. He opens and closes doors and climbs onto furniture to symbolize his power over the bewildered spectators.

In the darkened, cavelike club, charged with tension, the audience sits hunched over, tense, breathless, their eyes fastened on the weird figure in the center of the magic circle. While the tribe looks on with fearful absorption, the medicine man puts himself into a trance in preparation for the terrible struggle with the tribal demons (anxieties). And then—when the performance is over and the "unspeakable" has been shouted forth—there is mingled with the thunderous applause a sigh of release. Purged of their demons by the *shaman*, the tribe has been freed, for the moment, to "hunt the prey and in general fight reality."

6. PLAY

> *. . . to be allowed . . . to live symbolically, spells true freedom.*
> —THOMAS MANN: *Confessions of Felix Krull*

Man is the most social of animals—out of desperate need and exuberant play. As they grow up, other mammals unlearn to play—man never does. In this, he is ever an infantilized ape—and one capable of a maturity of such richness, depth, and complexity as no other mammals can attain. Play, even in its most complex and esoteric manifestations—the brilliant leaps of the scientist reconstructing the universe, the soaring poetry of the creative artist, the fabulous beguilements of the master confidence man—draws ever from and ever renews the great and inexhaustible forces of the unconscious, linking man to his evolutionary past, projecting him into a future ever-changing yet ever the same, and also lifting him beneficently out of the stream of time altogether into the joy of an unbounded *now* of total absorption. Play is as polymorphous as the infantile sexuality at its root. In its widest sense, play can be found anywhere: A sober businessman plays the market. A tout dopes his racing form. Astronauts prance and prank in outer space. A party comic mimics the great. TV hucksters sport with magic tornadoes, witches, and doves. A wily jurist ingeniously stretches the elasticity of a silly law. A professional comic livens racial struggle with wit. Gallows humor emerges even from the horrors of the concentration camp. A scientist schemes to "bug" the latest marvel of electronic brain. A paleontologist perpetrates a fantastically elaborate hoax. A writer grinds out sex-and-sadism thrillers for fun and money and gloats as scholarly pundits plumb his nonexistent symbolic depths. A factory crew races to meet its quota in an hour or two, to conspicuously loaf the rest of the day, and mock the planning brains above. Teen-age boys play ball for forty hours at a stretch to prove it can be done. A meek accountant builds a replica Mayan temple in his backyard. An office staff is busy laying bets on the boss's amorous intrigues.

Play can be found in, and thus confound, all of its supposed antitheses. It isn't work? But work can be the highest play, for the scientists we have seen through Roe, the artists through Schneider, the shaman through Róheim, the comic through Lenny Bruce, and any man who loves the tasks that bring his daily bread. Play is not serious? But who is more seriously devoted than the chess wizard at his game, the expert golfer on the green, the vacationing mathematician with his system at the Vegas wheel? Play doesn't matter? Tell it to the Harlem domestic who plays a number every day and dreams of that duplex in the Bronx—but don't then also try to tell her she has no fun from the daily game! Tell it also to Géza Róheim who finds in every major cultural invention of man an artifact of play. To Watt who "reinvented" an ancient Greek toy. Or to any inventor who has ever tinkered in a cluttered shed.

Play eludes any one definition that will satisfy all the thinkers who have tried to plumb its nature and significance. Freud sees play as those activities devoted to satisfaction of the pleasure principle rather than devotion to utility or the reality principle. He also finds in children's play (among other things) the conversion of passive experiences (even unpleasant ones) into active ones in play—as in the case of the child who has been forcibly examined by the doctor afterward playing at being the doctor himself for little brother or sister, as defenseless against him as he was against the physician.[56]

Elsewhere Freud deals at many points with *children's* play, seeing it, for example, as the prototype for adult daydreaming and similarly of the poet's or novelist's imaginative creations.[57] However, he does not deal with adult play generally (in fact he does not define the activity of the poet or novelist as play, and tends to take the surprising view that adults do not play at all, at least not in the sense that children do).

G. H. Mead sees in children's play the means by which the child develops a sense of the self, through the make-believe of taking the role of the other. Piaget finds children's games provide clues to the development of notions of morality in the child.

[56] Sigmund Freud, *Collected Papers* (London: The Hogarth Press, 1952—originally 1931), Vol. V, "Female Sexuality," p. 264.
[57] *Ibid.*, Vol. IV, "The Poet and Daydreaming," pp. 173-83.

Johan Huizinga sees play as a "voluntary activity or occupation executed within certain fixed limits of time and place according to rules freely accepted and absolutely binding, having its aim in itself, and accompanied by a feeling of tension, joy, and the consciousness of difference from 'ordinary life.' " [58]

Roger Caillois finds Huizinga's definition at once too broad and too limiting.[59] To consider play, he argues, as necessarily excluding any material interest ("having its aim in itself") would exclude from play all games of chance and betting. He also finds in Huizinga's treatment so great an emphasis on competitive games, contest, agon, as to leave out whole areas which are certainly play, such as the pursuit of vertigo by whirling, swinging, sliding, aerial or wheeling acrobatics, and so on, and the activities Caillois calls mimicry—the donning of masks, impersonations, masquerades, and the like.

Huizinga and Caillois do agree about certain characteristics of play: the perfectly voluntary nonobligatory character of the activity —one can stop when one wants, start when one wants; separation from ordinary life, and being fixed within definite limits of time and space, defined and fixed in advance; tension or uncertainty, the course and results are not predetermined. Caillois also qualifies play as *unproductive* (rather than not pursuing material gain) in that it creates neither goods nor wealth, nor new elements of any kind, and except (as in gambling) for the exchange of property among the players, ends in a situation identical to that prevailing at the beginning of the game. He insists on the characteristic of being "governed by rules" i.e., by conventions that suspend ordinary laws (though the play pursuing vertigo does not seem to fit this qualification entirely).

Caillois then classifies play activities into these four types:[60]

> . . . *depending on whether, in the games under consideration, the role of competition, chance, simulation or vertigo is dominant. I call these* agon, alea, mimicry, *and* ilinx *respectively. All four indeed belong to the domain of play. One plays football, billiards, or chess* (agon); *roulette or a lottery* (alea); *pirate, Nero, or Hamlet* (mimicry); *or one produces in oneself, by a rapid whirling or falling movement, a state of dizziness and disorder* (ilinx). . . .

[58] Johan Huizinga, *Homo Ludens: The Play Element in Culture* (Boston: Beacon Press, 1955), p. 28.

[59] Roger Caillois, *Man, Play and Games*, trans. by Meyer Barash (New York: Free Press of Glencoe, 1961).

[60] *Ibid.*, pp. 12-13.

> [*Games*] *can also be placed on a continuum between two oppo-*
> *site poles. At one extreme . . . turbulence, free improvisation,*
> *. . . carefree gaiety . . . designated* paidia. *At the opposite ex-*
> *treme . . . arbitrary, imperative and purposely tedious conven-*
> *tions. . . . I call this component* ludus.

In Caillois' view any particular play activity may combine two or more of the four distinct elements of agon, alea, mimicry, and ilinx in various ways. But certain combinations are much more likely than others, and of the six possible pairs (taking only two at a time, since three or four together are rarer combinations) Caillois finds that two are inherently improbable, two are "contingent," and two are "fundamental." Because of the mutual incompatibility of the two elements, the combination of agon and ilinx is impossible, and so is that of alea and mimicry. Next alea and ilinx may be contingently combined, as in the vertigo induced in "compulsive" gambling; and agon and mimicry are combined in any contest which is also a spectacle. But the fundamental combinations are agon with alea (as in games where skill and chance are equally and complementarily at work), both requiring an absolute equity and thorough subjection to rules, and mimicry with ilinx, the combination producing a "sorcerizing" effect which is at the heart of the sacred.[61] The applicability of this latter combination to shamanism is obvious. However, Caillois does not explicitly consider shamanism a form of play, but rather an institutional complex in which the basic forces of mimicry and ilinx (simulation and frenzy) are powerfully concentrated, so much so as to give a characteristic stamp to a whole type of culture or society. This society is named by Caillois "*société à tohu bohu*," roughly translated by Barash as "Dionysian" essentially in the sense of Nietzsche followed by Benedict. For Caillois, then, the elements agon, alea, mimicry, and ilinx are ways of classifying types of play, but they are not limited to play. They, in fact, are basic components of any kind of cultural force or social structural pattern. Nor do the characteristics which Caillois asserts are definitive of play—freedom, voluntariness, separation, time-space limitation, tension, and uncertainty—even if all insisted on in combination (which may in fact not be true of some play activities), apply exclusively to activities clearly recognized by participants and observers alike as play, for they appear in apparently other activities as well. Consequently, we are back to our recognition of the ambiguity of demarcating play from

61 *Ibid.*, pp. 71-79.

work, play from the serious, in fact also play from "reality," and it may be more adequate to follow Huizinga rather than Caillois in finding "play elements" in practically all areas of culture—law, art, religion, war, politics—and in fact as the creative force in all of these areas.

Psychodynamically, the continuum that Caillois sees as a dimension running through all the four kinds of play, that from *paidia* (turbulence, carefree gaiety) to *ludus* (arbitrary regulation) can be seen as parallel to the distinction between the pleasure principle and the reality principle,[62] or to that between id and ego (though assuredly the correspondences are far from exact). Romping tumult provides free expression of id impulses, always with the potential danger that destructive as well as erotic (body-gratifying) elements will be released, while the self-imposed regulation of *ludus* shows the ego actively constructing its world and directing behavior toward it. *Vertigo* type of play (*ilinx*) involves release from the normal equilibrium of the body, which in its more complex forms, such as trance and ecstasy, give the feeling of contact with or immersion into extraordinary cosmic or supernatural forces, in other words, the great reservoir of the unconscious—significantly above and out of the normal processes of time, as the unconscious is. Its *paidia* forms (Caillois

[62] There are admittedly some difficulties here. Freud saw *all* play as antagonistic to "reality," hence one can deduce that it is all under the influence of pleasure principle only. It is improbable that any human activity could be exclusively under the dominion of either the pleasure principle or the reality principle; but if "reality principle" is interpreted to mean *any* kind of imposed limitations, then it can include the arbitrary self-imposed and voluntarily accepted regulations of *ludus*. Then play activities can be classified according to the degree to which they dominate in combinations of various kinds with a theoretical "pure" *paidia* or activity according to pleasure principle only. It may be asked, Is all of this discussion really anything more than purely verbal translation from the concepts of one system (Caillois') into those of another (Freud's)? The answer is that while Caillois' categories, in an improvement over Huizinga's almost exclusive concentration on agonistic forms of play, do include and clarify the other three elements, and do distinguish the valuable dimension of *paidia-ludus*, they do not come to grips with the basic motivational forces involved, in terms of the intrapsychic structure of human beings. They are reminiscent of the social psychologist W. I. Thomas' classic "four wishes"—security, response, recognition, and new experience—which nicely label certain conscious desires without relating them in any way to personality *structure*. (I am in no way attempting to equate Caillois' four "elements" with Thomas' four wishes; they deal with quite different kinds of problems. I only mean to point out common inadequacies of both classifications for the kind of task undertaken in this book.) My effort here is to show how the infusion of psychoanalytic perspectives deepens the contributions Caillois and Huizinga have made by relating them to a systematically psychodynamic view.

lists children's whirling, swinging, etc.) are almost free id expression. Its more ludic forms, such as skiing and tightrope walking, add the ego gratification of conquest over the usual constraints of gravity and space as well as over the threats of vertigo itself. *Alea* involves a deliberate passive submission of oneself to the inscrutable forces of the universe—fate, luck, destiny—and reflect one kind of attempt of the ego to come to terms with mysterious forces over which it has no "realistic" control. It can also be an exhilarating release from all the regularized and routinized forms of control to which human beings are subject in any society. In this sense it constitutes defiance of the reality principle. *Mimicry* provides another kind of break-out from the constraints of everyday reality, one that is rooted in the process of forming and discovering a self through the taking on of roles. It "plays with" the basic problem of identity by allowing the expression of otherwise restrained or suppressed unconscious potentials in the as-if characters adopted for the moment in the mimicry play. It can be a powerfully creative cultural force, as Caillois recognizes, because it keeps open channels to unconscious forces that may be denied expression in the "everyday life" of the society. *Agon* provides for a channeling of all of the resources, conscious and unconscious, into performances goaded into peaks of skill and virtuosity by the element of contest or competition, the effect the more exhilarating as the results have no obvious "utilitarian" value in reference to the prevailing "realistic" demands of everyday life of the society concerned. These play forms too (like mimicry) may have enormous culture-creating capacity—not in their aims, but rather as it were, as unintended consequences. In all of these there is special pleasure in the tension between freedom and order, where the order itself (as in complex arbitrary rules of the game) partakes of freedom in that the rules are freely accepted as conventions as well as (and therefore) absolutely binding.

The work-play of the shaman is clearly a mimicry-ilinx complex, as is that of a comic like Lenny Bruce. That of the artist also lies in this terrain, to the extent that his work involves the creation of illusions and spectacles that connect with the unconscious of the audience, or produces the controlled vertigo of great poetry or painting that whirls the spectator or auditor out of the world of everyday reality. The artist's relation to the mimicry-ilinx complex is more intricate in that he both creates and breaks through illusions and reveals by his disguises. He skirts the chaos potential of ilinx with exquisite con-

trols. In our kind of culture he may involve himself in agonistic con-
tests with other artists, but these are extrinsic: the great artist is *sui
generis*, in direct relation with his audience without need of competitive elements. The scientist's work-play might be classified as *agon* if
the element of skill and ability rather than that of competition is
emphasized. If we stretch an interpretation, the scientist can be seen
as pitting himself against the antagonist constituted by the great
unknown and in that sense engaging in agonistic encounter. *Alea*
enters into his kind of work-play, in the significant role of "chance"
discoveries (which are really the convergence of a unique concatenation of circumstances with a prepared and disciplined mind). If Caillois is right in defining modern cultures as dominated by the *agon-
alea* complex and suppressing *mimicry-ilinx*, then it should not be
surprising that scientists are among the culture heroes of such societies. In turn, the business executive should be regarded as an even
purer type of the *agon-alea* combination: most distinctively of any
of those we have been discussing, business executives epitomize the
ethos of competitive encounter, tempered and spiced by chance.
Their arena of work-play is intricately bounded by space-time and by
conventional regulations of great complexity, and they are keyed up
and enlivened by challenge and contest.

The following selection extends the sociology and psychodynamics
of play into another area of activity, rather neglected by the insightful analyses of Huizinga and Caillois—that of crime and delinquency.

Play elements in delinquency

In recent years two illuminating essays on play have been published:
Johan Huizinga's *Homo Ludens*[63] and Roger Caillois' *Man, Play and*

This is a revision of two papers, "Play Elements in Delinquency" and "The
Conflict Gang as an Agonistic Institution," presented, respectively, at meetings
of the Eastern Sociological Society and the American Sociological Association
in April and August 1961. It is published here for the first time.

For the record, the original version of this paper was written in 1957. Since
that time, some of the sociological specialists in delinquency have reintroduced
discussion of, or allusion to play aspects, in some form, into the professional
literature in this field. See David J. Bordua, "Delinquent Subcultures: Sociological Interpretations of Gang Delinquency," The Annals of the American
Academy of Political and Social Science, November 1961, 338: pp. 120-36; and
David Matza and Gresham Sykes, "Delinquency and Subterranean Values,"

Games.[64] Huizinga, seeing play primarily as *agon* or contest, finds the play element in many phases of culture: law, language, war, philosophy, art, and poetry, drawing broadly on historical and primitive cultures.[65] He sees play in archaic rituals such as initiation ceremonies still practiced in many primitive societies, in medieval tournaments, in legal forms grown out of ordeals and wagers, and in other agonistic encounters. He portrays the enormous elaboration of such agonistic encounters in classical Greek and in medieval European civilizations.

Caillois finds Huizinga's study too exclusively concerned with agonistic or contest forms of play, and he broadens the discussion to distinguish four different kinds of elements in play: *agon* (contest, competition, much as used by Huizinga); *alea* (chance, luck); *mimicry* (simulation, wearing of masks, disguises, etc.); and *ilinx* (vertigo, voluptuous panic in equilibrium disorder). Caillois applies these categories, and their various combinations, not only to analysis of obviously playful activities such as games, but also (like Huizinga) to characteristics of whole institutional complexes like shamanism.

Our purpose here is to show what light these ideas may shed on the phenomenon of juvenile delinquency in modern societies. Our thesis is simply that various forms and aspects of delinquency are richly infused with one or other of the four kinds of play that Caillois distinguishes, and that viewing delinquent activities thus helps illuminate their psychology and sociology, their relationship both to the psychodynamics of the participants and to the patterns of the culture in which they live.

Thrasher, studying hundreds of gangs in Chicago back in the 1920s, found that they typically developed as *spontaneous play groups* of young boys responding to universal childhood needs. In a

American Sociological Review, Vol. 26, No. 5, October 1961, pp. 712-19, which deals with the quest for excitement, thrills, and "kicks"—clearly play aspects, though not treated as such—as part of a pattern of values operating in a "subterranean" way throughout modern American culture, in opposition to the official values emphasizing work.

The word "reintroduced" is used since Frederick Thrasher's The Gang (Chicago: University of Chicago Press) clearly derived delinquent gang activity from street play back in 1927.

[63] Huizinga, *op. cit.*
[64] Caillois, *op. cit.*
[65] Huizinga, *op. cit.*

street environment offering many attractive and exciting opportunities for fun and adventure, these play groups carry on a great variety
of activities which they choose and direct for themselves. Many of
these activities are illegal, but many are not. The high degree of
autonomy in these activities is predicated on "weak social controls"
from the conventional order—parents, teachers, police.

David Bordua, discussing Thrasher's analysis of the gang, contrasts the perspectives on gang delinquency provided by the more
recent theorists, Albert Cohen, Richard Cloward and Lloyd Ohlin,
and Walter Miller particularly, and summarizes as follows:[66]

> *All in all, though, it does not seem like much fun any more to be a
> gang delinquent. Thrasher's boys enjoyed themselves being chased
> by the police, shooting dice, skipping school, rolling drunks. It was
> fun. Miller's boys do have a little fun, with their excitement focal
> concern, but it seems so desperate somehow. Cohen's boys and
> Cloward and Ohlin's boys are driven by grim economic and psychic
> necessity into rebellion. It seems peculiar that modern analysts have
> stopped assuming that "evil" can be fun, and see gang delinquency
> as arising only when boys are driven away from "good."*

With Bordua we may well wonder whether the reality of delinquency has really changed in the forty years since Thrasher's studies,
or whether it is only the point of view of the theorists, since the
latter do not, as Bordua notes, provide any detailed documentation
at all comparable with Thrasher's. Let us assume for this paper that
the reality has in fact not much changed and pursue Thrasher's observations about play with the more searching categories that Caillois and Huizinga have since provided, as well as with some of the
conceptual distinctions developed by the more recent sociological
theorists of delinquency.

The concept of the delinquent subculture is by now a staple in
sociology. It was most powerfully formulated by Albert Cohen in his
Delinquent Boys where he refers to that segment of delinquency
carried out primarily by male adolescents of lower or working class,
organized in definitely structured gangs, sharing a common pattern
of largely illegal activities and an approach to the world revolving
around and justifying these activities. The delinquent subculture

---

[66] Bordua, *op. cit.*, p. 136. The references by Bordua are to Albert K. Cohen,
Delinquent Boys (New York: Free Press of Glencoe, 1955); Walter Miller,
"Lower Class Culture as a Generating Milieu of Gang Delinquency," *Journal
of Social Issues*, 1958, Vol. 14, pp. 5-19; Richard Cloward and Lloyd Ohlin,
Delinquency and Opportunity (New York: Free Press of Glencoe, 1960).

concept was further differentiated by Richard Cloward and Lloyd Ohlin in *Delinquency and Opportunity* who distinguish within the range of phenomena that Cohen refers to, three distinct subvarieties: criminal, conflict, and retreatist subcultures—essentially, stealing gangs, fighting gangs and drug-using gangs. Though the critical response of specialists to the Cloward-Ohlin differentiation strongly questions whether delinquents in reality are that sharply split into three such distinct varieties, the distinction may still be valuable for heuristic purposes, and we shall so use it here. We propose, then, to analyze the play elements—of each of Caillois' four types—that appear in each of the three delinquent subcultures, or if you will, the three major kinds of delinquent activities.

PLAY IN THE CRIMINAL SUBCULTURE

Activities in what Cloward-Ohlin call the "criminal subculture" include a whole range of pleasurable pastimes many of which bring the youngsters into conflict with the law, even at an early age. These include playing truant from school, staying away from home all night, turning over garbage cans and other acts of petty and sometimes not so petty vandalism, and stealing of various kinds, from swiping fruit from outdoor stands, shoplifting from dime stores, to more distinctly organized and lucrative theft such as stealing hubcaps from cars and (usually at a later age) burglaries from houses. That a lot of this, if not all, is clearly fun (if other things too) can hardly be doubted.

Cohen describes a scene like this:[67]

> *A group of boys enters a store where each takes a hat, a ball, or a light bulb. They then move on to another store where these things are covertly exchanged for like articles. Then they move on to other stores to continue this game indefinitely.*

Cohen in this passage clearly recognizes the activity as play, but he then moves on to other aspects, since he has other axes to grind. One of these axes, however, does concern us: i.e., that a lot, if not all, of such juvenile stealing is essentially *nonutilitarian*. It does not serve specific material needs. As the particular example clearly indicates, the boys are not stealing for the material rewards they can get from these goods, but rather for the fun of the activity itself.[68] Steal-

[67] Cohen, *op. cit.*, p. 26.

[68] There has been a good deal of challenge to this view of Cohen's in the subsequent delinquency literature, the critics arguing that in fact a lot of the stealing is precisely for the material rewards, even to satisfy basic needs such as

ing for the fun of the activity itself clearly qualifies for Huizinga's characterization of play as a "voluntary activity . . . having its aim in itself" or for Caillois' characterization of play as "Free . . . the playing is not obligatory . . . [and] unproductive: creating neither goods nor wealth. . . ."

Let us take another example. Consider the self-history of Sidney, given in Clifford Shaw's *The Natural History of a Delinquent Career.*[69]

Sidney tells how he first started stealing, at the age of seven:[70]

> *I became acquainted with a boy named Joseph . . . who lived a few doors from where I lived. He was about four years older than I was and knew a lot. He knew so much about life and I liked him, so I made him my idol.* [Joseph showed him how to steal fruit from sidewalk stands.] *. . . Never a thought occurred to me as to whether it was right or wrong, it was* merely an interesting game. *The apple or the orange didn't make as much difference as the getting of them. It was the taking them that I enjoyed. . . . I found as much fun and enjoyment in grabbing a potato or an onion as to grab anything else.*
>
> [*The proprietor soon caught on and started watching the boys closely.*] *This only made the game more interesting, and it began to require real skill to get away with anything. Often after this he would chase us for a block or two in order to teach us a lesson, but he never did. This is when it started to get real good, and you couldn't keep us away after that. The chases added spice to our little game. . . . I never stole when I was by myself. The kick came when there was some one with me and the fun could be mutual. It was a* merry exciting pastime *that interested me to the exclusion of all others. . . .*
>
> [*Later, venturing to the Loop*] *Joseph taught me to shoplift, and* most the things we stole were useless. . . . *The store detectives*

hunger, where the food stolen provides a crucial part of the diet of the kids, or where stolen objects are systematically sold to fences known to the young thieves and by regular arrangements. Some of the critics even stretch the term "utilitarian" to include satisfaction of *any* kind of needs of the thief, but this kind of verbal magic simply makes the word synonymous with "functional," allowing one to argue then that all activities are "utilitarian" in some way. Cohen's point, however, that in many cases the stealing activity is satisfying in and for itself, is still valid and important. It applies not only to the nonmercenary stealing, such as his example shows, but can also be true in cases where the stolen objects have an *additional* material value.

[69] Clifford Shaw, *The Natural History of a Delinquent Career* (Chicago: University of Chicago Press, 1931).

[70] *Ibid.*, pp. 57-59, 66, 68, 70. Italics added. (These and later quotations reprinted with permission of the University of Chicago Press.)

started following us, but we didn't even worry about them. It seemed we always saw them first, and it was a simple matter to dodge through the store and lose them. . . . [If caught by a store detective, he learned to cry his way out of it. Once, however, he was arrested, and spent the evening in jail, but he did not reform.]

I had been in jail and I was now a jailbird. I wished I knew of some other things to do that was as interesting to do, so that I couldn't be arrested any more; but I didn't know of anything else to do. I grew more wary and kept a keen watch for the house detectives and made more of an effort to get away from them when about to be apprehended.

[*Still later, with another gang of boys, older than himself:*] *We would all go into a store and while one of us would ask for some article that we knew wasn't kept in stock, the rest of us would scatter and see what we could steal.* [Editor Shaw's footnote here: "Although it is clearly a form of stealing, the boys in certain neighborhoods commonly regard it as a game or sport."]

The numerous references to "game," "fun," and "interesting pastime," in these passages are clear enough indications of play and of the fact that the delinquent child himself saw them as such. The *kind* of play is indicated by the fact that once merchants or peddlers or store detectives started to go after the boys, the "game" became all the more exciting and interesting. Here is *agon*, a contest encounter: the boys pitting their wile and guile and lithe young bodies against the enemy, or more properly the antagonist, that is, someone who opposes your efforts but against whom you feel no hate, for he is a necessary part of the game. True, strictly in agon, the contest should be according to fixed rules and arbitrary conventions freely decided on and/or accepted by the participants in advance, and the arena and time of action would be clearly demarcated from ordinary life. In a sense, though, these encounters with merchants or detectives *are* rule-bound, for the merchants and detectives have been cast willy-nilly into their pursuer roles, in which they follow the conventions of protectors of private property, but also, implicitly, the conventions of the "cops and robbers" game the youngsters have drawn them into. The pursuit does nothing at all to deter the children from repeating their crimes. Far from it, it encourages them to repeat the game by adding that much more relish to it. The tension and uncertainty are exhilarating. This too is crucial to *agon*: it intensifies the development of skill, here not only in stealing itself, but in escaping getting caught.

There is another kind of *agon* in the activities of youthful criminals, and that is contest among themselves. They challenge each other to see who can get the biggest hauls from their thieveries, who can carry off the most daring provocation of the authorities.

Alea appears among such youngsters to the extent that they participate in gambling among themselves, but in that aspect it is not nearly as important a part of the criminal subculture as is *agon*. In a more general sense, it is a part of the delinquent's perspective on the world: by the time he is in his teens, any aware youngster in the lower-class environment recognizes that luck—for example, the chance fact of having been born rich or poor—plays an enormous part in what happens to one in life. So does luck play an important part in the outcome of the criminalistic *agon* encounters. (All of this is in accord, as Walter Miller has pointed out,[71] with general features of lower-class culture, in which "fate" is one of the "focal concerns" —a sense of man as the pawn of mysterious or magical powers: if the cards or dice come up right, or your lucky number comes up, things will go your way; if luck is against you, it's not worth trying.) *Alea* is thus a subsidiary concomitant of *agon*. Their combination Caillois regards as the essential underlying ethos of advanced societies (*sociétés à comptabilité*)[72] in contrast to societies whose cultures are dominated by simulation and vertigo (*mimicry* and *ilinx*) such as those primitive cultures where shamanism is prevalent. What is interesting about the way in which *agon* and *alea* appear in the delinquent (and adult criminal) subcultures is that they are in many ways only outcast versions of the *agon* and *alea* of the respectable world, where we also find efforts to compensate for the inequity with which the contest must be waged by stretching the rules in such forms as "white-collar crime"[73] cheating on examinations and income tax, and more importantly, the emergence of new forms of *agon* with their own special conventions in the form of various "arrangements" between representatives of the law and denizens of the criminal world. In the younger delinquents there is a more spontaneously (less rule-bound and less cynical) playful approach to *agon* and less emphasis on organized recourse to *alea* in such forms as gambling. In a sense this reflects a more hopeful or optimistic, less

[71] Miller, *op. cit.*

[72] Caillois, *op. cit.*, Chapter VIII. Barash translates this term "rational societies," using rational in the Weberian sense.

[73] See Edwin Sutherland: *White Collar Crime* (Chicago: University of Chicago Press).

fate-ridden view of the world than they are likely to have as they get older and know their way around better.

Mimicry—simulation, let's pretend, the donning of masks, and disguises—Caillois regards as less intimately combinable with *agon* than is *alea*, nevertheless, one that can be so combined. We find it so in the delinquent criminal subculture in such actions as Sidney's impersonation of a ruefully weeping child to elicit sympathy from store detectives or police—an impersonation that is particularly ironic in that the child is so perfectly "type-cast" for the part, hence so plausible, while so patently disguising the wily scheming thief that is his active self. Another instance of ingenious mimicry in juvenile crime is provided by still another account:[74]

> *Recently two children, a girl of twelve and a boy of nine, went around ringing doorbells in several apartment buildings on the East Side [of Manhattan]. They were dressed in Scout uniforms and said they were selling Scout cookies. Many people let them in, and while the girl was taking orders, the boy would ask for a drink of water, or a sharp pencil, or permission to use the telephone, and then a telephone directory—anything to get the cookie buyer out of sight— and while the victim was in the next room, the two of them would grab a wallet or whatever else was lying around. "They were only children," an adult victim said when they were caught. Nine and twelve is a little young (though a gang of child burglars in London is known to have included an infant of two), but burglary, like robbery and auto theft, is a crime of youth. . . ."*

A more general aspect of mimicry in juvenile crime is the fact that for some adolescents a "fling" at delinquency may be a phase of the searching for an identity so poignantly prevalent among adolescents in modern societies.[75] Here the boy is "trying on a part" and more or less convincingly wearing a mask which he half asks to be taken seriously.

When we turn to ilinx or vertigo, we find there is a great deal of this play element in juvenile delinquency of the "criminal" variety. Turn again to Sidney, of Shaw's account: he is describing his first visit to the Loop (downtown Chicago), to which he was taken by his friend Joseph. The boys stole the money from a neighborhood store to pay their El train fare. Sidney describes his feelings:[76]

[74] Susan Black, "Reporter at Large: Burglary One," *The New Yorker*, Dec. 7, 1963, p. 92.

[75] *Cf.* Erik H. Erikson, "The Problem of Ego Identity," *Psychological Issues*, Vol. 1, No. 1, Monograph 1, 1959, p. 131.

[76] Shaw, *op. cit.*, pp. 61-63.

I was about to experience my first ride in an elevated train on the first occasion that I was to enter the Loop. Nothing at home or at school equaled this joyous occasion. . . . When we arrived at the Loop . . . it was a new world, a fairyland that seemed real. . . .
[*In the department stores, they rode escalators and elevators, visited toy and sporting goods departments feasting on the variety of new experiences, but stealing nothing on this first trip. Sidney was happily overwhelmed by the big booming confusion of everything.*]
. . . we made plans for future visits to the Loop. The impression in my mind of the Loop and its big stores were a general disorder to everything. Wild bedlam reigned everywhere and system was unknown. Even the traffic policemen were not taken too seriously. People dashed across the street continuously at every opportunity whether traffic was with them or against them. I know to us the traffic policeman was merely a nuisance. To mix with the crowd, and to struggle from the one interesting thing to the other, always seeking something more interesting and receiving many pleasant surprises, was one thing that I never grew tired of, no matter how many hours or how many days I spent at it.

Of his later visits to the Loop with another gang of boys, he writes:[77]

We went places and did things merely for the fun that was in it. It was, I admit, a somewhat distorted sense of humor. We would enter a store, and if we saw eggs anywhere, we would try to steal them. Sometimes one of us would have a pocket full of eggs and one of the boys would slap the pocket of the one who had the eggs and cause us all to run out of the store laughing gleefully. Sometimes one of us would put an egg in a strange boy's pocket while the other one would smash it. Then we would all run off and pull the same trick on another boy. It was very funny to stick gum in one another's hair, and to stick burning matches to each other's skin afforded us great pleasure. We would pry open the rear door of small theaters and either sneak inside where we would cause a disturbance, or we just merely let out a loud shout or threw tin cans into the show. To sneak on the elevated and ride around the Loop was an adventure, and we were always disorderly on the train.

Here is vertigo in its innocuous forms and then veering over into its destructive potential. Here is reveling in *disorder*—the very opposite of play (*agon*) according to strictly regulated conventionalized rules self-imposed and accepted by the players. Sidney is exhilarated, excited, almost ecstatic, by the first ride on the El (an equilibrium-threatening experience), then even more so by the mardi-gras kalei-

[77] *Ibid.*, p. 70.

doscopic atmosphere of the Loop, the multiplicity of new experiences bombarding the senses. The intoxicating atmosphere of this environment is at first itself sufficient vertigo satisfaction: Sidney and his older pal did not steal on the first trip. Later two kinds of transformations occur in this excitement-laden milieu: One is an extension of disorder into the activities of the gang of boys themselves, their mischievous antics and pranks on each other, disturbances they create in theaters, trains, and stores (activities which are endlessly reinvented by boisterous youngsters of today, as almost any ride on a New York subway will attest).

These activities were evidently encouraged by the anonymity, diversity, and general disorder of a downtown metropolis. This is turbulence extended, though not very far, into release of id impulses of a destructive nature. (Here are the "malicious" and "negativistic" qualities of the delinquent subculture as seen by Albert Cohen.) The other transformation is the extension of earlier local neighborhood agonistic encounters in thievery in the stores, now to the "big time" of the downtown department stores. For Sidney, then, *agon* in the form of stealing, imposes a kind of order of Sidney's own upon this vast confusion of potential gratifications. Sidney thus maintains and controls an exquisite tension between order and disorder; stealing as a game places himself and particular others in definite parts in an agon-drama for which he, in his way, has written the script, leaving much to chance, uncertainty, and the thrill of danger.

The courting of self-destruction by physically dangerous exploits forbidden or frowned on by parents or other authorities is a common activity of boys in this culture, whether they come to be defined as delinquent for it or not. (The ambiguity and mushiness of the label "delinquent" is by now a commonplace.) Activities such as swimming in a dangerous current, hitching rides on the back of buses or trolley cars, racing hot-rods or just ordinary fast and reckless driving of regular cars, are familiar examples, as are almost any feats of endurance and skill that constitute validations of masculinity in a culture where submitting oneself to the mother's demands for caution and propriety is profoundly felt as a threat to a young man's sexual identity.

Vertigo or *ilinx* in Caillois' classification is closely akin to what Joseph Campbell calls the "Chaos Principle," [78] a principle of cul-

[78] Joseph Campbell, *The Masks of God: Primitive Mythology* (New York: Viking Press, 1959), p. 274.

ture constantly at war with a principle of order. In Freud's terms, what we are concerned with is the "seething cauldron of the id." The turbulent, mischievous, and at times quite destructive antics of delinquents like Sidney and his pals share the qualities of slapstick comedy and low farce, found in Punch and Judy shows, and in primitive folklore, the almost ubiquitous figure of the "Trickster." [79] The analogies of delinquency to the primitive figure of the Trickster are sufficiently rich and complex to merit a detailed discussion. Space permits only a very cursory treatment here.

Trickster figures appear in the legends or myths of primitive peoples of many parts of the world. For example, the Papuas of Waropen (New Guinea) tell of the Divine Trickster, Uri, who is both older brother and younger brother, and also a snake or a bird, or a woman.

> Uri is a lying, deceitful, lecherous giant with an enormous penis and overwhelming passion. In one story he is a stand-in for the Creator, but lacking miraculous powers of his own, he depends on trickery. He is always playing crude practical jokes, but finally gets his come-uppance by dying himself the victim of another's coarse prank, by which his liver is drawn out of his anus and eaten. Still in the death struggle, he kicks loose several small islands which come floating down from the back country where he died and now grace the landscape.[80]

Half a world away, we find the Trickster figures of the North American Indians. For example, the Winnebago Trickster has a whole series of adventures and misadventures.[81]

> He carries his enormously long penis in a box on his back, taking it out on occasion to send it across the waters to cohabit with the chief's daughter. When he sends it to probe a hollow tree-trunk, it is almost gnawed to pieces by Chipmunk, and Trickster ends up with one of only standard human size. He is carried off by a giant bird, later takes vengeance by changing himself into a deer and tricking Hawk into penetrating his anus, thus killing the bird and giving himself a fancy tail. He encounters the talking bulb, and defies its prophecy that "whoever eats me, will defecate"; he eats and mocks; then breaks wind, ever more stupendously, exploding the whole town of log houses that have been piled on him to hold him down; then his defecation starts and also takes on superhuman proportions; he ends up scrambling on a mountain of his own ex-

[79] Paul Radin, *The Trickster: A Study in American Indian Mythology* (New York: Philosophical Library, 1956).

[80] G. Held, *Papuas of Waropen* (The Hague: 1957), pp. 282-302.

[81] Paraphrased from Radin, *op. cit.*, pp. 3-53.

*crement. He is duped at times by Coyote, by Mink, by Bear, etc.,
and dupes each of them in turn. He craftily acquires the skills of
muskrat, snipe, woodpecker, pole-cat, in getting food by trickery
and fraud. He also removes obstacles in the Mississippi and re-
locates a waterfall for human good.*

Elsewhere in North America, Trickster appears in many guises: he is
the greedy hungry Raven, tricking others out of food; or lecherous
Mink, conniving to steal females from all his friends; or the inept
social-climber Blue-Jay, busy putting on status-seeking airs; or he is
Coyote, who is all three: greedy, lascivious, and an arriviste. Or he is
the Great Hare, or Master Rabbit, the Indian prototype of the Afro-
American syncretism, Bre'er Rabbit. But Trickster may also be the
culture-builder, if only accidentally. For example, Raven, when very
thirsty, steals all the water; escaping his pursuers, he carelessly spills
the water all over the world, and so we have lakes, rivers, and
oceans.[82]

Joseph Campbell summarizes the import of the Trickster type of
hero as follows:[83]

> *This ambiguous, curiously fascinating figure of the Trickster ap-
> pears to have been the chief mythological character of the paleo-
> lithic world of story; a fool, and a cruel lecherous cheat, an epitome
> of the principle of disorder, he is nevertheless the culture-bringer
> also. And he appeared under many guises, both animal and human.
> . . . [Campbell gives North American Indian examples] In Europe
> he is known as Reynard the Fox, but also, on a more serious plane,
> he appears as the Devil. . . . In carnival customs of Europe, this
> figure survives in the numerous clowns, buffoons, devils, etc. . . .
> who play the roles, precisely, of the clowns in the rites of the Indian
> Pueblos and give the character of topsy-turvy to the feast. They
> represent, from the point of view of the masters of decorum, the
> chaos principle, the principle of disorder, the force careless of taboos
> and shattering bounds. But from the point of view of the deeper
> realms of being from which the energies of life ultimately spring,
> this principle is not to be despised.*

Here then, returning to Caillois' terminology, is the *mimicry-ilinx*
complex of primitive cultures. The corresponding aspect of the criminalistic delinquent subculture may thus be seen as a kind of survival

[82] Franz Boas, "Folktales of the North American Indians," *Journal of American Folklore*, Vol. 27, 1914, pp. 374-410. Reprinted in Boas, *Race, Language
and Culture* (New York: The Macmillan Company, 1948). Paraphrase by this
author from pp. 465, 472, 473, 474, 479, of the latter edition.

[83] Campbell, *op. cit.*, pp. 273, 274, 275. Other familiar counterparts in
European lore and literature are the figures of Til Eulenspiegel, Peer Gynt, and
Bertold Brecht's *Baal*.

of central facets of primitive or "Dionysian" culture into a modern world whose legitimized institutions give central place to the *agon-alea* complex of mastery and social placement by the combination of competition and chance, or merit in productive work along with the chance factors of heredity. Dynamically, it is the defiant challenge by polymorphous sexual-destructive forces of the id, over the attempts of rational self-control and social respectability of the ego and superego imposed or developed by the established order. (We shall return to these themes after consideration of the conflict and retreatist subcultures.)

PLAY IN THE CONFLICT SUBCULTURE

In the delinquent subculture of fighting or "bopping" gangs, fighting between antagonistic gangs is, of course, the central defining activity, and in a sense the focal point of existence. The phenomenon can be seen as an almost pure case of *agon:* "a contest, an engagement between two groups of antagonists, executed within certain fixed limits of time and place, and filled with feelings of tension, joy, and the consciousness of difference from 'ordinary life.' " [84]

Contest—the battle of wits and nimble bodies against cops and, more ferociously, against rival gangs—is the essence of the bopping gang's culture. Many of the gang members cannot even imagine a world in which such conflict gangs do not exist: "It's the way the world is—always going to be gangs. Always going to be fighting. Nobody's going to stop it," a bopping boy told the journalist Harrison Salisbury.[85] The "rumble" is the apogee of the bopping gang boy's existence. It is *agon* in exactly Huizinga's or Caillois' sense. Internally and toward each other, the fighting gang's life is extensively regulated by rules and customs, exacting comformity from the members. The fights with other gangs may be arranged with an etiquette as ritualistic as that governing combat for Plains Indian war parties, medieval European knights, or the Samurai of old Japan.

"Heart" is an agonistic concept: it means the irrational willingness to risk injury or death in combat. It is the delinquent fighter's analogue of the idea of heroism so important in other agonistic institutions. The demonstration of "heart" brings "rep"—*honor.* For bopping boys all this is deadly serious—often literally so. So too with other forms of agonistic encounter. Serious, yes; instrumental, no.

[84] Huizinga, *op. cit.*, p. 30.
[85] Harrison Salisbury, *The Shook-Up Generation* (New York: Crest Paperbacks, 1959), p. 19.

Tension and uncertainty of outcome are essential elements of *agon*. These are evident in the fighting of bopping gangs. The gang boys live in a world of tense uncertainty and agonizing risk, where a possibly casual encounter might erupt into violence at any moment. The fights, while rule-bound, are also the occasion for release of enormous amounts of pent-up destructive energy. "Heart" both dramatizes and intensifies this element of risk, and it provides the chance for assertive triumph over danger. The rumble can be ecstasy.

The fierce ingroup loyalty of the members of these gangs and their sharp self-demarcation from other gangs and from the rest of society also mark the gangs as agonistic structures.

The quasi-military[86] trappings are also interesting. Some fighting gangs have the marks of an elaborate internal organization. For example, the Cobras, a Brooklyn gang reported by Salisbury in 1958,[87] claim to have a president (in charge of public policy, domestic and foreign relations, and strategy), a vice-president (chief of staff), a war-counselor (war plans, intelligence, tactics), a gunsmith or armorer (weapons and logistics). The gang also has a junior branch (the "Little People") with a similar top echelon, but subject to overall control by the "Big People." The pattern of fighting is reminiscent of agonistic qualities of medieval warfare or tournaments mixed with some of the weaponry and ambush tactics of World War II and the Korean war. Many of the gang names are appropriately warlike or suggestive of fierce marauding hordes: Warriors, Huns, Vikings, Comanches, Demons, Killers. Many are echoes of the medieval order: Crusaders, Viceroys, Lords, Dukes, and interestingly, Chaplains, Bishops.[88]

Gang battles as well as truce talks take place at specially appointed places, conforming to *agon's* requirement of specially demarcated

[86] "Quasi-military" rather than "military" is used because careful firsthand studies indicate that the organizational structure is very fragile, contrary to the impression that the active boys, especially leaders, like to give. Leadership and ranks may be quickly decimated by arrests and reform school or prison sentences following an especially bloody rumble, defection to other gangs, etc., and a good deal of the membership figures that would be given by a gang leader turn out to be boys only vaguely on the periphery of the gang, though often mobilizable for a big rumble. However, claims by some New York gang leaders that they could mobilize an "army" in the tens of thousands from all over the city, are discounted by expert observers as bravado pretensions. Sustained organizational capacity and power by leaders as well as sufficient long-term discipline by members, are evidently lacking. See Lewis Yablonsky, *The Violent Gang* (New York: The Macmillan Company, 1962), Ch. 13.
[87] Salisbury, *op. cit.*, p. 22.
[88] *Ibid.*, p. 22.

space for the agonistic encounter. The sacredness of particular space appears also in the mystique of the "turf"—the particular area of officially public space (certain city blocks) that the gang claims as its own and will defend to the death. The relationship of the "turf" to the gang does not fit any modern legal theory of property: hence solid citizens are outraged at the gang's often violent enforcement of its territorial claims, aghast at the idea that a teen-age boy may not walk freely through what are officially public streets. In effect the gang sees the territory as a sacred place: between it and the gang there exists some special mysterious bond, separate from "ordinary life." The term "turf" itself suggests the medieval idea of a mystic attachment of men to a physical space, in contrast to the modern legal view of land as a completely alienable *thing*.

Mimicry is abundantly evident in the fighting gangs. Names of the gangs and of the boys themselves are indicative. The gang name gives the boys a powerful group identity rich in suggestive imagery. Besides those suggestive of marauding hordes, or high status in the medieval order (already mentioned) others are suggestive of exotic cultures, high status, ferocity or valor in any combination: Egyptian Kings, Royal Niles, Comanches, Cherokees, Sioux (pronounced Cy-ox); dangerous wild animals, real or mythical, are common: Scorpions, Dragons, Jaguars, Tigers, Cobras, etc.[89] Significantly, whereas several American Indian tribes are represented in these names (evidently honoring an image of them as ferocious fighters derived from movies and TV), none of the names connotes the Subsaharan African ancestry of so many of the fighting gang boys, and Egyptian (the nearest geographic approximation) is used only with a regal appendage. That the name of the gang represents an attempt at a radical identity transformation seems quite evident from all of this. The gang name given to the boy himself is further indication: it distinguishes the boy's gang identity from that imposed by the family, the school, the courts, or other agencies of the wider society, over which the boy has no control. Often this gang identity is the most important identity the boy has, and it may be the only name by which he is known at all in the gang world. "Favorite *noms de gang* include Blood, Snake, Leadpipe, China, Knobby, Hatchet, Killer, Geronimo, Cochise, Diablo, Rocky, Moto, Johnny the Bop, Vice, Dice, Goat, Savage, Wolf, and Saint."[90] Ferocity and exoticism again appear. While the centrality of the gang, its name, and the boy's gang

[89] *Ibid.*
[90] Salisbury, *op. cit.*, p. 29.

nickname, to the boy are suggestive of the poverty of the rest of these boys' lives, our concern here is with their value as *mimicry*. Alongside whatever utilitarian value may be attributed to the nicknames by the gang members[91] is the important element of make-believe, mystical participation, of theatrical game. Throughout the subculture of the conflict gang, we can find this self-dramatizing quality: the militaristic and organizational pretensions, the touchiness about "rep" for oneself and for one's gang, the identification with exotic or ferocious beings, the mystique of the "turf," the costumes and insignia reminiscent of medieval heraldry or the totemic emblems of Australian aborigines. In fact, their mimicry shows parallels or analogues to a great variety of cultures, primitive or historical, to anything *but* the formal institutions of a representative democracy.

There are elements of vertigo too—the ecstasy attainable at the height of an especially violent rumble. Many gang boys report that during a rumble is the only time they "really feel alive." (This is a devastating commentary on the quality of the "ordinary life" available for these boys.)

Thus, despite surface indications to the contrary, the conflict gang's life is rich in play, in a combination of *agon* and *mimicry*, with touches of *ilinx*, in a culture form radically at odds with the official trends of the society in which they live.

PLAY IN THE "RETREATIST" SUBCULTURE

Cloward and Ohlin consider the turning to narcotics as a distinctive subvariety of delinquent subculture. (Since adolescent narcotics users typically engage in criminal activities to get their supply of drugs, and since a great proportion of them were already involved in criminal activities before they took to drugs,[92] the distinctiveness of the narcotics subculture from the criminal subculture is problematical, but unimportant for our present purposes. Similarly Cloward-Ohlin's treating it as a "retreatist" way of life, following a line of

---

[91] Salisbury seems credulously to accept the gang rationale that the nicknames are designed to prevent enemies (police, parole officers, rival gangs) from penetrating real identities and tracing participants in rumbles—as though police dossiers do not list a long string of aliases along with a criminal's "legal" name! *Ibid.*, p. 23.

[92] Harold Finestone, "Narcotics and Criminality," *Law and Contemporary Problems*, Vol. 22, Winter 1957, pp. 69-85.

analysis initiated by Merton, is open to a challenge[93] which does not concern us here.)

The world of the young drug addict can be seen as very largely a world of play. In fact, of the three varieties of delinquent subculture, this one most forcefully and dramatically exhibits the play phenomenon at the core of its pattern. Harold Finestone, in a very perceptive paper, "Cats, Kicks, and Color," [94] has explicitly applied Huizinga's analysis of play to a population of over fifty male Negro heroin users in their late teens or early twenties in Chicago. He finds these young men to conform rather closely to one distinctive social type, the "cat," and the "cat's" life is almost pure play, in Huizinga's sense. In his zestful pursuit of kicks, the "cat" is ever at play. Play is freedom: the "cat" avoids all conventional restraints. Play is outside "ordinary life": the lower-class Negro addict is already outside the serious life of the society and reactively separates himself even more, rejecting anything conventional as "square." He totally rejects legitimate and scheduled work and boss authority and devotes himself to a self-consciously cultivated world of play. He provides for himself not by work but by a variety of "hustles"—illicit but nonviolent means, scheming, conning, intriguing, extorting, pimping, and so on. The hustle is one of his forms of *agon* against the conventional world. He cultivates the esoterica of his world: a discriminating taste in clothing, jazz, and lingo; a studied "cool" in the face of any contingency. Above all, he is ever in pursuit of "kicks"—pleasurable, even ecstatic experiences, the more unconventional the better, whence the special value of the heroin "high." His perpetual battle with the forces of conventional society—to get his supply of drugs and to protect the secrecy of esoterica—put him into endless agonistic encounter, full of tension, uncertainty, and zest. This is agonistic play to the fullest.

While some parts of Finestone's portrait of the Chicago Negro "cat" of the early 1950s may not be applicable to other young heroin addicts who are white, or live in other cities, in more recent years[95] enough of the characteristics seem to be generic and relatively stable in the pattern of adolescent drug use to enable us to discuss the

[93] See Victor Gioscia: "Adolescence, Addiction and Achrony" in this volume, on pp. 341, fn. 77.
[94] Harold Finestone, "Cats, Kicks, and Color," *Social Problems*, Vol. V, No. 1, 1957, pp. 3-13.
[95] See Gioscia: *op. cit.*, and his sources, especially I. Chein, *et al.*, *The Road to H.* (New York: Basic Books, 1964).

whole youth-drug complex as an entity, in relation to play, with Finestone's "cats" as a special example.

Applying Caillois' more differentiated concepts of play, we find the addict delinquent displaying an abundance of *agon* (as indicated) and of *mimicry* as well, but his special distinction as compared to the criminal or conflict delinquents is his dramatic cultivation of *ilinx*. *Mimicry* appears in the Chicago "cats" in their self-conscious construction of a distinctive identity around a specially refined sartorial style, their distinctive lingo and advanced-jazz cultivation, and the phenomenon of "cool." The cat in his self-dramatization maintains an image of himself and his peers strikingly at odds with the image of him maintained by conventional society and especially by the agents of law and order (the "dope fiend," or the image of some well-meaning social scientists who see him as only an "escapist"). He has constructed a role, indeed a whole drama, which denigrates, even denies, conventional "reality" and, in turn, is seen as "unreal" or "illusional" by conventional society. Further he cultivates the arts involved in the mimicry complex—deception and manipulation of others—in the versatile conning activities that make up his "hustles"—putting something over on respectable society.

The ecstasy of drugs is the high point of his existence: it takes him "out of this world." [96] It is the ultimate in a whole variety of "kicks" the "cat" pursues. Here is *ilinx* or vertigo, via paranormal, chemico-psychic states. How defiant this orientation is, as a central approach to life, to the basic patterns of modern culture, has been pointed out by Gioscia's paper. Here we can add that it is the centrality of the addict's particular play pattern of *ilinx and mimicry*, spiced with a particular style of *agon* (very different from that pursued in conventional work-play) that marks the addiction life style as profoundly oppositional to the central patterns of modern culture.

PLAY AND DELINQUENCY: REPRISE

I have tried to show how play, in various manifestations and in the several varieties distinguished by Caillois, is profoundly involved in the subcultures of delinquency in modern society. Only where gambling is a major part of the activities of the denizens of the criminal subculture, is *alea* a significant component of these play elements in delinquency. Otherwise, the patterns are various combi-

[96] See Gioscia, *op. cit.*, for the significance of this in reference to *time*.

nations of *agon, mimicry,* and *ilinx.* All three appear in both the criminal and narcotic subcultures, but with very different emphases: for the criminal—*agon, mimicry,* and *ilinx* in that order of importance, with *agon* dominant; for the narcotic—*ilinx* by far the dominant element, and *agon* and *mimicry* about equally in a secondary place. For the fighting gangs, *agon* is the central element, with some aspects of *mimicry* secondary.

All show the basic components of play—freedom, autonomy, zest, fun, spontaneity, separation from "ordinary life," tension and uncertainty of outcome, nonutility and unproductiveness, make-believe, and some self-imposed system of order or regulation constantly vying with the breakthrough of underlying chaos. In fact, one could say that play in its diverse forms is so central to all the patterns of delinquency as to make this general aspect a key factor in the unsettling or subversive quality perceived in delinquency by conventional society. The cultural norms of the latter demand a centrality for *work* in life, with play relegated to a subordinate—and at that, *utilitarian!*— role of recreation to lighten the burden of work and prepare the workers for renewed disciplined efforts in the sequel. If an ordinary grown-up man puts his intelligence and talents into "fun and games" he may be rebuked as frivolous. For a sizable segment of the population to make play the center of their lives, however, will be felt as subversive to the order of the universe. The conventional disapprovers of the delinquent worlds seem to have divined, at some subliminal level perhaps, that none of these delinquent life styles accepts the central organization of life in society around the *agon-alea* complex that is basic to all modern technological societies. Instead we find the eruption of dangerous vertigo elements (most dramatically in the addicts) or of *agon* forms recalling a pre-industrial society (the bopping gangs) with corresponding mimicry ingredients. These are eruptions of *mimicry-ilinx* combinations suggesting a persistence of or return to a kind of society lacking the fruits of modern "progress" (of rational organization, systematic scientific pursuit of knowledge and its applications in utilitarian ways, of rationalized law and order) and displaying instead an immersion in the irrational and mysterious and the strange and dangerous outer boundaries of experience, the world of shaman-trance and spectacular-audience-awe.

This essay does not pretend to be a general theory of juvenile delinquency in modern society. Its goal is only to point out some essential elements of delinquency as a set of culture patterns that have been obscured in prevailing sociological and psychological formulations. Nor does it intend to imply that such elements of delinquency as brutal gang killings or the depredations of a desperate heroin addict are nothing more than harmless fun and games. Vicious and brutal delinquency often is. Repressively conformity-binding it may well frequently be. Still the delinquent subculture does appear to be some kind of answer to all the forces repressive of the play impulse in the larger culture today. Creature and expression of social disinheritance and psychic discontent, it can well be called "rebellion without a cause." Its defiance of respectable society is dedicated to no program for change of institutions or even milder social melioration. Nor is it dedicated to anything resembling established religious codes, much less to radical political action. The delinquent subculture seeks only satisfaction of the impulse of the moment, and in this it is engaged primarily in play. This itself is a major act of rebellion in this culture.

7. CONCLUSION

In this chapter we have explored various facets of the relationship of personality, social structure, and culture to the activities of work and play. In our treatment of work, we have deliberately chosen occupations or activities that are likely to be particularly absorbing and resonant for the personality, activities into which a person can throw himself or immerse himself almost completely. In the light of such occupations, the problem of the dividing line between work and play is particularly puzzling. Hence, the movement of the discussion in this chapter has been by barely perceptible transitions rather than by a sharp cleavage of work and play. We have tried, by this device, to capture some of the actual texture of reality in this complex and fascinating sphere. We thus moved from the psychodynamics of the business executive, with some cross-cultural asides comparing American and Soviet versions, to the psychodynamics of the different varieties of research scientists, thence to their nearby kin, the creative artist and thence by obvious association to that undifferentiated all-round professional, the primitive shaman. The shaman in turn brings us back to the modern world by that superficially improbable figure of the nightclub comic, as epitomized in the early work of Lenny Bruce, who, to the humanist seems very like a shaman in modern guise. How each of these deals with the basic forces of the unconscious, with the id impulses, and with their relationship to the forces of rational control and creative mastery, is a persistent concern through these discussions, though dealt with in varied ways by the different authors represented. The concern with the interplay of unconscious and conscious forces, of id with ego and superego, takes us back to the essential problems of *play* and its manifold relationships to the whole texture of human activities, however seriously or frivolously defined. In this discussion, we return to the considerations of human infantilization that concerned us in Chapter One of this book, to universals of human problems rooted in the evolutionary history of man, and reflected in myriad guises in the many cultures of the world. We have drawn upon the insights and categories of a number of humanistic thinkers—Huizinga, Caillois, Campbell prominently among them—and tried to relate them to the psychodynamic analysis of the Freudian perspective and the social-structural and cultural analyses of sociology and anthropology. (Many of these connecting links, at this stage, are necessarily sketchy or impressionistic, and are to be considered as prologue to further work.)

Our principal manner of approach has been to keep in dialectical tension primary opposing forces that seem to be central to the topics under examination: the ambiguous opposition of work and play, of regulation and freedom, of concentrated discipline in work with free spontaneity, of id versus ego forces, of unconscious depths versus conscious controls; of ilinx-mimicry versus agon-alea in the realms of culture and play; of principles of order against principles of chaos.

Also as in the other chapters, we have tried to keep in simultaneous view both primitive and modern societies. Again we have found that when we look for modern analogues of primitive institutions, they appear most compellingly in "subterranean" or "deviant" or "problematical" phases or aspects of culture or social structure—in an obscene or outrageous comic, in delinquents and drug addicts, more sublimely, in the creative artist. This is perhaps a selectively biased view, but we shall explore its further implications in the last chapter of this book.

Selected Bibliography

Barnard, Chester I. *The Functions of the Executive.* Cambridge: Harvard University Press, 1938.
A "classic" treatment of the nature of the executive's role.
Bauer, Raymond A. "The Psychology of the Soviet Elite: Two Case Histories," in C. Kluckhohn, H. Murray, and D. Schneider (eds.), *Personality in Nature, Society and Culture,* rev. ed. New York: Alfred A. Knopf, 1952.
Two distinct personality orientations in high-status Soviet Russians.
Bensman, Joseph. *Dollars and Sense.* New York: Macmillan Co., 1967.
Profound analysis of dilemmas of work in advertising, academia, social work, and poverty programs.
Caillois, Roger. *Man, Play and Games.* Translated by Meyer Barash. New York: Free Press of Glencoe, 1961.
Major recent philosophical analysis of play.
Calhoun, D. *et al. Personality, Work, Community: An Introduction to Social Science.* Philadelphia: J. B. Lippincott Co., 1953 and later editions.
The section on work contains intriguing selections on the psychology and sociology of several occupations: salaried employees, miners, waitresses, and entrepreneurs.
Campbell, Joseph. *The Masks of God: Primitive Mythology.* New York: Viking Press, 1959.
Valuable not only for the analysis of the shaman and trickster, but generally illuminating on the whole problem of work, play and the sacred.
Caplow, Theodore and Reece J. McGee. *The Academic Market Place.* New York: Basic Books, 1959.
A sociological study of how college professors get, leave, or lose their jobs.
Denney, Reuel. *The Astonished Muse.* Chicago: University of Chicago Press, 1959.
Insightful essays on many facets of play, leisure, and popular culture in America.
Devereux, George. "The Origin of Shamanistic Powers as Reflected in a Neurosis," *Revue Internationale d'Ethnopsychologic Normale et Pathologique.* Vol. 1, 1956, pp. 3-13.
Relation of shamanism to neurosis.
Gomme, Alice B. (ed.). *Traditional Games of England, Scotland, and Ireland.* 2 volumes. New York: Dover Publications, 1964. (First published 1894).
One of the few detailed ethnographies of play for large-scale societies.
Huizinga, Johan. *Homo Ludens: The Play Element in Culture.* Boston: Beacon Press, 1955.
Major contribution on the relationship of play to culture.

Klein, Melanie. "Psychoanalytic Play Technique: History and Signifi-
cance," in Klein *et al.*, *New Directions in Psychoanalysis*. New York:
Basic Books, 1955.
Use of play as means of tapping dynamic trends.
Koestler, Arthur. *The Yogi and the Commissar and Other Essays*. New
York: The Macmillan Company, 1945.
Contrasting life ways built into these roles.
Kris, Ernst. *Psychoanalytic Explorations in Art*. New York: Interna-
tional Universities Press, 1952.
Many aspects of art and the artist dynamically explored.
Larrabee, Eric and Rolf Meyersohn (eds.). *Mass Leisure*. New York:
Free Press of Glencoe, 1958.
A variety of probings into the worlds of play.
Lasswell, Harold D. *Power and Personality*. New York: W. W. Norton
& Co., 1948.
This and Lasswell's earlier *Psychopathology and Politics* (Chicago:
University of Chicago Press, 1930) significant applications of psycho-
analytic approach to various kinds of political leaders, strangely very
little followed up in others' researches.
Lessa, William A. and Evon Z. Vogt (eds.). *Reader in Comparative
Religion: An Anthropological Approach*. 2nd edition. New York:
Harper & Row, Publishers, 1965.
In Part 10, "Shamans and Priest," good discussions of shamanism in a
number of primitive tribes.
Merton, Robert K. "Bureaucratic Structure and Personality," Chapter V
in *Social Theory and Social Structure*. New York: Free Press of Glencoe, 1949.
Poses basic problems of relationships between bureaucratic settings
and personality functioning.
Miller, Arthur. *The Death of A Salesman*. New York: Viking Press,
1949.
Though much more than that, this significant modern drama is a
study in the psychology of an occupation representative of major
themes of this culture.
Mills, C. Wright. *The New Men of Power*. New York: Oxford Univer-
sity Press, 1948.
Probing study of labor leaders, valuable for analogies and contrasts
with business executives.
Neumann, Erich. *Art and the Creative Unconscious*. New York: Harper
and Row, Publishers, 1966.
Four significant essays.
Parsons, Talcott. "The Professions and Social Structure," in *Essays in
Sociological Theory*. New York: Free Press of Glencoe, 1949.
A major sociological approach to the professions.
Rank, Otto. *Art and Artist*. New York: Alfred A. Knopf, 1932.
A maverick Freudian's deep explorations into the psychology of the
artist.

Riesman, David, Nathan Glazer, and Reuel Denney. *The Lonely Crowd*. New Haven: Yale University Press, 1950.
Includes interesting analyses of work and play under changing characterological emphases.
Roe, Anne. *The Making of a Scientist*. New York: Dodd, Mead & Co., 1953.
————. *The Psychology of Occupations*. New York: John Wiley & Sons, 1956.
These are further explorations by the major recent psychologist to deal with occupations.
Rosenberg, Bernard and Norris Fliegel. *The Vanguard Artist*. Chicago: Quadrangle Books, 1965.
Excellent sociological-psychodynamic analysis of leading artists of today.
Schneider, Daniel. *The Psychoanalyst and the Artist*. New York: International Universities Press, 1950.
A profound psychoanalytic exploration into the nature of the artistic creative process. (Also available in paperback.)
Shostak. A. and William Gomberg (eds.). *Blue Collar World*. Englewood Cliffs, N. J.: Prentice-Hall, 1965.
Various papers explore the psychology of contemporary manual workers.
Swanson, Guy E. "Agitation Through the Press: A Study of the Personalities of Publicists," *Public Opinion Quarterly*, 1956. Vol. 20, pp. 441-56. Reprinted in N. and W. Smelser (eds.), *Personality and Social Systems*. New York: John Wiley & Sons, 1963.
In this interesting study, Swanson found that male editorial writers (on a college newspaper) showed characteristics more oral-dependent, anal-expulsive, and phallic-aspiring than business staff and sports writers on the same paper, confirming expectations of the dynamics of a publicist personality derived from Lasswell's work.
Whyte, William H., Jr. *The Organization Man*. New York: Simon and Schuster, 1956.
Middle management in the large corporation critically dissected.
Wilson, Robert N. (ed.). *The Arts in America*. Englewood Cliffs, N. J.: Prentice-Hall, 1964.
Various efforts in the developing "sociology of the arts."
Wolfenstein, Martha. "The Emergence of Fun Morality," *Journal of Social Issues*. Vol. 7, No. 4, 1951, pp. 15-25.
The dilemmas produced when "play" paradoxically becomes a kind of imperative.

SIX

Personality in extreme situations

It is an understatement to say that our present age is an era of extreme situations. We have witnessed in our lifetime the unparalleled cruelties of man to man in the unprecedented bestialities of the concentration camps and in the atomic bomb devastations of Hiroshima and Nagasaki. Since World War II the further technological developments of nuclear weapons confront the world with the possibility of total destruction by hydrogen bomb warfare. On a smaller but still terrifying scale, more localized wars, terroristic uprisings, "national liberation" movements and counterterrors, persisting concentration and forced-labor camps, terrorist suppressions of minorities in many lands, continue the long record of man's destructiveness to man. Alongside this is the continuing impact of disasters both natural and man-made. Technological progress multiplies the possibilities of "accidental" disasters deriving from the very fruits of man's technological mastery of the material world—airline crashes, shipwrecks, train wrecks, gas explosions, devastating fires. And ironically in the midst of technological developments that would have astounded men of a mere century ago, modern man is still incapable of protecting communities from devastation by the age-old disasters of earthquake, drought, flood, hurricane, tornado, volcanic eruption, avalanche, or even raging storms of rain, hail, or snow.

How do human beings deal with such extreme situations? For countless millions we will never know: we cannot interview the dead. From and about survivors we now have a growing body of accounts. We shall focus here on personality in relation to social forces in two of the many types of extreme situation faced by men in recent times—the Nazi concentration camps and disasters ranging from natural to manmade.

1. BEHAVIOR IN CONCENTRATION CAMPS

In the now considerable and agonizing literature documenting the horrors of the Nazi camps of concentration and extermination of 1933-1945, one firsthand account from a prisoner survivor from the relatively early phase of the camps (1938-1939) stands out for its combination of psychological clarity and social perspicacity, Bruno Bettelheim's observations of himself and fellow prisoners in Dachau and Buchenwald, first published in 1943. This paper (presented here in a version abbreviated to about half its original length) is itself a moving tribute to the enormous potential for autonomy in man, the capacity to resist personality disintegration in the face of long-sustained extremity of assault and deprivation. Bettelheim's account is especially valuable for its specification of which prisoners undergoing such experiences were, and which were not, capable of resistance to the destructive personality transformation evidently designed and intended by the concentration camp institution: here psychological and sociological acuity brilliantly combine. It is no detraction from the value of Bettelheim's paper as a contribution to the social psychology of extremity and as a document of heroic inner freedom, to recall that the horrors of the 1939 camps were still relatively benign or humane compared to the total dehumanization of the camps under the full extermination policies of the later part of World War II.[1]

The concentration camp institution was, of course, not limited to Fascist versions of totalitarianism as is shown by the growing number of accounts of the Soviet camps, especially significant during the Stalin regime. Alexander Solzhenitsyn's *One Day in the Life of Ivan*

---

[1] See Eugen Kogon, *The Theory and Practice of Hell* (New York: Farrar, Straus & Giroux, 1946); David Rousset, *L'Univers Concentrationnaire* (Paris: Pavois, 1946), records of the Nuremberg Trials, and of the Eichmann trial; Hannah Arendt, *Eichmann in Jerusalem* (New York: Viking Press, 1964) among other accounts.

Denisovich[2] gives in fictional form an especially vivid picture of life in such a Siberian camp around 1950. Partial analogues are to be found in the "relocation camps" into which American citizens of Japanese descent were herded during World War II, and even by a tragic irony in the temporary camps housing the masses of new immigrants to Israel in the early days of its independence, as well as by countless camps into which civilians have been concentrated in many lands, as "revolutionary" or "wartime precautions." "Brainwashing" of war prisoners and other captives by Chinese Communists and other revolutionary regimes in many parts of the world, extend the analogies. Camps of prisoners of war, prisons generally, and mental hospitals, all in turn provide further analogies, as recognized in Erving Goffman's brilliant essay on "Total Institutions." [3] Still it is scarcely to be doubted that the Nazi concentration camps provide the extreme and epitome of this horrifying human phenomenon.

Individual and Mass Behavior in the Concentration Camp
BRUNO BETTELHEIM

The author spent approximately one year in the two biggest German concentration camps for political prisoners, at Dachau and at Buchenwald. During this time he made observations and collected material, part of which will be presented in this paper. . . .

An effort will be made to deal adequately with at least one aspect of [the camps], namely with *the concentration camp as a means of producing changes in the prisoners which will make them more useful subjects* of the Nazi state. . . .

With the setting-up of concentration camps the Gestapo appears to seek various goals, one of which seems to be to produce changes in the personality of the prisoners. An effort will be made to understand how this is done by means of an historical account of what happens in, and to the prisoners in the camp. The collecting of data is viewed as an example of private behavior of one prisoner who develops this behavior as a mechanism to be better able to survive in the camp.

[2] Alexander Solzhenitsyn, *One Day in the Life of Ivan Denisovich*, trans. by Max Hayward and Roland Hingley (New York: Frederick A. Praeger, Publishers, 1963).

[3] Erving Goffman, *Asylums* (New York: Doubleday & Company, 1961).

Reprinted in condensed form, with permission of the author and the journal, from Bruno Bettelheim, "Individual and Mass Behavior in Extreme Situations," Journal of Abnormal and Social Psychology, Vol. 38, October 1943, pp. 417-52.

THE INITIAL SHOCK

In presentation, the initial psychological shock of being deprived of one's civil rights and unlawfully locked into a prison may be separated from the shock of the first deliberate and extravagant acts of torture to which the prisoners were exposed. These two shocks may be analyzed separately because the author, like most of the prisoners, spent several days in prison without being exposed to physical torture before being transported into the camp. This transportation into the camp, and the "initiation" into it, is often the first torture which the prisoner has ever experienced and is, as a rule, physically and psychologically the worst torture to which he will ever be exposed. . . .

The prisoners' reactions on being brought into prison can best be analyzed on the basis of two categories: the socio-economic class to which they belonged and their political education. . . . Another factor of importance was whether they had been previously acquainted with prisons, due either to criminality or to political activities.

Those prisoners who had previously spent time in prisons, or who expected to be imprisoned due to political activities, resented their fate, but somehow accepted it as something which happened in accordance with their expectations. It may be assumed that the initial shock of finding oneself imprisoned expressed itself—if at all—in a change in self-esteem. But it might be said that the self-esteem of the former criminals, as well as that of the politically educated prisoners, was rather heightened by the circumstances under which they found themselves in prison. They were, as a matter of fact, full of anxieties as to their future and as to what might happen to their families and friends. But, despite this justified anxiety, they did not feel too badly about the fact of imprisonment itself.

Persons who had formerly spent time in prison as *criminals* showed their glee openly at finding themselves on equal terms with political and business leaders, with attorneys and judges, some of whom had been instrumental earlier in sending them to prison. This spite, and the feeling of being equal to these men who up to now had been their superiors, helped their egos considerably.

The *politically educated prisoners* found support for their self-esteem in the fact that the Gestapo had singled them out as important enough to take revenge on. The members of different parties relied on different types of rationalizations for this building-up of their egos. Former members of radical-leftist groups, for example, found in the fact of their imprisonment a demonstration of how dangerous for the Nazis their former activities had been.

Of the main socio-economic classes, the lower classes were almost wholly represented either by former criminals or by politically educated prisoners. Any estimation of what might have been the reaction of non-

criminal and nonpolitical members of the lower classes must remain conjecture and guesswork.

The great majority of the *nonpolitical middle-class prisoners,* who
were a small minority among the prisoners of the concentration camps,
were least able to withstand the initial shock. They found themselves
utterly unable to comprehend what had happened to them. They seemed
more than ever to cling to what up to now had given them self-esteem.
Again and again they assured the members of the Gestapo that they
never opposed Naziism. In their behavior became apparent the dilemma
of the politically uneducated German middle classes when confronted
with the phenomenon of National Socialism. They had no consistent
philosophy which would protect their integrity as human beings, which
would give them the force to make a stand against the Nazis. They had
obeyed the law handed down by the ruling classes, without ever questioning its wisdom. And now this law, or at least the law-enforcing agencies,
turned against them, who always had been its staunchest supporters.
Even now they did not dare to oppose the ruling group, although such
opposition might have provided them with self-respect. They could not
question the wisdom of law and of the police, so they accepted the behavior of the Gestapo as just. What was wrong was that *they* were made
objects of a persecution which in itself *must* be right, since it was carried
out by the authorities. The only way out of this particular dilemma was
to be convinced that it must be a "mistake." These prisoners continued
to behave in this way despite the fact that the Gestapo, as well as most
of their fellow prisoners, derided them for it. . . .

The great desire of the middle-class prisoners was that their status as
such should be respected in some way. What they resented most was to
be treated "like ordinary criminals." After some time they could not help
realizing their actual situation. Then they seemed to disintegrate. The
several suicides which happened in prison and during the transportation
into camp were practically confined to members of this group. Later on,
members of this group were the ones who behaved in the most antisocial
way; they cheated their fellow prisoners, a few turned spy in the service
of the Gestapo. . . .

Members of *the upper classes* segregated themselves as much as possible. They, too, seemed unable to accept as real what was happening to
them. They expressed their conviction that they would be released
within the shortest time because of their importance. The upper-class
prisoners never formed a group; they remained more or less isolated, each
of them with a group of middle-class "clients." Their superior position
could be upheld by the amount of money they could distribute,[4] and by

---

[4] Money was very important to the prisoners because at certain times they
were permitted to buy cigarettes and some extra food. To be able to buy food
meant to avoid starvation. Since most political prisoners, most criminals, and

a hope on the part of their "clients" that they might help once they had been released. This hope was steadily kindled by the fact that many of the upper-class prisoners really were released from prison, or camp, within a comparatively short time.

A few upper-upper-class prisoners remained aloof even from the upper-class behavior. They did not collect "clients," they did not use their money for bribing other prisoners, they did not express any hopes about their release. The number of these prisoners was too small to permit any generalizations.[5] It seemed that they looked down on all other prisoners nearly as much as they despised the Gestapo. In order to endure life in the camp, they seemed to develop such a feeling of superiority that nothing could touch them.

As far as the political prisoners are concerned, another psychological mechanism became apparent at a later time, which might already have played some part in the initial development and which, therefore, ought to be mentioned. It seems that many political leaders had some guilt feeling that they had fallen down on their job, particularly the job of preventing the rise of Nazi power either by fighting the Nazis more effectively or by establishing such water-tight democratic or leftist class rule that the Nazis would not have been able to overcome it. It seems that this guilt feeling was relieved to a considerable degree by the fact that the Nazis found them important enough to bother with them. . . .

Summary.   It seems that most, if not all, prisoners tried to react against the initial shock by mustering forces which might prove helpful in supporting their badly shaken self-esteem. Those groups which found in their past life some basis for the erection of such a buttress to their endangered egos, seemed to succeed. Members of the lower class derived a certain satisfaction from the absence of class differences among the prisoners. Political prisoners found their importance as politicians once more demonstrated by being imprisoned. Members of the upper class could exert at least a certain amount of leadership among the middle-class prisoners. Members of "anointed" families felt in prison as superior to all other human beings as they had felt outside of it. Moreover, the initial shock seemed to relieve guilt feelings of various kinds, such as guilt feelings originating in political inactivity, or inefficiency, or in acting badly to one another, and for casting aspersion on friends and relatives in an unjustified way. The reason why it was either relieved or did not develop was the actual punishment the prisoners had to endure.

---

many middle-class prisoners had no money, they were willing to make easier the lives of those wealthy prisoners who were willing to pay for it.

[5] The author met actually only three of them, a Bavarian prince, member of the former royal family, and two Austrian dukes, closely related to the former emperor. It is doubtful whether there were at any time more than three of these prisoners in the camps.

THE TRANSPORTATION INTO THE CAMP AND THE FIRST
EXPERIENCES IN IT

After having spent several days in prison, the prisoners were brought
into the camp. During this transportation they were exposed to constant
tortures of various kinds. Corporal punishment, consisting of whipping,
kicking, slapping, intermingled with shooting and wounding with the
bayonet, alternated with tortures the obvious goal of which was extreme
exhaustion. For instance, the prisoners were forced to stare for hours into
glaring lights, to kneel for hours, and so on. From time to time a prisoner got killed; no prisoner was permitted to take care of his own or
another's wounds. These tortures alternated with efforts on the part of
the guards to force the prisoners to hit one another and to defile what
the guards considered the prisoners' most cherished values. For instance,
the prisoners were forced to curse their God, to accuse themselves of vile
actions, accuse their wives of adultery and of prostitution. This continued for hours and was repeated at various times. According to reliable
reports, this kind of initiation never took less than twelve hours and
frequently lasted twenty-four hours.

The purpose of the tortures was to break the resistance of the prisoners, and to assure the guards of their own superiority. This can be seen
from the fact that the longer the tortures lasted, the less violent they
became. The guards became slowly less excited, and at the end even
talked with the prisoners. As soon as a new guard took over, he started
with new acts of terror, although not as violent as in the beginning, and
he eased up sooner than his predecessor. Sometimes prisoners who had
already spent time in camp were brought back with a group of new
prisoners. These old prisoners were not tortured if they could furnish
evidence that they had already been in the camp.

It is difficult to ascertain what happened in the minds of the prisoners
during the time they were exposed to this treatment. Most of them became so exhausted that they were only partly conscious of what happened. In general, prisoners remembered the details and did not mind
talking about them, but they did not like to talk about what they had
felt and thought during the time of torture. The few who volunteered
information made vague statements which sounded like devious rationalizations, invented for the purpose of justifying that they had endured
treatment injurious to their self-respect without trying to fight back. The
few who had tried to fight back could not be interviewed; they were
dead.

The writer can vividly recall his extreme weariness, resulting from a
bayonet wound he had received early in the course of transportation and
from a heavy blow on the head. Both injuries led to the loss of a considerable amount of blood and made him groggy. He recalls vividly, nevertheless, his thoughts and emotions during the transportation. He won-

dered all the time that man can endure so much without committing suicide or going insane. He wondered that the guards really tortured prisoners in the way it had been described in books on the concentration camps; that the Gestapo was so simple-minded as either to enjoy forcing prisoners to defile themselves or to expect to break their resistance in this way. He wondered that the guards were lacking in fantasy when selecting the means to torture the prisoners; that their sadism was without imagination. He was rather amused by the repeated statement that the guards do not shoot the prisoners but kill them by beating them to death because a bullet costs six pfennigs, and the prisoners are not worth even so much. Obviously the idea that these men, most of them formerly influential persons, were not worth such a trifle impressed the guards considerably. On the basis of this introspection it seems that the writer gained emotional strength from the following facts: that things happened according to expectation; that, therefore, his future in the camp was at least partly predictable from what he already was experiencing and from what he had read; and that the Gestapo was more stupid than he had expected, which eventually provided small satisfaction. Moreover, he felt pleased with himself that the tortures did not change his ability to think or his general point of view. In retrospect these considerations seem futile, but they ought to be mentioned because, if the author should be asked to sum up in one sentence what, all during the time he spent in the camp, was his main problem, he would say: *to safeguard his ego in such a way, that, if by any good luck he should regain liberty, he would be approximately the same person he was when deprived of liberty.*

He has no doubt that he was able to endure the transportation, and all that followed, because right from the beginning he became convinced that these horrible and degrading experiences somehow did not happen to "him" as a subject, but only to "him" as an object. . . .

All the thoughts and emotions which the author had during the transportation were extremely detached. It was as if he watched things happening in which he only vaguely participated. Later he learned that many prisoners had developed this same feeling of detachment, as if what happened really did not matter to oneself. It was strangely mixed with a conviction that "this cannot be true, such things just do not happen." Not only during the transportation but all through the time spent in camp, the prisoners had to convince themselves that this was real, was really happening, and not just a nightmare. They were never wholly successful.[6]

6 There were good indications that most guards embraced a similar attitude, although for different reasons. They tortured the prisoners partly because they enjoyed demonstrating their superiority, partly because their superiors expected it of them. But, having been educated in a world which rejected brutality, they felt uneasy about what they were doing. It seems that they, too, had an

This feeling of detachment which rejected the reality of the situation in which the prisoners found themselves might be considered a mechanism safeguarding the integrity of their personalities. Many prisoners behaved in the camp as if their life there would have no connection with their "real" life; they went so far as to insist that this was the right attitude. Their statements about themselves, and their evaluation of their own and other persons' behavior, differed considerably from what they would have said and thought outside of camp. This separation of behavior patterns and schemes of values inside and outside of camp was so strong that it could hardly be touched in conversation; it was one of the many "taboos" not to be discussed.[7] The prisoners' feelings could be summed up by the following sentence: "What I am doing here, or what is happening to me, does not count at all; here everything is permissible as long and insofar as it contributes to helping me to survive in the camp."

One more observation made during the transportation ought to be mentioned. No prisoner fainted. To faint meant to get killed.

THE ADAPTATION TO THE CAMP SITUATION

Differences in the response to extreme and to suffering experiences. It seems that camp experiences which remained within the normal frame of reference of a prisoner's life experience were dealt with by means of the normal psychological mechanisms. Once the experience transcended this frame of reference, the normal mechanisms seemed no longer able to deal adequately with it and new psychological mechanisms were needed. The experience during the transportation was one of those transcending the normal frame of reference, and the reaction to it may be described as "unforgettable, but unreal."

The prisoners' dreams were an indication that the extreme experiences were not dealt with by the usual mechanisms. Many dreams expressed aggression against Gestapo members, usually combined with wish fulfillment in such a way that the prisoner was taking his revenge on them. Interestingly enough, the reason he took revenge on them—if a particular reason could be ascertained—was always for some comparatively small mistreatment, never an extreme experience. . . .

On the terribly cold winter night when a snow storm was blowing, all

---

emotional attitude toward their acts of brutality which might be described as a feeling of unreality. After having been guards in the camp for some time, they got accustomed to inhuman behavior, they became "conditioned" to it; it then became part of their "real" life.

[7] Some aspects of this behavior seem similar to those described in literature as "depersonalization," still there seem to be so many differences between the phenomena discussed in this paper and the phenomenon of depersonalization that it seemed not advisable to use this term.

prisoners were punished by being forced to stand at attention without overcoats—they never wore any—for hours.[8] This, after having worked for more than twelve hours in the open, and having received hardly any food. They were threatened with having to stand all through the night. After about twenty prisoners had died from exposure, the discipline broke down. The threats of the guards became ineffective. To be exposed to the weather was a terrible torture; to see one's friends die without being able to help, and to stand a good chance of dying, created a situation similar to the transportation, except that the prisoners had by now more experience with the Gestapo. Open resistance was impossible, as impossible as it was to do anything definite to safeguard oneself. A feeling of utter indifference swept the prisoners. They did not care whether the guards shot them; they were indifferent to acts of torture committed by the guards. The guards had no longer any authority, the spell of fear and death was broken. It was again as if what happened did not "really" happen to oneself. There was again the split between the "me" to whom it happened and the "me" who really did not care and was just an interested but detached observer. Unfortunate as the situation was, they felt free from fear and therefore were actually happier than at most other times during their camp experiences. . . .

The psychological reactions to events which were somewhat more within the sphere of the normally comprehensible were decidedly different from those to extreme events. It seems that prisoners dealt with less extreme events in the same way as if they had happened outside of the camp. For example, if a prisoner's punishment was not of an unusual kind, he seemed ashamed of it; he tried not to speak about it. A slap in one's face was embarrassing, and not to be discussed. One hated individual guards who had kicked one, or slapped one, or verbally abused one much more than the guard who really had wounded one seriously. In the latter case one eventually hated the Gestapo as such, but not so much the individual inflicting the punishment. Obviously this differentiation was unreasonable, but it seemed to be inescapable. One felt deeper and more violent aggressions against particular Gestapo members who had committed minor vile acts than one felt against those who had acted in a much more terrible fashion.

The following tentative interpretation of this strange phenomenon should be accepted with caution. It seems that all experiences which

[8] The reason for this punishment was that two prisoners had tried to escape. On such occasions all prisoners were always punished very severely so that in the future they would give away secrets they had learned, because otherwise they would have to suffer. The idea was that every prisoner ought to feel responsible for any act committed by any other prisoner. This was in line with the principle of the Gestapo to force the prisoners to feel and act as a group, and not as individuals.

might have happened during the prisoner's "normal" life history provoked a "normal" reaction. Prisoners seemed, for instance, particularly
sensitive to punishments similar to those which a parent might inflict on
his child. To punish a child was within their "normal" frame of reference, but that they should become the object of the punishment destroyed their adult frame of reference. So they reacted to it not in an
adult way, but in a childish way—with embarrassment and shame, with
violent, impotent, and unmanageable emotions directed, not against the
system, but against the person inflicting the punishment. A contributing
factor might have been that the greater the punishment, the more one
could expect to receive friendly support which exerted a soothing influence. Moreover, if the suffering was great, one felt more or less like a
martyr, suffering for a cause, and the martyr is supposed not to resent his
martyrdom. . . .

It seems that if a prisoner was cursed, slapped, pushed around "like a
child" and if he was, like a child, unable to defend himself, this revived
in him behavior patterns and psychological mechanisms which he had
developed when a child. Like a child he was unable to see his treatment
in the general context of the behavior of the Gestapo and hated the
individual Gestapo member. He swore that he was going "to get even"
with him, well knowing that this was impossible. He could develop neither a detached attitude nor an objective evaluation which would have
led him to consider his suffering as minor when compared with other
experiences. The prisoners as a group developed the same attitude to
minor sufferings; not only did they not offer any help, on the contrary
they blamed the prisoner who suffered for having brought about his
suffering by his stupidity of not making the right reply, of letting himself
get caught, of not being careful enough, in short accused him of having
behaved like a child. So the degradation of the prisoner by means of
being treated like a child took place not only in his mind, but in the
minds of his fellow prisoners, too. . . .

Differences in the psychological attitudes of old and new prisoners.
In the following discussion we refer by the term "new" prisoners to
those who had not spent more than one year in the camp; "old" prisoners are those who have spent at least three years in the camp. As far as
the old prisoners are concerned, the author can offer only observations
but no findings based on introspection.

It has been mentioned that the main concern of the new prisoners
seemed to be to remain intact as a personality and to return to the outer
world the same persons who had left it; all their emotional efforts were
directed toward this goal. Old prisoners seemed mainly concerned with
the problem of how to live as well as possible within the camp. Once
they had reached this attitude, everything that happened to them, even
the worst atrocity, was "real" to them. No longer was there a split be-

tween one to whom things happened and the one who observed them. Once this stage was reached of taking everything that happened in the camp as "real," there was every indication that the prisoners who had reached it were afraid of returning to the outer world. They did not admit it directly, but from their talk it was clear that they hardly believed they would ever return to this outer world because they felt that only a cataclysmic event—a world war and world revolution—could free them; and even then they doubted that they would be able to adapt to this new life. They seemed aware of what had happened to them while growing older in the camp. They realized that they had adapted themselves to the life in the camp and that this process was coexistent with a basic change in their personality. . . .

There was, of course, considerable variation among individuals in the time it took them to make their peace with the idea of having to spend the rest of their lives in the camp. Some became part of the camp life rather soon, some probably never. When a new prisoner was brought into the camp, the older ones tried to teach him a few things which might prove helfpul in his adjustment. The new prisoners were told that they should try by all means to survive the first days and not to give up the fight for their lives, that it would become easier the longer time they spent in camp. They said, "If you survive the first three months you will survive the next three years." This, despite the fact that the yearly mortality was close to 20 percent.[9] This high death rate was mostly due to the large number of new prisoners who did not survive the first few weeks in the camp, either because they did not care to survive by means of adapting themselves to the life in camp or because they were unable to do so. How long it took a prisoner to cease to consider life outside the camp as real depended to a great extent on the strength of his emotional ties to his family and friends. The change to accepting camp life as real never took place before spending two years in camp. Even then everyone was overtly longing to regain freedom. Some of the indications from which one could learn about the changed attitude were: scheming to find oneself a better place in the camp rather than trying to contact the outer world,[10] avoiding speculation about one's family, or world affairs,[11] con-

[9] The prisoners in charge of a barrack kept track of what happened to the inhabitants of their barrack. In this way it was comparatively easy to ascertain how many died and how many were released. The former were always in the majority.

[10] New prisoners would spend all their money on efforts to smuggle letters out of the camp or to receive communications without having them censored. Old prisoners did not use their money for such purposes. They used it for securing for themselves "soft" jobs, such as clerical work in the offices of the camp or work in the shops where they were at least protected against the weather while at work.

[11] It so happened that on the same day news was received of a speech by President Roosevelt denouncing Hitler and Germany, and rumors spread that

centrating all interest on events taking place inside of the camp. . . .

Changes in attitudes toward one's family and friends.   The new prisoners were usually those who received most letters, money, and other signs of attention. Their families were trying everything to free them. Nevertheless, they consistently accused them of not doing enough, of betraying and cheating them. They would weep over a letter telling of the efforts to liberate them, but curse in the next moment when learning that some of their property had been sold without their permission. They would swear at their families which "obviously" considered them "already dead." Even the smallest change in their former private world attained tremendous importance. They might have forgotten the names of some of their best friends, but once they learned that the friends had moved they were terribly upset and nothing could console them. This ambivalence of the new prisoners in relation to their families seemed to be due to a mechanism which was mentioned before. Their desire to return exactly the person who had left was so great that they feared any change, however trifling, in the situation they had left. Their worldly possessions should be secure and untouched, although they were of no use to them at this moment.

It is difficult to say whether the desire that everything remain unchanged was due to their realization of how difficult it might be to adjust to an entirely changed home situation or whether it finds its explanation in some sort of magical thinking running approximately along the following lines: If nothing changes in the world in which I used to live, then I shall not change either. In this way they might have tried to counteract their feeling that they were changing. . . .

As a matter of fact, although most families behaved decently to those family members who were in the camp, serious problems were created. . . . they found difficulties in finding employment because a family member was suspect; their children had difficulties at school; they were excluded from public relief. So it was only natural that they came to resent having a family member in the camp. Their friends did not have much compassion for them, because the German population at large developed certain defense mechanisms against the concentration camp. The Germans could not stand the idea of living in a world where one was not protected by law and order.[12] They just would not believe that the prisoners in the camps had not committed outrageous crimes since the way they were punished permitted only this conclusion. So actually a

---

one officer of the Gestapo would be replaced by another. The *new* prisoners discussed the speech excitedly, and paid no attention to the rumors, the *old* prisoners paid no attention to the speech, but devoted all their conversations to the changes in camp officers.

[12] See earlier discussion of the rationalizations of middle-class prisoners.

slow process of alienation took place between the prisoners and their families. . . .

Old prisoners did not like to be reminded of their families and former friends. When they spoke about them, it was in a very detached way. They liked to receive letters, but it was not very important to them, partly because they had lost contact with the events related in them. It has been mentioned that they had some realization of how difficult it might be for them to find their way back, but there was another contributing factor, namely, the prisoners' hatred of all those living outside of the camp, who "enjoyed life as if we were not rotting away. . . ." But even this hatred was very subdued in the old prisoners. It seemed that, as much as they had forgotten to love their kin, they had lost the ability to hate them. They had learned to direct a great amount of aggression against themselves so as not to get into too many conflicts with the Gestapo, while the new prisoners still directed their aggressions against the outer world, and—when not supervised—against the Gestapo. Since the old prisoners did not show much emotion either way, they were unable to feel strongly about anybody. . . .

Hopes about life after liberation. Here the prisoners embarked a great deal on individual and group daydreams. To indulge in them was one of the favorite pastimes if the general emotional climate in the camp was not too depressed. There was a marked difference between the daydreams of the new and old prisoners. The longer the time a prisoner had spent in camp, the less true to reality were his daydreams; so much so that the hopes and expectations of the old prisoners often took the form of eschatological or messianic hopes; this was in line with their expectation that only such an event as the end of the world would liberate them. They would daydream of the coming world war and world revolution. They were convinced that out of this great upheaval they would emerge as the future leaders of Germany at least, if not of the world. This was the least to which their sufferings entitled them. These grandiose expectations were coexistent with great vagueness as to their future private lives. In their daydreams they were certain to emerge as the future secretaries of state, but they were less certain whether they would continue to live with their wives and children. Part of these daydreams may be explained by the fact that they seemed to feel that only a high public position could help them to regain their standing within their families.

The hopes and expectations of the new prisoners about their future lives were much more true to reality. Despite their open ambivalence about their families, they never doubted that they were going to continue to live with them just where they had left off. They hoped to continue their public and professional lives in the same way as they used to live them. . . .

REGRESSION INTO INFANTILE BEHAVIOR

The prisoners developed types of behavior which are characteristic of infancy or early youth. Some of these behaviors developed slowly; others were immediately imposed on the prisoners and developed only in intensity as time went on. Some of these more or less infantile behaviors have already been discussed, such as ambivalence to one's family, despondency, finding satisfaction in daydreaming rather than in action.

[Such regression represents, by our definition, a mass phenomenon: i.e., evidently it would not have taken place if it had not happened in all prisoners. Prisoners accused those who would not develop a childlike dependency on the guards as threatening the security of the group—a realistic view since the Gestapo punished the whole group for individual members' misbehavior.] Even during the transportation the prisoners were tortured in a way in which a cruel and domineering father might torture a helpless child; . . . the prisoners were also debased by techniques which went much further into childhood situations. They were forced to soil themselves. In the camp the defecation was strictly regulated; it was one of the most important daily events, discussed in great detail. During the day the prisoners who wanted to defecate had to obtain the permission of the guard. It seemed as if the education to cleanliness would be once more repeated. It seemed to give pleasure to the guards to hold the power of granting or withholding the permission to visit the latrines. (Toilets were mostly not available.) This pleasure of the guards found its counterpart in the pleasure the prisoners derived from visiting the latrines, because there they usually could rest for a moment, secure from the whips of the overseers and guards. . . .

The prisoners were forced to say "thou" to one another, which in Germany is indiscriminately used only among small children. They were not permitted to address one another with the many titles to which middle- and upper-class Germans are accustomed. On the other hand, they had to address the guards in the most deferential manner, giving them all their titles.

The prisoners lived, like children, only in the immediate present; they lost the feeling for the sequence of time, they became unable to plan for the future or give up immediate pleasure satisfactions to gain greater ones in the near future. They were unable to establish durable object-relations. Friendships developed as quickly as they broke up. Prisoners would, like early adolescents, fight one another tooth and nail, declare that they would never even look at one another or speak to one another, only to become close friends within a few minutes. They were boastful, telling tales about what they had accomplished in their former lives, or how they succeeded in cheating foremen or guards, and how they sabotaged the work. Like children, they felt not at all set back or ashamed when it became known that they had lied about their prowess.

Another factor contributing to the regression into childhood behavior was the nonsensical work the prisoners were forced to perform. . . . They felt debased when forced to perform "childish" and stupid labor, and preferred even harder work when it produced something that might be considered useful. There seems to be no doubt that the tasks they performed, as well as the mistreatment by the Gestapo which they had to endure, contributed to their disintegration as adult persons. . . .

THE FINAL ADJUSTMENT TO THE LIFE IN THE CAMP

A prisoner had reached the final stage of adjustment to the camp situation when he had changed his personality so as to accept as his own the values of the Gestapo. A few examples may illustrate how this acceptance expressed itself.

The Gestapo considered, or pretended to consider, the prisoners the scum of the earth. They insisted that none of them was any better than the others. . . .

The prisoners found themselves in an impossible situation due to the steady interference with their privacy on the part of the guards and other prisoners. So a great amount of aggression accumulated. In the new prisoners it vented itself in the way it might have done in the world outside the camp. But slowly prisoners accepted, as expression of their verbal aggressions, terms which definitely did not originate in their previous vocabularies, but were taken over from the very different vocabulary of the Gestapo. From copying the verbal aggressions of the Gestapo to copying their form of bodily aggressions was one more step, but it took several years to make this step. It was not unusual to find old prisoners, when in charge of others, behaving worse than the Gestapo, in some cases because they were trying to win favor with the Gestapo in this way but more often because they considered this the best way to behave toward prisoners in the camp. . . .

Old prisoners who seemed to have a tendency to identify themselves with the Gestapo did so not only in respect to aggressive behavior. They would try to arrogate to themselves old pieces of Gestapo uniforms. If that was not possible, they tried to sew and mend their uniforms so that they would resemble those of the guards. The length to which prisoners would go in these efforts seemed unbelievable, particularly since the Gestapo punished them for their efforts to copy Gestapo uniforms. When asked why they did it, they admitted that they loved to look like one of the guards.

The identification with the Gestapo did not stop with the copying of their outer appearance and behavior. Old prisoners accepted their goals and values, too, even when they seemed opposed to their own interests. It was appalling to see how far formerly even politically well-educated prisoners would go in this identification. . . .

The writer asked more than one hundred old political prisoners the following question: "If I am lucky and reach foreign soil, should I tell the story of the camp and arouse the interest of the cultured world?" He found only two who made the unqualified statement that everyone escaping Germany ought to fight the Nazis to the best of his abilities. *All others were hoping for a German revolution, but did not like the idea of interference on the part of a foreign power.*

When old prisoners accepted Nazi values as their own, they usually did not admit it, but explained their behavior by means of rationalizations. For instance, prisoners collected scrap in the camp because Germany was low on raw materials. When it was pointed out that they were thus helping the Nazis, they rationalized that through the saving of scrap Germany's working classes, too, became richer. When erecting buildings for the Gestapo, controversies started whether one should build well. New prisoners were for sabotaging, a majority of the old prisoners for building well. They rationalized that the new Germany will have use for these buildings. When it was pointed out that a revolution will have to destroy the fortresses of the Gestapo, they retired to the general statement that one ought to do well any job one has to do. It seems that the majority of the old prisoners had realized that they could not continue to work for the Gestapo unless they could convince themselves that their work made some sense, so they had to convince themselves of this sense.

The satisfaction with which some old prisoners enjoyed the fact that, during the twice daily counting of the prisoners, they really had stood well at attention can be explained only by the fact that they had entirely accepted the values of the Gestapo as their own. Prisoners prided themselves on being as tough as the Gestapo members. This identification with their torturers went so far as copying their leisure-time activities. One of the games played by the guards was to find out who could stand to be hit longest without uttering a complaint. This game was copied by the old prisoners, as though they had not been hit often and long enough without needing to repeat this experience as a game.

Often the Gestapo would enforce nonsensical rules, originating in the whims of one of the guards. They were usually forgotten as soon as formulated, but there were always some old prisoners who would continue to follow these rules and try to enforce them on others long after the Gestapo had forgotten about them. . . .

Other problems in which most old prisoners made their peace with the values of the Gestapo included the race problem, although race discrimination had been alien to their scheme of values before they were brought into the camp. They accepted as true the claim that Germany needed more space (*Lebensraum*), but added "as long as there does not exist a world federation," they believed in the superiority of the German race. It should be emphasized that this was not the result of propaganda on the side of the Gestapo. The Gestapo made no such efforts. . . .

Among the old prisoners one could observe other developments which indicated their desire to accept the Gestapo along lines which definitely could not originate in propaganda. It seems that, since they returned to a childlike attitude toward the Gestapo, they had a desire that at least some of those whom they accepted as all-powerful father-images should be just and kind. They divided their positive and negative feelings—strange as it may be that they should have positive feelings, they had them—toward the Gestapo in such way that all positive emotions were concentrated on a few officers who were rather high up in the hierarchy of camp administrators, but hardly ever on the governor of the camp. They insisted that these officers hid behind their rough surfaces a feeling of justice and propriety; he, or they, were supposed to be genuinely interested in the prisoners and even trying, in a small way, to help them. Since nothing of these supposed feelings and efforts ever became apparent, it was explained that the officer hid them so effectively because otherwise he would not be able to help the prisoners. The eagerness of these prisoners to find reasons for their claims was pitiful. . . .

After so much has been said about the old prisoners' tendency to conform and to identity with the Gestapo, it ought to be stressed that this was only part of the picture, because the author tried to concentrate on interesting psychological mechanisms in group behavior rather than on reporting types of behavior which are either well known or could reasonably be expected. These same old prisoners who identified with the Gestapo at other moments defied it, demonstrating extraordinary courage in doing so. . . .

CONCLUSION

It seems that what happens in an extreme fashion to the prisoners who spend several years in the concentration camp happens in less exaggerated form to the inhabitants of the big concentration camp called Greater Germany. It might happen to the inhabitants of occupied countries if they are not able to form organized groups of resistance. The system seems too strong for an individual to break its hold over his emotional life, particularly if he finds himself within a group which has more or less accepted the Nazi system. It seems easier to resist the pressure of the Gestapo and the Nazis if one functions as an individual; the Gestapo seems to know that and therefore insists on forcing all individuals into groups which they supervise. Some of the methods used for this purpose are the hostage system and the punishment of the whole group for whatever a member of it does; not permitting anybody to deviate in his behavior from the group norm, whatever this norm may be; discouraging solitary activities of any kind, etc. The main goal of the efforts seems to be to produce in the subjects childlike attitudes and childlike dependency on the will of the leaders. The most effective way to break this influence seems to be the formation of democratic groups of resistance of independent, mature, and self-reliant persons, in which every member backs up, in all other members, the ability to resist. If such groups are not formed, it seems very difficult not to become subject to the slow process of personality disintegration produced by the unrelenting pressure of the Gestapo and the Nazi system.

2. REACTIONS TO DISASTER

The second paper of this chapter takes up the problem of human reactions to disaster, drawing upon accounts and analyses of behavior in a whole range of disasters, ranging from a carbon-monoxide poisoning afflicting most of the workers in a small factory, to the extremity of the atomic bombings of Hiroshima and Nagasaki in 1945. In this paper the concentration is on psychodynamic interpretation of the reported reactions, and its linkage to role structure, to the implicit "social contract" of organized society, and to some of the general trends of modern industrialized societies.

This paper, in an almost inevitable consequence of the process of intellectualization, analysis, and generalization, necessarily lacks a feeling of vivid direct confrontation with the horrors of a disaster as directly experienced. Probably this can be said of any attempts at plumbing by analysis and systematic interpretation into the meanings of human reactions—perhaps keeping at a distance by intellectualization is a necessary defense against being emotionally overwhelmed by the events and experiences under consideration.[13]

[13] The author and other members of the Disaster Research Team of the National Opinion Research Center at the University of Chicago 1952-1954, found themselves using this and a number of other psychological devices, only partly consciously, to protect themselves from overwhelming affect in dealing with the highly charged data of others' experiences of disaster. One such mechanism was a kind of ghoulish professionalism—probably also developed by journalists who frequently deal with disaster—according to which certain catastrophes were rated as "great" or "lovely disasters" entirely in terms of their offering us research opportunities—usually roughly correlated with the extent and suddenness of destruction—a scale of values almost exactly the reverse of what we would ordinarily use in our "civilian" capacity. Another mechanism was a heightening of ghoulish or "sick" humor, according to which we delightedly seized upon and read to each other any "funny" or grotesque incident recounted in the interviews or heard about in the field, such as the ludicrous locations some survivors found themselves in during or after a tornado or the "quaintness" of expression of victims from an alien subculture (in this case uneducated rural Southerners of Bible-belt intensity). Retrospectively, while many of the survivor victims about whom we jested would have been scandalized and affronted by our ma-

Psychosocial dynamics in disaster

This paper attempts to interrelate depth dynamics of reactions to disaster with certain sociological dimensions: behavior in reference to social roles and the problem of "social contract."

By "disaster" we are referring to large-scale catastrophic events like tornadoes, floods, earthquakes, and atomic bombings—events that bring destruction and suffering to a community on a large scale and in a brief compass of time. A brief definition with sociological emphasis is the following:[14]

> A disaster is an event, concentrated in time and space, in which a society or a community undergoes severe danger and incurs such losses to its members and physical appurtenances that the social structure is disrupted and the fulfillment of all or some of the essential functions of the society is prevented.

This kind of definition emphasizes that the event must refer to a relatively large-scale social unit, and be disruptive rather generally to

---

cabre levity, it seems clear that these devices were necessary protective mechanisms to keep us from being overwhelmed with the affect that would be evoked by the "natural" tendency toward identification with other suffering human beings. The affective explosiveness of the subject matter probably also helps explain why a considerable expenditure of research on disasters (in America at least) has so far resulted in relatively little in the way of penetrating analyses that combine psychoanalytic and sociological depth that should have been expected by the numbers of talents of each of these types that have addressed themselves to these questions.

The writer is indebted to the psychologist Stanley Rosenman for assistance in the preparation of this paper, but the responsibility for the resulting formulations presented here rests, of course, entirely with the present author. Dr. Rosenman has also generously granted permission to draw upon parts of an earlier paper written in collaboration with the present author: Stanley Rosenman and Robert Endleman, Personality and Role Behavior in Disaster: A Thematic Approach, prepared for the National Opinion Research Center Disaster Research Project, University of Chicago, 1952. Unpublished, 128 pp.

The empirical disaster studies most frequently referred to in the present paper are those in which the author participated as a member of the Disaster Research Project of the National Opinion Research Center, University of Chicago, 1952-1954. They are reported in Eli Marks, Charles Fritz, Robert Endleman, Enrico Quarantelli, Rue Bucher, Leonard Schatzman, and Dotsie Earle, Human Reactions in Disaster Situations. Report No. 52 (Chicago: National Opinion Research Center, University of Chicago, June 1954), 3 volumes, 950 pages. (Available in microfilm from NORC.) For brevity, this report is hereafter cited as "NORC."

[14] Adapted from R. Endleman, "An Approach to the Study of Disasters." Unpublished paper, National Opinion Research Center, Disaster Research Project, 1952.

such essentials of social functioning as biological survival, the maintenance of order, the sustaining of socially validated meanings, and the continuance of socially required motivations to action.[15] By contrast, no matter how traumatic or personally catastrophic, an event occurring to only an individual or to small groups while not generally disturbing the social fabric, will not be defined as a disaster in these terms. (Significantly, studies have shown that human reactions to such events as the latter—e.g., an accident killing several members of one's immediate family—follow patterns quite different from those to disasters of community or wider scope. Basically, personal accidents or catastrophes tend to isolate the individual or small group in their suffering, while community disasters draw people into a community of suffering and loss, with important consequences to be discussed.)

Disasters in the sense used, of course, differ importantly from one to another: natural or manmade, "momentaneous" or "crescive" in onset, focused or broad in scope, greatly or only slightly destructive in effect, and differing in precipitating agent (flood, fire, explosion, hurricane, tornado, earthquake, etc.). Necessarily, then, any general discussion of disaster behavior cannot be equally valid for all of these different types of event; hence the following discussion concentrates on broad similarities, but inevitably some of the formulations are more applicable to certain kinds of disaster situations than others.

Mostly since 1950, sociologists and social psychologists have made relatively systematic studies of a large number of peacetime community disasters or serious accidents. This has been done largely in the United States, but a few studies have been made in other countries as well.[16] For the most part, these studies have concentrated on the

---

[15] Though it lacked substantial danger to life or destruction of property, the great transit strike of New York City of January 1-12, 1966, comes close to qualifying as a disaster in these terms, so widely proliferating were the disruptive effects on social and economic life of the whole metropolitan region. Less qualifying for the status of disaster, though geographically much more widespread, was the electricity blackout of large sections of the northeastern United States and parts of Canada, of November 9, 1965, where danger to life and property was minimal, and proliferation of disruption limited by the relatively brief duration. Studies of such emergencies would, however, provide valuable adjunctive data for disaster studies.

[16] Chapman, in a 1962 publication surveying the disaster research to that date, counts well over a hundred events studied. They include 20 tornadoes, 13 fires and explosions, 12 floods, 12 hurricanes and typhoons, 8 earthquakes, 8 toxicological incidents, 5 threatened or realized epidemics, 4 airplane crashes, 3 blizzards, 2 mine disasters, as well as 6 miscellaneous emergencies plus 6 false air-

sequence of behavior in such community disasters as tornadoes, floods, explosions: what kind of behavior occurred, in what frequencies, by what segments of the population, and with what subsequent verbalization of feelings and attitudes. They have dealt with such questions as who acted effectively in rescue and relief work; who were relatively controlled or uncontrolled in their actions and emotional expression; who helped or impeded rescue, relief, or restoration work; what patterns of cooperation or conflict appeared. Psychological considerations in such studies have tended to be restricted to conceptualizations such as "definition of the situation" or "relative deprivation," rarely with deeper psychodynamic dimensions.

By contrast, psychodynamic efforts, such as Wolfenstein's *Disaster*[17] or the essays on disaster in the psychoanalytic literature, do not deal with frequencies or role or other social distributions of the dynamic patterns of response portrayed. Nor do they attempt a linkage of the psychodynamic with sociological elements, except in incidental or passing reflections. Hence, works showing frequencies and distributions of particular actions or reactions have not generally been linked with psychodynamic interpretations.

The gap between the two kinds of writing is not entirely surprising. It is almost impossible to extrapolate from frequencies or distributions of certain types of behavior, to frequencies or distributions of certain psychodynamic constellations. Any item of behavior or verbalization—e.g., "very active in rescue work" or "expresses negative feelings toward neighbors"—can mean any one or combination of different things at the psychodynamic level. A man works hard all night following a tornado that struck his town, digging victims from out of the wreckage: what are the depth-psychological meanings of his behavior? Is he expiating guilt for not having been hurt himself?

---

raid alerts and 11 civil defense exercises. These studies used over 14 thousand interviews or questionnaires. In addition, research on four World War II bombings involved over 7 thousand interviews or questionnaires.

See Dwight W. Chapman, "A Brief Introduction to Contemporary Disaster Research," in C. W. Baker and D. W. Chapman (eds.), *Man and Society in Disaster* (New York: Basic Books, 1962), p. 5. This paper gives a general survey of disaster research to that date. A comparable brief general source is Charles E. Fritz: "Disaster," in R. Merton and R. Nesbit (eds.), *Contemporary Social Problems* (New York: Harcourt, Brace & World, 1961), pp. 651-94. Both papers refer extensively to the published (and much more extensive unpublished) disaster literature available to their dates.

[17] Martha Wolfenstein, *Disaster: A Psychological Essay* (New York: Free Press of Glencoe, 1957).

Is he desperately denying his own terrified reactions experienced during impact? Is he reveling in the chance to play a hero's role denied him in "ordinary" life? Is he getting sadistic gratification from seeing and handling horribly mangled bodies? Is he expressing positive generous feelings released by the fact that the catastrophe has gratified his repressed hostilities? Any one or combination of these may be true, but we do not know which without a careful personality study of the man in the context of the event. Conversely, the same psychodynamic constellation—e.g., expiation of guilt for having been less hurt than others—may be expressed in a number of different behavioral or verbalized forms, such as agitated rescue work, exaggeration of one's own injuries, or prayer to a merciful Deity.

Since no systematic research that I know of has integrated these two kinds of approaches, the following essay, though drawing on an extensive range of sources, represents a necessarily exploratory attempt.

GENERAL PATTERNS OF DISASTER REACTION

In order to place in context any discussion of role variations and of elements of social contract in disaster reactions, we need a brief delineation of the general range of variations in reaction to disasters.

Remote danger. Generally, worry about and preparedness for a remote disaster are rare, even in communities subject to a chronic threat, for example, of tornadoes, earthquakes, or mine disasters. The basic psychological mechanism here is *denial:* denial of the danger, denial that it will hit here, or if it does, that it will hit me and my family.

Imminent threat. Even when a disaster threat is imminent, or warnings have been given, the time taken to take such cues or warnings seriously is highly variable, many persons (not all) continuing to deny disaster threat until the moment of impact itself. In most persons disaster cues tend to be assimilated to a "normal" context as long as possible. For unfamiliar disasters this may be up to the moment of impact. Accordingly, precautionary activity during this imminent period is quite variable also, some of it delayed so long that it is even more maladaptive to the disaster danger than no precautionary activity at all.[18] In the context, some of the precautionary action is reasonable; some of it is suggestive only of magical propiti-

[18] NORC, Vol. I, pp. 303-19, 502.

ation; and some has both elements. Some is oriented entirely to oneself, some to the protection of others as well. Sharing the danger with others may hasten accurate appraisal and reasonable precautionary action or foster continuation of denial. In either case, anticipatory anxieties may be either allayed or heightened by the interaction.

Impact. In disasters of momentaneous impact (tornadoes, earthquakes, bombings, explosions) most victims initially imagine themselves either the only ones hit or at the very center of the destruction. Generally, people tend to take actions protecting themselves first, other close family intimates next, others present next, and possessions usually last. In the context of available perceptions, these actions *tend* to be generally reasonable and adaptive[19] though *ex post facto* analysis may prove otherwise. Very rare is *panic,* in the technical sense of acute fear marked by loss of self-control and antisocial and irrational flight. Though it does occasionally occur, its frequency nowhere approximates popular and folklore expectations.[20] Also rare is the extreme loss of self-control: the general pattern is some kind of maintenance of self-control, even through extreme emotional reactions to the critical danger. Both control, and degree and kind of emotional reaction tend to vary according to roles, to the social situation, to the amount of forewarning, as well as idiosyncratically by personality trends.

Immediate post-impact. Large percentages of those physically intact, though momentarily stunned and bewildered, tend to recover self-control rather rapidly and quickly set about to extricate themselves, look to the safety of kin, intimates, neighbors, and others, and search for missing intimates. Many help rescue others and serve in various aspects of relief. Most such activity is initially uncoordinated. Again in contrast to popular expectations of mass panic and "irrational," maladaptive, and egoistic reactions, a major feature of behavior in this phase is community self-help and mutual aid, most of the more critical of this being accomplished before outside formal aid and relief and rehabilitation arrives. Distribution of such self-help and mutual aid activity is, of course, highly variable, by role, situation, and individual personality. So too are the emotional intrapsychic meanings of such action. A common concomitant feeling is a

[19] This finding may, however, be at least partially an artifact of the fact that we did not interview the dead.
[20] NORC, Vol. I, p. 503. See also Wolfenstein, *op. cit.*, for a perceptive analysis of why panic should be so much more intensely *expected* than it actually occurs. Part II, Chapter 5.

great expansion of positive feelings toward others and heightened sense of community solidarity under stress: a phenomenon called by one author the "post-disaster utopia." [21] Such mutual aid is also variable in efficiency and effectiveness as well.

In the variety of different, often contradictory emotional reactions in the immediate post-impact period, one syndrome has been persistently reported, in one form or other, in all disasters studied. This "disaster syndrome" involves absence of felt emotion, lack of response to present stimuli, inhibition of outward activity, docility, and undemandingness. Persons in this state are described as "dazed," "shocked," "stunned," "stupefied," "almost in a state of mental paralysis," and, negatively, as "*not* screaming or crying," "*not* hysterical," or "*not* feeling real." Clinically this state can be seen as a temporary *depression*.[22] Due to the variability of classification of reactions in different studies, we can arrive at only approximate notions of the frequency and distribution of this syndrome. (Relevant role elements are discussed in the following section.) Other probable determinants are degree of danger during impact, and severity of loss, as in the death of a close loved one in the disaster.[23]

Post-impact emotional reactions are not only variable interindividually. There is also commonly a rapid alternation of feelings within the same individual: alarm, exhilaration at having escaped, invulnerability feelings, great helplessness, fluctuations of hope and despair.

Aftermath. In the longer-range subsequent period, the "post-disaster utopia" of great mutual aid and solidarity feeling inevitably declines. More formal longer-term aid by outside agencies evokes new definitions of "relative deprivation," frequently with hostile feelings about the apparently inequitable distribution and bureaucratism involved in such aid. Property loss, earlier denied significance (feeling "lucky to be alive") now takes on more importance.

Few of the inhabitants of a disaster-stricken area move away. The decision to rebuild one's destroyed home, however, is least likely for those who have suffered the most extreme losses in the disaster (death of very close kin or severe injuries to oneself and household family members).[24]

Other aftermath reactions include obsessive reliving of the disas-

[21] Wolfenstein, *op. cit.*, Part II, Chapter 6.

[22] *Ibid.*, p. 78.

[23] NORC, Vol. I, p. 501, considering the "shock-stun" reaction classified in that study, as an approximation of "disaster syndrome."

[24] NORC, Vol. I, p. 501.

ter in memory and the opposite, repression of it by amnesia or at least avoidance of all reminders, a magical denial device. Great need for subsequent re-exposure in memory tends to be proportional to lack of antecedent preparation. Preoccupation with things undone during the disaster resonates with other, earlier, nondisaster-related sins of omission.

The disaster tends to bring to the fore implicit beliefs about overall or supernatural powers and man's relation to them, re-evoking infantile beliefs in intentional causation by anthropomorphized powers. And for the religious in Western cultures, disaster poses the problem of evil: Why does God let such things happen?

ROLE DIMENSIONS IN DISASTER REACTIONS

With this general picture of typical disaster reactions in mind, we can explore variations in reactions according to social roles and attempt some linkage with psychodynamic themes. We shall consider especially the following kinds of roles: (1) men in responsible kinship roles; (2) men in responsible occupational roles; (3) women in responsible roles; (4) the aged.

Men in responsible kinship roles. By our cultural standards, a man who is a husband and father is expected to be active, to be supportive of his dependents, generally to be in control of his emotions in difficult situations, especially where his dependents' needs are involved, to give priority to his dependents' needs over his own, and to be capable of "rising to the occasion" to help the community as well as his own family. To fulfill such expectations well, validates a man's image of himself as an adult, as a male, as a husband, and as a father. The different elements of such an image, however, may have greater or lesser centrality in a man's feelings about his ideal and his real self, and may be abetted or contradicted by a variety of dynamic elements in his total personality structure. Drives toward mastery may largely support this role constellation, but they may also contain elements of self-assertion or individualization that work against supportive or cooperative activities. The impulse for individual survival may also counteract supportive or protective action for the benefit of others. Strong dependency needs may seriously interfere with the capacity to help "weaker" others in extremity, while strong empathic identification with victims or underdogs may drive a man in a crisis into actualizing a rescuer or savior role.

The validation by men of the responsible husband-father role in a disaster can be seen in a number of the findings of the systematic community studies. The NORC study of an Arkansas tornado found that "male household heads with dependents" differed from those without dependents and from persons in "all other household roles"—i.e., women, with or without dependents, and children—in the following ways:[25]

> . . . in displaying more controlled adaptive behavior and greater protectiveness toward others, before and during the impact of the storm . . . Also . . . a higher frequency of community-oriented activity after the storm, both . . . emergency (e.g., rescue) and in later postimpact aid to disaster victims. They also gave indications of higher "morale" in more positive attitudes about post-impact problems and a greater tendency to understate their deprivations.

The NORC studies also found such differences to be generally true in several other disasters studied (airline crashes, an earthquake, a mine explosion, and others).[26] Another study found that adult men, particularly fathers of families, were more controlled and more rationally effective in rescue operations, than teen-age boys, in a different tornado-struck community.[27] Since the NORC Arkansas study also found that persons who suffered the greatest personal loss in the disaster (death of intimates, severe injury to self or close kin) gave little post-impact aid to others and showed low post-impact "morale," we may infer that the controlled, active, helpful husband-fathers did not include men who had had severe losses and that such rescue activitists may see themselves as having been effective (by their precautionary and protective actions before and during impact) in aiding their families' survival. These same men tend also to report less of the "incapacitating" emotional reactions (shock-stun or expressive-hysterical) during and after the storm. Evidently, then, their activity before and during the disaster *validates* their responsible family role. This is further confirmed in the survival results. Not only may their "illusion of invulnerability" be thus maintained, but something like a savior fantasy is realized. Such a fantasy may, in turn, evoke guilt feelings over the hubris implied; and these, in turn, can be assuaged by throwing oneself into rescue activities for the community in general, once one's own family's safety is assured.

[25] NORC, Vol. I, p. 500.
[26] *Ibid.*, p. 508.
[27] William H. Form and Sigmund Nosow, *Community in Disaster* (New York: Harper & Row, Publishers, 1958, pp. 40-47).

These men are found to show (or at least to report) less of the "disaster syndrome" in the immediate post-impact, and less longer-range incapacitating symptoms of psychophysiological varieties, than persons in other role positions. Thus their post-impact rescue and other aid activities further validate responsible-male role images, and their "morale" is relatively high—they feel comparatively good about the experience.

This, however, is but one composite picture of men in responsible family roles. Other findings from the systematic NORC study modify this picture. For example: "Males more often took a directing or initiating role ('leadership') during the storm *if they were the only adult male present*, and also reported somewhat greater emotional agitation in such situations." [28] This finding gives some sense of the emotional cost during impact of the family-head leadership role. Also it indicates that the presence of other adult males both reduces the tendency of an adult male to take a leadership role (i.e., one validating adult male role images) and reduces the emotional impact of the disaster force. The pattern suggests that a man, intensely frightened by the raging disaster power, feels somewhat protected by the presence of other men and less impelled to take initiating action, presumably because, in effect, the presence of other men divides the adult male responsibilities. By contrast, when he finds himself the only man with women and children, terror for his own safety conflicts with the need to aid, support, and protect the others, and the resulting emotional reaction is strong, though not necessarily enough to immobilize the man.

Further, not all men in such family-responsible roles do behave in controlled adaptive ways, aiding and protecting their dependents. Some fail to notice warning signs until less than a minute before impact. They are then caught in the midst of belated precautionary or protective activities that make themselves and their families even more vulnerable. Such inattention may frequently indicate that the supportive husband-father role is not salient in the man's underlying self-image. Rather the disaster situation may bring to the fore, or intensify, strong deeper dependency feelings. Sometimes it may mobilize guilt feelings (of origins unrelated to the disaster) to the point where the man abandons himself to helpless submission to the pun-

[28] NORC, Vol. I, p. 500. Note that the social situational category used here is not the same as "male household heads with dependents," but the two would overlap considerably.

ishing power. Since direct expression of such feelings by men is so strongly tabooed by our culture, a corresponding effect may be brought about by means less obvious than overt collapse into helplessness. He may carry out apparently well-intended but effectively ill-advised protective or precautionary actions which do not in fact protect his family; or he may get himself isolated from them in another part of the house, in a frantic or belated precautionary measure.

Similarly, immediately after impact, some family heads do display the "disaster syndrome" of shock, stun, bewilderment, even where they and their families emerge unhurt. Such momentary depressive reaction may involve unacknowledged guilt feelings over impact-period reactions reflecting dependency, submissiveness, or simply failure to live up fully to adult male responsibilities. They may then "recover" and attempt to reassert the responsible adult male role by helping in rescue activities. In these cases their work may be chaotic, disorganized, and generally ineffective. This may be especially the case where the man is faced with a role conflict—for example, get help for a slightly injured family member or help rescue trapped neighbors or others in more desperate need. Here the "helping" behavior may be particularly disorganized and ineffective. If the man recognizes this, his guilt feelings may be further intensified, with subsequent effects in incapacitation, reduced energy or will to work, and a variety of psychophysical symptoms in the aftermath.

Thus while the culturally prescribed role of the male family head may be a general guideline to what to expect of man in a disaster situation, it is insufficient without a consideration of the intrapsychic meanings of the role for each particular man in question. Behavior consonant with the role demands is not explained by the role itself, for this leaves unexplained the deviant cases. Even the conforming cases may include roughly similar kinds of behavior and affect deriving from a number of *different* underlying psychic constellations. The common element would be role-validation by playing it reasonably effectively, thus strengthening those underlying trends that support the role and weakening contradictory trends. On the other side, antagonistic dynamics such as strong dependency feelings, hitherto masked or kept under control, may prevent validation of the required role during the disaster and take its toll afterward in the ways described. Otherwise expressed, the men who are defective in active supportive action for their families during impact, who are

overwhelmed with affect during the disaster, or by the "disaster syndrome" afterward, may be realizing a fantasy role or "latent role" by
such behavior.

Men in responsible occupational roles. Many occupational roles
also include culturally validated expectations of taking over, directing,
and supporting others or giving them special aid in emergency. Obvious examples are doctor, policeman, and schoolteacher. Disaster
studies tend to confirm that such persons tend to act in more self-
controlled, adaptive and helpful ways at all phases of a disaster. The
NORC studies found that persons with "disaster-related skills"
(medical, hospital personnel, policemen, firemen, etc.) perceived
and correctly interpreted disaster cues earlier and hence acted more
adaptively before impact; were more self-controlled, adaptive and
helpful to others during impact; and more frequently than others
assumed informal leadership roles both in immediate and in later
post-impact periods as well as showing higher morale and few incapacitating symptoms still later on. Intrapsychic dynamics comparable to those of the effective fathers can be postulated here, and a
consolidating role-validation process inferred.

The following case provides a good instance showing interrelations of psychodynamic patterns and responsible occupational role.

> *In a tornado in Worcester, a bus was overturned. The driver of*
> *the bus describes his feelings at the moment that it was happening:*
> *"I thought it was the end of all of us. . . . At one point I im-*
> *agined leaving my family an' I could even imagine the funeral they*
> *were holdin' for me. . . . But the thoughts were always in my*
> *mind of holding on and bein' able to stand up and get out of there*
> *an' help. . . . I can't ever remember stop thinking of what to do*
> *after."*
> *Afterwards this bus driver worked hard and valiantly to rescue*
> *injured passengers from the battered bus. ". . . I lost part of my*
> *thumb and it was hanging from the end. An' the thing that was*
> *making me the most impatient of it all was trying to get that piece*
> *of thumb outa people's faces as I was workin' on them. An' I kept*
> *trying to bite it off and feelin' if I could only remove it. It kept*
> *bothering me so much. An' a little thing like that after the great*
> *tragedy that had just struck! It seems funny now that those things*
> *you remember so clearly."*
> *After he had brought the injured bus passengers to the hospital*
> *and given them over to the care of medical personnel, explaining*
> *the injuries of each: "A nurse came up to me, an' she took me by*
> *the thumb an'—this is the part that I'm almost ashamed to relate—*

that when she took me by the thumb I keeled over, an' evidently I landed on the floor down there." [29]

This bus driver evidently regards it as part of the responsibility of his work role to look out for the welfare of all his passengers and to get them out of the damaged bus after the impact. He vividly imagines his own death, and then fantasies his family's holding the funeral for him—thus activating his husband-father role, though in the totally helpless and final position of being the object of bereavement. Helplessness in the face of the disastrous force, however, is quickly counteracted immediately afterward when he emerges not too seriously injured and able to activate his responsible driver role. By his rescue work he puts aside his own impact-period terror and any self-concern for his injury, which he reacts to at the time not as a frightening loss of a body part, but rather as a minor nuisance impeding the work he has to do. His responsible role thus gives him the context for useful helping activities which defend him from fully reacting to the extremity of the disaster and to his own danger and damage, denying that he himself was helpless or is now less than intact by focusing on the *others* who are injured or trapped. The defensiveness of this pattern is evident in his fainting in the hospital once he had completed the work of displacing his concern onto the others by getting them to competent aid. This defensive resource now exhausted, his own terror is now too dangerously close. He wards it off by loss of consciousness.[30]

It is interesting here that the threatened breakthrough of the extremity of affect appropriate to the danger he has been through, and to the injury he has suffered, occurs fairly soon after the end of the impact period—here as soon as the bus driver has completed the particular rescue task he assigns himself, one defined by his role responsibilities toward his passengers. The timing then is at least partly a function of the *kind* of responsible role the individual has: here a rather limited one as bus driver. This case is in contrast to those of some medical doctors who effectively rise to meet their role responsibilities in care for the injured and dying in the wake of the disaster. There the immersion in helping work—thus warding off anxieties about oneself—may be considerably more prolonged. Perhaps a "classic" case is that of Dr. Michihiko Hachiya who survived the

[29] Disaster Research Project, Psychiatric Institute of the University of Maryland. Interviews with disaster victims. Cited in Wolfenstein, *op. cit.*, pp. 98-99.
[30] Psychodynamic aspects of this interpretation follow Wolfenstein, *op. cit.*

atomic bombing of Hiroshima.[31] Though seriously injured, Hachiya never let out of his awareness his responsibility as Director of the Hiroshima Communications Hospital. He constantly rebuked himself for taking his colleagues' medical care attentions, instead of actively giving care to other injured; did all he could from his hospital bed to keep up direction of the hospital under the extreme demands made on it; tried to get up and about and back to active helping work well before his medical condition allowed; agonized over the moral dilemmas of the hospital's not being able to meet all of the conflicting and unprecedented demands; and constantly resisted, in the best tradition of rational science, the temptations to accept irrational rumors and anxiety-derived interpretations and prognostications, such as the statement, widely circulated in Japan in those first weeks after the bombing, that Hiroshima would be uninhabitable for seventy-five years, an interpretation contradicted by the evidence of his senses as he stayed and worked in the remnants of the ruined city.

But we may note that not all persons in responsible occupational roles act in such controlled, adaptive, and helping ways. Following are two examples where they did not.

A policeman who came into a badly damaged section of tornado-struck Worcester, is described by a doctor, as follows:[32]

> *He was overwhelmed by what he saw, as I interpret his behavior, and he just ran around. He was just running around and I don't know what he thought he was doing, that is, I don't know what he did. I'm sure he thought he was doing the best he could, but he didn't do anything.*

The doctor himself had started out to be helpful, confident of having special professional capacities to do so. His rescue activities turn out in fact to be hasty, disorganized, and not very efficient. He dashes from one victim to another evidently "trying to undo all the damage at once." [33] He uses inappropriate materials for a tourniquet, while better ones are at hand. He tries to get uninjured but dazed survivors to help him lift injured persons. He is then overcome by the frustrated feeling that "there was nothing you could do." Here

[31] Michihiko Hachiya, *Hiroshima Diary*, transl. by W. Wells (Chapel Hill: University of North Carolina Press, 1955).

[32] Disaster Research Project, Psychiatric Institute of the University of Maryland; quoted in Wolfenstein, *op. cit.*, p. 117.

[33] Wolfenstein's interpretation, *op. cit.*

then is a man who starts out acting on a self-image as a competent and relevantly trained professional, then being overwhelmed by the enormity of the damage. His role-defined self dissolves; and the picture of futile frustration shows an image of himself not much unlike that he gave of the totally ineffective policeman.

Women in responsible roles. Our cultural standards allow women more open expression of dependency and of emotional reaction in danger, stress, or pain than men. But also, women responsible for dependents, e.g., mothers of young children, are expected to keep self-control to give emotional support and reassurance to the dependents. The expectations and demands are thus at least partially contradictory. Such contradictions are reflected in the findings of such systematic studies as the NORC Arkansas tornado research:[34]

> *During impact, females with dependents were as other-protective as the males with dependents, but also had the most intense affective reactions and a higher frequency of expressive behavior, praying, and dependency on others. They also show a higher frequency of immediate postimpact emotional reactions—including the "shock-stun reactions"—and of physiological, psychosomatic, and psychological disturbances in the later postimpact period. On indices of postimpact morale they showed the lowest frequency of positive attitudes about problems of postimpact aid and rehabilitation (especially about disruption of community services); felt most affected by the disaster in a long-range sense (as expressed in "feeling changed"—religiously or otherwise—since the storm); and gave the most supernaturalistic "explanations" of the disaster.*

The same study also found that females more often took a "leadership" role during impact when there were children present. Findings from other studies showed similar trends.

The impact-period behavior reported here seems paradoxical: both protective toward dependents (children or old folk) and emotionally expressive ("hysterical," etc.) and dependent on others. Since the findings indicated are statistical trends, they do not tell us to what extent the same individual women were both protective toward others and "hysterical." Expressive behavior would seem to deny a level of self-control necessary to be protective and supportive toward others, and post-impact "disaster-syndrome" reactions, with

[34] NORC, I, p. 500. The comparisons referred to in statements of "more" and "most" are with males in any household role, and adult females without dependents.

their depressive implication, suggest that some of the reported protective behavior represents an idealized later reconstruction indicating how they felt they should have acted but did not, and therefore felt guilty about it.

A comment by Wolfenstein on one interview is relevant:[35]

> [A] *mother tells the interviewer: "When the storm hit . . . I just prayed to the good Lord to bring me through and let me see my kids alive and well." The interviewer rephrases this: "I see, you were thinking of your children." The woman . . . replies: "I certainly were, and the thought of myself never entered." What the woman had at first said was that she prayed for both herself and her children. The interviewer, by acknowledging only her concern for her children, succeeds in activating the feeling of guilt that one has thought of oneself at all (perhaps because at that moment one had thought of oneself above all), so that she quickly affirms that "the thought of myself never entered." If in the moment of extreme danger the feeling occurs that the loss of loved ones would be less unbearable than the loss of one's own life, there is apt to be shame and guilt for such feelings afterwards.*

This interpretation suggests possible dynamics that may have been operating in many of the women of Arkansas to contribute to the combination of reported protective behavior toward dependents, and expressive behavior—crying, wailing, praying. Guilt reactions after the storm, indicated in "disaster syndrome" ("shock-stun") and possibly also in the later post-impact disturbances, suggest these women were not as supportive and helpful to their dependents during impact as they say, or as they think they should have been. At the same time there is less culturally defined role pressure on themselves to deny having had "hysterical" reactions during the storm. Another line of interpretation, not entirely divergent from the one just given, would be that the combination of protective activity and emotional expressiveness-and-dependency aptly reflects the conflicting role expectations of women with dependents. To the extent that they did behave protectively and supportively toward their children this is accomplished against strong feelings of terror for one's own survival. Much of the "expressive behavior" summarized in the statistical trends in fact consisted of praying, and this was frequently done by gathering the children around her in a close huddle in a spot chosen with an eye to maximizing protection. The praying itself

---

[35] Wolfenstein, *op. cit.*, p. 97. The case quoted is from interviews by the Waco-San Angelo Disaster Study, Disaster Study, University of Texas.

is, of course, an intense expression of dependency, not upon a human, but upon a supernatural protector. Where the prayer is for one's own survival, though also for the children's—a common reaction in these disasters, as in the example discussed—guilt feelings may ensue. These in turn reflect the conflicting role demands. These women's greater resort to later supernaturalistic interpretations of the disaster indicates a continuing pressure of such conflicts and guilt feelings into the post-disaster period. The central content underlying these supernaturalistic references is: God is punishing us (me) for our (my) sins. And "sins" here may well include thinking of oneself before one's children, and not actually having acted protectively enough for them.

In the period immediately after the tornado, the prevalence in these women of the "disaster syndrome" reactions may reflect not only guilt about impact-period behavior and feeling, but also a continuation into the post-impact period of conflicts inherent in the role of mother with children, exacerbated by the social situation. If no one in the family was missing or badly hurt, and the family was together during impact, the typical post-impact situation was one where the mother stayed with the children, giving what comfort and support she could muster, while the father took off to help in rescue and other aid work for the broader community, leaving the mother both with responsibilities and without the reassuring and supportive presence of the husband. In such situations, the women were also denied the opportunity for dealing with their own guilt feelings by expiatory community rescue work which was done mostly by the men. The drive toward activity to master the traumatic impact of the disaster itself, would for these women, remain frustrated. While staying with and comforting children would serve to validate the supportive mother role, it could be felt as a much more passive kind of behavior. These women's later "least positive" attitudes toward relief and rehabilitation aid also reflect continuation of emotional turbulence toward the whole disaster experience, and specifically a feeling that their own dependency needs have been very inadequately satisfied. Though many of these same women in the early post-impact phase (providing they and their families emerged unhurt) typically insisted to people offering help, "Never mind, we're O.K. Help some of the others who need it more," later they give voice to many complaints of inadequate aid from the agencies, as compared with aid given to others, or complained about the agencies' bureaucratic procedures. Their persistent physiological, psycho-somatic, and psychological disturbances not only reflect continuing irresolution of the emotional stress and conflicts of the disaster period itself, but may also dramatize an exaggerated feminine dependency: "If I feel this sick, people have to take care of me" and an implicit plea for release from maternal responsibilities which are "just too much after all I have been through."

Role validation and the dynamic mechanisms enabling it turn out then to be much more difficult for the women with dependents than for the men in comparable responsible roles. Part of the reason for this would appear to be that the cultural definition of the role itself is internally ambiguous and contradictory. The emotional costs of such strain are evident throughout the whole sequence.

The aged. It is by now a commonplace that the aged in modern societies are in a peculiarly disadvantaged position—both compared to their own situation when younger ("in the prime of life") and compared to that of the aged in more traditional societies where age itself confers esteem on the assumption that longevity gives a greater accumulation of the wisdom of the generations. Rapid change in industrial societies makes the aged easily obsolete in their thinking and adaptations—commonly so in the eyes of the younger, frequently in their own eyes as well. For men it means extrusion from the world of gainful work, the most important single basis for adult male status in the society. For women it means loss or decline of sexual attractiveness, one of the central foci of feminine identity, and, as offspring are grown, independent and departed to their own family households, loss of maternal responsibilities, the other central basis of the adult feminine self. The shift from a position of responsibility and support for others to one of at least partial dependency on them, further exacerbates the situation for both sexes. According to the demographic facts of life (or death) the women are likely to have the further difficulty of being left widowed for many of their last years.

In modern societies, then, the aged are in a particularly dependent, helpless, and vulnerable position in relation to disaster. It is only by a kind of irony that we can speak here of role *validation*, since basically there is little "role" at all for the aged in the sense of definite positive behavioral expectations. They are expected to be *acted upon*, rather than acting. Disaster should rather, then, be seen as *dramatization* of the "role-less" role of the aged. In fact it turns out that they are more vulnerable to the dangers of disaster than younger adults: they are more likely to become physical casualties of the disaster, either directly during impact itself or indirectly through protracted effects such as decreased resistance to illness, exposure, and other post-disaster stresses.[36] Part of this greater vulnerability is a product of greater likelihood of social isolation and hence lesser chance of receiving adequate warning of the impending disaster, or in certain kinds of disasters with longer-term warning, greater reluctance to evacuate a danger area. Related to this and to post-impact reactions as well is the fact that the aged are likely to have greater attachments—symbolic and emotional—to locale and to their specific dwellings, especially if these are places where they have lived for many years. Thus aged survivors who have lost everything materially are less likely than younger counterparts to be reconciled to this loss with the feeling that "property has been exchanged for life" and "we are lucky to have gotten out alive." Rather the feeling of deprivation occasioned by such loss is likely to be more intense than for younger persons. We find depressive or despairing reactions such as these: "Everything we'd acquired, saved for, for forty years—all gone in a moment—who can start over at our age and replace all that?" Loss of items of no great material value but of irreplaceable symbolic worth—mementos of special moments of the past, wedding gifts, treasured photographs or diplomas, and such— these may be especially and unconsolably painful to the aged. These people rarely have the energy, capacity, or will to rebuild and start over, and many deaths in the longer-term post-disaster period, apparently unrelated to any disaster injuries as such, may represent a demise hastened by the psychological effects of disaster losses.

Understandably, the effects even for physically unhurt older survivors are exacerbated by the relative rarity of their being physically active in helping with rescue or other aid work in the post-impact period.[37] This trend represents a further dramatization of the relatively helpless, dependent, and passive position of the aged in disaster.

There is no clear-cut evidence whether these difficulties in disaster are greater for older women than for older men. Considering the

[36] H. J. Friedsam, "Older Persons in Disaster" in Baker and Chapman, *op. cit.*, p. 179.

[37] These and the other "trends" indicated in this section, are from "tentative generalizations" offered by Friedsam, *op. cit.*, on the basis of careful study of all references to the aged in disaster studies to that date (1962).

greater likelihood that older women would be widowed (*before* the disaster) than older men, one would expect that they would.

Here we can draw upon what amounts to anecdotal case study data and explore some of the possible "deeper" dynamics involved. The Arkansas tornado studied by the NORC team again provides case material. In this community where the prevailing religious beliefs are a strongly fundamentalistic version of Protestantism, religious imagery of the disaster was highly expectable and seemed to be especially strong for aged widows who survived the storm. For some of these God, who had caused the disaster force, seems to be equated with a combination husband-and-father figure. In some cases this meant God is a punishing father visiting this disaster upon me and thus expressing his great concern with me, even his love for me. In one case, the widow spoke of how wonderful God is and, in almost the same breath, spoke of how inadequate her late husband was by comparison.[38] In these instances the disaster tended to be accepted in a very fatalistic manner. The theme seems to be, "If God takes me, that is, if the disaster kills me, then I shall be in rapturous ecstasy. The disaster expressed His love for me." On the other hand, "If the disaster spared me while it struck others, this proves God found me more worthy than my rivals: I therefore rejoice in this token of God's love of me." One otherwise sweet and kindly old woman expressed regret that she was too decrepit to go down to the morgue in order to see how bruised the bodies were. Here the confirmation of the illusion of invulnerability also appears, along with scarcely disguised aggression against the dead.[39]

This picture of dramatized passivity and dependency, however, is not the only theme of the aged, or aged women specifically, in disaster. A different constellation is one where the older woman is the focus of the reuniting of various members of the extended family after the disaster—a role more likely assumed if her house is intact

[38] NORC Interviews re Arkansas tornado, 1952.

[39] Such responses are of course not confined to the aged, nor to American disaster survivors. A younger woman survivor of the atomic bombing of Nagasaki, the following day greeted an elderly woman as follows: "Well Grandma Muriuchi, God must love both of us, mustn't he? I'd never thought I was such an especially good person but I guess I must be after all, for it was only God's special grace that I wasn't burned to death, they must have made God angry, mustn't they? They must have provoked him to wrath. You must be a good person too, Grandma. You've just been hurt a little." T. Nagai, *We of Nagasaki: The Study of Survivors of the Atomic Wasteland* (New York: Duell, Sloan & Pearce, 1951).

and the dwellings of her children and grandchildren have been damaged or destroyed. "Where intact, the mother-daughter relationship tends more than any other familial relationship to structure intergenerational contacts in pre-and post-impact evacuation and in search activities." [40]

Thus in effect for many older women, the disaster situation revitalizes those elements of the mother role that emphasize protecting, giving comfort, and providing a reassuring hearth to the troubled, even where the children are fully grown and themselves parents of families—and this especially for their *daughters*. A number of significant themes converge here. The mother-daughter involvement may be a *reciprocal* protective and comforting one, in which each reinforces in the other as well as herself the profound feeling that it is the womenfolk who are the basic locus of comfort and response in an emergency situation. In each also there is probably a revitalization of infantile dependency needs which can be legitimately gratified in this context: for the mother because she is old and thus has a claim to a greater expression of dependency than a woman in her prime; for the daughter simply because she *is* the "child" of her mother. And in each the possible psychic costs of such dependency are reduced by being in turn able to provide some comfort and affective response, if not specific material aid, to the other. As Friedsam notes:[41]

> . . . it is the mother-daughter relationship which is ubiquitous. One is reminded of Peter Townsend's[42] emphasis on the mother-daughter relationships in his study of old people in a lower-class section of London. His contention that there is a "special unity between grandmother, daughter and daughter's child," that "the family system of care is largely built around these three," and his illustrations of how the system functions, particularly in "many of the emergencies of life" are reflected over and over in the disaster protocols.

The situation of older men presents different problems. They are less likely than older women to be the extended-family focus of refuge; and they are also significantly less likely than younger men to engage in active rescue work, or even searching, or later post-impact aid and rehabilitation toward the community generally. Sheer limi-

[40] Friedsam, *op. cit.*, p. 179.
[41] *Ibid.*, pp. 162-63.
[42] Peter Townsend, *Family Life of Old People* (London: Routledge & Kegan Paul, 1957).

tations of physical strength, energy, and stamina may partly explain these differences, but frequently older men themselves simply attribute such inactivity to age itself, without necessary reference to physical condition, so that it appears that a question of role definition is involved. The orientation of such men is not to the wider community, but to the family group, but apparently without the depth of affective involvement of the older woman, especially to her grown daughters.

There is also some indication in the existing studies that where supernaturalistic interpretations are readily available in the general cultural or subcultural context of the disaster-stricken population, older persons may be more likely to resort to such interpretations. The NORC studies again provide pertinent examples, older widows being particularly vocal in expression of the belief that the tornado was "God's will" and the like. (See the particular case cited in the following section.)

DISASTER, PERSONALITY, AND SOCIAL CONTRACT

Disaster, if sufficiently widespead, shatters existing social order. It shatters the implicit contract according to which social life is normally possible: If one restrains expression of his disruptive or antisocial impulses and drives, if one imposes on himself the culturally-validated moral constraints, if one follows the accepted social rules, then he will be protected by society and given the full range of allowed gratifications. In disaster, protection is lost: familiar sources of comfort or enjoyment are transformed into dangerous inimical forces—walls that provide comfort and warmth become deadly crushing weights, windows onto the bright outdoors become lethal missiles of flying glass, sheltering roofs become murderous massive weights, useful gas becomes poisonous fumes, wires that brought "miracle" conveniences become dangerous tangled obstacles and threats; friendly kin and neighbors become mangled bodies evoking horror and disgust, blocking escape from entrapment or taxing one's damaged capacities to help, needing from you the nurturance, comfort, and aid you so desperately want or need yourself. The familiar is torn asunder. The sheer physical landscape may be unrecognizable, pulling out from under one even these elementary props for everyday orientation to the world. One can count on not even the very existence, let alone the normal responses, supports, and exchanges of the persons of one's everyday world. Reality is radically changed. One has been bombarded by many violent, destructive stimuli in a sudden massive assault. If physically unscathed, one may emerge from the destruction at first seeing no one and feeling one is the sole survivor in this sea of destruction.

Disaster thus represents a crisis of social contract. There are numerous ways that this crisis may be dealt with by individuals in disaster. One might offhand expect that shattering of the social contract by the massive impact of a disastrous force would necessarily lead to a great release from those constraints which are part of the bargain between personality and the social order, leading to a variety of anti-social and expediently egoistic behavior, release of aggressions against others, abandonment of moral obligations, sensual orgies, and the like. Though all of these have been variously reported (mainly in journalistic accounts) in a variety of disasters, they do not appear to be common or frequent reactions, judging by the accumulating studies done by social scientists, with adequate precautions against being taken in by overdramatized accounts. Even the memoir and journalistic accounts of the almost holocaustal disasters of the atomic bombing of Hiroshima and Nagasaki do not appear to indicate nearly as much of anti-social behavior as one could expect of so vast a disruption of normal life. And the social science studies of peacetime disasters such as tornadoes and earthquakes and the World War II studies of bombings of English and German cities show relatively little of anti-social conduct like looting, interpersonal aggressions, or debauches. (Admittedly, looting would be hard to verify in the wake of such an event as a tornado, where missing goods might either have been destroyed by the storm or scattered to the winds, or in fact looted from relatively "intact" wreckage of houses. Perhaps the social scientific accounts exaggerate in the direction opposite to that of the more melodramatic journalistic accounts.)

Other alternative responses are possible. During impact, there may continue to be denial that the social contract has in fact been broken: the disaster force itself may be assimilated into the powerful figure or force with whom the implicit contract has been made, and one's own guilt or worthiness interpreted in terms of what the disaster force does to one. Here may be invoked magical propitiation, in modern societies most commonly in the form of prayer to the powerful force, the Deity.

After impact, the social contract may be experienced not as abrogated entirely (which would justify release of all constraints) but rather as having been reformulated, i.e., rewritten, under new terms. Such "rewriting" may be felt in several positive ways. An individual who emerges unscathed may feel that he has proved to himself that he can undergo a terrifying and dangerous experience and take it. Therefore, he can, in effect, "write a new contract" with the powers that be, based upon the resulting improvement of his own "bargaining position" vis-à-vis the larger powers, and perhaps vis-à-vis other human beings as well. The fluid situation following impact may also be seized as the opportunity for asserting new roles and relationships previously impossible to assume, hence allowing the individual to formulate a new contract with the community. Or a person may make a kind of reformulation that attempts to assimilate the disaster experience generally to the "old" contract with the powers that be, while recognizing new formulations of contract existing, if not for oneself, then for others in the community. This kind of process is vividly seen in some of the older women who survived the 1952 Arkansas tornado, who tried to fit their fundamentalistic religious beliefs into the observed outcomes of loss and damage as distributed in the community. The following is an interesting case in point. This is a 70-year-old woman who was in the immediate impact of the tornado:[43]

> [*Following an account of various close friends and acquaintances killed in the tornado, while she and her husband and daughter were spared:*]
>   *We're lucky that God, the Good Lord, was with us. We've been good to the church and I believe that goes a long ways in the Lord taking care of you. I think the good Lord gives us credit for all those things, and they's people in the church last Sunday that never was known to be in church. We never have seen 'em in church before. And I guess they never did nothing in the cause of Christ. And I just want to praise the Lord that he did take care of us. We called on Him, and He—but I don't wait till the storm. There's never a night pass over my head that I don't read a chapter and pray for all my friends and for everybody.*
> [INT.: *"How did you feel when you were so scared?"*]
>   *. . . I just felt like the Lord was going to be with me. I just had a feeling that with all three of us calling on the Lord—we were two or three gathered together, asking in His name . . . and I believe that. That's Scripture.*
> [*"Did any of your family members get hurt?"*]
>   *No ma'am, my son in Judsonia and his family was saved, and I*

[43] From NORC Disaster Research interviews, 1952.

believe it's because they went to church and was trying to live right. I just believe I guess there's some good people blowed away, but there's some that wasn't all right. Still if they was going to take the people that wasn't living right, looks it took this depot outfit down here. That's always lived down there. I've said several times—I just look for a bad storm to strike near—funniest thing in the world. ["Do you feel the community life of this town has changed?"]

It's changed them. They found out there's a high power and they going to church. The Central Baptist Church is just full of people that we never did know to go to church before. I say that, and I don't say it to hurt anybody's feeling. They need something to wake them up. I think these things are sent to wake people up.

Here we have the magical propitiation during impact, with intense concern to keep the whole experience assimilated to the theology of a good God and people getting their just desserts. Having survived herself and her own family also, she can experience the contract as having been honored, at least in saving their lives. Then, however, she has to engage in some nimble mental gymnastics to make sense of the tornado impact in terms of the implied contract of her theology, since some of the "good" and "deserving" people did in fact get killed and some of the sinful and undeserving were exasperatingly spared. The hubristic complacency expressed here about her survival is almost exactly like that of the Japanese Christian woman quoted above (from Nagai). In effect, also, the tornado has allowed her to emerge in a partially new role, that of a person who has been religiously right (both accurate and moral) thus holding a superiority over the partakers of a Johnny-come-lately churchiness, toward whom she expresses verbal aggression, followed by guilt—"I don't say it to hurt anybody's feelings." This is also a good case of dramatization and validation of this woman's social role, in this case a religious one.

POST-DISASTER UTOPIA

At the opposite pole, almost, from the breakthrough of anti-social impulses in the wake of disaster is a temporary post-impact pattern which has been reported in a great many disasters studied. "Post-disaster utopia" refers to an exhilarating feeling of great positive expansiveness toward others, great loving neighborliness to everyone in the community, and a refreshing feeling of the democratization of life caused by the disaster's impartially destructive force. This can be seen as a reformulation of social contract, a revitalization of certain elements of the pre-existing value system not previously realized in everyday practice ("brotherly love," care and support for all members of the community, and the like). In a sense it says that the ideal social contract conditions, which the prior state of the community violated in many ways, may have a chance to be put into effect, now that the disaster has destroyed, or put out of commission, so much of the "superstructure" of the previously prevailing society. Guilts and hostilities have been drained off by the disaster itself, and naïve positive feelings toward others can be directly expressed without formality or embarrassment. In the extremity so much help is obviously and directly needed and can be directly and unceremoniously supplied by any impelled to do so. Tasks are too urgent to allow the delays and obstacles of usual bureaucratic formalities, and this provides an exhilarating release both to those getting the help and those giving it. In crisis people can step into demanding roles otherwise attached to high positions, without the dreary preliminaries of qualifying examinations and adaptation to complicated organization and rules. Clothing, possessions, and other such differentiating insignia become meaningless in the urgent concern with the starkest essentials of survival and the recognition in such extremity of the equally naked vulnerability of all human beings. The disaster has produced an extremely fluid situation in which "everything is possible" and the constraints and obstructing and deadening effects of many of the normal social processes are suddenly removed. One aspect of "post-disaster utopia" is the recognition of disaster as the "great equalizer." It is well expressed by Ignazio Silone, who writes, in reference to a devastating earthquake which in 1915 destroyed a large part of his Italian province, killing about fifty thousand people:[44]

> An earthquake buries rich and poor, learned and illiterate, authorities and subject alike beneath its ruined houses. Here lies, moreover, the real explanation of the Italians' well-known powers of endurance, when faced with the cataclysms of nature. An earthquake achieves what the law promises but does not in practice maintain—the equality of all men.

Comparative studies, of course, show that the phenomena Silone refers to are not limited to Italy, but are probably close to universal. Disaster disrupts whole systems of roles based on differentials of wealth, prestige, and power and the competitive race for these goals

[44] Ignazio Silone, in Richard Crossman (ed.), *The God that Failed* (New York: Bantam Books, 1952), p. 93.

that characterizes most modern societies. Disaster is thus a kind of *deus ex machina* that in one stroke ushers in a kind of ultimate democracy. Thus it may be a source of considerable gratification, especially to those who before held "have-not" positions in the status hierarchy. While it can be conversely disturbing to those previously "on top," even for them it can have gratifying power, in relieving any guilt felt for the advantages they held in the prior inequalities—again, especially in a society like America where the individualistic "rat race" is countered by a philosophy of universal basic dignity—in a never-ending dialectic of great psychic cost. Some of the smilingly accepting—even welcoming—responses of people previously well off who lost all their property in the disaster may thus not only express the theme of having exchanged property for life, but may also reflect euphoria at having been stripped of the symbols and burdens of status differentials. If disaster forces one to "start over from scratch" in a material sense, it can also suggest the exhilarating possibility of doing so also in role and personality dimensions. In Western cultures this resonates with primitive Christian values of complete equality in a materially rudimentary setting, and the values, of more recent historical epochs, of sloughing off decadent excrescences to pit oneself in a rough demanding life against new frontiers. Here we find both the theme of stripping oneself to the essentials of the personality, in a sense a radical confrontation with the deepest elements of oneself, along with immersion into loving cooperative ties on a level of equality. A disaster may, *for a time*, provide opportunities for both of these realizations, for different persons.

Such democratization then amounts to a radical reformulation of the social contract on terms felt as very gratifying by large numbers of persons.

Another aspect of rewriting of the contract may be a feeling of release from being bound to material things. The following is a good example. A doctor who survived the atomic bombing of Hiroshima writes:[45]

> . . . *Besides, we had no radio [diary date 14 August, 1945, 8 days after the bombing]. To me, this was something of a blessing, for being without some of the so-called advantages of civilization gave me a freedom of spirit and action others could not enjoy with their telephones, radios, and newspapers. Having lost everything in the*

[45] Hachiya, *op. cit.*, p. 75.

*fire and being now empty-handed was not entirely without advan-
tage. I experienced a certain light-heartedness I had not known for
a long time.*

In a similar vein, Hachiya describes his own condescending and
ironic reaction to a Tokyo businessman friend who at the time of
the Emperor's announcement of surrender (August 15, 1945) was
frantically trying to convert his currency to material assets, to avoid
his wealth being "frozen" by the conquering enemy. Hachiya, having lost everything material and feeling miraculously lucky to have
escaped with his life, felt a superior amusement at his friend's frantic
concerns.

The generality of disaster, and its democratizing effects, can have
profound effects on the person's idiosyncratic reaction to the impact
and immediate post-impact situation. For example:

> *(After the 1915 earthquake that hit our town) A neighbor of ours,
> a woman who kept a bakery, lay buried, but not hurt, for several
> days after the earthquake, when her house had fallen down . . .
> she was greatly distressed, so much so that when a rescue party
> wanted to drag her out of the ruins, she absolutely refused. She
> calmed down, however, and quickly regained her strength and her
> wish to live and rebuild her house, the moment she was told there
> had been an earthquake and that an enormous number of other
> houses had collapsed as well.*[46]

Perhaps this woman's suicidal despair, despite absence of personal
injury, was a reaction to a great burden of guilt, according to which
she felt the destruction of her house as punishment personally directed against herself. The subsequent information that her house
(and hence herself) had not been singled out for special destruction,
she apparently feels as a release from her guilt, and hence a dis-
pensation to go on living—and her energies, until then bound up
in her despair, are released for the rebuilding task. Thus the realization of the generality of the disaster suddenly provided this woman
with an entirely new contract with the powers that be, nullifying the
old one according to whose implicit terms the woman evidently felt
she had nothing left to do but die.

The phase of post-disaster utopia, of recognizing disaster as the
"great equalizer of mankind," thus provides a situation where individual potentialities and previously suppressed inner dynamics may
come to the fore and find a variety of realizations. Roles only dimly

[46] Silone, *op. cit.*, p. 95.

felt before may become dramatized, their underlying dynamic sources brought into a new and salient position. Previously guilt-inhibited potentials for action may be released. And discoveries of previously unrecognized positive qualities in others may in this phase heighten positive fellow feelings and produce a sense of suddenly found or renewed solidarity. A new social contract is felt to be in force with genuine dedication to the ideals of the old.

In time, however, this post-disaster utopia inevitably breaks down: negative feelings recuperate, volunteer workers tire, and different (more normal) relative deprivation feelings are reasserted. Victims now start to compare themselves with others better off, others who receive more aid or more undeserved aid. Negative feelings are reawakened by bureaucratic procedures of formal relief agencies and policies of such agencies of giving aid not according to losses but according to remaining resources available. While earlier, property has been exchanged for life—"no matter we lost our worldly goods, we are lucky to be alive"—now property starts to count again, and one starts to feel how much worse off he is than he was before. The decline of the post-disaster utopia is inevitable in any case, both psychologically and sociologically. The experience of disaster arouses fantasy expectations of compensation impossible to gratify—partly arising from the similarity of the immediate post-impact period to a kind of "kingdom of heaven" where all men are loving, a condition impossible to sustain as more routine life is re-established. And sociologically, the social structural fluidity is bound to give way to more routinized ways of meeting needs once the worst emergency is past, and supplies, resources, and personnel become more "normally" available. Here we find again the powerful human capacity to "normalize" a situation—seen earlier in the prevailing tendency to deny the pre-disaster warning cues and assimilate them to an everyday context. Now normalization takes a different form. Improvised medical techniques and personnel are no longer defensible once the urgency of crisis is gone. Spontaneous individual aid to stricken neighbors seems less justified (and more onerous), once normalized agencies for aid have arrived. Persons' routine needs are pressing once again, and a semblance of the former social order is re-established. So too, the temporary ideal social contract of the "utopia" period now gives way to the grayer world of more venal considerations and compromises.

3. CONCLUSION

These two papers show us some of the human repertoire of behavior in situations of extremity. In each case the paper hurriedly passes over those who were the extreme victims—those who died—and concentrates on those who survived. (This imbalance too is a measure of the emotional difficulty of the human scientist in dealing with death.) The survival reactions to the different kinds of extreme situations show some interesting common features. The most prominent is "the domestication of extremity"—the assimilation of the extreme experiences, by one device or another, to a framework having some familiar contours, or at least to one with which the survivor victim can at least cope and somehow "keep going." The mechanism of denial is critical in this process. The concentration camp prisoners could manage to withstand the most brutal physical tortures and the devastation of the most basic sense of worth by denying that this was really happening to themselves, or to themselves as subjects. It could only happen to themselves as objects looked at with a kind of strange detachment. Another form of denial was the feeling that none of the events were "real"; it was in effect happening in another world or dimension which did not really count. And at some point the real "I" would return to his earlier familiar world and the whole concentration camp experience would be wiped out. Beyond that—and presumably those who could not muster this much illusion simply perished the more quickly—the "domestication of extremity" involved a concentration on getting through from one day to the next, including a constant busy calculation of minute advantage in every situation. Evidently most persons who did survive carried behavior to the point of profound personality change, even to assimilating the values, attitudes, and behavior of the Gestapo guards. Very few could carry through such "domestication" and at the same time preserve core elements of the former self to retain some basic dignity and strength, as Bettelheim himself was able to do.

In the disaster situations—which are usually of sudden onslaught and relatively brief in their most destructive phase—mechanisms of denial are used during all phases of the disaster; remotely prior phases, immediate pre-impact, impact itself, and the post-impact period. One important form of denial—the concentration on rescue and other helping work immediately after impact in an impersonal, almost detached way—implicitly denies that anything widely devastating has happened, and temporarily protects the worker from a great access of unmanageable affect. Another form of denial is the enormous self-restraint exhibited by many disaster victims, in preventing themselves from giving in to strong emotional expression of any kind. This again denies that anything extreme has occurred, a patent illusion in the face of the surrounding devastation and loss of life. The folk phrase—tremendously frequent in post-disaster statements by survivors—that "it was just one of those things," conveys the great effort to assimilate the extraordinary to the ordinary, and thus to "domesticate the extremity." The extent to which communities—a least in peacetime natural disasters—rally to handle their own immediate problems of disruption, rescue, aid, and the first stages of the re-establishment of order, also represents ways of denying the severity of what happened by rebuilding and re-establishing the town as quickly as possible. Similarly, the prevalent decision to stay in or return to the disaster-stricken town afterward suggests a willful wiping out of the disaster experience, and demoting it to the status of a minor irritation and interruption. Rhapsodists may exalt such behavior to the status of "testimony to the strength of the human spirit." But there are two elements in such reactions that deserve attention which they usually do not get. One is the centrality of illusion in such denial reactions, which occurs to such an extent that it may appear to be a precondition for survival, especially psychological survival, through an extreme experience. The other is the way in which such processes of domestication of extremity fit into general patterns of modern culture, where the existence of extremity (in the form of persisting damaging institutions and situations of a very pervasive kind) and the probability of sudden violent extremity in the form of manmade disasters, is in effect part of the very landscape of existence itself. The domestication of disaster where it does occur in a sudden concentrated form, then, tends very diffusely to make for an "adjustment" to the more generally pervasive quality of extremity throughout modern life, especially since World War II and the "perfection" of absolute weapons of destruction.

There is an impressive similarity and resonance among each of the following: the detachment of affect from experience resulting in a feeling of unreality, used as a defense mechanism by the concentration camp prisoners when exposed to the most brutal of tortures and humiliations; the denial and refusal of affect on the part of disaster survivors intent upon keeping that "old calm feeling," of rescuers who saw without any emotional reaction whatever the mangled bodies of kin, friends, and acquaintances, and of those doggedly rebuilding after the storm; the dead-pan affectlessness of the hero of Camus' *The Stranger* who kills without understandable motive and totally without conscious feeling and undergoes the subsequent legal processing in an utterly detached, feelingless, and robotlike manner; much of the atmosphere of the popularity of "sick humor" in the period since World War II; the tone of the presentation of and interest in human sexuality in popular literature. The latter is a quality that is almost antiseptically behavioristic, superficial, and concentrated on sheer physicality, at the expense of exploration of any of the human meaning or emotionality of the "interactions" being described (Kinsey's use of "outlet" as the unit for counting sexual behaviors is likewise symptomatic at the "scientific" level). In other words the whole pattern of behavior constitutes a kind of dogged mechanical exploration to the outer edges of extremity while refusing to deal with it by any kind of affect whatever. In each case the grotesque and horrifying is made commonplace. There is a startling parallel between an incident that occurred in a Nazi concentration camp and a fantasy routine of "sick" humor of Lenny Bruce: A prisoner was being subjected to all the variations of brutality a group of Gestapo guards could invent to wreak upon him; as a culmination, pressed by a very full bladder, one Gestapo man proceeded to urinate all over the prisoner, from head to toe, while his companions roared with gleeful laughter. In the Lenny Bruce routine (recounted in Goldman's paper reprinted in the preceding chapter), Bruce informs the audience that he is going to urinate over them, does not do so, but tells how the previous audience reacted, with the punch line, "Shut up Harry, he does it real cute!" In the same vein, Hannah Arendt's point about Eichmann is precisely the linkage of the most ghastly of atrocities to the mindless, very ordinary, mediocrity of a man.

We may wonder then, if the atrocities of the camps and the extremities of actual experience of disaster, have not been outdone by the pervasive domestication of extremity that is so widespread a part of life of the postatomic age.

SELECTED BIBLIOGRAPHY

Baker, C. W. and D. W. Chapman (eds.). *Man and Society in Disaster.* New York: Basic Books, 1962.
A valuable collection of papers on many aspects of disaster behavior.
Cohen, Elie. *Human Behavior in the Concentration Camp.* New York: W. W. Norton & Co., 1953.
A psychodynamic analysis by a survivor.
Elkins, Stanley. "Slavery and Personality," in Bert Kaplan (ed.), *Studying Personality Cross-culturally.* New York: Harper & Row, Publishers, 1961.
An illuminating comparison of the psychology of the Negro slaves and that of concentration camp survivors.
Frankl, Viktor E. *Man's Search for Meaning: An Introduction to Logotherapy.* Boston: Beacon Press, 1959.
Includes reflections on this psychiatrist's concentration camp experiences.
Goffman, Erving. *Asylums.* New York: Doubleday & Company, 1961.
Sociological analysis of mental hospitals, including the essay on "Total Institutions," which defines the common elements of extremity in asylums, prisons, and concentration camps.
Hachiya, Michihiko. *Hiroshima Diary.* Translation by W. Wells. Chapel Hill: University of North Carolina Press, 1955.
A harrowing account of the atomic bombing and the survivors.
Janis, I. L. *Air War and Emotional Stress.* New York: McGraw-Hill Book Co., 1951.
A psychologist's careful analysis of emotional effects of World War II bombings on English and German populations.
Kogon, Eugen. *The Theory and Practice of Hell: The German Concentration Camps and the System Behind Them.* New York: Farrar, Straus & Giroux, 1946.
A thorough account of the whole system by a Buchenwald survivor.
Marks, E., C. Fritz, R. Endleman, E. Quarantelli, R. Bucher, L. Schatzman, and D. Earle. *Human Reactions in Disaster Situations.* Report No. 52, 3 volumes. Chicago: National Opinion Research Center, University of Chicago, 1954.
(Available in Microfilm from NORC.)
Intensive systematic analysis of reactions to a tornado in Arkansas and smaller scale studies of several other peacetime community disasters. One of the most detailed sources in disaster literature.
Nagai, T. *We of Nagasaki: The Study of Survivors of the Atomic Wasteland.* New York: Duel, Sloan & Pearce, 1951.
Devastating firsthand account.
Rousset, David. *L'Univers Concentrationnaire.* Paris: Pavois, 1946.
A moving account of the concentration camps by a survivor.
Solzhenitsyn, Alexander. *One Day in the Life of Ivan Denisovich.* Trans-

lated by Max Hayward and Roland Hingley. New York: Frederick A. Praeger, Publishers, 1963.
A fictionalized firsthand account of life in a Soviet labor camp in the 1950s.

Wallace, Anthony F. C. *Tornado in Worcester: An Exploratory Study of Individual and Community Behavior in an Extreme Situation.* (Publication No. 392. Committee on Disaster Studies, Disaster Study No. 3.) Washington, D.C.: National Academy of Sciences, National Research Council, 1956.
Introduces the concept of the "disaster syndrome."

Wolfenstein, Martha. *Disaster: A Psychological Essay.* New York: Free Press of Glencoe, 1957.
A major effort to apply psychodynamic analysis to disaster behavior, drawing on the studies made by others to that date.

SEVEN

Shared dynamics and psychopathology: the transcultural problem of normality

We come now full cycle to problems raised in Chapter One: the view of social institutions and collective behavior as collective transformations of common intrapsychic problems and culturally "validated" solutions to these problems. We are concerned with the interplay of psychic life as social product and social life as product of common psychodynamics. In earlier chapters we have considered some of the universal psychosocial problems of man as a product of certain distinctive evolutionary processes; and as recurrently embroiled in the interplay of persons and institutions through the inevitable involvements of socialization and its critical institution, the family. We have examined some of the variables involved in the socialization of a child and also have hypothesized how the institutional arrangements of the family in different societies and communities have affected personality development. Next we considered the problem of psychosocial transitions in the life cycle and probed in some depth into one of these transitions, the critical one from childhood to adulthood. Our next concern was to explore dimensions of the interplay between the psychodynamic and the social in the interrelated worlds of work and play and in extreme situations that provide a kind of "test" of personality and of society.

In this chapter we turn to the intricate questions of collective "psychopathology." We shall be concerned with the psychodynamic dimensions of social movements, the interplay of individual and collective psychology in different types of leadership, the patterning of psychopathology by the stamp of differing ethnic subcultures, the "problem of illusions" in psychopathology and culture, and then the general problem of "normality" and culture seen from a perspective that attempts to transcend the dilemmas of cultural relativism to formulate a *trans*cultural (rather than *cross*-cultural) psychodynamic. Some of the main theoretical problems involved have been sketched in the first chapter, and have been alluded to in other portions of the book. Here we shall try to bring them into central focus.

Are the Dobuans "paranoid," as a whole society? Are the Hutterites collective "depressives"? Was Nazism a collective madness of the whole German people? Or is any society "crazy" when viewed from the premises of some radically different society? Or are some societies "crazier" than others, or only differently crazy—by some view independent of all of them? Can there be such a view, one unfettered by the biases of any one particular culture? Are some groups within a society identifiably and collectively "mad" from a perspective that is more than a mere distillation of the parochial prejudices of others in the society who are not among their members? Such questions have been opened up by the development of the more probing analysis of psychodynamic processes ushered in by Freud and of the relativistic view of cultures brought by recent anthropology.

It may be well to start with some examples in detail. "Social movements"—religious, economic, political—provide a good point of departure. Cults, sects, organized movements for political, social, or economic liberation, movements to propagate some way of life deviant to the surrounding culture, even artistic, educational, or entertainment "crazes" are of dramatic interest for the intensity and exclusiveness of involvement of their participants in goals, sets of beliefs, and styles of acting and feeling that appear to outsiders as strange, exotic, or frightening or as bizarre, irrational, and "crazy." We can posit a general formulation that such a cult or movement attracts to its way of life persons who are in some ways in a similar or common situation and who correspondingly have some similar or common psychic problems. In turn, the cult or movement sets in motion for its participants certain collective processes which consolidate for the "true believers" who remain in the movement, a kind of "solution" to these problems. This makes the movement for the participant a viable and satisfying way of life that has centrality, intensity, and exclusiveness. Correspondingly, the cult or movement repels or even actively extrudes potential or tentative or temporary joiners for whose psychic problems the movement does not provide "solutions," or for whom it intensifies, exacerbates or complicates their problems in various ways. We can also ask, about those who do find commitment and psychic resonance in a cult or movement, not only what positive values does it serve for them but also what are its psychic costs? In these lights, the question "Are the cultists crazy—individually or collectively—or not?" is a misleadingly simplified one. Instead we may reformulate the query in different and more searching terms: "What pre-existing psychological elements or tensions (pathological, pathogenic, or whatever) lead into recruitment into a particular cult or movement? What psychodynamic processes are set in motion by the interindividual and collective experiences the person undergoes in the life of the cult, and how do these solve (or not solve) his pre-existent problems? How do they confront the convert with new or reformulated dilemmas and provide solutions for these—or not, as the case may be? What psychic mechanisms—projection, displacement, denial, and so on—does the new collective experience set in motion in individual members? How do these contribute to his finding a viable way of living in the world—and at what costs? And importantly, are irrational elements intrinsic to these processes or only the "accidental" concomitants of a particular cult in a particular time and place and society?

1. COLLECTIVE PSYCHODYNAMICS

To deal with such questions concretely, we present two case studies, one of a messianic Judaeo-Christian religious cult and one of the religio-nationalistic movement called the Black Muslims. Aaron and Joan Katcher are a psychiatrist and anthropologist husband-wife team who conducted a "participant-observation" study of a small messianic religious cult in an Eastern city. Their study documents the development and structuring of a variety of paranormal experiences—hallucination, spirit possession—and the use of "double-bind" and other internally contradictory communication techniques (evidently not deliberate or conscious), and the illusionary belief systems of the cult. The authors go to pains to argue the distinctiveness of these phenomena, in the cult context, from analogous phenomena appearing in individual psychosis. As they see them, the cult beliefs and experiences are "adaptive" for the participant members. Their description also gives a sense of the psychic costs involved in such adaptation, regardless of whether one excludes the participants from the category of "psychotic."

The second paper, by political scientist Michael John Parenti, deals with the Black Muslim movement. He shows how this movement serves a critical psychosocial need of its communicants—their need to reconstruct their identity. Again we find the combination of cognitive absurdities (in the dogmatic belief system) and adaptive or reconstructive values in the experience for the adherents. The critical role of politico-social myths and symbols in the reconstruction of personality is well developed in this paper. True, as Parenti indicates, the question of the historical accuracy of the Muslim myths is irrelevant to their psychological function for the adherents. True, also, as Parenti says, "Muhammad's sacred tale is no more implausible and actually less adorned than that found in Genesis and Revelation." It is illusion, nonetheless, and as such, an important part of the psychosocial process of such movements.

The Restructuring of Behavior in a Messianic Cult

AARON HANNA KATCHER AND
JOAN HALL KATCHER

The behavior occurring within a small urban religious cult will be described and the induction and regulation of that behavior related to the social structure and patterns of communication within the cult. Both the ecstatic experiences of cult members and their interpretation of events would be considered aberrant by the society at large. Members had visions exposing sin and sexual perversion within the congregation, were possessed by the Holy Ghost, and suffered physical attack by the Devil and perverts under his command. The prophet had repeated visions of Christ and acted as a medium through whom Christ spoke. As this behavior was induced in new converts, direct observation of the conversion process provided an excellent example of the restructuring of individual behavior by a small social group. Observation of cult interaction also provided information about processes controlling and stabilizing halluci-

Original paper published here for the first time. The research involved was supported in part by a United States Public Health grant. Aaron Hanna Katcher is Associate Professor of Psychiatry and Medicine in the University of Pennsylvania School of Medicine. Joan Hall Katcher is an anthropologist pursuing advanced study at the University of Pennsylvania.

nation and possession, and aiding the maintenance of a highly aberrant world view in a somewhat hostile larger society.

The cult has as its primary structural element a dyadic relationship: an intense, ambivalent dependency relationship between prophet and convert. The convert is continually subjected to paradox and contradiction within statements, between statements, and between statements and behavior both in his relationship with the prophet and in the total context of cult activities. Yet veiled or implicit instructions for resolution are hidden within this communication. The convert is threatened with death should he sever the dependency relationship. His anxiety can be reduced only by progressive increase in dependency, selective perception of ongoing events, and interpretation of his life history in terms of the cult world view. The environment provided by the cult continually reinforces that world view and encourages the convert's progressive commitment. It is our conclusion that, given the varying susceptibility of individuals, this kind of social structure and communication is highly significant in the induction of marked changes in behavior.

The cult studied was a small Judaeo-Christian Pentecostal group, located in a large city on the Eastern Seaboard of the United States. Both authors were participant observers, attending once or twice weekly for a five-month period in 1959. The extreme suspiciousness of the cult's prophet forced the writers to claim identities as potential converts rather than as investigators. No spurious credentials were offered; information given was correct but incomplete. Members knew that the authors were a married couple expecting a child. A. K. was a physician engaged in cardiovascular research; J. K.'s claim to be an anthropology student was seen as mildly pretentious and then ignored. Prayer sessions were held in our home and members had access to A. K. in his laboratory. Members were active in interpreting our behavior in terms of their own world view. As a result, the anxiety generated in the investigators by their covert role did not distort their relationship with the members, for it approximated the air that guilty sinners were expected to have. This situation did not permit the use of objective tests or structured interviews, but was ideal for observation of the dynamics of the conversion process.

At the time it was studied the cult was affiliated with no other religious group and had held regular services in a permanent meeting place for four years. It was organized around its founder and prophet, Emmanuel, and consisted of between fifty and sixty baptized members. Of these, an inner core of about twenty was distinguished by long service and positions of trust. A fringe of twenty to thirty supporters, potential converts and provisional members was in a constant state of flux, with individuals either being baptized, or more frequently, being cast out of the group. Individuals who attended once or twice and did not return were said to be envoys of the Devil sent to inhibit worship, and irregular attendance was poorly tolerated. Those who wished to remain in association had either to maintain movement toward baptism or accept forced dissociation by curse. Thus, all individuals who had the right to do so were likely to be in attendance at the Sunday afternoon and evening and Wednesday evening services. All those baptized were adults, children only rarely attending services.

The prophet was Jewish and had received his childhood religious training in an Orthodox synagogue. Baptized members included two white Roman Catholic converts, both female; five Jewish converts, all male; six Negro Protestant converts, both male and female; the remainder of the congregation was of white Protestant background. Although the numbers of men and women were roughly equal and about one half the adults were married, the inner core was predominantly male, and single Jewish males were held to be favored by God. Most members were between the ages of twenty-five and forty. All males were employed, but none was startlingly successful and there were no evidences of high income. However, seventeen had at least some college education; these included one physician, three engineers, two former naval officers, and one former Presbyterian minister. Not all members were local residents; the prophet and some elders drove as far as 500 miles for weekend services. Most of the nonmembers in attendance were Negro residents of the immediate neighborhood. A. K. as male, Jewish, and a physician was immensely desirable as a convert, while J. K., female and Protestant, was permitted to slip into the pattern of worship and attendance with much less attention.

In order to provide orientation, a brief description of cult doctrine and the physical setting of the services will be provided. However, the writers' primary concern in this paper lies with analysis of the patterns of communication within the cult rather than with the historical sources of elements of doctrine or ritual. Formal doctrine is justified exclusively by reference to the Old and New Testaments with emphasis on the Pentateuch, Daniel, and Revelations. The Trinitarian doctrine and the Roman Catholic Church are tools of the Devil. God has a corporeal body, but has revealed himself thus only rarely to men—once to Moses, once to Joshua as an angel, as Jesus, and several times to the prophet of the cult. Christ, hence, is God and the Jews' unacknowledged Messiah. His second coming is imminent, but the precise date has not yet been announced by the prophet. In preparation for His coming, the Lord is permitting His elect few to prophesy, to work miracles, and to heal and kill in His name. The congregation constantly does battle with the Devil, who assaults them in person and in the form of the homosexuals, perverts, whoremongers, prostitutes, and sinners who try to invade the service. The outside world is the Devil's domain. Although the member is forced to enter it to earn his livelihood and support the church, he relies on his own sanctity, his resident Holy Ghost, and the miraculous power of the prophet to make him successful and to preserve him from sin and harm. The stated *raison d'être* of the cult is not proselytization and conversion but to please the Lord with exaltation of His name while awaiting the second coming.

The cult owns two adjoining three-story brownstone buildings in a now decayed downtown residential area. These contain living space for some members, a communal dining hall and kitchen, and a long narrow "upper room" where services are held. The Sunday afternoon service lasts from three o'clock until 5:30, is followed by a communal meal and then by an evening service which lasts from 7:30 until 11 or 11:30 o'clock. Each service has the qualities of a drama. There the Ghost descends, the presence of the Devil is revealed, lapsed converts are expelled, the sick cured, and death called down on those who sin against the Ghost. The congregation sits on small hard chairs in a very crowded hot and stuffy room. There is no pulpit; the prophet speaks from the floor in front of a visually complex altar area filled with Jewish and Christian ritual objects. This area is backed by full multicolored silk drapes thrown into deep relief by complicated lighting. The prolonged periods of hymn singing are accompanied by an orchestra containing horns, cymbals, tambourines, accordion, piano, organ, and harp. This exposure to moderate but prolonged physical discomfort and sensory overstimulation undoubtedly aids in producing perceptual distortion.

The central figure in the services is the prophet Emmanuel. He is a short, stout, middle-aged Sephardic Jew, with no distinctive physical characteristics. He was raised in an Orthodox Jewish family and given a religious education, received Bar Mitzvah and became a member of the Synagogue in his teens. His father died while Emmanuel was very young, and his mother is remembered as being an affectionate, overprotective woman who permitted him little privacy or solitude. The crucial moment of his life came when he was seventeen and thinking of becoming engaged. He was converted to the Christian faith by an elderly Negro woman who pressed a Bible into his hands and revealed to him the sin he had committed the night before. He broke his relationship with his girl and began a program of prolonged religious meditation in his attic. Within a month he was rewarded with his first vision of Jesus. On multiple occasions Christ appeared before him, kissed him, danced with him, talked to him in baby talk, and gave him the power to prophesy and to have visions. His behavior during the following years was undirected. He attended several colleges without taking a degree and spent periods erratically wandering and preaching. In his early thirties he made some converts in a small rural college who were to remain with him, forming the inner core of the present cult. They traveled over the East Coast preaching and staying with whoever would keep them. Finally Emmanuel was given divine instructions to cease his wandering and raise the House of the Lord in the city in which the cult is now located.

Emmanuel speaks with a high-pitched nasal voice and a slight lisp, and for dramatic effect he occasionally assumes the stereotyped accent and mannerisms of Central European Jews. In his sermons he shifts from intense emotional barrages to high comic relief. He freely abandons all dignity to give impressions of the bewilderment of the believer before an arbitrary God. With almost vaudevillian technique, he enacts the insanity of the believer to the world, the world to the believer, and the incompatibility of the demands of City Hall and Heaven. Kirkegaardian fear and trembling are evoked with baggy pants and a stage Yiddish accent. He has comic charisma. On the other hand, in the same hour-long sermon, he may not only describe God's wrath, but revivify and embody it. The following example, excerpted from our notes occurred during a long evening service which had deviated from the usual pattern.

> The prophet kneeled on hands and knees in front of the congregation to pray. He began to rock back and forth, moaning and calling to Christ to reveal Himself. His verbalizations became more indistinct, and he began to make violent retching motions. Between spasms of dry retching, Christ began to speak through him in falsetto, threatening to vomit up the impure congregation. This behavior was sustained, faded, and Christ left. As the prophet rose and turned to the congregation, one of the elders in the front row (a thirty-year-old chemical engineer) fell to a crouched position on the floor. While the prophet violently castigated the backsliding of an unnamed member, the elder became more and more disturbed. He crouched tightly, his head hidden under clenched arms, his back turned to the prophet. He remained crouched while the service was terminated, when he and the prophet withdrew immediately. Response in the congregation was politely bland, and no mention was made of the foregoing circumstances. We were told later by the prophet that the elder had been thinking of women's breasts during the service.

Cult members engaged in behavior considered aberrant in our society and maintained a distinctive world view. (World view is used here to refer to a subcategory of culture which states values and provides rules for the extension of meaning to events.) Small subsocietal groups tend to develop world views which are differentiated in greater or lesser degree from that of the larger society. Cult members believed that events were infused with a deeper meaning which was not accessible to nonbelievers. So difficult of access was this meaning that often only the prophet could elucidate it. The prophet and cult members were aware that both the behavior occurring during services and the interpretations of that behavior made by members differed from the behavior and reality judgments of outsiders. They knew that their actions and beliefs might be accounted insane, and had their own criteria for differentiating their ecstatic experiences from "crazy" behavior. While from the investigators' scientific world view, cult members were subject to cognitive distortion in their interpretation of reality; from the cult's viewpoint, all of humanity save the small body of true believers suffered from severe cognitive distortion.

While members consistently professed to interpret ongoing events from a stance which was different from the outsider's, the authors noted both that the interpretation of single events shifted over time and that there were behavioral regularities upon which members never commented. It was possible for the observers to construct implicit rules which were predictive but in direct conflict with the explicitly affirmed values of the group. For example, members believed that possession by the Holy Ghost was determined by God only in response to the sanctity of the recipient. We observed that possession experiences were initiated and terminated by the activity of the prophet during limited periods of the service. The rule "Possession occurs in response to the direction of the prophet" directly contradicted the cult affirmation that possession was purely a Divinely initiated experience.

The convert also must learn to ignore components of the behavior of other members which are incompatible with their social identities within the group. Available identities were limited and stereotyped. Males, especially sexually continent males, were believed to be in a state of greater purity, while women were expected to play, and in fact did play, passive and minor roles. Men who differed widely in personality structure were spoken of only in terms of the limited number of attributes which formed the ideal identity. The prophet was seen as humble, loving, and egalitarian and his great hostility and position of supreme authority received no verbal recognition. In general, behavior in conflict with cult identity was ignored or recognized in denunciatory visions.

Our notes indicate that some events were misremembered or reinterpreted within short periods of time although members would have denied it. It was our conclusion that consensual validation of cause and meaning was reached not so much by reference to detailed internal models as by reference on the part of individuals to the prophet for cues. The cult interpretation of events, past and present, rationalized present behavior, sharply limiting and directing individual action in a way which resulted in the maintenance of a social structure which was not directly recognized by the participants.

As noted above, members believed that their behavior intermittently was determined by supernatural activity. The descriptive term "dissociated state" is used to refer to this behavior indicating that it is dissociated from the activity of the normal ego without implication of its etiology.[1] Intermittent possession by the Holy Ghost was highly valued, for it constituted direct and tangible evidence of the extension of God's grace and the spiritual cleanliness of the recipient. It was shared by most members currently in good grace. Commonly following long periods of hymn singing to loud music with rhythmic hand waving, possession consisted of sudden convulsive body movements, slight doubling up with flexion of hip and knee, clonic arm movements, and violent jerking of the head. Forced expiration against a partially closed glottis produced straining noises and explosive utterances of single words, most commonly "Poppa" and "Jesus." In periods of high excitement there was a rapid stuttering repetition of incoherent syllables.

A substantial proportion of the membership, but not the entire group, experienced the permanent presence of the Ghost. It initially entered their bodies "as a baby is born," continued to reside in their bellies, and rose to counsel them in times of distress. It took the form of an inner voice, but members insisted it was distinct from their own personalities. Possession by the Devil also occurred, but its expression was not as obvious or stereotyped as possession by the Ghost. At some services when the Ghost did not descend, members experienced malaise, nausea, or stomach cramps, subsequently attributed to the presence of the Devil. Possession by Christ, as described above, was experienced only by the prophet.

More direct evidence of God's grace than possession by the Ghost was the ability to have a vision of another person's sin. "If God loves you, he will give you something on somebody." Visions were described as "open" and "frank"; they were said to occur in three-dimensional space and not inside one's head. Frequently, the hallucination was auditory and even tactile as well as visual, but it was most commonly described as appearing like "the image on a television set." While visions sometimes occurred during service, they most frequently occurred while the member was alone. Not all visions revealed sin; a more restricted group of members also experienced visions of some symbol of the Godhead, e.g., the Ark, the Mercy Seat, or golden fish. This kind of vision was perceived as intensely pleasurable rather than fear inspiring, and was reported by only three members during the period of investigation. The prophet alone experienced visions of Christ. Twenty-one current visions were reported to us by the prophet or the persons who experienced them during the five-month period of investigation, twelve experienced by the prophet and nine by six other members. At least seven more members had had visions in the past. Of the twenty-one current visions, fifteen were revelations of sin in a present or past member of the congregation or visitors.

These forms of altered experience were not distributed randomly

[1] A. F. C. Wallace, "Cultural Determinants of Response to Hallucinatory Experience," *A.M.A. Arch. Gen. Psychiat.*, 1:58-69, 1959.

among members of the congregation. Everyone present at service indicated at least tacit acceptance of the cult world view. In conversation, visitors were actively solicited to indicate explicit belief. Visitors and potential converts were not expected to experience possession or have visions, and those who did so spontaneously were discouraged from returning. Possession by the Ghost was often interpreted as a token of Divine acceptance, and such possession was a minimal requirement for baptism. The distribution of other forms of altered behavior was more limited and paralleled the hierarchical structure of the group. Individuals experiencing the more restricted forms also experienced all the more common forms and tended to be persons of greater power and responsibility in the cult. The prophet experienced most of the visions, and visions of Christ and possession by Him were his prerogatives, as already noted. Group dynamics also limit the content and targets of visions. No member currently having visions was denounced by another's vision, and so far as known, no one has ever seen the prophet in a compromising vision. In contrast, the most frequent targets of visionary denunciation were new converts and visitors. Of the fifteen denunciatory visions that occurred during our stay, only four exposed baptized members. Of the seven persons producing the twenty-one visions, only two were women, experiencing between them three visions, all of divine symbols. No woman was reported ever to have produced a vision of the sin of another person. More control on visionary activity is provided by the practice of reporting all visions to the prophet for interpretation. The prophet alone decides on their meanings and action to be taken. Only after his decision can a member freely describe his experience.

Cult members contact potential converts by passing out literature on populous downtown street corners. Most individuals accept the proffered tract and walk rapidly by. The individual who remains to talk is presented with communications that are intensely emotional and contain contradictory elements. The member greets him with warmth and interest and is willing to answer his questions and arguments at great length. He is offered contact with a religious leader of miraculous power, who can bestow the gift of eternal salvation, a gift not to be found elsewhere. At the same time he is told that the cult does not want converts, for its members practice a "dog eat dog" religion with each interested only in his own salvation. As the prospect is invited, he is warned that sinful persons approaching the congregation are in danger of exposure, damnation, and perhaps sudden death. These contradictions at the verbal level are paralleled by similar ones at the nonverbal level. The warmth, receptivity, and friendliness of the members' greeting is opposed by the intense anger and hate displayed as they tell stories of the fates of nonbelievers in this world and at the day of judgment. An image constantly used which expresses the ambivalence of the proffered relationship is blood: salvation is obtained by drinking blood; the faithful are covered by the blood; the Horsemen of the Apocalypse ride to the withers in blood. The only element of nonverbal communication which is not contradicted is that the prospect is of immense personal interest to the cult members.

The ambiguity of the potential convert's situation is increased when he learns that his not yet fully repentant state gives the Devil access to the congregation, and that the conversion experience almost always includes revelation of his sin in a vision given by God to a cult member. Thus to become accepted he must first become, in a sense, hateful to the congregation. The divine power he seeks is a potential vehicle of attack. While he is subject to these communications, both privately and in the prophet's sermons, the potential convert views the constant drama of visionary denunciation, repentance and acceptance, or failure and expulsion. During our stay three provisional converts were expelled, another (a Jewish dentist) was being kept in disciplinary ostracism because he persisted in keeping a mistress, two new converts were finally baptized, and four visitors were expelled from services, one bodily.

The use of visionary denunciation in conversion can be illustrated by describing the authors' experience. For a period of several months we were permitted passively to attend services without gross alterations in our behavior. Then the prophet began making more detailed inquiries into our lives, and we felt that a response was expected which we were not making.

One Sunday we did not attend services but remained at home. V., the physician who was continually near us during the services, spoke to J. K. by phone to inquire after A. K. J. K. replied that A. K. was visiting his father, who was ill. The next evening V. called again, to suggest that A. K. come promptly, as someone had "got something." Upon calling A. K.'s father it was learnt that at the appropriate time an unknown man had called asking for him. The authors conferred, and predicting that a confession would be required of A. K., chose an appropriate sin. A. K. went to meet with the prophet and V. He was told only that another member, S., had had a vision of his sin, and that he had better confess the sin. Upon A. K.'s confession of having visited a prostitute the prior evening, the prophet became possessed by Christ, who threatened to vomit A. K. up out of the congregation if he did not repent. A. K. was told that his father's life might be taken by God if he remained in sin. Finally, he was told to return home, to confess to J. K., and not to contact any cult member until the following Sunday service. At that time although the sin was public knowledge, the congregation was cordial. After the service, J. K. was requested to see the prophet, V. and S. Asked if anything unusual had happened to her husband, she responded with his confession. For the first time, the vision was recounted. S., while at home, had had a vision of A. K.

standing with an unidentified woman who was naked from the waist down and with her "bottom" toward him. In the vision A. K. spoke, saying, "I shall clean my house from bottom to top." The prophet also recounted that at A. K.'s confession he had unknowingly repeated those very words. A. K. had not said those words but when V. was asked by the prophet to confirm this small miracle, V. replied "Well, yes, that was the gist of it." However, a week later, when the story was recounted to others in our presence, V. immediately and emphatically responded, "Those were his exact words." Following the service after which the vision was discussed, it was suggested that A. K. spend long hours in prayer asking for a vision indicating forgiveness. A. K. was also asked to spend more time in discussion with the prophet and to stimulate this contact the prophet held a prayer meeting at the authors' home. At the termination of this meeting the prophet had a vision of a bloody dagger, point downward, suspended over A. K.'s head.

At this point the authors judged that further attendance at the cult was impossible, and the association was terminated. No effort was made by any cult member to get in touch with us. The material that follows is drawn from our prior observations of other converts.

The contradictions communicated within the cult are unresolvable within conventional reality. In the face of such communication and the continued threat of rejection, the individual who wishes to remain with the cult must begin to suspend rational judgment and increase his dependency upon the prophet and cult members for direction and instruction. Because that instruction itself is contradictory, he cannot develop a rationale for coping with their behavior, but remains in continual need of verbal and nonverbal cues. Following initial denunciation, confession, and repentance, the convert is permitted to satisfy his augmented dependency needs by spending extended periods of time (up to eight hours consecutively) with the prophet. He is urged to remember and confess all his past sins and is advised to spend long hours in solitary prayer, begging God for a vision or a descent of the Ghost as a token of forgiveness. This process itself increases anxiety since discussion of his previous life of necessity reveals more behavior accounted sinful by the cult. Decrease of anxiety within the relationship can be achieved only by greater dependence upon the prophet for behavioral cues. Any spare time is spent with baptized members who throng about him discussing his and their own conversion experiences. During these probationary periods converts are always accompanied by an experienced cult member, and it was our impression that two potential converts are not permitted to converse. Behavior acceptable to cult members receives continual reinforcement, and it is during this period that the convert reinterprets his life history in terms of the cult world view. He is also liable to have his first experiences with possession by the Ghost.

Even following an experience of the Godhead, the convert is not accorded unqualified membership. He continues to spend hours with the prophet and elders and is expected to make his behavior progressively more in accord with the cult ideal, to place more of his affairs under the prophet's direction, and to restrict or eliminate competing social ties. Many of the exemplary tales of the cult involve the efforts of the families of converts to destroy their faith. The prospective convert is told explicitly that he should abandon all other social life and warned that he may come in conflict with his family. The prophet may require him to change his job or residence. In effect, he progressively severs social contact with individuals who could support or recall his old sense of self, becoming more estranged from the world and more dependent upon the prophet and cult. Severance of this dependency relationship is equated with death.

The identity to which the convert must conform or face severe penalties embodies contradictory elements similar to those inherent in the communication which induced his conversion. The believer must be sinless but is encouraged to have visions of sin in others. He must perceive the prophet as motivated by and generating only love of God and man, yet he must also accept and endorse the punishments of death, expulsion, and public denunciation meted out by the prophet. He must behave in such a way within the cult as places him in danger of being accounted insane by the rest of the world. He must account the rest of the world insane, yet he must master its intricacies without protest in order to earn his living. The only way these contradictions can be resolved is that the convert learn to deny or misinterpret his own feelings and those of others.

Previous discussion has indicated the way in which contradictory communication aids in increasing anxiety and dependency and in decreasing critical judgment. Contradictory communication also functions in directing the convert toward use of the psychic mechanisms of projection and denial. For example, the believer must avoid all acts or thoughts of sex apart from the performance of the connubial act (even then he is enjoined "not to be a pig in bed"). At the same time he is constantly exposed to minute prolonged and emotionally charged monologues on sexual sin, which include recounting of the prophet's visions of the act itself. Moreover, he is exhorted to be attuned to the possibility of deviant sexual behavior in those around him. If he is to be favored of God, he must have visions about others. At no time is he allowed to handle the problem by sexual activity or repression. Either he must deny the meaning of his own feelings and those of others, or he must learn to project his unacceptable feelings on others. Although denial is permissible within the cult, projection is the method which permits fullest participation in highly rewarded activity and the greatest utilization of the cult world view as an explanatory system for the events of one's life. Altera-

tion in behavior in the form of perceptual distortion and finally hallucination progressively commits the convert to the cult, making defection
more difficult. It appeared that converts who reached baptism rarely
defected.

The dynamics of the conversion process can be summarized at a more
generalized level. Individuals choosing to associate themselves with the
cult are in some sense dissatisfied with their current state. They may be
unsuccessful, alienated, anxious, guilty, suffering from neurotic or psychosomatic disability, or simply conscious of a sense of meaninglessness.
This state, common to individuals in many cultures who seek esoteric
religious experience and to those who seek psychotherapy in ours, has
been described by Stunkard [2] as the *nonadapted state*. Wallace[3] has
identified a similar period of disability preceding the experience he terms
mazeway resynthesis. Cult members offer such an individual an immediate, intense personal relationship, and a defined position within a cohesive social group. Within this context he is offered access to great power
and a means of effecting transition from his current negative state to an
idealized identity.

The communications with which the potential convert was presented
are emotionally intense and contain contradictory elements on both
verbal and nonverbal levels. The consistently uncontradicted messages
are those indicating that his worst possible fate is to leave the field, a
move which is irrevocable. This pattern of communication renders old
patterns of interpreting messages and choosing responses ineffective and
inhibits the formation of a new consistent response set, with the result
that anxiety is intensified. In order to maintain association and reduce
anxiety, the convert must intensify his search behavior, becoming increasingly dependent upon the prophet and members for small clues,
verbal and nonverbal, to correct responses. The threat of visionary denunciation and the requirement for confession of sin and reinterpretation of life experience provide the prophet with a means of modulating
anxiety and aid the convert in internalizing the cult world view. Reinforcement of the convert's previous response set through social relationships in the larger society is attenuated. The intensity of his dependency
upon the prophet decreases the need for contact with individuals outside
the cult. He is given direct instructions to break ties with family and
friends. The identification of cult behavior by the outside world as
"crazy" defines other relationships as threatening and to be avoided.
Once accepted as a convert, the individual can identify with the prophet

[2] A. Stunkard, "Motivation for Treatment: Antecedents of the Therapeutic
Process in Different Cultural Settings," *Comprehensive Psychiatry*, 2:140-48,
1961.
[3] A. F. C. Wallace, *Mazeway Resynthesis: A Biocultural Theory of Religious
Inspiration*, Translated. New York Academy of Sci. Ser. II, 18:626-38, 1956.

and other converts through proselytizing activities, possession experiences, and visionary denunciation of others. Instructions for resolution of contradiction direct the convert toward the psychological mechanisms of projection and denial. The dependency relationship, contradictory communication and reinforcement by the group are particularly significant in the restructuring of individual behavior by the cult.

Descriptions of intense dyadic relationships in which the subordinate member is subjected to severe contradiction are to be found in accounts of diverse social groups which claim or are claimed to be capable of radically altering behavior, perception, or cognition. These include, with or without a reinforcing group environment, the analyst-patient relationship, Alcoholics Anonymous, Synanon (an organization for the recovery of dope addicts), Chinese thought reform,[4] John Rosen's institutional therapy for schizophrenia,[5] and the Eastern mystical religions, Buddhism, Vedanta, and Tantra. The close descriptive similarities in institutions with such diverse rationalizations for their efforts attest to the efficiency of the technique. The present cult is distinguished from some of the above groups by its use of contradiction to stimulate the defense mechanisms of projection and denial.

Numerous recent studies[6] have analyzed interaction in families with a diagnosed schizophrenic member. In these studies, many of the patterns of communication and organization which we noted to be significant in the conversion process have been stigmatized as psychopathological or even as etiologic of schizophrenia. In particular, a symbiotic dependency relationship and paradoxical communication including "double binds" have been indicated. A double bind is a message which is contradicted by concurrent communication at another logical level.[7] The contradictory messages within the cult include but are not limited to double binds. The question arises whether the behavior of cult members can be said to be diagnostic of mental illness or even psychotic. Paranoid schizophrenics commonly elaborate belief systems similar to the prophet's. In our society, dissociated states are labeled "hysterical," and hallucination is almost exclusively restricted to individuals classified as schizophrenic. While it is not feasible here to enter the complex problem of the defini-

    [4] R. J. Lifton, *Thought Reform and the Psychology of Totalism* (New York: W. W. Norton & Company, 1961).

    [5] A. E. Scheflen, A *Psychotherapy of Schizophrenia* (Springfield, Ill.: Charles C. Thomas, 1961).

    [6] See S. Fleck, "Family Dynamics and Origin of Schizophrenia," *Psychosom. Med.*, 22:333-44, 1960; I. Ryckoff, J. Day, and L. C. Wynne, "Maintenance of Stereotyped Roles in the Families of Schizophrenics," *A.M.A. Arch. Gen. Psychiat.*, 1:93-98; L. Schaffer, L. C. Wynne, J. Day, I. M. Ryckoff, and A. Halperin, "On the Nature and Sources of the Psychiatrists' Experience with the Family of the Schizophrenic," *Psychiatry*, 25:32-45, 1962.

    [7] G. Bateson, D. Jackson, J. Haley, J. H. Weakland, "Toward a Theory of Schizophrenia," *Behav. Sc.*, 1:251-64, 1956.

tion of mental illness, it is possible clearly to distinguish cult behavior from psychosis.

Psychotic behavior usually is meaningless to others, is stimulated by internal fantasy rather than communication from the environment, and is marked by a high degree of disorganization.[8] The meaning of cult behavior is not at all private and is subject to consensual validation, for its appropriateness and validity can be determined by appeal to other members and the prophet. Unlike the man with a cat phobia who finds that no one shares his belief that cats are dangerous, the convert finds that the entire group shares his estimation of the power of the Devil and can teach him how to modify his behavior in order to protect himself. Cult behavior is highly controlled by small cues from the environment. All persons interviewed stated that they had not experienced possession or visions prior to contact with the cult. In fact, individuals who spontaneously manifested such behavior without prolonged contact were called "crazy," and Negro visitors were discouraged partially because their possession experiences were not susceptible to close control. As noted above, the occurrence and prevalence of all forms of altered behavior was organized.

Psychotic behavior and symptoms of mental disease are so labeled because they interfere with the functioning of the individual within society. Within the cult context, possession and hallucination are highly adaptive, providing a means of obtaining approbation and satisfaction of important life goals. There is evidence that conversion and cult membership improved individual performance in the society at large. Most members stated that their physical health, job performance, and personal behavior improved following conversion. Since all members were employed, it is probable that they were able to confine aberrant behavior to the context within which it was rewarded. Cult members were well integrated in a social network, while schizophrenic patients are characterized by an inability to integrate themselves in any group.[9] Although the families of the schizophrenics studied in the literature were active in maintaining some of their aberrant behavior, they were chosen for study because even the family had labeled their behavior as "crazy" and extruded them, permitting hospitalization. Cult members were precisely those who had not been extruded but had been able to meet demands for the regulation of their behavior. The analysis of cult process indicates that contradictory communication in the context of a symbiotic dependency relationship, while disruptive of pre-existing behavior patterns, can restructure behavior in an organized fashion. Behavior of cult members

[8] B. A. Rashkis, "The Organization Factor as an Explanatory Principle in Functional Psychosis," A.M.A. Arch. Neurol. and Psychiat., 60:613-19, 1938.

[9] R. Sommer and H. Osmond, "The Schizophrenic No-Society," Psychiatry, 25:244-55, 1962.

may be distinguished not by its disorganization or maladaptive character, but by the restricted number of choices available to individuals.

Black Nationalism and the Reconstruction of Identity
MICHAEL JOHN PARENTI

> *To be a person identical with oneself, presupposes a basic trust in one's origins—and the courage to emerge from them.*
> —Erik H. Erikson

Of the strange sects nurtured in American soil, few have attracted more attention in recent years than the "Nation of Islam," more popularly known as the "Black Muslims." [10] At a time when Americans are moving toward an integrated society, the Muslims advocate racial separation; while others preach brotherhood, the Muslims teach that the white man is a "devil," while Americans, white and Negro, look to the Judaeo-Christian deity for guidance, the Muslim faithful pray to Allah. Most of America places its faith in traditional democratic procedures, but the Muslims obey the messianic and authoritarian leadership of their "Messenger," Elijah Muhammad. Many Negroes strive for acculturation in the mainstream of American society, but the Muslim Negroes determinedly remain apart, dressing their women in strange gowns, praying strange prayers and advocating a separate nation of their own.

Because of the ostensibly revolutionary and fantastic tenets of this sect, observers periodically have denounced the Muslim movement as a black equivalent of the Ku Klux Klan, a "lunatic fringe" group, and a danger to domestic tranquility.[11] Before we share such apprehensions, a dispassionate investigation is in order. The Nation of Islam, it is suggested herein, is primarily striving to create a new identity for a people

Original paper published here for the first time. Michael John Parenti is on the faculty in Political Science at Sarah Lawrence College.

[10] The best full-length study of the Muslims to date is E. U. Essiem-Udom, *Black Nationalism, A Search for an Identity in America* (New York: Dell, 1964.) Other titles worth mentioning are C. Eric Lincoln, *The Black Muslims in America* (Boston: Beacon Press, 1961); Louis Lomax, *When the Word Is Given* (New York: World, 1963).

[11] See, for instance, A. B. Southwick, "Malcolm X: Charismatic Demagogue," *Christian Century*, Vol. 80, June 5, 1963, p. 741; C. Eric Lincoln, "Extremist Attitudes in the Black Muslim Movement," *Journal of Social Issues*, Vol. 19, April 1963, pp. 82-83; *New York Times* editorial, March 14, 1964. For an analysis suggesting that the Muslims are moving toward a more moderate position in American society despite the occasional vehemence of their rhetoric, see my "The Black Muslims: From Revolution to Institution," *Social Research*, Vol. 31, Summer 1964, pp. 175-94. For a sympathetic treatment of the movement, see William Worthy, "The Nation of Islam; Impact and Prospects," *Midstream*, Vol. 8, Spring 1962, pp. 26-44.

who have been deprived of any worthwhile self-identity. That the Muslims have succeeded in this endeavor will be shown in the pages below. Whether the new black nationalist identification is to their credit or discredit, whether it is a desirable phenomenon for American society or for the civil rights movement or even for the individuals participating in the Muslim organization would depend on one's value presuppositions and expectations. The present investigation does not assay an evaluative conclusion, rather it is guided by a nonnormative interest in the following questions: What are the components of this new identification, and by what actual methods and mechanisms has such a remarkable racial, quasi-religious, nationalistic reidentification been accomplished?

THE SEARCH FOR A PAST AND A FUTURE

Just as a patient on the analyst's couch, attempting to ascertain "Who am I?" and "What is wrong with my present condition?" begins a journey into his past, so do a people trying to find a new identity and purpose look to their history. What is true of individual identity appears true of collective identities: to see what is wrong with our present predicament, we must rediscover the past; to decide who we are, we must ascertain who we were.[12] Few people have been so alienated from a sense of cultural heritage and historical origin as the American Negro. In the words of a prominent Negro sociologist:[13]

> Reduced to a chattel in an alien land, the enslaved Negro was not only "detribalized" as the African who has had contact with European civilization, but he was annihilated as a person. . . . The enslavement of the Negro in the United States destroyed not only his family ties and his household gods; it effaced whatever memories of the African homeland that had survived the Middle Passage. The destruction of a common tradition and religious beliefs and practices reduced the Negro to a mere "atom" without a personality or social identity.

The two centuries of bondage were followed by a century and a half of white oppression which left the Negro economically and socially deprived and burdened with a deep feeling of racial inferiority.[14] Today there remain millions in this Negro Lumpenproletariat, living in desolation and squalor, beset by every known kind of social pathology, from whose ranks have emerged the thousands who embrace Elijah Muhammad's vision of a grandeur that was Islam.

[12] Cf. Hans Kohn, Prophets and Peoples (New York: The Macmillan Company, 1946), for a study of rising nationalisms that document this observation.
[13] E. Franklin Frazier, Black Bourgeoisie (New York: Free Press of Glencoe, 1962; Collier Books edition), p. 114.
[14] Ibid., also A. Kardiner and L. Ovesey, The Mark of Oppression (New York: W. W. Norton & Company, 1951), for further documentation.

This Muslim vision bears a striking resemblance to the eschatologies propagated by revolutionary-religious and nationalistic mass movements throughout the centuries. First, there is the state of original purity and bliss: the first man whom God (Allah) created was black, indicating that "blackness" was the true expression of Allah's beauty and virtue and "whiteness" the antithesis. Then came the Fall: the black man was obfuscated and enslaved by the Devil incarnate, i.e., the white man who is a corrupt replica of man contrived by Yakub, the evil universal adversary of Allah. But there came the Message: a Messiah and his followers, the Black Muslims led by the Messenger Muhammad, who saw through the Devil's machinations and who, armed with the truth of Islam, purged themselves of the white man's corruption.[15] (The Message was brought to Muhammad by Allah, himself, in the person of one W. D. Fard who appeared in Detroit during the 1930s.) The Muslims will lead the chosen from their present bondage to a terrestrial paradise, an autonomous Muslim nation.[16] The black man finds happiness and redemption in a land of his own but the blue-eyed white devil will meet his Nemesis in the Armageddon, when the wrath of Allah is delivered upon him. From then on the black man, i.e., all nonwhites, will rule the earth.

Whether the prophet be Treitschke, Dostoevsky, or Hitler, Moses, Mazzini, or Mussolini, or Elijah Muhammad, the myth of the past and the illusion of the future remain a remarkably consistent nationalistic mass movement formula.[17] To convince an alienated people of their worth and unity, one must remind them of their sacred origin. To explain the disheartening realities of their present plight, one must convince them of their natural superiority, and ferret out corruptors and devils. To gird them for the trials ahead, one must reveal a glorious destiny foreordained since the beginning of time. Past, present, and future intermingle in one expression of Divine Intent.

That such myths, be they revived from an earlier day or invented anew, are wanting in historical accuracy, is a consideration of minor importance when compared with the function they serve in creating a new collective pride and individual self-respect. However preposterous Allah

[15] Muhammad writes: ". . . It has been written that God would choose the rejected and the despised. We can find no other persons fitting this description in these last days more than the so-called Negroes in America." *Muhammad Speaks*, September 27, 1963.

[16] For accounts of the Muslim eschatology see Essiem-Udom, *op. cit.*, pp. 140-59; Lincoln, "Extremist Attitudes . . ." *op. cit.*, pp. 80-81; Elijah Muhammad, "What the Muslims Believe," reprinted in every issue of *Muhammad Speaks*.

[17] Kohn, *op. cit.*; see also Karl Popper, *The Open Society and Its Enemies*, Vol. I (New York: Harper & Row, Publishers, 1963), for a discussion of "Theistic historicism," i.e., "the theory of the chosen people which assumes that God has chosen one people to function as the selected instrument of His will, and that this people will inherit the earth" (p. 8).

and Yakub may appear to the disinterested observer, Muhammad's sacred tale is no more implausible and actually less adorned than that found in Genesis and Revelation. In any case, the Muslim eschatology affords the believer an answer to the question "Who am I?" He is not "a nigger up from the Southlands," but a creation of Allah striving for redemption, an "Asiatic black," a member of that great nation of Islam whose adherents stretch clear across the world, part of that great rising tide of mankind, Allah's colored races, as opposed to Yakub's whites.[18] The roles have been reversed: the white man is now the "minority" with his back to the wall, the cursed and the misbegotten; the black man is the chosen. The psychological impact of all this should not be underestimated. The ghetto Negro had never quite heard the likes of it before.

REHABILITATION

The Muslim myth does not serve as a battle plan directing nonwhites toward some cataclysmic confrontation with whites, although too many alarmed critics have leaped to that conclusion. Its real function is a reconstruction of social identity. As Essiem-Udom concludes, after an intensive study:[19]

> The eschatology of the Nation of Islam shows the black nationalists' desire to free themselves from the exploited image of blackness and hence from the deep feeling of self-rejection, cultural alienation, an social estrangement which pervade and corrupt the personalities of the Negro masses. It expresses the nationalist's need to attach himself in a positive way to something worthy and esteemed, some center of power, some tradition and, generally, some "central ideal" capable of endowing his life with meaning and purpose. It offers hope in a future, one in which blackness will no longer be despised. In part, this vision of the future inspires the Muslims to pursue their life activities with courage and unbending determination.

The practical effects are quite astounding. Drug addicts, alcoholics, criminals, and despairing slum dwellers in general, many whom social workers and community leaders had tacitly declared beyond help, have been rehabilitated by joining the movement.[20] Men who heretofore lived shiftless or illicit lives, now were employed at honest jobs (the first in

---

[18] Worthy quotes one Muslim convert: "It was not enough to hear that a few of us were great. I no longer felt I was a nobody. It was a re-birth. . . . The teachings of Islam began to take hold." Op. cit., p. 32.

[19] Essiem-Udom, op. cit., p. 141.

[20] This rehabilitation phenomenon is well-documented in Ibid., Chapter 4, and in the testimonies offered by Muslims in "What Islam Has Done for Me," a feature now appearing in every issue of Muhammad Speaks; see also Claude Brown, "Ally Bush," Dissent, 10, Summer 1963, p. 265 and Worthy op. cit., pp. 31-32.

their lives, for some), conscientiously marrying and raising families, obeying the law, saving money, and faithfully contributing a tithe to Black Islam. In obedience to the teachings of Elijah Muhammad, they abstain from drink, drugs, and tobacco, refrain from gambling, promiscuity, dancing, long vacations, idleness, excessive sleeping, lying, and stealing. Muslim women are devotedly domiciled, thrifty, and keepers of fastidiously clean homes.[21] Muslims are forbidden to spend money frivolously, and are committed to pooling their resources to help themselves and each other. The result is a healthy living standard even in the ghettoes where most Muslims dwell. The movement has, in its own strange way, repaired some of the irreparable and saved some of the damned.

ORGANIZATIONAL AND INSTITUTIONAL SUPPORTS

Aware that faith alone does not always work this extraordinary transformation, the Muslims buttress their belief system with a host of organizational controls and psychologically fortifying symbols.

One problem faced by the "cured" addict or ex-convict is that upon release he is often thrown into the same pathological environment that brought him to his difficulties. By the same token, the slum dweller may entertain no serious thoughts of improving his lot because he is surrounded by others similarly, and seemingly hopelessly, situated. This problem of emerging from a social milieu while being perpetually subjected to its contaminations is partly solved for the person entering the Muslim Nation. Former unsavory companions are eschewed and new group relationships with others living the regenerated, inspired life are established.

The neophyte is assisted, encouraged, and disciplined by an elaborate organization within the Brotherhood. Frequent visits to Muslim temples are required to hear the Message from a dedicated and vigorous clergy. Temple "investigators" mediate disharmonies in families or among members, or refer disputes to the appropriate officers, while a well-disciplined elitist security force (Fruit of Islam) guards against attacks from outside enemies and heterodoxy within Muslim ranks. Muslim publications, the most popular being *Muhammad Speaks*, filled with inspirational messages and articles on the Negro's struggle and on the activities of the organization and individual Muslim brothers are distributed and read regularly by the faithful. There are women's auxiliaries to teach domestic skills, child care and a woman's proper role in the home, summer camps for Muslim children, accredited Muslim grade schools, community centers for adolescents, employment training and housing agencies for Muslim families, and modest but prospering Muslim retail and service businesses.

[21] Essiem-Udom, *op. cit.*, p. 121ff.; Lincoln, *The Black Muslims in America*, *op. cit.*, pp. 17-18, 24, 60-64.

Presiding supreme over this small empire is Elijah Muhammad, whose alleged messianic wisdom and strength are an inspiration to the rank and file.[22] It is not long before the novice comes to share the admiration and loyalty his brothers express toward the Messenger and the emotional comfort and security that is associated with such devotion. Membership in the Nation, then, is not something exercised in one's spare time; it is a total commitment to Islam. Every day is lived with the consciousness of one's new Muslim identification.

THE FUNCTION OF SYMBOLS

The search for a collective identity, as we have observed, necessitates a reconstruction of past, present, and future. Collective myth, however, is refortified by symbols which furnish a reified object for mass loyalty and a concrete expression of a sometimes almost transcendent realm of aspiration. Every nationalism has its flag and its god or gods around which the faithful may rally. For the Muslims, Islam provides some of the necessary accessories: Allah, the star and crescent, the black nationalist version of the Koran, and the Islamic tongue, which some Muslims make a sincere attempt at mastering.

Of greater importance is the "symbolism of the self" utilized by the collectivity for the benefit of its individual members. The search for an identity is often expressed by the adoption of appearances and practices that are meant to symbolize the self. Thus, a desire to be the bohemian may include the wearing of old clothes, long hair and sandals, a new speech pattern, a taste for avant-garde arts and a Greenwich Village apartment. But these appurtenances are not merely symptomatic of the new social role, they become an important, and often, sole, means of expressing it. Symbolic appearances and practices, by becoming fortifying and substantive expressions in their own right, not only signify a way of life, to a great extent they *are* that life. One might say there is no such thing as a "mere symbol"; for something to be a symbol, it must take on meaning.[23] In much of their practice and ritual the followers of Black Islam may seem, at worst, cultist, at best, laughable. But if we keep in mind that an individual's name, appearance, deportment, and tastes are part of what identify him to himself and others, then such things are symbolically functional and must be transformed and redefined for the

---

[22] Lomax, *op. cit.*

[23] This could explain the rigidity and ostensible triviality of many ideologues on the question of symbols. For example, congregations have suffered schisms over disputes about stain glass windows. A seemingly minor decorative question is really a fight over symbols, which in turn is a struggle having fundamental religious implications. Thus, such windows may "symbolize" the church's position toward "Popery" and "idolatry" and a host of related theological questions. One might also think of the secular religion of nationalism and the Canadian dispute over the design of the national flag.

sake of a new identity. Either by conscious design or shrewd instinct, this is exactly what the Muslims do.

Initiation into the Muslim society is designed to facilitate and dramatize withdrawal from the "dead world," i.e., the Negro world, which means above all an eradication of labels and attributes associated with Negro stereotypy. The neophyte learns that he is not, nor was he ever, a Negro, his "real" nationality being "Muslim" or "Asiatic." The term "Negro" is rarely used by Muslims except in the expression "the so-called Negro" indicating that it is an appellation fabricated by the white slavemasters centuries ago and lacking in historical legitimacy.

What is true of the group name is true of individual names. The black men in their generations of captivity lost their original identities and were given names by their masters, or themselves adopted white names when emancipated. This slave name is discarded as an important step toward independence from the "dead world," and replaced by an initial or, more commonly, the letter "X." Some Muslims have been accorded the high honor of receiving their "real" Islamic names from Muhammad.[24] This rejection of former names and the appellation of "Negro" is of no minor importance to the membership. One Muslim minister, commenting on American Negroes who retain their "slave names," observed: "They don't even know who they are." [25] To the question "What's in a name?" the Muslims seem to answer, "A man's identity."

In Islam, one's apparel is no longer a matter of personal taste. Muslim men must dress conservatively in suits, ties, and white collars. The women usually wear headdress and full white habit covering arms and legs. These "uniforms" have several indentificational functions. The disheveled or flamboyant appearance represented in the lower-class Negro stereotype is replaced by a sober neatness which both expresses and strengthens a new sense of dignity. The rather archaic dress of the female perhaps emphasizes the protected, sequestered, and obedient role she plays vis-à-vis her male counterpart. The uniformity, as in the military, heightens a sense of group cohesion and affords a readily detectable commonality. Brothers can be differentiated from others.[26]

---

[24] One such notable is heavyweight champion Cassius Clay who is now Muhammad Ali. Elijah Muhammad himself is another, who has his "real" surname. Muslims of lesser renown usually use a numbered X, thus, James X, James 2X, James 3X, etc. At some future day Allah will bestow upon them their lost names.

[25] Quoted in Essiem-Udom, op. cit., p. 225.

[26] In a study of another sect, J. A. Hostetler, Amish Society (Baltimore: John Hopkins Press, 1963), the author writes: "The horse and buggy, the beard of the married man, and the styles of dress—all take on symbolic meaning. All Amish know that this is the accepted way of doing things, and symbolism becomes an effective means of social control as the nonconformist can quickly be detected from the conformist." (Pp. 132-33.)

One's appreciation of racial physical appearances also changes considerably. The Negro suffering from a "slave mentality" and a lost identity accepts Caucasian standards of personal attractiveness, but the black man who becomes a Muslim learns differently: black skin is truly the most appealing; kinky hair is "strong hair"; Negroid features are the highest human representation of Allah's beauty; nonwhites are the only desirable mates. The observation volunteered by one female correspondent to *Muhammad Speaks* is typical: "The handsomest and most beautiful and congenial people in the world are the black and brown people— African and Asian types. Even white policemen resent and are jealous of our men." [27] The Islamic faithful have no need for skin bleach, hair straightener, and other cosmetic contrivances. The black man is invited to love rather than hate his own skin. What we are witnessing here is a whole reversal and reconstruction of racial aesthetics.

It seems, from what has been said thus far, that not only their achievements but the people themselves become symbolic: along with name and appearance, one's very deportment is instrumental in identity reconstruction; Muslim self-composure is to be maintained at all times. Boisterous behavior and displays of unrestrained emotion are interdicted. Brought into Muslim company, the novice immediately grasps that he is to listen quietly to any music, and not sway or croon. Other people, including whites, are to be treated courteously, and women are to be accorded the utmost respect. Followers are taught that violence for any reason other than self-defense is forbidden; hence, no member of Islam is allowed to carry weapons or bear arms, and consequently, Muslims are conscientious objectors. It should not be overlooked that in the various cities subjected to racial violence and looting during the summer of 1964, not one of Muhammad's followers was implicated. The Muslims seem to practice what they preach.[28]

In all behavior, the Muslim represents the antithesis of the chortling, carefree, razor-wielding Negro stereotype; if anything, he is a black replica of the self-constrained and self-consciously respectable white bourgeois.

The "reborn" black man is one who respects and cares for his body as

[27] *Muhammad Speaks,* August 28, 1964.
[28] "I have been teaching for the past years . . . that we carry no arms and we do not seek to win victory with arms," Muhammad has said; see Gertrude Samuels, "Feud Within the Black Muslims," *New York Times Magazine,* March 22, 1964, pp. 17, 104-07. Worthy quotes a "New York Police Department spokesman" as saying: "The Muslims don't carry weapons. If they did, we'd arrest them. They are a well-behaved group." *Op. cit.,* p. 39. The assassination of Malcolm X, allegedly perpetrated by some of Muhammad's followers, proves the exception to this rule. The restraints governing relations with the wider community are suspended when dealing with heretics. This is often the case with true believer movements.

a gift from Allah; therefore, the foods prescribed by the Nation of Islam are wholesome and nourishing (for example, whole wheat rather than white bread). The manner of eating (only one daily meal, with the entire family ceremoniously brought together) is designed both to avoid overindulgence and to stabilize domestic life, in sharp contradistinction to the haphazard eating schedules and unhealthy dietary habits of many lower-class Negroes.

Of equal interest are the proscribed foods: as a true Muslim, one is divinely forbidden to touch pork, sea food, or other scavenger creatures. Corn bread, black-eyed peas, collard greens, possum, coon, and other standard Southern fare reminiscent of past "slave habits" are also strictly prohibited. Hence, even in what and how the Muslim eats, he receives an answer to the question "Who am I?" His dietary laws are one more means of bolstering the new identity while eradicating the old.

What that new identity means for the rest of American society remains an important question.[29] But one thing is certain: it is neither what the white man is nor what he has believed the Negro to be. Witness the admonition from Elijah Muhammad to "Stand yourself up and look—with your eyes not the white man's," and to "get away from the idea of depending on others to do for us what we can do for self. Fear, cowardice, and laziness are our greatest enemies." [30] In so many words, Muhammad teaches: To feel inferior results in acting inferior and is the outgrowth of believing the white man's view of yourself. Pleading for his acceptance is another way of waiting for him to liberate you. Free yourself of the slave mentality. Love yourself and you will not need the white man's love. Muhammad's greatest desire, it seems, is not racial war but racial self-reliance and separation. His peculiar "program" perhaps best sums it up. Some of the points read: "Separate yourselves from the slave master. Pool your resources, education, and qualifications for independence. Stop forcing yourselves into places where you are not wanted. Make your own neighborhood a decent place to live. Rid yourselves of the lust of drink and learn to love self and kind before loving others. . . . Build your own homes, schools, hospitals, and factories. Do not seek to mix your blood through racial integration. Stop buying expensive cars, fine clothes, and shoes before being able to live in a fine house. Spend your money among yourselves."

It is a curious fact that this "extremist" movement which blames the whites for the downfall and enslavement of the Negro, nevertheless, does recognize that blacks are at least partly responsible for their own continued plight and, therefore, must take it upon themselves to better their lot, independently of the wider society's approval and good will. This

[29] See Parenti, "The Black Muslims: From Revolution to Institution," *op. cit.*, for some prognostications.
[30] *Muhammad Speaks*, November 22, 1963.

idea that the present major responsibility for betterment rests not with the white man but with the black man is one of the less obvious points, often overlooked, that distinguishes the Muslims from most militant civil rights groups.

CONCLUSION

The Black Muslims provide us with one of the clearest examples of how individual psychic identifications and political or religio-nationalistic collective identifications interact in one and the same dynamic. In "submerging" himself in some authoritarian body which promises a collective redemption, it is questionable that the individual necessarily "sacrifices" or "loses" his individual self, as is often stated;[31] rather he may well emerge, for better or worse, with a revivified sense of self. By constructing collective identity through the use of myth, symbol, and organization, the Muslims revitalize individual identity. Not the psychotherapist, but the representatives of a black nationalist movement performed the remarkable rehabilitation of criminal drug addicts. Conversely, the symbolic and primary-group supports operating at a personal level of interaction reaffirm the collective self and fortify the very organization which creates and propagates the collectivity. In emerging nationalisms—perhaps especially those born of intense racial suffering—it would seem that the search for an individual identity and a collective identity, the search for person and people, self and society, are inseparable.

It has often been observed that various peoples "identify" with causes, and leaders, or "seek an identity" in one movement or another. The main purpose of this paper was to demonstrate empirically *how*, that is, by what actual means and mechanisms an awakening and reconstruction of individual-group identification is effected.

The Negro who journeys into Black Islam embarks upon no whimsical passage. He must first attend several temple meetings and register with a Muslim secretary. He must demonstrate literacy in a letter of application before he is even considered as a candidate for membership. He must wait to receive lessons and instructions from other members. Doctrinally infused with a new zeal and confidence, and a new sense of means and goals, he is endowed with a new name and nationality, a new past and future, a new manner of dress, deportment, and diet, a new appreciation of racial physical attributes, new supporting social relationships and institutionalized obligations and loyalties, and immanent in all this, a new set of life values. Everything is designed to impress upon him the fact that he is making a momentous life decision; the passage from a "dead world" into a reborn world, from a dead self to a real self.

Through the use of eschatological myth, messianic leadership, organi-

31 See Eric Hoffer, *The True Believer* (New York: New American Library, 1958).

zational direction of personal life, institutional structuring of social life, and the fabrication and mobilization of symbols, this black nationalist movement has, among a limited population, perpetrated a revolution. We will fail to comprehend its nature as long as we search for what are probably nonexistent Muslim arm caches. The revolution is one of racial aesthetics, moral regeneration, and psychocollective identification. As such, it is of truly remarkable dimension, having repercussions, for better or worse, well beyond the confines of Black Islam.

Discussion

These two papers provide a vivid picture of two variations on collective transformation of common psychic stress, each showing a subculture providing a viable adaptation for the personalities of the members. Each shows certain collective psychodynamic and social processes working simultaneously for the consolidation of the cult or movement as a social organization and for the reintegration of the personalities of the participants around clearly identifiable values and a distinctive life style. Each shows both rewards and costs to the personalities of the members.

In both cases recruitment into the movement is based on a negative psychological condition in the potential convert—some kind of "nonadapted state," dissatisfaction with life, alienation or degradation of some kind. Why this particular cult or movement and not some other is a significant question which cannot be answered (for these two cases) from the available data. The collective processes set in motion once the convert is in the organization show certain important differences between the two situations, but also there are certain broad similarities which have been reported in other social movements as well. The similarities are the following: The member's attention and concern are monopolized by the movement: the movement is no mere pastime, but a way of life. The member is kept in direct interaction with other members a great deal of his time, and even when not with them, is led to think and feel about all his other relationships in terms of the newly learned norms, symbols, and beliefs of his cult. The concomitants are the active interest, concern, social support, and discipline provided by the other members of the movement, with the combination of primary group satisfactions and restrictions that this involves. The latter means a radical limitation of behavior choices available to the convert—a gratifying simplification of life. The collective relationships constantly reinforce the new identity of the member. Related to this is the radical ingroup-outgroup process. This ingroup-outgroup process does several things. It solidifies identity by contrasting it with polar opposites—"people possessed by the Devil" or "people who don't know who they are—the so-called Negroes." It also provides a channeling of aggression—aggression derived from the prior degraded state of the convert (and whatever idiosyncratic psychic tension he brings with him to the new experience) and aggressions aroused by the very collective processes of inducting the new member into the cult. In both these cases considerable authoritarian control over the member by his newly accepted leader is involved.

The Katchers' study reveals collective processes which involve psychological mechanisms usually considered pathological—extreme dependency, the anxiety that is heightened by double-bind communication and the dilemma of heightened focusing on sexuality without allowing either direct expression or repression (hence the extreme use of the mechanism of projection), as well as the collectively structured use of the parapsychic states of vision and spirit possession.

The "costs" in each case involve the acceptance by the members of an objectively preposterous set of beliefs, each set in its own way documenting the infinite capacity of man to "believe at least six impossible things before breakfast." The mythology may be—as both the Katchers and Parenti aver, in each case—"adaptive" or "functional" for the believers, but it is still irrational. Therefore, it confronts us with the dilemma of how far such irrationality needs to be "accepted" as a "necessary cost" of adaptation, or more positive personality identity, or whatever other values are perceived and to derive from the cult or movement experience. Another—and *different*—cost for the cult member is the necessity to come to terms with being *considered* "crazy" by the outside world. (This is not the same problem as the irrationality or nonrationality of the belief system itself; it is rather the question of how the "others"—i.e., noncult members—*define* the cultists, which may or may not focus on the elements of mythology that are *objectively* out of line with history or current reality. The "craziness" of the cultists from the outsiders' view is simply in how their beliefs and actions depart from the outsiders' *own*.)

A third type of "cost" lies in the radical restriction of choices the convert faces in consequence of his membership. This is of course an ambiguous "cost"—depending upon what values one emphasizes. On the one hand it can be seen as limiting or precluding the possibility of the converts arriving at some "more rational" solution of his problems—for example in reference to the handling of sexuality in the case of Emmanuel's disciples. On the other hand, a serious consideration of the socially *available* alternatives open to the convert—especially in Parenti's example of the Negro *Lumpenproletariat*—may lead to the conclusion that the cult membership has a stronger claim to human dignity than the existing alternatives and hence the restriction of choices that it involves is hardly a cost but a boon.

On the other side are the rewards available to the member, most signally the transformation of social identity with all the enormous gratifications this entails. In both of these cases, also, by an apparent paradox, the consolidation of the partially deviant identity as cult member also entails an improved social adaptation to the wider society, judged by its norms of respectability regarding work, sex, and family life.

2. PSYCHODYNAMICS AND LEADERSHIP

The examination of cults and movements involves a consideration of the social psychology of leaders and followers. In both of the case studies we found a definitely charismatic leader who is the central focus for the organization and for individual members' psychic orientation to the movement. Katchers' analysis of the Emmanuel cult shows the significance of direct personal dependency on the cult leader in the transformation dynamics of the members. In the Black Muslims, the sheer size to which the movement has now grown has made direct personal interaction with the leader, Elijah Muhammad, impractical for most of the followers, but indirectly the personalized appeal is maintained by Muhammad's printed inspirational messages and by local religious leaders functioning as intermediaries.

We can turn now to a more general consideration of the dynamics of relations between leaders and followers. The following paper by Fritz Redl explores the depth elements in ten types of situation involving a group and one "central person" (or leader).

Group Emotion and Leadership

FRITZ REDL

Freud called the person around whom the group formative process crystallizes the "leader," following a well-rooted linguistic habit. However,
since 1921, quite a few things have happened which make all more sensitive to the tremendous differences of meaning which this word assumes
under certain circumstances. This investigation, especially, led to the discovery of a number of types of group formation, which do occur "around
a central person," but for the designation of which the word "leader"
simply does not lend itself. It is therefore necessary to begin with a ter-
minological correction, reserving the word "leader" for only one type of
role of the person central for group formation and relationships with
members, giving different names to the other forms.

By *central person* is meant person "around whom" group formative
processes take place, the "crystallization point" of the whole affair. . . .

The term *central person* designates the one through emotional relationship to whom the group formative processes are evoked in the
potential group members.

Ten types of "leadership"—ten different roles which this *central person* may play in group formation—can easily be distinguished.

The object of this investigation must be recognized as the study of
drive-relationships and emotional procedures within each member of a
group, on the basis of which group formative processes are evoked.

All the *Ten Types* presented deal with group formation "around" a
central person. The difference between the ten types lies in the different
role of the central person for the basic processes of group formation.

TYPE 1: "THE PATRIARCHAL SOVEREIGN"

Illustrative example.   This group is composed of approximately ten-year-
old children, most of whom are just at that point in their "childhood"
immediately before the outbreak of preadolescent symptoms. In charge
of them is a teacher who fits the following description: "He is an elderly
gentleman of stern but not unfriendly exterior, decided but fundamentally mild in his manner. He stands for 'order and discipline' but they
are values so deeply ingrained in him that he hardly thinks of them explicitly, nor does it occur to anyone to doubt them in his presence. He
believes in good and thorough work, knows very clearly what he expects,
and leaves no doubt about it in the minds of his students." The atmo-

*Reprinted by special permission of The William Alanson White Psychiatric
Foundation, Inc. and of the author, from Fritz Redl, "Group Emotion and
Leadership," Psychiatry, Vol. 5, 1942, pp. 573-84. Copyright held by The Wil-
liam Alanson White Psychiatric Foundation, Inc. Also included in Fritz Redl,
When We Deal with Children (New York: The Free Press, 1966).*

sphere of the classroom may be easily described. The children accept his values without question. Their emotions about him are a mixture of love and adoration, with an element of anxiety in all those instances in which they are not quite sure of his approval. As long as they behave according to his code, they feel happily secure—sheltered. Thoughts and imaginations which do not comply with his code are suppressed in his presence. The jokes he makes, or acknowledges, are funny. If one youngster who is not quite so ready as the others to concentrate his filial adoration upon this type of a teacher makes unfitting remarks, unruly gestures, or shows lack of submission, the others will experience a deep feeling of moral indignation—even though they may have enjoyed this youngster's jokes a few minutes previously during the recreation period. . . . Behind the happy security felt in his presence there is a nagging fear of its loss which streams into awareness every once in a while without apparent cause.

Explanation. These youngsters love their teacher, but that is not all that occurs. Their love is of a type which leads to "identification." It would be absurd to say that they want to be like their teacher, but they want to behave so that their teacher will approve of them.

Formula. These children become a group because they incorporate the "superego"—conscience—of the central person, into their own. On the basis of this similarity between them, they develop group emotions toward each other.

TYPE 2: "THE LEADER"

Illustrative example. This group of boys are between fifteen and seventeen years of age. Most of them are far beyond their preadolescence— at the verge of transition from earlier adolescence into later adolescence. The teacher in charge of them is, or has the appearance of being, very young. He has an attractive exterior. He is somewhat juvenile but not too unpleasantly so in his views and behavior. He also stands for "work and discipline," and gets his youngsters to comply without much outward pressure. However, the basis on which he gets them to accept his authority is a little different. He differs from the patriarch mainly in that he strongly sympathizes with the drives of the children. They are clearly aware of it. He plays a dual role in his teaching. In his own superego, he is identified with the order and the demands of the school which he represents; but he is keenly aware of the instinctual demands of the youngsters. In order to combine both he has to display considerable technical skill. If he succeeds, he makes his class feel secure and happy; if he fails, they are frightened either of him or of their own drives. . . .

Explanation. A central person of this kind appeals to the love emotions as well as to the narcissistic[32] tendencies in the children. However,

---

[32] *Ed. note:* i.e., "self-interested."

it would be difficult to say that they put the teacher in the place of their "conscience." Rather they place him in the other part of their superego, in what is usually called their "ego-ideal," which means that they start wishing to become the type of person he is.

Formula. The children become a group because they incorporate the teacher's personality into their ego-ideal. On the basis of this similarity they develop group emotions toward each other. This formula coincides most closely with that of Freud in *Group Psychology and the Analysis of the Ego.*

TYPE 3: "THE TYRANT"

Illustrative example. This is a class of children approximately ten years old, near the verge of preadolescence. In charge of them is an elderly, or middle-aged teacher, among whose motives for teaching were one or both of the following: He is compulsively bound to repeat a certain pattern of "discipline" against the children because this is the only way he can prove late obedience to some of the demands of his own parents; or, his most intensive drive satisfactions lie in the direction of sadism, and he has to use the children as objects for that purpose. This teacher will not "stand for" anything, but has to "impose" some kind of capricious "order" or "discipline" all the time. . . . In short, there is a "regular tyrant" in charge of this class. Everyday psychology might tempt one to expect children to hate the teacher and fight him as much as they dared. . . . The entirely different reaction from the youngsters is surprising. These children submit easily. They rebel against the silly pedantry of this tyrant less vehemently than other groups do against the reasonable demands of their beloved leader. Nor do they submit only temporarily. What they show is genuine "identification." How strong is this identification? This is illustrated by the youngster who does dare to rebel in such a class. He has a difficult time. He has everyone against him, the teacher, the other youngsters, and himself.

However, one difference seems obvious. The emotional relations these youngsters develop among themselves seem less intensive than in the other illustrations. Children of such classes develop little "comradeship" —unlike those who just hate their teacher without identifying with him —and they seem to be afraid of each other, and distrustful. They seem to fear that too much intimacy might endanger the successful repression of their hostility and might force them to realize what cowards they are.

Explanation. Doubtless, the identification of these children with their tyrant is genuine. He is the central person for that group. Unlike the two previous illustrations, this identification occurs from a different motive. It is not love which causes them to identify, but fear. Of course, not all fear leads into identification, but it does in the type just described.

Formula. These children incorporate the superego of the central person into their own by way of identification, the outgrowth of fear of the aggressor, and on this basis establish group emotions between each other.

TYPE 4: THE CENTRAL PERSON AS LOVE OBJECT

Freud mentioned an example of group formation which he exempted from the leadership type. It fits into the pattern according to the broadened concept of the *central person* I have introduced.

> *Imagine a number of women who are in love with a singer or pianist and crowd around him after his performance. Certainly each of them would prefer to be jealous of all the others. However, considering their large number and how impossible it is for them to reach the aim of their infatuation, they resign and instead of pulling each other's hair, they act like a uniform group. They bring ovations to their idol in common actions and would be glad to divide his locks among themselves.*[33]

The life in the school class furnishes two similar examples for illustration.

Illustrative example. There is a group of sixteen-year-old girls in a class of a girls' high school. In charge of them is a male teacher—young, attractive, but narcissistic enough so that they are not too greatly frightened sexually from the outset. It is known that in some such cases "the whole class falls in love with him." From that moment on, they will act like a group in many ways along the line of Freud's example. Despite their infatuation for him, it would not be surprising if the teacher complained that he had trouble with discipline—that these girls did not obey him or follow his wishes without pressure. It seems that this kind of "being in love" with the central person does not make for "identification" described in Type 2.

Explanation. There is no doubt that the group emotional symptoms are genuine and that the teacher is playing the role of the central person without whose presence this type of group formative process would not have been evoked. However, it is also evident that these central persons could not be called "leaders" by any interpretation of the term—that the other children do not "identify" with them. Nor do they incorporate their central person's standards. The central person remains "outside" but does call out a display of group emotional symptoms in these children.

Formula. The children choose one and the same person as an object of their love, and on the basis of this similarity they develop group emotions between each other.

[33] Sigmund Freud, *Group Psychology and the Analysis of the Ego* (London: Hogarth Press, 1922). 134 pp.

TYPE 5: THE CENTRAL PERSON AS OBJECT OF AGGRESSIVE DRIVES

Illustrative example. A type of teacher similar to the one described under the heading of "tyrant" is less intensive in his sadism, less superior in the rest of his personality traits. He is in charge of a group of rather problematic adolescents in a school setup which is so well regimented through an established system of suppressive rules that no one dares to rebel, because it would be too futile. These children obey their teacher under the constant application of pressure. They behave sufficiently well to keep out of trouble, but they do so grudgingly. They neither identify with the teacher nor with what he represents. Their relationship toward him—with the possible exception of a "sissy" in the class—is one of intensive hatred, of piled-up aggression which is kept from exploding only by their reality-insight. And yet, although they do not identify with the teacher, the emotions they develop toward each other will be truly positive and strong. The amount of "comradeship" these children display is enormous—greater than in any of the other groups. He who dares to identify with the hated oppressor is an outcast—arouses a lynching attitude in the rest of the class. Their feeling toward him is one of moral indignation, but its content is different from the other examples. It is moral indignation "from beneath," to use one of Nietzsche's terms.

Formula. The children choose one and the same person as an object of their aggressive drives and through this similarity develop group emotions about each other.

TYPE 6: THE ORGANIZER

Illustrative example. In a class of approximately thirteen-year-old boys there are five who find clandestine enjoyment of the cigarette as a symbol of adulthood. And yet, all five are of the type who have decided worries about how they can obtain cigarettes. They have neither the money to buy them, the courage to do so, nor the impudence to steal them from their fathers. Preadolescent revolt against adult concepts of what a good child should be has not progressed far enough. A new boy, for whom smoking is no great problem, enters the class. He neither invites, instigates nor encourages the others in this enterprise. They all know that he can get the desired cigarettes for them if they but ask. I have seen cases where hardly any other factor was involved. The boys neither loved nor admired this youngster; on the contrary, he was rather looked down upon as socially inferior. They did not fear him nor did he use any direct or indirect pressure upon them. Yet, by the mere fact of getting them the cigarettes, they suddenly eventuated into a regular "group," held together on the basis of their participation in the same forbidden pleasure.

Explanation. Perhaps this example seems more complicated—less credible—than the others, being unaccustomed to finding this function of the organizer isolated. Usually, it is coupled with other roles which the central person assumes for the potential group members. Although there are not many clear examples of this type, they cannot be reduced to any of the other types because neither love, hatred, nor identification is involved.

Formula. The central person renders an important service to the ego of the potential group members. He does so by providing the means for the satisfaction of common undesirable drives and thus prevents guilt feelings, anxieties, and conflicts which otherwise would be involved in that process for them. On the basis of this service, the latent undesirable drives of these youngsters can manifest openly. Through this common conflict-solution, group emotions develop in the interpersonal situation.

TYPE 7: THE SEDUCER

Illustrative example. In a group of thirteen-year-old boys, six, involved in "group masturbation," are apprehended. The first superficial examination by school authorities reveals apparent, unequal participation. Some were onlookers, none were mutually active; all agreed that one of them was the "leader" of the gang. After thorough investigation the following situation was revealed. The obvious "culprit" was most "actively" engaged in masturbation. He was the "first to start it." However, he was not at all active in encouraging the others to join or to perform likewise. He was a little more developed than any of them; he masturbated freely at home without special guilt feelings. Masturbation meant something entirely different for him than for them, nor did he need the group from the standpoint of sex satisfaction. He gained nothing from the group situation, except prestige. He was not homosexual in the usual sense of the term, more surprising, perhaps, is the fact that the others neither especially loved nor feared him. They were more infantile than he. They had sufficiently conquered their anxieties about sex curiosity to take the first step in active experimentation on a highly pregenital level. However, they might not have done so alone, since that would have made them feel guilty about it. Actually, they used this boy for the purpose of "seduction." They needed him, and the group situation allowed them to overcome their restrictions. Only after he was the "first one to do it" were they ready and able to join him.

Explanation. The example beyond doubt represents group formation through the existence of a central person. In this case the potential group members had much in common before the group formative processes began. It is also evident that they did not start before the central person committed the "first act." Apparently what evoked the group emotional reactions was the fact that these central persons committed an "initiatory" act. Through this act, the satisfaction of undesirable drives became possible in others, who would otherwise not have openly expressed them. This concept of the "initiatory act" is not an invention but the description of a procedure observed so frequently in school and adult life that it does not require proof. It needs, however, to be explained. Thus far, I do not attempt to show why the "first act" may have such magical power over other people's suppressed drives. . . .

What occurred in these children is here described. There is a strong increase in the intensity of drives. . . . The personal superego of these children remains strong enough to suppress any possibility of the drives becoming overt. The ego of these children is in a predicament. Pressed with equal strength from oppressed drives and super-ego demands, it knows not what to do. Anxiety and uneasiness are the usual emotional accompaniments of such disturbances to balance. It is on the basis of such a situation that the effect of an "initiatory act" seems to take place.

Formula.   The central person renders a service to the ego of the potential group members. He does this by committing the "initiatory act" and thus prevents guilt feelings, anxieties, and conflicts. On the basis of this service, the latent drives of these children manifest openly. Through this common conflict-solution, they develop group emotions.

TYPE 8:   THE "HERO"

Illustrative example.   This is the same tyrant-group described under Type 3—where all the children were fully identified with their oppressor —at a later interval. These children have developed further into preadolescent rebelliousness. . . . The tyrant now begins to make deplorable mistakes. He chooses, for example, one child as the preferable object of his sadism and persecutes him more and more persistently. The others almost pity the child, but pity would imply criticism of their tyrant, and that would tend to revive their own dangerously rebellious feelings against him. So, they hold as tightly to their protective identification with the oppressor as they can. However, one of them has more courage. Something in his history makes him less able to endure this—or, perhaps, his insight into the real dangers implied by rebellion dwindles more rapidly. In any event, he is one day unable to tolerate the teacher's attack upon his victim. This boy defends his colleague and is considered "fresh" and reckless. The whole class gasps with surprise. They expect something fearful to happen. Surely the teacher will kill that child, or lightning will strike out of the clear sky. But no avenging stroke of lightning descends to quell the rebellion. The teacher is evidently too surprised or frightened momentarily to know what to do. When he demonstrates his fury, it is too late. The "hero" has worked his miracle. All the youngsters have altered their sentiments, at least secretly. Now they adore him and even start identifying with him. He takes his punishment, but remains victorious.

Explanation. The situation is similar to the one previously described, but events now move in the opposite direction. These youngsters suffer similarly from a number of suppressed tendencies—such as just rebellion in favor of a suffering colleague—however, they are too fearful of the realistic consequences of such feelings. Their personal cowardice hinders them from doing what they feel is right, but what would have awful consequences for them. Again the hero commits the "initiatory act." Through his demonstration of courage the others suddenly discard anxieties and dare—if not to act, then, at least, to feel what their own standard of justice has long wanted them to experience.

Formula. The central person renders a service to the ego of the potential group members. He does so by committing the "initiatory act" and thus saves them anxieties and conflicts. The "initiatory act," however, leads in the direction of moral values versus cowardly self protection this time. On the basis of this service the undesirable tendencies toward cowardly submission in these children are conquered. Through this common conflict-solution group psychological emotions are evoked.

TYPE 9: THE "BAD INFLUENCE"

There are children in many classes who are constantly being accused of being "undesirable elements" by all teachers, parents, and other children, too. And yet, they can scarcely be accused of "having an evil" influence. Usually what they are accused of is unclear, but it is assumed that their mere presence in the classroom affects the others badly— "brings out the worst in them." And yet it would be embarrassing to say how they do this. Accusations made against them often have to be withdrawn, because no definite basis exists in fact. Nothing can be proved. Sometimes, admittedly, these children are not so difficult to manage; they are better than the influence they are accused of having on the others. Fundamentally, this is an accusation of seduction through magic. Apparently belief in the infectiousness of something within these children seems absurd, and yet, it is not. The background upon which the accusations are made is usually true. These children do affect the others, not overtly—quite in contrast to the "seducer type"—but, by their presence in the same room, something happens to these youngsters which makes them unruly, full of "dirty" ideas, or just difficult to manage. What supports this?

Illustrative example. In a botany class of eleven-year-old children, a word is mentioned which reminds those who "know" of a sex situation. About a dozen are preoccupied with associations of this sort. When the word is mentioned, they all look at one boy, then at each other. They grin. He grins back. The whole room at this moment, is divided in two. The threads of this little clique are spread like a net over it. Next day a nearly identical situation recurs. However, that boy happens to be absent from class. Nothing happens. The children fail to make the same association as the day before. Their little "gang" remains submerged in the group without interruption.

Explanation. This type again is very similar to that of the "seducer"; the difference, however, rests in the technique used for "seduction." Nothing like the "initiatory act" is implied here. . . .

With the inner constellation of the potential group members similar to that described in the seduction type, it can apparently be said that they possess a number of undesirable drives which seek expression; their superego is in command of the situation, so that satisfaction of these undesirable drives is impossible without the penalty of remorse and anxiety; and, the ego of these children is in a "bad jam," squeezed between the urges of their drives and the demands of a strong superego.

The inner constellation of the "bad influence" type of a central person is different from that of the group members. In him there is no conflict. His drives in the same direction do not set loose conflicts and problems for him. He faces them and does not care. Alertness, on the part of the others to this event seems sufficient encouragement for the expression of what they had just been trying to suppress. . . .

Formula. The central person renders a service to the ego of the potential group members. He does so by virtue of the "infectiousness of the unconflicted personality constellation upon the conflicted one." Through this, he saves them the expense of guilt feelings, anxieties, and conflicts. On the basis of this service, the latent undesirable drives of these children can manifest openly. Through this common conflict solution, these children develop group emotions in relationship with each other.

TYPE 10: THE "GOOD EXAMPLE"

Illustrative example. The same class as the one mentioned in the previous example contains another group of boys who "gang up" with each other even more intensively than do the undesirable ones. Nevertheless, the teacher would hesitate to call them a "gang" or even a group. They are just a bunch of very good friends, he would say. However, one of them is the obvious center, and he "has a marvelous influence" upon the others. They are much nicer when he is around. If pressed, the teacher could hardly explain how that boy manages to influence them for he obviously does nothing. In looking at this group more closely, the following situation is discovered. These children are not "friends" in the personal meaning of this term. All are at that stage where they are full of new curiosities of which they are afraid, because they would feel guilty in satisfying them. This one boy, however, is far removed from any undesirable thought or act.

Explanation. The inner constellation in the potential group members shows a number of undesirable drives seeking expression; the superego is decidedly against this but scarcely able to maintain its position for long, and the ego is in a "bad jam" about how to maintain balance in such a situation. The inner constellation of the central boy in this situation contains no conflict of this kind. The mere idea of expressing undesirable thoughts in his presence is impossible. So, the group moves closer to him; in his presence they feel secure. What they fear is their own drives; what they look for is some support for their endangered superego. The situation is the exact reverse of the Bad Influence example.

Formula. The central person renders a service to the ego of the potential group members. He does so by virtue of the "infectiousness of the unconflicted personality constellation upon the conflicted one." Through this, he saves them the necessity to face their own drives of which they are afraid, and conflicts resulting from this. This time, however, the solution leads in the direction of moral values instead of undesirable drives. On the basis of this service, the children can suppress their undesirable drives according to the command of their own superego. Through this common conflict solution they develop group emotions in the relationship with each other. . . .

THE ROLE OF THE CENTRAL PERSON FOR THE GROUP FORMATIVE PROCESS

THE CENTRAL PERSON AS AN OBJECT OF IDENTIFICATION

On the Basis of Love

Incorporation into conscience .... Type 1
Incorporation into the "ego ideal" .... Type 2

On the Basis of Fear

Identification with the aggressor .... Type 3

THE CENTRAL PERSON AS AN OBJECT OF DRIVES

As an object of love drives .... Type 4
As an object of aggressive drives .... Type 5

THE CENTRAL PERSON AS AN EGO SUPPORT

Providing means for drive satisfaction .... Type 6
Dissolving conflict situations through guilt-anxiety assuagement

Through the technique of the initiatory act in the service of drive satisfaction .... Type 7
and in the service of drive defense .... Type 8

Through the "infectiousness of the unconflicted personality constellation over the conflicted one" in the service of drive satisfaction .... Type 9
and in the service of drive defense .... Type 10

The description of 10 different group psychological patterns under "type" headings does not effect a compulsively logical separation between them. In fact, they are not rigid "types" of groups so much as they are typical *trends* in group formative processes. Simplification and abbreviation may have made the types seem much more final and exclusive than they are meant to be. The 10 "types" are *auxiliary concepts for exploratory purposes only*. Holding them toward practical life situations should help to show certain trends in them that might not otherwise have been discovered. That is all they are good for. Nothing could be more wrong than to extrapolate practical group experience into any one of these "types," as though any one real group situation would ever be a clear exemplification of them.

Discussion

Redl's analysis, though taking its example almost entirely from situations involving children or adolescents in schools, can be fruitfully applied to any kind of group situation crystallized around one central person, and as Redl makes clear, any actual situation may involve any combination of these different dynamics. More detailed information on the Emmanuel cult and on the Black Muslims, for example, would enable us to analyze their inner dynamics from the viewpoint of Redl's categories, and the analysis could be fruitfully applied to such extreme situations as the concentration camps and various disaster situations examined in Chapter Six. A significant aspect of Redl's type of analysis is to show how collective phenomena are the products not only of pre-existing common psychic problems of the participants, but are *emergent* in a specific situation in a way which is post facto understandable and susceptible of this analysis, but *not predictable* from knowledge of the pre-existing common psychic orientations alone. The common psychic stresses may have very different outcomes depending, sometimes, on the mere presence of a certain type of central person, who may do nothing overtly to affect the situation. In other cases, the situation may change because of particular kinds of action by the central person. Neither outcome is predictable from the presence or actions of the central person without the prior existence of certain commonly experienced psychic stress for at least a large proportion of the members of the collectivity. On a national scale, for example, the peculiar hideous institutions of Nazism are explainable neither by the common psychic orientations of the German people of the time alone, nor by Hitler alone. The emergent phenomena involve a release in action of psychic potentialities not allowed expression prior to or without the particular group formation. Some of this behavior may be strongly aberrant from the values of surrounding observers and from the values otherwise held by the group members themselves, even values which to some considerable degree have been internalized by these members. It can be adaptive, as in the senses in which the Emmanuel cult members' visions and paranoid projections are seen by the Katchers as adaptive. It can also be quite maladaptive, in the sense of heightening problems of reality orientation, at least to some portions of the social world (as where courageous defiance of a tyrant brings severe penalties). Or it can be any kind of combination of adaptiveness and maladaptiveness. The mechanisms used (for example, paranoid projections of "bad" impulses onto outgroups) may involve elements ordinarily regarded as psychopathological in individual clinical study. Yet any of these mechanisms may serve for the individuals and groups involved in ways, which, from some viewpoints, can be seen as an improvement of their individual or collective well-being. The import of this discussion is to further question the adequacy of regarding such group processes as some kind of collective madness and to throw wide open the whole question of what constitutes normality or abnormality, and this not only in a cultural-relativistic framework.

3. SUBCULTURES AND PSYCHOPATHOLOGY

Another approach to the problem of collective or communal forms of psychopathology is to examine whether behavior patterns or ways of living in the world that are by wide consensus seen as psychopathological show distinctive variations in either mechanisms or content (or both) according to variations in the subcultures in which the individuals were primarily socialized. Do Poles become psychologically "sick" differently from Swedes? Suburbanites differently from slumdwellers? Children of bohemians differently from children of solid burghers? The following paper presents the detailed results of such a comparison, in this instance involving Italian and Irish male schizophrenics. Anthropologist Marvin K. Opler and clinical psychologist Jerome L. Singer studied essentially matched samples of forty Irish and thirty-seven Italian male patients in a large New York City psychiatric hospital. Hypothesizing the differences they would expect to find on the basis of substantial cultural knowledge of the forms and interaction patterns of Irish and Italian families, the authors found that these hypotheses are substantially confirmed by the detailed anthropological, psychiatric and clinical test observations of these seventy-seven men. The paper also presents some cogent discussion on the general problem of the interrelations of psychopathology and culture.

Ethnic Differences in Behavior and Psychopathology: Italian and Irish[34]

MARVIN K. OPLER AND JEROME L. SINGER

This paper questions the adequacy of current psychiatric terms and concepts applied in therapy or prevention. It presents unique findings on cultural differentiation in respect to *both* content and aetiology of schizophrenic disorders.

Papers by Bierer and Rennie in the first issue of this journal stressed social and cultural factors in manifestations of mental illness. Ever since Bleuler's descriptions of a group of schizophrenias, or Meyer's stressing of *ranges* in illness categories, the search for a variable typology of illness rather than airtight entities has been the trend. Just as Bierer and Rennie have signalized the possible importance of social and cultural factors, Diethelm's paper on "The Fallacy of the Concept: Psychosis" argues similarly for ranges and subtypes, and suggests the interrelated operation of biological, psychological, and environmental factors (1, 2, 7).

The present study continues the senior author's previous research with schizophrenics at Morningside Hospital in Portland, Oregon, a Federal institution for persons from Alaska. These patients were Eskimos, Aleutian islanders, Tsimshian and Tlingit Indians, and Alaskan whites.

Reprinted, with permission, from Marvin K. Opler and Jerome L. Singer, "Ethnic Differences in Behavior and Psychopathology: Italian and Irish," The International Journal of Social Psychiatry, Vol. II, No. 1, Summer 1956, pp. 11-22. This paper is part of the research of the senior author (Professor Opler) on "Urban Studies in Mental Health."

34 The authors wish to acknowledge the stimulus of Dr. T. A. C. Rennie, Director of the Community Mental Health Research Study, of which this is a part. In initiating this sub-study, the senior author wishes to thank Dr. Harvey J. Tompkins, as Chief of the Neuropsychiatric Section of the Veterans Administration, who facilitated arrangements for this study. This research was in part supported by a grant from the National Institute of Mental Health of the National Institutes of Health, United States Public Health Service. Gratitude is also expressed for support from the Milbank Memorial Fund, the Grant Foundation, the Rockefeller Brothers Fund, and the Corporation Trust Company.

While they did not provide large or adequate samples for study, they nevertheless brought into focus sharp contrasts in cultural backgrounds, in acculturation processes, and consequently in psychological functioning. In 1942, the senior author formulated the theory of distinct cultural differences in both normative behavior and in psychopathology based on these cases and particularly on field research in Ute and Apache Indian tribes. The work was published as "Psychoanalytic Techniques in Social Analysis"(4). In the present study, the same perspectives apply. First, mental illness is not a collection of airtight entities, since cultural realities define variables in family, social, and economic structures and functions as these influence normative behavior or psychopathology. Second, the concept of psychosis is misleading if, by it, one means a single category of closely related disease entities. If environmental factors such as the pace or extent of acculturation, or the specific kinds of value conflicts in a society, operate in behavior at all, they will show Olympian unconcern whether that behavior is disordered or not. In fact, schizophrenias will highlight cultural conflicts. Third, cultural and personality functions are inevitably connected since it is culture which provides a family or an individual with systems of value, patterns of thought and action, the language and symbols, and even characteristic styles of interpersonal relations to which we all must constantly refer.

In this study we avoid the unfortunate tendency of some anthropologists to overlook statistical aids to research. Instead, we drew two samples of Irish and Italian patients, controlling variables: (a) age, from 18-45; (b) sex, male; (c) religion, Catholic (although aware of historical and expressive differences in Irish and Italian Catholicism); and (d) provenience from urban areas of New York City. Before drawing these samples, the senior author collected a nonsignificant series of cases of Irish and Italian males and females from two other hospitals and supplemented these with Irish and Italian interviews from an area of the city. The purpose was to formulate clearly our hypotheses about behavior and psychopathology in each cultural group. Men and women were included in the exploratory case studies in order to learn details of Irish and Italian cultural stress systems in families. In this, a knowledge of the feminine, as well as masculine, role was thought to be important.

These preliminary case collections and anthropological interviewing in New York led to the prediction of distinct differences in dynamic variables between the cultural groups and for each age and sex unit within the group.

To test hypotheses, the author conducted a census of four contiguous hospital buildings (one "Admissions Building," two "Continued Treatment Buildings," and a fourth "Privilege or Open Ward Building"). Controlling for age, sex, religious background and provenience from New York, as above indicated, he drew total samples of 40 Irish and 37

Italian male patients. Dr. Opler, as senior investigator, studied these patients for a period of a year from the time the census was conducted (March, 1954) to the following March. Objective criteria for inclusion in the study added the stipulation that they must be cases without record of cerebral damage and that they should be of the first, or immigrant, generation; second, or children of immigrant, generation; or of the third generation. Within these limits, the senior investigator studied all psychiatric records and interviewed the 77 subjects. A unique aspect of the research included the senior investigator's recommendation, after his study, of each patient to the clinical psychologist, Dr. Singer, for independent testing with a battery of thirteen psychological tests including Rorschach, T.A.T., Sentence Completion, Porteus Maze, and other instruments appropriate to the hypotheses erected. While the senior investigator studied all subjects, for the independent check of psychological testing we independently determined that some patients had to be eliminated from testing as not being in sufficient contact. Ten Irish and 7 Italian patients were therefore psychiatrically and anthropologically studied by such independent consensus. The senior author could make ward observations of their behavior, study their previous history of illness and total psychiatric records, and interview them.

This smaller group of 17 patients in no way influences our findings adversely, but would seem to be concordant with the trends reported here, except in being more out-of-contact and having, in the records, only previous psychological testing by an incomplete battery. Despite similarities to those reported upon here as being psychologically tested, they were too deeply enmeshed in illness or deterioration to be included in current testing. The age limitation of 45 was helpful in eliminating an approximately equal number of similar patients whose chronicity and deterioration would only have produced a barrier to an efficient research process. In the study of the original 77 patients by Dr. Opler, as with those too old to fall within the sample, research procedures included thorough scrutiny of total psychiatric records from relevant clinical institutions, supplemented where advisable by discussion with the psychiatrists and in all instances with the social worker, the nurse, or the aide. The senior investigator also inspected social history records on the families, nurses' notes, ward ratings, records from occupational therapy, etc. The anthropological interview of the 77 subjects then followed, with suitable caution as to psychiatric requirements in the particular case and for making off-the-ward observations on appearance and manner, for eliciting points of psychodynamic interest, and for obtaining life-history data from the perspective of anthropology. Since the study continued for a year, one from each group departed on trial visit before testing was accomplished by the clinical battery, and the remainder were contraindicated for testing as being too ill. Of these 17, it is significant that 5 in each group, Irish and Italian, were too ill to go through testing, but a larger number of Irish patients (4) refused to be tested, in contrast to the one Italian who declined in that group. Chronicity and contra-indication for testing yielded matched samples of 30 Irish and 30 Italians available for total psychiatric, anthropological and psychological study, and an additional 10 Irish and 7 Italians who could be studied by psychiatric and anthropological means alone.

In the matched samples studied by all three methodologies, we were fortunate in having all relevant variables rigidly controlled. The mean age of Irish (32 years of age) matched the mean of the Italian sample (30.5). For last year of educational grade completed, an Irish mean of 10.5 matched the Italian 10.9. The Wechsler averages on I.Q., again by means, showed no differences in intelligence of an Irish sample of 108.4 and an Italian of 105.5. The means for first year of hospitalization were 1949.8 in the Irish sample and 1949.5 in the Italian. Numerical counts of marital status revealed that 25 Irish and 22 Italians were unmarried. Thus the variables controlled were age, sex, educational level, intelligence, and first year of hospitalization. Marital status was approximately controlled, with the Irish showing only a slight and possibly culturally influenced excess of celibacy of two predominantly celibate groups. As to control of regional differences in the independent variable of cultural difference, we were also fortunate in that all but one of the Italians had ancestral lines from Southern Italy or Sicily; all Irish traced ancestry to the "southwest" counties of Ireland. The one North Italian proved to be an interesting variation on psychodynamic and cultural patterns of this sample.

To test whether socio-economic status was similarly controlled, the senior investigator used family and individual composite ratings of a cluster including income, education, housing, and status. Both samples were comparable in being composed of families and individuals showing the same degree of economic, educational, housing, and status deprivations. A lower-class position was occupied by 23 Irish and 21 Italians. Irish had 5 lower-middle-class members to 6 Italian, equalizing those below middle-class position to a total of 28 Irish and 27 Italian. Actually, of 30 in each group, only 2 Irish and 3 Italian *families* could be called middle class, since the patient as a consequence of illness had downgraded from parents in comparisons of status and earning power. Neither investigator could find discernible shifts in patterns of illness as described below when we compare the majority in each group of economically deprived patients with the smaller number in each of the higher socio-economic level.

In respect to generation level, 19 (or two-thirds) of each group were second generation, and have, consequently, foreign-born parents. The 2 Italian and 4 Irish patients of the first, or immigrant, generation do not in the least contrast with the second-generation citizens born in the United States. Besides this apparent resiliency or continuity in the effects of cultural background extending to children of immigrants, a notion of the strength of traditional cultural fabrics which anyone may glean from historical study is here substantiated by reference to the third-generation groupings of cases. Seven Irish and 9 Italians, all born of citizen parents and reflecting two continuous generations in this country, follow the same trends. In psychological and dynamic characteristics of behavior patterns, they do not form a common group with novel differences from first and second generation. Instead, on comparison, they retain characteristics of their own ethnic group and resemble, most surprisingly, both first and second generations without variation.

The central problem of typology in mental illness required a new approach. Earlier approaches were complicated by two extreme positions. One position failed to recognize the importance of diagnoses and prognostic indicators, while, at the same time, realizing the tremendous overgeneralization involved in major classifications of psychotic or neurotic disorders. To escape this overgeneralization, we insisted on the current or increasing awareness that "behavioral events are multidetermined" (Stainbrook), or that schizophrenia is "not a disease, but a way of life" (Sullivan). The second problem of illness typology was to avoid arguing for a monistic aetiology, so characteristic of the nineteenth century (10). Here, of course, we had in mind the work of Stainbrook indicating additional historical determinants of contemporary diagnostic terms. But we also had in mind the work of Rennie on varying prognoses in psychoneurotic illnesses (6). To this pluralism of influences upon, and balances within, personality, we added a ten-point system for profiling our cases and developing a factor analysis in each case of interest to the senior investigator. The ten points were hypotheses for testing expected differences in illness history and symptomatology of two contrasting cultural groups. Since each of the following ten characterisics represents, in Irish or Italian patients, a point of cultural variability, we present them as variables or dichotomies between the two groups. A factor analysis reserved for monographic description by the senior author will be presented elsewhere, since it indicates the balance of forces within each case and has more direct aetiological significance.

Variable 1 dealt with primary hostility or primary anxiety (tinged with fear and hate). The question was whether one or the other was felt by the patient predominantly, and whether this was felt more markedly in relationships with mother or with father and their respective surrogates. Normative cultural standards led to the hypothesis that the central female figure in the Irish family, the mother, could instill primary anxiety and fear toward female figures. In the Italian family setting, we hypothesized that primary hostility would be felt toward both paternal and maternal figures, but particularly toward the more domineering fathers or older male siblings. These hypotheses grew out of anthropological observations that the central figure in Irish families is more likely to be a controlling figure on the distaff side, while fathers, especially in straitened economic circumstances, are frequently by contrast shadowy and evanescent. In Italian families, the cultural value system sets greater store on paternal and older sibling dominance and at the same time reinforces more direct expressions of emotions whether positive or negative in male assertions of authority. The acting-out of feelings, and the distinct Italian cultural emphasis on expression from "the heart," would bring hostility to the fore in any poorly developed parent-child relationships.

Variable 2 dealt with the resolution, or typical balance, in homosexual trends. The senior investigator hypothesized, both from psychiatric literature and previous cultural studies on the two groups, that the consequences of the first factor, the different emotional valences toward parent of own and opposite sex in each cultural group, implied an eventual, but inevitable, variation in sexual identification. An Irish male patient beset with anxiety and fear of female figures early in life, and lacking possibilities of firm male identifications with a father, would later experience the sexual repressions and socio-religious definitions of marriage and sexuality for which his culture, with its high celibacy rates, protracted engagements, and sin-guilt emphases, is justly famous. In extreme instances, all this spells a final anxious and fearful lack of positive sexual identification, varying in a continuum from repressed and latent homosexual balances through to added displacements and distortions that are either pallid asexuality or fearful and bizarre misidentifications. Since the culture does not condone sexual expression, or postpones and then rigidly defines it in marriage, the senior investigator hypothesized latent homosexual balances for this group, no overtly sought interpersonal manifestations, and a facade of asexual misogyny varied only by the most personalized and bizarre female identifications.

The dynamics of Italian sexuality in general favor overt expression at all costs, and where negative identification processes involved the greater degree of overt hatred against any symbolizations of an adult male role, frank nonidentification with males followed. Consequently, we hypothesized overt homosexuality for Italians, some becoming overtly "feminized," as proved to be the case, and few able to maintain the latent balance.

Variable 3 dealt with the central tendencies in each culture for channeling emotional expression. The senior investigator hypothesized values in Italian culture stress freer expression of emotions. In average behavior or in the largely healthy projection of art forms, this intensity and lability can become a most endearing trait. But in negatively identified and primarily hostile patients, behavioral expressions for disturbance include impulsiveness, less inhibition in acting-out hostility toward self or others, and motility disorders. Where the illness had proceeded long enough, such motility phenomena as catatonic outbursts, oscillations between hyperactivity and underactivity, or the inability effectively to time action, thought or emotion could take over. In contrast to this overtly disturbed behavior, the Irish patient, we hypothesized, showed fewer disturbances in motility behavior, but far greater indulgences in the fantasy substitute for action; the Irish when ill would grossly err on the side of fantasy life for which his culture is famous. In comparisons, since the Irish defensively utilize the fantasy layer (as defense); the Italian would express defeat and hostility in catatonic excitements, mood swings, impulsiveness, and motility disorders.[35]

The fourth dichotomy (Variable 4) is a consequence of the preceding variables. Italians, whether in personal history, ward rating, or in course of illness when hospitalized, would mostly evidence behavioral disorders, including assaultiveness, suicidal attempts, property destruction, or temper outbursts. The Irish, on the other hand, would be preoccupied with masturbation sins and sexual guilts, but generally remain passive and compliant, or, if indulging in compensatory fantasies, would be quietly withdrawn in thought. Oral aggression and sullen anger could be expected rarely on the surface. In addition, Irish patients would present fewer behavioral problems in previous history or in ward behavior. Far from being assaultive, they would at worst show one or two ineffectual departures from quiet, passive conduct. Yet their sense of inadequacy and private aspirations would evidence a weaker and more paranoid ego-development.

Variable 5, testable in personal history or in such psychological instruments as Sentence Completion, would show Italian males (if not females) rejecting or disdainful of authority, and Irish compliant (sometimes with verbal or actual compliance, plus resentment and "passive resistance").

Variable 6 hypothesized an Italian male with greater oral dependency features traceable to early, more positive, relationships to the mother. The Irish, incorporating greater hostility toward the maternal figure in their oral emphasis, would therefore be of a more oral-aggressive type. However, in this dichotomy, the senior author, not overly impressed by the value of zonal fixity theories in the schizophrenias, where reality contacts are broken, noted both cultures tended at many points to give the green light to aggressive behavior, expecially early, oral forms of aggression. For the normative and later Irish standard, we may think of Joyce and Shaw as exemplary or excellent artistic expressions of the power of

[35] The complexity and importance of these cultural factors, fantasy, and motility usage have led the authors to describe this variable or dimension elsewhere. Cf. Opler and Singer, "Contrasting patterns of fantasy and motility," *J. Abn. and Soc. Psychol.*, 1956.

the word or of thought respectively. Italian orality quickly and directly conveys emotions as in Italian speech, literature, or opera. Reference to anthropological data supported the feeling of the senior author in hypothesizing a mixture of oral-aggressive features in both groups to be determined by individual case history in each instance. This later proved to be the case. For this variable, no statistically sound dichotomy occurred separating dependency from aggressive features, although, as expected, the Irish showed greater oral preoccupation consequent upon their greater degree of oral deprivation.

Variable 7 predicted that Irish patients, with their fantasy, their latent and repressed homosexuality, and their "sex-is-sin" feelings of guilt, would build up fixed delusional systems. The Italians, by contrast, with their tendency to express and act out behavioral problems, might provide greater difficulties in institutional management, but their delusions, if any, would be fleeting or changeable, and less often of the highly systematized, paranoid type.

Variable 8, on the other hand, predicted more frequent somatic and hypochondriacal features in complaints of Italian patients, whose body image, though certainly disturbed, would be at least a more realistic remnant of the human body. Indeed, realistic bodily emphasis is a feature of Italian culture, and hardly a feature of its Irish counterpart. Somatic emphases among the Irish, if present at all, are not hypochondriacal as with Italians; instead, they fit the more delusional framework of distorted body image and are bizarre and extravagant remnants of a notion of the human body. Therefore, Irish show absence of somatization and Italians a greater preponderance of this feature.

Variable 9, alcoholism, is based on the premise that alcoholism is not itself a mental illness (3). The senior author, from his studies of cases including this feature, preferred to regard it as a symptomatological addition to other, more deep-seated, personality disturbances. Again, however, the expectations of greater disturbance in the mother-child role for the Irish male, their more inadequate ego structure on the side of assertiveness, and the possibility of greater oral-aggressive needs, suggested that in these schizophrenic processes, alcoholism would be found additionally in Irish and would be absent in the Italian counterpart. Normative cultural data reinforced this prediction, and the foreign and domestic statistics on alcoholism in each group made this an easy construction.

Variable 10 predicted a totally different psychopathology of schizophrenia for each cultural group. Stainbrook in studies of schizophrenia in the Bahian region of Brazil demonstrates how one has to study psychopathology of behavioral disease in each society (9). E. S. Carpenter, in the 1954 volume of the same journal, makes the same point concerning schizophrenia among Eskimos. Our point is that, in mental illnesses, dynamics and content are always interrelated and both have cultural determinants. Different cultures provide differing family structures, or social reference groups, but they also provide reference points of another type which influence behavior. The cultural *system*, its values, language, economy, expressive symbolism, and kinds of interpersonal relationships always play a role in individual adjustments, whether these are healthy or disturbed in type. Patients, like all people, have *cultural* backgrounds, and we must take these into account if we are to understand them at all.

All patients in our sample were schizophrenics, but this group of illnesses covers a range of phenomena. Just as no two cultures produce identical norms of behavior, so the symptoms and structure of schizophrenia vary as between Italian and Irish males. Italian patients, even where we found them labeled as schizophrenics with paranoid reaction, fell into a particular range not shared with Irish. There were many with prominent schizo-affective features, who had elated periods of overtalkativeness, manneristic behavior, or grinning and laughing hyperactivity. In some, overactivity merely showed as generalized catatonic excitements with confusion. In mood swings, depressed and quiescent periods easily gave way to bizarre mannerisms, assaultiveness, inept suicidal attempts, or to becoming laughingly excited. Practically all showed so much affective coloring that the classic schizophrenic categories scarcely fitted them. Excitable, fluctuating and periodic overactive affects were the consistently outstanding feature. In planning work with these patients, in surveying their institutional management problems, or in reflecting upon their dynamic histories or therapeutic needs, these were the major considerations for this cultural and class group.

Variable 10 showed the Irish typology in schizophrenia to be more often the reaction with paranoid features. Since no two cultures produce identities in normative behavior, their role positions can be said to vary. Irish resistance to role identification with the parent of the same sex (father) was seen as being not merely a fixation in a stage of Oedipal striving, but as having the more characteristic imprint of anxiety in relations with persons of the opposite sex, ordinarily mothers and older sisters. Here the whole modulation of the system of affect becomes different. In Freudian language, cathexes are never achieved without containing anxiety toward females, and the shaping of basic personality has stamped into it such feelings as male inadequacy, the masculine protest, hostility toward females, and the kind of latent homosexual feelings which produce a further sense of sin and guilt, and an incompletion of self-image, or self-esteem, which fosters paranoid projections. In Irish cases, while no actual homosexuality had occurred in life history, the patient's identification was so blurred that his body image was destroyed. One such systematically fantasied the lower front of his body covered with a vitreous aqueous apron. The connotations of this delusional covering were certainly feminine and were spoken of in terms like "flowing," and having "periods, affecting my thoughts through connection with the apron." In most cases, weakness, inadequacy, suspicions, and hostility were aimed at the self as "the rejected male" and then projected as a safeguard against forbidden extremes of self-hostility and annihilation toward others who came to be conceived of as essentially persecuting, feminine, hostile, and threatening figures. Actual bodily somatizations and realistic hypochondriases were rare. Delusions were fixed in paranoid channels, and layer after layer of childish fantasy and distortion used to preserve the system intact. These were the quietly anxious men, paranoid and hostile, who showed a record of molestation of small girls, avoidance of immature males or mature females, *vagina dentata* delusions, or the settled hebephrenic stance of a good, shy boy, fearful of anything which will separate him from the protection of the ward or his well-ordered delusional system.

We have described the tenth variable in somewhat greater detail since Variables 2, 4 (a) and (b), 5 (a) and (b), 7, 8, and 9 are summarized below. Variables 1 (Family Structure), 3 (Fantasy-Motility), and 6 (Orality) are described above and will be summarized in Conclusions. Tables 7.1-7.7 show a surprisingly high degree of confirmation of our hypotheses.

Obviously, Variable 10 is difficult to dichotomize since it covers a total descriptive pattern of cultural types in schizophrenias. As a concluding category, or culturally influenced diagnosis, it is appropriate here to summarize the basic differences in psychodynamics and psychopathology together for each group. For the first variable, we found the social role positions of family members, particularly the mother and the father, developed by cultural values and standards. In the gamut of past and present emotional responses to each parent or their surrogates, we found one outstanding (along with elder siblings of the same sex as this parent) as having involved the patient in severe and negative emotional overreactions. With Italian males, more direct feelings of hostility flooded up from shallowly repressed levels, so that *repulsion* from the father, elder brother (or surrogate authority figures) was dominant and often poorly controlled. In the balance of relationship to both parents, this linked to subtle rejecting or seductive roles of the mother. With such repulsion from male role, homosexual tendencies were active in two-thirds of the Italian cases and had been, indeed, overtly practiced. Little inhibition or poor control marked this rejection of a male identity. Italians were constricted or limited in their use of fantasy, but high in impulsiveness, acting out, and emotional overflow. In ward behavior, incomplete suicidal attempts, periodic and destructive assaults and motility outbursts came from this group. Few showed sin or guilt preoccupations connected with sex, as did the Irish. The acting out of impulses or a

TABLES

Table 7.1

FACTOR 2: HOMOSEXUALITY TYPES

	Latent	Overt	Total
Irish	27	0	27
Italian	7	20	27
TOTAL	34	20	54

Prob. = 3/1,000,000,000

Table 7.2

FACTOR 4(a): SIN, SEX, GUILT IDEOLOGY

	Present	Absent	Total
Irish	28	2	30
Italian	9	21	30
TOTAL	37	23	60

Prob. = 3/10,000,000

Table 7.3

FACTOR 4(b): BEHAVIOR DISORDER

	Present	Absent	Total
Irish	4	26	30
Italian	23	7	30
TOTAL	27	33	60

Prob. = 8/10,000,000

Table 7.4

FACTORS 5(a) & (b): ATTITUDE TOWARD AUTHORITY

	Compliant	Rejecting	Total
Irish	24	6	30
Italian	9	21	30
TOTAL	33	27	60

$e = 450/895 = .50$
$\chi^2 = 15.0$ (Significant at .001)

Table 7.5

FACTOR 7: RELATIVE FIXITY OF DELUSIONAL SYSTEM

	No	Some	Total
Irish	7	23	30
Italian	20	10	30
TOTAL	27	33	60

$e = 390/895 = .44$
$\chi^2 = 11.6$ (Significant at .001)

Table 7.6

FACTOR 8: SOMATIC (HYPOCHONDRIACAL) PREOCCUPATION

	Present	Absent	Total
Irish	13	17	30
Italian	21	9	30
TOTAL	34	26	60

$e = \dfrac{-240}{\sqrt{795,600}} = \dfrac{-240}{892} = -.27$
$\chi^2 = 4.20$ (Significant at .05)

Table 7.7

FACTOR 9: ALCOHOLISM

	Present	Absent	Total
Irish	19	11	30
Italian	1	29	30
TOTAL	20	40	60

$e = \dfrac{540}{\sqrt{720,000}} = \dfrac{540}{849} = .64$
Prob. = 4/10,000,000

background of socio-pathic escapades was frequent for Italians in childhood or in youth. They were rejecting or ambivalent toward authority, as they had been early in life toward the usual authoritarian father or punitive older male sibling. Their expressive lability contrasted with the Irish patient's rich and extensive fantasy, the latter preoccupied with sin, guilt, and masturbation fears and able to act out impulses only briefly in the disturbed stages of the onset of illness.

Among the Irish the father was an evanescent figure and, in conformance with the mother's controlling role in Irish families, primary anxiety (with some fear and hostility) was directed in about two-thirds of the cases toward the female figure. In only 3 cases of the 30 did the Irish father appear more centrally, and in these instances the entire pattern of illness shifted over to the Italian model in every detail. In one of the three, the Irish mother had died when the patient was 3. Of course, the unconcerned and evanescent father was resented to an extent, but this merely added to the prospect of latent homosexuality. Irish asexual and latent homosexual trends would show up repeatedly in such systematized delusions as "the fear of drinking milk with sperm in it" lest one "become pregnant," or of suffering from some *vagina dentata* episode. With maternal problems looming larger for the Irish, oral fixations were slightly more marked in this group as a whole than in the Italian sample.

Otherwise, beyond parental problems and sexual identification, our dichotomies are clearly contrasting in each detail and lead consequently to the final diagnostic difference. They are therefore arranged in a kind of temporal order of adequacy. Certainly the sexual identification problem which ends in overt homosexuality in the Italian patients represents cultural emphases on sexuality, expression of deeply felt emotion, and acting out of impulse, but note the destructive assertions of older male relatives are still there. The strength of anger in emotional lability, motor excitements, or flaring up of affect can throw the patient into confusional affective states, as in the catatonics (one-third of the Italian sample), or into the schizo-affective excitements which are somewhat parallel (the other two-thirds). In the Irish sample, the expansion of fantasy and the inhibition on acting out led to latent homosexual and asexual trends, and on to the paranoid compensations against ultimate feelings of weakness and isolation.

CONCLUSIONS

The search for monistic aetiology, and failure to recognize overgeneralization in major classifications of psychoses and psychoneuroses, are corrected by noting that Italian and Irish patients differ in their psychogenetic and psychodynamic pattern. Each group illustrates the sociocultural variability stressed by field data of the cultural anthropologist. Distinctive effects of family organization, social group, and cultural experience are differentiated. In addition, we are led to extend the earlier purely psychogenetic searches for a unitary, single theory of behavior and psychopathology to the point of recognition that the energy distribution of physiological drive mechanism is always mediated by family systems, the values, and the symbols of the cultural group into which one is born.

While culture is not a mold completely determining kinds of affect associated with parental and sibling relationships, or the exact quality of self and sexual identifications, it does favor certain stress systems and sanction given styles of emotional expression (Variables 1, 2 and 3). The fourth and fifth variables are composite effects of these cultural patterns applied to male role positions in subjects marked by immaturity or incomplete enculturation according to normative standards. Variables 6 to 10 express the final disturbances in personality functioning in logical order leading to a description of the total contours of the schizophrenias in each cultural group.

In the profiles of a representative and controlled set of samples for each group, equalized or matched for age, sex, religion, New York City provenience, educational level, year of hospitalization, intelligence, cultural region, generation, and socio-economic status, each author independently determined:

1. The primary problem of male Irish patients is concerned with a dominating, rejecting mother to whom sons are "forever boys, and burdens." This is introjected in part and strongly repressed as both hostility and fear. The result is a defensive layer of anxiety. In discussions, ventilation of this affect and awareness of its origin relieved the patient. Among Italian patients, there was a conflict of a less repressed kind concerned primarily with father and male siblings. Hostility was only partly repressed. Ventilation was again beneficial.

2. Sexual confusion varies from latent homosexuality and misidentification in the Irish to a stronger, active nonidentification of the Italians, in overt homosexuality.

3. Fantasy and motility usage, reported on elsewhere, are here found to be inversely proportionate, both between the groups and in individual cases. The Irish utilized the former, the Italian the latter.

4. Twenty-six Irish showed no evidence of acting-out behavior. Twenty-three Italians showed repeated and marked evidence. On the other hand, sin-guilt ideology was a preoccupation of 28 Irish; it did not concern 21 Italians.

5. Twenty-four Irish were compliant to authority, and almost the same number of Italians were noncompliant.

6. Oral characteristics with both dependent and aggressive features were stronger in the Irish and relatively weak in the Italian.

7. Delusional fixity occurred in a ratio greater than 3 to 1 for Irish, while exactly two-thirds of the Italian cases showed no fixity whatever and the remainder had slight, scattered, and changeable delusions in only half the instances.

8. Italians led in somatic preoccupations (hypochondriacal complaints).

9. Italians were drinkers, but non-alcoholism marked this group with one exception. Alcoholism was prevalent in Irish.

10. The total balance of defenses in fantasy and withdrawal for the Irish versus motility and poor control for the Italian varies markedly between the groups, as does the descriptive diagnostic type.

While these patients from different cultural settings do not characterize the best or even the average norms of their respective cultures, they illustrate distinctive cultural patternings in illness processes. While, to some extent, Cannon, Wolff, and Funkenstein have stated the physiological consequences of emotional states, and Freud the emotional and organic consequences of the human ability to symbolize, the contribution of this paper is to demonstrate relationships between the various necessary biosocial levels of investigation. The contributions of psychiatry, anthropology, sociology, and psychology were independent. It is of interest that D. H. Funkenstein's work on hostility states directed outward versus anger directed inward could be extended, on an organic level, to cultural groups. If culture influences types of family organization and the social experience and role position of its carriers, its deepest reflection will occur on any and all biosocial levels as evidenced in norms of behavior and in types of psychopathology.

REFERENCES

1. Joshua Bierer, "The validity of psychiatric diagnostics," *Int. J. Soc. Psychiat.*, 1955, 1:22-30.
2. Oskar Diethelm, "The fallacy of the concept: psychosis," in P. Hoch and J. Zubin, editors, *Current Problems in Psychiatric Diagnosis.* (New York: Grune & Stratton, 1953.)
3. Oskar Diethelm, *Etiology of Chronic Alcoholism.* (Springfield, Ill.: C. C. Thomas, 1955.)
4. Marvin K. Opler, "Psychoanalytic techniques in social analysis," *J. Soc. Psychol.*, 1942, 15:91-127.
5. Marvin K. Opler, *Culture, Psychiatry and Human Values.* (Springfield, Ill.: C. C. Thomas, 1956.)
6. T. A. C. Rennie, "Prognosis in the psychoneuroses: benign and malignant developments," P. Hoch and J. Zubin, editors, *Current Problems in Psychiatric Diagnosis.* (New York: Grune & Stratton, 1953.)
7. T. A. C. Rennie, "Social psychiatry—a definition," *Int. J. Soc. Psychiat.*, 1955, 1:5-13.
8. J. L. Singer and M. K. Opler, "Contrasting patterns of fantasy and motility in Irish and Italian schizophrenics," *J. Abn. and Soc. Psychol.*, 1956.
9. Edward Stainbrook, "Some characteristics of the psychopathology of schizophrenic behavior in Bahian society," *Amer. J. Psychiat.*, 1952, 109:330-35.
10. Edward Stainbrook, "Some Historical Determinants of Contemporary Diagnostic and Etiological Thinking in Psychiatry," in P. Hoch and J. Zubin, editors, *Current Problems in Psychiatric Diagnosis.* (New York: Grune & Stratton, 1953.)

Discussion

This paper demonstrates conspicuous differences in both mechanisms and content of psychic illness between otherwise matched
members of two distinct subcultures within the United States. The
interplay of subculturally normative family patterns and the kinds of
pathological processes is clearly highlighted. Irish males, coming
from families that are "typically Irish" in the sense of mother-
domination, weakness and evanescence of the father, and massive
sex-is-sin preoccupations, and a culture which gives great weight to
fantasy, show their "schizophrenic" pathology primarily in great anxiety in relation to the dominating rejecting mother, in sexual confusion in latent homosexuality and sexual misidentification, in compliance to authority, in resort to elaborated fantasy often to the point
of paranoid delusional systems with great emphasis on the sin-guilt
ideology, in alcoholism, and in fantasy and withdrawal as the main
defenses. Italian males, by contrast, coming from families with a
domineering authoritarian father supplemented by similarly domineering older brothers, and with a culture pattern favoring free expression of emotions, and of sexuality specifically, and high motility
expression, showed sexual conflicts centering on the father, sexual
misidentification being expressed in overt homosexuality, a high degree of acting-out behavior and very little fantasy, great emotional
lability and little delusional development, great bodily preoccupation (as in hypochondriacal complaints), resistance to authority, with
high motility and poor self-control. The "versions" of illness in the
two cases are so distinct, and this in line with subcultural variations
in points of common psychic stress, as to make almost meaningless
the common diagnostic category into which all these patients were
classified. (This study does *not* purport to say that all Irish families
produce sons with this constellation of problems, nor all Italian families sons with this other constellation, but only that where pathological processes do set in, they tend to follow lines of both content and
mechanisms distinctively in line with the normative and behavioral
patterns of families of the respective subcultures. In all of these cases
the patient's behavior, ideation, and emotional responses were such
that members of their own subcultures, as well as hospital psychiatrists, defined them as "crazy"—that is, beyond the range of acceptable variation within the subculture concerned.) While the "normal"
Irish male, product of comparable Irish families, is evidently not so
burdened with strong latent homosexual trends or deep sexual mis-

identifications, nor given to rigid and systematized delusional systems of a paranoid nature, nor so repressedly compliant to authority, we may raise the question of whether the symptomatology displayed by these Irish male schizophrenics is but an exaggeration and intensification of processes that are common to the whole subcultural group. In fact, this is what we would have to hypothesize, if we take seriously the dramatic demonstration of the influence of subcultural differences on pathology made by this paper. Similarly for the Italians: the "normal" male product of the typical Italian-American family is presumably not overtly homosexual, nor given to the degree and kind of acting-out behavior, defiance of authority and hypochondriacal preoccupations displayed by these schizophrenics; but would he not, according to the cultural-psychiatric analysis of the Italian family, be susceptible to trends in these directions? The typically high alcoholism rates of "normal" (at least not manifestly psychotic) Irish males, and the typically high lability of emotional expressiveness of Italians generally, are certainly relevant data for such a discussion.

The problem of what "really" constitutes "psychopathology" has certainly not been solved, and the more we have of sophisticated studies interrelating cultural, social, and psychodynamic elements, such as the Opler-Singer piece, the more complicated the question of "normality" becomes. We shall now continue its discussion from yet another angle of vision: the problem of illusions.

4. THE PROBLEM OF ILLUSIONS

The belief of the adherents of the Emmanuel cult described by the Katchers, that they suffered physical attack by the Devil and by perverts at his command, is not merely a bit of exotica, strange, silly or "crazy" to the surrounding Americans of that Eastern city—it is patently an illusion. Similarly the elaborated "history" and "anthropology" of the Nation of Islam with its interesting mythology of the origin and dispersion of races, is not only a rival of exotic beliefs to be found in primitive tribes, but patently inaccurate by objective standards of the relevant sciences. Such illusions may have important psychological functions and "adaptive value" for the believers as Katcher and Parenti show. However, for our present discussion the central point is that they *are* in fact illusions. Similarly, the "delusional system" of a paranoid schizophrenic—that there is an enormous, complicated, and convoluted plot afoot in the world to subvert or destroy his special genius, that all the doctors, nurses, attendants, fellow patients, and visitors to the hospital are in on this plot and carrying on elaborate masquerades to do so—is called "delusional" not just because it does not happen to correspond to the beliefs of the others around the patient who call themselves "sane" but because it has no correspondence to objective verifiable reality. (This is not to rule out the possibility, of course, that the paranoid has, in fact, and in a partial sense correctly, perceived unconscious hostilities of others around him, and also, overt negative reactions of others to the patient's provocative behavior, in a kind of self-fulfilling prophecy. Still the systematization into a plot theory is identifiably out of line with outer reality.)

Similarly, if Trobriand Islanders or Australian aborigines dogmatically state that sexual intercourse has nothing to do with conception, which is rather caused by the entrance of an appropriate spirit into the vagina of the woman, we are confronted not only with a bit of amusing esoterica, but with a statement demonstrably false to reality. In this kind of instance, the "sophisticate" who imagines that cultural relativism teaches that all kinds of beliefs are not only possible, but equally valid, that it is only a matter of what culture you were brought up in, is quite mistaken, as compared with the more naïve observer who declares the Trobrianders or Australians just plain wrong. The same can be said for practically all elements of mythologies or other religious beliefs of peoples the world over and all through history. The enormous preoccupation with sex as something sinful, that has pervaded all Judaeo-Christian religions and the associated doctrinal beliefs certainly partake of such an illusional system, and the pathogenic potential of this set of illusions has been central in the whole development of modern psychodynamic understandings. If such beliefs are so common in "peculiar" religious subcultures within our wider one, in primitive cultures very generally, and in many phases of our own religious traditions, may they not also be true of most elements of most cultures in all times and places?

The anthropologist Weston La Barre certainly thinks so:[36]

[36] Weston La Barre, *The Human Animal* (Chicago: University of Chicago Press, 1954), pp. 233, 234. (These and the following excerpts reprinted with

The sad situation is that homo sapiens, *the "knower," knows a great many things that are not so. The folklores of the world consist primarily in such things—indeed, perhaps the bulk of all human beliefs is in things that are not only not so, but cannot possibly be so. . . . The ability to know things that are not so is an extraordinary and unique perculiarity of man among animals, and arises out of the profoundly inter-individual nature of his being.*

La Barre goes on to give some very telling examples of illusions which are not only patently such, but also quite dangerous to the interests or even the continued existence of the society believing them. The Koryak of Siberia believe that they must yearly sacrifice their dogs, for otherwise the gods who "own" the various species of wild animals will not send them as food for the Koryak. Actually, in their subarctic environment, dogs are an essential for human hunters' survival, hence the Koryak by their sacrifice actually decrease rather than improve their survival chances. The African Dinka believe that members of the totemic Crocodile clan can swim the upper Nile without being harmed by crocodiles, since crocodiles are their blood relatives; hence, Crocodile clan members, armed with this spurious peace of mind, are likely to swim in crocodile-infested waters oftener than other Dinka, thus producing a higher mortality rate from this cause. We can present endless examples of such illusions from primitive tribes. According to our ideology of progress, we tend to imagine this cannot be so for a modern sophisticated society. Any careful examination, however, reveals quite otherwise. For the simplest example, our racial mythologies rob modern America of the use of the abilities of vast numbers of potentially talented Negroes. (A more detailed case study of the impact of illusions in a modern society follows, in the next section.)

If every culture is built up of beliefs, many of which are clearly illusions, and if illusions are also an important part of the pattern of psychic illness, then what relationship can we see between culture and pathology? Here La Barre is again very helpful. He discusses the relationship among the primitive, the child, and the psychotic as follows:[37]

> But primitive people (primarily for lack of writing) lack sufficient "communication" with their own intellectual history to be

---

permission of the University of Chicago Press. Copyright 1954 by the University of Chicago.)
[37] La Barre, *op. cit.*, p. 243.

able to have much perspective on or moral sophistication about their problems—just as a child lacks the experience of a long life-history, which might help him to get bearings on himself and his predicaments. Psychotics in a sense are still imprisoned in their childhood: they are still using now-inadequate old ways of solving new problems, and they are relatively cut off from the other humans and a current clear experience of the real world, both of which might help them with their problems. Now primitive men (those who lack writing) are not children. Nor are they psychotics either. Each of these—primitive, child, and psychotic—is in a different human situation or predicament, and may not immediately be compared with any other. But all of them share three things in their predicaments:

1. They do not have (or have not yet achieved) an adequate communication with their fellows—other tribes, intellectual predecessors, and contemporary age-mates respectively.
2. They have too small a stock of technological solutions and ego-controls relative to their unresolved life-problems.
3. And they have insufficient critically assessed large knowledge of the real world as it is, relative to the great amount of special edited "knowledge" of "reality" they have got from the few immediate humans who have shaped them.

This means that in each case, when feeble ego-controls fail, they must fall back on magical control of reality—the sacred cult, the daydream, and the psychosis—though in other ways primitives, children and psychotics are vastly different. In their relative inexperience of the variety of humans and of human beliefs, they all tend to turn inward upon their own limited resources: the primitive to his sacred tribalism, the child to his narcissistic self and body, and the psychotic to the inward resources of his autistic thinking.

Then, in considering what anthropologists call the "culture hero" (that is, the successful innovator, often credited with inventing all the tribe's major technical arts and religious institutions), La Barre poses the question of whether a particular psychotic might not in a different culture be considered a culture hero. He continues:[38]

Qualitatively there is no discernible difference in content between a culture and a psychosis. The only objective or operational criterion is quantitative; the number of their respective communicants . . . cultures and psychoses are identical in these ways: qualitatively, in being symbol-systems; functionally, in being anxiety-allaying; and also operationally, in being mere human hypotheses to be tested by reference to the real world.
Indeed, psychotics and the bearers of a culture are further alike

[38] *Ibid.*, pp. 245-46.

in refusing to put belief to the test, or in not being aware of why reality testing of belief is necessary . . . both . . . alike mistake their needed beliefs for Nature.

We shall return to further implications of this radical position in the last part of this chapter. At this point our focus is on the element of illusions: La Barre is arguing that any culture, like any psychosis, is an illusional system, different mainly in that it is shared, or consensually validated, by large enough numbers of people, constituting most if not all the population of a society. Any such imputation of illusional status to a belief or system of beliefs rests, of course, upon some criterion of assessment. To be able to argue that all cultures are illusional—or at least contain illusional elements in their central premises—means to have a standard of judgment that is independent of the belief system of any one particular culture, such as our own. To emphasize: what La Barre is saying is not only that all other cultures embody illusions (and in that sense are "crazy") when viewed from the standpoint of our own Western culture of today, but rather that all, *including our own*, are illusional from some universalistic perspective—and that perspective is perforce the viewpoint of naturalistic science. This perspective has, of course, been at the core of the whole iconoclastic development of science, and notably, for our present discussion, of the developments in the study of mankind whose giant exemplary figures are Marx and Freud. The whole thrust of such science has been to challenge and demolish illusions Western man has cherished about himself and about human beings in general, whether they be the intricate devices by which we protect ourselves from confrontation with the powerful forces within our unconscious selves or the obfuscations of socially validated ideologies.

5. SHARED ILLUSIONS IN MODERN AMERICA

Idol breakers of the illusions of modern America have not been wanting. Regarding our economic mythologies, the works of Thorstein Veblen (*The Theory of the Leisure Class, The Theory of Business Enterprise,* and other works), of Thurman Arnold (*The Folklore of Capitalism*), and more recently of David Bazelon (*The Paper Economy*) all attempt to expose the ultimately nonrational or irrational bases of our beliefs about our economic system, beliefs which serve to buttress certain economic institutions but which on inspection prove to be radically at variance with the ways in which this system actually operates. Many other scholars have elaborated on such themes; others have focused on the disjunction between our political myths and the actualities of political power as it functions in the United States; still others on the hollowness of formal Judaeo-Christian religious beliefs in relation to the actual lives of the people. From sociologists, perhaps the most cogent dissection of the gap between illusional beliefs and social actualities in a concrete situation is to be found in Arthur Vidich's and Joseph Bensman's *Small Town in Mass Society*, a detailed analysis of community life in a small upstate New York town they call Springdale.

Illusion and reality in Springdale[39]

The public rhetoric of Springdale proclaims this 3000-population town as a nice friendly place to live, a place where everyone is treated on a level of equality, a community that is democratic and equalitarian, that maintains local autonomy and direct democratic control of its own affairs by its own citizens, and where opportunity for successs is open to all. All of these illusions are contradicted by daily reality. Springdalers believe they have local autonomy: in fact their affairs are subject to intricate and pervasive control by myriad agencies of the wider mass society—by the federal government in its various agricultural-economic programs, and its regulation of many markets and prices; by the state government in its educational, road, and other public works policies and expenditures; by state, regional, or federal agencies and organizations in religion, education, entertainment, and a host of other facets of daily life; by the pervasive influence of the mass media which reflect the wider society far more than purely local influences. The myth of direct democratic political control is countered by the reality that all important political questions are determined or limited by agencies outside the local community and by the fact that wherever there is local political

[39] This section is a brief summary of the final chapter of Arthur Vidich, and Joseph Bensman's *Small Town in Mass Society* (Princeton: Princeton University Press, 1958). Summarized by permission of Princeton University Press. Copyright 1958 by Princeton University Press.

decision-making, only two groups—businessmen and modern prosperous farmers—actually have any active participation rather than the whole community, and here only on issues of local law, taxes, and roads. Whole sections of the community—the "old aristocrats," the industrial workers, the traditional farmers, the "shack people," and most of the professionals—have no part in the decision-making processes. The illusion of intimate communitarian, organically satisfying rural community life is countered by the reality of myriad local class and other barriers, schisms, antagonisms, and hostile personal gossip dividing and pitting people against each other. The illusion of an easy-going noncompetitive life confronts the reality of a high degree of competitiveness required of all but the very top and the very bottom—that is, the old élite and the shack people—of the population of the town. The rhetoric of equalitarianism is countered by the reality of very definite class distinctions not unlike those commonly found in towns of all sizes across America. The success goal enjoined upon all, and the notion of opportunities being open to all, is contradicted by the reality of the unavailability, to all but a few, of the means of achieving such success. All the conventions of social intercourse in Springdale enforce verbal obeisance to and acknowledgment of the community illusions and avoidance of any confrontation with the pervasive realities negating the illusions.

The persistence of both the mythologies and the contradicting realities thus involve the inhabitants of the town in a constant set of social-psychological dilemmas, for which in turn a limited number of rather stylized "solutions" are found by individuals, as modes of adjustment to the paradoxical situation. Many of these solutions, in turn, find social validation in the norms of community life and of social intercourse in the daily round. Even relatively idiosyncratic solutions in the form of pathological behavior disorders, withdrawal into privatized activities, or autonomous ritualization of a narrowed repertoire of respectable activities tend to get absorbed into the mainstream of the life of the rural community. That is, they tend to be assimilated to community notions of "normality," and as such to provide no threat to the public ideology. The class deviancy represented by the déclassé life of the shack people, who give up respectable aspirations and disavow the public values, is insulated from having effect upon the public myths by making them wherever possible socially invisible and where not, marking them off as an open warning of the fate of those who slide out of the net of community values. Otherwise the people maintain an active involvement in the community life and ritual affirmation of its values and illusions.

They employ several major techniques of adjustment: the repression of inconvenient facts, the mechanism of particularization, the redefinition of events intrinsically incompatible with the illusions to a version that sustains the illusions, the falsification of memory and scaling down of personal goals, and in some cases the private surrender of illusions without public confrontation. While unavoidably aware of particular circumstances or events which could be seen as contradicting the public ideology—for example, the necessity to gear a local policy to a state subsidy, or the impact of an outside economic decision on nearby industry affecting the workers' lives—the implication of such events is not confronted, and there is a steadfast refusal to generalize from the specific instance to general trends which contradict the myths. Redefinition of reality is seen when, for example, the location of a state-supported road (determined of course at a state, not a local level) is reinterpreted as a victory of the small town over the metropolis. Inconvenient facts are typically suppressed or repressed, maintaining the illusions and personal self-satisfaction. The glaring contradiction between youthful normatively supported success aspirations and the harsh realities of failure or only extremely modest achievement by middle life, is dealt with by falsification of memory, forgetting the earlier aspirations or redefining them more in line with the subsequent present reality, and by pervasive scaling down of goals. The contradiction between the myth of the friendly communitarian social life and the actuality of personal hostilities, back-biting, vicious personal gossip, and so on, is dealt with by suppression of its realization, by denial, by particularization, accompanied by fervent public affirmation of apparently confirming evidence, and particularly, by the maintenance of the ritual code of etiquette in social intercourse which rigoruosly avoids any indication of sentiments of disenchantment. Finally, a major part of life in the town is given over to developing forms and techniques of avoiding any confrontation with one's self, since any sustained reflection on and analysis of one's life realities is bound to threaten the maintenance of the public illusions. The techniques of self-avoidance are manifold. Constant, sustained, and exhausting work is the major one—work carried to a point where economic utility or necessity cannot rationally be adduced as its justification; other mechanisms are a pervasive and constant round of sociability—

much of this in the context of formal religious organization; absorption in sports and other recreations; automatization of life into an endless round of ritualized activities set by the clock, the calendar, and the weather; and very generally, in all kinds of mechanisms for the externalization of the self. These various mechanisms all intermesh in a pattern where the public illusions are constantly reinforced by reiteration and social validation.

Discussion

It would be somewhat extravagant to take Springdale as a microcosm of all of modern America. Some of its features are idiosyncratic to itself, but others are probably paradigmatic for small rural towns at least of its region, if not for the country as a whole. Some aspects do have a relevance that is nation-wide, if not even to the whole of Western culture, as in the conflicts between "Protestant-ethic" work and success values and contradicting realities and between democratic communitarian values and the realities of class stratification.

What is especially valuable in Vidich's and Bensman's study is its well-documented demonstration of the pervasive power of beliefs patently contradictory to a reality open to the observation of all the participants—more than that, a reality that is the very web and texture of their daily lives. The study also documents the personality *costs* of the maintenance of the illusions: Springdale citizens, probably not unlike large portions of the populations of modern societies, are revealed as engaged in a series of persistent complicated and compulsive adjustment techniques that are scarcely different from the convoluted defensive maneuvers of the neurotic, at least, if not the psychotic. It is not unreasonable, therefore, to consider the townsfolk as exhibiting a socially stylized neurosis, or a series of different but interrelated and functionally similar socially stylized neuroses. The awareness of illness is prevented from recognition individually or socially by its very prevalence (that is, the statistical normalcy of the disease process) and by its constant social validation as the proper way to live in the world. Applying La Barre's kind of tests, in fact, one could even go further and argue that this is even a culturally validated kind of psychosis, to the extent that it is unamenable, or at least is highly resistant, to any kind of reality testing, much like the delusions of the paranoid schizophrenic.

With this, we can move to a broader consideration of the illusions of Western man. We present a condensation of a major seminal essay by historian-sociologist Benjamin Nelson.

The Future of Illusions

BENJAMIN NELSON

I

If I were asked how one could become a psychoanalyst, I should answer, through the study of his own dreams.—Sigmund Freud

In Western society, as in any other, those who allow themselves or are permitted to express the representative thoughts of the culture have characteristically been constrained to function in one or another of the following roles:

1. The *pontiff* or *priest*.—At every time there are individuals who play the role of pontiff or priest whose central prerogative and responsibility is to administer the *sacra*—the precious utensils and ideals of the culture—and to protect the holy mysteries, the so-called *arcana*, from the obtrusive gaze of illiterate and aggressive masses. It is not at all necessary that these guardians of the holies be men of the cloth. They may be persons of various professions—political, commercial, educational.

2. In reaction to this systematic protection or concealment of the mysteries of the culture, there have arisen in moments of great stress prophets whose role it becomes to *expose the mysteries* and to *conjure up a vision* of a world where men would see each other face to face, no longer as through a glass darkly. There is no prophet in the Western world who will not play the part of *conjurer*, who will not present to men's eyes the vision of a *utopia* in which happiness will abound, conflict cease, unity pervade, and self-interest disappear. Again, prophets are not necessarily whirling dervishes or overstimulated hermits. They may also appear in the guise of businessmen, secondary school teachers, lawyers, politicos, journalists, and, even, college professors.

They will differ markedly among themselves in the degree in which they are animated by what Nietzsche called *resentment*. But, there seems reason to suspect that all such conjurers have had some portion of resentment and all have had more than an insignificant measure of illusion.

What roles have there been—are there—in our culture for persons

Reprinted from Benjamin Nelson, "The Future of Illusions," Psychoanalysis, Vol. 2, No. 4 (Spring-Summer, 1954), pp. 16-37, by permission of the publisher and the author; this abridged version has been approved by the author. (The journal is now called Psychoanalytic Review.) *Another version of this paper, slightly revised by the author, appears in: Contemporary Civilization Staff of Columbia College,* Man In Contemporary Society *(New York: Columbia University Press, 1955), Vol. II, pp. 959-79.*

who desire neither to conceal nor in any aggressive and resentful fashion to expose the premises of the culture? What parts lie available to men who are concerned to tell man plain truths about some of the balky and intractable aspects of his fate here below and to persuade him wisely to use such resources as wisdom suggests to improve his lot, to the extent that it can be improved?

There have been no recognized roles for such activity in Western culture, except those of the clown or court fool and the privy councilor, both, it will be observed, confidential intimates of the king.

It is interesting that in the Orient a role has long existed in the form of the *sage* who considers it his responsibility to make man aware of the character of the persistent or recurrent truths about himself and his culture and to protect him from the excesses of nihilistic concealment and nihilistic exposure. The Western world has characteristically not had much room, if any, for sages. . . .

Through the history of so-called Western civilization, both in the Orient and Occident, one detects the paramount importance of planetary or cosmic myths of apocalypse, utopia, and final renovation, to which I shall henceforth refer as *apocalyptic cosmism* and *futurism*. The fascination over men's minds exerted by these overpowering dreams of a final and perfect rebirth is readily discovered in the successive philosophies of history and destiny-ideas of Western civilization. The whole of history, human and natural alike, has been conceived to exhibit either inevitable degeneration or inevitable and infinite progress—both, however, to be climaxed by a Millennial Age and final redemption.

There are any number of versions of the Heavenly City in Western culture, ranging from the ecstatic worshippers of Dionysus and the consecrated secret brotherhoods of Pythagoreans to the devotees of millennial communism in our own day. The variations in the faiths and liturgies of these sects are too numerous to mention. Here one must be content to recall only the major groupings: the early Christian communities described in the Acts of the Apostles; the Montanists, the Donatists, the new millennialists of Asia Minor described by Eusebius; the medley of Messianists, Adamites, Flagellants, Millennialists, Perfectionists, and spiritual Franciscans who appear in the Middle Ages; the Anabaptists of Munster, the Diggers and Fifth Monarchy Men in England, the Hutterites, Shakers, Quakers, Mormons (and in some respects even the early New England Puritans) of the early modern era; and latterly, the devotees of Communism, Fascism, Nazism, Pan-Slavism, Pan-Islamism, and other exponents of national or international dreams of collective redemption. . . .

Other versions of these myths of final redemption have escaped notice because of the seeming absence of transcendental metaphors in their promise and program. We must not deceive ourselves into thinking that these necessitarian and inevitabilist views are peculiar to the present Soviet state, the self-styled Eastern democracies, or Oriental culture as a whole.

As a noted German Church historian, Ernst Benz, has recently remarked, Russian and Western European conceptions of man, though differing in detail from time to time, appear to belong together in a kind of dialectical tension. Both anthropologies, Eastern and Western, he remarks, are rooted in the same evangelical message and are complementary rather than exclusive. . . .

Western culture is Judaeo-Christian to the core and reveals at every turn the insistent emphases of European Christianity. Russian culture, whatever its excesses, is no less Judaeo-Christian and reveals the insistent emphases of the Byzantine and Russian churches. Both, in their different ways, are permeated by chiliastic eschatologies, millennial expectations of God-manhood (theosis) symbolized in the mystery of the Incarnation. Both have developed versions of cosmic brotherhood of man and their sacramental oneness in an undivided state of community.

As one might anticipate, especially ingenious versions of eschatological thought are found in the writings of Hegel and Marx, who form a bridge between Western thought and Russian thought. . . .

Academic observers of the history of society have largely been deceived about the rhythms and characteristics of the cultural evolution of the so-called West. In their oversimplified and evidently distorted notions about intellectual and social progress, they have failed to recognize the dominance under different guises of the gospel of apocalyptic cosmism and futurism. The present ways of periodizing the history of Western civilization make the error of supposing that liberal intelligence steadily advanced at the expense of ancient myth in the eras of the Renaissance, the Reformation, the French, American and Industrial Revolutions. A more sober view would at once suggest that these very designations prove the persistence of the myth of rebirth, of renovation, of apocalyptic futurism. . . . Two observations deserve to be made in this connection:

1. The various forms of individualism which are so often supposed to have been and still to be at war with one another can readily be seen to reveal an inner affinity. Their oppositions are the result of contingent rather than structural circumstances. Solipsistic individualism in its various versions has been one of the two dominant strains in Western culture. (As must already be apparent, familialistic collectivism has been the other.) There is a most peculiar affinity between the religious individualism of a St. Paul and the economic individualism of a Herbert Hoover. It would be easy to show that the so-called "rugged economic individualism" of some American "captains of industry" is more than an illustration of brutal self-assertion in the economic sphere. If it were merely that, it would be easy for culture to set limits to its actions. To the contrary, rugged economic individualism is principally an exhibit of a religious dream in secular guise. Any study of the life histories of the

rugged individualists in our culture will readily show the crucial importance of the influence upon them of individualistic religious conceptions.

2. The notion that mythic futurist ideas and magical habits of mind disappeared with the advance of sober science and rational knowledge can now be described as a sheer misreading of the facts. We are indebted to the late Carl Becker for having proved so ingeniously that the eighteenth-century philosophers who supposed that they were exploding superstitions themselves designed a new Heavenly City with not substantially different materials.

We should go far astray, indeed, if we looked for cosmism and futurism only among sectarian enthusiasts. Some of the most dynamic myths of recent days have been those which have been masquerading in the guise of "level-headed" realism, efficient management, and experimental science. . . . [For example] the belief that technical power, so-called scientific management, organized intelligence combined with social engineering, will inevitably yield economic plenty, the more abundant life, and the eternal enjoyment of the (Four?) Freedoms of Man. In these hopes we recognize the myth of Prometheus Bound and Unbound, the dreams of Roger Bacon and Francis Bacon, the vision of the American, Frederick Winslow Taylor—the prophet of the stop-watch and the slide rule—and his fellow worker in the vineyards of the Lord, Frank Gilbreth. . . . Between them, Taylor and Gilbreth established the logic of the mechanized industrial universe—time-motion analysis, and its attendant schemes, the belt-conveyor, the speed-up, the vast expansion of administrative personnel, and so forth.

Moving versions of all these myths—of Prometheus Bound and Unbound, of Paradise Lost and Paradise Regained—will be found in Marx, whose strategic importance for the modern era lies in his incredible power to synthesize myths ancient and modern, as well as to depict the unsavory realities lying behind the mythical pretensions of others. . . .

II

For there is a path to a world more beautiful, trodden in all ages and civilizations, the easiest and also the most fallacious of all, the dream. A promise of escape from the gloomy actual is held out to all; we have only to color life with fancy, to enter upon the quest of oblivion, sought in the delusion of ideal harmony—Johan Huizinga

These myths can be ultimately traced, I would guess, to men's nostalgic reminiscences of childhood. Since it seems evident that a great number of persons are utterly unwilling to admit the differences between rational goals and self-contradictory illusions, it might not be amiss to rehearse some observations made in a related connection by the master interpreter of dreams, Sigmund Freud.

"There is no one," Freud somewhere observes, "whose life is likely to be more difficult than he who presumes to awake people from their dreams." Such attempts, he explains, have been made three times in the history of modern European culture, once by himself, twice by men he regarded as predecessors, Copernicus and Darwin. . . . Copernicus' heliocentric hypothesis rudely disturbed men's images of their place in the universe. All sorts of convictions appear to collapse as a result of his suggestion that the earth revolves about the sun. Before the great fabric of institutions which rested on these convictions could be adjusted to the new outlook, Bruno had to die at the stake and Galileo bow before the Inquisition. . . . The Darwinian argument [of the evolution of species] appeared to cast doubt upon the centrality of man's position in the "Great Chain of Being." Man appeared no longer to be the monarch of creation, the summit of the animal kingdom, but simply another mortal animal who had descended from lower species. . . . [It] was almost impossible for great numbers of men, scholars as well as laymen, to accept the suggestion of man's humanity, his animal origin, his mortality. The Darwinian teaching is still not universally accepted. . . .

The third episode in the awakening of man to reality, said Freud, involved himself. And his presumption, Freud suspected, might come to be considered as perhaps "the unkindest cut of all." For what did Freud do but suggest that man was not master in his own house—that is, that man's conscious mind was in the grip of unconscious drives and memory traces and that the conscious self (the Ego) was very far indeed from being the captain of the individual's destiny? How can any considerable number of people be persuaded to believe that? . . .

To round out this long digression and draw the moral from Freud's revealing venture into history: Western culture has been acutely suffering from the domination of two seemingly distinct, but actually dynamically related, dreams:

1. The dream of the ecstatic, orgastic union of parents and children—this dream expresses the nostalgia of all who have been bred in the family. Where, one might ask, is the family in which fathers and sons, mothers and daughters, brothers and sisters have actually enjoyed an uninterrupted state of undivided community? Surely we must admit in our more sober moments that our childhood was not one of unmixed bliss. Why, then, do men permit themselves to dream against all evidence that the future holds the promise, if only we apply the right key to a state of *utter harmony for all mankind?* The belief in this myth has already had the most tremendous consequences. Now that the range of "civilization" has become planetary, the risks to be run have grown to cosmic proportions and the price of failure has come ultimately to be tantamount to the common ruin of all.

2. The second dream is the dream which we find reflected recurringly in the philosophy of absolute individualism, or what I prefer to describe

as solipsism. In the solipsistic view, only the "I" is real. No one or nothing else here below is held to have reality, only the self. This myth, also, I would guess, originates in the experience of the child—except that this time, the ever-selective consciousness organizes the memories of misfortune and ends by adopting an unqualified resentment against authority, whether rational or irrational. The child remembering in this case is the child who has rejected the authority of father and mother, who wishes to be utterly alone and independent of constraint.

These two myths, in their extreme forms, have dominated the whole of Western culture. Now I may be asked, how can society proceed without dreams? Must not youth be allowed to dream? Can old men live if these particular myths are shorn of their romance? I should hope that all men, young and old, might learn to orient themselves meaningfully to reality, without the illusory consolations of contradictory dreams; if they cannot, then they must be prepared, like the alcoholic derelicts in Eugene O'Neill's *The Iceman Cometh*, to waste their lives in neurotic aggressions against themselves and others. If, at the present turn in history, the masses and classes alike cannot forego the luxury of such delusions, our civilization and culture have no future whatever. Is it so difficult to perceive the fact that the *price of illusion* has multiplied a thousand-fold during the last century? Even before the notion of an atomic bomb was ever dreamed of, Freud wrote in the last pages of his *Civilization and Its Discontents* (1930): "Men have brought their powers of subduing the forces of nature to such a pitch that by using them they could now very easily exterminate one another to the last man." Is it not clear that all of us—the "children of light" as well as the "children of darkness"—now have dreadful toys with which to play out our dreams of love and hate?

These myths—of Prometheus and Paradise—are common in the United States and the Soviet Union. They are now penetrating China and India, as they have already penetrated Japan.

Tomorrow, they may reign everywhere.

Wherever these myths take hold, they are accompanied, willy-nilly, by a new concept of human action and association which carried to its extreme can have no other end than the bureaucratic mentality and way of life: the notion of *impersonal* (bureaucratic) service to an *impersonal* (bureaucratic) end. The religious roots of this conception in Western religion will be familiar to those who have encountered the profound writings of Max Weber.

The mythical elements in the "secular" dreams of Paradise have managed to escape notice because they have been unconsciously secreted into the interstices of the dominant systems of economic and social thought and continue to be fashionably outfitted in the latest vocabulary of science. . . .

Thus both cultures, Russian and American, are persuaded in the last analysis of the *ultimate* reconcilability of interests, and the overcoming of conflict through communication. In the former case, the perfection of community is felt to demand the maximizing of *the intensity of the bond* which unites men one to another. Total communion, which I call *Unanimism*, is felt to be necessary for true community, and total community is felt to be necessary for true communication. In the case of our own land, community is supposed to develop as the outcome of a *willed* association of individuals who choose to communicate with one another. Community is presumed to follow inevitably upon the enlargement of the area of communication. . . .

Our culture has been beset from the very beginning, and is beset today, by an inability to distinguish between apocalyptic visions and plausible and fruitful ideals. In this connection, one could cite the interesting illustration provided by the Swiss writer, Denis de Rougemont, in his challenging book, *Love in the Western World.* Since the twelfth century, de Rougemont argues, Western man has been under the domination of a myth of perfect and uninterrupted happiness through romantic love. . . . The pursuit of the perfection of romantic love has been assumed to know no other consummation than death. Perfect fulfillment occurs only in what Richard Wagner calls the *Liebestod*, the love-death. Is this not striking evidence of the grim ending which accompanies every human attempt to organize life on the basis of utter self-transcendance?

Another example of the permeating of our ideas by chiliastic aspirations would be the idea of "freedom from want, . . . [an idea that is] a jungle of confusions and illusions. So long as man preserves his humanity, so long indeed as he continues to be an animal, whether or not rational, he will continue to entertain wants which are incapable of satisfaction.

The notion of freedom from want would seem innocent enough did it not so readily lend itself to the proliferation of just those illusions I have been describing. There are many who suppose that human productivity has now expanded to the point of guaranteeing a minimum subsistence to all peoples of the world. . . . The notion of "freedom from want" makes the absurd postulate that wants remain stable. [On the contrary, their mobility, known to Plato and Aristotle, has been more recently restated by the sociologist Emile Durkheim and the economist Frank H. Knight.] How can there be "freedom from want" when wants show so aggressively a tendency in our present culture to expand more rapidly than men's productive powers? If wants could be kept stable while the improvements of science and economic organization continued to promote ever larger outputs of goods and services, it might be possible for men to achieve something comparable to what may be implied in the essentially mythical phrase "freedom from want." But if wants were kept stable, could one be sure that the gross output would expand?

In any case, it is a sheer delusion to imagine that the only or even the most important source of human unhappiness at the present time is economic need. Our public discussions would gain greatly if more men were to perceive the myths involved in the notion of freedom from want.

To say that human life and culture, wherever they occur, are likely to reveal recalcitrant or recurrent features is not to say that men must resign themselves to live unloved or loveless lives, empty of joys and fulfillments. It is merely to say that human and social organisms may be expected to exhibit limits to their perfectability. The frank facing-up to this fact is the best antidote I know for moderating the threat of the endless recurrence of what I have called *apocalyptic futurism*.

III

To rest upon a formula is a slumber that, prolonged, means death.
—Oliver Wendell Holmes, Jr.

. . . Another illustration of the price men are now paying for the luxury of illusions [is the idea of] "freedom from fear." It hardly needs saying that it has been very difficult for the Western imagination, overstimulated as it has been by millennial expectations, to acknowledge the fact that men die. As Freud observed, the *Id* does not know of death and will not hear of it. Today, as millions face the prospect of death, our journals of opinion and newspapers carry comforting stories . . . that scientists frankly do not understand why men die and are now entertaining the hope that they can be made to live forever, as apparently some of the micro-organisms do. It is difficult not to see in this simply another instance of the persistent dream of eternal life. One wonders how, if things are to be as they are, if the pace of life is to remain as most men now describe it—"simply killing"—how it can be anticipated that they will want to live as long as science trusts they can be made to live.

Another recent article reports that Professor Harold Urey, whose exploits in the creation of the atomic bomb are well known, has finally become persuaded that human life exists on other planets. . . . The revival, at the present time, of the old notion of a plurality of worlds has a transparent poignancy. . . . Bruno died at the stake in the year 1600 principally because his visionary imaginings conflicted with the prepotent assumptions concerning the divine plan for human and superterrestrial existence. We today have somehow escaped the limits of the older drama and in any case our need is so much greater. If we must perish, will it not be a consolation to know that on some other planet the great game in which we have been engaged will continue to be played under more fortunate auspices?

Not so easy, however, is the elimination of "want and fear." Those who live by science fiction have for many decades now assumed the likelihood of life on other planets and, indeed, have painted grim tales of interplanetary warfare. One of the most profound studies along these lines, which provides as brilliant a rendering of modern myths as can be found anywhere, can be read in the pages of a too little known Russian novel *We*, completed in 1922 by Eugene Zamiatin, forerunner of Aldous Huxley and George Orwell. It is no accident that the plot of the work centers in the massive preparations made by the people behind the "Green Wall," evidently the Communists, to bring happiness to the deluded people who live on the other side of the moon. What shall we say to this fable concerning the "freedom from want?"

The classes have known no better than the masses how to escape the production of illusions. Those who have held power, rank, and station in the Western world have either generally not cared, nor known how, to protect culture from the spread of illusions. Characteristically, in both the Orient and the Occident, ruling cadres have insisted upon establishing one or another version of the illusion of Paradise. In the modern world they have insisted that Paradise was already available here below or could readily be achieved with no great effort. One is reminded of the behavior of the Romans in the so-called Golden Age of the Antonines, from 96 to 180, A.D., when aspirants to favor sought so desperately to conceal from themselves and from their mighty patrons that the Great Empire was at the very brink of destruction. . . .

The wealthy and the mighty deceive themselves by building Palaces of Pleasure which are inevitably called by the names of Versailles and Sans Souci, whether they be in the Ile de France, le Cap d'Antibes, or Miami Beach. Wherever established classes congregate, they irresistibly exhibit their desire both to protect the mysteries of the society from the uninitiated and to conceal from themselves the evidence of its impending disintegration.

One who wishes to understand how profound are the illusions accepted and encouraged by the more favored classes at the present time has only to spend a weekend with the travel section of the blessedly abundant Sunday edition of *The New York Times*. How desperate is the effort to find, if not for a week, then at least for a weekend, some hideaway which is stocked with the world's goods and all of the dreamt up pleasures . . . [these ads] are now directed to all mankind without discrimination. Conrad Hilton is one of the great religious virtuosi of our time. A world structured like ours must have its Paradise, if only for a weekend. "Heaven can wait. This is Paradise."

The highest strata build their castles on the cliffs; the middle classes painfully fashion their glass menageries in the flats; the least favored groups learn to dull their anxieties with the aid of strong draughts of heady pleasure—sadism, sex, and unblended whiskey. All alike lust for the Palaces of Pleasure . . . taught by those more fortunate in circumstance and by those who purvey the seemingly boundless supply of marvels over the mass media. Already the peoples of Asia and Africa are demanding to possess a full complement of the miraculous fruits of our productive system—our gleaming gadgets.

This cry on the part of everyone everywhere for an improved standard of living would surely merit our sympathy and support or would at least appear utterly innocent were it not so evidently tainted at its source by resentment and therefore destined to involve all mankind in the greatest of risks. The so-called "underdeveloped" nations of the world have served notice that they will no longer suffer foreign investment in the development of their resources. They will no longer endure "colonialism" and "imperialism," but insist upon possessing their own "arsenal of production," their own stock of absolute weapons. New contestants are flocking to enter the race for material supremacy whose goal becomes daily more difficult to fathom.

Unless now inconceivable miracles of social invention occur in the very near future, we are all destined to reap the harvest of a new crop of industrial wars. . . . In the name of self-determination, all peoples are claiming control over their own resources and their own destinies—all of this being urged in the name of Justice. The maxim which prevails everywhere has become *Fiat Justitia, Pereat Mundus*—"Let there be justice, though the world perish."

Twice already within the present century, mankind has been embroiled in wars between those nations which were relatively early to industrialize and those which for one or another reason entered the race later in the day. It is not surprising that the laggard countries—especially those whose "economic progress" was long delayed by the hold of the feudal and familialistic institutions—have adopted the most stringent economic and political centralization in the hope of more rapidly outdistancing their more favored competitors. . . . The new element in the situation, which now involves the world in the risk of common ruin, is the latter-day perfection of the technology of warfare. . . .

Throughout the Western world, but especially in the United States, the situation has a peculiar poignancy. Here, those most favored by circumstances do not actually know how to embody in their way of life a pattern which will cause them to be admired and respected both at home and abroad as truly representative of culture's highest ideals. . . . [For whatever reasons] there simply does not exist in the United States of America any body of persons who in any consistent way know how to act as paradigms or representative exemplars of our most precious values. There is no use blaming this upon the ravages of mass society. Long before the masses invaded the inner sanctum, the classes had abdicated. Mass men now traffic in the holy of holies.

These historical reveries have, for the moment, one primary purpose:

to document my conviction that the present threat is only the first in a long new series of threats which are not likely to diminish in intensity and scope unless and until the peoples of the world manage to discover new ways of defining their expectations and scaling their values. I repeat, I have no desire to suggest that the present threat is not one of immense magnitude. What I protest is the assumption that its outcome will be decisive and the likelihood of its early recurrence negligible. These are hard words, but hard times call for hard words and there is surely nothing to be gained by the perpetration of still further illusions. Those concerned to conserve and promote free culture have great explorations to make, and it will take no one knows how much time to make them tolerably well. During that indefinable interval, our culture may expect regularly to be challenged by the thrusts of the devotees of apocalyptic and redemptive cosmism. *The least that one can do to assist in the works of reconstruction is to desist from giving sanction and encouragement to the spread of illusion.*

IV

If you have no will for human *association, I tell you that you are exposing civilization to the fate of dying in fearful agony.*
—Pierre Leroux

It seems to me evident, in short, that Western society is now in the midst of deep convulsions, the sources of which are obscure to most if not all of us. These convulsions did not originate in 1914, 1917, 1933, or 1945, nor will they end in any foreseeable future. These are convulsions which stem from the evident incapacity of our society to achieve patterns of integration which artfully orchestrate the multitude of conflicting wants, needs, and interests which men and groups in the modern world have come to experience. The available schemes of association are either lapsing into anomic disorder or are being found to impose the killing yoke of uniformity. . . .

Liberal society recurrently runs the risk of underintegration and absence of compelling loyalties and coherent motivations. Totalitarian society offers us no other prospect than that of overintegration, the substitution of mechanism for spirit. The killing yoke of undivided oneness—*Unanimism*—is thrust at us because we cannot bear the ravages of total absence of community—*Inanimism*.

Intermediate ways which would allow for varying balances of individuality and community, between personality and social framework, have yet to be found. Numerous experiments have been conducted among small groups in various lands. All of these attempts have repeatedly run into difficulties either because they have adopted excessively simple views of man's ambiguous nature or because they have assumed the absolute necessity of single systems of belief and utter unity in the organization of motivations. I know of no modern or recent experiment in community, however elevated its articles of faith, which does not have totalitarian features or propensities.

Patterns of total integration, which frustrate man's stark pursuit of elemental joys, deny the evidence of man's variety, and abort or stereotype their mysterious groupings for creative novelties, are doomed to destruction. It makes no difference whether these schemes of total integration take the form of a vision of a cosmic brotherhood, a totalitarian race-nation-state, or a consecrated sectarian brotherhood within the pores or on the frontiers of a hateful civilization.

This much we know. No society can long survive if each of its members in the last analysis call himself "I" and regards all others as a kind of inanimate "They." No society can long survive if each "I" is compelled to shout "We" in utter unanimity to the point of surrendering all sense of self and freedom. Eugene Zamiatin was prophetic in entitling his novel *We*. Throughout the world today, wherever disintegration is held in check by bureaucracy, men are compelled to cry "We." It must be apparent that men wish neither to have to say "I" all of the time nor "We" all of the time, but that they are seeking blindly without guidance or direction for ways of achieving relationships which are mutualistic— ways which affirm the reality and validity of, yet seek to orchestrate the differences between, the *mine* and *thine*. . . .

May one not hope that schemes of reciprocity will arise in which, to paraphrase the writings of Martin Buber, the *I* and *thou* will echo to one another's integrity, where *ego* will not remain indifferent to or tyrannize over the *alter*, and the *alter* will not subordinate and constrain the *ego*, where men would be related as persons, rather than as objects. Such a society would inevitably be a personalist society, a community in which persons would strive to achieve *patterns of reciprocity* with one another. . . .

It hardly needs saying that such mutualistic communities will also be plagued by conflict. Conflict is the very heart of life, resulting not simply from the malevolence of others, but also from the fact that men of the best will in the world seem to suffer from what William James called "a certain blindness" in perceiving the vitalities of others. . . .

If all of this has been so well known for so long a time, how, we are again brought to ask, does one explain the persistence of the delusions which mark both the Communist and solipsistic schemes of social order? . . .

In the spirit of Freud, we may seek them in the nuclear experiences of men when they were children in the bosoms of their families. As earlier suggested, both of the myths under discussion bear evident traces of their derivation from nostalgic and regressive infantile reminiscences, if indeed, they do not go even further back. It is not by accident that the collectivist dream has generally described itself as the *Brotherhood of Man*, whether or not under the Fatherhood of God. I am also saying that the image of society founded upon the flight of the child from the home is also derived from infantile reminiscences. There is no child who has not longed for liberty, who has not suffered from arbitrary restraint, who has not longed for complete independence to do and live as he chooses. When this illusion becomes the cornerstone of social order, it produces utopian dreams of anarchism and the not-so-utopian realities of "capitalist" society. . . . If the family has persisted for so many millennia and will persist so many more, it must be because it has managed to provide satisfactions and to perform functions which are not adequately perceived by either the Communists or the absolute individualists. The family is perhaps as significant an example of *mutualism* as Western society has known. It is evident that the secondary environment cannot, must not, be modeled too closely upon the image of the family, whether patriarchal or matriarchal, but it is also evident that a society which does not in some way embody the mutualistic strains of a family will simply not endure. I do not dare to speculate how we must proceed to develop the new patterns of integration so evidently needed for our time.

To summarize:

If our cosmos is to have a future, it must learn to do without its two most persistent illusions, apocalyptic cosmism and redemptive futurism. Mankind must cease to dream of building a utopian society which will transcend the bonds of time, the taint of place, and the limits of political society. It must learn to accept the fact that there never has been and never will be an undivided wholly consecrated community here below or anywhere else in this cosmos where men are constituted as they are now and will, so far as anyone can tell, forever be. It is the illusion of cosmism which persistently generates the illusion of futurism; it is the illusion of futurism which persistently generates the illusion of cosmism. Our culture stands now in peril of destruction because of the intensity and aggressiveness of those who entertain these intertwined illusions. . . .

May one anticipate that men in the Orient and the Occident alike can soon learn to live meaningful lives, without continually embracing overmastering myths which drive them on relentlessly to the achievement of unobtainable goals? It seems unlikely. . . .

It is not suggested that illusions of all sorts can be permanently eliminated from all minds in all corners of the cosmos. Illusion is inexpugnable and the comforts which illusion provides are doubtless imperative for the very persistence of organized life. It would probably be the height of illusion to anticipate that all illusion could be eradicated. It is simply being suggested that the scope, the intensity, the range, the magnitude, the dynamism of illusion be checked in the interest of the preservation of human society. To repeat our refrain: *if the cosmos is to have a future, it must learn to do without apocalyptic futurism.*

REFERENCES

More recent writings of Benjamin Nelson, pursuing the themes introduced in the present paper, are the following:

"Social Science, Utopian Myths and the Oedipus Complex," *Psychoanalysis and the Psychoanalytic Review* (henceforth Psa. R.), 45, No. 2, Summer, 1958, pp. 120-26.
"Introductory Comment on Norman O. Brown's 'Apocalypse,' " *Harper's Magazine,* May, 1961, pp. 46-47.
"Phenomenological Psychiatry, *Daseinsanalyse* and American Existential Analysis," *Psa. R.,* 48, No. 4, Winter, 1961, pp. 3-23.
"Sociology and Psychoanalysis on Trial: An Epilogue," *Psa. R.,* 49, No. 2, Summer, 1962, pp. 144-60. (Forms part of symposium *Psychoanalysis and the Social-Cultural Sciences,* ed. B. Nelson as a special issue of the *Review.* Contributors include: T. Parsons, A. Vidich and J. Bensman, D. Wrong, and M. Stein.)
"(Jean Genet's) *The Balcony* and Contemporary Existentialism," *Tulane Drama Review,* 7, No. 3, March, 1963, pp. 60-79.
Comment on Herbert Marcuse's "Industrialization and Capitalism," *Max Weber und die Soziologie heute.* Ed. O. Stammer. Tuebingen: J. C. B. Mohr, 1965, pp. 192-201. (The Max Weber Centenary at Heidelberg, April 30, 1964.)
"Self-Images and Systems of Spiritual Direction in the History of European Civilization," *The Quest for Self-Control: Classical Philosophies and Scientific Research.* Ed. S. Z. Klausner. New York, Free Press of Glencoe, 1965, pp. 49-103. (Includes extensive bibliography.)

6. TOWARD A TRANSCULTURAL PSYCHODYNAMIC

We return at this point to the basic question of the nature of "normality." Are all the Dobuans "paranoid?" The question asks since most, if not all, Dobuans are intensely suspicious of their neighbors, suspecting them of all kinds of evil magical machination against oneself, may we not say that the whole society is "paranoid"—in the clinical sense of entertaining illusions of others' persecution? The standard answer of relativistic anthropology is: No, because in fact to suspect your neighbors of such expressed hostilities is in fact, in Dobu, to be oriented to reality. It is quite likely that neighbors (members of other clans, etc.) are really practicing dark magic against oneself; hence the suspicion is reasonable and likely to be valid in fact. But it turns out that the "black" (hostile) magic of the Dobuans is at least in major part a product of the familiar "self-fulfilling prophecy." The extent to which the suspicion of others' black magic against oneself is justified in reality, is itself a product of the extent to which one believes such a proposition, and acts accordingly—that is, by practicing black magic against the supposed antagonists oneself. A suspects B of practicing black magic against A, and he proceeds to practice black magic against B. Then B with a perfectly reasonable (and likely to be accurate) suspicion that A is practicing black magic against B, proceeds to practice (to the extent available to him) black magic against A. What we have then is a version of the "paranoid pseudo-community." [40]

Corresponding questions can be raised about other topics previously considered in this book. Are the members of the Emmanuel cult collectively insane? Are the Black Muslims communally mad? Is Nazism a collective psychosis of the whole German people of 1933-1945? Do the survivors of the concentration camps survive by virtue of undergoing a temporary (or perhaps not so temporary) psychosis in which they systematically blot out or distort reality in order not to be totally overwhelmed by the horrible experiences they are undergoing? Are the co-participants in narcotic addiction undergoing a collective experience of insanity, facilitated by collectively validated responses, and insulated from the "normal" world by the special processes of time-isolation marking them off from the everyday "square" world of people who have never experienced the "anesthetic revelation"? Are the Springdalers, unbeknownst to themselves, victims of a culturally stylized psychosis in which the illusions dictated by their parochial social ideology dominate over the hard facts of social reality available to all of them but recognized by none, presumably because to recognize these realities would be too painful and traumatic, compared to the uneasy world of illusion in which they allow themselves to be uncomfortably ensconced? Are we all so thoroughly immersed in the illusions of *apocalyptic cosmism* and *futurism* (as Nelson contends) that we are in effect psychotic in relation to the realities of the limitations of man and society? Are we therefore destined to enact yet further variations on these irrational utopian notions and hence to create further collec-

[40] See N. Cameron, "The Paranoid Pseudo-community" *American Journal of Sociology*, Vol. 49, pp. 32-39, 1943, reprinted in N. Cameron, *The Psychology of Behavior Disorders* (Boston: Houghton Mifflin, 1947), pp. 437-39.

tivistic or individualistic horror in our institutions? Are we thus basically insane? Some of our most profound artistic observers would say yes to all of these—witness Lewis Carroll, whose fantasies disguised as nursery stories and rhymes probe the crucial irrationalities of our culture, or Jonathan Swift, who tears to shreds the respectable fabrics masking the horrid nakedness of our culture and countless artists, greater and lesser, contemporary, before, and since.

Weston La Barre—cultural anthropologist, and hence the shaman-intermediary between the "way-out" artist and the "down-to-earth" scientist of culture—has gone to the root of things in his provocative argument that the only basic difference between a culture and a psychosis is the number of people involved. A culture is just as irrational and just as rational as a psychosis: only, enough people are involved, mutually reinforcing each others' illusions to make a culture the "common sense" of life experience for thousands or millions of people; it is based just as thoroughly on illusion as the most extravagant delusions of the most "way-out" paranoid schizophrenic to be found in any asylum. His examples, some of which have already been cited, can be multiplied *ad infinitum*. More glaring examples can be selected from primitive societies, where their presuppositions depart more dramatically from our own. But innumerable ones can also be cited from any "higher" civilization, our own quite prominently, though not exclusively, included. Springdale is only a quiet, modest case.

Norman Brown, Herbert Marcuse, and Géza Róheim—inheritors of the "radical" wing of Freudianism—would emphatically agree. These interpreters radically disagree with the easy optimism of the "neo-Freudians"—Kardiner, Fromm, Erikson, Horney, and myriad disciples, or "revisionist" adjustmentist-oriented psychoanalysis—by questioning the notion of health as adjustment to the social order and by insisting on the radical conflict between the forces of Eros and those of *any* established social order, and hence the basically tragic view of the insoluble dilemmas of man in society. Brown insists on the existence and persistence of the "basic neurosis" of man —a neurosis (or psychosis) that is "built in" to the basic relationship of the individual human being to *any* extant variant of human institutions. He scoffs at any easy progressivism that assumes that human institutions could be tinkered with in such a way as to give some optimal expression to basic human needs and desires, and hence minimize conflicts and neurotic, self-defeating mechanisms in man. Marcuse comparably berates the "neo-Freudians" with a compromising adjustment psychology that would make peace with existing repressive institutions. He proposes, contrary to Freud's pessimism, but in line with one reading of *Civilization and Its Discontents*, that, while cultures hitherto have been marked by strong if not extreme repression of the underlying potentialities of man, these need not be considered as representative of all that is humanly possible, but should rather be viewed as culture institutionalizing "surplus repression." Marcuse posits, by contrast, a culture in which only minimal repression is necessary, allowing much fuller scope and utilization of the powerful forces of Eros in man. (Utopianism dies hard, as Nelson in another context observes. Still Marcuse can be read with profit for his harsh and pessimistic evaluation of contemporary culture, in terms of a radical Freudian view, and his posing of possible alternatives. Brown is not so sanguine, seeing in the ever-changing, yet ever-the-same repressive cultures of mankind, repeated yet variant versions of the "basic neurosis of man." Neither is content with seeing such neurotic or psychotic involvements as basically "culture-bound" as the neo-Freudians, with their emphasis on cultural variability, tend to maintain.)

The case studies we have examined—from the exoticisms of the Emmanuel cult and the Black Muslims, to the horrors of concentration camp existence (and the glories of survival therein) and the potentialities of psychological survival in disaster, from the illusion-built structures of communality in the Israeli Kibbutz, to the arcane timeless illusions of the drug addicts studied by Gioscia—all testify to the enormous, almost inevitable power of illusions, to their essential necessity for the persons involved, to survival, to any kind of well-being in living-in-the-world. In each case the outsider can look on in a kind of fascinated amalgam of horror and admiration at the dramatic combination of enormous costs and impressive survival and victory over enormous odds. In our view, taught by the dialectic of opposites, we can ignore neither the "victories" nor the "costs," neither the "survivals" nor the powerful "degradations." To glorify, to legitimate illusions over the outsiders' "hard-headed realism" would be to surrender the weapons and achievements of science and to submit ourselves to the dark world of magic and mysticism of primitive and other bygone times (whose remnants are all too glaringly still all around us, but certainly not to be embraced)—a world in which reality-testing would be ruthlessly suppressed (as witness the struggles for Copernican truths, not to mention Darwinism and Freudianism in more recent times). The alternatives are harder to discern and state, as Nelson's essay movingly attests. But one thing is certainly clear: the line that must be followed is the line of Copernicus, Darwin, and Freud, pursuing and questioning all illusions by the method of naturalistic science.

The nature of psychological "normality"— a transcultural view

Is it possible, then, to posit a view of "normality" in human beings that comes to terms with the complexities we have considered in the course of the essays and papers of this book? Such a view of "normality" must come to terms with the nature of the human animal in all his biological and evolutionary aspects and in all the social and cultural involvements that make him distinctively human. It must take into account the perpetual paradoxes of the human situation— the inevitability and the arbitrariness of socialization in its diversities and commonalities; the inevitability and arbitrariness of the human involvement with language and symbolism, again in all its diversity and universality. It must also face the peculiar dilemma of being human: that to be human at all we must be socialized by other human beings, and hence in the modes of a particular arbitrary culture, learning its peculiar modes of communication. A part of that human dilemma is that any particular culture necessarily suppresses a large part of human potentiality, but that potentiality still tends to break, in some way, through the barriers of parochial culture, linking man with man of any time and place, most impressively in the life and work of great artists or virtuosi. How define "normality" in the face of the enormous, if not infinite variety of possibilities in man, from oriental mysticism to Olympian activism, from rabelaisian sensuality to pauline asceticism, from apollonian equilibrationism to dionysian diffusion, from cerebration to vegetation to muscularity, and on through the many dichotomies or trinities of possibility?

THREE CONCEPTIONS OF NORMALITY

We may for heuristic purposes reduce the possible number of ways of thinking about "normality" to the Western magic number of three: we shall call these, for convenience, the *statistical*, the *cul-*

tural, and the *transcultural* conceptions of normality. Briefly, the statistical view of normality looks at empirical reality and asks "What *is?*" and "How frequent?" The statistically normal is the average—the midpoint in a range of variations, the arithmetic or other type of mean of a range of scores, or the most popular, or modal, score or type within a range of actually appearing possibilities. The *cultural* refers to what is expected or desired by the standards of a particular way of life of people in a particular society or subsociety. The *transcultural* refers to some standard or ideal which refers to human *potentiality*, based on the nature of human biology and human social condition, regardless of norms of actual statistical occurrence or the dictates of any particular cultural or subcultural tradition. These each need to be explicated in some detail.

Statistical normality. The simplest to describe, and the simplest norm to apply to any existing personality or culturally pervasive pattern of personality is the statistically normal. Its reference is always to what actually exists in some given empirically observed situation at some particular point in time and place. This normal is the *average*, in whatever mathematically statistical method the average happens to be computed. Statements such as "The *typical* Parisian is scornful of traffic and tax laws and insufferably arrogant toward foreigners who don't speak his language"—whether empirically true or not—are couched in the language of statistical normality. Similarly, the proverbial American who "owns .58 of a house, 1.4 cars, and has 2.7 children" is a construction of statistical normality. So, too, are the statements that the "average Springdaler is enmeshed in the illusions of local autonomy and democratic communality" and "the typical Puerto Rican man of middle-class San José is torn by the contradictions between traditional status and current realities." Other examples of statistical normality are statements such as "The average Dobuan married man or woman engages in adulterous relations at least once a month" or "The average American cheats at least a little on his income tax." The "average" or "typical" may be something susceptible of mathematical computation, such as *mean* (arithmetical, or in more complex cases, geometrical average) as in "the *mean* income of a group of 1,327 householders studied in this survey" (the total income of all of them divided by 1,327); or the *median* (the middle score in a range of scores, in this example, the 664th score in income, in the array of 1,327 scores arranged in order of magnitude); or the *mode*—meaning as its name implies, the most fashionable, or the most popular, or mathematically, the most frequent, of scores, of incomes, of behaviors, or patterns of behavior, or the whole patterns of personality configuration—as in the conception of "modal personality structure" as used in the Inkeles paper on Soviet character types. If all, or a majority, of Springdalers, or Kibbutzniks, or Samoans, or Hutterites, follow a particular personality pattern, this can be described as the statistical norm of the society or community or subsociety in question—regardless of how this personality pattern measures up against the cultural ideals of the particular group in question or how it squares with any psychiatric notions of the "ideally healthy personality." America is famous for its addiction to statistical conceptions of normality—but perhaps this is a canard, for it is likely that *all* societies are concerned with people being "very much like everyone else" (apart from being like the culturally ideal) and the penalties for "standing out from the crowd" are proverbial in countless societies in the world, if not in all. Needless to say, a *valid* statement of statistical normality, such as "The typical Italian has great emotional lability," can be distinguished from a prejudiced stereotype—for example, "All Jews are crafty money-grubbers"—only by being based on some solid and technically careful empirical research, as opposed to popular "common-sensical" conceptions which may be widespread in particular communities, but may in fact be quite inaccurate as a description of the people involved.

The statistically normal may thus deviate strongly from the ideals of a particular culture, and it may also contain elements that psychiatrically are considered pathological.

The abnormal—from a statistical point of view—means simply the atypical, or the unusual. In other words, any form of behavior or any configuration of total personality that is different from that of the majority or the modal trend of the society or group under consideration would be so classified. What is statistically abnormal in one social context may of course be statistically normal in another, and vice versa—a superficial and ephemeral example being the Brooks Brothers suit in lower-east-side-bohemia and tee-shirt-and-dungarees on Madison Avenue; or more subtly, a fastidious book-keeping personality in a longshoreman's union hall, or a volatile method-actor at a funeral-directors' convention. Similarly, the person who "*over*conforms" to certain special norms of a culture may be (in fact, is likely to be) statistically abnormal for the groups within which he lives—the proverbial extreme example being the saint. Or the statistically abnormal may be the person who falls at one extreme end of a distribution of certain kinds of talents or capacities, such as the idiot or the genius, or a tone-deaf mute compared to Arnold Schönberg, each being a case of statistical abnormality.

Cultural normality. The cultural conception of normality has a quite different point of reference: the norms or ideals of a particular culture or subculture. Thus the culturally normal Zuni is restrained, highly self-controlled, constantly dedicated to an "apollonian" middle way. He is noncompetitive, highly cooperative, peaceable, slow to anger or other violent emotion, measured and sedate in his behavior. (There may of course be no actual Zuni, living or dead, whose real personality and behavior fit this description.) Behaviorally, the culturally normal can be described as the person who conforms to the norms of his culture generally, and to those of the particular subcultures and special situations in which he ordinarily moves and lives. This may be further specified, as Merton[41] does, as accepting the culturally prescribed goals of a particular society or subsociety, and also the institutionally prescribed means for reaching these goals. This is exemplified by the proverbial American who seeks success by hard work, ability, and a crafty sensitivity to available legitimate opportunities. Or it may be specified as fitting into or approximating closely a culturally desirable personality or character type, as suggested by David Riesman's notion of the "other-directed man" [42] or Erich Fromm's related conception of the "marketing personality" [43] or whatever other formulation may be suggested by popular or intellectual imagination, of a particular time and place. The culturally normal, in this sense, may of course coincide with a statistically normal type, or it may not. Research is necessary to determine whether and to what extent they do coincide.[44]

[41] Robert K. Merton, "Social Structure and Anomie," in *Social Theory and Social Structure* (New York: Free Press of Glencoe, 1949).

[42] David Riesman, Nathan Glazer, Reuel Denney, *The Lonely Crowd* (New Haven: Yale University Press, 1950).

[43] Erich Fromm, *Man for Himself* (New York: Holt, Rinehart and Winston, 1947).

[44] This rather obvious point needs to be made, for most of the studies which have attempted formulations of prevailing or normative "types" such as Riesman's and Fromm's cited just above, or for primitive societies, characterizations of personality trends—such as Margaret Mead's of Samoans, Manus of New Guinea, Bali, and so on, or Cora DuBois' of the Alorese, or almost any of the culture-personality studies—have tended to confuse these two kinds of state-

Another conception of the "culturally normal" is that of the "adjusted" personality. The Springdaler who accepts the standardized illusions of its small-town rhetoric, who works hard in the belief that this will really bring success, who follows carefully the intricate rituals of social conversation that Vidich and Bensman have described, and who sedulously avoids confronting himself with the contradictions of his immediate social reality, is in this sense a culturally normal ("adjusted") man for Springdale in that particular age. The fundamentalistic Arkansan tornado victim who constructs a self-pleasing rationale of the distribution of disaster damage and death along lines emphasizing the basic goodness and justice of God, is acting in an "adjusted" way to the tornado from the point of view of the most relevant elements of his community—regardless of how irrational his "rationale." The ritualistic petty bureaucrat in a government office and the highly automatized assembly-line worker are each "adjusted" to their occupational situation, thus providing a culturally normal personality response. By contrast, a highly obedient and disciplined child in a "Summerhill" school is not. A psychopathic personality may be highly adjusted, thus culturally normal, in the role of a confidence man, while an hysterical neurotic may be highly maladjusted in the role of a social welfare investigator.

The culturally normal may also include adjustment to certain "deviant" types provided these are rather definitively institutionalized: a classic case is the *berdache* of many Plains and other American Indian tribes. There the personality trends which would be culturally very "maladjusted" in reference to the more central and standard roles for adult males, may gain recognition and social validation in the *designated* aberrant role, and thus be drawn in, as Benedict shows,[45] to the range of acceptable and culturally approved alternatives for personality expression.

From the *cultural* perspective on normality, "abnormality" would then consist of deviancy (except in roles that are institutionalized, as just discussed), delinquency, failure, extreme overconformism, inno-

---

ments; we are frequently at a loss to know whether the author is attempting to describe *typical* (that is, statistically normal) kinds of behavior or character, or is simply describing the norms of expected or ideal personality or character types (culturally normal). One might as well accept Pauline ideas of the "good Christian" as a description of actual Christians of the time of Saint Paul!

45 Ruth Benedict, *Patterns of Culture* (Boston: Houghton Mifflin, 1934 and many later editions).

vationism of all kinds, withdrawal or apathy, or "maladjustment" of all kinds. Deviancy may consist of rejecting, or simply not regarding as important, the culturally prescribed goals or the institutionalized means for achieving these goals, or both. Delinquency would be culturally abnormal to the extent that illegitimate means are used to strive toward acceptable goals. Overconformity (what Merton calls "ritualism") would involve an extreme emphasis on the *means*, to the detriment or underplaying of the goals which they were culturally intended to reach. Apathy, withdrawal, or "retreatism" would be rejection or withdrawal of affect and value from both the culturally prescribed goals and the institutionalized means. And radicalism would involve attempts to transform both the goals and means in terms of some alternative formulations of the ideals of the culture.[46] All of these possibilities are subject to many further variations if one considers a plurality of possible goals as well as a plurality of possible means as all falling in some way within the normative structure of a particular culture. Such analysis would also require a further extension of the implicit relativism to enable the analyst to see some kinds of personality configuration and related behavior patterns as being conformist within a certain goals-means context, and simultaneously highly nonconformist within another, both contexts being simultaneously, though differentially relevant within a particular society at a particular time.[47]

Another way of formulating "abnormality" according to the cultural perspective on normality, is to refer to the "maladjusted"— examples of which have already been given. A person may be maladjusted because he cannot fit his personality constellation—his particular pattern of drives, defenses, and integrations—into the prevailing requirements of his cultural milieu. He is or feels "out of tune," "out of line," or just plain "out of it" in relation to the expectations of the people around him, in his work, in his family life, in his recreation, in any other sphere of his life, or in all of them. A person who would be well-adjusted as a Zuni would be painfully maladjusted in the "rat-race" of a Madison Avenue advertising agency or in that of a typical academic department in a modern university. Or a person may be maladjusted in a general sense if his

[46] These formulations derive from, and are a slight modification of, Merton's in *op. cit.*

[47] An example of analysis along these lines is to be found in some of the discussion of drug addiction in Gioscia's paper in Chapter Four.

personality does not fit well into what Riesman has referred to as the "characterological needs of his society." A simple example, in the form of anachronism within a single society, would be an American whose personality is molded around the maxims of Benjamin Franklin trying to live in a society oriented around the hedonistic values of Miami Beach.

It is obvious from this whole discussion that what is culturally "normal" or "abnormal" in particular behavior, or more importantly, in the whole personality orientation, can be determined only by reference to the specific values, norms, and ideals of a particular culture, or subculture, or even of a particular kind of situation. It is historically and cross-culturally variable. This perspective points to the possibility that the same kind of personality pattern can be highly adjusted to one subculture or one type of occupational or other situation, and simultaneously, or in quick succession, highly maladjusted to another subculture or situation, all within a brief span of the person's life experience. In fact, one could say that this state of affairs is typical (that is, *statistically* normal) for the conditions of our modern, pluralistic, and fast-changing society. Correspondingly, in the chronology of one person's life cycle, personality configurations developed during socialization in one period and in one particular milieu, may turn out to be highly adjusted or conformist in certain contexts in adult life, but highly maladjusted or nonconformist in certain others. Or one may find oneself having undergone a socialization process appropriate to an earlier era (as, for example, by parents and teachers considerably older than a typical single-generation older parent, and in a culturally "backward" region of the country) peculiarly maladjusted to adulthood demands of a later time and more "advanced" or "sophisticated" milieu.

Being *culturally* normal or abnormal has no *necessary* relationship to being *statistically* normal or abnormal, although frequently in given empirical cases the two may go hand in hand. In many cultures, being "just like everyone else" (statistically normal) *may* carry an aura of cultural prescription, or failing to live up to some culturally prescribed ideal may be perceived as so general (statistically normal) a condition that one is absolved from feeling any special sense of failure or sin or guilt about the matter. Still, the two sets of standards are analytically quite distinct. One may recognize oneself as statistically abnormal, for example, by being an unusually pre-eminent "success," while feeling oneself in effect an epitome of cultural normality in the sense of having fulfilled to a high degree generally recognized cultural imperatives. In fact, the expression "He is just like the rest of all of us poor sinners" shows implicit recognition, at the folk level, of the distinction between the two sets of standards. The implication is clear that the person talked about is, perhaps, to be tolerated and given our sympathetic understanding, but not that he is to be admired. The error of mistaking these two sets of standards for each other, or of coalescing them into a single concept, prevents us from searching out the complex relationships between the two in a given cultural situation.

Similarly, the cultural perspective on normality is not to be confused with a psychiatric orientation in terms of "health" and "illness." Much of the writing in the vein of "adjustment psychology" tends to make this confusion and to use such terms as "neurotic" and "maladjusted" almost interchangeably. Theoretically, and in a great many cases in reality, one may be highly "adjusted" and severely "neurotic"—or even "psychotic" as in the case of a person who has made his peace with long-term incarceration in a mental hospital, a prison, or a concentration camp, or in any of the less obvious variations on prisons to be found in the putatively "free" society. Conversely, one may be highly maladjusted to a particular culture or subculture in which one lives, and *not* be neurotic or psychotic in the clinical senses in which these terms are ordinarily psychiatrically used. Bettelheim's way of surviving in the concentration camp is a most dramatic example: he did not become "adjusted" to the camp, as older prisoners he describes commonly did by adopting the norms and reaction patterns of the Gestapo guards; his stubborn resistance to this kind of process of personality change marked him as highly "maladjusted" to the culture of the camp and can only be seen as the very opposite of illness in a psychiatric sense. It is quite true that an individual may be both highly maladjusted and highly neurotic at the same time. In such a case, the maladjustment—being out of tune with the surrounding world—may exacerbate some of the neurotic trends, such as extreme infantile dependency, magical warding off of contacts with other persons, or extreme ritualization of behavior. At the same time, the neurotic involvements may further intensify a person's maladjustment to the world around him. Still the two elements are analytically distinct. What characterizes a person as neurotic may *not* be those elements that characterize him as maladjusted in his particular milieu. More important, the personality trends required of an individual to be adjusted to a particular milieu may actually be severely neurotic in clinical terms. The whole analysis of Springdale clearly points to the adjustment patterns of those townsfolk as involving a severe neurotic constriction, as already pointed out, and perhaps even elements of psychotic delusion.

The cultural view of normality represents an enormous expansion or extension of perspective that is clearly the product of the prevailing wave of cultural relativism by which the cultural anthropologists of the twentieth century have extended and enriched the implicit relativism of cross-historical studies that earlier, historical scholarship provided. Where historians gave us the possibility of recognizing the diversity of standards provided by the variety of epochs of larger civilizations, the anthropologists vastly extended this perspective by showing us the hundreds of differing cultures of the surviving primitive tribes of the world—cultures whose range and type of variation from the historically familiar was vastly in excess of the variety provided by the historically known civilizations of "high" (i.e., literate) cultures. Such an expansion of perspective opens up our sensitivity to the enormous range of potentialities in man that may be capitalized upon or institutionalized in different kinds of settings: the special kind of "normality" of the epileptoid institutionalized as a shaman in many primitive societies, the almost anarchic individualistic prowess of the Plains hunter-warrior, the highly ritualized obsessive-compulsive sobriety of a Pueblo priest, the special managerial dignity of an Iroquois matriarch, the exquisite amalgam of grace, control, and trance of a Balinese girl dancer, the stolidity and resilience of an Eskimo wife, the paranoid misanthropy of a Dobuan sorcerer, the lithe and totally noncerebral sensuality of a Polynesian maiden.

Such cultural relativism taken to its extreme means there are no standards of judgment for evaluating behavioral configurations or total personality patterns, except by reference to the norms of the cultures or subcultures in which they appear. Indeed, cultural relativists among the anthropologists have made it a virtue that they "pass no judgments" on the culturally patterned behaviors they describe, implying (often even insisting) that it is improper or impossible to make any valid value judgments about behavior or personality. In their view one can only describe how the behavior or the personality is evaluated by the members of the tribe in question. Ruth Benedict's famous *Patterns of Culture* can be regarded as in truth the very manifesto of this "new" relativistic anthropology: there is no universally applicable standard of normality and abnormality; all is in flux and can be understood only in the context of its own particular culture, and each culture, no matter how small and otherwise insignificant the population who practice it, has its own intrinsic "validity" that cannot be measured by the standards of any other. In this ultimate democracy of nonevaluation, each of the hundreds of different cultures revealed to us by anthropology is distinct and unique, in effect a world of value unto itself. According to this view, it is futile, even wrong, to try to evaluate some cultures as "better" or "worse" than others: all, by the very fact of their existence and persistence at least over some span of time, have an intrinsic value distinctively their own.

This radical "non-judgmentalism" can be seen as a meritorious corrective for hasty ethnocentric (usually negative) judgments of other (usually primitive) cultures commonly made in the recent historical past by lay observers or practitioners who are not anthropologically oriented, such as missionaries, traders, and a miscellany of other exploiters of the "simple primitives." It is a battle cry against allowing ourselves to be immersed in the premises and prejudices of our own contemporary culture, in our views of other peoples and other times. Carried to its full logical extension, however, it has led to some strange intellectual results.

The thought dilemmas to which total cultural relativism can lead are already evident in its manifesto itself. When Benedict writes of the early Puritans of the American colonies as appearing to us today as almost psychotic, there is more than a hint that she is not merely reporting the relativity of conceptions of normality, but is in fact slipping into a kind of judgment, clearly an evaluative one, of the Puritans, from a viewpoint that is not only an ethnocentrism of present-day American culture, but implies some transcending standard of evaluation. Similarly, Benedict, writing in 1934, could not quite bring herself to treat the then contemporary development of Nazism in Germany as just another culture whose exotic blooms we must regard with detachment, to learn from it something more about the lovely diversity of man. From a strictly cultural-relativistic point of view, these notes could be regarded as pardonable lapses of an intrepidly voyaging mind into ethnocentric and contemporocentric thinking that even the most sophisticated anthropologist cannot always avoid falling into, being like everyone else a product of her own culture. But to dismiss them thus is to miss the potentiality in these notes, for a different, more intellectually demanding, and more transcendent view—a view not reached by a cultural relativism that stops close to the behavioristic level of cultural description and analysis, rather than venturing into culture's psychic depths.

As La Barre eloquently points out, it is no mere ethnocentric prejudice to regard as "worse" than others cultures by which men systematically destroy whole segments of their own population, cultures that minutely divide men against each other (the Indian caste system), cultures that systematically threaten their own small tribe with extinction through practices that attempt magical rather than realistic control over nature, cultures that imprison the talents of whole segments of their population within ritualistically narrowed life paths, cultures that destroy or neutralize potential culture heroes of particular psychic types, and on and on. We return to La Barre's radical anti-relativistic formulation: culture and psychosis differ only in the number of their adherents. The standard of judgment in each case is *trans*cultural and not cross-cultural as is the nonevaluative position of the relativists. The corollary of the culture-psychosis equation is that some cultures, like some psychoses, are more harmful than others; or put positively, some cultures are more beneficent than others. Some cultures provide more or better channels for the potential of breaking through destructive illusions and magical self-manipulations (the autoplastic approach to the world typical of psychotics, very young children, and the cultures of many magic-ridden societies). And clearly that potential has to do with the avenues for rationality, for naturalistic science, for reality-testing, and for the self-expression of "deviants" who somehow see through the prevailing mythologies and are able to effectuate their vision into change of the culture to more rational ways. (I am fully aware that there are pitfalls in all these criteria, and Nelson's paper attunes us to the possibilities of continued illusionary elements in such dreams and ideals.)

Transcultural normality. These verbal peregrinations preface an attempt to formulate a third perspective on normality that tries to find a way out of the morass of "non-judgmentalism" to which the cultural-relativistic view, we believe, inevitably leads. The features of such a view have already been touched upon or implied in much of the previous discussion in this chapter and earlier in the book. This view attempts some universalistic criteria according to which behavior, personalities, and ultimately cultures as well can be evaluated in a way transcending both ethnocentrism and relativism. The viewpoint can be charged with ethnocentrism in the sense that it necessarily derives from perspectives developed especially in Western culture, but the charge must be tempered by the recognition that it is from those elements of Western culture that are most universal in their *intended* (if not achieved) approach to mankind—i.e., the perspectives of naturalistic science, which knows no ethnic or national boundaries. It is the very science that gave us earlier the enrichment of the relativistic view. The criteria to be developed derive from a view of man that emphasizes his *universal* problems, problems stemming from the nature of man as a human animal, in all the evolutionary implications of that term[48] and in all the implications that refer to the pan-human social dilemmas of man as faced in every human society. Thus we refer to the peculiar problems of infantilization of the human social animal, in all its ramifications, and the problems of man's peculiar sexuality. We refer to the constant unresolved conflicts of the conscious and unconscious forces, of libidinal strivings against inevitable cultural limitations, of the drives of Eros toward ever-widening unions with others in the world as against the opposite drives that Freud called the "death instinct." (Slater has lucidly redefined the latter as a tendency toward dissociation, contraction, and simplification to its ultimate end of return to its origin point of nothingness.)[49] We refer to the conflict between attempts at solutions by magical manipulation of one's own and others' bodies (autoplastic) as against those that work toward mastery of external reality (alloplastic). And to the conflict between the constantly regressive tendencies of man to retain or return to the modes of satisfaction of infancy, as against those drives toward maturation and growth, mastery of new experience, and integration of earlier levels of adaptation into later more appropriate (present-reality-oriented) ways of adapting to "oneself-and-the-world."

According to this view, modes of dealing with one's world (oneself, the others of one's world, the world of surrounding nature) that perpetuate infantile omnipotence fantasies are relatively more "sick" ways, regardless of the degree and extent of their social validation in the magics and illusions of the tribe, the community, or the nation. Illusions are but the cognitive side of such a process; the need for

[48] See Chapter One for the development of this theme.
[49] Philip E. Slater, "On Social Regression," *American Sociological Review*, Vol. 28, No. 3, June 1963, pp. 339-64.

them, rooted in the paradoxical amalgam of infantile omnipotence and infantile dependency, and the need perpetually to restore that "paradise lost" are the larger dynamic configuration. Where a whole culture's ways of dealing with the world are deeply imbedded in such an infantile configuration, we are justified in speaking of the whole culture as "sick"—and hence of all individual personalities who are adjusted to such a culture as "sick," hence abnormal in this dynamic sense. We may wish to distinguish "sickness" in this sense from individualized neuroses or psychoses where the ideational content of the illness and the emotional mechanisms being used separate the individual from the conformists or adjusted of his society, his ideas and reactions being "crazy" from their limited culturally relative viewpoint as simply not coinciding with their own (likely to be equally, though differently, illusionary) views. But it is the dynamic similarity, rather than the extent of social consensualization, that primarily concerns us here. If a distinction need be made, we can call one form a culturally patterned sickness (and being such, seldom recognized as such by its victims) and the other an individualized sickness. Either may as effectively block the individual personality from contact with its deeper potentialities, or even from some of its most elementary possibilities of gratification. Either certainly will block any far-reaching understanding of itself and its possible resources, thus blocking off their possible use in life-enhancing, mutually joining kinds of contact. Psychiatric discussions which accept some of the basic notions of culturally patterned illness still often argue that the individualized illness is the more destructive in the ways it isolates the sick person the more effectively, and the more progressively, from productive contacts with his fellows. Even this proposition can be questioned if one tries to evaluate, as La Barre poignantly does, a psychotic process as itself a means—often a desperate last resort—for delving into one's inner depths in a way which a life-limiting culture does not allow within any of its standard symbolisms or frames for emotional expression. Thus severe individualized illness may be a commentary and critique on the culture itself and its paucity of resources or channels for certain special kinds of sensitivities. The psychotic in his special private symbolism has in effect done far more than any ordinary "adjusted" person ever does, that is, he has invented his own language, and is but blocked from taking the next critical step (the step taken by the artist, as Schneider showed)[50] of finding a way to make this language communica-

50 See Chapter Five.

ble to sharing others—and even a handful of such others could transform the individualized psychosis into a subculture, a potential nucleus for a transformation of the wider culture, or a whole new way of seeing or living in the world.

There are a variety of other kinds of limitation and constriction deriving from different stages of a child-becoming-man's working through the multiple conflicts that mark the human condition. The elaborate development of certain kinds of "solutions" to the critical problems of any particular phase—e.g., in zonal terms, the anal stage, or the phallic stage—may be proliferated through the whole fabric of a culture, as in the enormous elaboration of anal reaction formations, projections, displacements, and so on, in many aspects of the whole texture of modern Western culture, as Norman Brown has so tellingly documented.[51] Correspondingly, Géza Róheim has analyzed the psychodynamics of the culture of the tribes of central Australia as a hyper-elaboration of "solutions" to the phallic phase, which is demonstrated in their hyper-masculinity obsessions, their defensive patriarchal institutions, their inadequate efforts to convince themselves of biological equality with women, their obsessive divisions of the sexual roles.[52] Other cultures exhibit a hyper-development of punitive superego formations, involving an intense underlying anxiety, with superego-dictated and highly constricted behavior. This behavior instead of alleviating the anxieties intensifies them. The Puritan phase of our own culture and the Pueblo Indians are prime examples of this. Clearly, by these criteria, conformity or "adjustment" to such cultures represents a culturally stylized illness of the first order.

All such discussion, then, implies a standard of health by which such illness can be gauged. How may we formulate such a standard that transcends Western ethnocentrism and yet avoids a formulation of hopelessly impossible to realize ideals of a kind that Nelson has cogently identified as still futher elaborations of the illusions of Western man? We know no really satisfying answer to this question. We can construct some kind of synthesis of the thinking of major dynamic analysts of personality-in-culture of recent decades and still suspect that we continue to be hopelessly culture-bound or indulging in impossible dreams, or both. However, the effort needs to be

[51] Norman Brown, *Life Against Death* (Middletown, Conn.: Wesleyan University Press, 1959).

[52] Géza Róheim, *Psychoanalysis and Anthropology* (New York: International Universities Press, 1950), pp. 41-150. Compare the discussion of Róheim's views of the Australian initiation ceremonies in Chapter Four above.

made. Our guides in this journey are clearly these: Freud himself, the towering figure of all explorations into the depths of man; Géza Róheim, the anthropologist-psychoanalyst whose searing explorations into the inward being of many primitive tribes as well as ourselves has been expressed, unfortunately, in a language so frequently extravagant, overconvoluted and arcane as to repel most potentially sympathetic students; Weston La Barre, who has probably gone the farthest among anthropologists in synthesizing physical and cultural anthropology, linguistics, and psychoanalysis; Norman Brown, whose *Life Against Death* is indeed the most probing psychoanalytic view of all history to be produced thus far; and Herbert Marcuse, whose *Eros and Civilization* offers some ways out of the dilemmas of Freud's *Civilization and its Discontents*, ways which may, as Benjamin Nelson argues, themselves contain utopianistic illusions.

First, any standard of the "healthy personality" must perforce include some general indications of the nature of the social order in which such a man can or must live. By this I do not mean the cultural-relativistic notion that we can specify "health" only in relation to a given society, but rather that we cannot take any particular society of present or past as *given*, but rather must regard a great variety of social and cultural orders as potential and possible, in any of which some kinds of patternings of *relatively more* healthy personality may develop. We can specify, however, certain general characteristics of such societies, as in a sense, necessary conditions for the potentialities of relatively more healthy personalities. These general conditions can be summmarized by the term *pluralism*—a structure of sufficient looseness and diversity as to allow for multiple kinds of developments of a great variety of personality types. In its nature, a pluralistic kind of society could itself take a variety of forms, which could allow for constantly changing internal configurations.

Within such a society a variety of detailed forms of personality could develop. The common general features would be (1) a direct contact with the basic organic experiences of the human animal, rather than having conscious awareness of them mediated by the standards of arbitrary authority figures; (2) the capacity to build on the successive solutions to the central psychosexual problems of the successive libidinal stages and to minimize, or mitigate the effects of the inevitable conflict aspects of each of these stages; (3) the capacity to utilize the psychic transformations—sublimations, displacements, projections, and so on—developed through these successive stages in ways that combine "creative thrust and creative mastery," keeping sufficiently open the channels to the great well of the unconscious, along with sufficient ego-control to direct its forces into constructive relationships and mastery of the material world; (4) the capacity to utilize libidinal forces in creative relationships with other human beings and to limit the inevitable potential of using others to project onto them an image of a controlling other limiting one's autonomy; and (5) the capacity to counter the development of negative authority images (a process that could probably never be totally avoided) with more realistic perceptions—based upon sufficient security that the child can learn to tolerate moderate degrees of realistically dangerous or hostile qualities in the surrounding world. Such a personality would learn not to have impossible expectations of others and the world, without in doing so having to dam up the wellsprings of fantasy and the reservoir of the possible in the unconscious. This criterion involves a conception of an intricate and subtle interplay of conflicting forces in the personality ever changing in their configuration, thus allowing for changing emphases of impulse and order, self-absorption and immersion into social relatedness, and so on. This parallels the notions of social order embodied in the idea of a pluralistic and dynamic society. Not the absence of conflict (impossible anyway) but the capacity to tolerate certain degrees of it and to deal with, work with, and transform such conflict in productive ways, the details of which can never be specified in advance— this is the criterion in mind. Neither abject dependency nor an autonomy based on lonely isolation would dominate the mode of interrelatedness with others.

The quality of such a personality needs also to be specified in terms of relationship to the social order since it is axiomatic that we cannot become human at all without society and culture; paradoxically, we must do so in the context of a particular society and culture of a particular time and place, and hence be limited by its limitations. But as discussed earlier in the book,[53] socialization is never total or complete, and the impact of the social order is always far from absolute or consistent upon the personality. There is an inevitable looseness of interplay between the two, probably the more in more complex and particularly, in more pluralistic societies. Therefore, a specification of what would be ideally healthy in personality

---

[53] See Chapter One, especially Wrong's paper on oversocialized conceptions of man.

must take into consideration the problematics of any relationship between individual and social order in any society, and the more so in what from our view would be the more ideal kind of social order, i.e., a pluralistic kind of society. The ideally healthy personality would have a flexibility and resilience in orientation to the persons and objects representing the constraints and limitations of the social order. He would be able to perceive the boundaries of the imperatives of the social order, be able to make subtle distinctions as to the relative intensity of different kinds of moral and social regulations and of the differential weights of specific constraining persons and forces. He would have internalized significant parts of these moral constraints, but not to the point of punitive superego formations that reactively mobilize aggressions aroused in more infantile contexts. He would have relatively greater direct access to such aggressions and capacities to express them in socially useful or at least socially harmless activities such as competitive athletics or actively motile mastery over materials of the physical world. He is able to recognize, and to utilize, areas of discretion where the social contract makes no direct prescriptions or proscriptions on behavior, thus leaving ranges of choices free. And he is maximally free to exercise such choices according to the idiosyncracies of his own powers, talents, and capacities.

Such a personality does not have to feel that society dictates *all* his behavior so that he must compulsively conform to all its demands; nor on the contrary does he need reactively to defy conformity for the sake of defiance itself, nor that in order to be "free" he must have an infinite range of choices in his personal behavior and thus not be bound by any social norms whatever. Such capacity, in turn, implies a degree of ego strength according to which the personality need not feel he is constantly pitting himself against antagonistic or constraining forces in society, even though he realistically recognizes that social order does involve some constraints. He is capable of some balance between internalized constraints built into superego formation and reality-oriented expediency that questions the absolutism of any societal norms. He has capacities to live and adapt himself without sacrifice to his own basic needs and values, to a variety of social situations and social forms, in a society that is changing and far from absolute in its demands, but variable in its possibilities. He is able to keep some kind of intricate mechanism at work which is attuned to changing possibilities afforded by the social world, but attuned to these not as Riesman's other-directed man as cues to dictate his own behavior, but rather as information sources to guide his choice of lines of pursuit in relation to his own personal goals and aspirations.

Such a personality potential is intimately tied up with the existence of some form of pluralistic society. Such a society would have room for a great multiplicity of socially valued roles for players representing a great variety of psychodynamic configurations. In maximizing a diversity of personalities, such a social order would necessarily be relatively loose, maximizing freedom if necessary at the expense of order. In leaving open whole areas of values for a variety of formulations, in contrast to absolutistic insistence on a single tightly knit scheme of values, such an order would of necessity seem insufficiently protective and insufficiently satisfying to dependency needs of those personalities who were relatively more arrested at such infantile trends. These would be the "costs" of such a social order. Another possible cost would also derive from the relative looseness of the value structure, and that is anxiety occasioned by the very existence of great diversity, making it more difficult for some to get definitive bearings. On the other side, the multiplicity of roles available for different individuals, and even for the same individual at different times or occasions, would allow for maximization of the diversity of psychic configurations not only between individuals, but also within any one individual personality. The multiplicity of different configurations being given expression for any one person, far from being a pathological condition, could be a highly creative one where the gratification of different, even contradictory, needs in one role allows the individual to turn refreshed (that is, with freer access to his energies) to other roles.

The temptation of social thinkers to construct Utopias is evidently continuing strong; while succumbing to it in a modest way here, we have attempted to do so in a manner that avoids the pitfall of constructing some absolutistic hypothetical system—attempts toward realization of which could only produce totalitarian potentials or intensify those already existing in modern culture. We have also tried to keep in mind what has been learned about the enormous recalcitrance of certain basic kinds of conflicts in human beings, recurrent throughout all manner of societies and cultures. We have tried to think in terms of "relatively more healthy" rather than in the absolute terms of "*the* healthy personality"—stressing that the key to human possibility is in the very fact of human diversity. And we have tried constantly to see such personality in the context of social order, anticipating the costs as well as advantages of the kind of social order that would be *optimally* compatible with the diversity of personality trends here posited as desirable.

The contrast of this kind of view with the cultural relativistic one should be patent. It is an explicitly evaluative one, where the value scheme is constructed in relationship to our view of the best knowledge now available about the universal nature and problems of mankind. The conception serves then as a measuring rod for the analysis and evaluation not only of different personalities, but of different cultures, in their potentialities for this strange and improbable animal, man.

SELECTED BIBLIOGRAPHY

Key Works

Brown, Norman O. *Life Against Death*. Middletown, Conn.: Wesleyan University Press, 1959.
Analysis of the "universal neurosis of mankind." Traces the psychopathological roots of the "rational" institutions of science, technology, and bureaucracy, in effect all the core elements of modern industrialized society.

Freud, Sigmund. *Civilization and Its Discontents*. Translated by Joan Riviere. London: Hogarth Press, 1930 and many later editions.
Freud's gloomy analysis of the inevitable psychodynamic costs of civilization. See especially Brown and Marcuse for further dialogue on these themes.

Fromm, Erich. *The Sane Society*. New York: Holt, Rinehart and Winston, 1955.
A neo-Freudian view of the psychopathology of modern society. In his concept of "culturally patterned defect," he shows how one can be culturally normal ("adjusted") while psychiatrically sick.

La Barre, Weston. *The Human Animal*. Especially Chapter 13. Chicago: University of Chicago Press, 1954.
A major critique of neo-Freudian relativism on the issue of normality and mental illness.

Marcuse, Herbert. *Eros and Civilization*. Boston: Beacon Press, 1955.
A "radical" Freudian view, challenging Freud's idea of the inevitability of repression for civilization. Sees modern civilization as a special, and modifiable, case involving "surplus repression."

Róheim, Géza. *Psychoanalysis and Anthropology*. New York: International Universities Press, 1950.
The fullest development as yet of a radical psychoanalysis of culture applied both to primitive societies and modern civilization.

Other Significant References

Adorno, T. W., et al. *The Authoritarian Personality*. New York: Harper & Row, Publishers, 1950.
The dynamics of a type of personality pathology of great social relevance in modern society; relates ethnic prejudice, jingoistic nationalism, and authoritarian political belief to inner personality dynamics and their familial origins. (See also plethora of critical appraisals of this work, e.g. Christie and Jahoda.)

Bateson, Gregory, Don Jackson, Jay Haley, and John Weakland. "Toward a Theory of Schizophrenia," *Behavioral Science*. Vol. 1, 1956, pp. 251-64.
Relates this type of pathology to "double-bind" communications in infancy. Very relevant for the analysis of collective psychoses such as cult movements.

Benedict, Ruth. *Patterns of Culture*. Boston: Houghton Mifflin, 1934, and many later editions.
The last two chapters the "classic" case for the "cultural view of normality."

Christie, Richard and Marie Jahoda (eds.). *Studies in the Scope and Method of "The Authoritarian Personality."* New York: Free Press of Glencoe, 1954.
Some of the more significant appraisals and "continuities" of the Adorno, *et al.*, studies. Edward Shils' paper a significant extension to include "authoritarianism of the left" neglected in the Adorno work.

Cohn, Norman. *The Pursuit of the Millennium*. New York: Harper Torchbooks, 1961.
A dynamically informed historical study of "revolutionary messianism in medieval and Reformation Europe and its bearing on modern totalitarian movements." A moving documentation of collective psychoses in action.

De Rougement, Denis. *Love in the Western World*. Translated by M. Belgion. New York: Harcourt, Brace & World, 1940.
Thoughtful analysis of the influence of the myth of romantic love on Western culture.

Devereux, George. "Normal and Abnormal: The Key Problems of Psychiatric Anthropology," in J. Casagrande, and T. Gladwin (eds.), *Some Uses of Anthropology: Theoretical and Applied*. Washington, D.C.: The Anthropological Society of Washington, 1956.
A significant formulation of a post-relativistic view of "normality," synthesizing rich anthropological and psychoanalytic perspectives.

Dollard, John. *Caste and Class in a Southern Town*. Garden City, N.Y.: Doubleday Anchor, 1957. (Original publication, New Haven: Yale University Press, 1937.)
Includes psychodynamic interpretations of Negro-White relations as of the time of the study, the late 1930s.

Eaton, Joseph and Robert J. Weil. *Culture and Mental Disorders*. New York: Free Press of Glencoe, 1955.
Mental disorder among the Hutterites, compared with other populations. Explodes the notion of the absence of mental illness in this communitarian sect.

Freud, Sigmund. *The Future of an Illusion*. Translated by W. D. Robson-Scott. London: Hogarth Press, 1928.
The irrational roots of religion.

————. *Group Psychology and the Analysis of the Ego*. Translated by J. Strachey. London and Vienna: International Psycho-Analytical Press, 1922.
The seminal source work for all studies of shared dynamics in group behavior.

Fromm, Erich. *Escape from Freedom*. New York: Holt, Rinehart and Winston, 1941.
Traces the rise of totalitarian movements like Fascism to a psychic need to "flee from freedom" aroused by modern secularization. A

primary inspiration for the researches into the "authoritarian personal-
ity" (see Adorno).
Goffman, Erving. *Asylums*. Garden City, N.Y.: Doubleday Anchor,
1961.
These sociological essays on American mental hospitals may lead us to
raise the question, "Who is more insane, the inmates, the keepers, or
the institutions responsible?"
Horney, Karen. *The Neurotic Personality of Our Time*. New York:
W. W. Norton & Co., 1937.
A major formulation of the "neo-Freudian" position emphasizing so-
ciocultural elements in the etiology of neuroses in modern society.
Kennedy, David. "Key Issues in the Cross-Cultural Study of Mental
Disorders," in Bert Kaplan (ed.), *Studying Personality Cross-Cul-
turally*. New York: Harper & Row, Publishers, 1961.
A thoughtful recent discussion.
Kluckhohn, Clyde. *Navaho Witchcraft*. Papers of the Peabody Museum
of American Archaeology and Ethnology. Vol. 22, No. 2. Cambridge:
Harvard University Press, 1944. Reprinted Boston: Beacon Press,
c1963.
One of the most careful studies of the incidence, distribution, and
functions of a culturally patterned illusion, in the anthropological lit-
erature.
Leighton, A. J., Clausen, and R. Wilson (eds.). *Explorations in Social
Psychiatry*. New York: Basic Books, 1957.
Many significant contributions.
Leighton, A., *et al. Psychiatric Disorder among the Yoruba*. Ithaca,
N.Y.: Cornell University Press, 1963.
A major effort to analyze mental illness in a non-Western culture,
involving a thoughtful confrontation of Western psychiatry with
tribal conceptions of mental illness.
Meerloo, Joost A. M. *Delusion and Mass-Delusion*. Baltimore: Williams
& Wilkins, 1949.
A psychoanalytic essay.
Meyers, Jerome K. and Bertram H. Roberts. *Family and Class Dynamics
in Mental Illness*. New York: John Wiley & Sons, 1959.
An important contribution to the analysis of sociological elements in
psychiatric disorder.
Murphy, Jane and Alexander Leighton (eds.). *Approaches to Cross-
Cultural Psychiatry*. Ithaca, N.Y.: Cornell University Press, 1965.
Studies on problems of identifying the mentally ill in different cul-
tures, and relations between personal and sociocultural factors in dis-
order. Field studies of Eskimos, Navahos, Mexicans, and Nova Sco-
tians. (A continuation of the Cornell studies of the Leighton group.)
Opler, Marvin K. (ed.). *Culture and Mental Health: Cross-Cultural
Studies*. New York: The Macmillan Company, 1959.
A valuable collection of studies.
Ranulf, Svend. *Moral Indignation and Middle Class Psychology*. New

York: Schocken Books, 1964. (Original publication, in Danish, Copenhagen: Levin and Munksgaard, 1938.)
Though weak on psychodynamic interpretation, an interesting and contentious essay arguing that moral indignation and disinterested drive toward punishment are peculiarities of middle-class psychology. To the extent valid, this shows a set of culturally standardized illusions of a broad segment of modern society.

Reich, Wilhelm. *The Mass Psychology of Fascism*. Translated by Theodore Wolfe. New York: Orgone Institute Press, 1946.
First published in German in 1933. Deep analysis of the collective psychodynamics of Nazism at the very outset of Hitler's regime.

Riesman, David, Nathan Glazer, and Reuel Denney. *The Lonely Crowd*. New Haven: Yale University Press, 1950.
A widely influential essay on changing American character proposing a conception of the "autonomous" character structure, somewhat analogous to the transcultural standard of normality.

Róheim, Géza. *Magic and Schizophrenia*. Bloomington: Indiana University Press, 1962.
A posthumously published work showing the relationship between these two phenomena.

Rose, Arnold (ed.). *Mental Health and Mental Disorder*. New York: W. W. Norton & Co., 1955.
Good collection of papers toward a social psychiatry.

Slater, Philip E. *Microcosm: Structural, Psychological and Religious Evolution in Groups*. New York: John Wiley & Sons, 1966.
A major contribution to the psychodynamic analysis of group processes, with significant linkages to primitive rituals and myths. [Unfortunately was not available until after the manuscript of the present volume was completed.]

Slater, Philip E. "On Social Regression," *American Sociological Review*. Vol. 28, No. 3, June 1963, pp. 339-64.
A brilliant analysis of societal and psychodynamic needs to prevent or limit regression (e.g. diadic or monadic withdrawal, or to nirvana immersion), and their bearing on important institutionalized taboos.

Srole, Leo, T. Langner and others. *Mental Health in the Metropolis*. New York: McGraw-Hill Book Co., 1962.
The most thorough epidemiological study of mental health and disorder in a modern population. Samples the whole population of midtown Manhattan. Sophisticated integration of psychiatric and sociological survey techniques.

Teicher, Morton. "Windigo Psychosis," in Verne F. Ray, (ed.). *Proceedings of the 1960 Meeting of the American Ethnological Society*. Seattle: American Ethnological Society, 1961.
Synthesis of field data by many observers on a disorder involving cannibalism, found among Chippewa and Cree Indians. Significant for the question of whether Western psychiatric concepts can deal with apparently distinctive types of psychosis.

Vidich, Arthur and Joseph Bensman. *Small Town in Mass Society*. Princeton: Princeton University Press, 1958.

The documentation of the illusions of the "Springdalers," a major piece of sociological analysis.

Wallace, Anthony F. C. "The Institutionalization of Cathartic and Control Strategies in Iroquois Religious Psychotherapy," in M. Opler (ed.). *Culture and Mental Health*. New York: The Macmillan Company, 1959.

A keen analysis of changing styles of emotional illness and correspondingly of psychotherapy, in two periods of Iroquois history.

Wegrocki, Henry J. "A Critique of Statistical and Cultural Conceptions of Normality." in C. Kluckhohn, H. Murray, and D. Schneider (eds.). *Personality in Nature, Society and Culture*. New York: Alfred A. Knopf, 1956.

Argues that "abnormality" can be determined only by the function of the mechanism or characteristic for the personality, thus rejecting statistical and cultural formulations.

Weinstein, Edwin A. *Cultural Aspects of Delusion: A Psychiatric Study of the Virgin Islands*. New York: Free Press of Glencoe, 1962.

The interplay of cultural and psychodynamic elements in delusions.

Wheelis, Allen. *The Quest for Identity*. New York: W. W. Norton & Co., 1958.

A psychiatrist's sensitive exploration into the changing psychic costs and dilemmas of identity over the past few generations in America.

Worsley, Peter. *The Trumpet Shall Sound: A Study of "Cargo" Cults in Melanesia*. London: MacGibbon and Kee, 1957.

Fascinating study of a millennarian movement arising under the impact of European culture upon the tribal peoples of Melanesia.

Subject Index

abnormal, 582–3, 584–5
abortion, 94
abreaction, 402
absent father pattern, 310–11, 319
acceptance-seeker, man as, 45–6
achievement drive, 188–9, 199–200, 205–8, 215 355–6, 362, 373
achrony, 330 ff, 342–6
acting out, 409, 545, 548
activity drive, 358, 479
adaptive behavior, 206, 453, 500, 513, 525, 538
addiction, narcotic, 330–45, 437–8; and social deficit, 336; as puberty rite, 338
adjustment, 199, 379, 457, 460–2, 493, 561–2, 584, 587
adolescence, 204, 330–46, 409, 528–9; in Kibbutz, 165–71
adult-child relations, Kibbutz, 154–7
adulthood, Kibbutz, 170, 172
aesthetic distance, 413
affection-authority balance, 193–5
affective functioning, 219, 224–5
affectlessness, 493–4
affiliation need, Russian, 214–15
age grades, 272–3
aged, the, 262, 480, 481–4; in disaster, 481–4; like very young, 263
"ages of man," 262
aggression, 64, 66, 328–9, 344–5, 372–3, 375, 399, 412, 452–3, 458, 482, 525, 531, 545, 552; alcoholic, 123–4; of executives, 358; in Kibbutz, 142, 166; in Puerto Rico, 92–

aggression (continued)
9, 107–9, 122–5
agon, 417–18, 420–2, 426–30, 433–4, 436–9
agon-alea complex, 421, 433, 439
alcohol, 123–4, 546
alea, 417–18, 420–2, 427–8, 438
Allah, 516–17
ambiguity, 204–6, 246–8, 293–4, 508; resolution of, 246–8
ambivalence, 217, 293–4, 317, 319, 339–40, 457, 507; re family role, 111–12, 117, 121, 147–8, 457–8; re sex identity, 313–14; re regime, 226
American folklore, satirized, 414
American Indian, 264–5
American socialization, personality patterns of, 184, 186, 189–201, 202–10, 235–8; cf. Kibbutz, 202–9; cf. Soviet, 235–8
American society, as type, 186–7; homogenizing forces in, 186–8
Americanadians, 186n
Amish, 128n, 520
anal-compulsive character, 53
anality, 459
analogues of tribal ways, 441
anarchism, 575
"anaesthetic revelation," 330
Anglo-Saxon Protestantism, 188
anonymity in mass society, lack of in Kibbutz, 176
anthropological viewpoint, 541, 555, 580 ff, 588 ff, passim

Name Index